WORLD STUDIES

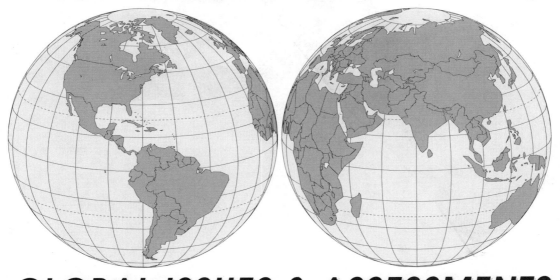

GLOBAL ISSUES & ASSESSMENTS

© Copyright 1995

N & N Publishing Company, Inc.

18 Montgomery Street   Middletown, New York 10940

(914) 342 - 1677

Hard Cover Edition: ISBN # 0-935487 24 7

Soft Cover Edition: ISBN # 0-935487 62 X

3 4 5 6 7 8 9 BMP 9 8 7

Printed in the United States of America, Book-mart Press, NJ

SAN # 216 - 4221

WORLD STUDIES

GLOBAL ISSUES & ASSESSMENTS

The World is a complex mixture of cultures, religions, political and economic systems, geographic and social problems.

Authors:

Sue Ann Kime

Regina O'Donnell

John Osborne

Editors:

Wayne Garnsey and **Paul Stich**

Cover Design, Illustrations, and Artwork:

Eugene B. Fairbanks

N & N Publishing Company, Inc.
18 Montgomery Street
Middletown, New York 10940
(914) 342-1677

Special Appreciation

Dedicated to our students, with the sincere hope that

WORLD STUDIES — *Global Issues & Assessments*

will further enhance their education and better prepare them
with an appreciation and understanding of the people
and historical events that have shaped our world.

Special Credits

Thanks to our many colleagues who have contributed
their knowledge, skills, and years of experience to the making of our endeavor.

To these educators, our sincere thanks
for their assistance in the preparation of this manuscript:

Cindy Fairbanks
Kenneth Garnsey
Gloria Tonkinson

Special thanks to the staff of the New Rochelle Public Library.

WORLD STUDIES – Global Issues & Assessments was developed on an Apple Macintosh. Word processing was done in Microsoft's *Word* with the *American Heritage Dictionary* and *The New Grolier Multimedia Encyclopedia* as resources. Graphics and illustrations were drawn in Deneba's *Canvas*. Original line art and photos were reproduced with a Microtek scanner and scanned and modified in *Adobe Photoshop*. The format, special designs, graphic incorporation, and page layout were accomplished with *QuarkXPress* by Quark Inc.

High resolution scans and film were produced by John Spear, Spear Printing, Washingtonville, New York. Special technical assistance was provided by Frank Valenza and Len Genesee of Computer Productions Unlimited, Newburgh, New York.

To all, thank you for your excellent software, hardware, and technical support.

Table Of Contents

FORWARD

WORLD STUDIES – Global Issues & Assessments presents a fresh approach to learning for both students and teachers. Underlying the text are three frameworks to meet contemporary instructional needs:

- The **Conceptual Framework** incorporates twelve global concepts and eleven world issues with the text and activities.
- The **Learning Standards Framework** correlates basic learning objectives.
- The **Assessment Framework** provides a system of measuring learning objectives.

These frameworks support the total learning process. They define tasks to help students grasp the underlying meaning of each event. They provide tools to dissect and analyze complex relationships. Spending some time understanding these frameworks will make the World Studies course more meaningful and rewarding.

THE CONCEPTUAL FRAMEWORK

Twelve key concepts and eleven world issues furnish the foundation for *WORLD STUDIES – Global Issues & Assessment*. The concepts are universal building blocks to a firm knowledge in social studies. The issues are the critical concerns of people all over the globe. Together, they present the essential questions that must be resolved for humanity to progress. Special icons embedded in the text alert readers when the concepts and issues are being discussed. Relevant charts in the appendices contain explanations and selected examples of these concepts and issues.

Twelve Key Concepts:

Change
Choice
Citizenship
Culture
Diversity
Empathy

Identity
Interdependence
Justice
Power
Scarcity
Technology

Eleven World Issues:

Terrorism
Population
War and Peace
Human Rights
Hunger and Poverty
World Trade and Finance
Environmental Concerns
Political and Economic Refugees
Energy, Resources, and Allocations
Economic Growth and Development
Determination of Political and Economic Systems

THE LEARNING STANDARDS FRAMEWORK

As American education undergoes broad changes, much attention centers on the *process* of learning. Often, traditional instruction concentrates heavily on content study. Many educators now recommend that basic standards and learning outcomes should be the focal point of the classroom. Therefore, the substance and activities of learning spring from these learning standards. The learning standards are the basis for the questions, and the skill activities of this text are as follows:

Learners should understand that:

- ... human values, practices, and traditions are diverse, yet all people face the same global challenges.

- ... different national, ethnic, religious, racial, socioeconomic, and gender groups have varied perspectives on the same events and issues.

- ... interdependence requires personal and collective responsibility for the local and global environment.

- ... the ideals of democracy and human rights constantly evolve in the light of global realities.

- ... civic values and socially responsible behavior are required of members of school groups and local, state, national, and global communities.

Learners should be able to:

- ... analyze and evaluate differing views of historic, social, cultural, economic, and political events, eras, ideas, and issues.

- ... present their ideas both in written and oral form in a clear, concise, and properly accepted fashion.

- ... analyze and evaluate the effects on societies caused by human, technological, and natural activities.

- ... employ a variety of information from written, graphic, and multimedia sources.

- ... monitor, reflect upon, and improve their own and others' work.

- ... work cooperatively and show respect for the rights of others to think, act, and speak differently from themselves within the context of democratic principles and social justice.

THE ASSESSMENT FRAMEWORK

"The primary purpose of the social studies is to help young people develop the ability to make informed and reasoned decisions for the public good as citizens of a culturally diverse, democratic society in an interdependent world."
– National Council of Social Studies, 1993

As schools redefine their mission, social studies instruction needs new ways of assessing academic performance. Schools require more than on-demand multiple choice testing. Constant performance analysis requires assessments that are intrinsic as opposed to disembodied testing events. Assessments must encourage active, in-depth understanding and application of knowledge in new and complex situations. Instead of numerical ratings, newer directions call for cumulative course portfolios that have long-range diagnostic use.

PHILOSOPHY OF ASSESSMENT

While *WORLD STUDIES – Global Issues & Assessments* contains traditional short-range measurement tools, each unit concludes with a long-range performance assessment. The premise is that content instruction is important, but learning standards require broader methods of evaluation. With this in mind, the authors and editors developed an assessment framework based on the following assumptions:

Assessments should:

- ... be based on learning standards determined by the educational institution's overarching goals. The assessments offered here reflect universal goals. Still, the tasks lend themselves to modification in accordance with goals that local communities and states establish for students.

- ... be learner-centered. Students construct their answers and apply skills. Instructors find this useful because it shows inherent knowledge as opposed to luck or guesswork.

- ... be varied. They offer a wide array of opportunities to show learning (e.g., oral presentations, displays, research writing, role playing, debates).

- ... be as authentic as possible. They are open-ended to allow for application of skills, knowledge, and strategies.

- ... develop students' abilities. They enhance conceptual analysis and communication skills.

- ... allow for individual differences. They are flexible, permitting instructors to build on students' different experiences and backgrounds.

The assessments in *WORLD STUDIES – Global Issues & Assessment* are not merely a measure of student achievement and mechanisms for public accountability. By embodying the ideas listed above, they provide opportunities to explore many dimensions of knowledge. They evaluate what students know and can do. They measure the extent to which students:

- can manage and organize data
- make linkages between specific data and larger issues
- view issues from multiple perspectives
- solve problems
- think critically

Clearly, the assessments presented in this book are designed for course portfolios. Most are worthy of inclusion in graduation portfolios or as exit pieces.

CAUTIONS AND CONSIDERATIONS

Performance-based assessment is not new. Still, its principles and perspectives require deliberation and experimentation. *WORLD STUDIES – Global Issues & Assessments* offers the assessment instruments as models and guides. Of course, they must be adapted to individual learning environments. Educational authorities recommend performance assessments be developed, appraised, and refined among colleagues, staff, and the community.

Though placed after specific units in this book, the assessments are relatively generic. Most can be altered easily and used elsewhere in the course.

Few instructors will employ all these assessments. Each school environment is different. Instructors (perhaps with student input), should decide the number, nature, and weighting. Some instructors complete two or three units, then stop to focus class time on the assessment of those units. At the outset, students might be allowed to choose from any of the assessments in those several units.

Many details on evaluation should be decided before undertaking the assessments. How will peer evaluation be combined with instructor evaluation? How will each standard in an evaluation grid be weighted? On interdisciplinary assessments, how will observations of colleagues, parents, or outside experts be used?

FLEXIBILITY IN ASSESSMENT CRITERIA

The *WORLD STUDIES – Global Issues & Assessment* performance assessments include evaluation standards so that students know the expectations and standards. Yet, translating individual student performances into achievement standards must be developed within the specific learning environment.

On each assessment, the scoring grid accompanying the evaluation items (*Standards* to be evaluated) was left blank intentionally. Appropriate choice of scoring descriptor terms is a matter left for instructor, collegial, or administrative decision. Selection of appropriate terms ("minimal," "satisfactory," "distinguished," etc.) can also vary with the nature of a particular assessment. The table below offers suggestions for scoring descriptors that might be inserted in the blank grids.

Sample Scoring Descriptors for Evaluation Grids
Numerical scores or letter scores can be used as well as the descriptor words.

Category 1	Category 2	Category 3	Category 4	Category 5
Poor	Fair	Good	Very good	Excellent
Unacceptable	Minimal	Satisfactory	Mastery	Superior
Unsupported	Competent	Elaborated	Proficient	Distinguished

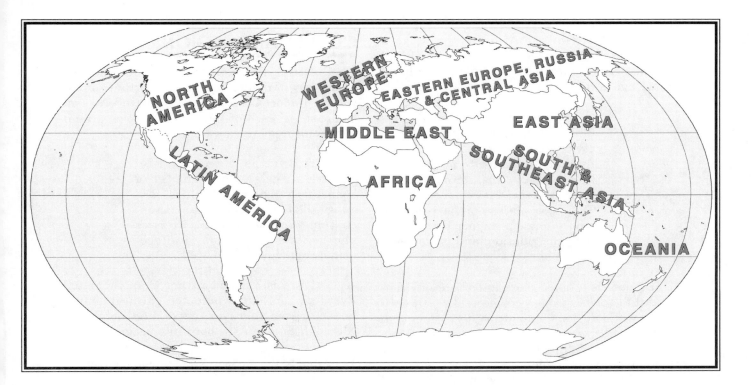

INTRODUCTION

OUR INTERDEPENDENT WORLD

Most students (or adults, for that matter) know very little about the people and countries outside their own region. Still, most people have economic, educational, diplomatic, and even family ties throughout the world. Widening horizons is one purpose of world studies. Students should learn of other people's achievements, concerns, and needs. There is a definite need for cross-cultural awareness.

Examining global regions' historic, political, social, and economic development, people begin to see that human needs are similar. Yet, differences in **environment** (the setting in which people live) create different cultural identities and differing perspectives.

Studying global regions helps students understand that all people have made contributions to world cultures. This course takes students through Africa, South and Southeast Asia, East Asia, Oceania (Pacific Rim), Latin America, North America, Middle East, Western Europe, and Russia, Eastern Europe, and Central Asia.

MAPS AND THEIR USES

Maps are critical in understanding the global environment. They portray some of the reasons for the differences among people. It would be wise to review the maps on the pages of this section to note the regions, their sizes, and positions. Throughout the book, various maps provide a closer look at each of the regions.

Maps have many uses. They provide a wide variety of information such as landscape and water-forms (**topographical** maps), climate, vegetation, population distribution (**demographic** maps), and political boundaries. Note, maps have limitations, and one should always be on the alert for changes and distortions.

Relative distances on the globe have begun to shrink through numerous transportation and communication advances. This produces more interaction of the world's people and causes a more interdependent world. People's lives may depend on their knowledge of resources of other regions.

REGIONS

A **region** is an area with some common physical, political, economic, and/or cultural features. A region could be as small as a neighborhood or as large as a continent. Global regions define units of study which help build knowledge of the world.

DIVERSITY

Each of the nine global regions discussed in this book has a variety of characteristics. Each can be further divided into subregions. For each region, many factors have influenced its current status. This book places emphasis on the environment's impact on the culture, distribution, and movements of people.

Climate is a much more important environmental factor than most people realize. In each of the world regions, climate is a key factor in shaping culture and the progress people have made throughout history. Geographers know that climate is a complex area of study. The text and maps of each unit employ an adaptation of the standard climate classifications of Wladimir Koppen (see Africa: CLIMATIC FEATURES key and map example below).

CULTURE AND REGIONS

Culture is a term that refers to a people's whole way of living. It is also important to realize the impact on a region of past events and tradition. In each of the global regions, a number of cultures are viewed.

A culture is a way of life. Culture is made up of a number of elements: religion and values, language, history, social organization, customs and traditions, literary and artistic expression, and economic organization.

CULTURE

Culture is learned rather than inherited. Every person learns accepted cultural characteristics from relatives, peers, and neighbors. Although humans are born into racial and ethnic groups, their behavioral habits are formed according to the ways of their regional culture.

Throughout history, the movements of people caused **cultural diffusion**, the spreading of cultural patterns from one group to another.

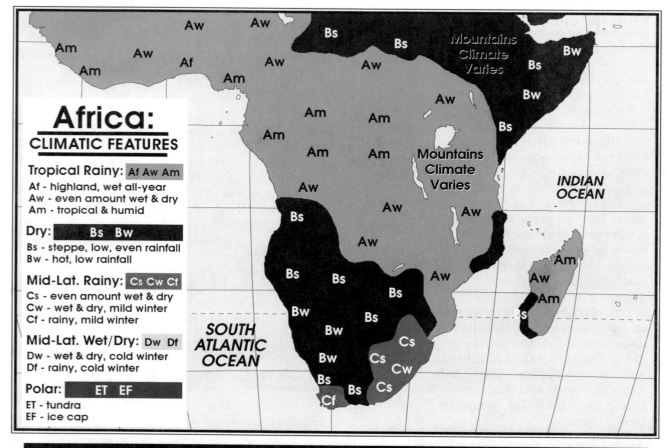

Africa:
CLIMATIC FEATURES

Tropical Rainy: Af Aw Am
Af - highland, wet all-year
Aw - even amount wet & dry
Am - tropical & humid

Dry: Bs Bw
Bs - steppe, low, even rainfall
Bw - hot, low rainfall

Mid-Lat. Rainy: Cs Cw Cf
Cs - even amount wet & dry
Cw - wet & dry, mild winter
Cf - rainy, mild winter

Mid-Lat. Wet/Dry: Dw Df
Dw - wet & dry, cold winter
Df - rainy, cold winter

Polar: ET EF
ET - tundra
EF - ice cap

In the modern world, technology and global interdependence increase the speed and extent of cultural diffusion. Often, culture is adapted or changed to meet the needs of a group. However, no single culture exists today that has not been affected by cultural diffusion. The world increasingly moves toward a global culture.

STUDYING WORLD ISSUES

Throughout this world studies course, major world issues illustrate connections among the regions. They include War and Peace; Overpopulation; Hunger and Poverty; Political and Economic Refugees; Environmental Concerns; Economic Growth and Development; Human Rights; World Trade and Finance; Determination of Political and Economic Systems; Energy, Resources, and Allocations; and, Terrorism.

These issues show that people live in a world of global interdependence. Global regions can be studied separately, but issues interlock people's lives. A global perspective provides a better understanding of the world and its wide variety of peoples and cultures.

QUESTIONS

1   Environment refers to the
1   setting where humans live
2   climates of the Earth
3   waterways around the globe
4   natural resources of a region

2   A people's way of life is called
1   values
2   survival
3   culture
4   density

3   A world political map will show
1   the Earth's climate
2   vegetation regions
3   land-forms on the Earth
4   national boundaries

4   One factor that regions of the world have in common is
1   highly educated populations
2   high standards of living.
3   interdependence
4   smooth transportation and communications networks.

5   Which of the following might a topographical map of South America reveal?
1   where the majority of people live
2   temperatures near the Equator
3   location of major mountain ranges
4   patterns of cultural diffusion

ESSAY

The 20th Century witnessed numerous technological changes which have created greater global interdependence.

Areas of Interdependence

- Trade
- Defense
- Health
- Education
- Economic Development

Choose *three* of the areas listed above. For *each*, discuss how a recent technological advance has had a positive or negative effect on global interdependence.

ASSESSMENTS IN WORLD STUDIES

A course in world studies is a journey. Traveling through the regions of the globe broadens perspectives about people, but it also offers a chance to gain life skills.

As partners in this world studies journey, students and instructors share a common bond. Instructors become guides to point out important perceptions for student travelers.

Travelers use mileposts to measure progress on a journey. In the world studies journey, the mileposts are the major assessments at the end of the units.

In this world studies book, each assessment measures progress in reaching basic **learning standards**. These standards are clearly set forth and shape the **student tasks**. The standards also determine the **evaluation** design of the assessment.

Milepost markers such as the one above indicate the assessments. The markers show that standards, task, and evaluation are linked to measure progress on the journey. Instructors can help students measure their learning progress by guiding them with these markers.

INTRODUCTION
ASSESSMENT
SKILL: COOPERATIVE ORGANIZATION

This evaluation involves small group and class discussion work to set up a notebook for the course. Notebooks serve many purposes. The instructor will discuss the major uses for the notebook in this class. The following is a short list of suggested notebook functions:

- Annotated list of library sources
- Assessment records
- Bibliographies
- Biographical profiles
- Book reports
- Collection of articles on world studies current events, global issues, technological advances, etc.
- Collections of maps, graphs, charts
- Cross-regional comparisons
- Cultural sketches
- Homework assignments
- Interviews and surveys
- Items for final assessment portfolio
- Map references
- Minutes of cooperative group activities
- Notes on daily lessons
- Notes on films or TV programs assigned
- Outlines for oral presentations
- Peer and instructor evaluation reports
- Preparation for reports
- Questions for test and quiz reviews
- Reports and questions on reading assignments
- Reports on field trips
- Simulation reports
- Study guides

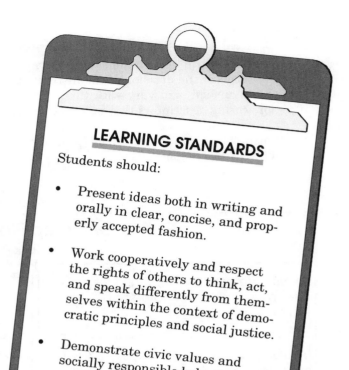

LEARNING STANDARDS

Students should:

- Present ideas both in writing and orally in clear, concise, and properly accepted fashion.

- Work cooperatively and respect the rights of others to think, act, and speak differently from themselves within the context of democratic principles and social justice.

- Demonstrate civic values and socially responsible behavior as members of school groups.

STUDENT TASK

Participate in a group and class discussion to decide on an organized system for taking notes for the world studies course.

DETAILED PROCEDURES

A   According to instructor's specifications, obtain a three-ring binder, a set of index dividers, and a packet of loose-leaf paper.

B   Take notes on instructor's discussion on the range of class activities planned for the year.

C   Use notes to participate in a group that generates a plan for organizing an ongoing evaluation of the course notebook. Select a spokesperson to present your group's plan to the class.

D   Participate in a class discussion and vote to decide the best plan for assembling and monitoring the notebook.

EVALUATION

The scoring grid next to the evaluation items was left blank intentionally. Choice of appropriate category terms is the decision of the instructor. Selection of terms such as "minimal," "satisfactory," and "distinguished" can vary with this assessment. The table on page 10 offers additional suggestions for scoring descriptors that might be inserted in the blank grids.

"Rating Of Group Plans" involves peer ratings. "Instructor Rating of Class Discussion" is completed by the instructor.

Rating Of Group Plans – Evaluation Grid
(Task Part "C")

	Category 1	Category 2	Category 3	Category 4	Category 5
Evaluation Item a Does plan identify and organize a variety of notebook categories?					
Evaluation Item b Does plan provide for note-taking for the various activities outlined by the instructor?					
Evaluation Item c Is the plan presented clearly and effectively?					

Instructor Rating Of Class Discussion – Evaluation Grid
(Task Part "D")

	Category 1	Category 2	Category 3	Category 4	Category 5
Evaluation Item a Does class demonstrate socially responsible behavior?					
Evaluation Item b Does class proposal combine a variety of elements from group presentations?					
Evaluation Item c Is class proposal realistic and comprehensive, yet practical?					

ADMINISTRATIVE GUIDELINES

1   Discuss with class the range of activities the class will experience in the world studies course. Also, discuss the different record keeping skills students need in the course.

2   Discuss role of students in peer evaluation of class discussions.

3   Set up student groups (Part C). Discuss cooperative learning group expectations, procedures, and how they are evaluated.

4   Have groups put plans on board in outline form so that they are available during the discussion.

5   Discuss the weighting of peer v. instructor ratings in the final scoring of the activity.

6   Explain how the notebooks will become part of the long-range student portfolio evaluation.

1 Africa

apartheid
cultural diversity
desertification
exploitation
imperialism

overpopulation
pan–Africanism
Scramble for Africa
slave trade
subsistence

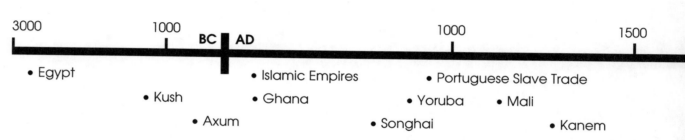

| 3000 | 1000 | BC | AD | 1000 | 1500 |

- Egypt
- Kush
- Axum
- Islamic Empires
- Ghana
- Portuguese Slave Trade
- Yoruba
- Mali
- Songhai
- Kanem

Time-line is not drawn to scale.

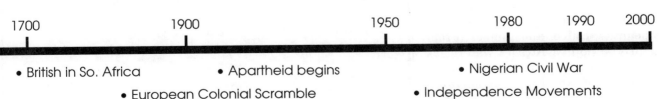

| 1700 | 1900 | 1950 | 1980 | 1990 | 2000 |

- British in So. Africa   • Apartheid begins   • Nigerian Civil War
    • European Colonial Scramble   • Independence Movements
    Anti-apartheid Movement •

Time-line is not drawn to scale.

UNIT ONE: AFRICA

I. PHYSICAL AND HISTORICAL SETTING

A close relationship exists between the climate and physical features of Africa and the cultures and economies which developed there. This unit deals mainly with sub-Saharan Africa. The northern area will be treated in Unit Seven, The Middle East.

SIZE AND LOCATION

Africa is the second largest continent in land mass. It is three times the size of the continental United States. The Equator bisects the continent. It is bordered on the west by the Atlantic Ocean and on the east by the Indian Ocean. To the north and the northeast are the Mediterranean Sea, Suez Canal, and Red Sea. Africa's southernmost land tip is the Cape of Good Hope. Its natural resources and exports are important to the world's economy. They include petroleum, gold, copper, diamonds, cobalt, cotton, peanuts, coffee, and lumber. From early antiquity, Africa's waterways have been avenues of cultural exchange among civilizations. Merchants from India and Southeast Asia reached East Africa long before the Europeans.

PHYSICAL FEATURES

Europeans once called Africa the "Dark Continent," because its interior was unknown and mysterious. Geographic features and the climate worked together to keep Africa an enigma. These factors also limited Africa's development, isolated its interior peoples, and contributed to the development of multiple cultures.

Topographically, the continent's basins and plateaus vary greatly. Africa's average elevation is higher than most other continents; nearly 90% of its land is at least 500 feet (152 meters) above sea level. This general plateau structure is broken by few mountains: the Atlas Mountains in the northwest and the Drakensberg Mountains in the southeast.

Also, five basins interrupt the plateau structure. The largest, the **Zaire River Basin** (once called the Congo), is in the center of the continent. North of the Zaire Basin are the **Nile, Chad**, and **Niger Basins**. To the south lies the **Kalahari Basin**, a huge desert wasteland. The Nile, Niger, and Zaire Rivers drain into the seas.

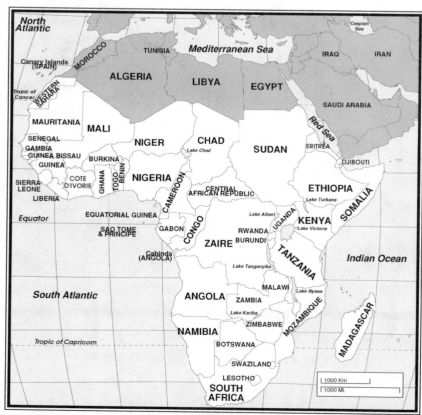

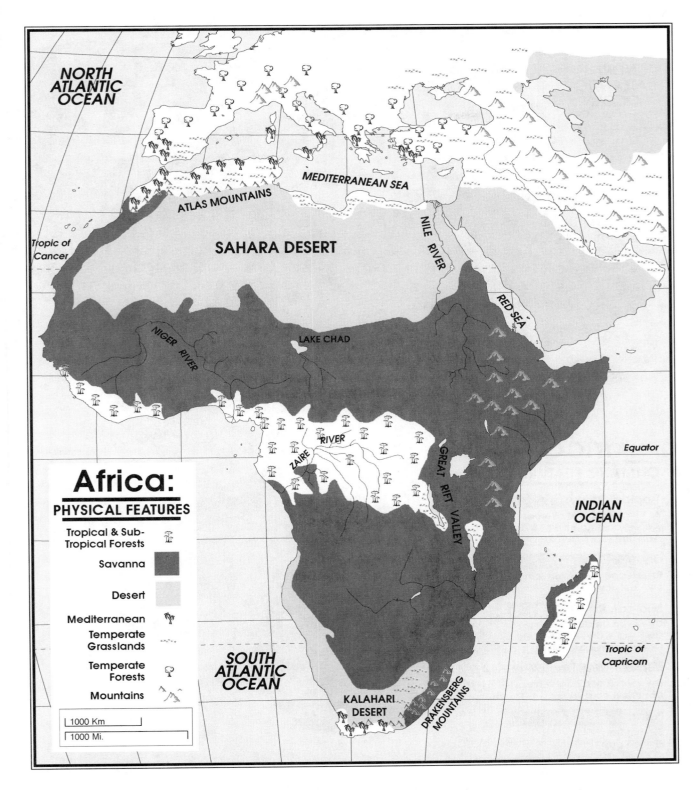

Africa:
PHYSICAL FEATURES

- Tropical & Sub-Tropical Forests
- Savanna
- Desert
- Mediterranean
- Temperate Grasslands
- Temperate Forests
- Mountains

1000 Km
1000 Mi.

Also breaking the African plateau is the **Great Rift Valley**, a 3,000 mile (4,828 km) long crack in the Earth's surface running along the east coast and south through Eastern Africa. This deep valley has channeled human migration in north-south patterns in East Africa.

The world's largest desert, the **Sahara** (3.2 million square miles), lies across North Africa. Today, it is mostly uninhabitable. Some groups survive in a nomadic existence (constantly moving about, seeking food). One such people are the Tuareg. They search for oases (small fertile

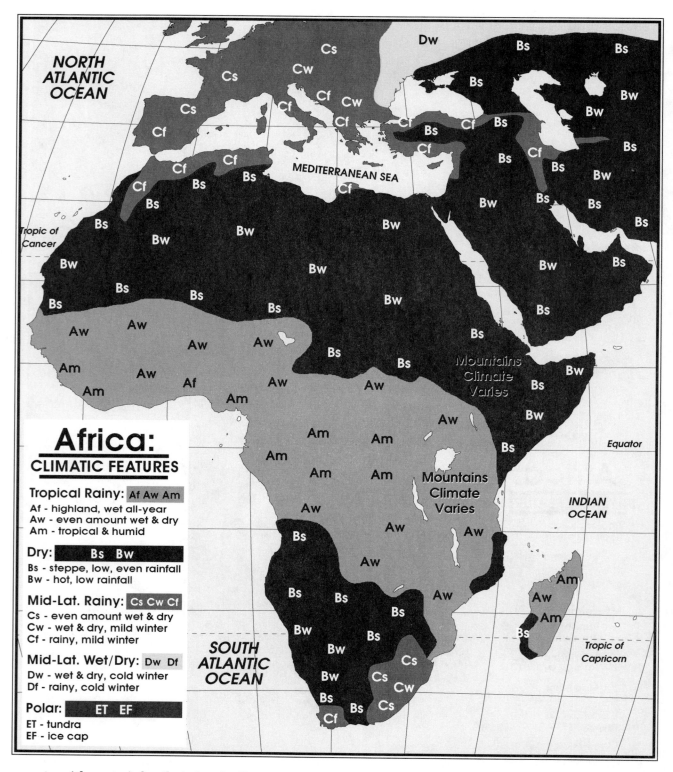

Africa:
CLIMATIC FEATURES

Tropical Rainy: `Af Aw Am`

Af - highland, wet all-year
Aw - even amount wet & dry
Am - tropical & humid

Dry: `Bs Bw`

Bs - steppe, low, even rainfall
Bw - hot, low rainfall

Mid-Lat. Rainy: `Cs Cw Cf`

Cs - even amount wet & dry
Cw - wet & dry, mild winter
Cf - rainy, mild winter

Mid-Lat. Wet/Dry: `Dw Df`

Dw - wet & dry, cold winter
Df - rainy, cold winter

Polar: `ET EF`

ET - tundra
EF - ice cap

---

spots with water) for their herds. Beginning in the early centuries A.D., Arab traders crossed this great barrier of desert in search of the products of sub-Saharan Africa.

Geographers determine the type of climate of an area by the amount of annual rainfall it receives and by its **latitude** (distance north or south of the equator). Since most of Africa lies in the tropics, Koppen's *Type A* and *Type B* climates prevail.

• **Tropical Rainy** (**Am** and **Aw**), rain forest, climate dominates West Africa and Equatorial

Africa. A small amount of rain falls each day, and the average daily temperature is in the 80°F (27°C) range. The soil is leached (minerals and nutrients have been washed away by constant rainfall). It is not good for commercial agriculture. This thickly vegetated area comprises about 15% of Africa's land mass. Central Africa is home to the **Pygmy** people, who are small in stature (4 ft to 4 ft 8 in [122 to 142 cm]). They are hunter/gatherers, living off the land.

- **Steppe** or **Savanna** (**Bs**) is another climate type found in tropical latitudes. It is sometimes called Tropical Grassland. In Africa, it covers about 40% of the continent and is found in the regions bordering the tropical rainy areas: the Sudan, central, and southern regions. Many groups here are labeled **Bantu** because of their linguistic classification. Savanna climates suffer from high temperatures similar to the rain forest but have more dry periods. Still, rainfall is sufficient to support rough grasses and some trees. Soil is dry and infertile for farming unless it is irrigated. Savannah is big-game "safari" country, home to nomadic hunters.

- **Deserts** and **semi-deserts** make up another 40% of Africa's land mass. Geographers classify their climates as **Tropical Dry** (**Bw**) – warm all year, scant rainfall only in summer. The **Kalahari** and **Namib** Deserts are home to the Bushmen and Hottentots who speak the Click language.

Africa's climatic picture shows that approximately 85 to 90% of its surface is unsuitable for agriculture. During the 1980's, African nations suffered terrible droughts, making hunger and poverty major concerns.

CULTURAL DEVELOPMENT

The history of human existence in Africa seems to go back farther than that of people most everywhere else. Until recently, western civilization's awareness of Africa's past was blinded by its definition of history being confined to literate societies.

A number of modern historical tools have opened the African past:

- **Archeology** is the study of human existence by means of its physical remains. It has given archeologists information as they studied the pyramids of Egypt and the stone structures of Zimbabwe.

- **Radiocarbon Dating** is a scientific method of determining the age of once-living organic matter by measuring its **Carbon 14** content.

- **Oral Traditions** are myths, legends, and anecdotes that provide entertainment and education for the young and preserve traditions.

- **Written Records** give historians information about Muslim traders and settlers from as early as the 9th Century A.D.

Anthropology is the study of the origins and development of human culture. The discoveries of anthropologists in Ethiopia, Kenya, and Tanzania suggest that modern humans first emerged in Africa. In 1959, in Olduvai Gorge, Tanzania, **Mary Leakey** made one of the most well known finds in modern anthropology. She discovered the 1.75 million-year-old remains of *Homo habilis* (able man). In 1972, **Richard Leakey** found an older skull with a larger brain capacity than *Homo habilis* in Kenya. Four human bones, estimated to be over 3 million years old were discovered in the region in 1974.

African tales and genealogies provide oral histories of tribal chiefs. One important event of pre-literate Africa tells of the fall of the **Hittite Empire** of North Africa in 1200 B.C. The migrations of its skilled ironsmiths brought plows, hammers, and swords to peoples to the south.

Myths and legends provide identity and continuity to Africa's past. Much of this literature has now been recorded. It is an important source of information for scholars of African history. Literature also expresses the African perception of the forces of the world that affect their lives, including animal tales, myths, legends, proverbs, and episodes from the lives of the people.

CULTURAL PATTERNS OF ANCIENT AFRICAN CIVILIZATIONS

(for geographical locations, see map on page 29)

CIVILIZATION	TRADE: PRODUCTS	TRADE: TECHNOLOGY	TRADE: REGION
Kush 2000 BC	iron products, gold, ivory, spices	ironworking center of the ancient world	Egypt, Red Sea, Mediterranean Sea
Axum 300 AD	iron products, gold, ivory, spices	ironworking center of the ancient world	Egypt, Greece, Rome, Semites of Arabia
Ghana 300 AD	salt, gold, slaves	metal weapons, metal tools, jewelry	across Sahara to North Africa
Zimbabwe 1100 AD	cattle, grains, gold, ivory	metalworking, dry stone building techniques	India, Indonesia
Mali 1200 AD	cattle, grains, gold, ivory, slaves	cloth, jewelry, metal tools	North Africa, Arabia, Mediterranean Sea
Kongo 1300 AD	slaves	metalworking, pottery, coppersmithing	slave trade with Portugal
Songhai 1400 AD	salt, cattle, gold, slaves	cloth, jewelry, metal tools	North Africa, Arabia, Mediterranean Sea

Geography and climate have been obstacles to cross-cultural contact. Geographic features have led to the creation of over 800 culturally distinct societies and languages. African geography resulted in cultural diversity that gave rise to distinct early civilizations (see **Ancient Civilization Chart above**).

BARRIERS TO DEVELOPMENT

Although Africans have shown skill and success in adapting crops and animals to their environment, serious limitations still remain:

- Scarcity of water – Much of the land's infertility is due to climate. Lack of capital to expand irrigation hinders progress.

- Limited use of natural resources – Africans lack technological training, equipment, and surplus capital to develop their various natural resources.

- Pervasiveness of insect pests – An example is the tsetse fly that carries the "sleeping sickness." It greatly limits the effectiveness of horses, oxen, and human labor in sub-Saharan Africa.

- Lack of access to markets – Because of waterfalls and rapids, rivers are unfavorable to transportation and communication. Mountains, deserts, and rain-forests are also barriers. In addition, there is a shortage of wheeled vehicles.

- Reliance on traditional methods of production – Lack of modern technology, equipment, and training compound problems.

RELIGION AND CULTURE

TRADITIONAL INFLUENCES

African religions are inseparable from traditional social and political order. They vary widely but have certain basic characteristics:

- Ancestor worship – Forbearers are considered a living part of the tribal community.

- Reinforcement of family group associations – One's lineage and membership in a clan is important. **Lineage** is the tracing of one's

CULTURAL PATTERNS OF ANCIENT AFRICAN CIVILIZATIONS

SOCIAL UNITS	RELIGION	GOVERNMENT	CIVILIZATION DECLINE
family (reflects Egyptian influence)	blend: Kushite and Egyptian gods	kingdom under divine pharaoh	succeeded by Axum, c. 250 AD
family (reflects Egyptian influence)	Coptic rite, Christian c. 100 AD	kingdom	evolved into Ethiopia
matrilineal clans and tribes	tribal religions	divine king	Muslim conquest
clans: Bantu people	tribal religions	divine king	European conquest, c. 1660 AD
matrilineal clans and tribes	Muslim	empire divided into provinces	Muslim conquest, c. 1300 AD
tolerated clans: Bantu people	Christianity (introduced by Portuguese c. 1840)	elected king, empire divided into provinces	civil wars over slave trade
matrilineal clans and tribes	Muslim	empire divided into provinces	European conquest, c. 1550 AD

ancestry to a common forebearer. A **clan** is an association of lineages. In traditional African culture, one belongs to a family, the family to a clan, the clan to a tribe, the tribe to a nation. Lineage is important, causing individuals to associate with others who honor the same common ancestors.

- Divine Rulers – Chiefs were not merely political rulers, they were considered lesser gods or priests in charge of ceremonies worshiping ancestral deities. People identified with the special connections their chiefs had to ancestors. This enhanced the powers of the chieftains in social and political matters.

- Common divinities – There was a belief in a supreme being who created life. It was associated with concepts of good and evil and had great healing powers. Lesser deities and invisible forces held the power of life and death over mortals.

- Ritual ceremonies – Local diviners believed to have supernatural powers presided at rituals of birth, puberty, and death. Charms and amulets offered protection to the individual. Evil acts were to be avoided because they dishonored the lineage.

ISLAMIC INFLUENCES

In the 7th Century A.D., **Islam** overwhelmed Christianity (which had been slowly spreading throughout northern Africa). It spread across the Sahara with Muslim traders. By the 11th Century, the larger West African empires, like **Ghana,** were converted to Islam for the following reasons:

- Islam's diversity tolerated many of the practices of traditional African religions, allowing Islam to spread rapidly.

- Islam influenced tribal life. It undermined some of the divine power of chiefs and witch doctors.

- Islam brought increased trade and knowledge to West Africa. **Hausa** city-states of the 14th Century and West African Islamic kingdoms such as Mali became **theocratic.** In theocratic societies, religious leaders ran the government. The most famous of the Muslim rulers of Mali was **Mansa Musa** (1312-1332). He made the fabled city of **Timbuktu** a leading center of Islamic learning and wealth.

Islamic influence is seen across Africa. The more decorative Mosque at the left is in the city of Mombasa, Kenya. At the right, a group of worshipers pray at a Mosque in the countryside near Diemoul, Senegal.

In the 19th Century, the Muslim Fulani tribe of northern Nigeria began a **jihad** (holy war). It ended in their domination of the area. Islam became a powerful force along the southern reaches of the Sahara but never entered the central or southern areas of Africa, except for traders along the east coast.

In the modern era, aggressive Islamic missionary activity played an important role in the drive of certain African nations for their independence from colonial rule.

CHRISTIAN INFLUENCES

Christianity also had an ongoing impact on many areas of Africa. In the early Christian era, Greek-influenced **Coptic Christianity** spread rapidly into the upper Nile area (Nubia and Ethiopia). This area later resisted Islamic conversion while the predominance of the **Roman Catholic Church** along the Mediterranean coast of Africa was overwhelmed by the Muslims' jihad.

There was some Portuguese missionary work along the sub-Saharan coastal regions in the 16th and 17th Centuries. Still, southern Africa was not the focus of Christian missionary work until the 19th Century. The Christian influence is greatest today in South Africa, Zimbabwe, and Tanzania.

Independent African Christian Churches emerged in opposition to European colonial rule. They incorporated Christian missionary teachings with native religious concepts. These movements are sometimes referred to as "Ethiopianism" or "Zionism." (Christian "Zionism" is not to be confused with the 19th and 20th Century nationalistic movement for a Jewish homeland discussed in Unit 7.)

TRADITIONAL AFRICAN ART

The forms of African art were strongly influenced by the traditional social structure and tribal religions. Often, the arts represented instruments of social control. Body painting and tattooing gave identity to clans, tribes, and families. Not one African society has been found to be without some form of art. There are three major art forms of sub-Saharan Africa:

- **Visual Arts** include wood-carving, terra cotta figures, metalworking, stone, ivory, and bone carving. Use of gold was limited to leaders. Masks were used in ritual ceremonies. Figurines, sometimes symbolizing ancestors, were used at funeral, fertility, and healing rites. The Benin and Ife bronzes are examples.

Photos by David Johnson, 1992

Dances are a major part of cultural art forms across Africa. The above photos show the Oku people in the Kilum Mountains of Cameroon involved in a traditional masked dance.

- **Music and Dance** are art forms that have always been a vital part of traditional activities. Early paintings from 6000 – 4000 B.C. depict dancers and men playing instruments. These ancient instruments included drums, gourds, stringed bows, harps, lutes, and whistles. African music is polyrhythmic, employing two or more rhythms at the same time. Hand-clapping supports the dancers. Important events in family and tribal life were usually accompanied by ritual dancing.

- **Architectural Forms** reflected an interplay of natural environment, available technology, and prevailing religious, social, and political institutions. Examples ranged from round mud-huts with cone-shaped thatch roofs to the famous stone fortress-temples of Zimbabwe. Typical tribal homes were built from local materials and reflect the traditional life of the village.

QUESTIONS

1 Which of these newspaper reports best illustrates a major problem of Africa?
   1 *Africa Lacks Deep Water Ports*
   2 *African Economy Dependent on Foreign Technology*
   3 *Chinese Experience Difficulty with African Transport System*
   4 *Rail Travel More Dependable in Africa Than in Asian Countries*

questions continued on next page

2 Which problem is common to emerging nations in Africa?
1 exhaustion of natural resources
2 interference by the United Nations in internal affairs
3 continuing oppression by European colonial powers
4 scarcity of technically trained persons

3 An *archeologist* is a scientist who
1 studies the physical remains of ancient civilizations
2 paints and sculpts ancient humans
3 builds stone bridges
4 studies the habits of migratory animals

4 In discussing the relationship between humans and their environment, which of the following statements would be valid? The environment
1 limits human actions
2 is unimportant in urban areas
3 only controls humans in rural areas
4 can be fully controlled by humans

5 Heavy rainfall and high temperatures are constant throughout the year in the Zaire Basin. Which climate does this describe?
1 Tropical Rainy
2 Mediterranean
3 Tropical Desert
4 Savanna

6 Long periods of drought, high temperatures, and grassy vegetation are found in the Sudan. Which climate does this describe?
1 Tropical Rainy
2 Mediterranean
3 Tropical Desert
4 Savanna

7 The soil of Africa may be generally described as
1 highly productive
2 similar to the "Great Plains" of the United States
3 too rocky for agriculture
4 largely infertile

8 Africa's tribal cultures are
1 in close contact with the outside world
2 closely related to religion and tradition
3 forerunners of capitalistic economies
4 forerunners of the Islamic religion

9 Early African religions resembled modern world religions in the belief in
1 ancestor worship
2 a creator of the universe
3 charms to drive off evil spirits
4 the divinity of the ruler

10 The absence of which of these presents the greatest barrier to Africa's development?
1 dangerous animals
2 technological knowledge
3 lineage
4 Zionism

11 In sub-Saharan Africa, the introduction of Islam eventually
1 brought increased trade
2 destroyed tribal religions
3 isolated cultural growth
4 stopped communications among tribes and clans

12 Which aspect of a society would an anthropologist study in depth?
1 development of self-image, causes of insanity
2 family patterns, legends, festivals
3 problems of scarcity, production of goods
4 results of opinion polls

ESSAYS

1 Until recently, Western Civilization was basically unaware of African cultural achievements.

a Identify *two* historical tools which reveal African history.

b List and explain *three* reasons why Africa enjoyed a varied cultural history before the age of European exploration.

2 Africa suffers from several barriers to development. Select *three* different African nations and discuss how geographic factors and the absence of technology affected their development.

II. DYNAMICS OF CHANGE

FALL OF THE LATER AFRICAN KINGDOMS

A number of kingdoms existed in Central Africa in the late Medieval Period (see Ancient Civilization Chart in previous section). In most cases, the coming of European traders led to downfall of the African kingdoms.

- **Kanem – Bornu** was an Islamic state northeast of Lake Chad. It was overthrown by the French by the end of the 19th Century.

- **Hausaland** (Hausa city-states) was a Saharan Islamic state west of Bornu. It was conquered by the Fulani and eventually fell to the British.

- **Benin**, **Yoruba**, and **Ashanti** disintegrated because of the slave trade. They were incorporated into the British colonies of Gold Coast, Togo, and Nigeria.

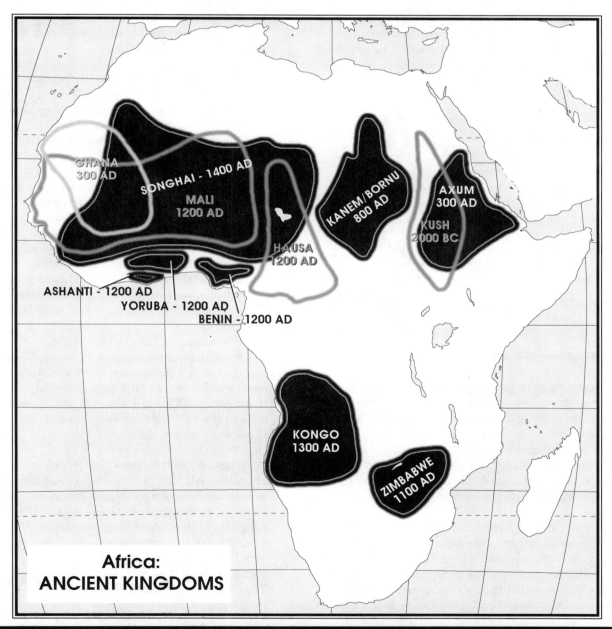

GHANA 300 AD

SONGHAI - 1400 AD

MALI 1200 AD

HAUSA 1200 AD

KANEM/BORNU 800 AD

AXUM 300 AD

KUSH 2000 BC

ASHANTI - 1200 AD

YORUBA - 1200 AD

BENIN - 1200 AD

KONGO 1300 AD

ZIMBABWE 1100 AD

Africa: ANCIENT KINGDOMS

- **Kongo** (modern Angola) was also destroyed by the slave trade. It fell to the Portuguese.

- **Zimbabwe** was conquered in the 19th Century. It was renamed "Rhodesia" after **Cecil Rhodes**, the great "Empire Builder" of British East Africa. Upon independence, Northern Rhodesia was renamed Zambia, and Southern Rhodesia, Zimbabwe.

SLAVERY AND THE SLAVE TRADE

Slavery has existed since the dawn of humankind. It has been traced from the Roman Empire to ancient China. During the 12th Century A.D., Muslim traders began to take captive Africans back to sell in Arab lands. Later traders, whether black, white, or of mixed race, became intensely motivated by monetary rewards.

SLAVE TRADE WITH THE AMERICAS

The trade in slaves increased tremendously by the mid-16th Century due to the demands of the agricultural economies of European colonies in the New World. Slaves were used on the large-scale sugar and tobacco plantations of the Western Hemisphere.

From the 1500's to the early 1800's, Europeans became highly involved in buying slaves (sometimes called "black ivory"). In return for guns, whiskey, and utensils, African chieftains sold prisoners captured in battles with rival tribes. The transactions took place in

fortresses constructed by slave traders along the coast. The Dutch, Portuguese, Spanish, and English became the major transporters. Their ships dropped surviving slaves for plantation owners in South and Central America, the Caribbean, and the southern colonies of North America.

TRADITIONAL SOCIETY SUFFERED

Slavery had a number of destructive effects in West African society:

- **Social Upheaval** – Slavery brought the largest and longest forced migration of people in history. Millions were sold into slavery over three centuries.

  - **Violence** – Slavery led to an escalation of violence. Proud kingdoms deteriorated into civil warfare to capture prisoners to be sold to the coastal slavers. Slavers themselves recruited natives to go on raiding parties.

  - **Social Collapse** – Slavery was a major cause in the collapse of traditional African social and political order. African art, culture, and prosperity suffered. Slavery dispersed millions of young, healthy individuals to other parts of the world. This made the people of Africa easy prey for European governments to conquer and colonize.

  - **Prejudice** – Slavery left a legacy of racial prejudice against Africans. Those engaged in the trade searched for justification by instilling a sense of inferiority in their victims. This left a heritage of bitterness in the relationship between the Europeans and Africans.

- **Political Adjustment** – Many African kingdoms fell victim to political realignment as new sources of wealth and power emerged from the slave trade. As the Hausa Kingdoms fell to the Fulani, old trans-Saharan trade routes deteriorated. West African coastal states such as **Benin**, **Yoruba**, and **Ashanti** rose in the 18th and 19th Centuries.

ABOLITION OF THE SLAVE TRADE

Gradually, the evils of slavery gave rise to an abolitionist movement in Western Europe and the United States. Among the forces that produced the anti-slavery drive were an emphasis on the doctrine of the **Natural Rights of Man** and **Humanitarianism**. Both grew out of the 18th Century **Enlightenment**. Also, a large wave of Christian missionary zeal during the 19th Century added moral and financial commitment to the movement.

In 1808, the *U.S. Constitution* ended the importation of slaves. (The United States did not abolish slavery until the end of the Civil War in 1865.) In 1833, Parliament abolished slavery in the British Empire. While the slave trade ended officially in West Africa in the early 19th Century, an illegal trade continued for many years.

The abolition of the slave trade disrupted the African economic structure once more. Many tribes and states had become dependent on the revenue from salve trading, neglecting other industries. The Industrial Revolution of the early 19th Century created a need for raw materials. European nations used industrialization as an excuse to begin the imperialistic conquest of Africa.

THE ERA OF IMPERIALISM

Europe was able to dominate sub-Saharan Africa because of trade and technological superiority.

TRADE RIVALRIES

In the late 15th Century, trade rivalries among European nations led to a period of exploration. The Dutch, Spanish, Portuguese, English, and French set up commercial colonial settlements. Political colonies eventually emerged from private charter company posts along sea routes to the Orient. One example was Britain's **Royal Niger Company**.

THE SCRAMBLE FOR COLONIES

A second factor in the evolution of 19th and 20th Century European imperialism was indus-

trial capitalism. The factory systems and technical breakthroughs, including the application of steam power, created great demand for raw material and markets. Limited resources in Europe made conquest and exploitation of overseas territories more urgent.

However, movement into Africa's interior sections was slow. As late as 1880, Europeans controlled a relatively small area of Africa. Leopold II of Belgium announced that he was officially claiming the vast equatorial region known as the Congo (today's Zaire), setting off an intense "**Scramble for Africa**." In 1884 and 1885, the Berlin Conference divided the continent into colonial regions. By 1914, only the African nations of **Liberia** and **Ethiopia** remained independent.

OPPOSITION

The "Scramble for Africa" produced varied responses on the part of Africans themselves:

- **Violent opposition** took place in some areas. On their "**Great Trek**" into the interior of South Africa (1836), Dutch "**Boer**" settlers met fierce resistance from the Zulu people. It took decades before the British broke the power of the **Ashanti** in 1896.

- **Passive opposition movements** also emerged. Indian independence leader Mohandas Gandhi led nonviolent protests in South Africa in the 1890's. His resistance movement became a model for 20th Century nationalist movements.

- **Cooperation** did occur in some areas. Many tribal leaders agreed to become mercenaries in the pay of European conquerors. Also, the British followed an "indirect rule" approach. They preserved the power of traditional African chieftains as long as they followed English imperial policies.

EFFECTS OF EUROPEAN RULE

The period of European imperialistic dominance had negative and positive effects on the African continent.

Africa:
EUROPEAN COLONIES
Prior To WW I

- **Rampant Exploitation** – Exploiting natural resources such as minerals, lumber, and rubber did serious damage to the African economy and ecology.

- **Cultural Destruction** – Imperial rule was destructive to African culture. It destroyed communal land ownership, weakened family and tribal ties, led to forced labor, and abused Africans' rights. While Western political ideas were introduced, the white European minorities refused to extend these political freedoms to Africans. Westernized legal codes separated older civil and religious laws, leading to abandonment of previous legal customs.

- **Physical Improvements** – While Western developments in medical care and nutrition lowered infant death rates, they also led to a population explosion that places a strain on African resources today. Improved transportation and communication in the zones of natural resource development opened previously remote areas.

- **Agricultural Changes** – Changes in agricultural practices increased production of cash crops needed in Europe. Yet, domestic staple crops were ignored, making Africans more dependent on importing food.

- **Economic Transformations** – Changing economies from barter to currency systems stimulated capital accumulation and trade. Yet, the change created gaps in wealth and increased social tensions.

- **Educational Improvements** – Expanding educational opportunity gave Africans a wider choice of career opportunities. Yet, some of the training was in areas unrelated to African needs, and it often downgraded tribal culture.

- **Unifying Influences** – Altering the African political, economic, and linguistic structures unified diverse groups into larger groupings. Yet, in dividing the continent, Europeans created national boundaries that cut across traditional tribal and clan lines. Even today some of these divisions remain sources of disputes.

QUESTIONS

1 Colonies acquired by imperialists would generally have
   1 great natural beauty
   2 a small population
   3 surplus investment capital
   4 good natural resources

2 European colonialism in Africa reached its height during the period just
   1 before the Franco-Prussian War
   2 before World War II
   3 before World War I
   4 after World War II

3 The fundamental cause of imperialism in the late 19th Century was the
   1 increase in merchant guilds
   2 outbreak of the French Revolution
   3 expansion of the Industrial Revolution
   4 desire for collective security

4 Historians writing about slavery could accurately state that it
   1 was first introduced in Europe
   2 was limited to areas of the Western Hemisphere
   3 seems to have existed in some form since earliest times
   4 has been abolished for many centuries in all nations

5 In 1914, which two nations controlled the greatest amount of African territory?
   1 Germany and Italy
   2 Portugal and Spain
   3 Belgium and the Netherlands
   4 France and Britain

6 *"We shall not ask England, France, Italy, or Belgium, 'Why are you here?' We shall only command them to get out!"* The speaker reflects African
   1 nationalism
   2 imperialism
   3 cooperation
   4 neutrality

7 *"We must bring the benefits of Western Civilization and Christianity to the less fortunate."* This idea has been used to justify
   1 imperialism
   2 nationalism
   3 socialism
   4 feudalism

8 Which was a major result of European imperialism in sub-Saharan Africa during the late 19th and early 20th Centuries?
   1 adoption of Islam as the dominant African religion
   2 decline of traditional African cultures
   3 strengthening of tribal organization
   4 beginning of slavery

ESSAYS

1 By 1914, only Liberia and Ethiopia remained independent of European control. Briefly discuss *three* reasons why European nations of the late 19th Century became interested in the continent of Africa.

2 Europe was able to dominate sub-Saharan Africa due to its technological superiority.

   a Discuss *two* ways in which colonies benefited from European imperialism.
   b Discuss *three* ways colonies were harmed by imperialism.

III. CONTEMPORARY NATIONS

In examining contemporary African nations and their cultures, a number of factors must be understood. European rule had a profound effect. Understanding the origins and development of nationalism and **Pan-Africanism** (an effort to promote continental unity) is important. The relationship between free and non-free societies is also important. Lastly, a majority of Africans are still dependent upon a rural-agrarian life style. This creates an ongoing clash of traditional and contemporary forces that shapes life on the continent.

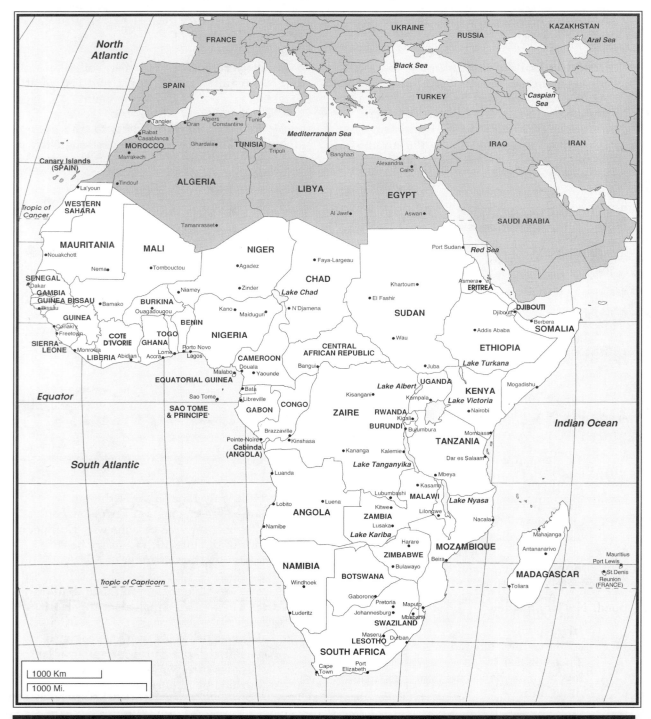

AFRICAN NATIONALISM

Full-scale colonial rule lasted for less than a century. Most of the continent achieved independence by the mid-1960's.

Early African nationalist movements were nonviolent, nonracial, and nonideological. They placed strong emphasis on human rights and dignity. Some of these independence movements reflected the influence of the American experience.

Nationalism is a strong feeling of unity for people desiring to control their own destinies. In Africa, nationalism had a distinct **anti-imperialist** character (a strong desire for freedom from foreign control). The main demand by early African nationalists was a greater voice in running their own governments.

An educated elite that had studied in Europe and America led African nationalist movements. While abroad, they had experienced human rights unknown in their homelands: the right to vote and hold political office, trial by jury, and freedoms of speech, press, and assembly.

 Returning to their homelands, these Africans felt humiliated when European colonial rulers would not accept them as equals. They saw their only recourse in political action to achieve self-government. With slogans like "Uhuru" (freedom) and "Self-government Now," Africans drove for independence. They wished to gain their rights and dignity and to break down economic and social discrimination.

From colony to colony, the transition from foreign to African leadership varied. Yet, a pattern soon developed. Nationalist leaders organized political parties. Africans looked upon the new leaders as emancipators and the fathers of their nations.

World Wars I and II accelerated the nationalist movements. During World War I, colonial governments recruited African villagers to work the mining and industrial centers. There, they learned of Western constitutional and electoral policies. During World War II, Africans served as troops for the colonial governments and provided necessary raw materials for the Allies. Colonial governments sent many Africans overseas. These Africans saw what freedom meant to others. The **Atlantic Charter**, proclaimed by American President Franklin Roosevelt and British Prime Minister Winston Churchill in 1941, encouraged many to seek self-determination. It stated that all people had the right to choose their own form of government.

After World War II, the *Atlantic Charter* ideals became the basis for the **United Nations Charter**. Together, these two documents promoted human rights and self-determination. Many of the Asian nations were given independence following World War II, but the Africans had to wait until the 1950's and 1960's to achieve either their freedom or independence.

World War II signaled the beginning of the end of colonial rule in Africa. The homelands of the European powers were devastated. They paid scant attention to their colonies. African nationalism gained strength. Political power shifted from the Europeans to the Western educated, urban-oriented African leaders.

Still, European colonial powers had not prepared most of the new African nations for governing themselves. Many of the leaders failed to maintain the support of their citizens.

Haile Selassie
(Ethiopia)

Kwame
Nkrumah
(Ghana)

Mobutu
Sesu Seko
(Zaire)

Jomo Kenyatta
(Kenya)

Julias Nyerere
(Tanzania)

ethnic groups. In each country, the minority Tutsi are about 15% of the population. Yet, their struggle for dominance has taken thousands of lives.

New African leaders also had difficulty balancing nationalistic loyalties with **Pan-Africanism**. Often, conflicts arose among neighbors such as Kenya and Tanzania in the 1960's and Nigeria and Ghana in the 1980's. While these rivalries intensified nationalism, they made regional African unity difficult.

Today, most African nations belong to the **Organization for African Unity (OAU)**. It was created in 1963 to help settle disputes and to promote common causes and a common defense of members' independence, but it has been largely ineffective.

CASE STUDIES

In this section, the patterns of emergence of four sub-Saharan African nations are examined: South Africa, Zaire, Nigeria, and Kenya. The case studies provide examples of the different problems facing nations in Africa.

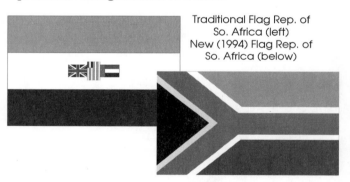

Traditional Flag Rep. of So. Africa (left)
New (1994) Flag Rep. of So. Africa (below)

Numerous **coups d'état** (military overthrows of governments) occurred, and authoritarian military groups seized power from their ineffective leaders.

In 1957, Britain's Gold Coast colony in West Africa became the first sub-Saharan colony to be released from European rule. Its charismatic nationalistic leader, **Kwame Nkrumah**, changed its name to honor the ancient empire of Ghana.

In the next decade, more than 35 African colonies achieved independence. In most, independence came without violence. Many followed Ghana's example taking names associated with great African kingdoms of the past.

Political problems occurred in the new nations. Unaccustomed to participatory democracy, disputes arose. Conflicts flared between tribal groups. For cultural reasons, many villagers had difficulty shifting allegiance from their traditional tribal units to national governments. Over the years this has led to civil war. Recent examples include ethnic violence in Rwanda and Burundi. These East African nations are divided between the Hutu and Tutsi

THE REPUBLIC OF SOUTH AFRICA

HISTORY

The Dutch established a naval outpost at the **Cape of Good Hope** in 1652. Dutch settlers, called Afrikaaners or Boers, expanded it into the **Cape Colony**. The British captured the colony in 1806, during the Napoleonic Wars. Wishing to preserve their Dutch culture, thousands of Boers migrated away from the British to the interior in the "**Great Trek**" of 1836. The Zulu people were overpowered by the Boers after years of fierce resistance. The Boers set up two independent republics: **Transvaal** and **Orange Free State**.

After the discovery of gold and diamonds in the late 1800's, British settlers began to migrate into the Boer territories, touching off skirmishes. They were encouraged by **Cecil Rhodes**, a British imperialist who wished to see a **Cape-to-Cairo Railroad** linking British territories along Africa's east coast. The result was the Boer War (1899 to 1902). Following their victory, the British formed the **Union of South Africa** (1910). It remained a self-governing member of the British Commonwealth until 1961, when it became the independent **Republic of South Africa**.

GOVERNMENT AND ECONOMY

South Africa is a parliamentary republic. It has an administrative capital in **Pretoria** and a legislative capital in **Capetown**. Its economy is one of the most prosperous on the continent. Its principal agricultural products are corn, wheat,  citrus fruits, and wool. Its most important natural resources are gold, diamonds, uranium, asbestos, iron ore, and coal.

RACIAL PROBLEMS

One of the nation's key problems has been "**apartheid**" (the government policy of total racial separation). When Britain took control of South Africa, it continued provisions in the Boer Constitution which supported segregation.

Later, the government instituted additional restrictions on the Bantu people. The ***Native Land Act of 1913*** forbade them to own land outside reservations. In 1950, the ***Groups Area Act*** divided 13% of South Africa's land among ten "homelands" for "coloureds," while the rest

Prior to the Constitutional reforms of the 1990s, apartheid policies supported white dominance and racial injustice.

of the country was reserved for whites. Until 1985, the government pursued a policy of forcibly relocating people to these reservations or "homelands."

In 1913, the **African National Congress (ANC)** began fighting against racial segregation. Well-known leaders against apartheid included Episcopal **Bishop Desmond Tutu** and ANC President **Nelson Mandela**.

Mandela became a symbol of defiance while serving a life prison term for leading anti-apartheid demonstrations in 1961. In 1989, a new reform government under Prime Minister **F. W. de Klerk** announced a more conciliatory policy. Early in 1990, de Klerk freed Mandela and legalized the ANC once again.

International sanctions were placed on the government in support of the anti-apartheid movement. Movements pressured international corporations doing business in South Africa to pull out of the country. Universities and other institutions divested themselves of stocks in these corporations.

The 1990's began on a note of optimism. The government lifted restrictive ***Pass Laws***, allowing peaceful protests, the legal recognition of numerous outlawed opposition groups, and the releasing of many imprisoned anti-apartheid leaders. The old constitution denied 73% of the population voting rights. Blacks could only vote for local leaders of their segregated Bantustan homelands.

In a 1992 referendum, 68% of the white voters agreed to abolish apartheid. In 1993, voters adopted a new constitution guaranteeing political equality. Mandela and de Klerk won the Nobel Peace Prize in 1993. Yet, South Africa's struggle for democracy had only begun. Tribal fighting and riots preceded the nation's first universal elections in 1994. Still, the nation went to the polls in astounding numbers in April 1994. The ANC won a majority of seats in the new all-race Parliament which chose Nelson Mandela South Africa's first black president. Former president de Klerk was elected deputy president. Mandela constructed a 30-member coalition cabinet from leaders of the ANC, de Klerk's nationalists, and Mangoshuthv Buthelezi's Inkatha (Zulu Nationalist) Party.

The cabinet faced problems of housing, employment, health care, and education that were the legacy of past apartheid policies.

ISSUE OF NAMIBIA

After World War I, administration of the former German colony of South-West Africa was given to the Union of South Africa. In 1966, the **South-West Africa People's Organization (SWAPO)**, a communist organization, began a guerrilla war against the South African-backed white minority government. In 1968, *U.N. Resolution 435* named the area Namibia and condemned South African efforts to block independence. Steady pressure from the U.N., the United States, SWAPO, and South African internal problems resulted in the formal withdrawal of the South African colonial government in 1990. Namibia became independent after a United Nations supervised election in 1990.

REPUBLIC OF ZAIRE

HISTORY

An American news correspondent, **Henry Stanley**, discovered the source of the Congo River in 1877 and opened the interior to conquest. Later, acting in service to an independent company headed by **King Leopold II** of Belgium, Stanley returned to make a series of treaties with tribal chieftains. They enabled Leopold to announce a **Congo Free State**. At the Berlin Conference in 1885, he claimed a vast central African area. It was this claim that set off the European "Scramble for Africa."

King Leopold was ruthless in his exploitation of the Congo. The lands were stripped of their raw materials. He levied a "labor tax" on the chieftains. Under it, they had to provide a number of workers every year for forced labor to private companies. The system was known for its excessive cruelty.

Growing criticism of these practices prompted Belgium to take over control of the colony before World War I. Belgium's harsh authoritarian rule provided little preparation of the colony for self-government. After World War II, a nationalist movement gained strength. Violent demonstrations began in the capital causing many European settlers to leave. Fearing a prolonged and costly struggle, Belgium moved rapidly to grant independence in 1960.

The republic's first democratic election was a shamble. Civil war broke out. The U.N. sent troops to keep order. A three-way power struggle began among **Moise Kapenda Tshombe**, **Joseph Kasavubu**, and **Patrice Lumumba**. Lumumba was removed as Premier and began an opposition movement in the southern provinces. Lumumba was killed in 1961.

Three years later, U.N. troops were withdrawn. Tshombe was elected President. Communist rebels began a slaughter in the South that caused the U.N. to enter the country again in 1965. **General Joseph Mobutu** seized control as the rebellion ended. Mobutu ordered "Africanization" of 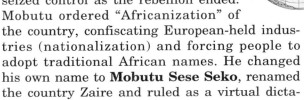 the country, confiscating European-held industries (nationalization) and forcing people to adopt traditional African names. He changed his own name to **Mobutu Sese Seko**, renamed the country Zaire and ruled as a virtual dictator.

The country did not prosper. In 1977, the government invited former industrialists to return, but two rather serious invasions by Angola-backed communist rebels discouraged European resettlement. Political challenges to Mobutu's autocratic rule continued to unsettle the country during the 1990's.

GOVERNMENT AND ECONOMY

Zaire's capital is **Kinshasa**. The country has a one-party republican form of government dominated by a strong executive. Its principal agricultural products are coffee, palm oil, manioc, sugar, cotton, cocoa, and bananas. Zaire is a land rich in mineral resources, and its major economic activities revolve around mining and processing raw materials. Chief among these minerals are cobalt (60% of the world's known supply), copper, zinc, industrial diamonds, tin, gold, silver, iron, and coal.

FEDERAL REPUBLIC OF NIGERIA

HISTORY

Nigeria has a rich history which dates back to the **Nok** culture (c. 700 B.C.). The advanced Mali and Songhai Empires existed there from the 12th to the 14th Centuries when Muslim influence prevailed in its northern region. Portuguese and British slave ships worked the coastal areas in the 15th and 16th Centuries.

By the 18th Century, the British controlled the slave trade. They seized Lagos in 1861. Most of Nigeria came under firm British colonial rule by the early 1900's. The British consolidated northern Muslim states into an administrative region. Still, Nigeria was carefully prepared for independence. The British acknowledged local self-rule after World War I. They set up a central government at Lagos to administer the federated nation. In 1960, Nigeria achieved independence and became a member of the British Commonwealth of Nations.

The Nigerian constitution guarantees respect for political, religious, and cultural differences among its many ethnic (tribal) groups. However, open hostility developed in the mid-1960's. Two coups and a series of political assassinations brought Nigeria's fragile federation to the brink of civil war.

In May 1967, the Eastern region, dominated by the **Ibo** people, seceded from the federation. It declared itself the **Republic of Biafra**. A civil war erupted which lasted two and a half years. Hundreds of thousands lost their lives from fighting and famine. The Ibo people finally surrendered in January 1970. The national government promised protection and restoration of political rights for all people.

In the 1970's, Nigeria's economic policy aimed at controlling its industrial, banking, and commercial interests and making the nation agriculturally self-sufficient. In 1979, it peacefully returned to civilian rule with a new constitution and competing political parties. For the last decade, succession of military coups destabilized the government, but a policy of modified socialism continued.

With over 100 million people, Nigeria has the largest population in Africa. It continues to rely on oil revenues for its economic and social improvements. Much of its overseas business is with the U.S. Nigeria is one of the few African nations to protest the communist nations' military advisors present in Africa. Today, Nigeria seeks to promote African unity.

ECONOMY

While Nigeria produces a variety of agricultural products from cacao to cotton and palm oil, petroleum has become the mainstay of its economy. (Most of the petroleum is traded to the United States and Britain.) Nigeria's major problem is its rapid population growth. (Current projections indicate it will reach 500 million by 2030.) Soil erosion, lack of productivity, desertification in the north, and a foreign trade tied to changeable oil prices all make the economic future seem questionable.

REPUBLIC OF KENYA

HISTORY

Several maritime city-states existed as early as the 8th Century in Kenya. **Faza** and **Mombasa** on the Indian Ocean conducted a spice and slave trade with Arab countries. In the colonial movement of the late 19th Century, Kenya came under the rule of Great Britain. The British developed the highland region with its rich agricultural farmland and pleasant climate. By the end of World War II, there were over 30,000 British settlers in this region.

Kenya's largest tribal group, the **Kikuyu**, resented this intrusion and organized a secret society to spread terrorism against the white farmers. Known to British settlers as the **Mau Mau**, the society's tactics to regain its lost lands were bloody and brutal. Yet, the society became the core of a strong nationalist independence movement. In over a decade, more than 12,000 people were killed before the British broke the movement in 1956.

The leader and hero of this nationalist movement among the Kikuyu was **Jomo Kenyatta**. He was jailed by the British for allegedly organizing the Mau Mau. Kenyatta denied these charges to the day he died.

In 1961, Kenyatta was released from prison, and the British agreed to majority rule for Kenya. In 1963, Britain granted Kenya independence. Kenyatta became the nation's first president. Under Kenyatta's leadership, European ownership of land and Indian control of commerce was phased out, and black Kenyans filled these positions. Kenyatta's power declined before his death in 1978.

At first, President **Daniel Moi's** regime allowed political freedom. Later, he began to use the military to silence opposition.

ECONOMY

Kenya's capital is **Nairobi**, a city of over one million people. It is located in the cooler western highland region of the nation. Kenya's economy is primarily agricultural. Coffee, tea, cotton, and sisal are exported to the rest of the world. There are limited amounts of natural resources including gold, limestone, sapphires, garnets, salt, and feldspar. Other economic resources include timber, hides, beef and lamb production, fishing, light industry, and tourism. Kenya has close economic ties to Western nations, but recent loan defaults by its government have jeopardized its future.

CULTURAL AND SOCIAL IMPACT OF THE WEST

The cultural impact of Western society on Africa has been significant in the latter half of the 20th Century as witnessed in the numerous changes in African life styles and world views. Also, European and American **ethnocentrism** (proclaiming one's own race or culture as superior) alienated many Africans. It caused them to search for their own heritage and to develop their own unique cultural identity.

The development of large towns and urban centers lures Africans from their tribal villages.

The modern city of Nairobi, Kenya

David Johnson, 1993

Migration weakens traditional lineage and kinship bonds. As Africans adapt to new ways, a transitional period occurs. People question the usefulness of the new ideas and institutions. The new ideas of nationalism and politics, technology, medicine, and religion pressure today's urban African to give up former tribal ways. This often creates generational conflicts in which the young reexamine and often discard former (tribal) traditions. **Extended families** (three or more generations under one roof) are no longer the norm in the towns and cities. The **nuclear family** (mother, father, and children) has replaced this traditional clan structure.

Today, many African couples practice family planning and limit themselves to only one or two children. This diminishes the lineage bond and the power of tribal chiefs. Also, the traditional practice of **polygamy** (having two or more wives) declined after World War I. **Monogamy** is more widely practiced in the urban areas.

The changing role of women is very evident in today's African urban centers. About 25% of urban African women are involved politically. Today, African women often pursue careers in medicine, education, law, and technology. Many rural village women, especially among Muslims, lead lives that are still centered at home. Yet, even in tradition bound villages, many women are assuming roles of equality.

As the hubs of government and industry, urban centers are also the centers of significant change in Africa. World views, gained through trade and telecommunications, influence people in the cities. As new generations of Africans

David Johnson, 1993

The Wolof people, Keur Mibarick Village, Senegal

TECHNOLOGY

grow up in urban centers, their education and experiences pull them further from the traditional ways. They are more interested in personal careers and national and international events than the life styles of ancestors in old tribal villages.

AFRICAN LIFE IN TRANSITION

African life is in transition. Still, the rural areas retain their traditional values. People have fierce loyalties to councils of elders and local chiefs. They still practice subsistence agriculture where family members learn to work together for the good of the whole group. Food is shared equally within the group whether the harvest is good or bad.

The group teaches children the importance of the family by sharing in the care of younger children or the elderly. They learn farming, fishing, herding, or trade skills. Initiation ceremonies, with elaborate rituals, signal the end of childhood and the beginning of adulthood. Such passage rituals strengthen tribal bonds.

Women have an important role in the tribal tradition. Women work in the fields besides sharing motherhood and household chores. They assume the task of preparing the next generation in the lineage system. Young girls have marriages that are prearranged by their families.

Today, new attitudes and values constantly clash with traditional tribal practices. Modern technology has found its way to the rural areas. Increased education, better communication (TV, radio, movies, and news media), and continual influence from the outside world place enormous pressure on traditional ways.

It remains to be seen how rapidly new attitudes and values will be accepted. Which ones will be assimilated and culturally diffused into a new life style is one of Africa's great challenges.

QUESTIONS

1 Which individual is correctly paired with the colonial area with which he was associated?
   1   Joseph Mobutu — Nigeria
   2   King Leopold — Transvaal
   3   Cecil Rhodes — Zaire
   4   Henry Stanley — Congo

2 The policy of apartheid in South Africa was
   1   imposed by the British after World War II
   2   advocated by the descendents of the Dutch
   3   proposed by Bantu leaders
   4   introduced by communists

3 A nuclear family consists of
   1   the bride, groom, and in-laws
   2   father, mother, and children
   3   several generations living under one roof
   4   all the people of the tribe

4 Tribal initiation ceremonies commonly occur
   1   at marriage
   2   between childhood and adulthood
   3   when a child is born
   4   when an elder makes a major decision

5 Once the scene of a brutal war between the British and Boer settlers, which country suffered from strife over racial inequality?
1 Zimbabwe
2 Nigeria
3 Republic of South Africa
4 Zaire

6 The custom of African men having two or more wives is called
1 monogamy
2 nepotism
3 polygamy
4 ethnocentrism

7 The Organization for African Unity (OAU) is best defined as an association
1 strictly for colonial powers
2 strictly for free trade
3 for settling disputes
4 for urban dwellers

8 Early African nationalist leaders were looked upon by their peoples as
1 terrorists
2 emancipators
3 social discriminators
4 traditionalists

9 The *United Nations Charter* helped promote nationhood for the former African colonies because it supported
1 self-determination
2 tribal religion
3 colonialism
4 imperialism

10 The first sub-Saharan African colony to achieve independence after World War II was
1 Nigeria
2 Kenya
3 Zaire
4 Ghana

11 Which situation is most similar to the practice of apartheid in the Republic of South Africa?
1 establishment of official state religions in Europe
2 economic oppression bringing about the American Revolution
3 government censorship of the press in communist nations
4 segregation laws in southern states in the U.S. (1860's -1960's)

12 The most heavily populated nation in Africa today is
1 South Africa
2 Zaire
3 Nigeria
4 Kenya

13 In the 1960's, U.N. forces were twice brought into this nation suffering from a violent civil war
1 Zaire
2 Kenya
3 Republic of South Africa
4 Orange Free State

ESSAYS

1 Imperialism in the 19th Century set the stage for continuing conflict in the 20th century. Describe how *three* of the following have affected African nations after European colonial rule ended.

- Tribal ties
- Coups d'état
- Nationalism
- Urbanization
- Race relations
- Technology
- Pan-Africanism
- The United Nations
- The (British) Commonwealth of Nations

2 The dramatic pace of urbanization in Africa in the last half of the 20th Century has caused African life to change significantly.

Aspects of African Life

- Status of women
- Tribalism
- Agriculture
- Education
- Religion

Choose *three* of the aspects of African life listed above. For *each* one chosen describe how it has been affected by urbanization.

IV. ECONOMIC DEVELOPMENT

Most African nations have achieved political independence. Still, most are **LDCs** (Less Developed Countries), and many obstacles remain for the countries searching for national unity and economic self-determination. Rapid population growth and its accompanying poverty cycle hamper economic and social development. Also, internal and external political and social forces undermine freedom and stability.

Rapid urban growth is one source of the problems that have emerged. Studying the problems, it also becomes evident that the new nations remain dependent on the Western World for trade, foreign aid, and food supplements. This dependency demoralizes and embitters relations with the industrialized nations of the world.

ECONOMIC INDEPENDENCE

When African nations were freed from colonial domination, most of the trained people in technical, business, and management positions were non-African. Most returned to their European homelands. Africa's new leaders realized that their nations' economies remained dependent on European markets. They had to seek new markets and create new industries. This required extensive capital investment. The prospect of going into debt to foreign lending institutions brought fear of **neocolonialism** (a new outside control of African life).

For this reason, much economic aid has been sent from international monetary agencies such as the World Bank and the European Union (Common Market). In this way, one nation does not overly influence the new nations' affairs. Still, banks and export companies of former colonial powers remain entrenched in many African nations.

Some African nations offer favorable incentives (cheap labor, tax breaks, and plentiful raw materials) to **multinational corporations** (major businesses that are involved in many nations) to attract investment and business.

URBAN INDUSTRIAL DEVELOPMENT

African nations have quickly learned that **subsistence agriculture** (producing for one's own basic needs) does not lead to economic growth. The result has been state-run corporations in urban areas. As population shifts from the countryside to the urban industrial centers, a labor force of skilled and semi-skilled workers emerges. A middle class develops, but many of these people have difficulty in finding adequate housing.

RECENT DROUGHT CONDITIONS

Agricultural failures and severe water shortages plagued nations of the **Sahel Region** (a drought-stricken area of West Central Africa) during the last two decades. Many nations that had sufficient food

Mossi women with traditional cultivation tools outside of Biba village, the Toma region, Burkina Faso

David Johnson, 1992

supplies are now dependent on food imports. This further drained limited investment capital, preventing significant development.

MIXED ECONOMIC SYSTEMS

Since independence, conflicting ideological and economic goals have created mixed economic systems. In **mixed systems**, elements of government control combine with free enterprise. Former colonial powers pressed new nations to adopt free enterprise market systems. In the 1970's and early 1980's, the Soviet Union, Cuba, and other communist nations offered aid to African countries following **authoritarian socialism** (strict government command).

Tanzania and Ethiopia adopted socialist economies. They promoted cooperation in nationalized industries by sharing profits with the work force. Yet, government controlled agricultural cooperatives and state controlled industries and marketing caused severe economic problems. Widespread shortages of vital goods and services occurred. Both now try to attract foreign firms, promising to renew efforts to achieve free enterprise and private ownership.

Other African nations such as Kenya and Nigeria reluctantly accepted programs of assistance from their former colonial masters and developed mixed socialist-capitalist economies.

More recently, the U.S. has assumed a greater role as a trading partner. For example, the U.S. buys almost 60% of Nigeria's oil. In most instances, cultural and ethnic diversity and nationalism limit efforts at regional economic cooperation or Pan-African cooperation.

The Republic of South Africa has the strongest and most diversified economy in Africa. Yet, South Africa's long history of racial and ethnic conflict serves as a major roadblock to economic growth. In the 1980's, many outside governments and multinational corporations debated **boycotting** South African goods and **divesting** their financial interests to bring pressure against the apartheid policy. As government changes and civil disturbances erupt, investors shy away and development slows.

David Johnson, 1992

Young Kapoata-Toposa child carries meager ration of corn home to the family – Southern Sudan

POPULATION PROBLEMS

Overpopulation is another serious economic condition that contributes to widespread poverty. Nations such as Nigeria  and Kenya have extremely high population growth rates. Traditional beliefs and pressures for large families in subsistence agricultural areas contribute to population growth. Families need children to work in the fields or tend the herds. In these areas, parents also look upon children as "social security" – a support system for their old age.

Many rural areas still lack access to proper educational and health services. Africans migrate to urban areas in search of employment opportunities. Yet, demand far exceeds the number of jobs, putting an additional burden on the cities.

Modern medicine has decreased infant mortality and increased life expectancy. This has led African population growth rates to be among the highest in the world. Agricultural production has not kept pace with this growth. The problem of hunger adds to the woes of the developing nations.

HUNGER & POVERTY

AGRICULTURE AND FOOD SUPPLY

All nations must manage the problem of maintaining an adequate balance between population and food supplies. Yet, the African LDCs face the dilemma of scarce food resources and high prices on imported food and other goods. African governments devote much of their time coping with this serious problem.

In African LDCs, the tremendous population growth has surpassed the growth in food production. Nations which once exported agricultural products now must import food.

IMPORTED AND DOMESTIC CROPS

African nations have three distinctly different types of farming: subsistence farming, cash crop farming (agricultural products sold to the urban areas and exported), and **mixed farming** (combination of subsistence and herding). The dominant exports are palm oil, coffee, tea, cacao, cotton, peanuts, and sisal (used for rope and cord).

Many African LDCs rely on only one or two cash crops. This can be a dangerous practice for a nation. Poor weather, a bad harvest, or falling prices in the world market, can easily bankrupt a nation's economy.

Families pickup their monthly allotment of corn at the Torit relief warehouse, Southern Sudan

To sell their surplus in the world market place, Africans must learn to make their land more productive and diversify their products. One hope was the scientific breakthroughs in agriculture of the 1960's, the **Green Revolution**. It encouraged new African nations to use improved seeds, fertilizers, and modern farm machinery to increase crop production.

Yet, the Green Revolution met resistance. Many traditional farmers were reluctant to change, especially when the new methods required an additional expense. Still, without change, the land cannot yield the surplus needed. The surplus is more than extra food. It must provide the capital needed for further development.

Most of the African nations are dependent on food subsidies from grain surpluses of the Western world. African diets have often been altered by this recent trend of food imports. African nations must take what is provided as foreign aid or purchase the least expensive foodstuffs. This often leads to a lack of proper nutrition and to medical problems.

DESERTIFICATION

Severe soil erosion in an area called the "Sahel" in West Africa accelerates the process of **desertification** (loss of available land to the desert). Combined with the severe drought in Mauritania, Mali, Niger, and Chad, this brought widespread starvation and death to the region's people and herds.

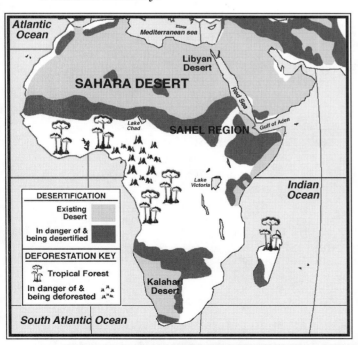

Atlantic Ocean
Mediterranean sea
Libyan Desert
SAHARA DESERT
Red Sea
Lake Chad
SAHEL REGION Gulf of Aden
Lake Victoria
Indian Ocean

DESERTIFICATION
Existing Desert
In danger of & being desertified

DEFORESTATION KEY
Tropical Forest
In danger of & being deforested
Kalahari Desert
South Atlantic Ocean

ENVIRONMENTAL CONCERNS

Near Keur Mibarick, Senegal, desertification
turned this once productive farmland dry and unusable.

ized countries to tradition-based agricultural systems in Africa is difficult.

Before African LDCs can achieve economic self-sufficiency, they must overcome all these barriers. Continued overpopulation, coupled with scarce food resources, is a major concern. Technical training and financial assistance must be brought in from the outside world to develop natural resources.

Urban growth must be controlled, or there will be a continuing breakdown of services and alienation of the people. African nations must find solutions to these problems in their own way while they search for national unity.

The disaster was not entirely created by nature. The region's farmers and nomads traditionally over-cut trees for firewood. They also maintained excessive camel, goat, sheep, and cattle herds which overgrazed the limited grasslands. They also over-cultivated the limited arable land. The local ecological balance was pushed beyond its limits. Accelerated desertification created a land unsuitable for human existence.

ADDITIONAL AGRICULTURAL PROBLEMS

African governments fail to provide enough financial incentives to their agricultural producers. In many cases, they created state-run monopolies that fostered an expensive and unproductive bureaucracy. Profits realized through improved agricultural production were often absorbed by these government officials. They rarely filter down to the farmers.

Also, in many areas there is a scarcity of water. Water retention projects such as irrigation and well drilling are costly. Thus, applying agricultural technology from the industrial-

RAPID URBANIZATION

The urbanization process in Africa provides a prime example of the ill effects of accelerated population growth in LDCs. Massive unemployment leads to shanty towns and poverty. It widens the gulf of inequality between wealthy and poor. In the early 19th Century, about three percent of the world's population lived in metro-

Locals work to slow the spread of the desert by building
a water retention dam – Yako, Burkina Faso Water Project.

Another problem is that rural workers lack the skills associated with modern industrial technology. This has caused high unemployment, and forced many migrants into slum areas. Within sight of these depressing shanty towns are thriving business districts and wealthy neighborhoods. This intensifies class divisions within the societies.

As long as cities continue to be the industrial hubs and the government centers for new nations, as well as the centers of modernity and change, it will be very difficult to control population shifts from rural to urban areas.

African youth was once content to live the traditional life of the rural regions. Today, young people face decisions about moving to the cities and gambling their futures on the opportunities (such as education, economic

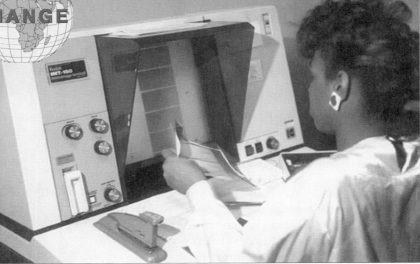

PhotoDisc Inc. 1993

PhotoDisc Inc. 1993

Change in Africa: Culture and traditional skills clash with modern technology and education.

politan regions. By the 21st Century, experts predict that more than fifty percent will live in cities.

African cities have a staggering growth rate. Along with the industrial economic development of the colonial era, nationalist leaders built impressive but sometimes useless modern buildings and services. They wished to showcase their achievements but ignored more basic economic reform. The waves of migrants drawn from rural areas continue to flood the cities searching for scarce jobs. This migration has created severe urban congestion and strained essential services (transportation, housing, sewage, etc.).

and social mobility). Their new mobility and rapid urbanization breaks down traditional social structures. The new urban dwellers encounter a culture that is very **cosmopolitan** (a wide mixture of cultural traits). This often results in personal identity crises, alienation, and frustration.

QUESTIONS

1   Neocolonialism results from the lack of
    1   development capital
    2   consumer industries
    3   religion
    4   aid for rural migrants

2   Desertification is caused by
    1   flooding of low-lying plains
    2   overgrazing, deforestation, and over-cultivating
    3   strip mining for gold
    4   over-mechanization

3   A new middle class in modern-day Africa consists of
    1   former tribal chieftains
    2   a military elite
    3   skilled urban laborers
    4   rural farmers

4   The Sahel is a region in Africa that over the past two decades experienced
    1   widespread drought
    2   massive earthquakes
    3   devastating floods
    4   extensive volcanic eruptions

5   One form of socialism recognizable in new African nations can be seen in
    1   the African Common Market
    2   the use of the American corporate form of business organization
    3   governmentally controlled economic development
    4   numerous collective farms and communes

6   Lower birth rates occur among the middle class of developing nations because
    1   governments offer couples financial incentives to limit families
    2   educational programs on family planning have become available
    3   tribal religions encourage modesty
    4   traditional extended family bonds are strong

7   A major reason for widespread overpopulation in developing African nations is
    1   a higher life expectancy rate
    2   government's subsidizing of larger families
    3   improved birth control
    4   poor medical facilities

8   A major cause of shanty towns has been
    1   a breakdown of essential urban services
    2   increased employment in cities
    3   increased social mobility
    4   the rural to urban population shifts

9   In new African nations, traces of colonial institutions remain most noticeably in
    1   rural areas
    2   banking industry
    3   military forces
    4   government bureaucracy

ESSAYS

1   Africa's economic development is tied to a number of conflicts.

Conflicts
- Traditional agriculture v. the Green Revolution
- Traditional values v. urbanization
- Independence v. close ties with former colonial powers
- Over-grazing v. desertification
- Socialist systems v. capitalist systems

Choose *three* of the above conflicts and discuss how *each* one affects the economic development of African nations.

2   Overpopulation in many newer African nations has contributed to widespread poverty.

a   Describe the causes of overpopulation in one specific African nation.

b   Explain how urbanization affects the population problem.

c   Show how the problems discussed in *a* and *b* affect African agriculture.

V. GLOBAL CONTEXT

The major global powers exert strong influence on Africa. It is very difficult for African nations to maintain policies of **nonalignment** (refusing to always be on the same side in all issues). The strategic location, vast size, and valuable resources of the African Continent are of global importance. Also, a large number of the nations are LDCs. They must seek capital and markets from among the developed nations. The complexity of the political, ethnic, and ancestral divisions throughout Africa makes the region even more volatile in a global context.

ALLIANCES AND LINKAGES

Many African nations maintain close diplomatic ties with the western world because of their persistent economic problems. Africans have to do a difficult balancing act among the eager industrial powers of the world. Modern African leaders realize that cooperation can insure their survival and progress.

1975 LOME (TOGO) CONVENTION

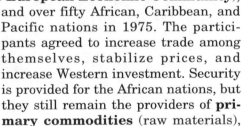

This promising economic trade agreement was signed by the **European Union** (formerly called the **European Economic Community**), and over fifty African, Caribbean, and Pacific nations in 1975. The participants agreed to increase trade among themselves, stabilize prices, and increase Western investment. Security is provided for the African nations, but they still remain the providers of **primary commodities** (raw materials), not finished products. In essence, they sell raw materials at low prices and then buy back finished products at high prices. A losing proposition.

THE GATT

African nations participate in the **GATT** (General Agreement on Trade and Tariffs). It is an ongoing U.N. – sponsored treaty series intended to create fair and equal international trade. It has not always favored LDCs. The 1993 negotiations in Switzerland brought major changes in the agreement. New provisions appear promising for Africa. They will eliminate unfair **tariffs** (import taxes) and should break down tax barriers to increased international investments in LDCs.

THE BRITISH COMMONWEALTH

Many of the former colonies such as Nigeria maintain close economic and cultural ties with Britain. More than a dozen nations use English as their official language. Most have joined the **Commonwealth of Nations** (a worldwide organization of former British colonies). It gives them the cooperative benefits of favorable trade agreements and shared social programs. Yet, Britain's internal problems have weakened the organization in recent decades.

THE UNITED NATIONS

African nations make up more than 33% of the U.N.'s members. This gives African nations a powerful voice and voting bloc in the General Assembly. The United Nations goal of self-determination for all peoples and its strong position on human rights encourages the emerging nations of Africa.

U.N. economic, educational, and social agencies provide assistance to African LDCs. Also, the African nations have used the United Nations as a world forum to insure that their needs are met by the wealthier nations of the world. U.N. financial agencies such as the **World Bank** and **International Monetary Fund** (**IMF**) provide loans and technical assistance for economic development in most African nations. They often arrange private investment for developing nations to co-finance major projects.

ORGANIZATION OF PETROLEUM EXPORTING COUNTRIES (OPEC)

OPEC (Organization of Petroleum Exporting Countries) is a global oil **cartel** (an association of global members which seeks to alter commerce in its favor). In the 1970's and early 1980's, it was successful in determining world oil prices and in promoting trade with the oil-dependent Western world. Nigeria and Gabon are two sub-Saharan nations which belong to this thirteen-nation group. In recent years, internal disagreements, realignments of power, energy conservation, and development of non-OPEC oil supplies have made the group less powerful.

FOREIGN INTERFERENCE

Even after independence in the 1950's and 1960's, peace did not always come immediately. The deep loyalties of certain nations led to direct foreign involvement in the new countries' internal affairs by the major powers. (The Zaire profile in Section III is a good example of this.) Others include:

FRANCE AND ITS FORMER COLONIES

France granted independence to most of its African colonies in the early 1960's. It gave assurance that it would not meddle in the new nation's domestic affairs. However, the French offered to assist their former colonies in foreign affairs and with finances and defense.

In Chad, a civil war erupted in 1966 between Northern Muslim rebels with close ties to Libya and their Southern Christian and **animist** (natural religion) countrymen. France sent troops to assist the Southern forces and restore order. Libya and Chad announced their intentions to unite in 1981. France led neighboring African nations in condemning the union. In 1983, France sent over 3,000 troops to Chad to stop Libyan-backed rebels. France and Libya continue to back different sides in the unstable situation.

COLD WAR RIVALRIES

Because of the presence of European colonial governments, African colonies became involved in both World Wars. After World War II, Europe involved Africa in the struggles of the Cold War between the Soviet Union and the Western democracies. As the African colonies moved toward independence, they became sites for the Cold War power struggles. The major communist nations at the time (China, U.S.S.R.) sent aid to communist groups in the newly emerging nations.

Into the 1990's, communist regimes still exist in several African nations, Angola, for one. This former Portuguese colony received its independence in 1974. A political power struggle grew into a full-scale civil war. The Soviets and Cubans backed a communist "Popular Movement." South Africa, the U.S., and European democracies backed the "National Union." During the 14-year war, the National Union became the **UNITA** guerrilla fighters, led by **Jonas Savimbi**. The Reagan administration gave $15 million dollars to Savimbi's cause. The two sides worked out a fragile truce in 1991. Savimbi lost a U.N.-supervised election in 1992 to José Eduardo dos Santos.

Another Cold War battleground involved the Horn of East Africa. In the drought-plagued nation of Ethiopia, the Soviet-backed communists overthrew the pro-Western Emperor Haile Selassie in 1974. The Soviets also backed a communist regime in neighboring Somalia. In the late 1970's, a territorial dispute erupted between Somalia and Ethiopia. Soviet and Cuban forces helped Ethiopia hold its Ogaden Province. In retaliation, Somalia expelled the Soviet and Cuban advisors and accepted U.S. aid. U.S. arms fell into the hands of local Somali warlords. They terrorized the countryside until the government collapsed in 1991. President Bush sent U.S. forces to assist the U.N. in relieving terrible famine resulting from the civil war. In 1993-94, the U.S. withdrew its forces after the warlords turned on the peacekeeping efforts. By 1994 the U.N. was working toward an uneasy truce in a national council made up of former warlords.

U.S. – AFRICAN RELATIONS

During the 1960's, American Presidents Kennedy and Johnson openly encouraged self-determination for all African peoples with financial aid and developmental assistance. Kennedy began the **Peace Corps** that continues to send volunteers to aid the development of educational, agricultural, and industrial programs.

American philanthropy has always been evident in Africa and is most noteworthy in the **Food for Peace Program**. It helped feed many nations faced with the prospects of massive starvation. Also, many promising African scholars were provided with tuition-free study at American universities. Most of the Americans serving in African nations are volunteers, not government officials. These volunteers serve in the spirit of humanitarian need, and it is through these people that a better understanding may be made between the U.S. and their African host nations.

In the tense years of the Cold War, the United States provided military aid to pro-western leaders throughout Africa. It built military communications bases in Kenya, Liberia, and Somalia. Pro-Western forces in the Congo (Zaire), Nigeria, and Angola received American military aid.

Racial discrimination has caused the largest strain in American-African relations. When photographs and stories of African Americans suffering discrimination in the U.S. are shown in the newspapers of Africa, it causes many Africans to think of the U.S. as a racist nation.

Fortunately, many African leaders have noticed the progress that has been made in American race relations. Some have been impressed that American democracy provides the mechanism to peacefully remedy injustice. Those feelings were reinforced when American businesses divested their interest in the Republic of South Africa as a protest against the past white government's racial policies.

AFRICA IN WORLD AFFAIRS

African nations are historically linked to the different world views of the West and the Third World. They are caught in the middle and unable to remain truly neutral. Most new nations chose non-alignment but were caught in global conflicts.

Their national policies stress a form of economic development which seeks full employment for Africans in agriculture  and industry. They must follow policies that bring direct benefits to their nation. They resent supporting the corporate economics of a multi-national corporations. It is a difficult balancing act. Capital for initial investment is often provided by such foreign investors. Developing the "keep-out-but-help-me" attitude is perplexing and, at times, irritating to the outside corporate world.

Increased sensitivity to racial issues must be a concern for any of the world's nations when becoming involved with African nations. Respect for human equality and human rights is the basic beginning to develop any relationship. These lofty aspirations contribute to peace and the development of the African nations.

The African Continent and its nations are strategically important to the entire world. The complex issues of racial policy and economic development must be addressed through masterful diplomacy. At present, the United Nations serves as the main international forum for African concerns.

QUESTIONS

1 Most African nations have foreign policies that favor non-alignment because they want to
  1   receive aid from only the communist world
  2   avoid entangling alliances
  3   remain loyal to their former European colonizers
  4   avoid a policy of neutrality

2 The Lome Convention in 1975 was a meeting of European, African, Caribbean, and Pacific nations which concentrated on
  1   education
  2   defense budgets
  3   trade agreements
  4   medical advances

3 The Commonwealth is a group of nations that are former British colonies which share
  1   extensive Christian missionary work
  2   the apartheid policies in South Africa
  3   a mutual defense alliance
  4   social and economic programs

4 What percent of U.N. members are African?
  1   twenty-five percent
  2   sixty-seven percent
  3   fifty percent
  4   thirty-three percent

5 Which sub-Saharan African nation belongs to OPEC?
  1   Republic of South Africa
  2   Somalia
  3   Angola
  4   Nigeria

6 African nations need loans from the World Bank and the International Monetary Fund because they want
  1   to build up military defenses
  2   capital for economic development
  3   to strengthen their ties with colonial powers
  4   to attract highly skilled professionals for their bureaucracies

7 During the Cold War, the U.S. sent aid to groups in Africa to
  1   spread Islam
  2   promote apartheid
  3   resist communism
  4   assure neutrality

8 The U.S. successfully used the Peace Corps in Africa to assist
  1   anti-communists guerrillas in local civil wars
  2   in developing native literature and art
  3   in educational, agricultural, and industrial development
  4   in developing a new form of military alliance

9 Which subject has caused the greatest strain in U. S. and African relations?
  1   repayment of loans
  2   the Peace Corps
  3   the Food for Peace Program
  4   the issue of racism

ESSAY

1 During the 1960's and 1970's, communism made steady inroads in Africa as nationalist leaders leaned favorably toward Marxism.

a Explain what aspects of this political philosophy were attractive to the Africans.

b Select *two* nations below and explain why communism had such a significant impact on the leadership of each.

   Nations
- Angola
- Ethiopia
- Somalia
- Tanzania
- Zaire

UNIT ONE: AFRICA ASSESSMENT

ISSUE: HUMAN RIGHTS

This evaluation offers individual library research and cooperative group analysis opportunities.

STUDENT TASK

Participate in designing, publicizing, and presenting a school display / demonstration on human rights in South Africa.

DETAILED PROCEDURES

Part One:

A. Submit a design for a library display / demonstration on the issue of human rights in South Africa. In a properly written plan:

    1 identify the content and the reasons for including it

    2 list all materials to be used in detail

    3 give details of all visual, written, and oral parts of the display / demonstration.

B. Present the plan to a group set up by instructor. The group evaluates individual plans. It combines elements from participants to fashion a group plan.

Part Two:

Instructor reviews group plans and selects one. Selected group sets up the display with the aid of the librarian and receives grade for participation.

Part Three:

Remainder of class groups produce the promotional aspects for the class's display / demonstration in the library. (Examples: handbills, public address announcements, posters, school newspaper articles, etc.)

EVALUATION

The scoring grid next to the evaluation items (on the following page) was left blank intentionally. Choice of appropriate category terms is the decision of the instructor. Selection of terms such as "minimal," "satisfactory," and "distinguished" can vary with this assessment. The table on page 10 offers additional suggestions for scoring descriptors that might be inserted in the blank grids.

LEARNING STANDARDS

Students should:

- Present ideas both in writing and orally in clear, concise, and properly accepted fashion.

- Understand that different national, ethnic, religious, racial, socioeconomic, and gender groups have varied perspectives on the same events and issues.

- Analyze and evaluate differing views of historic, social, cultural, economic, and political events, eras, ideas, and issues.

- Employ a variety of information from written, graphic, and multimedia sources activities.

- Understand that the ideals of democratic principles and human rights constantly evolve in the light of global realities.

- Work cooperatively and respect the rights of others to think, act, and speak differently from themselves within the context of democratic principles and social justice.

- Demonstrate civic values and socially responsible behavior as members of school groups, local, state, national, and global communities.

Part One (B) Peer Group Rating of Individual Plans

Table on page 10 offers suggestions for scoring descriptors.

Evaluation Item a Does plan identify and organize a variety of materials to convey problems?	Category 1	Category 2	Category 3	Category 4	Category 5
Evaluation Item b Does plan approach problems from many perspectives?	Category 1	Category 2	Category 3	Category 4	Category 5
Evaluation Item c Is the plan written clearly and effectively?	Category 1	Category 2	Category 3	Category 4	Category 5

Part Two: Instructor Rating of Group Plans

Table on page 10 offers suggestions for scoring descriptors.

Evaluation Item a Does group proposal clarify understanding of human rights issues?	Category 1	Category 2	Category 3	Category 4	Category 5
Evaluation Item b Does group proposal combine variety of presentation types for an appealing display?	Category 1	Category 2	Category 3	Category 4	Category 5
Evaluation Item c Is group proposal realistic, given available resources?	Category 1	Category 2	Category 3	Category 4	Category 5

Part Three: Peer/Instructor Rating of Promotions

Table on page 10 offers suggestions for scoring descriptors.

Evaluation Item a How informative are announcements and promotional materials?	Category 1	Category 2	Category 3	Category 4	Category 5
Evaluation Item b Are announcements and promotional materials graphically and verbally stimulating?	Category 1	Category 2	Category 3	Category 4	Category 5

ADMINISTRATIVE GUIDELINES

1   Survey library resources and discuss project with librarian and any other staff members that may be involved.

2   Arrange library time for students to explore display/ demonstration resources.

3   Discuss with class the range of media resources available. Discuss research procedures to follow in library session(s).

4   Set up student groups (Part One, B). Guide groups in evaluating individual display / demonstration plans .

5   Instructor option: involve students (and other staff) in selecting final display/ demonstration (Part Two).

6   Arrange with librarian for students to assemble, construct, and manage the display / demonstration.

7   Supervise class groups in taping of announcements, drawing of posters, and other promotions presented under Part Three while display group is involved in setting up display.

8   Instructor option: use peer rating of final display, or instructor can rate and issue a special portfolio commendation for participants in the final library display / demonstration.

2

Gandhi
monsoons   *castes*
Buddhism   *Hinduism*
non–alignment   *Himalayas*
mixed economy   *overpopulation*
self–government   *Green Revolution*

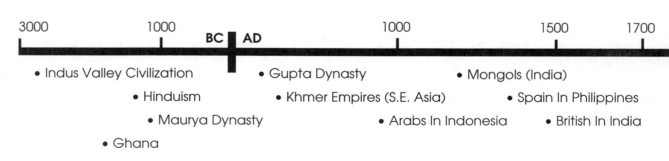

3000   1000   BC | AD   1000   1500   1700

- Indus Valley Civilization   • Gupta Dynasty   • Mongols (India)
    • Hinduism   • Khmer Empires (S.E. Asia)   • Spain In Philippines
    • Maurya Dynasty   • Arabs In Indonesia   • British In India
        • Ghana

Time-line is not drawn to scale.

South
& Southeast
Asia

1800	1900	1945	1965	2000

- Dutch Take Indonesia
- U.S. Takes Philippines
- French Take Indochina
- Gandhi's Independence Movement
- WW II
- India & Pakistan Independence
- French Defeated In Indochina
- Philippine Independence
- U.S. – Vietnam War •
- E. Pakistan Becomes Bangladesh

Time-line is not drawn to scale.

UNIT TWO:

S. & S.E. ASIA

This region stretches between the Persian Gulf and the Pacific Ocean. This vast southern portion of the continent of Asia encompasses a wide variety of people and cultures. It can be studied in two subsections: **South Asian Subcontinent**, in which the large nation of India will be the focus, and **Southeast Asia**, with seven nations on its large peninsula and two extensive island nations off its coasts.

I. PHYSICAL AND HISTORICAL SETTING

SOUTH ASIAN SUBCONTINENT

The South Asian Subcontinent's geographic characteristics and location had an enormous influence on the cultures and economies of this area. Today, it is the site of two large nations (Pakistan and India) and four smaller ones (Bangladesh, Bhutan, Nepal, and Sri Lanka). The area is a huge peninsula, jutting into the Indian Ocean with the Arabian Sea on the west and the Bay of Bengal on the east.

The South Asian Subcontinent is north of the equator, and its climate is generally of the "C" Type (Mid-Latitude Rainy). The major physical features of the region have a considerable effect on the climate.

The world's highest mountains, the **Himalayas**, extend 1,500 miles (2,414 km) along the northern reaches of the South Asian Subcontinent in three parallel ranges. **Summer monsoons** (prevailing summer winds) blow northeastward off the Indian Ocean, depositing a large amount of precipitation (see map pg. 60). The mountain barriers capture the rain. The water drains into three major river systems: the **Brahmaputra**, **Ganges**, and **Indus**. The **winter monsoons** blow southward from the dry Asian interior. While cooler, these winds are very dry.

South of the Himalayas, the **Indo-Gangetic Plain** spreads from Pakistan to Bangladesh. It has fertile, **alluvial soil** (rich in minerals) produced by the steady summer monsoon drainage off the mountains.

The **Deccan Plateau** occupies most of the central peninsula area. It holds much of India's

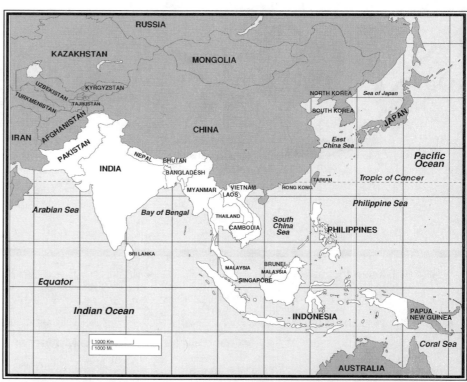

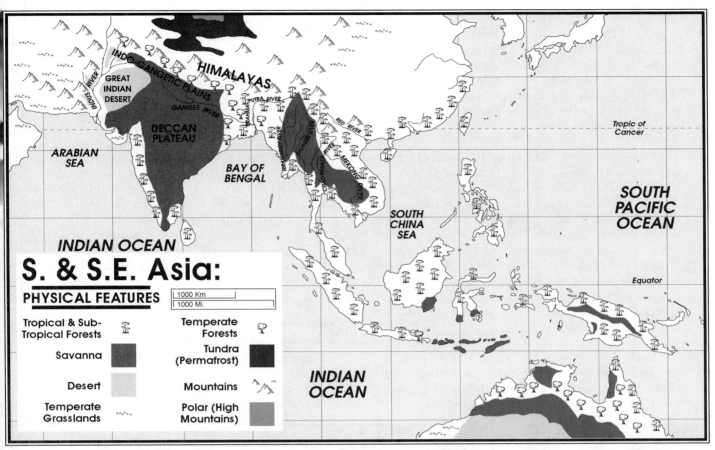

S. & S.E. Asia:
PHYSICAL FEATURES

Tropical & Sub-Tropical Forests		Temperate Forests	
Savanna		Tundra (Permafrost)	
Desert		Mountains	
Temperate Grasslands		Polar (High Mountains)	

1000 Km.
1000 Mi.

mineral wealth. Most of the population live in the narrow coastal valleys along the Deccan's edges, where the rainfall is heavy.

The South Asian Subcontinent's uneven rainfall has a decisive influence on the region. Life in the three major river valleys revolves around the summer monsoons. Insufficient seasonal accumulation often causes drought and famine. Too much rain causes flooding and destruction. The Indus River irrigates northwest India and Pakistan. Major crops along its route to the Arabian Sea include wheat, cotton, and vegetables. The Ganges and Brahmaputra flow through northern and eastern India ending in the Bay of Bengal. Products of their valleys include wheat, rice, jute, sugar cane, and vegetables.

SOUTHEAST ASIA

Geographic factors also shaped the cultures of Southeast Asia. The term "Southeast Asia" lends an impression of unity, but the area is culturally diverse. The term was coined by the Allied military command in World War II, when

the area was occupied by the Japanese. It is rugged, and the people are divided by mountains and rivers.

Southeast Asia is bounded by the South Asian Subcontinent on the west, China on the north, the Pacific on the east, and the Indian Ocean and Australia to the south. It is approximately 4,000 miles (6,437 km) east to west and 3,000 miles (4.828 km) north to south. It is divided into nine nations: Myanmar (formerly Burma – name changed in 1989), Thailand, Malaysia, Cambodia, Laos, and Vietnam on the mainland and the island nations of Indonesia, the Philippines, and Singapore.

Like the South Asian Subcontinent, the portion of Southeast Asia on the mainland is a vast peninsula jutting out into the Indian and Pacific Oceans. It has a rugged, mountainous terrain with its population clustered  around its river valleys. The north–south mountain ranges of the mainland divide the people. The mountains are responsible for the many cultures evolving in the area. The scattered islands of the south and east are another reason for cultural diversity. Among the islands, Singapore is a small island group, extending off the tip of the Malayan Peninsula. Indonesia and the Philippines are **archipelagos** (chains of islands that are really the peaks of undersea mountain ranges).

The rivers and surrounding seas are the connecting tissues of life in Southeast Asia. The most important river systems of the Southeast Asian mainland are the **Irrawaddy** and **Salween** in Burma, the **Chao Phraya** in Thailand, and the **Red River** in Vietnam. The longest of the area's rivers is the 2,800-mile (4,506 km) **Mekong**. It starts in China, flows along the border between Laos and Thailand, passes through the heart of Cambodia, and empties into the South China Sea at the southern tip of Vietnam.

Each river system has served as an avenue of contact for the people living in fertile river valleys. They remain the main areas of agricultural production and commercial avenues.

Half of the area of Southeast Asia is composed of seas and straits. These sea-lanes have provided easy access for the coastal inhabitants and island-dwellers. Examples of these traditional routes are the Gulfs of Thailand and Tonkin, the Java Sea, and the Luzon Strait.

As with India, monsoons dominate Southeast Asia's climate. The summer monsoons, blowing off the Indian Ocean from the south and southwest, are very wet. Some of the Southeast Asian winter monsoons blow from the Pacific and carry considerable moisture to the east coast and into the islands. Therefore, the region has more climatic variations (A and C types dominate) than the South Asian Subcontinent.

EARLY CIVILIZATIONS

The geographic features of the region, in particular the river valleys, contributed to South Asia's long history of disunity and the evolution of a variety of cultures.

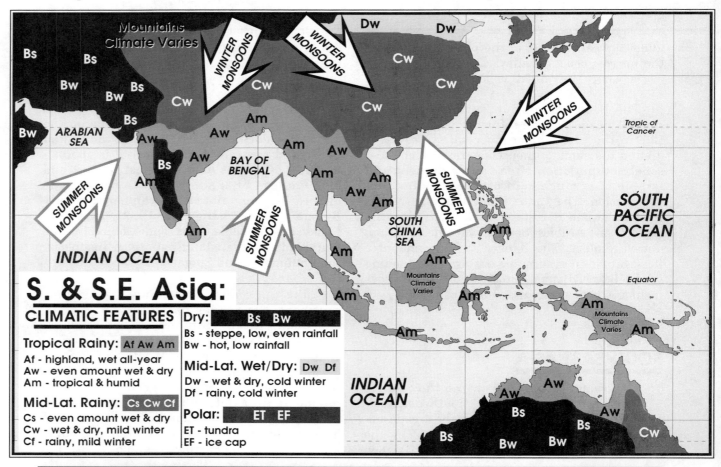

S. & S.E. Asia:

CLIMATIC FEATURES

Tropical Rainy: Af Aw Am
Af - highland, wet all-year
Aw - even amount wet & dry
Am - tropical & humid

Mid-Lat. Rainy: Cs Cw Cf
Cs - even amount wet & dry
Cw - wet & dry, mild winter
Cf - rainy, mild winter

Dry: Bs Bw
Bs - steppe, low, even rainfall
Bw - hot, low rainfall

Mid-Lat. Wet/Dry: Dw Df
Dw - wet & dry, cold winter
Df - rainy, cold winter

Polar: ET EF
ET - tundra
EF - ice cap

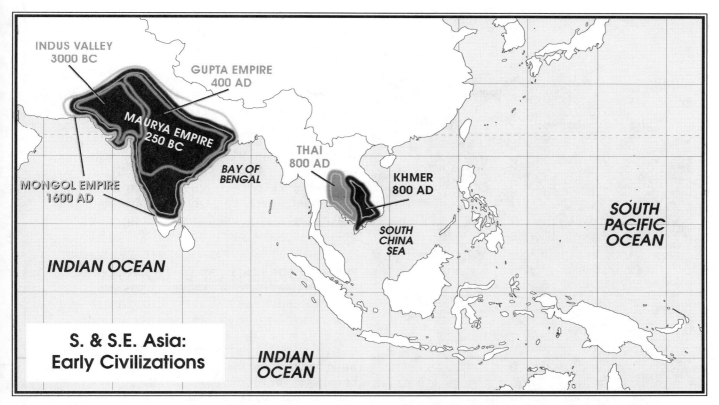

S. & S.E. Asia:
Early Civilizations

The Indus Valley is the birthplace of India's civilization. Two early city-states were **Mohenjo-daro** and **Harappa**. Their inhabitants raised rice, wheat, and cattle. Pottery and dwellings excavated by archaeologists at the sites of these cities date back to 3000 B.C.

The South Asian Subcontinent's history alternates between waves of conquest and stable periods with the conquerors being assimilated. The most common path of conquerors was out of Central Asia through the Khyber Pass and into northwestern India. Major invasions and empires include:

*   **Aryans** overran the region from 1500 to 500 B.C. They brought the **Sanskrit** language, the horse, and iron products.

*   **Hellenes**, under Alexander the Great, led an invasion in the 4th Century B.C., founded new cities, and spread Greek culture.

*   The **Mauryas**, under their great leader, Asoka, established an empire in the 3rd Century B.C. that unified most of the South Asian Subcontinent.

*   The **Gupta Dynasty** gradually dominated most of northern and central India from 270 A.D. to 500 A.D. and regenerated the classical arts and sciences.

*   **Thai** and **Khmer Empires** arose in Southeast Asia around 800 A.D. The two warred constantly until the Thais overran the area in the 16th Century. The Great Temples at Angkor Wat built by the Khmer are the greatest ancient architectural achievements in Southeast Asia.

*   **The Mongol (Mughal) Empire** was set up by Babur, a Muslim descendent of the Mongols of Central Asia from 1526 A.D. to 1857 A.D. Its great kings (Akbar, Jahangir, and Shah Jahn) ruled over a golden era of Indian cultural achievement, including the building of the Taj Mahal.

Long before the birth of Christ, Indians established a thriving trade with Arabia, Persia, and the east coast of Africa.  The Portuguese were the first Europeans to reach India. In the late 1400's, they established trade stations along the Indian coast and made it the gateway to the Orient.

David Johnson, 1991

The faithful Hindu followers wash at the edge of the river from the steps of the Pashupatinath Temple, Kathmandu, Nepal.

DEVELOPMENT OF HINDUISM

Since its origin around 3000 B.C., Hinduism has greatly influenced Indian society. While Hinduism allows for many variations, there are certain basic beliefs. Chiefly worshiped are **Brahma**, the creator; **Vishnu**, the preserver; and **Shiva**, the destroyer. A central belief is **reincarnation** (rebirth of the soul in another form of life).

Hindus believe in two key principles, Karma and Dharma. **Karma** is the idea that a person's actions carry unavoidable consequences and determine the nature of subsequent reincarnation. **Dharma** is the sacred duty one owes to family and caste.

Hinduism is more than a form of worship. It is a way of life. It has been a strong, unifying element in Indian culture. It plays a major role in daily life, determin-ing an individual's associations, occupation, and one's spouse. Today, 85% of Indians consider themselves Hindus.

The intertwining of the Hindu religion and the social class structure through castes created a stable and ordered society for centuries. Caste assignment was accepted as one's lot in a present incarnation. The most desirable castes, or varnas, were Brahman (priests), Kshatriya (warrior), Vaisya (merchant or farmer), and Sudra (laborers). The Untouchables were the lowest caste, prohibited from contact with others and assigned the most distasteful tasks.

DEVELOPMENT OF BUDDHISM

Two other major sects, **Buddhism** and **Sikhism**, began as movements to reform Hinduism. Buddhism emerged in the 4th Century B.C. It attempted to diminish the importance of **castes**, the rigid Hindu system of hereditary social groupings dictating one's rank and occupation. Buddhists believe that the cycle of reincarnation is broken when one achieves **Nirvana** (a perfect state of mind). Sikhism was founded in the 15th Century A.D. It rejects the caste system completely, teaching human equality.

The Buddhist movement had a profound effect on the Hindu social structure. Buddhism follows the basic beliefs set forth in the 6th Century B.C. by Siddhartha Gautama. He was a noble of north-ern India known as **Buddha**, or the Enlightened One. He issued the doctrines of the *Eightfold Path* and the *Four Noble Truths*. Through prayer-ful contemplation, Buddhists follow these rules to achieve Nirvana (state of enlight-enment).

PhotoDisc Inc. 1993

Buddha, Thailand

Hinduism And Islam Compared		
	Hinduism	**Islam**
Sacred Writings	*Vedas* - epics of the gods	*Qur'an* (*Koran*)
Social Organization	rigid castes	social equality
Dietary Laws	no beef or milk products	no pork or wine
Concept Of Duty	Dharma	Five Pillars
Position On Violence	Forbidden - no taking of any form of life	wars accepted
Pilgrimage	city of Benares	Mecca
Submission To Authority	family more important than individual	all submit to will of God
Afterlife	reincarnation as reward or punishment for actions and behavior	paradise, or punishment for evildoers

In the 3rd Century B.C., **Asoka** unsuccessfully sought to make Buddhism the established religion of the Maurya Empire. However, Buddhism did become popular in Asia. Through the zealous missionary work of its priests, the movement spread into Tibet, China, Japan, Korea, and most of the Southeast Asian peninsula.

DEVELOPMENT OF ISLAM

Islam spread rapidly in the Middle East and North Africa after its establishment in the 7th Century A.D. Waves of Muslim conquerors also moved eastward into Persia and the South Asian Subcontinent from the 8th to the 16th Centuries. The Hindu population resisted the Islamic faith of their rulers. This created instability for a long period.

Many of the Muslim rulers' difficulties stemmed from the fundamental differences between Islam and Hinduism. **Muhammad** (570–632 A.D.) was the originator and major prophet of the faith. God's (Allah's) revelations to Muhammad are recorded in Islam's sacred text, the *Qur'an* (*Koran*). Muslims must follow the doctrine of the *Five Pillars* (bearing witness, giving alms, praying five times each day, fasting during the holy month of Ramadan, and making a pilgrimage to Mecca). Islam was often spread through force by **jihad**, or holy war, against infidels (nonbelievers).

Arabian Muslim invasions began in the 8th Century followed by Turkish and Mughal (Mongol) Muslim attacks around 1000 A.D.

The first Muslim empire, the **Sultanate of Delhi**, was established in 1206 by **Qutb-ud-Din Aybak**. Each of its five dynasties were filled with bloodshed, tyranny, and treachery.

In the 16th Century A.D., the Mughal conquest provided the highest degree of centralization since Asoka's Maurya Empire, 3rd Century B.C. Under Mughal Emperor **Akbar** (1555-1605), efficient government, religious toleration, and culture flourished. Subsequent rulers were less able to keep the their empires under control. Fanaticism and civil war became frequent. An exception was Emperor **Shah Jahan** (1629-58). During his reign, religious strife diminished, trade expanded, and art prospered. Shah Jahan built magnificent palaces and buildings such as the famous **Taj Mahal**.

Islam came more peacefully to Southeast Asia. Around the 13th Century A.D., Muslim merchants spread trade along the Malay Peninsula and into the islands of Indonesia and the Philippines.

OTHER RELIGIOUS MOVEMENTS

Hinduism's long history was marked by numerous reform movements centering on the caste system and the individual's responsibility in the scheme of reincarnation.

Ghuru Mahavira founded a sect of Hinduism in the 6th Century A.D. called **Jainism**. It teaches that escape from the cycle of rebirth comes from correct faith, knowledge, and nonviolence to any living thing.

Ghuru Nanak founded **Sikhism** in the 15th Century A.D. It combines elements of Hindu and Islamic beliefs. It is monotheistic and holds to the equality of all men. Martyrdom of Sikhs was influential in changing this group into a cult of military brotherhood. Today, the Sikhs are known for their military skills. They form a large group within the Indian army, and some seek independence for their home province of Punjab, in northwestern India.

Reformers failed to bridge the gap between the two major religions. By the time that the Europeans arrived, the divisions in Indian society already were deep-seated and continued to be a source of friction.

QUESTIONS

1   Monsoons are seasonal
    1   prevailing winds
    2   grain harvests
    3   hurricanes
    4   religious rites

2   Which separates the South Asian Subcontinent from the rest of Asia?
    1   Pacific Ocean
    2   Deccan Plateau
    3   Himalayas Mountain Range
    4   Ganges Valley

3   Hinduism and Buddhism are similar in that both religions
    1   practice the belief in many gods
    2   provide followers with a rigid caste system
    3   stress attainment of a better life through spiritual rebirth
    4   follow the teachings of the same person as their basic belief

4   Which is an archipelago?
    1   Singapore
    2   Sri Lanka
    3   Vietnam
    4   Indonesia

5   Which religion is correctly paired with its major belief?
    1   Hinduism: one's present status in life is a merited incarnation
    2   Buddhism: an active life is preferred to contemplation of the hereafter
    3   Islam: one must worship a vast array of gods to achieve perfection
    4   Sikhism: the caste system is the key to eternal happiness

6   Which statement shows the major climatic difference between S. Asia and S.E. Asia?
    1   The annual rainfall in India is constant all year.
    2   The lack of mountains in Southeast Asia accounts for its dryness.
    3   The winter monsoons are wetter in Southeast Asia.
    4   India is too far from the Pacific to benefit from the summer monsoons.

7   Which statement about the role of religion in Indian culture is most accurate?
    1   Religious leaders have often held formal political offices.
    2   Religious differences have been the cause of division and conflict.
    3   Religion has historically had little influence on the secular world.
    4   Religious principles have seldom provided a base for civil laws.

ESSAYS

1   Geographic factors often have an important influence on a nation's or region's history, economy, and cultural diversity.

Geographic Factors:

- Khyber Pass   • Himalayas Mountains
- Monsoons   • Indo-Gangetic Plain
- river valleys   • Deccan Plateau

Select *three* of the above factors and discuss the influence of *each* on a South or Southeast Asian nation.

2   Discuss how Hinduism, Buddhism, and Islam have contributed to the culture of Southeast Asia.

II. DYNAMICS OF CHANGE

THE BRITISH CONQUEST

The Commercial Revolution of 16th Century Europe broadened trade opportunities for the British and other powers. It led to the exploitation of South and Southeast Asia. In 1612, the Mughal emperor granted commercial rights to **British East India Company**, a government-chartered trading monopoly. As competition arrived from the Netherlands, Portugal, and France, the emperors often found themselves caught in violent commercial struggles.

In the 18th Century, the British interests won out over other European commercial enterprises. Parliament funded better organization and military assistance. During the Seven Years' War, **Sir Robert Clive** commanded European and Indian soldiers (sepoys) hired by the East India Company. He led a series of military expeditions which ousted the French. His 1757 victory at Plassey led to effective political control over the vast riches of the Ganges Valley by 1765. Superior sea-power allowed British forces to move quickly to different areas on India's coasts. Clive made alliances with local Hindu princes who were not loyal to the Islamic Mughal rulers. Offers of financial gain caused many Indians to join the British forces as mercenaries. Parliament gave Clive's successor, **Warren Hastings**, the title of Governor-General (1773–1785).

The British policy of expansionism, as well as British insensitivity to Indian traditions and religious practices, increased tensions. After the **Sepoy Mutiny** (1858) by Hindu and Muslim mercenaries, Parliament replaced the East India Company and brought the South Asian Subcontinent into the British Empire.

BRITISH COLONIAL RULE

British authority was not based on dominance of a religion. As such, it was able to unify the diverse Indian society. The British imperialists also minimized their role in local affairs. They used a "divide and conquer" strategy to control opposition from local princes. Also, they employed Indians, especially Hindus, in many capacities. The Hindu acceptance of fate (Karma) and loyalty (Dharma) made them easier to work with than Muslims.

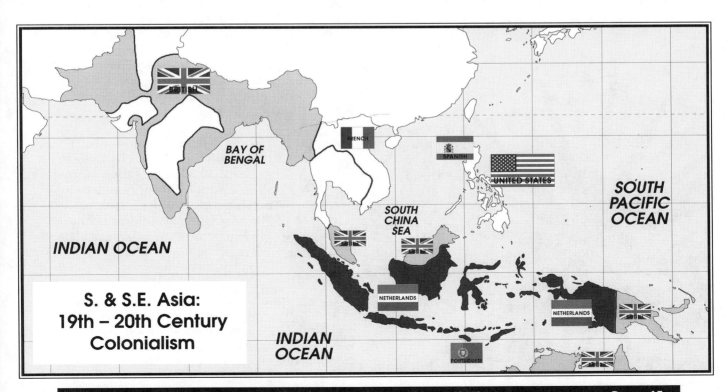

S. & S.E. Asia:
19th – 20th Century
Colonialism

Gradually, changes were introduced under the British imperialists. These changes consolidated their power rather than improving conditions for India's population. As in Africa, the imperialists improved transportation and communication systems and exploited the human and natural wealth of the colony. The needs of the "mother country" superseded those of the colony.

Indians joined other subjects of the British Empire in traveling and studying in England and other countries of Europe. The exposure they received to Western political ideas laid the groundwork for 20th Century independence movements. Returning to India, these individuals organized opposition to their second-class status as citizens.

The British maintained that the people were uneducated and unfit for self-government. The people saw themselves and their national resources as being exploited. During this period, several Asian leaders encouraged bloody riots and confrontations with colonial authorities. However, the British were too strong militarily, and the revolts were quickly crushed.

In 1906, out of reaction to the British division of Bengal province into Muslim and Hindu sections, an **All-India Muslim League** was founded under the Aga Khan.

LIMITED SELF-GOVERNMENT

Western-educated Indian nationalist leaders were at first rebuffed by Britain when they sought democracy. Later, the British made a series of small concessions when the opposition became more organized.

The British Parliament passed the **Morley-Minto Reforms** in 1908-09. Named for the British Secretary of State and the Viceroy of India, the reforms allowed more native participation in colonial government. These actions were in response to agitation by the **National Congress Party**. The party was founded in 1885 to expand self-government. In the early 20th Century, the movement's goals changed to seeking total independence for India.

MOHANDAS GANDHI (1869-1948)

The charismatic Mohandas Gandhi became the central figure in India's independence movement. He united the intellectuals and the masses. He dramatized the desire of the National Congress Party to use independence to relieve poverty. Gandhi emphasized that the spiritual and moral strength of Indians was superior to the materialism of Western society. He advocated *passive, nonviolent resistance* to British rule. He championed social justice and equal rights for untouchables. He wanted Indians to think of themselves as citizens of a unified nation first and as Hindus or Muslims second.

In 1919, British suppression of a demonstration in Punjab touched off riots. In 1920, Gandhi seized on the public's sense of outrage at the **Amritsar Massacre**. "Mahatma" ("Saintly One") Gandhi urged nonviolent passive resistance. The British imprisoned him.

Gandhi was famous for his hunger strikes and for organizing economic boycotts of British cotton goods. He encouraged Indians to spin and weave their own cloth ("**cottage**

Colonialism In India And Southeast Asia		
	India	**Southeast Asia**
Foreign Power	Great Britain	France, Britain, United States, Netherlands, Portugal, Spain
Involvement In World War II	Aided in Allied efforts against Axis	Entire region conquered by Japan
Commercial Domination	British and Indian merchant groups	Chinese dominated mainland trade

industries"). The spinning wheel became a powerful symbol of protest. (Today, it is incorporated in the Indian flag.) In 1930, he led the **Salt March**. In a symbolic protest against the British tax system, thousands joined him in gathering salt from the sea.

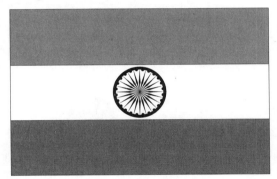

The British Parliament responded with the *Government of India Act* (1935). It established a federal constitution giving India a measure of **autonomy** (self-rule).

BRITISH WITHDRAWAL

Events of the 20th Century, especially the two world wars, weakened European imperialism in most areas of the world. The Indian National Congress stated it would not aid Britain's war effort unless India was granted independence. In 1942, Gandhi began the third of his campaigns for freedom. He and other leaders were jailed until 1944. In 1947, the British Parliament finally granted India independence with membership in the British Commonwealth.

As independence drew closer, it was obvious that a single, united nation would not satisfy Hindus and Muslims. The British yielded to Muslim pressure and agreed to **partition** (divide) the South Asian Subcontinent into Hindu India and Muslim eastern and western sections of Pakistan. **Muhammad Ali Jinnah (1876-1948)** was the founder of a movement to create the independent Muslim nation of Pakistan. He protested Hindu domination, and he resigned from the All-India Congress to help form the **Muslim League**. In the 1920's and 30's, he and his followers agitated for the partition of India into Hindu and Muslim sectors. In 1947, Jinnah became the first Governor-General of Pakistan.

Myanmar (Burma) was another of the areas controlled by Britain. It was acquired in the 1880's to block French imperial expansion westward from Southeast Asia. Burma received independence in 1947 and elected not to join the British Commonwealth.

COLONIALISM IN SOUTHEAST ASIA

Most of Southeast Asia came under European control by the end of the Imperial Era of the 19th Century. There were many similarities with the Indian experience, including the lack of political unity and of rivalry between different cultures. These similarities made conquests by Europeans easier. The pattern of casual commercial contact, missionary work, and increased political control was similar. However, the chart above notes several differences in the colonial pattern. It helps explain why the two areas had very different experiences after achieving independence.

VIOLENT REVOLTS

SOCIAL CONFLICTS

ECONOMIC PROBLEMS

POLITICAL CHAOS

BRITAIN

The Europeans left South & Southeast Asia many unresolved problems. The newly independent countries were ill-prepared to govern themselves. Many of these LDCs still view the former imperial powers with suspicion and blame them for many of their current problems.

DETERMINATION OF POLITICAL & ECONOMIC SYSTEMS

The end of World War II provided impetus to the independence movement throughout Southeast Asia. There were psychological effects to seeing the Western colonizers defeated by an Asian power. In addition, while guerrilla resistance fighting against the Japanese received little help from the colonial powers, it added strong momentum to independence movements.

The Philippines were promised independence in the early 1940's by the United States. Independence was postponed because of the attack on Pearl Harbor and the entry of the U.S. into World War II. Following the War, independence was granted to the Philippines. In 1949, the Dutch left Indonesia.

On the mainland, a series of bloody wars broke out in the Indochina region. In 1954, the French colonial empire crumbled. Laos, Cambodia, and North and South Vietnam were created as France left Southeast Asia.

QUESTIONS

1 Which statement is most consistent with the political views of Mohandas Gandhi?
   1 Not until the last Englishman has left India will I put down my sword.
   2 To protest injustice is to use one's time unproductively.
   3 Independence is a goal we may seek but never attain.
   4 Opposition to evil is as much a duty as is cooperation with good.

2 During the era of 19th Century European Imperialism, the central theme of colonial economies such as India's became
1 the exportation of raw materials
2 commercial investment and banking
3 heavy industry
4 agricultural communes

3 In the 18th Century, Robert Clive established British rule in India by means of
1 military victories
2 alliances with the Portuguese
3 peace treaties with the Dutch East India Company
4 promoting religious equality

4 While struggling for independence in the 20th Century, Indian strategy emphasized
1 terrorism
2 assassinations
3 troop mutinies
4 nonviolence

5 Which would historians consider a cause of disunity in 20th Century India?
1 abolition of castes
2 popular government
3 high literacy rates
4 religious conflict

6 Despite their size and large populations, both India and S.E. Asia were easy victims of European imperialism because they
1 lacked strong, unified governments
2 had no organized religions
3 wished to obtain Western technology to advance
4 lacked sufficient food supplies

7 A major reason the British government was able to consolidate its rule over the South Asian Subcontinent in the 18th and 19th Centuries was that it
1 was the dominant power on the European continent
2 used its Southeast Asian colonies as an invasion base
3 was on friendly terms with the Islamic rulers
4 gave strong backing to its private commercial companies

8 Which was a major result of World War II in South and Southeast Asia?
1 France replaced England as the dominant colonial power.
2 Islam replaced Hinduism as the official religion of India.
3 The East India Company gave up control to the British Parliament.
4 The European powers could no longer control their colonies.

9 Muhammad Ali Jinnah wanted the separate state of Pakistan because of
1 language difficulties
2 possible economic barriers
3 fear of Hindu domination
4 the example of Burma

ESSAYS

1 The 20th Century was a time of turmoil for the South Asian Subcontinent.

a While some revolutions have expressed the power of the pen, Gandhi's revolution in India expressed the power of an idea. Explain.

b Explain fully how India freed itself from imperialistic control in the 20th Century.

c Briefly describe *one* specific cause of serious disagreement in the 20th Century between India and Pakistan.

2 Imperialism declined in South and Southeast Asia after World War II.

a Why had the people of India and Southeast Asia been such easy prey for European imperialism?

b Why did imperialism decline in Southeast Asia after 1945?

c Discuss the post World War II relationship between one S./S.E. colony and the mother country.

III. CONTEMPORARY NATIONS

PARTITION OF INDIA

Independence and the separation of India and Pakistan caused considerable disruption. People in both areas protested having to leave their homes. The forced population exchange not only accentuated the religious hostilities, but also increased poverty, famine, disease and displacement of the people. As independence drew near, over 200,000 were killed in riots.

Gandhi himself was a victim of this violence. A Hindu fanatic, incensed by the idea of religious equality, assassinated Gandhi in January 1948. "The Saintly One's" death ended any hope for religious calm on the South Asian Subcontinent.

Nor did partition solve the territorial disputes between the two rival nations. Even today, two areas in the mountainous northwest are problems. **Kashmir** and **Jammu** are Muslim states claimed by both countries. Currently, they are part of India. When **Punjab** was divided in 1947, an estimated five million Hindus and Sikhs moved into the Indian sector.

Tara Singh, a powerful Sikh leader, demanded special status for Punjab as a semiautonomous **Sikh** homeland. The Sikh military contribution during a 1960 war with Pakistan persuaded then Prime Minister Indira Gandhi to divide Punjab into three regions. The Sikhs hold a majority in one.

NEW INDIAN GOVERNMENT

India is an example of a newly independent country adapting its previous colonial form of government (see chart top of opposite page).

The British legacy moved India toward a multiparty Parliamentary democracy. One major difference is that India's Constitution is formally written. The British system evolved as a series of acts and traditions compiled over the centuries. In India after independence, several revisions of the basic structure of the Indian government took place. The 1950 constitution created a parliamentary form of federal republic. It included many social and economic goals. These goals included free, universal education up to 14 years of age; prohibitions against discrimination because of race, religion, caste, sex, or place of birth; enfranchisement of citizens over twenty-one.

British And Indian Government Systems Compared		
	British System	**Indian System**
Legislature	bicameral: hereditary House of Lords, elected House of Commons	bicameral: Council of States (Rajya Saba); Council of People (Lok Saba elected every 5 yrs.
Head Of State	monarch (hereditary)	president (elected, 5 yr. term)
Executive	prime minister & cabinet selected by majority of House of Commons	prime minister & cabinet selected by majority of both houses of legislature
Parties	two major parties: Conservatives & Labour Party	two major parties: Congress Party and Lok Dal

PROBLEMS OF INDEPENDENCE

Many difficulties faced the leaders of the new nation. The popular slogan *"Unity in Diversity"* became a guideline for the early leaders. It meant that India wished to preserve individual freedom while maintaining a strong federal union among its many different states and cultures. Cultural diversity often leads to conflict. The reasons for clashes vary. Some revolve around religion, but dress, language, and even eating habits can become controversial. One difficulty has been that while the constitution recognizes 15 different languages, **Hindi** and **English** are the official languages.

Jawaharlal Nehru, a follower of Gandhi in the Congress Party, became the first Prime Minister. Gandhi and Nehru were both committed to unifying the Indian people. Gandhi championed rights for the untouchables and fought for religious toleration. He worked to elevate the role of women in political affairs. Nehru tried to break down traditional Hindu discrimination regarding women's rights to own property, to obtain divorces, and for widows to remarry.

SOCIAL CHANGE IN INDIA

India's social problems often block economic progress. The traditional village life remains central to India's social structure. Loyalty to local tradition makes it difficult for the central government to develop national unity. After independence, the central government tried to institute land reform measures, hoping to break the local power of large landholders and provide even distribution among citizens. The landholders' power rests in 550,000 **panchayats** (village councils) made up of tradition-bound elders.

PhotoDisc Inc. 1993

Elephants are still used for transportation and agriculture work, indicating both the widespread rural poverty among the lower classes and a resistance among South and Southeast Asians in shedding their traditions and ancient culture.

Unemployment is high. Annual per capita income in 1992 was only $380 (cf. approx. U.S. per capita = $22,000). Land tenure programs give more land to small farmers. Yet, more than half the farms in India today are one acre or less. Such small-scale subsistence agriculture cannot supply the kind of harvests India needs annually.

Rural poverty causes continual migration to urban areas. Since 1960, cities have grown at three times the rate of rural areas. Crowded slums, poor sanitation, inadequate housing, disease, and crime abound. Yet, city life has torn down

The Hindu caste system is also a problem. Despite efforts to abolish castes at the national level, traditional villages still maintain them. Assignment of local housing and selection of panchayat members still reflect castes.

Population issues also plague India and Pakistan. For decades, the South Asian Subcontinent has supported a population increasing at one of the highest rates in the world. The most crucial problem facing India is the rapid rate that food supplies are diminishing compared to the demands of the increasing population.

In 1952, India was the first country to adopt a nationwide **family planning program**. In addition to a high birthrate, improved medical care has increased life expectancy. Efforts to control the population have been unsuccessful. There has been a steady increase. There are both traditional and religious reasons for this.

In labor-intensive subsistence agriculture, large families are a necessity. Technological progress in farming lags, and farm families continue to grow. Family loyalty is still strong. Those children who migrate to India's cities are expected to send contributions home. Hinduism teaches that having children is virtuous. In fact, when a parent dies, a son is needed to light his parent's funeral pyre.

PhotoDisc Inc. 1993

Breaking with tradition, modern Indian women are taking more responsible positions in the workplace.

some of the old caste traditions. Increased mobility and modern communication systems tend to destabilize its rigidity. Radio, television, newspapers, and cinema have a unifying effect. Economic freedom for women has lessened the necessity for arranged marriages.

The continued population growth (nearly a billion) adversely affects the economy, urban development, and the general quality of life in India. The country does not have the natural or financial resources to provide many basic consumer goods.

Identity in South Asia is still based more on cultural groupings than on national or political loyalty. For instance, the government has often rebuffed the Sikhs' demands for greater freedom in the Punjab. Tensions increased there in 1984. Nehru's daughter, Prime Minister **Indira Gandhi**, ordered the army to storm the Gold Temple of Amritsar, a symbol of Sikh independence. Sikh insurgents were using the temple as a refuge. The action was viewed by India's 14 million Sikhs as a sacrilege. In October of that year, Mrs. Gandhi was assassinated by two of her Sikh bodyguards. Riots against the Sikhs broke out all over India.

Rajiv Gandhi became Prime Minister after his mother's assassination in 1984. He restored order, but Sikh uprisings brought another clash at Amritsar in 1988. The following year, opponents forced Rajiv from office on corruption charges. In 1991, this grandson of Nehru was assassinated while campaigning for reelection.

Kashmir presents a similar problem. Hindu leaders dominate this area in which the population is mainly Muslim. It caused the first of a series of **Indo-Pakistani Wars** in 1948. The United Nations attempted to settle the dispute, but wars broke out again in 1965 and 1971. In 1972, another partition took place, but it did not settled the issue.

INDEPENDENT PAKISTAN

Pakistan has also experienced difficulties achieving economic and social reform as an Islamic republic. It has been plagued with both internal and international problems.

During the colonial period, Muslims gained little experience in self-government. The British controlled the entire South Asian Subcontinent through the Hindu majority. The Muslims were poorly prepared to govern when Jinnah's request for a separate Muslim nation was honored in 1947.

Governing the two sections of Pakistan, separated by over 1,000 miles (1,609 km) of Indian territory, presented a major obstacle. The two sections were different geographically and economically and had different interpretations of some Islamic concepts. Prime Minister **Ayub Khan's** ruling group in West Pakistan wished to modernize the country and had liberal views of Islamic law.

In East Pakistan, the Muslim fundamentalist majority resented Khan's modernizations, because most expenditures went to the West. When Khan left office in 1969, East Pakistan began refusing to pay taxes to the central government in the West. The government sent troops to East Pakistan, setting off civil war. East Pakistan declared its independence as **Bangladesh** (the nation Bengal). Thousands were killed, and millions escaped to India. India entered the war helping Bangladesh win independence in 1972.

Political violence also disrupted Pakistan in recent times. In 1988, President **Zia ul-Haq's** plane mysteriously exploded with the U.S. ambassador aboard. **Benazir Bhutto** became Pakistan's first woman Prime Minister in 1988. She was forced from office in 1990 due to corruption charges against some of her cabinet ministers. She returned to office in 1993. Recent political turmoil revolves around returning to fundamental Islamic law and toning down Western modernization.

INDEPENDENCE IN SOUTHEAST ASIA: THE FRENCH EMPIRE

Amid background struggles by the major world powers after World War II, the nations of Southeast Asia took different routes to independence.

The French dominated the **Indochina Peninsula**. Three nations eventually emerged from a long and bloody series of struggles: Vietnam, Laos, and Cambodia.

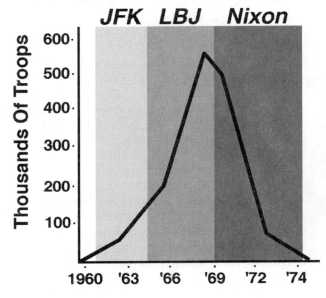

SOCIALIST REPUBLIC OF VIETNAM

The country runs along the eastern coast of the Southeast Asian mainland peninsula. It is bordered by China on the north, the South China Sea to the east, and Laos and Cambodia to the west. Communist revolutionary leader **Ho Chi Minh** (1890-1969) fought against the French before and after World War II. During the war, he organized a guerrilla resistance against the Japanese. This experience accelerated the drive for independence. As they retreated from Indochina, the Japanese proclaimed **Bao Dai** as Emperor of Vietnam, but nationalist insurgents rushed to assume power before the French could return.

Ho Chi Minh headed the communist **Vietminh** Party. He called for the establishment of the Democratic Republic of Vietnam. A north Vietnamese Vietminh state was recognized as a member of the French Empire in March 1946, but within months, the French attacked it and began an eight-year war. By 1953, the United States was paying over 80% of the costs of this struggle, viewing it as necessary to contain the spread of communism. In 1954, the French withdrew after the fall of the fortress at **Dienbienphu**.

A 1954 peace conference in Geneva divided Vietnam at the 17th Parallel into a northern Vietminh state (capital: Hanoi) and South Vietnam (capital: Saigon). Ho Chi Minh became president in the north and Emperor Bao Dai led the south. Almost immediately, **Viet Cong** communist insurgents began guerrilla activities in South Vietnam. The U.S. sent military aid and advisors to help the South resist communist aggression. **Ngo Dinh Diem** deposed the emperor in a 1955 coup. Diem proclaimed himself President of the **Republic of South Vietnam**. In 1960, Buddhist leaders began to protest discrimination by Diem's Catholic regime. Diem's dictatorial rule lost both U.S. and popular support. In 1963, the military led a **coup d'état** (forceful overthrow) against Diem that ended in his assassination.

America was drawn deeper into the Vietnam War. In 1964, President **Lyndon B. Johnson** ordered combat troops into the region. By 1968, the war had become so unpopular with many Americans that Johnson decided not to run for reelection. **Richard Nixon** promised to end the war. However, he ordered increased U.S. military aid and broadened the war by bombing Viet Cong supply bases inside Cambodia. In the U.S., antiwar protests became more widespread and violent.

Nixon finally began slow withdrawal of American troops. South Vietnamese troops bore more and more of the fighting. Simultaneously, Nixon ordered heavy bombing of Hanoi and North Vietnamese harbors. Eventually, secret peace talks brought about a cease-fire agreement in 1973 which resulted in complete withdrawal by the United States.

North Vietnamese troops swiftly moved into the South. They captured Saigon in April 1975 and unified the country under a communist government. During the 1990's, Vietnam engaged in sporadic border clashes with China, a traditional enemy.

CAMBODIA

Cambodia is also located in the south-central area of what was called **French Indochina**. It is bordered by Laos and Thailand on the north and Vietnam on the east and south. The French were pushed out of the area by the Japanese in World War II. Japan brought Prince **Norodom Sihanouk** to the throne.

After the war, the French allowed Sihanouk to remain and in 1953, granted independence. In 1963, Sihanouk attempted to secure neutral status as the war in Vietnam intensified. He was overthrown by a coup headed by **General Lon Nol**.

North Vietnamese troops infiltrated Cambodia in 1970, threatening its capital at Phnom Penh. U.S. President Nixon ordered a force of U.S. and South Vietnamese troops into the country to help with the fighting.

David Johnson, 1991
Khmer Refugee Camp at Khao I Dang, Thailand, September 1991

The 1973 Vietnamese cease-fire included a withdrawal of foreign troops from Cambodia, but fighting between government troops and communist **Khmer Rouge** insurgents continued. Lon Nol was overthrown in 1975. A communist government under Premier **Pol Pot** began a massive purge and resettlement of political opponents which resulted in a terrible blood-bath with nearly 4 million casualties.

From 1977 to 1985, civil war raged in Cambodia, spilling into neighboring Thailand. **Heng Samrin**, a former Khmer Rouge leader backed by North Vietnam and the Soviets, emerged victorious. Samrin temporarily gave the country the ancient name **Kampuchea**. In 1992, U.N. peacekeepers entered to oversee national elections. Prince Sihanouk emerged as head of a weak coalition in the Spring of 1993.

Although life is slow and relatively quiet, there are few luxuries such as electricity, sewage disposal, and running water for these rain forest people in Mom Village on the Thailand - Myanmar border.

LAOS

The **Lao People's Democratic Republic** is a land-locked nation on the Indochina peninsula, surrounded by China on the north, Vietnam on the east, Cambodia on the south, and Thailand and Myanmar (Burma) on the west. In 1950, France granted Laos independence within the French Union. The next year, Prince **Souphanouvong** launched a communist **Pathet Lao** movement. Aided by the Vietminh, the Pathet Lao invaded Laos in 1953. They gained two provinces in the North.

After the 1954 Geneva settlements, Pathet Lao influence grew. In 1957, Souphanouvong joined an uneasy coalition government led by a rival prince, **Souvanna Phouma**. Armed conflict broke out between the two factions which lasted until 1961. The war in Vietnam increased foreign influence in Laos. The Vietminh ran supplies through Laos to communist insurgents in South Vietnam. The U.S. and South Vietnamese attempted to block them. In 1975, the Pathet Lao overthrew the weak coalition, and Souphanouvong became president of a communist state. In the 1990's, Laos, like Cambodia and Vietnam, slowly moved toward a less rigid socialism with broader free market reforms.

INDEPENDENCE IN SOUTHEAST ASIA: ISLAND NATIONS

Outside the French colonial area of Indochina, the pattern of independence was somewhat different. Island nations of the Indian Ocean and the Pacific emerged from Dutch, British, and American colonial rule.

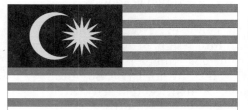

MALAYSIA

Malaysia is at the southern tip of the Malay Peninsula. Japan overran the British Malay colonies in World War II. Yet, wartime resistance groups forged a strong sense of national unity. When British rule returned after the war, the nationalists challenged it in 1948. The nationalist movement provided a foundation for building independence.

In 1957, the nationalists formed the **Federation of Malaya** (Malaya, Singapore, North Borneo, and Sarawak) with its capital at Kuala Lumpur. The country renamed itself **Malaysia** in 1963, but Singapore withdrew in 1965. The country was troubled by insurgents from Indonesia until 1965 and then by anti-Chinese riots because of the economic dominance of that group. During the 1970's, the country took in most of South Vietnam's "boat people" fleeing the communist takeover in their country.

Evidence of the large Chinese influence in Singapore is seen in this Chinese Market.

THE REPUBLIC OF SINGAPORE

Singapore proclaimed itself an independent republic after leaving the Malaysian Federation in 1965. It consists of one main island and 54 smaller ones off the Malay Peninsula between the Indian Ocean and the South China Sea. Prime Minister **Lee Kwan Yew** led the anti-British movement in the late 1950's when Singapore joined the Federation of Malaya. It left the Federation because of agitation against its Chinese majority. Still, Singapore remains closely tied to Malaysia commercially and through military alliances.

THE REPUBLIC OF THE PHILIPPINES

The Philippines is an archipelago nation lying in the Pacific some 500 miles (805 km) off the southeastern coast of Asia. The islands were ceded to the U.S. as a result of the Spanish-American War in 1898. In 1935, they were granted commonwealth status and were preparing for independence when World War II broke

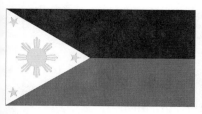

out in the Pacific. The Japanese captured the islands but were forced out by the Allies in 1945. In July of 1946, the nation received its independence.

President **Ramon Magsaysay** (1953-57) directed successful military actions against the **Huks**, communist guerrillas who constantly stirred up landless peasants.

Subsequent presidents were relatively weak until **Ferdinand Marcos** emerged in 1965. Marcos ruled as a dictator for over 20 years. Most of this time, the country was under martial law partially due to a Muslim secessionist rebellion in the south. In 1981, Marcos lifted martial law and restored parliamentary rule. Massive demonstrations began against Marcos' regime. They intensified after the assassination of opposition leader **Benigno Aquino**.

By 1986, most of the military joined the opposition backing the widowed **Corazon Aquino**. They forced Marcos into exile. Two

major problems remained: communist insurgency and pockets of discontented troops. Opponents attempted several coups, but Aquino managed to keep the country democratic. She stepped down in May 1992, and her ally, **Fidel Ramos**, became president.

PhotoDisc Inc. 1993

Terraced rice fields on rugged Indonesian Island mountain side

THE REPUBLIC OF INDONESIA

Indonesia is also an archipelago nation of over 13,000 islands (half are inhabited). Until the Japanese invasion in 1941, it was an integral part of the Kingdom of the Netherlands. The Dutch attempted to restore colonial rule in 1945. After a four-year struggle, nationalists won independence in 1949. The new nation became a "guided democracy" under the dictatorial rule of President **Sukarno**. Sukarno's troops, fearing too many concessions to communist opponents, helped to remove him in 1965. Violent anticommunist riots swept the country.

PhotoDisc Inc. 1993

Without modern transportation, Indonesians use their traditional trucking – water buffalo and cart.

Since 1967, Army General **Suharto** has ruled as president. Oil-rich Indonesia remains a strong anticommunist state. In 1975, Indonesia attacked and annexed the Portuguese colony of Timor, but the mistreatment of the native population has caused considerable criticism of the government.

QUESTIONS

1 Which is viewed as India's most serious problem?
1 protection of its oil resources
2 communist insurgency
3 Sikh terrorism
4 overpopulation

2 Why would the new nations of Asia distrust Western powers?
1 Western nations have opposed their entry into the United Nations.
2 Russia has sent troops to block their independence movements.
3 Most Western nations have sponsored communist insurgencies.
4 Western nations formerly controlled them as colonies.

3 After independence from the Netherlands, President Sukarno ruled the Republic of Indonesia as a "guided democracy." Actually, it was a
1 colony
2 dictatorship
3 religious state
4 communist government

4 Punjab and Kashmir have been problems since India's early nationhood because
1 widowed women cannot own property
2 the people want a separate communist government
3 they remained under British colonial rule
4 of religious struggles

5 Language diversity is a major problem for
1 Singapore
2 India
3 Laos
4 Vietnam

6 A major problem in the agricultural development of India is
1 tradition v. technology
2 British trade boycotts
3 huge food surpluses
4 collective farms

7 As the first prime minister of India, Jawaharlal Nehru sought to
1 break down traditional discrimination regarding women's rights
2 end the communist rebellions in his country
3 institute a caste system
4 have all Indians accept the Hindu religion

8 Communism has been successful in Asia because
1 Asians feel indebted to former colonial powers
2 coalition governments are common
3 poverty and inequality are widespread
4 most nations are archipelagos

9 Which change has taken place in South and Southeast Asian political life since independence?
1 more countries have monarchies
2 women play active leadership roles
3 less religious friction occurs
4 castes have been the basis for political parties

10 Which was a problem for Pakistan in its early nationhood?
1 domination by Christians
2 communist revolutionary activities
3 control of sea lanes
4 territorial division

11 Which contributes to South Asia's population problem?
1 overproduction of staple crops
2 the rapid pace of industrialization
3 urbanization changing women's roles
4 medical technology decreasing death rates

12 The first president of South Vietnam, Ngo Dinh Diem, lost popular support because of his administration's
1 collaboration with the communists of North Vietnam
2 corrupt and dictatorial rule
3 attempt to make Buddhism the national religion
4 desire to unite all former French colonies under his leadership

13 The rivalry between India and Pakistan led to India's military intervention in the
1 Buddhist-Muslim War
2 Bangladesh independence movement
3 Vietnam Conflict
4 Sikh Rebellion

14 The economy of Singapore is dominated by
1 Chinese merchants
2 Buddhist priests
3 British imperialists
4 communist insurgents

15 India is considered an underdeveloped nation because it
1 is divided into two separate regions
2 is dominated by Sikhs
3 has a low standard of living
4 follows communist doctrines

16 Which European nation was involved in independence struggles in Indochina from 1946-1954?
1 Netherlands
2 France
3 Spain
4 Britain

17 The Vietnamese communist leader who fought both the French and Japanese was
1 Sukarno
2 Aquino
3 Bao Dai
4 Ho Chi Minh

18 Which is a problem to India's development?
1 increasing agricultural and industrial productivity
2 increasing population of subsistence farmers
3 expanding religious diversity
4 establishing greater power for local village councils

19 The United States became involved in supporting the French in the Indo-Chinese independence movements because
1 it supported Christian missionary work
2 it wished to eliminate French economic competition
3 it was committed to containing communism
4 the movements were essentially democratic

20 In 1947, India adopted a parliamentary form of government. This event reflects the influence the British had in
1 ending religious conflicts in India
2 continuing the caste system
3 preventing partition of the South Asian Subcontinent
4 introducing some Western institutions to India

ESSAYS

1 The Indian government has attempted reform and social change since independence was granted in 1948. Progress has often been hampered by traditionalists.

 a Why has the government tried to control the population growth?

 b Discuss *three* reasons why India's population growth continues.

2 Democracy has been difficult to establish in Southeast Asia.

 Nations

 • The Philippines
 • Indonesia
 • Vietnam
 • Cambodia (Kampuchea)

 Choose *three* of the nations above and discuss why each has had difficulty in achieving democracy.

IV. ECONOMIC DEVELOPMENT

THIRD WORLD CONDITIONS

Since independence, economic development has been the most crucial challenge to "Third World" or **LDCs** (less developed countries) like India. The imperial system kept control of national resources and decision-making in the hands of British policy makers, giving Indians little experience. India was often forced to import its most commonly used items from elsewhere in the British Empire. As a result, the economy could not meet the population's basic needs once independence arrived.

Some segments of the Indian economy are managed by government agencies in the socialist manner, while some are based on free enterprise. This **mixed economic system** reflects the varied views on economic life held by diverse leaders. Still, the majority of India's agriculture and industry is managed by the private sector.

The government invests public funds in railroads, irrigation, power production, steel, nonferrous metals, basic chemicals, and heavy machinery. Leaders use democratic means to promote development. Gandhi wanted small—scale craft production in the nation's villages. However, Prime Minister **Jawaharlal Nehru** (1947 through 1964) stressed development of Western-style heavy industry and electric power plants. Wealthier classes supported free enterprise. In recent years, the government eased its management of the economy. Still, the Hindu philosophy of "less is more" holds the economy back.

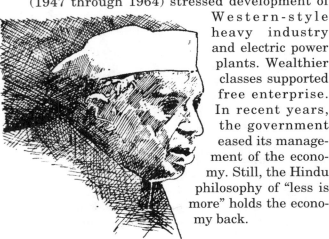

Jawaharlal Nehru

DECISION-MAKING IN LDCs

Because the economic systems of the modern world are interdependent, the choices of LDCs in South and Southeast Asia are highly sensitive to global conditions.

Basic or heavy industries such as mining, nuclear and conventional energy production, and transportation are extremely important for LDCs. The Indian government has attempted to develop these basic industries through a mix of state-run (socialist) projects, while supplementing private projects with government funds and encouraging private efforts.

India's growing urban middle class also encouraged expansion of consumer goods production. Its cotton goods industries expanded to meet domestic needs, but the industry is also dependent on foreign markets, especially in the more developed nations. The rise and fall of textile exports make India's economy dependent on economic conditions abroad.

Less developed countries must also compete at home with the exports of more developed nations. When a country's products are not as attractive to consumers at home or abroad as those of other nations, the domestic economy suffers.

Developed countries are powerful enough to manipulate world markets to the disadvantage of competing LDCs. "Trade war" tactics such as **"dumping"** or **"hoarding"** can undermine the economies of the LDCs. When another nation dumps goods, it greatly increases the supply and forces world prices down, driving out competing nations. Japan has done this frequently. Hoarding is holding supplies back to artificially create scarcity and drive prices up. OPEC did this in the last few decades. Both tactics can have disastrous effects on vulnerable LDC economies, due to their nondiversified industry.

To indicate the extent of the LDC economic problems, the table (next page) compares **annual per capita Gross Domestic Product** (per capita GDP = GDP divided by population) of the countries of South and Southeast Asia with some of the more developed nations.

1993 Per Capita GDP Compared	
South & Southeast Asia	**Developed Nations**
Bangladesh $200.00	Austria $20,895.00
India $380.00	Israel $12,5000.00
Pakistan $380.00	Japan $19,500.00
Philippines $720.00	Switzerland . .$21,700.00
Vietnam $230.00	U.S.A. $22,470.00

*(Gross Domestic Product ÷ population = share per person c. 1993)

ECONOMIC PLANNING

Decisions made by India's leaders today will affect both the country's standard of living and its future status in the world. India's role as a power in Asia and among the Third World LDCs depends on its leaders' ability to develop modern industrial capacities. As a mixed system, the economy combines elements of free market and command systems.

Despite the Green Revolution's technological advances, much of S. & S.E. Asia's agriculture remains labor intensive.

Free market systems (capitalism) operate through privately owned firms according to the relationship of supply and demand in the economy.

Government planning and operation of the economy constitute **command systems**. Since independence, the Indian government has indicated a desire to reduce dependence on outside nations.

Beginning in 1951, India's planners set official production goals in a series of national five-year economic plans. The first plan placed

emphasis on agricultural development. The second focused efforts on heavy industry. The third (1961-66) was a revision of the first because food shortages became life-threatening.

AGRICULTURAL ADVANCEMENT

"The Green Revolution" is a term social analysts apply to a worldwide effort to focus scientific and technological efforts on overcoming food shortages and starvation in LDC's. Thanks to the Green Revolution, India now uses hybrid wheat and rice seeds which are superior to older types. This has allowed the country to build up grain surpluses in recent years. However, as in many LDCs, the technological problem in India is intertwined with social and economic difficulties.

TECHNOLOGICAL PROGRESS

India has managed significant gains in technological progress since independence. It is now the tenth largest industrial power in the world in terms of **GNP** (Gross National Product – total value of goods and service produced annually). Major industrial production includes jute fiber, processed food, steel, heavy machinery, and cement. This rapid growth unevenly effects the standard of living.

David Johnson, 1991

As is true in most all of S. & S.E. Asia, farming is labor intensive and primitive – Ox plowing on Damak farm, Nepal.

- cultural and religious traditions affect the raising and utilization of certain animals (pork is banned by Muslims, and beef and dairy products are banned by Hindu custom)
- shortage of and resistance to animal or chemical fertilizers
- lack of capital for improvement and mechanization
- land held in tiny parcels
- acceptance of famines as natural

Two distinct classes are emerging. An educated urban class prospers, while the rural poor class declines.

INDIA'S ECONOMIC STRUGGLE

India's economic planning goals caused it to borrow heavily from the developed world. Besides debts to Britain and other Commonwealth nations, India relies on grants and food supplies from the United States. In 1955, Nehru also began accepting Soviet assistance. The government now encourages privately owned foreign companies to build plant facilities if they complement government planning goals.

The 1970's were exceptionally bad years. Drought and crop failures forced importation of food, and the increase in oil prices drained investment capital. Today, the economy is growing at a healthier rate (8% in recent years), but India still suffers from an **imbalance in trade** (imports exceeding exports). Today, India's major trade is with Japan, Saudi Arabia, and the United States.

DEVELOPMENT ELSEWHERE

Continued domestic and foreign problems plague the other economies of this region.

- **Vietnam**, **Laos**, and **Cambodia** suffer from the long years of fighting. The per capita income of communist nations is generally very low. Their economies are **agrarian** (agricultural). Farms are owned collectively not individually. Most socialist economies follow strict plans, with the labor force expected to achieve set production goals. Still, the economic collapse of the Soviet Union in the late 1980's modified the perspective of communist states. Vietnam recently signaled desires for broader trade relations with the U.S. and other Pacific Rim nations. Questions about Vietnamese accountability for the fate of American prisoners of war has hampered trade relations.

- **Indonesia** achieved independence in 1949. President Sukarno launched a nationalization program. The government confiscated personal and commercial property from the Dutch and other foreigners. After General Suharto's military control began in 1967, some private enterprise was allowed to reemerge. Still, the government of Indonesia controls major industries, such as petroleum production.

Industrial Growth in Steel and Cement Construction: This rapid growth has had an uneven effect on the standard of living throughout India and South Asia.

PhotoDisc Inc. 1993

PhotoDisc Inc. 1993

City of Singapore and Harbor: With its high per capita income, Singapore has the leading economy of the South and Southeast Asian region. The city-state of Singapore with its strict laws and harsh punishment for criminal behavior is virtually crime-free and very clean with no slums and no unemployment.

- **Singapore's** $13,900.00 (1991) per capita income made it second only to Japan's in Asia. It has a free-enterprise industrial economy with petroleum refining, rubber processing, and electronics prominent. Only 10% of its land is under agricultural production.

- **Malaysia** is also a free-enterprise system, but the imbalance of wealth in the hands of the urban Chinese minority has caused the government to institute costly rural development programs.

- The **Philippines** also follow capitalist economic principles, but the per capita income is low. Only 12% of the population is engaged in industry. Major products are sugar, timber, nickel, coconut products, bananas, and textiles.

The Southeast Asian nations are often linked commercially to Japan. Its investment capital can be found throughout the  region. Japanese industries purchase much of the raw material produced, especially petroleum, rubber, tin, and bauxite. Japan exports heavily to these areas, especially its electrical products. These nations also use Japanese shipping and financial services.

QUESTIONS

1   Which person is correctly paired with the economic development theory he favored?
    1   Suharto — Marxist revolution
    2   Gandhi — trade imbalance
    3   Nehru — five-year plans
    4   Sukarno — free enterprise

2   Third World nations are dependent on the developed nations for
    1   financial resources
    2   raw materials
    3   agricultural workers
    4   cottage industries

3   "Cottage industry" was a system in which
    1   overseas trade was discouraged
    2   piecework was done by hand craftsmen
    3   agriculture was the only means of making a living
    4   workers contract for their wages

4   What has been an important result of the Green Revolution?
    1   Agricultural productivity has increased.
    2   Slavery has been abolished.
    3   Large estates have become unprofitable.
    4   Commercial farming has become collectivized.

5   India's first economic five-year plan emphasized
    1   military production
    2   development of heavy industry
    3   improvement of food supply
    4   production of consumer goods

6   Currently, which situation in developing nations of South and Southeast Asia hinders efforts to raise their standards of living?
    1   continued high rate of population growth
    2   cold winters
    3   inability of scientists to increase crop yields
    4   rejection of Western technology by nationalist leaders

7   The term LDC is used primarily to refer to a country that
    1   lacks extensive natural resources
    2   has Christianity as its established religion
    3   is in revolt against control by communist foreign powers
    4   has underdeveloped industrial and financial resources

8   Which is common to current economic development in South and Southeast Asia?
    1   exhaustion of natural resources
    2   interference by the U.N.
    3   oppression of European imperialists
    4   imbalance of trade

9   Which is the primary reason why India often has difficulty adding to its supply of capital equipment?
    1   Most members of its professional classes emigrate.
    2   It has a scarcity of unskilled labor.
    3   Its government tends to promote a free market system.
    4   Much of its productive capacity is used to provide the bare necessities.

10 Which is the major problem facing many developing nations today?
    1   resolving conflicts between church and state
    2   adjusting traditional life to new technological advancements
    3   gaining political independence from colonial powers
    4   obtaining membership in the United Nations

11 Which situation has brought about changes in traditional Indian society?
    1   existence of cultural isolation
    2   establishment of local governments
    3   dependence on subsistence agriculture
    4   increase in industrialization

12 To which situation has the growth of industrialization in many South and Southeast Asian nations led?
    1   weakening of family and village ties
    2   reductions in the standard of living
    3   strengthening of ethnic loyalties
    4   increase in the influence of traditional religions

13 Which is most characteristic of a command economy?
1 resources are allocated by government direction
2 a variety of economic incentives encourage private business growth
3 there is a high rate of unemployment
4 prices are set by interaction of consumers and producers

14 An economic structure in which there is both private and government ownership of industry is known as
1 collectivization
2 mixed economy
3 free enterprise
4 command system

Base your answers to questions 15 through 17 on the opinions below and on your knowledge of the social studies.

Speaker A: Increased contact among nations and peoples is characteristic of our times. A single decision by OPEC or a multinational corporation can send ripples of change throughout our global society.

Speaker B: If the last 500,000 years were divided into lifetimes of years, there would be 800 such lifetimes. Humans spent the first 650 of these in caves, and the most important changes occurred only during the final lifetime.

Speaker C: If we are to survive, all passengers on our Spaceship Earth must participate in efforts to solve the issues that threaten humankind: poverty, resource depletion, pollution, violence, and war.

Speaker D: We must understand that no single culture's view of the world is universally shared. Other people have different value systems and ways of thinking and acting. They will not see the world as we do.

15 Which concept is discussed by both *Speakers A and C*?
1 self-determination
2 nationalism
3 conservation
4 interdependence

16 Which statement best summarizes the main idea expressed by *Speaker B*?
1 Humans have always had to deal with many changes in their lives.
2 The rate of change has increased rapidly in the 20th Century.
3 Throughout history there has always been great resistance to change.
4 Conditions in the modern world are better than in any prior era.

17 *Speaker D* indicates a desire to reduce
1 ethnocentrism
2 globalism
3 social mobility
4 religious tolerance

18 A chronic problem facing most Asian countries since World War II has been a shortage of
1 natural resources
2 unskilled labor
3 investment capital
4 markets for agricultural products

ESSAYS

1 The Industrial Revolution continues to change the world.

Choose *three* specific countries from South and Southeast Asia and describe *two* ways in which each has attempted to meet the challenge of industrializing.

2 Technological problems are intertwined with social and economic difficulties in India.

Describe *three* ways religious and cultural traditions have affected the economic development of India.

V. GLOBAL CONTEXT

Since independence, various foreign policy issues have affected South and Southeast Asian nations. Their international policies today are largely the outgrowths of many factors in their recent experience.

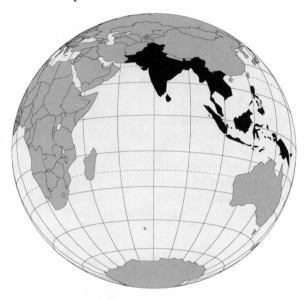

GEOPOLITICS

Historically, the political and strategic concerns of South Asian countries have been shaped by their relationships with major world powers. European colonial powers in the region, the People's Republic of China, the former Soviet Union, and the United States influenced foreign policies.

After independence, India's leaders committed the nation to a policy of nonalignment. Nehru wished to devote the nation's attention to domestic development. India accepted U.S. economic aid under President Truman's *Point Four Program* for less developed countries. However, in 1954, Nehru refused to join **SEATO** (Southeast Asia Treaty Organization), a U.S.–sponsored multilateral security agreement to help nations resist communism. A year later, he began accepting aid from the Soviet Union.

After being defeated by India in the 1948 war over Kashmir, Pakistan moved toward alliances with the west. President Ayub Khan joined SEATO in 1954. The following year, Khan committed his nation to membership in **CENTO** (Central Treaty Organization). CENTO was an alliance of Britain and several Middle Eastern nations, including Turkey and Iran. Both alliances were weak. Yet, when war with India broke out again in 1965 and 1971, Pakistan held its own with the military equipment and training it received from the west.

The major powers have had a direct impact on events in South and Southeast Asia. France fought to retain its Indo-Chinese colonies after World War II. Britain retained strong ties through its Commonwealth. Japan is the most influential economic power.

The United States attempted to restrain the communist takeover of South Vietnam. As a result of the nine years of the Vietnam War, the U.S. suffered 57,702 dead and 153,303 wounded. U.S. foreign policy in Southeast Asia was based on the **Domino Theory**. The feeling was that a communist victory in one of these small, weak states would lead to other nations falling. After the U.S. withdrawal from Southeast Asia, Vietnam, Laos, and Cambodia did fall to communist insurgents who had received aid from Red China and the U.S.S.R.

Thailand, once a strong U.S. ally and SEATO member, requested withdrawal of U.S. military personnel and bases after the fall of Vietnam and Cambodia. In 1975, SEATO disbanded. The following year, Thailand reached a formal diplomatic accommodation with communist Vietnam.

The Domino Theory: American foreign policy in Southeast Asia was influenced by the political idea that if one of these nations fell to communism, its neighbors would follow.

India's Cold War Policies			
	United States	**Soviet Union**	**Red China**
1950's	Nehru feared Western colonialism more than communist aggression. He refused defensive treaties with the West.	Negotiated aid treaty in 1955.	Generally friendly relations until 1959. After Tibetan revolt, China occupied territory in north India.
1960's & 1970's	Accepted arms from U.S. to defend against Chinese. Suspicious of continued U.S. aid to Pakistan.	Continued cordial relations. Technological assistance accepted.	Fought with China, lost more territory.
1980's	U.S. – Red Chinese detente and U.S. aid to Pakistan strained relations	Soviet invasion of Afghanistan cooled friendship.	More cordial and friendly relationship after Soviet action in Afghanistan.

INDIA'S FOREIGN POLICY

During the Cold War Era, India used many strategies to avoid superpower conflicts (see chart above).

Rather than taking sides during the Cold War Era, India tried to lead the LDCs as a neutral bloc. India played a role in shaping the United Nations General Assembly's policies. While it condemned the nuclear arms race of the superpowers in the Cold War, India developed nuclear weapons of its own. It is also in an intense nuclear weapons competition with its neighbor, Pakistan.

PAKISTAN'S CONCERNS

External threats have modified Pakistan's foreign policies. The border wars with India and the Indian interference during the secession of Bangladesh moved Pakistan to ally itself with Western nations. The 1979-1991 Soviet occupation of neighboring Afghanistan increased its security fears.

FOREIGN POLICY AND CULTURAL DIFFERENCES

Hostility to imperialism and superpower interference are not the only concerns of Southeast Asian nations. Ancient rivalries and cultural differences must be taken into account. Cambodia has long been the target of invasion from people in the area of Vietnam. Similarly, most Southeast Asian countries have historically been invaded by China and remain prejudiced against those of Chinese ancestry living in their countries. Such hostilities caused Singapore to leave the

General Foreign Policy Alignments		
Nations with Close Ties to the West	**Nations with Ties to Communist Countries**	**Neutral Nations**
Pakistan Philippines	Cambodia (Kampuchea) Laos Vietnam	Myanmar (Burma) India Indonesia Sri Lanka Thailand

PhotoDisc Inc. 1993

Opposing Dragon Motif On Singapore Wall
This artform is symbolic of the struggle between free enterprise and government
domination of economies in South and Southeast Asian countries.

Malaysian Federation in 1965. Traditional rivalries were also evident when, in that same year, Indonesia resigned its seat on the United Nations Security Council because rival Malaysia was admitted to U.N. membership.

QUESTIONS

1   The purpose of SEATO (1954-1975) was to solve problems through
    1   peaceful negotiation
    2   religious toleration
    3   free trade
    4   military defense

2   After gaining independence from Britain, India chose to
    1   end relations with all European nations
    2   not join the United Nations
    3   ally itself with the communist bloc
    4   steer a neutral course

3   The United States helped create SEATO after
    1   the communist victory over France in Vietnam
    2   India's defeat of Pakistan in Kashmir
    3   China's invasion of India in 1959
    4   the Soviet invasion of Afghanistan in 1979

4 Which is an example of Cold War neutrality?
1 attempt by France to hold its Indo-Chinese colonies after WW II
2 the 1979 Soviet invasion of Afghanistan
3 U.S. sponsorship of the SEATO alliance in 1954
4 India's decisions to avoid SEATO and CENTO

5 Which event strained Chinese-Indian relations?
1 impositions of tariffs
2 India's adoption of a pro-Western foreign policy
3 border disputes
4 India's participation in the Vietnam War

6 Newly formed nations sometimes choose to remain nonaligned because they
1 wish to ignore world problems
2 are concerned with internal problems
3 believe U.N. involvement might hamper relations
4 combine both public and private economic planning

7 The "domino theory" on communist insurgency in Southeast Asia held that
1 India would seek to become a major world power
2 cultural rivalries would be a continual source of friction
3 imperialism would be a constant threat
4 when one small nation falls, others will follow

8 For much of Southeast Asia, the decades since World War II may best be described as a period of
1 economic independence
2 cultural isolation
3 social unification
4 political instability

9 Which Cold War event strained relations between India and the Soviet Union?
1 the Soviet invasion of Afghanistan
2 the Soviet take over in Bangladesh
3 Indira Gandhi's assassination
4 Soviet-Chinese raids on the Indian border

10 Which nations are closely tied to the west?
1 Vietnam, India
2 Pakistan, the Philippines
3 Laos, Thailand
4 Indonesia, Cambodia

ESSAYS

1 Discuss an issue of conflict for *each* of the following pairs of nations.

- Indonesia — Malaysia
- India — Pakistan
- Singapore — Malaysia

2 Since World War II, the South and Southeast Asian region felt numerous influences by outside nations.

Outside Influences

- CENTO
- SEATO
- Soviet activities in Afghanistan
- Chinese activities in Tibet
- American Domino Theory

Choose *three* of the above influences and discuss how each affected specific nations in South and Southeast Asia.

UNIT TWO: S. & S.E. ASIA ASSESSMENT

ISSUE: THE EFFECTS OF IMPERIALISM

This two-part assessment offers individual library research and debate opportunities.

STUDENT TASK

Research and debate a position on imperialism.

DETAILED PROCEDURES

Part One:
Choose (or instructor assigns) a colony or mother country. For each area, instructor designates a student to investigate the positive effects and a student to investigate the negative effects of the imperial era. Compose a set of notes for use in debate.

Part Two:
Present notes in a debate format:
- 5 minutes for the oral presentation of positive effects of imperialism.
- 5 minutes for the oral presentation of negative effects of imperialism.
- 2 minutes for rebuttal for each side.

LEARNING STANDARDS

Students should:

- Understand that different national, ethnic, religious, racial, socioeconomic, and gender groups have varied perspectives on the same events and issues.

- Analyze and evaluate differing views of historic, social, cultural, economic, and political events, eras, ideas, and issues.

- Understand that interdependence requires personal and collective responsibility for the local and global environment.

- Understand that the ideals of democratic principles and human rights constantly evolve in the light of global realities.

- Work cooperatively and respect the rights of others to think, act, and speak differently from themselves within the context of democratic principles and social justice.

- Present ideas both in writing and orally in clear, concise, and properly accepted fashion.

EVALUATION

The scoring grid next to the evaluation items (on the following page) was left blank intentionally. Choice of appropriate category terms is the decision of the instructor. Selection of terms such as "minimal," "satisfactory," and "distinguished" can vary with this assessment. The table on page 10 offers additional suggestions for scoring descriptors that might be inserted in the blank grids.

Part Two: Debate Evaluation

Table on page 10 offers suggestions for scoring descriptors.

Evaluation Item *a* Does presentation use related data and analyze effect of imperialism on area?	Category 1	Category 2	Category 3	Category 4	Category 5
Evaluation Item *b* Does delivery make position clear and direct? Is there good eye contact? Are notes used appropriately?	Category 1	Category 2	Category 3	Category 4	Category 5
Evaluation Item *c* During debate, does student adjust and respond to arguments? Does student challenge positions of others?	Category 1	Category 2	Category 3	Category 4	Category 5

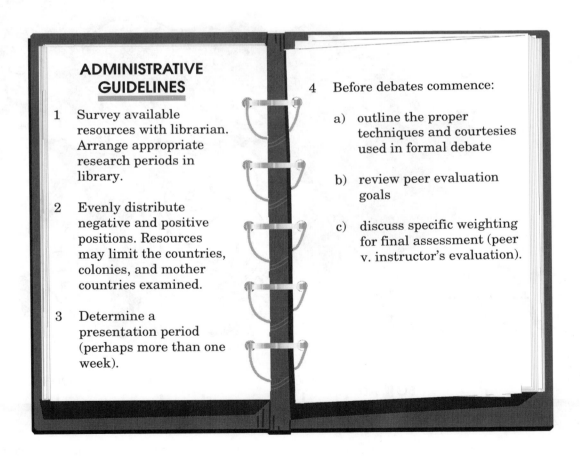

ADMINISTRATIVE GUIDELINES

1. Survey available resources with librarian. Arrange appropriate research periods in library.

2. Evenly distribute negative and positive positions. Resources may limit the countries, colonies, and mother countries examined.

3. Determine a presentation period (perhaps more than one week).

4. Before debates commence:

   a) outline the proper techniques and courtesies used in formal debate

   b) review peer evaluation goals

   c) discuss specific weighting for final assessment (peer v. instructor's evaluation).

3 East Asia

China

3000	500			800	1500	1700

BC AD

DYNASTIES: *Chin* •   • *Han*   • *Tang*   • *Mongol*   • *Manchu*

• Confucius   • Shintoism   • Feudal Japan   • European spheres

• Yaoi (Japan)   • Buddhism   • Tokugawa Shogunate

Time-line is not drawn to scale.

Japan

Shinto
dynasty
feudalism
Hiroshima
Long March
gang of four
Confucianism
expansionism
ethnocentrism
nuclear umbrella

cultural revolution
Great Leap Forward
Tiananmen Square

1900   1950   2000

- Japan industrializes
- Boxer Rebellion
- Republic of China
- Russo-Japanese War
- WW II
- Communist China (Mao)
- Democracy in Japan
- Chinese Cultural Revolution
- Deng Xiaopong

Time-line is not drawn to scale.

UNIT THREE:

EAST ASIA

I. PHYSICAL AND HISTORICAL SETTING OF CHINA

Many elements have shaped the culture of China. To understand China today and the actions of its government toward other nations, it is necessary to look at the cultural forces which shaped Chinese society.

PHYSICAL FEATURES

Geography has always posed a great challenge to China's evolution. There is a strong relationship between China's physical environment and the development of its civilization.

GEOGRAPHIC ISOLATION

China's topography and location isolated it from other civilizations. The **Altai Mountains** in the north, the **Himalaya Range** in the west and south, and the **Gobi Desert** in the north are formidable barriers. They separated China from the influence of the cultures of Europe and South Asia. To a lesser extent, the Pacific isolated China from the island people of Japan and Taiwan. In some instances, the separation discouraged Chinese movement outside its borders. In other cases, the physical barriers discouraged invasion by outsiders. The result of both was isolation.

RIVERS AS KEYS TO CIVILIZATION

Civilization in China began over 4,000 years ago in the major river valleys: first in the **Huang** (Yellow), then in the **Chang** (Yangtze), and **Xi** (West). Gradually, the civilization expanded outward from the river valleys. The major river valleys are also the heart of China's agricultural economy. They provide the basic framework for the growth of Chinese population and culture. The **Brahmaputra**, **Irrawaddy**, and **Mekong** descend from the mountains of the south. Yet, they are not navigable until they reach into South Asia. They played a greater role in the development of South and Southeast Asia than in the development of China.

PREVAILING WINDS

In China, **summer monsoons** blow off the Pacific and carry large amounts of moisture to the southeast coast. Flooding is common in this region during the wet months. Dry, frigid **winter monsoons** blow southward from the cold tundra and taiga regions of Siberia and the Gobi Desert. They keep most of the interior regions of the north very dry.

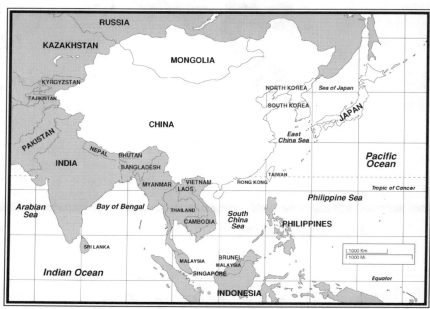

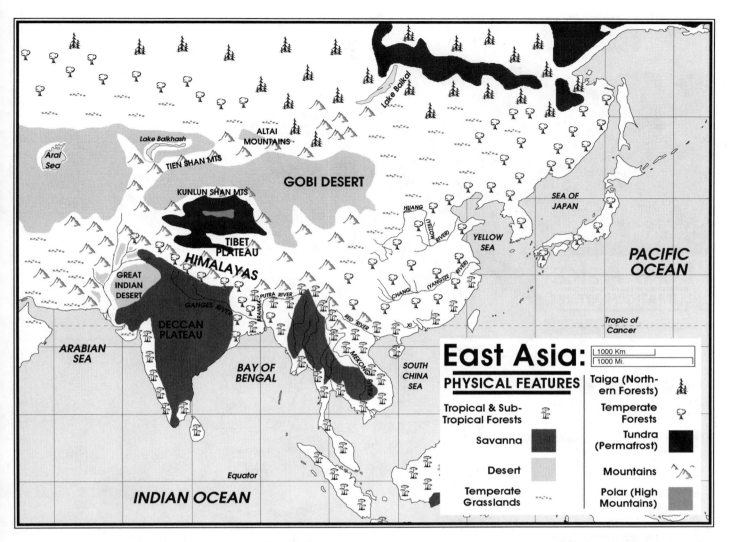

East Asia:
PHYSICAL FEATURES

Tropical & Sub-Tropical Forests		Taiga (Northern Forests)
Savanna		Temperate Forests
Desert		Tundra (Permafrost)
Temperate Grasslands		Mountains
		Polar (High Mountains)

RECURRING DROUGHTS AND FLOODS

Much of North China receives low, irregular rainfall. Irrigation canals are necessary throughout the area. Droughts often lead to famine and death. In the central and southern parts of China, major rivers frequently cause floods. The Huang River has flooded so often through the centuries that it is called "China's Sorrow." Recent regimes made substantial efforts to control this river's destructive nature by constructing dams, run-off trenches, and irrigation canals.

DEMOGRAPHICS AND CULTURE

While China's three million square miles seems large, the ruggedness of the terrain make much of it uninhabitable. Most of its 1.2 billion people live in the river valleys and along its Pacific coastal plains.

POPULATION DENSITY

Over 90% of China's people live on less than one-half of the land. The mountainous West has a very low density while the eastern river valleys have very high density. **Shanghai**, the major port on the Chang, has over 12 million inhabitants.

China has the largest population of any nation. India is a very close second with nearly a billion. Still, China's rate of growth has slowed, while India's is accelerating. China's population density (317 pop./sq mi) is also less acute than India's (782 people per sq. mi.). Unlike India, China's population is very homogeneous. Despite the constant influx of non-

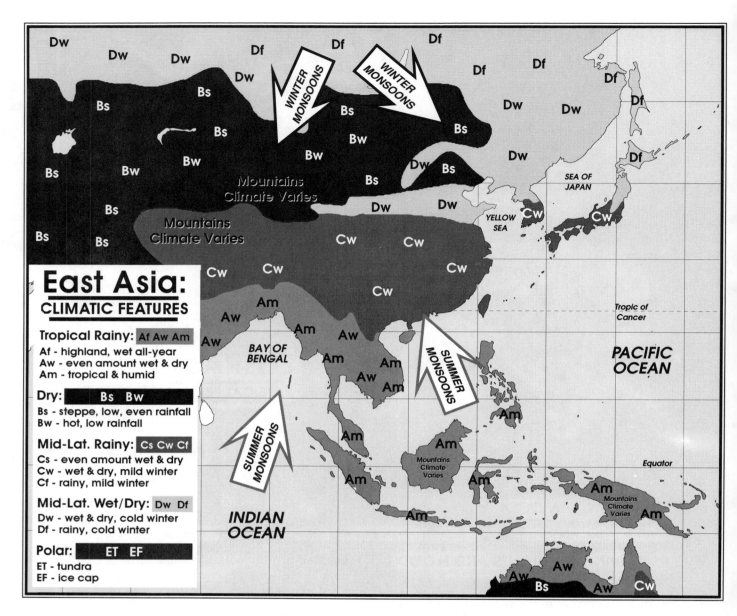

East Asia: CLIMATIC FEATURES

Tropical Rainy: Af Aw Am

Af - highland, wet all-year
Aw - even amount wet & dry
Am - tropical & humid

Dry: Bs Bw

Bs - steppe, low, even rainfall
Bw - hot, low rainfall

Mid-Lat. Rainy: Cs Cw Cf

Cs - even amount wet & dry
Cw - wet & dry, mild winter
Cf - rainy, mild winter

Mid-Lat. Wet/Dry: Dw Df

Dw - wet & dry, cold winter
Df - rainy, cold winter

Polar: ET EF

ET - tundra
EF - ice cap

Chinese invaders throughout its history, it has not suffered the ethnic and religious strife of India.

ISOLATION AND ETHNOCENTRISM

Ethnocentrism is a form of prejudice. It means viewing all other cultures as inferior to one's own. Traditionally isolated, the Chinese referred to their country as the **Middle** or **Central Kingdom** because they believed it to be the center of the world. They ignored foreign cultures, regarding them as "barbarian" or uncivilized. Physical factors favoring the formation of such a homogeneous culture and an ethnocentric attitude include:

- settlement and isolation in the deltas and river valleys

- ease of local contact with other settlements afforded by a network of rivers

- discouragement of Western infiltration

RELIGION AND PHILOSOPHY

The homogeneous cultural unity of China's people allowed ancient systems of thought to grow uninhibited for centuries. Certain modes of thought and behavior became monolithic. Physical isolation and intellectual resistance to outside ideas entrenched philosophies such as Confucianism in China's civilization.

Basic Tenets Of Confucianism

- Humanity is the center of heaven and earth.
- Human nature is essentially good.
- Cultural wisdom demands respect for age and authority.
- Success of the state depends on proper conduct of the ruler.
- The family group is the foundation of society.
- An ordered society, in which all know and do what is expected of them, is necessary.

CONFUCIANISM

In the 6th Century B.C., the philosopher Confucius' thought came to dominate Chinese social organization, political structure, and educational system and became the very foundation of Chinese civilization.

Confucians taught that society would be orderly if everyone knew his/her proper rank (place). In descending order of importance, the social classes were scholars, peasants, artisans or craftsmen, and merchants. "The Five Human Relationships" are found in the *Analects*, a collection of Confucius' sayings which are the guide to correct behavior.

Confucian philosophy taught that society was in harmony if everyone performed their proper duties. If the ruler was good, his people would naturally follow his example and also be good. The ruler was the "Son of Heaven." If he was just, he received a **mandate** (right or command to rule) which came from heaven. If he was unjust, he was denied the mandate. The people had the right of rebellion against an unfair ruler.

During the 3rd Century B.C., a number of philosophies emerged that challenged the three centuries of Confucian dominance.

Yin & Yang: Symbol of Chinese religious and philosphical tradition representing negative and positive life forces. (above center)

TAOISM

The **Taoist** philosophy revered nature, self-knowledge, simplicity, and nonaction. It held a person should follow instinct and not live a highly organized or activist life. If the natural order were upset by humanity, troubles would develop.

LEGALISM

Legalism developed in response to the lawlessness which plagued China. According to legalism, punishment should be very severe for even minor offenses. Legalists believed the best government was one in which the ruler had great authority. They viewed war as good for society because it required even more obedience and submission to the ruler's commands.

BUDDHISM

Buddhism, introduced from India, widened contacts with the non-Chinese world through pilgrimages to India and Southeast Asia (for greater understanding of Buddhism, see Unit II, Section One). Chinese Buddhists launched missionary trips to Korea and Japan. It remains the predominant religion in the western Province of Tibet.

The Five Human Relationships

1	Ruler and Subject	The first person is the superior and is to set a good example and take care of the inferior. The second person, the inferior, owes respect and obedience to his/her superior.
2	Father and Son	
3	Husband and Wife	
4	Older Brother and Younger Brother	
5	Friend and Friend	Friends are social equals who owe each other respect and courtesy.

THE GREAT DYNASTIES

In order to rule successfully, a political system must be responsive to its society's needs and desires. During key periods, strong dynasties implemented the main social philosophies and created a centralized rule.

CHOU (ZHOU) (1027 - 222 B.C.)

The Chou (Zhou) people invaded China's coast from the northwest. They set up a court **bureaucracy** (powerful body of civil servants) and a network of feudal territories. The outlying feudal lords warred in later ages. This weak-ened the Chou Dynasty for conquest by the Ch'in. Still, the later period produced Confucianism and Taoism.

CH'IN (QIN) (221 - 210 B.C.)

Lawlessness and social decline during the late Chou Era led to scholars developing **legalism** under the Ch'in. The Ch'in Dynasty lasted only fifteen years. Still, its adherence to legalist principles greatly changed China. It conquered the warring lords, united China, and created the first emperor (Shih Huang-ti). Its central government structure survived under succeeding dynasties. The Ch'ins began construction of

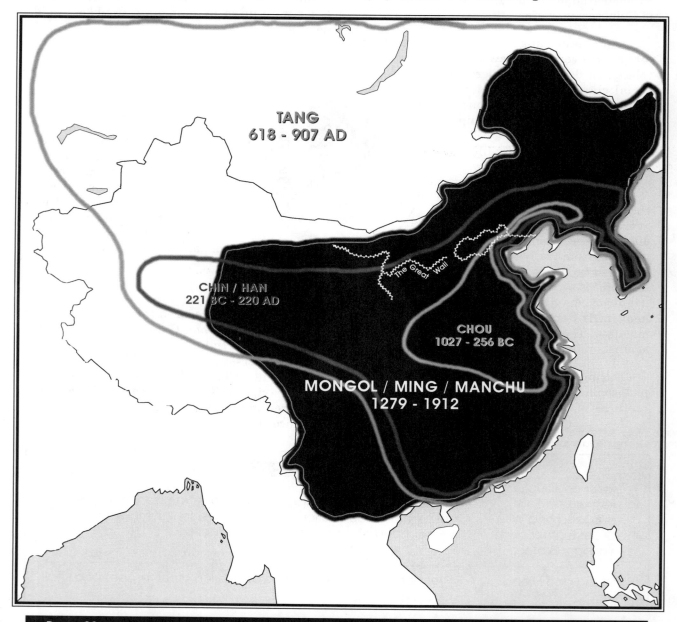

TANG
618 - 907 AD

CHIN / HAN
221 BC - 220 AD

The Great Wall

CHOU
1027 - 256 BC

MONGOL / MING / MANCHU
1279 - 1912

The Great Wall Of China: Constructed during the Chin Dynasty (221 B.C. - 210 B.C.)

DETERMINATION OF POLITICAL & ECONOMIC SYSTEMS

the **Great Wall**, regulated coinage, and standardized writing.

HAN (210 B.C. - 220 A.D.)

The Han Dynasty blended legalist structure with Confucian tradition. The major legalist contribution of strong central government remained, but the Hans banned the philosophy itself.

A main Han contribution was the establishment of the civil service examination system. Workers were needed to direct the empire's expanding bureaucracy. These government workers took competitive examinations, testing their knowledge of Confucianism. To prevent any one bureaucrat from becoming entrenched in his office, no official served in the province of his birth or served in any province longer than three years. In this period, a calendar was drawn up, sunspots recorded, and paper and the seismograph were invented.

T'ANG (618 - 907 A.D.)

T'ang rulers Li Yuan and T'ai-tsung reunited the empire after four centuries of fragmentation. Domestically, T'ang rulers revived Confucianism as the dominant philosophy and stressed the civil service examination system. Chinese society served as a model for Japanese, Korean, and Southeast Asian people. Literature and the arts flourished. The imperial armies conquered parts of today's Korea and Tibet.

After the T'angs established strong central government, their soldiers expanded the empire into Mongolia, Tibet, and the vast deserts of Central Asia. Trade along the **Silk Route** continued to flourish long after the T'angs declined.

MONGOL (YUAN) (1279 - 1368 A.D.)

For almost a century after the fall of the T'angs, Mongols from the north ruled China. The Mongol (Yuan) Dynasty, led by **Genghis Khan** and his successors, maintained contacts

Genghis Khan

with the world. One famous emissary from Europe was **Marco Polo**, an Italian visitor to the court of Kublai Khan. Mongol rule was successful for a time as it adopted Chinese form and tradition. In the 14th Century, the Mongols were overthrown by a native peasant group, the Mings.

MING (1368 - 1644 A.D.)

The Mings committed themselves to restoring Chinese traditional society. They reinforced ethnocentric tradition, regarding all outsiders as barbarians. The Mings were absolute rulers. They reduced the power of the civil service. They built magnificent courts at Beijing and encouraged cultural advancement.

The Ming Dynasty expanded China's regional influence. The Mings financed expeditions throughout Southeast Asia and even to the east coast of Africa. In the 15th Century, China had a substantial navy and armed forces of over 27,000 men. However, most contacts with Europe reinforced China's ethnocentric attitude toward foreigners.

MANCHU (1643 - 1912 A.D.)

Northern invaders from Manchuria conquered the Mings and established the Manchu (Ching) Dynasty. As with earlier conquerors, the Manchus preserved Confucian society. They organized the **tributary system**, in which conquered regions were required to send tribute (gifts) to Manchu overlords. Until the 19th Century, the Chinese continued to absorb invaders. They dominated Manchuria, Nepal, Mongolia, Burma, Thailand, Laos, Vietnam, and Korea.

During the 19th Century, the Manchu Empire declined. Modern Chinese history was shaped by the Manchu policies toward the

Western world. The Manchus treated the Europeans as inferiors, and displayed attitudes ranging from indifference to hostility.

QUESTIONS

1 Taoist philosophy taught humanity would only attain peace and happiness by
　1 accepting its lot in life and by not struggling against nature
　2 depending entirely on the government
　3 fighting to reform the nation
　4 seeking glory and wealth

2 In which river valley did the first Chinese Civilization develop?
　1 Yellow
　2 Mekong
　3 Yangtze
　4 Xi

3 Confucianism encouraged its followers to
　1 experiment with science
　2 travel to foreign countries
　3 respect traditional customs
　4 conquer East Asia

4 Western contacts with China can be traced to the famous merchant who visited Mongol China,
　1 Li Yuan
　2 Genghis Khan
　3 Confucius
　4 Marco Polo

5 Genghis Khan is remembered as a famous conqueror who
　1 united China under Mongol rule
　2 introduced Buddhism
　3 created the basic philosophy of China
　4 isolated China from the outside world

6 China fortified its northern border to
　1 protect Silk Route
　2 provide irrigation
　3 withstand barbarian attacks
　4 permit flood control

7   While China currently has the world's largest population, its problems are less severe than India in terms of
   1   density
   2   scarcity
   3   immigration
   4   urbanization

8   In Confucian society, a member of the "elite" class would be the
   1   soldier
   2   farmer
   3   scholar
   4   landlord

9   Regarding China's population distribution
   1   approximately half live in rural areas and about half in cities
   2   90% or more of the people live in less than half of China
   3   the largest cities are clustered in the west
   4   10% live in rural areas and 90% live in cities

10 The heart of China's agriculture over the centuries has been the
   1   winter monsoon season
   2   protection of the interior mountains
   3   slow population growth
   4   fertile river valleys

11 "China's classical period (1027 B.C. - 220 A.D.) produced its greatest philosopher. His rules for correct behavior set the pattern of China's society for 2,000 years." Who is described here?
   1   Lao Tze
   2   Genghis Khan
   3   Chiang Jiang
   4   Confucius

12 The strong ethnocentrism encountered by European traders in early 19th Century China was primarily due to China's
   1   economic superiority
   2   artistic excellence
   3   historic geographic isolation
   4   overwhelming military strength

13 Social control in traditional China was chiefly the function and responsibility of the
   1   established church
   2   extended family
   3   central government
   4   village communes

14 In Chinese history prior to the 20th Century, cultural traditions were transmitted primarily by
   1   the government
   3   the schools
   2   the family
   4   invading foreigners

15 Which was an important teaching of Confucians?
   1   Intellectual knowledge is secondary to one's emotions.
   2   The family group can often hinder the smooth functioning of the society.
   3   All persons must accept and perform their duties in society.
   4   Those who have military power have earned the right to govern.

16 Traditional society such as ancient China was most likely to
   1   discourage rapid population growth
   2   reduce the influence of the emperors
   3   emphasize the individual over the group
   4   accept only limited social change

ESSAYS

1   Geography has been a major influence on Chinese history.

   a   Explain how China's geographic isolation shaped its culture.

   b   Discuss the effect that China's three major rivers have had on the country's development.

2   Confucian, Taoist, and Legalist ideas influenced the development of Chinese civilization from earlier times.

   a   Describe the *three* philosophies which appeared during China's early history.

   b   Describe *two* qualities an ideal person would have according to these early philosophies.

II. DYNAMICS OF CHANGE

During the years since 1850, the Chinese people have experienced almost constant social upheaval, war, and political unrest.

RELATIONSHIPS WITH THE WEST

China disagreed with the Western powers on the conduct of international relationships. It had a different perception of what constituted justice in these relationships.

WESTERN INTEREST IN CHINA

Chinese tea, silk, porcelains, and various luxury goods were in great demand in the West. A growing number of merchants and missionaries tried to enter China. The 19th Century saw the rise of European Imperialism and the desire for Western capitalists to open China's markets and purchase its raw materials.

CHINA'S LIMITED INTEREST IN TRADE

Although contact with Europeans became more frequent, official foreign relations were limited. China continued to regard its civilization, culture, and knowledge as superior to that of the West. Its Manchu rulers wished to protect its culture from "barbarian influences." They were not interested in utilizing Western ideas or products. Manchu officials restricted European ships to one port, Canton. They demanded bribes and treated the Westerners as inferiors.

OBJECTIONS TO THE TRIBUTE SYSTEM

One major area of friction between China and the outside world was China's insistence on the **tributary system**. This was the act of showing homage to the Emperor by bringing gifts and performing the **kowtow** (deep ceremonial bow). By 1795, Westerners were demanding diplomatic relations based on equality.

THE WEST CARVES UP CHINA

Despite the fact that the Chinese invented gunpowder in the 6th Century, the low priority placed on technological development, especially in arms, compromised their power.

China's traditional ways of repelling foreign domination proved ineffective against industrialized nations. Events that led to the final humiliation and defeat of the Manchus included:

- **The Opium War** (1839 - 1842) – In order to upset China's **favorable balance of trade** (more exports than imports), Britain sold Indian opium to the Chinese. When the Manchu government destroyed British opium stored in Canton, a war began in which British warships and military firepower defeated the Manchus.

- **Unequal Treaties** – Chinese acceptance of the first of a series of unequal treaties ended the **Opium War**. By the  *Treaty of Nanking* (1842), China ceded the island of Hong Kong to Britain and opened five treaty ports to foreigners. More unequal treaties with Britain, France, and the United States followed. China was forced to accept **extraterritoriality** (by which foreigners were not subject to Chinese law), allow foreign gunboats in its waters, and accept the right of foreigners to set tariffs. The treaties from 1842-1860 reduced the Manchus' prestige and helped ignite over a half-century of peasant uprisings. The most serious was the **Taiping Rebellion** (1850-1864).

- **Spheres Of Influence** – The technologically superior European forces made China open its trade. They created **Spheres of Influence**. These were diplomatic agreements that carved up a weaker people's territory into areas dominated by an imperialist nation. European powers also forced China to accept Christian missionaries.

Their presence and humiliation of treaty ports functioning as centers of Western culture caused frustration to grow.

- **Sino-Japanese War** (1894-1895) – Perhaps China's greatest shock was delivered by another Asian nation, Japan. The Sino-Japanese War ended Chinese claim of dominance in East Asia. Japan easily won Taiwan and the Liaotung Peninsula and gained a sphere of influence over Korea.

RESPONSE TO IMPERIALISM

DETERMINATION OF POLITICAL & ECONOMIC SYSTEMS

Imposing Western and Japanese political, economic, and social demands upset the Chinese. Yet, Manchu attempts at reform and modernization failed.

ATTEMPTS AT WESTERN LEARNING

Economic concessions to the principal European powers convinced some Manchu officials that reforms were needed. An attempt was made to adopt Western technology without disturbing traditional Chinese social and political order. Between 1861 and 1895, the Chinese manufactured guns and steamships and constructed telegraph lines and railroads. Chinese students went to universities in Europe and the United States.

RESISTANCE TO REFORM

The **Empress Dowager**, who ruled first as a **regent** (governing for a child monarch) and later directly for 47 years, preferred to manipulate supreme power rather than institute reform. Resenting new Western ideas destructive to their power, Confucian bureaucrats reinforced the Empress' approach. Treaty concessions and peasant revolts drained the government's resources, further stifling reform.

OVERTHROW OF THE EMPEROR (1911 - 1912)

The final collapse of the Manchu Empire brought political confusion. The parliamentary government desired by **Sun Yat-sen** and other reformers was ineffective.

THE REPUBLIC OF CHINA

Throughout the 19th Century, opposition to the influence of Western nations grew. I-ho-Ch'uan ("righteous harmony fist"), a secret nationalist resistance movement nicknamed "the Boxers" by Westerners, led a rebellion in 1900. The Boxer Movement captured Peking (now Beijing) for several months. They isolated the Western diplomatic community and tried to force them out. A combined force of Germans, Russians, British, Japanese, Americans, and French managed to free the city and its rail links. After the Boxer Rebellion, the Manchus made more half-hearted attempts at reform.

In 1911, a middle class and student revolt became the final crisis for the Manchus. The revolution gained army support. Revolutionary spokesman Sun Yat-sen was abroad raising funds. He rushed home to try to take control.

THREE PRINCIPLES OF SUN YAT-SEN

Earlier, Sun Yat-sen (1866-1925) published his revolutionary speeches in *Three Principles of the People*. He drew support for a movement to create a democratic republic based on:

- **Nationalism** – the overthrow of all spheres of influence and the restoration of Chinese rule

- **Democracy** – the establishment of a democratic constitution and an elected President and Legislature

- **Livelihood** – the redistribution of the large estates

Sun Yat-sen

POWER

Sun tried to hold the army's support by choosing General **Yuan Shih-Kai** as president of the new Chinese Republic. The General dissolved the new legislature, bribed or murdered his opposition, and used the army to back his rule as a dictator until his death (1916). Sun Yat-sen and his followers formed the **Kuomintang** (Nationalist Party), dedicated to restoring the Republic of China.

CIVIL STRIFE AND THE WARLORDS

The local military dictator of each province was called a **warlord**. After General Yuan's death, no one was strong enough to unite China. The warlords ruled the provinces by terror and extortion. China was torn by the warlords' territorial wars. In the 1920's, Sun Yat-sen asked for Western help to defeat the warlords, but only the Soviet Union sent arms and military advisers.

NATIONALIST PARTY RULE (1928 - 1949)

To follow the history of the Nationalist Party is to understand the reasons for the communist triumph in China.

LEADERSHIP OF CHIANG KAI-SHEK

In 1924, the Kuomintang named **Chiang Kai-shek** its military leader. The following year, Sun Yat-sen died. Chiang became the full-fledged leader of the Nationalists. With help from the Soviets, Chiang broke the power of the warlords. He turned on the communists and tried to destroy them.

Chiang Kai-shek

NATIONALIST PARTY CORRUPTION

Under Chiang, the Kuomintang entrenched its power and tried to defeat the Chinese communists. Chiang abandoned the principles of Sun Yat-sen and allied with the wealthy who opposed land reform. Under his leadership, China became a military dictatorship with progress only in the areas of industrial growth.

RISE OF COMMUNISM (1920 - 1949)

Some of the opponents of Chiang turned to Marxist communism hoping to share the benefits of economic development equally among the workers and peasants. Marxism appealed to different classes of Chinese because it:

DETERMINATION OF POLITICAL & ECONOMIC SYSTEMS

- forecast the worldwide collapse of imperialism
- promised land reform and the end of poverty
- appeared successful in the large, backward nation of Russia
- promised industrial development and more employment
- rejected Confucian thought which supported acceptance of established authority
- had strong leadership

LEADERSHIP OF MAO ZEDONG

Mao Zedong emerged as the leader of the Marxist communist rebels at the time of the **Long March** (1934 -1935). This was the 6,000 mile (9,656 km) flight of the communists from southern to northern China in order to escape the Kuomintang Army (see map on opposite page).

Mao Zedong

The Long March survivors became the dedicated core of the Chinese Communist Party. Because of Mao's political and social programs, the party gained enormous strength among the peasants.

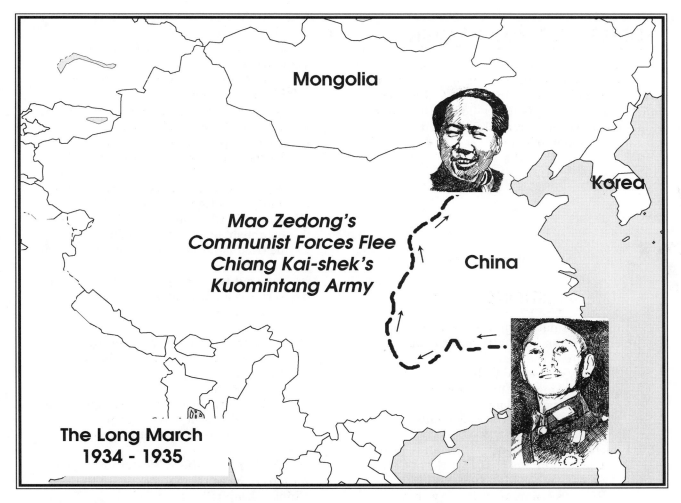

Mao Zedong's Communist Forces Flee Chiang Kai-shek's Kuomintang Army

Mongolia

Korea

China

The Long March 1934 - 1935

JAPANESE INVASION WEAKENED THE NATIONALIST GOVERNMENT

Japanese imperialism brought a halt to internal conflicts. Japan occupied the northern province of Manchuria (1931). In 1937, the Second Sino-Japanese War began with Japan's aerial attacks on Chinese seaports. Japanese armies marched into the Yellow and Yangtze Valleys. Chiang had to form a "united front" with Mao to fight the Japanese invasion. Each knew that civil war would resume once Japan was defeated. Much of the Nationalist Army was destroyed while fighting in World War II.

CIVIL WAR ESCALATES (1945-1949)

Kuomintang weaknesses in the 1940's set the stage for the communist victory in the Civil War. Chiang's corrupt and inefficient regime:

- made no effort to reform the country

- suppressed democratic ideals and alienated the intellectuals

- mismanaged American aid

- alienated business interests through misguided fiscal policies

- stifled business competition

- ignored peasant pressures for land during recurrent famines

As discontent with the Kuomintang grew, the communists gained support. In areas they liberated from the Japanese, communists divided the property among peasants, began political education programs, and raised the status of women. The Kuomintang Party lost, because it did not develop programs for economic and social reform.

PEOPLE'S REPUBLIC OF CHINA

Soviet communist leaders supplied Mao's forces with substantial amounts of weaponry. By 1949, Peking (Beijing) fell to the communists. Chiang and his forces fled to the island of Taiwan. Both governments claimed to be the legal government of China.

QUESTIONS

1 Imperialist nations in the 18th and 19th Centuries generally attempted to acquire or control areas that had
   1 highly developed technology
   2 undeveloped natural resources
   3 literate populations
   4 stable centralized governments

2 Which would be the most difficult to prove?
   1 The revolutions of 1911-1912 in China overthrew the Manchus.
   2 Russia's Communist Party were more ruthless than China's Communist Party.
   3 Mao Zedong came to power in 1949.
   4 China's population is larger than Japan's.

3 Which statement best applies to the Chinese Empire after 1885?
   1 The Chinese welcomed the economic imperialism of the Europeans.
   2 The Boxer Rebellion successfully drove out the Europeans.
   3 European powers carved China into "Spheres of Influence."
   4 The Open Door Policy of the United States ended imperialism.

4 Who led the Chinese government forces in the 1925-50 era against both Japan and the communists?
   1 Sun Yat-sen
   2 Mao Zedong
   3 Chiang Kai-shek
   4 Yuan Shih-kai

5 China was an easy victim of Western Imperialism despite its large size and population because it
   1 lacked effective central governments and technology
   2 was peace-loving and nonaggressive
   3 welcomed Western influence
   4 hoped to profit from lessons to be learned about Western science

6 The right of extraterritoriality in the 19th and early 20th Centuries allowed a Westerner in China to
   1 establish an export-import business
   2 be tried for crime under laws of his own country
   3 take out temporary Chinese citizenship
   4 serve as an advisor to the Chinese government

7 The Western nations became interested in China during the 19th Century because China
   1 had large reserves of oil
   2 had recently discovered large gold fields
   3 exported tons of surplus crops
   4 could serve as a market for trade

8 Which characteristic of Western European nations allowed them to dominate the Chinese Empire?
   1 rigid social class structures
   2 self-sufficiency in natural resources
   3 frequent political revolutions
   4 advanced technological development

9 The primary usefulness of the spheres of influence acquired by foreign nations in the late 19th Century was to provide
   1 aid for the Chinese in developing their industrial capacity
   2 assistance in resisting communist insurgents
   3 sources of raw materials and markets for the foreign nations
   4 new settlements for the growing Chinese population

10 During his regime, a basic aim of Sun Yat-sen was to
   1 declare war on Japan
   2 end foreign domination of China
   3 execute Christian missionaries
   4 overthrow the Dowager Empress

11 Philosophically, Chinese communists accepted the beliefs of
1 Marx
2 Gandhi
3 Sun Yat-sen
4 Confucius

12 A major reason for the defeat of the Kuomintang during the Chinese Civil War was that they lost the support of the
1 Buddhists
2 factory workers
3 army
4 peasants

13 Which best accounts for the lack of political unity in China between 1912 and 1937?
1 religious warfare
2 little popular loyalty to the central government
3 refusal of foreign powers to recognize the Chinese government
4 the declining strength of Chinese communism

14 One factor explaining the 1949 communist victory in China was that
1 the United States would not aid the Nationalists
2 Mao Zedong promised to drive out all foreign powers
3 Soviet Russia sent aid to Mao's forces
4 Japan had eliminated all of the Nationalist armies

15 During the late 1880's, imperialistic nations divided China into
1 plantations
2 communes
3 spheres of influence
4 independent city-states

16 The Long March is an important episode in the success of the communists because it
1 abandoned the principles of Sun Yat-sen
2 restored the Empress to power
3 rekindled devotion to Confucianism
4 strengthened the dedication of Mao's followers

ESSAYS

1 China fell victim to Western imperialism in the 19th Century.

a Why had the Chinese first placed restrictions on Western traders?

b Why are the Treaty of Nanking (1842) and others of that period referred to as "unequal"?

c Why were the Manchu attempts to reform China unsuccessful?

2 To know Chinese history in the 20th Century is to understand the reasons for the communist victory.

a Discuss the problems of the Nationalist-Kuomintang government in the 1930's.

b Why is the Long March important in this period of Chinese history?

c Marxist revolutionary philosophy deals with economic alteration in industrial societies. Why did the communist philosophy appeal to the Chinese peasants?

III. CONTEMPORARY CHINA

Under Mao Zedong's leadership, dramatic social, political, and economic changes occurred in China. Even greater change followed his death, as his successors wished to modernize China without his strict revolutionary ideology.

RULE OF MAO ZEDONG (1949 - 1976)

From the founding of the People's Republic of China until his death, Mao's vision of the Chinese Revolution dominated developments in China. He wanted to move China from its technological backwardness. At first, inflation was a problem, but the government managed to control it by the mid-1950's. Industrial production began to surpass pre-World War II levels. Mao's communists set up an authoritarian **command economy** that changed life in China.

DETERMINATION OF POLITICAL & ECONOMIC SYSTEMS

CHANGES IN AGRICULTURE

In rural areas, collective programs began to increase production. In **communist collec-tivization**, private ownership and wealth are dissolved. The government commandeers all resources (property, capital, labor) and reorganizes them. The government takes all products and profits and redistributes them according to the society's needs. Through collectivization, leaders hoped to:

- control the rapid population increases that strained food supplies

- generate capital to import needed industrial materials

- train workers in new technologies

- control the migration of rural labor to the cities

In 1958, Mao ordered collective farms to merge in an ambitious program called the **Great Leap Forward**. Villages were uprooted and people were moved into government controlled **commune** settlements of 20,000 people.

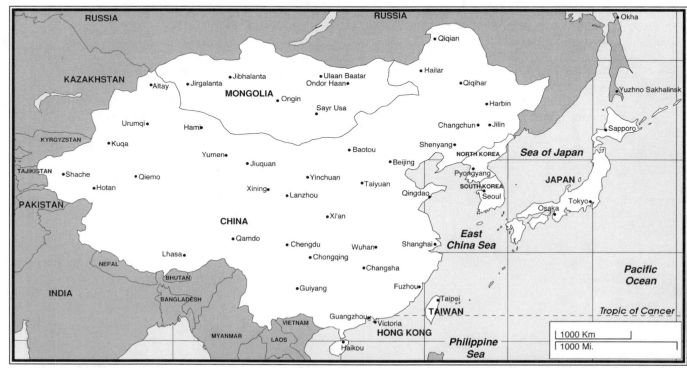

ECONOMIC GROWTH & DEVELOPMENT

CHANGES IN INDUSTRY

Under the Great Leap Forward, factories were formed into commune structures, also. Authorities forced long hours on workers to meet demanding goals. The major industrialization efforts of the communist regime included:

- implementing **Five Year Plans** which focused upon heavy industry

- expanding transportation facilities

- spreading industry more evenly throughout the country

- reforming the banking and financial systems

CHANGES IN THE QUALITY OF LIFE

The communist command system ignored individual freedom and personal choice. Still, its programs improved sanitation, medical facilities, and education. Reorganization and expansion of schools reduced illiteracy. Women received full equality with men. Although the peasants did not receive individual plots of land, they did enjoy a higher standard of living in the communes.

THOUGHT REFORM MOVEMENT

China became a **totalitarian state** (dictatorial regime that controls all aspects of life). To control the population, totalitarian leaders created a paranoid siege mentality. They spread unrelenting propaganda through media and education. This enabled them to regulate thinking and intensify the fear that became a foundation of domestic policies. The regime stressed constant alertness to internal and external dangers. It fostered dedication to communist ideals.

The government strengthened its position by:

- encouraging voluntary campaigns to improve production

- identifying all who agreed with Mao as "the People"

- labelling negatively as "landlords" and "capitalists" those who exploited the Chinese people in the past

- using psychological techniques to reinforce communist ideology and lessen ties with traditional Confucian thinking

- emphasizing literacy, particularly for adults

- employing "street committees" to provide surveillance of neighborhoods and disseminate propaganda

THE CULTURAL REVOLUTION

By the 1960's, the failure of the Great Leap Forward and Mao's disagreements with the Soviet Union caused a division in the Chinese Communist Party. Chairman Mao's brutal collectivization and heavy propaganda campaigns disturbed President **Liu Shao-qi** and others. A battle for the control of China erupted in 1965. It was more than a political struggle. It turned into a general purge involving education, gov-

PhotoDisc Inc. 1994

Contemporary Chinese Street Celebration

ernment, science, and culture and became known as the **Cultural Revolution**.

The Red Army supported Mao. Various party officials backed Liu Shao-qi. Mao ordered the removal of this opposition from power. He closed schools so that students could mobilize into political groups called the **Red Guards**. By 1968, the Army ended the street violence. Historians estimate as many as 20 million died in the ten-year struggles of the Cultural Revolution. Mao's repressive actions kept China on its revolutionary path. His *Quotations of Chairman Mao* condemned the old ways. The book became required reading throughout the country.

RESTORING WORLD STATUS

China's traditional image of itself as a great power influenced the national goals of the People's Republic. Starting in the 1950's, China's leaders sought influence over the newly independent LDC's of Asia and Africa. China represented itself as a successful model of a native revolution against imperialism. China assumed a preeminent position in East Asia. It became involved in the area's international questions. It supplied arms to both North Korea and North Vietnam in their struggles with the U.S.

PROBLEMS IN ACHIEVING GOALS

POPULATION INCREASES

A large population requires substantial resources for subsistence and makes development difficult. China's large population and the level of education within the country are both important factors affecting development. The communist government discourages early marriages and encourages couples to have only one child, but the population today exceeds 1.2 billion.

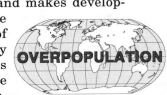

LIMITED AGRICULTURAL BASE

No more than one-third of China's vast territory is **arable** (capable of sustaining agriculture). Some characteristics of China's traditional agricultural pattern were:

- labor-intensive cultivation of small plots of land with almost no mechanization (labor was the cheapest factor in production)

- widespread primitive irrigation measures

- very little animal husbandry because of a lack of land for pasturage

The pressure to produce enough to sustain the largest population in the world has always been great. China's principal crops are grains (rice and wheat) and cotton. It does not enjoy the security of having large food reserves.

By 1990, in spite of intensive efforts to reform agriculture, only 11% of the land was used for agriculture, yet 75% of the labor force was engaged in agriculture. Annual per capita income was less than four hundred dollars.

PhotoDisc Inc. 1994

In China, modernization and mechanization have fallen behind the developed Western nations. Manual labor is the cheapest factor in production.

POLICIES AFTER MAO

TRIAL OF THE GANG OF FOUR

Following Mao's death in 1976, a power struggle began between moderates and radicals, led by his widow **Jiang Qing** and three conspirators. This "Gang of Four" tried to force a return to the violence of the Cultural Revolution. Moderate leader Deputy Premier **Deng Xiaoping** defeated the radicals and put them on trial in 1980. They were found guilty of undermining the party and government and were sentenced to life imprisonment.

In 1981, the Central Committee of the Chinese Communist Party issued a statement that Mao Zedong was responsible for the "grave blunder" of the Cultural Revolution. The years of the personality cult which idolized China's revolutionary leader were over.

POLICIES UNDER DENG XIAOPONG

In 1978, the moderates under Deputy Premier Deng announced **The Four Modernizations**, a plan to modernize China by the year 2000. Major improvements were forecast in four fields: agriculture, industry, science and technology, and military (see discussion in the next section).

Deng's moderates also initiated small changes in the legal system. While there has been some loosening of control, there is still little freedom of speech or press. There were also new education and cultural policies. China's Confucian tradition, rejected by Mao as unsuitable to modern China, was reevaluated by Chinese intellectuals.

Political struggles between hard-line communists and moderates continue. The moderate communist leaders wish to restore ties with China's past and adapt some cultural traditions to Marxism. Such areas include:

- a unitary pyramid of political control, traditional from the time of the Han Dynasty

- subordination of the individual to the group, with the communist state substituted for the family

In the 1980's, China expanded its cultural contacts with other nations. Ten thousand Chinese students were permitted to study abroad at foreign universities and technological schools. However, this program was modified after the student protests of 1989.

T'IANANMEN SQUARE MASSACRE

The new economic and social reforms and the intensified contact with the Western world triggered more and more political unrest, especially among the young. In the Spring of 1989, students held massive pro-democracy demonstrations in  Beijing's T'iananmen Square against the slow pace of Deng's reform. Party leader **Zhao Ziyang** was forced to resign from the leadership for failure to control democratic movement among the people. Premier **Li Peng**, with Deng's backing, unleashed troops on the demonstrators, killed many, and followed with harsh political repression, executions, and banishment of demonstration leaders.

In 1989, a Chinese student defies the government's power during pro-democracy demonstrations in T'iananmen Square ("Gate of Heavenly Peace"), Beijing

QUESTIONS

1 Soon after coming to power, the government of the People's Republic of China tried to make significant changes in the traditional family structure because
   1 it was an obstacle to communist plans for modernization
   2 there was too much decision-making power in women's hands
   3 the structure was based on Western values of self-reliance
   4 it did not encourage sufficient acceptance of authority

2 Which is a major reason why families are smaller in China today than in the past?
   1 Religious beliefs encourage small families.
   2 The government offers incentives for smaller families.
   3 Widespread disease and famines have reduced the population.
   4 Educational facilities are limited.

3 Which has been an effect of the communist revolution on the status of women?
   1 Women's legal rights have been diminished.
   2 Less emphasis is placed on women receiving higher education.
   3 There have been more employment opportunities for women.
   4 The percentage of women in domestic occupations has increased.

4 Which basic agrarian problem was collectivization of agriculture supposed to solve?
   1 a surplus of trained workers
   2 huge surpluses of agricultural produce
   3 inflation caused by overabundance of investment capital
   4 the flooding of rural workers into the cities

5 Which group achieved victory in the Cultural Revolution?
   1 Kuomintang
   2 Boxers
   3 Red Guards
   4 Gang of Four

6 Which factor is common to both Confucian and communist Chinese societies?
   1 decentralized government
   2 welfare of the group more important than the individual
   3 frequent internal conflict preventing stability
   4 stress on reverence for the past

7 Which is an accurate statement about art and music during the Cultural Revolution?
   1 Government programs fostered creative expression.
   2 Government banned all except Confucian expression.
   3 Government purged cultural activities.
   4 A special emphasis was placed on cultural diversity.

8 The fact that political controversy often occurs when governments try to solve complex economic problems indicates that
   1 proposed solutions often generate new problems
   2 the government should never interfere with economic life
   3 democratic governments handle economic decision-making best
   4 political and economic issues are not related

ESSAYS

1 Throughout history, leaders' ideas have affected their nations. In contemporary China, the ideas of Mao Zedong and Deng Xiaoping have led to profound change.

   a Discuss how Mao tried to reorganize China's economy and society.

   b Explain why "thought reform" was important to Mao's plan for remaking China.

   c Explain how Deng's plan for China's development differed from Mao's plan.

IV. ECONOMIC DEVELOPMENT OF CHINA

Struggles in China since Mao's death have unleashed a profound economic transformation. Today, China's leaders wish to move rapidly from an agrarian economy to an industrialized one. Yet the blending of private incentive into the older communist system presents problems.

ECONOMIC RESOURCES

HUMAN RESOURCES

Throughout its history, China relied on the use of human energy as the chief productive factor in the creation of wealth. Today's changing economic structures rely on technology and a labor force that can use it. To overcome its problems and modernize, China must train and retrain the vast labor force.

Terraced Millet Fields in China

PhotoDisc Inc. 1994

MINERAL RESOURCES

China has a very limited amount of the natural resources important in today's world. Known mineral wealth includes tungsten, antimony, iron ore, oil, and scattered coal deposits. Manchuria has one of the richest coal deposits in the world.

AGRICULTURAL RESOURCES

Agriculture is China's main source of income. Since no more than one-third of the land is arable, every acre must be carefully used. In southern China, extensive irrigation and **terracing** (carving planting areas out of the hillsides) have increased land use. Raising a sufficient rice crop requires intensive human labor. Because of its temperate, drier climate, northern China grows wheat, corn and soybeans.

Like India and the LDCs, Chinese agriculture must strain to feed a growing population – the world's largest. Beyond that, leaders must find a way to grow enough surplus to provide food for export. Exporting that surplus will furnish foreign currency needed for capital investment.

Natural resources help economic development. Still, sustaining a large population can drain available resources and can leave little for development. China is trying to utilize technology to overcome problems of scarcity in both food and consumer goods.

ECONOMY UNDER MAO

After their victory over the Kuomintang, the communists introduced an economic command structure. This caused far-reaching changes in the traditional landlord-peasant system to achieve greater production. To implement the command structure, Mao launched a Five-Year Plan in the 1950's that included:

- **Land Redistribution** – The communists took all land, farm animals, and equipment from landowners and gave them to the peasants. Many landowners were tried and executed.

- **Cooperatives** – In the early 1950's, the communists forced farmers to combine their lands and form cooperatives. The land was still considered privately owned, but the farmers had to work together. Farmers could sell a small part of their produce. Cooperatives proved insufficient to feed the city workers.

- **The Great Leap Forward** – In 1958, the communists established large scale agricultural communes. They forced excess peasants to labor in the factories, imposing heavy production demands. Although it managed a few significant economic gains, the program suffered from peasant resentment, mismanagement, and shortages.

- **The Commune System** – During the Great Leap, all the peasants' private property was merged into agricultural communes. Family living was all but destroyed. Communal space such as dining halls and dormitories replaced private homes. Each peasant received a government wage but could not sell any produce privately. Life was completely under the direction of the commune leaders. The commune system failed in the 1960's. Peasants hated the loss of their homes and privacy and resented the merciless work loads. Their resistance, plus disastrous weather conditions, forced the government to ration food and use scarce capital to import foreign grain.

- **Ideology Versus Expertise Controversy** – Some officials believed a person's loyalty to Marxist doctrine should be the first criterion for appointment to government positions. Other officials took another view and believed ideology should sometimes bend to knowledge and expertise. Mao's regime sided with the Marxist view. Expertise was sacrificed, and central economic planning suffered.

After Mao's death in 1976, the new leaders increased the reform movement. More moderate politicians permitted greater economic freedom, and planning experts employed limited capitalist methods.

THE FOUR MODERNIZATIONS

In 1978, the senior leader of China's communist oligarchy, Deng Xiaoping, announced the "Four Modernizations Program." The leaders hoped this plan would modernize communist China by the year 2000. The major departure from Mao's economic program was the use of incentives to encourage production. The plan included:

- The **Family Responsibility System** – In agriculture, the commune organization was disbanded in favor of family-directed farming. It allows the peasants to sell some produce for profit. This incentive steadily increased food production. The government allows small private enterprise in cities. This also has served to raise family and individual standards of living.

- **Local Management of State Factories** – In 1984, the government announced a series of reforms aimed at making industry more productive. The government cut back on central industrial planning. **Site-based management** allowed factory managers to decide the amount of goods to be produced, select workers, and set salaries. Rather than all profits being handed over to the central government, managers must pay a factory income tax. The remaining profits can be reinvested to expand production, add new workers, or raise salaries.

- **Stress On Consumer Goods** – Chinese industry now produces more consumer goods. Prices have risen steadily because of the law of supply and demand. Televisions and radios are top priority items. Making more consumer goods available also meets the goals of communist leaders to show the system can provide for the people.

- **Improved Global Relationships** – The leaders realize they will modernize more quickly and efficiently with technical help from the West. They have consistently worked to normalize relations with the free, capitalist countries. Today, among China's major trading partners are the democracies. Of its $76 billion in imports, China gets 16% from Japan, 38% from Hong Kong, and 7% from the United States. It also trades with Germany, Australia, and Canada.

New
China Trade
Policy:

"Swinging Doors"

TRANSFORMATION PAINS

Economic transformation from centralized command with state-run industries to decentralized market with private ownership is not easy. Russia, the former Soviet republics, and the nations of Eastern Europe struggle with this transformation. In China, a problem rests with leaders who want to convert the economy while retaining communist political control. Economic progress has the effect of raising people's expectations for freedom.

The 1980's showed enough economic success to cause demonstrations for greater freedom in Beijing and other industrial cities. The government repressed these outbursts with force, showing political freedom is not part of its plan. American calls for the revision of China's human rights policies have been rebuffed by China's leaders.

Still, the modernization plan shows progress. The World Bank reports annual Gross Domestic Product growth averaged above 8% in the 1980's. (U.S. GDP growth averaged less than 5% in the same period.) China's growth slipped after the T'iananmen Square Massacre in 1989. The global recession of the early 1990's suppressed growth to below 6%, but it went above 12% in 1992 and 1993. (Coming out of the recession, U.S. GDP growth was only 3-4% during those years.)

China still imports large amounts of Russian and Ukrainian military hardware and Japanese and U.S. electronics, high tech equipment, food, and consumer goods. Still, it exports $90 billion a year in textiles, shoes, and steel. Its exports now exceed the value of its imports, a positive sign of progress.

QUESTIONS

1   The recent encouragement of private enterprise in the People's Republic of China is a shift from that country's
1   mercantilism
2   command system
3   imperialism
4   free market system

2   A major consumer complaint about the centrally planned economy of Mao's China concerned
1   overemphasis on agricultural production
2   scarcity and the lack of variety of products
3   rapid fluctuations of prices
4   overproduction of consumer goods

3   Which is a characteristic of command economies?
1   Decision-making is concentrated in the hands of government officials.
2   Major industrialists make all economic decisions.
3   Colonial officials dominate the economic structure.
4   Consumer choices indicate use of economic resources.

4   Which is a current economic problem of the People's Republic of China?
1   internal interference by the United Nations
2   peasant rebellions
3   oppression by Western imperialists
4   lack of consumer goods

5   Which problem undermined Mao Zedong's goals in the Great Leap Forward?
1   landlord manipulation of food prices
2   overproduction and massive farm surpluses
3   peasant resentment and resistance
4   interference from the Kuomintang

6   Since the death of Mao Zedong, elements of which philosophy have been permitted in China?
1   socialism
2   fascism
3   totalitarianism
4   capitalism

7   A major difference between Chairman Mao's Great Leap Forward and Deng Xiaoping's Four Modernizations policy is the
1   creation of forced labor camps for dissenters
2   use of incentives to increase production
3   introduction of a pure free-market economic structure
4   importation of skilled labor

8   Which situation in the People's Republic of China best illustrates the concept of interdependence of nations?
1   expanded participation in international sports events
2   sale of textiles and steel by China to obtain technology from other nations
3   establishment of high protective tariffs
4   persecution of landlords by the government

9   A chronic problem for the People's Republic of China since 1949 has been a lack of
1   mineral resources
2   markets for agricultural produce
3   technologically skilled labor
4   government direction of the economy

10 In China, which best reflected Marxism in Mao's programs?
1   foreign influence over the economy
2   communal work teams in factories
3   small family-owned business
4   private ownership of small farms

ESSAY

1   Today, developing nations seek to improve the quality of life for their inhabitants through economic development. To achieve such improvement, the People's Republic of China must face decisions about modifying the way it makes basic economic decisions.

a   Define and compare the concepts of command economy and free-market economy.

b   Explain why the Great Leap Forward and the Commune system failed as command economic structures.

c   Discuss how China is modifying its command economic structure.

V. CHINA IN THE GLOBAL CONTEXT

Deng Xiaoping's present regime in China reorganized society, the economy, and the state toward the reasserting of the nation's role as a world power.

HISTORIC INFLUENCE

In terms of culture, China has been one of the world's leading civilizations. Evidence of this historic influence includes:

- **Literary Prestige** – Chinese writing developed over 3,500 years ago and began with the drawing of objects. Chinese script spread beyond its borders and was used by Koreans, Japanese, and Vietnamese. Although these civilizations later developed their own writings, they never discarded the concept of **pictographs** (pictures used for writing) and **ideographs** (pictures used for concepts or ideas).

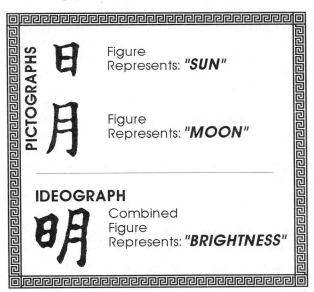

PICTOGRAPHS

日   Figure Represents: *"SUN"*

月   Figure Represents: *"MOON"*

IDEOGRAPH

明   Combined Figure Represents: *"BRIGHTNESS"*

- **Religious Impact** – During one of China's periods of disunity (220 - 581 A.D.) many Chinese adopted Buddhism. The Tang Dynasty persecuted Buddhists as the Confucian bureaucrat-scholars worried over its popularity. Buddhism never regained the number of converts it had previously.

Between the 7th and 9th Centuries, merchants and missionaries spread Buddhism to Korea and Japan.

U.S. RELATIONS WITH CHINA

In recent times, U.S. – Chinese relations moved from support to hostility to tolerance.

- **Civil War In China: 1945 - 1947** – At the end of World War II, as the Japanese withdrew from eastern China, the Nationalists and communists rushed to control the area. The armies of Chiang Kai-shek used material supplied by the United States during World War II to fight Mao's forces. In 1946, President Truman sent General **George Marshall** to negotiate between the communists and the Kuomintang to end the civil war. Neither side would compromise. The communists pointed to the U.S. supporting Chiang Kai-shek with military and economic aid. After thirteen months of frustration, Marshall returned to the United States without a settlement.

- **The Break-off Of Relations: 1949 – 1972** – After Mao's victory, China became a totalitarian state. Kuomintang supporters were arrested and many were executed. China broke diplomatic relations with the U.S. when America refused to recognize the People's Republic as China's legitimate government. The U.S. stationed its 7th Fleet off the coast of the Republic of China to prevent the invasion of Taiwan, where Chiang Kai-shek had retreated in exile.

- **Korean War (1950-1953)** – China and the U.S. clashed militarily in the Korean War. After World War II, the Korean Peninsula was divided at the 38th parallel. Soviet troops occupied the North. American troops occupied the South. Two separate governments developed. In 1950, communist North Koreans launched an invasion. It nearly pushed the South Korean Army into the

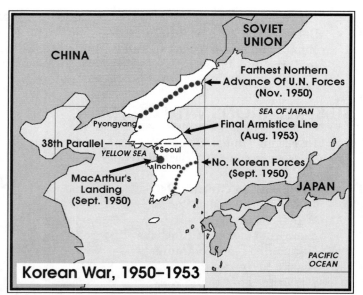

Korean War, 1950–1953

Map labels:
- CHINA
- SOVIET UNION
- Farthest Northern Advance Of U.N. Forces (Nov. 1950)
- SEA OF JAPAN
- Pyongyang
- Final Armistice Line (Aug. 1953)
- 38th Parallel
- YELLOW SEA
- Seoul
- Inchon
- No. Korean Forces (Sept. 1950)
- MacArthur's Landing (Sept. 1950)
- JAPAN
- PACIFIC OCEAN

sea. The U. N. Security Council condemned the aggression and voted to enter the war. The U.N. placed its force (American, South Korean, and 15 member nations) under the command of U.S. General **Douglas MacArthur**. The coalition quickly penetrated deep into North Korea. As the U.N. force drew close to the Chinese border, Red Chinese soldiers invaded Korea. This escalation of the war led to three years of heavy fighting. In 1953, a truce was reached and the division at the 38th parallel was restored.

- **Vietnam War** – An indirect Sino-American struggle took place during the Vietnam War. In the mid-1960's, as the United States dispatched soldiers and equipment to combat communist insurgency in South Vietnam, Red China aided North Vietnam and the southern Viet Cong rebels. After widening the war into Laos and Cambodia, President Nixon sent his aide, Henry Kissinger, to secret negotiations with Russia and Red China. After these discussions, public negotiations followed with North Vietnam. In 1974, American troops were finally withdrawn from Vietnam.

- **Relations since Mao** – China's diplomatic and trade relations with the U S. have improved since the late 1970's. Yet, there are areas of disagreement. The largest issue is the question of Taiwan. China claims the island belongs to the People's Republic while the U.S. still recognizes it as the

democratic **Republic of China** (Nationalist China), independent of the mainland. In 1982, the People's Republic agreed to cease hostilities if the United States pledged gradual reduction of military aid to Taiwan. China is also building its naval forces to strengthen its claims to oil-rich coastal islands claimed by Japan, Taiwan, Vietnam, and the Philippines.

RELATIONS WITH RUSSIA

From the days of the Chinese Emperors and the Tsars, there have been many sources of friction. They include border disputes, claims to the Amur River Valley, and support for the communist groups in Southeast Asia.

With the defeat of the Kuomintang in 1949, the Soviet Union welcomed China to the world stage as a second major communist power. In the four decades that followed, the friendship soured (see chart opposite page).

The two communist rivals clashed less frequently in the 1970's and 1980's. Internal problems preoccupied them. China strongly condemned the 1979 Soviet invasion of Afghanistan. In the late 1980's, Soviet President Gorbachev visited Deng to ease some of the tensions. They made some progress. Their wars of words eased. However, when Gorbachev resigned, most of the old problems remained. In the 1990's, the collapse of the Soviet Union and Russia's economic and governmental problems kept leaders from addressing problems. Russian President Yeltsin made several attempts to improve relations, but China remained suspicious of the new, unsettled republics on its borders (Kazakhstan, Tajikistan, and Kyrgyzstan).

THIRD WORLD RELATIONS

During Mao's regime, China tried to claim a leadership role among the poorer LDCs of the Third World. It gave aid and propaganda support to insurgent movements in Asia and Africa.

WARS OF LIBERATION

China is the strongest military power in East Asia. In

WAR & PEACE

Sino-Soviet Disagreements (1950's-1980's)

People's Republic Of China	Soviet Union
Mao defended Stalin's image, policies, and personality cult.	In 1956, Khrushchev attacked the policies of late Soviet dictator Josef Stalin.
Mao claimed Chinese communism was the true version of Marxism-Leninism.	Claimed to be true leader of world communist movement as oldest Marxist nation.
Rejected "peaceful coexistence" with Western democracies; supported spreading Marxist revolutions throughout the undeveloped world.	Promoted idea of "peaceful coexistence" and avoidance of nuclear warfare.
Detonated first nuclear bomb in 1964.	Refused to aid China in nuclear technology after 1959.
Denounced U.S.S.R. for refusing to help communist China against noncommunist India.	Sent aid to India in its 1961 border war with China.

the 1950's, Mao Zedong held the Marxist view that war with capitalism and imperialism was inevitable. He denounced the U.S. as a "paper tiger." China supported "wars of liberation" for the oppressed throughout the world. Chinese military aid and technical training were sent to struggling Marxist insurgents in Africa as well as other areas of Asia and the Pacific.

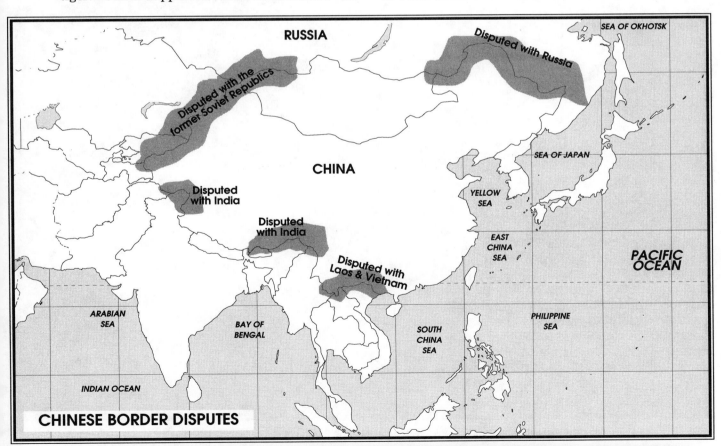

CHINESE BORDER DISPUTES

KOREAN AND VIETNAM WARS

Involvement in the Korean and Vietnamese wars showed that Mao Zedong intended that China play a major role in global affairs.

CHINA'S ROLE IN THE UNITED NATIONS

In 1971, the People's Republic of China was admitted to the U.N. It replaced the Republic of China (Taiwan) as the government officially representing mainland China. In addition to representation in the General Assembly, it also acquired Taiwan's permanent seat in the Security Council. Since that time, China has supported anti-colonialism and other Third World interests and often opposed resolutions of the Western democracies and Israel.

CHINA'S NEW STATUS IN THE PACIFIC

In recent years, the People's Republic of China reestablished itself as a force in Asian affairs. Its foremost trading partner is China's former enemy, Japan. Diplomatic relations between the two were reestablished in 1972. China exports agricultural products and clothing while importing electronics, machinery, and metal products from Japan.

The British Crown Colony of Hong Kong on China's southeast coast is a prosperous world

With the expiration of their Colonial Lease in 1997, the British will return Hong Kong to China.

PhotoDisc Inc. 1994

trading center. It has one of the strongest modern economies in East Asia and the Pacific Rim. China's Emperor permanently ceded it to the victorious British at the close of the first Opium War (1842). Britain and China reached an agreement in the mid-1970's that set a lease on Britain's possession of the island. The agreement states that the Chinese flag will be raised, but British social, economic, and legal systems will exist until the lease expires in 1997. Portugal agreed to a similar treaty with regard to the city of Macao for 1999. With the signing of these accords, China ended the divisions caused by 19th Century Imperialism.

QUESTIONS

1 In the 1970's and 1980's, the U.S. and the People's Republic of China moved toward establishing better relations mainly because
1 China democratized its government and sought to preserve human rights
2 both countries feared the rising industrial strength of Japan
3 the U.S. needed vital supplies of raw materials from China
4 both wished to balance the power of the U.S.S.R.

2 In the 1990's, Great Britain will return its Hong Kong colony to China. This planned event can be considered a victory of
1 free trade over tariff restriction
2 nationalism over imperialism
3 communism over capitalism
4 ethnocentrism over internationalism

3 A part of ancient China whose possession is a troubled issue for the U.S. and China is
1 Manchuria
2 Korea
3 Hong Kong
4 Taiwan

4 Since their victory in 1949, a major goal of China's communist leaders in Asia has been to bring about
1 peaceful settlement to all Asian conflicts
2 permanent U.N. control of disputed regions
3 establishment of China as a global power
4 ownership of the Korean peninsula

5 The introduction of Buddhism to Japan and Korea by ancient China is an example of
1 cultural diffusion
2 aggression
3 alliances
4 ethnocentrism

6 Which is an example of improved relations between the People's Republic of China and the United States?
1 sale of U.S. products in China
2 continued U.S. recognition of Nationalist China's government
3 increased U.S. support for Vietnam in its struggles with China
4 restrictions on Chinese immigration to the U.S.

7 The most accurate description of Chinese foreign policy today would be
1 deep friendship with former Soviet republics in the north and west
2 suspicion and coolness toward former Soviet republics in the north and west
3 deep friendship and military alliance with the United States
4 suspicion and increasing hostility toward the United States

8 During the 1950's, United States' policies toward the People's Republic of China were influenced primarily by
1 the existence of Soviet power over Eastern Europe
2 the fear of further communist expansion into critical areas of Asia
3 a close alliance between Japan and China
4 the stormy relationships between China and Vietnam

9 Which foreign policy did both Chinese and Soviet communist leaders use during the Cold War?
   1 They supported African and Asian "wars of liberation."
   2 They promoted peaceful coexistence with Western democracies.
   3 They provided aid for India against Pakistan.
   4 They remained neutral in Southeast Asian communist revolutions.

10 Even following the collapse of the Soviet Union after Gorbachev, China and Russia still have problems regarding
   1 whose communist system is better
   2 who should control Vietnam
   3 control of former Soviet naval bases
   4 their borders

11 The purpose of China's intervention in both the Korean and Vietnam Wars was to show the Chinese
   1 resistance to imperialism
   2 disdain for the United Nations
   3 intent to act as a regional power in Asia
   4 possessed advanced nuclear technology

ESSAY

The People's Republic of China is considered one of the world's major powers.

a Discuss *two* issues which have caused friction between the U.S.A. and China.

b Discuss *two* problems which caused friction between the communist regimes of China and the Soviet Union.

c Discuss communist China's policies toward less developed countries.

VI. PHYSICAL AND HISTORICAL SETTING OF JAPAN

Geography, climate, and location are keys to understanding the historical and cultural development of Japan.

LOCATION AND SIZE

Japan is an archipelago lying off the eastern coast of Asia. It extends 1,500 miles (2,414 km) Southwest to Northeast and covers over 142,000 square miles. Because it is an island nation, it has been able to isolate itself from invasion and commercial contact for long periods. This **insular behavior pattern** (separateness) is important to understanding Japanese culture.

FOUR MAIN ISLANDS

The three southernmost islands, **Honshu**, **Kyushu**, and **Shikoku**, are where Japan's civilization developed. **Hokkaido**, settled only in the 19th Century, is the northernmost island. It has a rough terrain and severe winters and is still considered a frontier area. Adjacent to the four main islands are about 3,400 smaller islands, many of which are uninhabited.

EDGE OF ASIAN CULTURE

Located off the eastern coast of Asia, Japan's extreme position compares with Britain's off the coast of Europe. Despite the geographic conditions that favored isolation, China greatly influenced Japanese civilization. Korea and the East China Sea served as the avenues of contact.

POLITICAL AND CULTURAL INDEPENDENCE

Japan's physical separation allowed it to observe and borrow selectively from other cultures without being overwhelmed by them. While Japan absorbed much of its culture from China and Korea, it was never controlled by these states.

TOPOGRAPHY, CLIMATE, AND RESOURCES

Physically secure boundaries and remoteness permitted the Japanese to develop a strong cultural identity and a tradition of isolationism. However, the lack of important resources in the

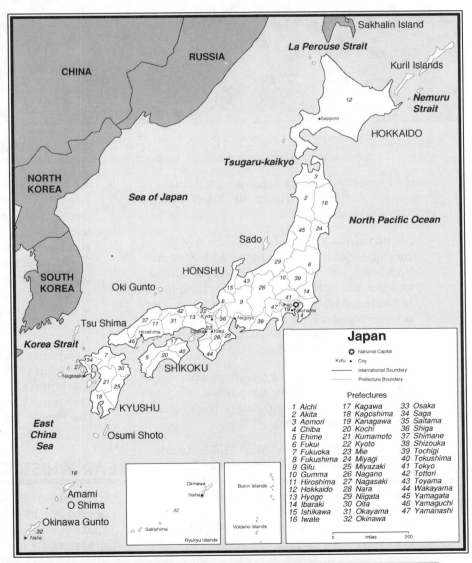

Japan

✪ National Capital
Kofu ● City
— International Boundary
--- Prefecture Boundary

Prefectures

1 Aichi	17 Kagawa	33 Osaka
2 Akita	18 Kagoshima	34 Saga
3 Aomori	19 Kanagawa	35 Saitama
4 Chiba	20 Kochi	36 Shiga
5 Ehime	21 Kumamoto	37 Shimane
6 Fukui	22 Kyoto	38 Shizouka
7 Fukuoka	23 Mie	39 Tochigi
8 Fukushima	24 Miyagi	40 Tokushima
9 Gifu	25 Miyazaki	41 Tokyo
10 Gumma	26 Nagano	42 Tottori
11 Hiroshima	27 Nagasaki	43 Toyama
12 Hokkaido	28 Nara	44 Wakayama
13 Hyogo	29 Niigata	45 Yamagata
14 Ibaraki	30 Oita	46 Yamaguchi
15 Ishikawa	31 Okayama	47 Yamanashi
16 Iwate	32 Okinawa	

0 miles 200

Mount Fuji, southwest of Tokyo, Honshu Island, is the highest mountain in Japan at 12,388 ft (3,776 m). Last erupting in 1707 A.D., it is now a dormant volcano. Mt. Fuji is visited by thousands of hikers and pilgrims each July and August and is held sacred by Japanese Buddhists. Its beauty has inspired artists and poets for many centuries.

modern era changed its behavior. A number of geographic factors contribute to this pattern of identity and isolationism.

- **Mountainous Terrain** – Eighty-five percent of Japan is mountainous with Mount Fuji being the highest. Agricultural land is at a premium. Since Japan has a high population density, it also looks to the sea to sustain its people. Fortunately, the waters surrounding Japan are among the world's richest fishing grounds.

- **Many Rivers** – Rivers are short with rapids and not used for navigation. They are important for irrigation, and in the modern era, for hydroelectricity.

- **Favorable Climate** – Mild Mid-Latitude Rainy Climate dominates the islands of Kyushu, Shikoku, and more than half of Honshu. The northern section of Honshu and Hokkaido are Mid-Latitude Wet-and-Dry Climate (**DF-Rainy, Cold Winter type**).

- **Lack of Resources** – Japan has copper and some small deposits of iron. Its coal deposits are not of the quality needed for steel production. About 90% of Japan's petroleum comes from Middle East imports. Japan's lack of natural resources was a major reason why it adopted aggressive policies towards Asian nations in the 20th century.

- **Frequent Natural Disasters** – Japan suffers from volcanic eruptions and periodic earthquakes. It is also frequently struck by typhoons (hurricanes) and tidal waves from the Pacific Ocean.

EARLY HISTORY

Little archaeological research took place prior to World War II. Information about early Japan is still incomplete and rests heavily on Korean and Chinese written records. It seems

that the earliest settlers came to Japan from Sakhalin Island and Korea. Later migrations from other Pacific islands and southeastern Asia reached Japan's southern islands. Significant cultural periods include:

- **Yayoi Culture** – Between 300 B.C. and 300 A.D., new invaders from the Asian mainland, the **Yayoi**, sailed to Japan. They introduced wet rice cultivation and bronzing and ironworking.

- **Tomb Period (300 - c. 650 A.D.)** – The **Tomb Culture**, most advanced of early Japan's societies, developed from the Yayoi culture. It took its name from the high mounds of earth which were the tombs of the local chiefs. It was during the Tomb culture that references to Japan are found in Chinese sources.

- **Yamato Clan Leaders** – By the year 220 A.D., there were about 40 tribal communities in the Japanese islands. For the next two hundred years, the **Yamato** of Honshu were the most powerful and were accepted as the first imperial clan. Japan's political organization was an outgrowth of these tribal and clan societies.

POWER OF THE IMPERIAL FAMILY

Chinese history is divided by dynasties. Japan's is divided by the family names which actually held power behind the emperor.

Scholars were appointed to write an official family history for the **Yamato** imperial family. The result was the *Nihongi* or *Chronicles of Japan*, finished in 720 A.D. According to this history, the emperor traced his ancestry to various **Kami**, "spirits," who had created the islands of Japan. With the acceptance of this myth, the emperors became regarded as divine and as the complete owners of all land. No one could question their authority.

The divine status of the emperor was enhanced by legends and folklore. Yet, imperial political power declined after 1000 A.D. The rise in influence of the military families in the 12th Century extended a feudal landholding system (see page 126) and undermined the emperor's authority. Examples of the military families' power include:

- The **Fujiwara Family** had enormous power from the 10th through the 12th Centuries.

- The **Tokugawa Shogunate** of 1603 - 1868 developed from feudal institutions.

The **Meiji Restoration** in 1868 nominally returned power to the emperor. Actually, the Meiji permitted the rise of a new coalition of political leaders, industrialists, and the military.

CHINESE INFLUENCE

The Japanese absorbed much from abroad. They adapted what they imported to suit their own needs and tastes. Indications of this in relation to Chinese culture include:

- **Early Contacts With Chinese Civilization Via Korea** – Korea was the bridge that transported Chinese civilization to Japan. During the reign of **Shotoku** (592-621 A.D.), students were sent to the "Middle Kingdom" (as China referred to itself) to study Buddhism, art, Confucian philosophy, and government.

- **Nara Period (710-794 A.D.)** – Scholars consider this the high point of Chinese influence in Japan. Nara was Japan's earliest capital city. It was patterned after the ancient Chinese capital, Chang-an. Nara's imperial court was strongly influenced by Buddhist monks. The Japanese eventually reacted to this domination. They built a new city, **Kyoto**, which served as the capital until 1868.

- **Japan Developed Script From Chinese Characters** – Written Japanese is partly based upon Chinese writing. Japan adopted pictographs and ideographs, but they found that Chinese writing did not meet all the needs of the Japanese language. In the 9th Century, Buddhist monks developed two writing systems in which the characters represented Japanese syllables rather than objects.

PhotoDisc Inc. 1994

Religion in Japan has been influenced by its neighbors China and Korea. Buddhism and Shintoism have been blended with the worship of nature.

spirit) and the worship of nature. Shintoism does not accept the existence of one personal, all-powerful God. Shintoism looks to the physical world for meaning and stresses the individual's duty to live in harmony with his surroundings. Shintoism serves to deepen the bond between the Japanese people, their family, and their nation.

KOREANS INTRODUCE BUDDHISM

Korean missionaries introduced Buddhism to Japan in 522 A.D. The Japanese branch of Buddhism used the Chinese language, ceremonies, and architecture, but it had no real influence among the common people in its early stage.

- **The Heian Classical Period (794-1185)** – Scholars consider this the point at which Chinese culture declined in Japan. The Japanese alternately encouraged and rejected outside contacts. During this time, Japan had less contact with China and adapted a broad variety of cultural borrowings.

Shinto has blended with Buddhism through most of Japan's history. Japanese religions became assimilations of several beliefs. A combination of Buddhism and Shintoism remains the major religious form today.

RELIGION

Isolation allowed traditional religion to predominate in Japan until late in its history. Shintoism and Buddhism were major influences.

SHINTOISM: "THE WAY OF THE GODS"

The development of **Shintoism** is an example of how physical geography and beauty influenced Japan's aesthetic values. Shintoism has no founder or sacred writings. It is a religion based on **animism** (belief that objects contain a

FEUDAL PERIOD (1185 - 1600)

DOMINANCE OF THE SAMURAI

During Japan's feudal period, power rested in the hands of military strongmen. The emperor's power declined noticeably. **Samurai** (the warrior class) governments replaced court nobles. The dominance of the warrior in feudal times made a deep impression on Japan's future. The power of the emperor's court declined as the samurai became the elite.

WORLD STUDIES – *Global Issues & Assessments*   N&N©

The real power in Japan was the warrior-noble who led the samurai. In 1185, a noble by the name of **Yoritomo**, obtained the title **Shogun** (military ruler) from the emperor. It became a hereditary title. The Shoguns deprived succeeding emperors of the power to select and control this supreme military ruler. Shoguns ruled Japan for 700 years.

Bushido, the Code of the Warrior, developed during the mid-17th Century. It was the guide to the ideal warrior, a blend of military discipline, Confucian thought, and Zen Buddhism. Bushido emphasized the Confucian stress on the individual's duty to his superior. **Zen Buddhism** was also popular among the samurai because its required meditation called for much self-discipline.

Late in the 13th Century, China's Emperor Kublai Khan launched armadas against Japan. Both fleets were heavily battered by typhoons. (This is the origin of Japan's **kamikaze**, meaning winds of the *kami* or divine winds). The surviving invaders were defeated by the samurai. At this time, only Japan, India, and Southeast Asia were able to withstand the power of China's Mongol overlords.

FEUDAL CULTURE

From the 13th to the 16th Centuries, trade flourished between China and Japan. Silk, porcelain, and pottery were imported from the Middle Kingdom in return for Japanese swords and lacquer ware. This commercial contact increased **cultural borrowing** and caused Japanese culture to bloom.

Two examples of artistic forms imported from China were flower arrangement and miniature **bonsai cultivation** (the technique of arresting the growth of trees). Another popular import was the Chinese tea ceremony. The Chinese-influenced landscape painting, scroll painting, and architecture of the **Ashikaga Shogunate** (1338-1567) have never been surpassed.

Japan developed two forms of drama during the feudal period. The **Noh** play, which arose in the 14th Century, dealt with Japanese myths and history. The second drama form was the **Kabuki**, which originated in the 16th Century. The Kabuki was directed towards the common people and was easier to understand.

The 16th Century samurai Matsuo Munefusa, known as Basho, developed haiku out of reverence for nature, in which he incorporated the spirit of Zen Buddhism. **Haiku** is a Japanese verse form expressing a single emotion or idea in which 17 syllables are arranged in lines of 5, 7, and 5 syllables. Over the years, haiku was refined by Buddhist and Taoist writers. Below is an example of this major genre of Japanese poetry:

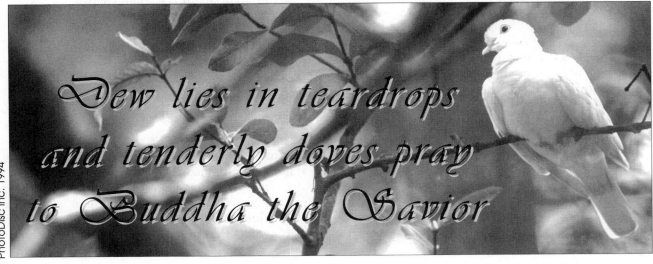

Dew lies in teardrops and tenderly doves pray to Buddha the Savior

PhotoDisc Inc. 1994

POLITICAL POWER SHIFTS

In the late feudal period, Japan suffered from internal wars. The **Ashikaga Shogun** was never able to exert much political control beyond Kyoto. From 1333 to 1600 A.D., peace and security declined. The local aristocracy, the **Daimyo** ("Great Lords"), fought among themselves for political supremacy.

MILITARY GOVERNMENT (1600)

In the early 17th Century, General **Tokugawa Ieyasu** won the battle of Sekigahara, one of the most decisive battles of Japanese history. He then created the last of the military dynasties of Japan, the **Tokugawa Shogunate** (1603-1868). **Edo**, later called **Tokyo**, became the center of Tokugawa government.

The Tokugawa Shoguns imposed a rigid social structure. In descending rank, the classes

were warriors, farmers, artisans, and merchants. All positions were hereditary and duties belonged exclusively to each class.

European contact with Japan increased in the 17th Century. Portuguese traders arrived in 1542 and gradually increased their numbers. Jesuit missionaries such as **Francis Xavier** accompanied the traders and converted many Japanese. Historians estimate that, by 1600, there were 300,000 Christians in Japan. Dutch traders arrived shortly thereafter and began trade wars with the Portuguese.

The Tokugawa Shogunate saw the Europeans as a disruptive threat to authority. Japanese authorities became fearful that Christianity and European traders would introduce social and political disorders, if not outright conquest. In 1639, a **seclusion** (isolation) policy emerged. The Shogun forbade missionaries to enter Japan on pain of death. Authorities also banned all contact with foreigners except for very limited Dutch and Chinese trade.

QUESTIONS

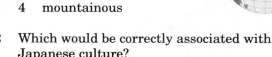

1   Most of the Japanese terrain can be described as
    1   desert
    2   steppe
    3   marshland
    4   mountainous

2   Which would be correctly associated with Japanese culture?
    1   cultural diffusion
    2   monotheism
    3   democracy
    4   social equality

3   By the 12th Century, Japan had
    1   accepted elements from Chinese culture
    2   driven out Christian missionaries
    3   conquered Korea
    4   begun to industrialize

4   Which figure would compare best to Japan's Shogun?
    1   a corporation president
    2   the President of the U.S.
    3   a military dictator
    4   a Christian missionary

5   What was the result of the Tokugawa Shogunate's seclusion policy?
    1   delayed Japan's development as a modern nation
    2   brought most of civilized Asia under Japanese domination.
    3   caused widespread competition with industrial nations
    4   brought about the golden age of Japanese art and literature

6   The heroes or elite of the Tokugawa Shogunate would have been
    1   scholars
    2   Shinto priests
    3   merchants
    4   samurai

7   Japan's suicide pilots in the WW II were named "kamikaze" after the
    1   most famous Shogun
    2   highest mountain peak of Japan
    3   chief Buddhist deity
    4   winds that destroyed Mongol armadas

8 Why did Japan isolate itself in the 17th Century?
   1 It feared European influence.
   2 Few Japanese were interested in Christianity.
   3 Europeans brought infectious diseases.
   4 It believed its civilization was superior to that of Europe.

9 Which represents Shintoism's major teaching?
   1 achievement of human perfection
   2 reincarnation of the soul
   3 love for fellow humans
   4 reverence for the land

10 Yoritomo, who became the first Shogun,
   1 outlawed further cultural borrowing from China
   2 took political power away from the emperor
   3 helped establish Christianity as a major religion
   4 began to build Japan into a modern industrial nation

11 Which island is one of Japan's main islands?
   1 Hong Kong
   2 Honshu
   3 Taiwan
   4 Korea

12 Korea, Japan's closest neighbor, has often served as a
   1 home for the Japanese Emperor
   2 buffer zone against European invasion
   3 climatic barrier
   4 bridge for cultural diffusion

13 The rivers of Japan
   1 originate near the seacoast
   2 all flow northward
   3 are important for hydroelectricity
   4 serve as ocean highways for many miles up-river

14 The geographic relationship of Japan to the continent of Asia is most similar to the relationship of which country to Europe?
   1 Spain
   2 Denmark
   3 Britain
   4 Italy

15 In the 16th Century, Francis Xavier altered Japanese culture by
   1 helping to develop its industrial base
   2 leading a joint-European military conquest of Japan
   3 establishing a French sphere of influence
   4 helping to introduce Christianity

16 Which natural resource is one of Japan's most crucial imports?
   1 diamonds
   2 copper
   3 oil
   4 silver

17 To which famous writing did the Japanese trace the divinity of their Emperor?
   1 *Chronicles of Japan*
   2 *The Analects*
   3 *Bushido*
   4 *Tales of the Genji*

18 The Daimyo or "Great Lords" of the 14th Century were involved in
   1 feudal wars for control of Japan
   2 spreading Chinese culture
   3 converting Japan to Buddhism
   4 defending Japan against European conquest

19 Asiatic invaders of Japan established the Yayoi culture. Which was not a feature of their civilization?
   1 feudalism
   2 rice cultivation
   3 bronze working
   4 use of iron implements

ESSAY

Identify *three* important geographic (physical) features of Japan. For *each* feature, show its relationship to the country's cultural development or history.

VII. DYNAMICS OF CHANGE

Japan's cultural borrowing and long-established sense of cultural identity spurred the drive for industrialization and modernization in the late 19th and 20th Centuries. As with other major powers, these forces also fed a nationalistic desire to achieve world power status.

ABANDONING ISOLATION

The power of the Shoguns weakened in the 19th Century. Enforced isolation finally broke down in the 1850's. At that time, U.S. President Franklin Pierce dispatched a naval expedition to negotiate a treaty to protect American sailors shipwrecked in Japan's territorial waters. Because of Japan's traditional hostility to foreigners, Commodore Matthew Perry's squadron of steamships was sent as a show of force. Perry also requested that Japan open its ports to American ships and trade.

Perry refused Japanese demands to sail away. Intimidated by the modern American warships, Tokugawa officials finally accepted the letter from President Pierce. Perry announced he would return in one year for the Japanese response. Japan acceded to American demands in the *Treaty of Kanagawa* (1854).

MEIJI RESTORATION (1868)

The signing of the Kanagawa Treaty hastened the decline of the Shogun. Many samurai resented the presence of foreigners. They wanted to unify behind the divine emperor in order to avoid the kind of imperialist experience the Chinese were having. Civil violence began, and the last of the Tokugawa Shoguns surrendered Edo to imperial forces in May 1868.

What followed was a remarkable period that became known as the **Meiji** (Enlightened) **Restoration**. Modified political power was returned to the emperor, and the last traces of Japanese feudalism dissolved.

Although the country considered the divine emperor restored, he was not the real power in Japan. The restoration was a form of political revolution. It freed power groups from feudal restrictions. It cleared the way for their participation in the economic modernization. The Meiji Constitution of 1889 created a parliamentary system. Yet, what developed was an **oligarchy** (power in the hands of a small group) and a highly centralized bureaucratic government.

This new government helped Japan modernize rapidly. The development of public education raised the literacy rate and created a large pool of skilled labor, accelerating progress. The bureaucracy oversaw the building of an **infrastructure** (transport and communication system) to accelerate industrialization.

The military and industrial groups oversaw the establishment of a powerful army and navy that eventually controlled the government.

INDUSTRIAL GROWTH

The political reorganization laid the groundwork for economic modernization. Yet, it revealed Japan's great economic shortcoming, a lack of strategic raw materials. That scarcity became a shaping force in Japan's international relations. The quest for raw materials led Japan along a dangerous path and into conflicts with others.

SINO-JAPANESE WAR

Meiji statesmen feared one of the Western imperialist nations operating in China would seize Korea from the decaying Manchu Empire. This growing unease and Japan's own realization of the need for natural resources led to the **Sino-Japanese War** (1894-1895). Japan's modernized forces quickly won. The **Treaty of Shimonoseki** (1895) granted Japan the island of Formosa (Taiwan) and a large indemnity (war damage payments). Korea became independent of China, and Japan began to create its own sphere of influence there.

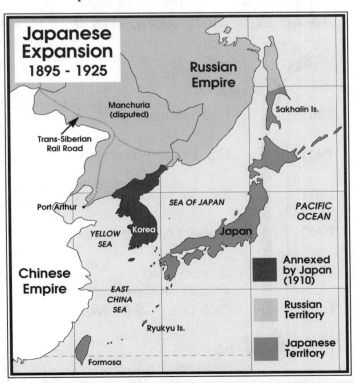

Japanese Expansion 1895 - 1925

Russian Empire

Manchuria (disputed)

Sakhalin Is.

Trans-Siberian Rail Road

Port Arthur

SEA OF JAPAN

PACIFIC OCEAN

YELLOW SEA

Korea

Japan

Chinese Empire

EAST CHINA SEA

Ryukyu Is.

Formosa

Annexed by Japan (1910)

Russian Territory

Japanese Territory

RUSSO-JAPANESE WAR

Japanese rulers also viewed Russian advancement in Asia with apprehension. Russia acquired a foothold in the Liaotung Peninsula and wanted Korea. Too often in the past, Korea had served as a launching place for foreign assaults on Japan. Meiji leaders feared any foreign power taking over Korea as a "dagger pointing at Japan's heart."

To block Russia from entering Korea, Japan launched a sneak attack on the Russian Pacific fleet anchored at Port Arthur and began the **Russo-Japanese War** (1904-1905). To the world's surprise, Japan defeated a Western power. Russia sued for peace. U.S. President Theodore Roosevelt mediated the dispute. With the **Treaty of Portsmouth**, Japan gained Port Arthur, territory in southern Manchuria, and the southern half of Sakhalin Island. In 1910, Japan annexed Korea, and neither China nor Russia could do more than protest.

WORLD WAR I AND THE 21 DEMANDS

In World War I, Japan joined the Allies and declared war on the German Empire. It seized German treaty areas in China and some small Pacific islands. During the war, Japan delivered **The 21 Demands** to the Chinese Republic (1915). If accepted, China would have become a Japanese protectorate. International outcry forced Japan to change its position. Yet, many of the demands were incorporated into subsequent treaties with China.

"GREATER E. ASIA CO-PROSPERITY SPHERE"

By the end of World War I, Japan was the dominant power in East Asia. Encouraged by success, Japanese nationalists proposed the creation of the **Greater East Asia Co-prosperity Sphere**, a new regional order. Under this imperialist plan, Japan offered to supply manufactured products and capital for underdeveloped areas. Korea, Formosa, and other less developed countries were to provide food and raw materials for Japan.

PRE-WW II EXPANSION

Japanese aggressions against weaker nations were modeled after earlier imperialist actions of Western powers. Between the two world wars, Japan continued this approach. The military / industrialist leadership **cabal** ("conspiratorial group") intensified its quest for raw materials, markets, and the rank of a world power.

Japan chips away at Chinese Territory.

After World War I, Japan became upset with discriminatory Western policies. For example, the Japanese resented the agreements of the **Washington Naval Arms Conference** (1922). It limited Japanese naval power in comparison to that of Britain, France, and the U.S.

Later, when Japan was hurt by the Great Depression, Japan ignored the 1922 limits and accelerated military output. The government-forced arms production stimulated the economy. This artificially enhanced arsenal opened the door for military conquest. A series of aggressive acts against Asian neighbors began. They revealed Japan's goal to become a supreme power in the Pacific.

In 1931, Japan alleged there was a Chinese attack on a Japanese train in Manchuria. Claiming riots were erupting, Japan used this **Mukden Incident** as an excuse to overrun the province of Manchuria and set up a puppet state, Manchukuo. The League of Nations created the **Lytton Commission** to examine Japan's conquest of Manchuria. Its 1932 report condemned Japanese actions. In answer, Japan withdrew from the League of Nations.

In the **Marco Polo Bridge Incident** in 1937, Japanese Army units on maneuvers clashed with Chinese soldiers at a bridge near Peking (Beijing). Blame was never assigned, but from this incident grew the **Second Sino-Japanese War** (1937-1945).

In 1940, Nazi Germany, Fascist Italy, and Imperial Japan signed the ***Tripartite Pact***. Commonly known as the **Rome-Berlin-Tokyo Axis**, it joined three aggressor nations. In reaction, the United States banned the export of war materials, scrap iron, and steel to Japan.

In 1941, Japan began seizing sections of Southeast Asia to gain vital rubber, tin, and oil supplies. The colonial powers were preoccupied. France and the Netherlands were already conquered by the Nazis. Britain was fighting for its survival. Japan met little resistance as it conquered the Asian and Pacific colonies of Europe.

U.S. officials denounced Japanese aggression in China and Southeast Asia. They could do little else. The war in Europe threatened and

Japanese Expansion Leads To An Explosion: World War II

1941	Pearl Harbor
1941	U.S. Trade Embargo
1941	S.E. Asia Conquered
1940	Joined Axis Powers
1937	Marco Polo Bridge Incident
1932	Quit League Of Nations
1931	Manchuria Mukden Incident

isolationist opposition was strong among Americans. In the summer of 1941, the Roosevelt Administration **embargoed** (refused to sell) trade of most strategic material with Japan, hoping to halt the Asian aggression.

On 7 December, 1941, American and Japanese diplomats met in Washington, D.C. to resolve tensions. In the midst of negotiations, news came of Japan's attack on the Pearl Harbor Naval Base in Hawaii. Over 2,000 Americans died on what President Franklin Roosevelt referred to as a "Day of Infamy." This surprise attack led to the American Congress declaring war against Japan.

WW II EXPANSION

The U.S. was unprepared for war. During the Depression, it had cut spending for the armed forces. In 1942, it had to raise and train an army to fight both in Europe and the Pacific. Japan launched a wide offensive capturing Hong Kong, Malaysia, Thailand, Burma, Indonesia, Philippines, and part of New Guinea. Still, the Allies managed to halt Japanese expansion at the battle of **Midway** (1942).

Allied defenses held in Australia. Allied commanders began offensive operations. They adopted an "island-hopping" strategy. This involved all-out assaults on key islands, with high Allied casualties. Other islands were cut off from supplies and left to "wither on the vine."

Fighting in the Pacific was brutal. Japanese soldiers, indoctrinated in Bushido, chose suicidal "banzai attacks" rather than face the dishonor of surrender. Over 1,200 Japanese became kamikaze pilots in 1944-45, sacrificing their lives by crashing bomb-laden planes into Allied ships.

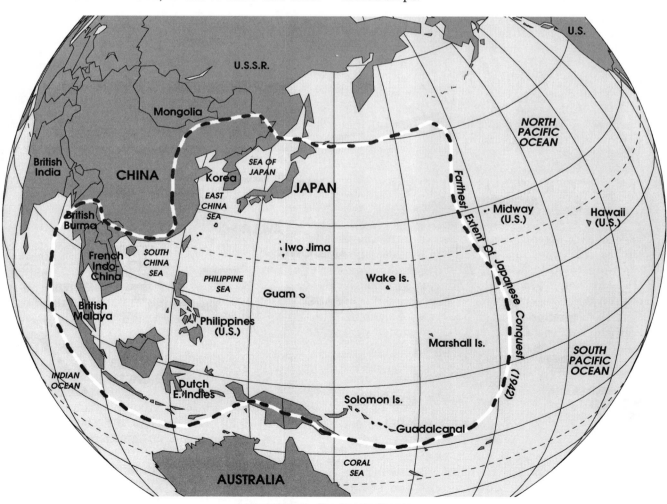

World War II – The Pacific Theater

By July 1945, the Allies pushed Japan to its home islands. They were sacred in the Shinto religion. The American military knew Japanese leaders would never surrender them. Commanders advised President Truman that Japan would have to be invaded. They projected hand-to-hand combat lasting another year. They estimated American casualties at one million. With this in mind, Truman decided to use a new secret weapon, the **atomic bomb**.

The military selected the city of Hiroshima as the target. It was obliterated, but Japanese leaders would not surrender until a second city, Nagasaki, was destroyed. On 2 September 1945, Japanese representatives signed the formal document of surrender. Truman claimed the loss of life in a conventional invasion (such as the one on D-Day, 6 June 1944 in France) justified the use of the bombs. No one could gauge the destructive force of atomic weapons in 1945. Still, as the world moves further from that era, some critics continue to question the wisdom of Truman's decision.

U.S. OCCUPATION OF JAPAN, 1945-1952

American troops occupied Japan until 1952. During this time, Japan's government was subordinate to the Supreme Allied Commander, General Douglas MacArthur, who was responsible for the sweeping reforms. The post-World War II occupation reforms had great economic, political, and social impact. They produced permanent change in Japan.

United States occupation led to the diffusion of some American ideas and practices into Japanese culture. American businesses sent advisors and technical help to restore the economy. Political advisors gave Japan a democratic government and social reform. They reestablished Japan in the community of nations. Key influences on Japanese government included:

- a limited monarchy

- reform of the parliamentary system

- elimination of military domination

- a new constitution in 1947

The new constitution included provisions for compulsory education, women's rights including suffrage, establishment and protection of rights of labor unions, and land reform.

QUESTIONS

1   Which denotes political power concentrated in the hands of a very few?
    1   representative democracy
    2   constitutional limited monarchy
    3   limited democracy
    4   an oligarchy

2   An important reform in Japan following World War II was the
    1   return to the Emperor the powers he had lost during the war
    2   recognition of Shinto as the state religion
    3   nationalization of industry
    4   adoption of a constitution which established democracy

3   Created before the outbreak of World War II, the Tripartite Pact linked Japan to the
    1   Communist nations
    2   Axis Alliance
    3   League of Nations
    4   East Asian Co-prosperity Sphere

4   Economic conditions in Japan during the period 1920-1940 contributed to the
    1   strengthening of parliamentary government
    2   growth of political stability
    3   rise of an expansionist party
    4   success of the League of Nations

5 China, weakened by concessions and economic privileges granted to foreign powers, became an easy prey for Japanese aggression. Which event best portrays this idea?
1 the Meiji Restoration
2 the Sino-Japanese War
3 the Pearl Harbor Attack
4 Perry's Expedition

6 During World War I, Japan
1 joined forces with Germany
2 participated in the war in order to gain territory
3 was forced into the war by direct attack on its land
4 declared its position only in the last year of the war

7 From 1865 to 1945, industrial Japan
1 exported large quantities of wheat
2 needed raw materials and markets
3 discouraged farming
4 wanted to maintain China's territorial integrity

8 Manchuria became a symbol of Japan's
1 attempts to aid underdeveloped regions
2 desire for empire
3 religious conversion to Christianity
4 experimentation with socialist government

9 One reason why modern Japan came into conflict with China was that China
1 possessed one of the oldest civilizations
2 was overpopulated
3 possessed natural resources
4 was too friendly with Russia

10 Which headline could have appeared during the first decade of the 20th Century?
1 *Treaty of Portsmouth Ends Russo-Japanese War*
2 *Lytton Report Condemns Japanese Aggression*
3 *War Ends - Japan Loses Empire*
4 *Rome-Berlin-Tokyo Axis Announced*

11 The Russo-Japanese War
1 resulted from the fear that Russia would control Korea
2 grew out of Japan's alliances in WW I
3 saw Japan fighting to defend China.
4 made Western powers force Japan to reduce its naval power

12 Japan's "21 Demands" were an attempt to
1 ally itself with Germany and Italy
2 gain entry into the League of Nations
3 establish a protectorate over China
4 defeat the United States at Midway

13 U.S. General Douglas MacArthur was the Allied Commander in World War II and
1 directed the postwar reconstruction of Japan
2 forced Japan to withdraw from the League of Nations
3 opened Japan to Western trade
4 supervised the Meiji Restoration

14 The Kanagawa Treaty in 1854 was responsible for "opening" Japan to
1 Russian conquest
2 Confucian philosophy
3 the East Asian Co-prosperity Sphere
4 Western trade, ideas, and technology

15 Which strategy did American commanders use in the Pacific from 1942-1945?
1 guerrilla warfare
2 island hopping
3 saturation bombing
4 naval blockade

ESSAY

The Industrial Revolution greatly changed the course of Japanese history.

a Explain how Western technology entered Japanese society in the 19th Century.

b Describe *two* changes made in Japan under the Meiji Restoration.

c Discuss how Japanese policy between the World Wars was designed to help the Japanese economy.

VIII. CONTEMPORARY JAPAN

Japan is a technologically advanced society, democratically governed and primarily urban.

POPULATION

Japan is a densely populated nation having 125 million inhabitants in an area about the size of California. The population growth rate has declined in recent years, but the population density is very high at over 850 persons per square mile in 1993 (U.S. = 83). Three fourths of the population live in urban areas. Its 1992, per capita Gross Domestic Product of $19,000 was among the five highest in the world. (U.S. GDP was $22,000.)

Because of its insular geography and centuries of seclusion, Japan's people are homogeneous. Although willing to adopt western methods for efficiency and modernization, they retain much of their traditional life. Japan reinforces the concept that westernization and modernization are not always synonymous.

PhotoDisc Inc. 1994

School Children, Tokyo, Japan

DEMOCRATIC GOVERNMENT

Postwar Japan's story is like that of the *Phoenix* of Greek legend which rose triumphant from the ashes. What emerged from the defeat and occupation after World War II was a new Japan. It moved dynamically ahead under a strong, democratic system of government.

The country is a constitutional monarchy under an **Emperor** and a two-house, democratic **Diet** (legislature). The Diet chooses the **Cabinet of Ministers**, whose members form the executive branch. The nation's chief executive is the **Prime Minister**, whom the Diet chooses from among the Cabinet members.

DETERMINATION OF POLITICAL & ECONOMIC SYSTEMS

There are a number of political parties in the nation. Recent scandals have unsettled the powerful **Liberal Democrats**, and several new

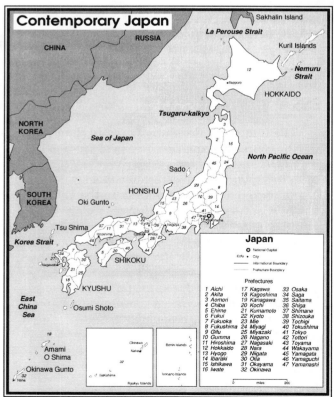

Contemporary Japan

CHINA
RUSSIA
Sakhalin Island
La Perouse Strait
Kuril Islands
Nemuru Strait
12
Sapporo
HOKKAIDO
NORTH KOREA
Sea of Japan
Tsugaru-kaikyo
Sado
North Pacific Ocean
HONSHU
SOUTH KOREA
Oki Gunto
Tsu Shima
Korea Strait
Nagoya
Tokyo
Yokohama
SHIKOKU
East China Sea
Osumi Shoto
KYUSHU
Amami O Shima
Okinawa Gunto
Okinawa
Naha
Bonin Islands
Volcano Islands
Ryukyu Islands

Japan

⊙ National Capital
Kofu • City
International Boundary
Prefecture Boundary

Prefectures

1	Aichi	17	Kagawa	33	Osaka
2	Akita	18	Kagoshima	34	Saga
3	Aomori	19	Kanagawa	35	Saitama
4	Chiba	20	Kochi	36	Shiga
5	Ehime	21	Kumamoto	37	Shimane
6	Fukui	22	Kyoto	38	Shizouka
7	Fukuoka	23	Mie	39	Tochigi
8	Fukushima	24	Miyagi	40	Tokushima
9	Gifu	25	Miyazaki	41	Tokyo
10	Gumma	26	Nagano	42	Tottori
11	Hiroshima	27	Nagasaki	43	Toyama
12	Hokkaido	28	Nara	44	Wakayama
13	Hyogo	29	Niigata	45	Yamagata
14	Ibaraki	30	Oita	46	Yamaguchi
15	Ishikawa	31	Okayama	47	Yamanashi
16	Iwate	32	Okinawa		

miles 200

reform parties have been formed. The country remains a strong, functioning democracy with far higher voter participation in elections than in the United States.

EDUCATIONAL SYSTEM

Japan places immense emphasis on education and enjoys a literacy rate of 99%. Japan produces a literate, skilled work force. Still, some Japanese criticize the pressure which the educational system places on youth. Japan's educational system is characterized by high standards and competitive examinations. To qualify for admission to high schools and universities, Japanese students must pass difficult examinations. Because a university degree is the major means to a good job and income, education is one of the most competitive areas in Japanese life. The number of university openings are limited, and competition is fierce.

PhotoDisc Inc. 1994

More Japanese and other Asian women are working in high tech fields. However, few females are in management positions in business, science, and government.

SOCIAL CONDITIONS

Public services lag in comparison to Japan's phenomenal industrial growth. The country has serious housing shortages. More public spending is needed in health care and pollution control. While the cities are overcrowded, there are few actual slums, and Japan enjoys a lower crime rate than the United States.

Socially, traditional male power and status as head of the family has declined. In post war Japan, work and loyalty to the employer became obsessions. There was less time devoted to family. Fewer marriages are arranged by family and friends. Yet, arranged marriages still account for over 50% of Japanese unions. The average age of bride and groom has risen to the mid or late twenties as more women are in the work force. Officially, women have been given equal

PhotoDisc Inc. 1994

Modern Japan has become a nation of industrialized high tech. Electronics lead its manufacturing output.

rights with men. Their status has risen, but traditional male dominance is strong in business. Few females are in leading positions in business, government, or science.

Employees identify intensely with their employers. Until the 1990's recession, Japan's paternal corporations offered lifetime employment until retirement at about age 55. As a result of this security, workers in Japan have not formed militant labor unions nor do they change jobs as frequently as Americans. However, job security has been shaken recently. Challenges from other Asian nations (see Pacific Rim in Oceania), shifts in the global economy, and recessions brought economic changes. Japan's great corporations have forced workers out and begun layoffs as they seek more efficiency. Traditional job security and workers' faith in the system have suffered.

IMPACT OF INDUSTRIALIZATION

The transition to a modern industrial state altered many aspects of Japanese society. Changing social conditions include shift to nuclear families in urban areas, declining birth rates, and decreasing support of household religious rites among the young.

Industrialization has not altered Japan's rich literary and artistic heritage. There is an ongoing popularity or Haiku (see page 129) and Japan's traditional art, reflecting nature, which enjoys great acceptance in the Western world.

Some of the most notable changes in Japan have been in the field of recreation. In particular, Japanese youth have become infatuated with American superstars, music, values, and materialism. Japanese flock to movies, watch television, and enjoy spectator sports. The effect of high-tech mass culture can be readily seen. There are more modern comforts and conveniences in most homes. The middle class of Japan has become more and more consumption oriented.

QUESTIONS

1 Which change in social living patterns has occurred in industrialized Japan since World War II?
   1 increased obsession with work
   2 lower standard of living
   3 decreased emphasis on material goods
   4 increased emphasis on hereditary status

2 The introduction of karate into the U.S. and baseball into Japan are examples of
   1 cultural diffusion
   2 aggressive behavior
   3 advanced democracy
   4 ethnocentrism

3 The best evidence that Japan has been greatly influenced by Western values and ideas is Japan's
   1 strengthening of the old family system
   2 efforts to increase the power of landlords
   3 insistence upon rigid job definitions and work rules
   4 adoption of parliamentary democracy

4 A major barrier to equal rights for women in Japan today is in
   1 the advancement to executive positions
   2 the ownership of private property
   3 political party enrollment
   4 the admission to higher educational institutions

5 The real political power today in Japan is held by the
   1 high military officials
   2 Shogun
   3 emperor
   4 legislature

6 Which characteristic best describes education in modern Japan?
   1 medieval
   2 religiously oriented
   3 dominated by militarists
   4 highly competitive

7 The government of contemporary Japan is a functioning
1 Federal union
2 constitutional monarchy
3 socialist state
4 democratic republic

8 Which factor helps explain the growth in Japanese industrial productivity since World War II?
1 emphasis on employment of unskilled workers
2 high rates of unionization
3 low tariffs
4 strong worker identification with employers

9 In which category of urban problems does the U.S. and Japan differ most?
1 crime rates
2 pollution
3 housing shortages
4 overcrowding

10 What is an accurate description of life in Japan today?
1 Japanese are still a rural people.
2 Japanese continue to isolate themselves from other nations.
3 Japanese have eliminated all social and economic classes.
4 Japanese are blending Western culture with their own.

11 Since 1945, Japan's economic success has depended primarily on its ability to
1 eliminate social welfare programs
2 expand its foreign markets
3 reduce domestic food production
4 increase its defense budget

ESSAY

Since 1945, industrialization has had a major impact on Japanese social, political, and economic forces and institutions.

Forces and Institutions

- Labor unions
- Public education
- Urbanization
- Women's rights
- Leisure activities

Select *three* of the items listed above. For *each* one, discuss *two* ways in which industrialization has had an impact on that force or social institution.

IX. ECONOMIC DEVELOPMENT OF JAPAN

Trade has been the lifeblood of modern Japan, crucial to its prosperity and growth.

POSTWAR ECONOMIC RECOVERY

In 1945, Japan was one of the most devastated nations in the world. One-fourth of its manufacturing capacity and communications network lay ruined. Its maritime fleet was devastated.

Occupation officials' economic goals included making Japan self-supporting and reducing the domination of farm and factory by the privileged few. To achieve these economic goals:

- American investments were provided to re-establish industry

- Land reforms were instituted to increase food production

- Contract incentives were given to labor unions

- Attempts were made to break up **keiretsu** (large corporations, formerly called zaibatsu) to encourage small, competitive industries

Japan's importance in Cold War politics changed rapidly after 1949. The communist takeover in China persuaded the United States to seek a new ally in Asia. Japan received over two billion dollars in aid and loans directed toward its economic reconstruction. Japan also benefited by selling much food and equipment to American forces in the Korean conflict (1950-1953).

This ship carrying finished products made in Japan is unloading in Port of Seattle, U.S.A. It will return to Osaka, Japan with unmilled timber from the state of Washington's forests.

PhotoDisc Inc. 1994

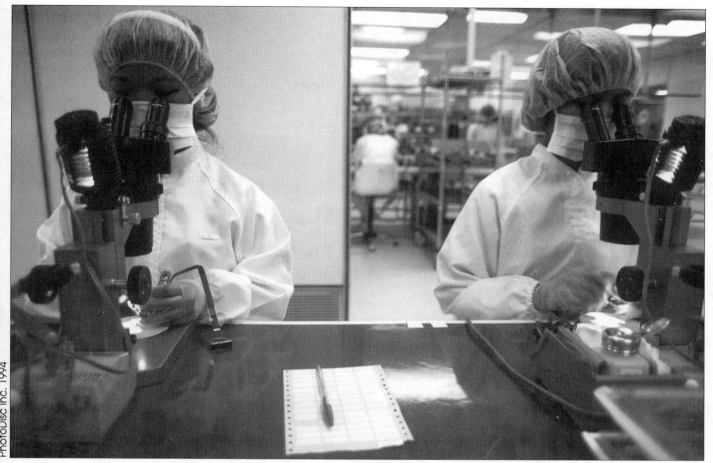

Technicians inspect integrated circuit chips in the "clean room" of a major Japanese computer manufacturer. In high tech as well as many other industries, Japan's corporations dominate global production and marketing.

Intense economic reorganization overcame the limited natural resources. Reasons for Japan's re-emergence as a great industrial power were:

- Technological innovation (New, efficient factories were built.)

- Abundant, highly skilled labor force (Japan's greatest resource has been its educated, highly motivated workers.)

- Substantial United States aid

CONTINUED GROWTH

Japan turned to advanced technology to improve its economic position in the world market. Freed from its prewar concentration on defense, Japan's industrial research and development made it a world leader in technology and trade. Its total production of goods and services is second only to that of the United States. The government industrial policies strengthened the **keiretsu** (formerly called zaibatsu). Giants such as Mitsui, Mitsubishi, and Fuji dominate the economy, and the government protects them from foreign competition.

Japan's corporations also dominate many global markets. Its electronics and other technology-related products, heavy industry, steel, machinery, and shipbuilding dominate world markets. Its automobile industry is one of the most profitable in the world, and although Japan's market share is falling, it sells nearly one fourth of the cars sold in the U.S.

CONTINUING PROBLEMS

Japan's export-driven economy and vast overseas direct investments link it to global economic conditions. Serious recessions in other industrial nations were reflected in Japan's own downturn in the early 1990's.

Japan enjoys a favorable balance of trade with most of the world. In the case of trade with the United States, Japan exports almost twice as much as it imports. According to the U.S. Dept. of Commerce in 1992, Japan exported nearly $90,000,000,000.00 to the U.S. and imported about $48,000,000,000.00 from the U.S.

The scarcity of raw materials and oil has always affected the pattern of economic development. Japan imports metal ore, raw materials, and food in large amounts from Australia and the underdeveloped nations of Southeast Asia. Because it is a major importer of fossil fuels, the Persian Gulf is a crucial waterway for Japan. Over 90% of its oil requirements are met by imports from the volatile Middle East. This makes Japan's economy vulnerable to unstable political conditions there.

Only 13% of Japan's land is used for agriculture, and only 9% of the work force, including fishermen, work to produce food. Major suppliers of food for Japan are the United States, People's Republic of China, Australia, and Canada. Japan learned it cannot sustain a rapidly growing population. In the 1980's, government programs led to a rapid reduction in birth rates. Japan's population continues to decline. It now has one of the lowest birth rates in the world. It is below that of the U.S., Canada, and most other industrial nations.

The population decline has caused a shortage of labor. Survival may require allowing more foreign labor into Japan. But, many critics fear that Japan's traditions and culture will suffer if immigrants flood the country.

Environmental issues also plague Japan's economic well-being. **Ecology** (preserving the natural environment) has become a major political issue among the younger generation of Japanese. They see conservation as vital to survival. Yet, cutting pollution and waste and recycling add to production costs causing large scale conflict with economic activities.

U.S. TRADE RELATIONS

The imbalance Japan experiences in its quest for raw materials and the United States' deficit in its trade with Japan show the **interdependence of nations** in the global economy. While Americans purchase many Japanese products, Japan has high tariffs and other restrictions to prevent domestic consumption of foreign goods. While the Japanese government supports its businesses with tax breaks and low cost loans, it also makes it difficult for foreign firms to prosper.

Japanese trade accounts for nearly half of the U.S. trade deficit. Japan's restrictions on

American products create many problems. Recent economic recessions caused increased tension between the two countries. U.S. Presidents place high priorities on working with Japanese leaders to reduce the trade imbalance. Both countries want trade to remain open, yet Japan's stubborn protective policies are difficult to negotiate. The U.S. has considered restricting Japanese imports in retaliation. However, often in the past this sort of trade warfare has back-fired, allowing other nations to gain advantages while the major powers hurt each other.

Japan needs to maintain a favorable balance of trade with some wealthier nations such as the United States in order to pay for the raw materials and oil it imports. In response to American threats of import quotas on its products, Japan's government promised to increase its defense spending, relax trade barriers for foreign businesses, and make its economy less export-intensive. Yet, it has often failed to follow through on these offers.

QUESTIONS

1 Japan is dependent on which unstable world area for its petroleum supply?
1 Western Europe
2 Indonesia
3 the Middle East
4 Mexico

2 Which is the best definition of the keiretsu?
1 philosophers who believe true knowledge can only be derived from science
2 a laboratory equipped by industrial corporations
3 one of the major corporations which control Japan's economy
4 an important principle of economics

3 What is a tariff wall?
1 high taxes on imported goods
2 a favorable balance of trade
3 alternate period of prosperity and depression
4 a barrier to stock brokers

4 How did the Korean War benefit Japan?
1 Communist expansion was broken in Asia.
2 Japanese industry sold to the American military forces.
3 Red China bankrupted its economy helping North Korea.
4 Southeast Asia looked to Japan for protection.

5 Which is the best explanation for Japan's current industrial success?
1 It needs to support heavy military expenses.
2 It has vast reserves of raw materials and fossil fuels.
3 The government plays a role in setting and supporting national goals.
4 It emphasizes individual achievement rather than group effort.

6 A chronic problem which has always faced Japan has been a shortage of
1 natural resources
2 unskilled labor
3 investment capital
4 markets for its manufactured goods

7 Which is a major supplier of food for Japan?
1 India
2 Bangladesh
3 Australia
4 Philippines

ESSAY

Today, Japan ranks among the world's top producers of goods and services.

Discuss *three* characteristics of the modern Japanese economy which have raised it to this status.

X. JAPAN IN THE GLOBAL CONTEXT

Following World War II, Japan has relied on its economic power rather than military strength in its global relationships.

ANTINUCLEAR POLICY

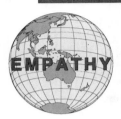

When nuclear tests are carried out by the world powers, protests follow from the Japanese government and general public. Many Americans today have empathy for the Japanese in their concern about nuclear warfare.

MILITARY STATUS OF JAPAN

Japan's 1947 Constitution outlawed the right to use force as an instrument of national policy. In part, Article 9 reads:

> "...the Japanese people forever renounce war as a sovereign right of the nation and the threat or use of force as a means of settling international disputes... In order to accomplish the aim... land, sea, and air forces... will never be maintained."

With the outbreak of the Korean War in 1950, the United States withdrew occupation troops from Japan. Japan was permitted to organize small army, navy, and air units.

One term of the *U.S.-Japanese Mutual Security Pact* (1951) was that the United States agreed to take the major responsibility for defending Japan. The treaty has been revised, but this essential provision remains in force.

Despite a steady military build-up, Japan insists its armed forces are only for its defense. Any attempt to amend Article 9 has been defeated as a majority of Japanese prefer to rely on the United States.

With U.S. protection, Japan has had to spend relatively little on defense, freeing investment capital for industry. As the Asian power structure has changed, the United States has pressured Japan to increase its defense spending. Japan has increased its armed forces. In 1992, the Diet (Japan's Legislature) passed legislation allowing limited use of Japanese forces to be used in international peacekeeping operations.

JAPAN'S ROLE IN WORLD ORGANIZATIONS

From the beginning of its modernization, Japan sought international influence. When the League of Nations condemned Japanese occupation of the Chinese province of Manchuria, Japan withdrew from that international organization (1932).

Although the Soviet Union regained territory from Japan at the close of World War II, the Soviets refused to sign a formal peace treaty. In 1956, the two nations resumed diplomatic relations. The U.S.S.R. permitted Japan to join the United Nations in 1956, although it disapproved of Japanese - U.S. defense arrangements.

ASIAN RELATIONS

While Japan may be dependent on other countries for resources, its industrial strength gives it power in international relations. It has overcome hostility in those parts of Asia it conquered in World War II.

Japan has paid reparations for war damages and given economic aid to Southeast Asian nations. Important trade relations exist with Japan dominating the economy of the region.

Trade with China grew after Japan lifted a trade embargo against Red China after the Korean War. Diplomatic relations were not instituted until 1972. Yet, the more open atmosphere since Mao has led to a thriving trade between the two former enemies.

Relations with South Korea were poor until 1965 when they set a World War II reparations figure and restored diplomatic relations. Japan agreed to pay for its exploitation of its former colony.

PhotoDisc Inc. 1994

Japanese Currency – Yen

ROLE IN GLOBAL ECONOMICS

Japan wields enormous economic strength. Japan's Gross Domestic Product is over $3 trillion. Japan participates in **G-7 Summit Conferences** (heads of state of the seven most powerful industrial democracies). It also joined in recent **APEC** (Asian Pacific Economic Conference) meetings to aid in developing the burgeoning markets of the Pacific Rim.

As global politics change, Japan's economic prominence will keep it in the forefront of world affairs. Its prominence as the most developed nation in the Pacific region will shape that region's future.

QUESTIONS

1   The purpose of Article 9 of the Japanese Constitution was to
    1   build an international police force
    2   establish high tariff walls
    3   outlaw war as an instrument of national policy
    4   abolish tariffs on grain

2   The United States gave economic aid to Japan after World War II to
    1   create an ally against the spread of communism
    2   strengthen Japan against British power
    3   help Japan socialize its industry
    4   raise the Japanese standard of living

3   Following the Korean War,
    1   Korea was unified
    2   Japan built up its armed forces
    3   communist influence in Asia ended
    4   Japan joined NATO

4   Which is most characteristic of Japan's foreign policy?
    1   voting with Russia in the United Nations
    2   spreading communist propaganda in Asia
    3   offering aid to communist Vietnam
    4   broadening trade relations in Southeast Asia

5   From which international organization, formed after World War I to preserve peace, did Japan withdraw in 1932?
    1   League of Nations
    2   Security Council
    3   Mandate System
    4   United Nations

6   Which event occurred last?
    1   Twenty-One Demands
    2   Japan's admission to the U.N.
    3   Bombing of Pearl Harbor
    4   Japan's surrender to the U.S.

7 According to the post-World War II peace treaty with the U.S., Japan
   1 was required to pay reparations
   2 retained ownership of Taiwan
   3 had the right of military self-defense
   4 could not trade with communist China

8 Which Asian nation, formerly an enemy of Japan, is now a major trading partner?
   1 People's Republic of China
   2 Cambodia (Kampuchea)
   3 Pakistan
   4 Vietnam

9 Japan's successful advancement to major global status proves which factor is critical for power and prestige?
   1 abundant natural resources
   2 charismatic leadership
   3 strong military
   4 technology

10 Japanese foreign policy toward other nations since 1945 has been generally motivated by
   1 social and humanitarian concerns
   2 a desire for isolationism
   3 a desire to spread its ideology
   4 economic advancement

ESSAY

Japan has significantly improved its foreign relations since the end of World War II. Discuss the status of contemporary Japanese relations with *three* of the following:

- Southeast Asia
- People's Republic of China
- Republic of (South) Korea
- Western Europe
- The United States of America

UNIT THREE: EAST ASIA ASSESSMENT

ISSUE: APPRECIATING CULTURAL DIFFERENCES

This three-part evaluation offers individual research and group interaction opportunities.

STUDENT TASK

Research and report on a common food dish and participate in presenting it to the class.

DETAILED PROCEDURES

Part One:
Research recipes commonly used in East Asia.
A   Select and copy 2 or 3 recipes from home, library, home economics, or members of a local Chinese or Japanese community. Note sources on recipe cards.
B   In class groups, share recipes and identify common ingredients.
C   Find library resources to clarify factors responsible for frequency of common ingredients.

Part Two:
Write a brief report discussing why key ingredients are common in the country. Include a list of sources consulted.

Part Three:
Work in group selecting and preparing recipes for a class dinner.
A   Select recipe.
B   Coordinate menu for class dinner with other groups.
C   Assign group members to buy ingredients, furnish equipment, and perform other preparation tasks.
D   Prepare and present recipe for class.

EVALUATION

The scoring grid next to the evaluation items (on the following page) was left blank intentionally. Choice of appropriate category terms is the decision of the instructor. Selection of terms such as "minimal," "satisfactory," and "distinguished" can vary with this assessment. The table on page 10 offers additional suggestions for scoring descriptors that might be inserted in the blank grids.

LEARNING STANDARDS

Students should:

- Present ideas both in writing and orally in clear, concise and properly accepted fashion.

- Understand that peoples' values, practices, and traditions are diverse, yet they face the same global challenges.

- Understand that different national, ethnic, religious, racial, socioeconomic, and gender groups have varied perspectives on the same events and issues.

- Analyze and evaluate the effects of human, techno- logical, and natural activities on societies.

- Work cooperatively and show respect for the rights of others to think, act, and speak differently from them- selves within the context of democratic principles and social justice.

- Employ a variety of information from written, graphic, and multimedia sources.

- Monitor, reflect upon, and improve their own and others' work.

Parts One and Two: Individual Effort

Table on page 10 offers suggestions for scoring descriptors.

	Category 1	Category 2	Category 3	Category 4	Category 5
Evaluation Item a Do recipes reflect common food ingredients?					
Evaluation Item b Does the written report explain popularity of ingredients?					
Evaluation Item c Does report display understanding of cultural differences in food selection?					
Evaluation Item d Has a list of sources been included?					
Evaluation Item e Is report written clearly and effectively?					

Part Three: Group Effort

Table on page 10 offers suggestions for scoring descriptors.

	Category 1	Category 2	Category 3	Category 4	Category 5
Evaluation Item a Does the group recipe reflect frequently used ingredients in an identified area?					
Evaluation Item b Does group show cooperation in assembling and production of recipe?					

ADMINISTRATIVE GUIDELINES

1 Survey library resources and discuss project with librarian.

2 Arrange library time for student research.

3 Discuss interdisciplinary approach with Home Economics Teacher, and /or involve parents in making physical arrangements (e.g., ingredients, utensils, and cooking equipment).

4 Advise production groups on availability of ingredients and degree of preparation difficulty (e.g., time, equipment).

5 Coordinate lessons on safety, preparation, service, and cleanup with other staff and / or parents involved.

4

Oceania
& The
Pacific Rim

Maori   *trusteeships*

outback   *the Four Dragons*

Aborigines   *missionary kingdoms*

50,000			800	1500	1700
	BC ▮ **AD**				

- Aborigines settle in Micronesia and Australia
- Polynesians settle in Eastern Pacific, Easter Island, and Hawaii
- Magellan: Age Of Exploration
- Capt. Cook's Expeditions

Time-line is not drawn to scale.

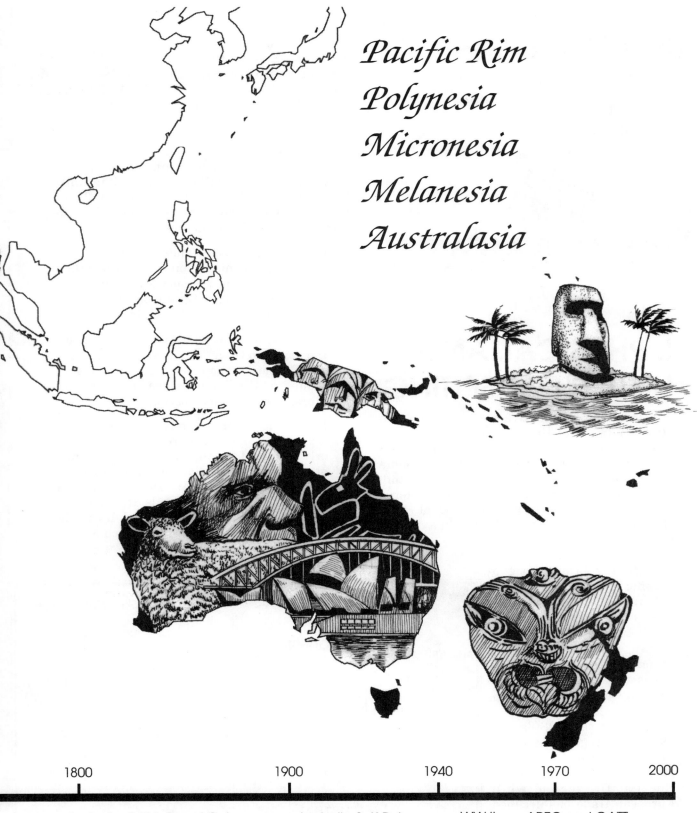

Pacific Rim
Polynesia
Micronesia
Melanesia
Australasia

1800	1900	1940	1970	2000

- Australia: British Penal Colony   • Australia Self-Rule   • WW II   APEC and GATT •
- European Colonialism   • Japanese Conquests
Independence: Island Nations •

Time-line is not drawn to scale.

UNIT FOUR:

OCEANIA

ECONOMIC GROWTH & DEVELOPMENT

I. PHYSICAL AND HISTORICAL SETTING

Oceania is a collective name for more than 30,000 islands of the Southern Pacific. The **Pacific Rim** is a new term embodying an economic and strategic region larger than Oceania. It includes all the areas with coastal lands along the Pacific in North and South America and Asia as well as the more traditional region of Oceania. Sections IV and V contain a detailed discussion of the Pacific Rim.

Oceania is more a geographic identification than a cultural one, as many cultures exist in the region. The southern part of the Pacific Ocean covers more than 30 million square miles. Its size is equivalent to the entire Atlantic Ocean.

During the 1980's and 1990's, the region has grown in importance. Economists point to the new commerce in the Pacific region while European trade has declined. They speak of the decline of **"The Atlantic Age"** and the rise of the **"Pacific Rim."** In the 1990's, U.S. exports to countries of the Pacific region surpassed those to Britain, Germany, France, and Italy. Section IV of this unit explores these changes in depth.

Because of its vastness, geographers divide Oceania into four geographic subregions: Australasia (Australia and New Zealand), Melanesia, Micronesia, and Polynesia. Those last three island subregions account for one-third of the Pacific Ocean area:

- **Melanesia** ("black islands") lies in the northeast Oceania region, just south of the equator. Melanesia's major island subgroups are Fiji, New Caledonia, the Solomon Islands, and New Guinea.

- **Micronesia** ("tiny islands") stretches across the northern Oceania, between Melanesia and Polynesia. Micronesia's four island subgroups are the Carolines, the Marianas, the Marshalls, and the Gilberts.

- **Polynesia** ("many islands") extends over many thousands of square miles in the easterly portion of Oceania. Polynesia appears on maps as a huge triangle or arrowhead pointed toward South America. Its northern point is the Hawaiian Islands. Its eastern point is mysterious Easter Island. Its southwestern point is New Zealand which is culturally British, but geographically it is part of Polynesia.

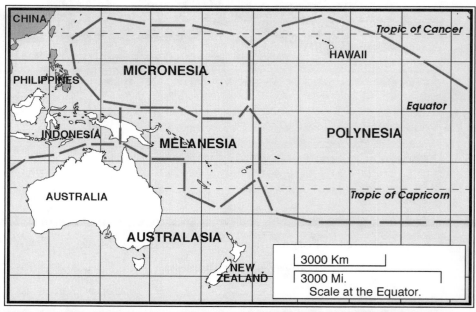

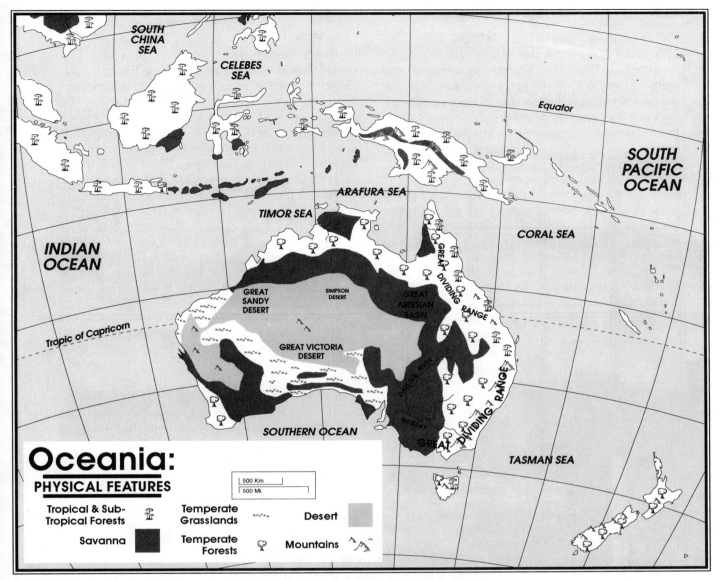

Oceania:
PHYSICAL FEATURES

500 Km
500 Mi.

Tropical & Sub-Tropical Forests	Temperate Grasslands	Desert
Savanna	Temperate Forests	Mountains

GEOGRAPHIC FEATURES

The islands of Oceania are of three geologic types: volcanic, coral, and continental. Polynesia has many volcanic islands. Geographers call them "high islands." They are mountain peaks rising from the ocean floor. Since they have fresh water and good soil, they often have large populations.

The highest proportion of coral islands lie in Micronesia. These islands are formed when coral sea life rings the peaks of sinking undersea mountain ranges. Coral can also cover narrow bands of land creating formations called reefs. The world's largest coral reef is over 1,250 miles (2,012 km) long. It is the **Great Barrier Reef**, off Australia's northeast coast. The conti-

nental islands of New Zealand, New Guinea, and Australia are large areas once part of a mainland formation. However, Australia is so large that geographers classify it a continent.

The dominant climate over Oceania is **Tropical Rainy** (Types **Am** and **Aw**). Most of Oceania lies close to the equator. The winds of the Pacific keep the air moist. Farther to the south, Australia's interiors have dry **Bw** desert climates in the interior and more temperate **C Types** on the coasts. Mountains in New Zealand cause variations in climate, but it still has a primarily **Cs** (mid-latitude marine or Mediterranean type) climate. In both countries, most of the population lives along the coasts.

Prevailing trade winds and the Doldrums along the equator have a primary effect on weather in Oceania. The clash of wind and water currents over the large stretches of ocean cause violent weather events. Typhoons (tropical cyclones) and **tsunamis** (tidal waves caused by undersea earthquakes) are frequent and dangerous.

The largest land area is Australia. It is almost the size of the 48 contiguous states of the U.S. The rugged topography and arid interior cause more than half of all Australians to live in its five largest cities along the southern and eastern coasts. Covering half the continent is the Western Plateau that Australians call "**The Outback**." It begins in the large, sparsely populated deserts of the plateau. The Outback continues into the dry Central Lowlands. The mountains of the **Great Dividing Range** separate the coastal plains from the Outback and keep the rains from reaching the interior. The narrow coastal rim of Australia enjoys good rainfall. This fertile area contains the main food producing regions. Australia's longest river system, the **Murray-Darling**, flows 2,000 miles (3,219 km) through the southeast. However, it is not a dependable source of water or transport because of the scant rainfall of the area.

New Zealand is a rugged, mountainous chain of islands lying 1,200 miles (1,931 km) off southeastern Australia. Its two largest islands are North Island and South Island. The latter

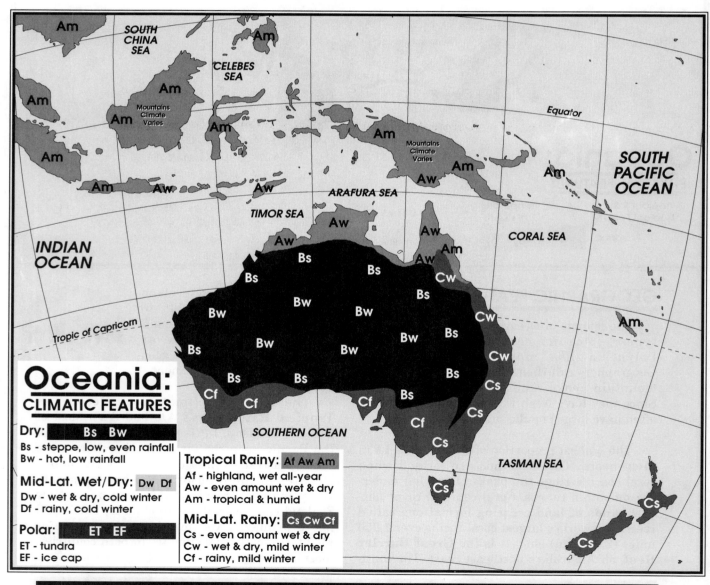

Oceania: CLIMATIC FEATURES

Dry: Bs Bw
Bs - steppe, low, even rainfall
Bw - hot, low rainfall

Mid-Lat. Wet/Dry: Dw Df
Dw - wet & dry, cold winter
Df - rainy, cold winter

Polar: ET EF
ET - tundra
EF - ice cap

Tropical Rainy: Af Aw Am
Af - highland, wet all-year
Aw - even amount wet & dry
Am - tropical & humid

Mid-Lat. Rainy: Cs Cw Cf
Cs - even amount wet & dry
Cw - wet & dry, mild winter
Cf - rainy, mild winter

Oceania is a world region of exceptional diversity and beauty. The Great Barrier Reef is the world's largest coral garden. Ayers Rock in Australia's outback seems to be a magnificent anomaly as it changes color with the time of day. Draining the rugged mountains of New Zealand's the Shotover River is the "playground" of both nature and New Zealanders.

contains the Southern Alps mountain chain. New Zealand enjoys a humid, cool climate, with many short rivers useful for hydroelectricity.

EARLY CULTURAL DEVELOPMENT

Early settlers reached the northernmost sections of Melanesia and Australia sometime between 30,000 and 50,000 years ago. The original settlers were migrants from South and Southeast Asia, moving slowly east toward Micronesia and into southeastern areas of Melanesia. They reached into Polynesia next, but the extreme area of Easter Island did not show settlement until 750 A.D. In some islands of eastern Polynesia, settlers from the Western Pacific arrived only a few hundred years before European explorers.

Vast distances between islands kept inhabitants isolated and led to much cultural variation. Over 450 languages are spoken in the islands of Oceania, but they have a common five vowel structure. Major cultural divisions include:

- Australia's nomadic **Aborigines** of the Outback are its earliest known inhabitants. Today, they are known for their music, dance, oral traditions, and the invention of the curved throwing weapon, the boomerang.

- Some 5,000 years ago, advanced Polynesian warrior groups called **Maori** arrived in New Zealand. Later, they resisted British imperialists before succumbing to modern technology and Western diseases in the late 19th Century.

- **Polynesians** spread over the Pacific evolving with wide cultural variety. Their litera-

Symbols of Polynesian culture show evolution of great variety.
Polynesian literature, visual, and performing art reflected their intricate ritual ceremonies.

ture, crafts, artistry, and performing arts reflected their intricate ritual ceremonies. Their visual arts such as sculpture, painting, and woodcarving portrayed the power and prestige of chiefs. However, climate and early European missionaries destroyed many artifacts of these earlier civilizations.

Much of Oceania was in a late Neolithic stage of development at the time of European contact. Many cultures did not survive their introduction to the Western world.

QUESTIONS

1   Which element appears most common in the remains of ancient Polynesian cultures?
    1   formal educational achievement
    2   religious ceremonies
    3   complex writing systems
    4   large, well-fortified cities

2   The geography of Oceania has created
    1   social cohesion
    2   widespread democracy
    3   political unity
    4   cultural diversity

3   Which is a result of topography and climate
    in Oceania?
    1   early and rapid industrialization
    2   the development of powerful nations
    3   diverse societies
    4   large-scale trade with Africa

4   Which condition is the major obstacle to
    economic development in Australia's
    Outback Region?
    1   reliance on a policy of laissez-faire
    2   use of strip mining to get natural
        resources
    3   lack of financial capital for development
    4   scarcity of water resources for crops

5   Which one of the following terms applies to
    a larger economic and strategic area than
    the traditional Oceania?
    1   Australasia
    2   Pacific Rim
    3   Outback
    4   Polynesia

6   The dominant climate over Oceania is Am
    and Aw (Tropical Rainy). Which element
    contributes to this?
    1   prevailing winds
    2   mountains
    3   deserts
    4   coral deposits

7   Oceania is often subjected to violent
    weather events. Which is a major cause of
    this?
    1   clash of wind and water currents
    2   mid-latitude marine type climate
        patterns
    3   all islands are active volcanoes
    4   mountainous terrain

8   In the 19th Century, the cultures of the
    Aborigines of Australia and Maori of New
    Zealand suffered from contact with
    1   famine
    2   Polynesian settlement
    3   natural diversity
    4   Western technology and disease

9   Most of Australia's settlement has been
    along the coasts because of their
    1   extensive river transportation systems
    2   closeness to the United States
    3   adequate rainfall
    4   cultural variations

10 Some economists speak of the end of the
    "Atlantic Age" and the rise of the "Pacific
    Rim" because
    1   U.S. trade with Pacific countries is
        increasing
    2   trade is easier where there is less
        cultural diversity
    3   the Pacific is less stormy than the
        Atlantic
    4   Oceania has more prosperity than
        Europe

ESSAY

Oceania is the collective name for more than
30 million square miles of ocean containing
30,000 islands. However, Oceania is more a
geographic identification than a cultural
one.

a   Why is this region so culturally diverse?

b   Identify *two* cultural groups that inhabit
    Oceania.

c   Explain how cultural diversity and the
    vast distances affected the development
    of the region.

In the 17th Century, Dutch traders made many discoveries. Some searched for "Tierra Australia Incognita," a legendary southern continent containing untold wealth. **Abel Janszoon Tasman** was an important explorer for the Netherlands. In the 1640's, he discovered New Zealand and other small territories.

There were clashes with inhabitants, but no prolonged hostilities occurred during this period. Early European explorers sought trade contacts, not territorial conquest.

18TH CENTURY:
WARRIORS AND MUTINEERS

Continued exploration revealed the vastness of the Oceania region. **Jacob Roggeveen** ventured into the Samoans. Later, he found mysterious ancient statuary on Easter Island in 1722. The interest aroused in Europe fueled important scientific explorations into the next century. Between 1740 and 1763, the War of Austrian Succession and the Seven Years' War interrupted explorations.

II. DYNAMICS OF CHANGE

The Commercial Revolution in Western Europe moved mariners to chart courses into unexplored waters. Mercantilists proposed setting up colonies. Governments sponsored ventures that brought wealth from far-flung regions. Western Europe's 15th Century "Age of Discovery" led to dramatic changes in Oceania.

DISCOVERY IN OCEANIA

16TH AND 17TH CENTURIES:
ADVENTURERS AND EXPLORERS

The Spanish explored for riches and wanted to spread Christianity. Between 1519 and 1521, **Ferdinand Magellan** led an expedition that eventually circumnavigated the globe. In the process, he discovered one of Polynesia's Tuamotu Islands. After his death, his crew reached the Caroline Islands. Shortly after that, Alváro de Mendàna de Niero discovered the Solomons, and Pedro Fernández de Quirós landed in the New Hebrides and New Guinea.

Captain James Cook, British Royal Navy
Explored Oceania Between 1768 & 1779

The Aborigine people had a unique form of culture, tradition, religion, and art. Behind the Aborigine figure (at left) is a part of a rock painting called the "Rock Painting of the Birth Scene." It is a story told in pictographs of the All–Mother, the old woman of the Northern Australian Myth, who in the form of a serpent arrived in Arnhem Land from the sea and gave birth to the Ancestors.

- Eugene Fairbanks, Artist

Britain emerged from these wars as the premier global sea power. British naval supremacy enabled **Captain James Cook** to launch extensive expeditions to Oceania from 1768 to 1779. Cook explored the Pacific from the Arctic to Antarctic. He became renowned as one of the Enlightenment's men of action. Cook claimed New Zealand and the eastern coast of Australia for Britain. Publication of the scientific journals of his three epic voyages was a major event in England.

While the Cook logs put to rest the dreams of a rich, unknown continent, they excited European interest in Oceania. Traders, whalers, and other adventurers descended quickly on Oceania. The guns they introduced permanently altered the lives of the region's people.

The most famous European settlers of the era were the mutineers of *HMS Bounty*. Since the 1789 incident on Captain William Bligh's ship, the descendents of the *Bounty's* crew have populated Tahiti and other islands of Polynesia.

19TH CENTURY:

MISSIONARIES AND PLANTERS

After the unruly early European settlement, came a change by Christian missionaries. Through the middle of the 19th Century, Christian sects from Europe and America sent missionaries to the Pacific Islands. They denounced local peoples' cultural differences, especially polygamy. When combined with the diseases, guns, and whiskey of the Western traders, the missionary influence undermined the authority of local chieftains. Missionaries moved from spiritual activities to taking political control. They helped the converted chiefs create "missionary kingdoms." Some areas such as Tahiti (1830) revolted. All outbursts resulted in more missionary control and the arrival of more European soldiers.

Trade increased as the missionaries imposed new order. Missionaries served as interpreters and sometimes as trade representatives. Western influence led to local demand

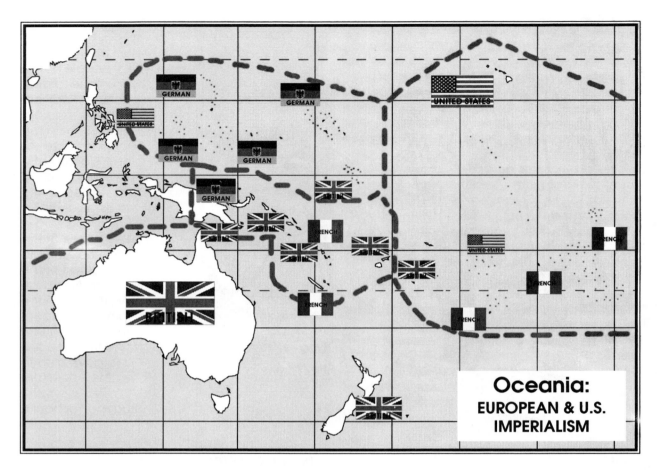

Oceania:
EUROPEAN & U.S.
IMPERIALISM

for clothing, hardware, and other tools. In return, Westerners demanded pearls and copra (coconut oil used for candles and soap). In the middle of the 19th Century, many Europeans set up plantations. Sugar cane became the primary crop. However, in the 1860's, the American Civil War caused shortages of cotton in the mills of Britain and France. Cotton plantations multiplied in Oceania.

Large-scale ownership and intensive working of the land created another cultural clash. Local people had a heritage of communal ownership. They limited production to local needs. Working dawn to dusk for wages did not interest them. Plantation owners manipulated laws to allow forced recruitment and even kidnapping. Farm tenancy disrupted village life and traditional social patterns even more.

Imperialism In Oceania				
Territory	**Britain**	**France**	**Germany**	**United States**
Australasia	Australia, New Zealand	none	none	none
Melanesia	Papua New Guinea, Fiji, Solomon Islands, New Hebrides (North)	New Caledonia, New Hebrides (South)	N.E. New Guinea	none
Micronesia	Gilbert Island	none	Nauru, Marianas, Carolines, Marshalls	Guam
Polynesia	Tonga	French Polynesia	Western Samoa	Hawaiian Is., Eastern Samoa

COLONIALISM IN AUSTRALIA AND NEW ZEALAND

European settlement had the most influence on Australia and New Zealand. After Cook's claims, Britain set up a colony in New South Wales in 1788. Among its earliest settlers were convicts sentenced to **transportation** (exile) for their crimes. In the 1600 and 1700's, the British had a penal colony in Georgia. However, U.S. independence forced them to look to Australia. For half the 19th Century, British courts sent convicts to **Botany Bay** as servants and laborers for the free British settlers. Many contemporary Australian families trace their roots to these prisoners.

In 1851, prospectors discovered gold near Sydney. Thousands rushed to Australia. Many Americans moved on to Australia after the California gold rush subsided. A few found gold, but many stayed to mine other minerals or raise sheep. Increasing numbers pushed into the hunting grounds of the Aborigines, forcing them farther into the barren interior. Life was hard, and the numbers of Aborigines declined.

In the 1880's, additional discoveries of gold brought another large wave of immigrants from all parts of the British Empire. Demands for self-government arose. By the end of the 19th Century, Parliament made Australia a self-governing dominion similar to Canada.

The Maori were Polynesian Warriors easily identified by their colorful body tattoos.

In New Zealand, the temperate climate, rich soil, and good fishing drew more settlers as the 19th Century progressed. At first, the Maori peoples tolerated them for the trade and Western goods they brought. They signed the *Treaty of Waitangi* granting British sovereignty in 1840. Still, a twelve-year war erupted in 1860, as the British settlers forced the Maori from traditional lands.

IMPERIALISM IN OCEANIA

The rapid industrialization in major European nations marked the third quarter of the 19th Century. Germany, Britain, France, and the Netherlands launched races to claim markets and colonies in Africa and Asia. The races naturally spilled into Oceania. Japan and the United States also joined the race. The increasing importance of raw materials, markets, and naval bases made the competition fierce. Disruption caused by missionaries and planters gave imperialist governments excuses for annexing nearly all Oceania by 1900.

The patterns of imperial control varied. Australia and New Zealand became self-governing dominions. Britain controlled their foreign affairs and defense. Elsewhere, the British used "crown colony" status. A crown-appointed colonial governor supervised an "indirect rule system." It allowed chiefs and local councils some administrative decision-making. Imperial German governors ruled as dictators, often ignoring traditional authorities. French governors ruled by decree but used an assimilation approach. It aimed at local people absorbing French culture. Like the British, the U.S. placed new territories under the rule of a governor but tried to work with local authorities. Usually, the net effect of imperialism was similar. It improved medical care, education, and agricultural production but destroyed the traditional culture.

IMPACT OF WORLD WAR I

Imperial rule in Oceania changed as World War I took hold of Europe. Early in 1914, British forces in Australia and New Zealand captured German New Guinea and Western Samoa. Japan occupied the Marianas, Carolines, and Marshalls.

After World War I, Germany lost its overseas territories. The new League of Nations directed powers occupying the Oceania territories to rule them as **mandates** (territories ruled by others until ready for independence). The League expected these mandates to be prepared for independence.

Some nations exploited the mandates. New Caledonia's nickel and Nauru's phosphates were taken without pay to local people. Other nations used permanent military forces to control the people. In the global Great Depression in the 1930's, sugar and copra prices varied. National budgets shrank. As in the imperial years, there was improvement in health and education. Colonial and military authorities reduced death rates for malaria, measles, and whooping cough. Literacy rates improved. Yet, progress toward economic and political independence was slow.

QUESTIONS

1   Which often causes cultural change?
1   strict enforcement of existing laws
2   maintenance of rigid class structures
3   continuation of traditional religious practices
4   introduction of new elements into an isolated society

2   Which change occurred in Oceania during the Age of European Imperialism?
1   The powers of local chiefs increased.
2   Emphasis on formal education decreased.
3   Industrialization created many large factory towns.
4   The Christian missionary influence expanded.

3   Which group traditionally held political power in much of Oceania?
1   religious leaders and landless peasants
2   chiefs
3   military warlords
4   Catholic Church leaders

4   European nations became interested in the Pacific Islands in the late 1800's to
1   obtain raw materials and new markets
2   promote socialist economic systems
3   remain isolated from other cultures
4   spread democracy throughout the globe

5   Which was an important effect of imperialism on Oceania?
1   Most Pacific nations developed self sufficient economies.
2   Europeans and Americans developed great respect for the cultures of others.
3   Most Pacific Islands became dependent on the imperialist mother countries.
4   Most Pacific Islands rejected democratic ideals.

6   Until the late 1500's, the Asian mainland and Oceania were similar in that both were
1   constantly overrun by hostile tribes
2   completely converted to Christianity
3   developing democracy
4   isolated from Europe and the rest of the world

7   Which of the following had the most influence on the history of Australia?
1   absence of warm water ports
2   abundant river systems
3   development from a British penal colony
4   lack of mineral resources

8   Japan and the United States joined the European race for colonies in Oceania in the late 19th Century because they needed
1   raw materials, markets, and naval bases
2   a homeland for excess population
3   to spread democratic institutions
4   to defend the area's independent countries

9   The success of Captain James Cook's 18th Century expeditions in Oceania resulted from
1   the need for penal colonies
2   the influence of the Enlightenment in Europe
3   Parliament taking power from the King
4   the loss of Britain's American colonies to France

10 Britain's emergence from 18th Century European wars as the premier global sea power led to
1 the industrialization of Oceania
2 increased colonization in the Pacific
3 democratic reform in Polynesian nations
4 loss of most French colonies in the Pacific

11 Which of the following brought many immigrants to Australia in the middle of the 19th Century?
1 two gold rushes
2 the need for cotton
3 the overthrow of British colonial government
4 industrialization

12 Which factors helped Christian Missionaries to move from spiritual activities to taking political control in the 19th Century?
1 the diseases, guns, and whiskey of the western traders
2 military resistance by local chieftains
3 armed crusades organized by church authorities in Europe
4 land reform for the peasants

13 In the 18th and 19th Centuries in Oceania, European concepts of colonialism led to
1 the rejection of Spanish culture
2 the growth of democracy in Oceania
3 opposition to the Catholic Church
4 exploitation of people and resources

14 Following Germany's defeat in World War I, how were its former colonies ruled by the victors?
1 as spheres of influence
2 as republics of virtue
3 as mandates of the League of Nations
4 as independent city-states

ESSAY

A number of global events influenced the development of Oceania.

Global Events

• Commercial Revolution in Western Europe
• European Enlightenment
• Imperialism
• Christian Missionaries
• World War I

Choose *three* of the global events listed. In discussing each event chosen:

a Identify the event in a global sense.

b Explain how it affected life in Oceania.

III. CONTEMPORARY NATIONS

WORLD WAR II – THE PACIFIC THEATER

BACKGROUND

Japan emerged as a major power in the Pacific Islands as the 20th Century unfolded. During and after the **Meiji Restoration** (1868-1912), it developed as a major military power. Simultaneously, Japan industrialized rapidly. With few natural resources, Japan strained to catch up to the major European nations and the U.S. The strain drove the nation's leaders to follow a path of aggression.

In the twenty years between the two world wars, Japan broadened its influence in Asia and the Pacific. It followed a policy of creating a **Greater East Asia Co-prosperity Sphere**. Under this imperial policy, Japan provided capital and manufactured goods to less developed nations. The underdeveloped nations provided food and raw materials to Japan. It applied this approach to its League of Nations' mandates. Japan treated the Mariana, Caroline, and Marshall Islands as its own colonies. It challenged British and French authority in their mandates. During 1941, Japan seized sections of Southeast Asia and then went into Oceania. It took over New Guinea and much of the Solomons. As the war progressed, Guadalcanal, Tarawa, and Iwo Jima were sights of some of the bloodiest battles in military history.

WAR IN THE PACIFIC (1941-1945)

The United States condemned Japan's aggression in China, Southeast Asia, and Oceania. It set up a trade embargo against Japan, blocking the sale of strategic resources. Open hostilities began 7 December 1941, when Japan launched a surprise attack against U.S. bases on Hawaii, Guam, Midway, and the Philippines. Japan quickly captured U.S. garrisons on Wake, Guam, and the Philippines. Attacks on the British in Malaya, Hong Kong, and New Guinea were equally successful. Japanese forces overran French Indochina and the Netherlands' East Indies (Indonesia).

Australian and New Zealand troops served with the Allies to hold off new attacks during the early stages of the  war. Eventually, 1.5 million troops fought in the Pacific Theater of the war. The Allies used an "island-hopping" strategy to win back large areas of Oceania. This was an all-out assault on certain strategic islands. The assault gave the Allies key bases to launch new offensives. They by-passed some Japanese-held islands in hope they would surrender as the war isolated them from Japan. Final victory came in August 1945, after the U.S. dropped atomic bombs on the Japanese cities of Hiroshima and Nagasaki.

Marines raise the American flag on Suribachi, Iwo Jima, February 1945.

Allied Victories In The Pacific Theater		
DATES	**BATTLE**	**SIGNIFICANCE**
May 1942	Coral Sea	Rebuilt U.S. Navy blocked conquest of Australia.
June 1942	Midway	Turning point of Pacific War; blocked westward advance of Japan.
Aug. 1942- Feb. 1943	Guadalcanal	Solomon Is. liberated.
Nov. 1943	Tarawa	Gilbert Is. liberated.
Jun.-July 1944	Saipan	Mariana Is. liberated.
July 1944	Guam	First American territory recaptured.
Oct. 1944	Leyte Gulf	First Kamikazes; Philippine Is. liberated by Allies
Feb.-Mar. 1945	Iwo Jima	Allies took strategic base to launch air/sea attacks on Japanese homeland.
Apr.-Jun. 1945	Okinawa	Allies took base to launch land troop invasion of Japanese homeland.

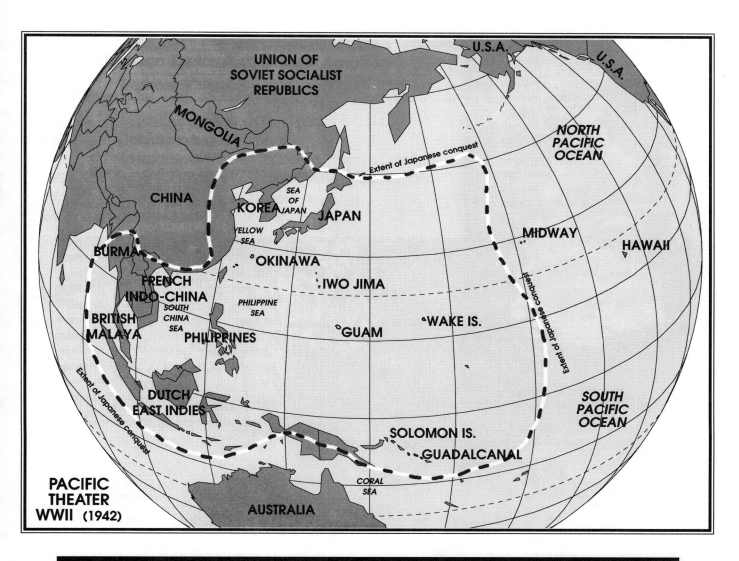

AUSTRALIA
NEW ZEALAND
FIJI
TONGA
NAURU
FRENCH POLYNESIA
VANUATU
REP. OF KIRIBATI
TUVALU
SOLOMON ISLANDS
MICRONESIA
PAPUA NEW GUINEA

Independence In Oceania

Territory	Britain	France	Germany	United States
Australasia	Australia -1901; New Zealand -1947	none	none	none
Melanesia	Papua New Guinea - (British northern half joined southern half League/U.N. trusteeship under Australia - independent, 1975); Fiji -1970; Solomon Is. - 1978; part of New Hebrides (became Republic of Vanuatu) -1980	New Caledonia remains a French possession with representation in French Parliament (Kanak people launched an independence struggle in 1980's)	Papua New Guinea (southern half League/U.N. trusteeship under Australia joined British northern half - independent, 1975)	none
Micronesia	Ellice Is. became Tuvalu -1978; Gilbert Is. (became Republic of Kiribati) -1979	none	Nauru Is. (League/U.N. trusteeship under Australia) -1968; Caroline Is. (U.N. trusteeship under U.S.; became Federated States of Micronesia -1991); Marshall Is. (U.N. trusteeship under U.S.; became republic -1991); Mariana Is. (U.N. trusteeship under U.S.; elected to become a U.S. possession - 1986)	Guam and Wake remain U.S. possessions; Palau is the last U.N. trusteeship administered by the U.S.
Polynesia	Tonga (became Kingdom of Tonga) - 1970	French Polynesia remains a French possession with representation in French Parliament.	Western Samoa (League/U.N. trusteeship under New Zealand) -1962	Hawaii became 50th state -1959

MARSHALL ISLANDS
WESTERN SAMOA
GUAM
PALAU
UNITED STATES

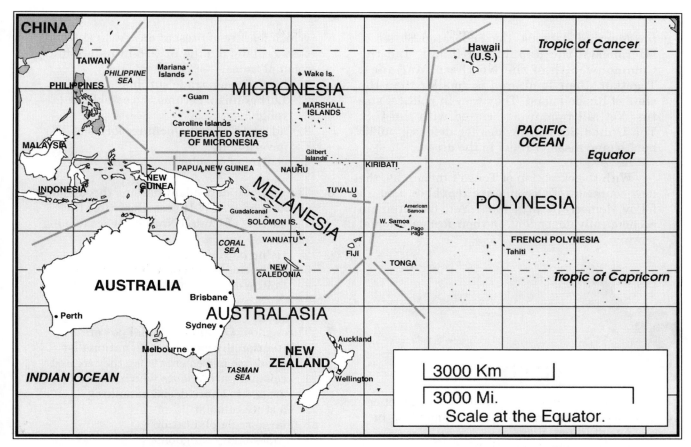

OCEANIA IN POSTWAR PERIOD

Globally, the Great Depression and two world wars weakened European powers. They lost control over their colonial empires. Nationalist movements worked for independence. Yet, there was little unrest in Oceania. Before World War II, most Western powers prepared their mandates and possessions for independence. France was an exception. It clung desperately to the illusion of empire.

Britain granted Australia independence in 1901. It became the first modern nation to introduce the secret ballot and grant women suffrage. Australia models its government on the British bicameral parliamentary system. Political power rests with the majority party in the lower chamber, the House of Representatives. The party leader becomes Prime Minister. The Senate, the Australian Parliament's upper chamber, has six-year terms. It is mainly a council of review of the representatives' work.

After World War II, the United Nations' Trusteeship Council replaced the League of Nations' mandate system. Britain and the United States easily accepted the idea of independence for Oceania's countries. France was more cautious. By 1980, most island groups of the region achieved independence. Some small, isolated islands remain dependencies of other nations. Easter Island remains a dependency of Chile.

U.N. TRUST TERRITORIES

After the Allied victory in 1945, the newly formed United Nations assigned the territories taken from the Japanese to Australia, New Zealand, Britain, France, and the U.S. The U.N. called the administrative assignments **trusteeships**. The idea was to guide and protect local people in preparing for nationhood.

The U.S. trusteeships were in three main island groups in Micronesia: the Marianas, the Carolines, and the Marshalls. They included over 2,000 islands now grouped in four separate areas (see chart opposite page): the Republic of the Marshall Islands, the Federated States of Micronesia, the Republic of Palau, and the Commonwealth of the Northern Marianas. Together, their land area is smaller than the state of Rhode Island. They vary in political status. Yet, all remain associated with the U.S. The United States provides for defense, public health, and disaster relief in the areas.

With the exception of Tonga's monarchy, the new countries of Oceania are republics, and all follow democratic principles. Yet, most remain economically dependent on their former colonial powers.

QUESTIONS

1 Which contemporary institution or practice most directly traces its development to the Age of Imperialism?
   1 subsistence agriculture
   2 extension of Islamic culture
   3 parliamentary government
   4 large diversified universities

2 Which term best describes the political conditions in Tonga, Fiji, and the Solomon Islands in the 1970's?
   1 isolationism
   2 mercantilism
   3 imperialism
   4 independence

3 Japan threatened many states in Oceania in the late 1930's and early 1940's because of their
   1 supplies of strategic natural resources
   2 support for terrorist groups
   3 economic competition
   4 attacks on the Japanese home islands

4 Since World War II, nations of Micronesia, Melanesia, and Polynesia have experienced an increase in
   1 economic isolation
   2 political independence
   3 large-scale civil wars
   4 colonial domination

5 Which feature of present day Australia and New Zealand did the British introduce in colonial times?
   1 large foreign trade surplus
   2 Lutheranism became the established religion
   3 adoption of parliamentary forms of government
   4 control of population growth

6 The rise of independent nations throughout Oceania after WW II best illustrates the
   1 success of United Nations peacekeeping forces
   2 rising power of minority groups
   3 decline of European colonial power
   4 failure of nationalist movements

7 Throughout Oceania, colonial powers unintentionally gave birth to nationalist independence movements when they created
   1 colonial parliaments which allowed local groups to share decision-making
   2 a state religion
   3 large-scale plantations
   4 "missionary kingdoms"

8 What was the purpose of the trusteeships the U.N. assigned after WW II to Australia, New Zealand, Britain, France, and the U.S.?
   1 annex them as full-fledged parts of the parent nations
   2 convert local people to Western religions
   3 use military force to end civil wars among local groups
   4 guide and protect local people in preparing for nationhood

ESSAY

As a result of World War II, most of Oceania was not only liberated from Japan but also from Europe and the United States.

Referring to the role of the United Nations Trusteeship Council, explain how these new nations gained self-determination.

IV. ECONOMIC DEVELOPMENT

ECONOMIC COOPERATION

World War II devastated the Pacific. Colonial economies received little help from their equally devastated mother countries. Still, European economic cooperation emerged. In the 1950's, the **European Coal and Steel Community** was formed which evolved into the **Common Market** and today's **European Union**. Western Europeans raised standards of living and increased production.

The dramatic economic improvement created a global model. Global leaders heeded these successes. In 1947, the United Nations formed **ECAFE** (Economic Commission for Asia and the Far East). It put the economic challenges of Oceania and East Asia in a global perspective. The **Colombo Conference**, called by India in 1955, and the **Association of Southeast Asia** (1961) made mutual economic plans for the region. Today, economists regard the Pacific

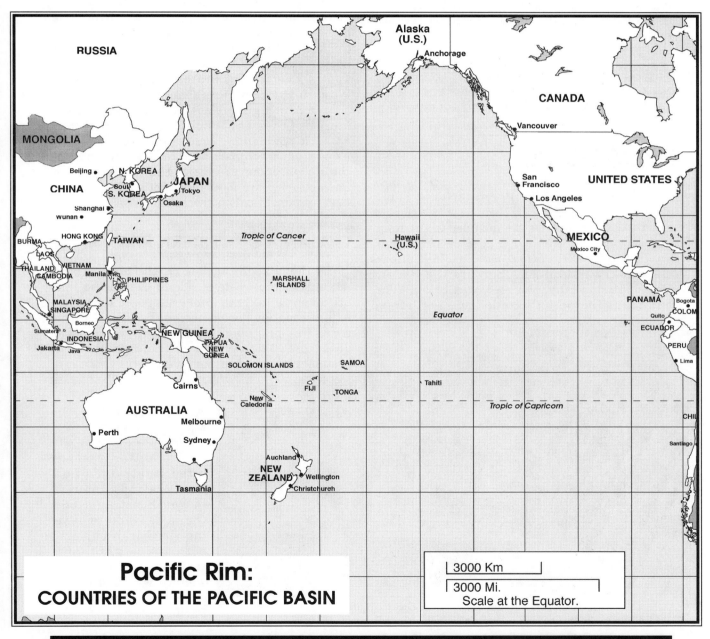

Pacific Rim:
COUNTRIES OF THE PACIFIC BASIN

3000 Km

3000 Mi.
Scale at the Equator.

region as significant. Hong Kong's $14,000 per capita GDP approaches Britain's ($15,000). The western area of Oceania is developing rapidly.

Two international organizations, the **World Bank** and the **International Monetary Fund**, now invest considerable sums in the region's future. The **IMF** estimates that $3.75 trillion, one half the growth of the world's production in the 1990's will come from Pacific countries. The growth rate in the Asia/Oceania region may be greater than that of Europe and the U.S. The reasons for this economic growth include:

- traditional emphasis on exports
- rapid emergence as a market
- attraction to foreign investors
- lower wages and fewer environmental restrictions

"THE PACIFIC RIM"

All this economic growth generated a new name for the region, the **Pacific Rim**. It is not a precise term. Authorities who use it differ on exactly which countries are included in the Rim.

In the broadest sense, the Pacific Rim can mean every nation that borders the Pacific Ocean. Historically, the area was called "The Far East." The westerly border runs north from

Australia to Russia. It includes Indonesia, Singapore, Malaysia, Thailand, Cambodia, Laos, Vietnam, the Philippines, Hong Kong, China, Taiwan, South Korea, and Japan.

Also in this broad sweep of the Rim is the entire Pacific coast of the **Western Hemisphere** (North and South America). This includes major economic powers such as the U.S. and Canada, and nations of growing importance such as Mexico, Colombia, and Chile.

Over half the world's people live in this broad configuration of the Pacific Rim. The globe's strongest military powers exist there. In the 1980's, world leaders predicted that the next century would be the "The Pacific Age." By the 1990's, the United States traded more with Western Pacific nations than with Europe. U.S. government figures showed 50% greater commerce across the Pacific than across the Atlantic. Currently, American businesses sell more products in Asia than in any other part of the globe. Among the major U.S. exports to the Pacific region are food, prescription drugs, cinematic productions, and recorded music.

OCEANIA'S "WESTERN RIM"

If the "Pacific Age" is on the horizon, the nations on the western side of the Pacific Rim are important. They could supplant the aging Atlantic nations' economic and political influence. This projection is not surprising to global observers. An overview of the area shows a gradual pattern of development.

AUSTRALIA AND NEW ZEALAND

World War II stimulated Australia's and New Zealand's interest in Southeast Asia and Oceania. While remaining British in culture, both areas gradually realized their economic welfare was tied to the outer reaches of the Pacific region.

Rutile (titanium dioxide) mine, Eneaba, Australia.
PhotoDisc Inc. 1994
Japanese companies control 12% of Australia's coal, iron, rutile, and nickel mines.

PhotoDisc Inc. 1994

In both Australia and New Zealand, wool is a major export.

Japan buys 50% of its iron ore and 17% of its natural gas from Australia. Japan is one of the three largest sources of foreign investment capital for Australia. The links between the two countries are very strong. Japanese companies control 12% of Australia's coal, iron, rutile, and nickel mines. Still, trade is broadening. Other Asian nations consume more than one-third of Australia's exports.

Australia buys nearly half its imported goods (machinery, autos, electronic equipment) from Japan and the United States. Recent figures from the Department of Commerce show U.S. consumers buy an annual average of $4 billion in goods from Australia.

World War II lessened Australia's dependence on Britain and strengthened its links to its own region. Signs of this included cancellation of its 1901 immigration restrictions designed to maintain a "White Australia." In 1973, the nation changed a policy excluding non-Europeans. The first Asians admitted were Vietnamese "boat people" escaping communism.

Because Australia's population is relatively sparse, it has higher labor costs than other nations of the Pacific region. Immigration is now seen as a force for economic improvement. Many of Australia's industries are labor intensive. Its mines produce raw materials sold to Pacific manufacturers (e.g., Japan, S. Korea, China). It produces aluminum ore, coal, and refined lead.

Wool is also a major export. Australia's **sheep stations** (ranches in the Outback) cover thousands of acres and produce one-third of the world's wool. It exports quantities of gold, tin, copper, and uranium. New petroleum and natural gas discoveries have drawn investments from Japanese and American firms. Australia is also a "bread-basket" country. It is a major grain exporter. Tourism is also important. One out of eight Australians work in the travel and tourism field.

Australia's largest customer is Japan. Nearly 40% of Australian exports go there.

New Zealand shares in the rising prosperity of the Pacific Rim. Its largest industry is sheep-raising. It does not have the mineral diversity of

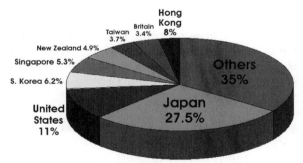

Hong Kong 8%
Britain 3.4%
Taiwan 3.7%
New Zealand 4.9%
Singapore 5.3%
S. Korea 6.2%
United States 11%
Others 35%
Japan 27.5%

AUSTRALIAN EXPORTS

China 3.1%
Italy 2.8%
Taiwan 3.6%
New Zealand 4.4%
Germany 6.4%
Britain 6.8%
Japan 18%
Others 35%
U.S. 23.5%

AUSTRALIAN IMPORTS

Source: Australian Bureau of Statistics (1992)

Trade Between Australia And Japan 1992 (In thousands of dollars; Australian Bureau of Statistics)		
Category	Imports from Japan	Exports to Japan
Machinery/Transport	6,580,330	$ 323,486
Manufactures	1,002,531	1,423,588
Chemicals	332,151	104,775
Food	43,162	2,200,749
Minerals	41,489	3,884,595
Fuel	16,228	4,607,137

its larger Pacific neighbor in the west. New Zealand is the world's largest exporter of lamb and the third largest exporter of wool (after Australia and Russia). New Zealand trades heavily with Australia and Japan. Britain and the United States also buy New Zealand's agricultural products. Recent figures from the Department of Commerce show U.S. consumers buy an annual average of $1 billion in goods from New Zealand.

SOUTHEAST ASIA

Moving northward along the Pacific Rim's western edge, Malaysia and Indonesia have growing economies. Rubber, petroleum, hardwoods, and minerals are important, but it is their expanding manufacturing that makes them attractive to investment. Their factories export high quality furniture and building materials.

Thailand and the Philippines export rice, corn, sugar, clothing, and shoes to the U.S., Japan, and Australasia. Both Thailand and the Philippines have suffered from recent political upheaval (see S. E. Asia Unit). Yet, their rates of economic growth exceed those of most European nations. Still, they are not as prosperous as "The Four Dragons" that dominate the Pacific Rim.

"THE FOUR DRAGONS" OF THE PACIFIC RIM

The NIEs (Newly Industrialized Economies) Singapore, Hong Kong, Taiwan, and South Korea have earned "The Four Dragons" nickname because of their astounding commercial

growth since the late 1980's. This growth owed its beginning to the unrestricted Western markets. Also, U.S. political and military aid contributed to growth in Taiwan and Korea. Low tariffs allowed these nations to compete in the developed countries. They marketed cheaper goods carried in discount chains (e.g., Wal–Mart, K–Mart, etc.). After World War II, grants from America helped to build new, state-of-the-art factories. Some of this industrial technology placed these countries ahead of the older industrial bases of Europe and the U.S. itself. Once they gained economic momentum, new capital from private investment poured into these countries.

In the high-spending 1980's, manufacturers in developed nations stopped competing with cheaper Asian-made toys, electronics, and clothing. South Korea's Hyundai autos and Goldstar appliances in the U.S. are examples. Some manufacturers in developed nations converted to higher quality, upscale products, leaving the cheaper product market wide open for the Dragons.

"The Four Dragons" that dominate the Pacific Rim.

Symbol of "The Four Dragons"

Singapore's location at the tip of the Malay Peninsula places it on the shortest water route between the Pacific and the Indian Oceans. The location makes this independent country an intermediary in the import-export trade. Japan's need for Mid-East petroleum has brought prosperity to Singapore. It has one of the highest standards of living in Asia due to shipping and financial services. Recent figures from the Department of Commerce show U.S. consumers buy an annual average of $9 billion in goods from Singapore.

Hong Kong launched large-scale competitive manufacturing in the 1950's. A good infrastructure, low taxes, and cheap labor attracted investors. International firms began locating in this welcome environment. More than 80% of Hong Kong's labor force works in manufacturing and finance. Clothing manufacture employs nearly 43% of the workers. Plastics, electronics, and textiles make up the bulk of Hong Kong's exports.

Hong Kong's free trade policy attracts wealthy shoppers from around the world. Freedom from tariffs leads to a brisk business in luxury items. Most recent figures from the Department of Commerce show U.S. consumers buy an annual average of $9 billion in goods from Hong Kong. The income earned from this

When recession hit the U.S., European, and Japanese markets in the early 1990's, consumption of more expensive high-end goods declined. Yet, consumers there continued to buy the cheaper products of The Four Dragons. The world economy slowed, but the European and American economies fared far worse than those of the Four Dragons. In addition, rising income from exports increased the spending power of Asians. Domestic markets grew as Asian workers bought more products. Trade within the region grew, too. Between 1986 and 1993, regional consumption of Pacific Rim goods rose from 31% to 43%.

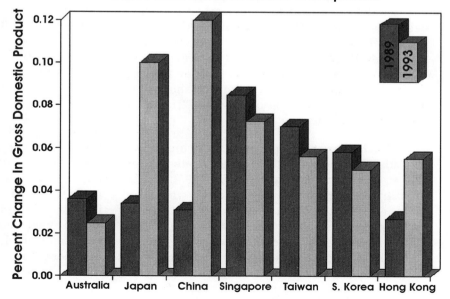

Gross Domestic Product Compared

Source: International Monetary Fund. (Gross Domestic Product is annual total of all goods and services produced within a nation. It discounts income from operations outside that country.)

Hong Kong City and Harbor

Textiles and shoes became important exports. S. Korea has been a major producer of sneakers and athletic shoes for global brands including Nike and Reebok. However, much of this business has been moved to Indonesia and Thailand for lower labor costs. S. Korea has also entered the automotive field and supplies parts to most United States and European companies. Electronic appliances are also a major export. Fishing, a traditional mainstay for S. Korea, also remains a major industry. Recent figures from the Department of Commerce show the U.S. buys an annual average of $18 billion in goods from South Korea.

economic growth raises the standard of living for many inhabitants. Many have become international investors in their own right. Still, there is fear because of Hong Kong being returned to Chinese rule in 1997.

Taiwan's expansion in the post-World War II Era came with aid from the United States. After the communists took over mainland China (1949), Taiwan's staunchly capitalist leaders received grants, loans, and military support from the U.S. This funding helped convert a labor intensive agricultural economy to manufacturing. Consumer product (plastics, electronics, and textiles) exports to America lead this economic change. Taiwan also exports iron and steel to other Pacific Rim countries. Taiwan's largest trading partners are Hong Kong and the United States. Recent figures from the Department of Commerce show that the U.S. buys an annual average of $21 billion in goods from Taiwan.

South Korea's expansion also came with considerable aid from the United States. After the stalemate of the Korean War (1950-1953), military support from the U.S. helped transform the poor South Korean economy. It moved quickly from subsistence agriculture to a manufacturing base. As the change occurred, former agricultural workers did not demand the high wages paid in developed countries. This kept production costs low and accelerated the economic change. South Korea's major trading partners are the United States and Japan.

THE SUPERPOWERS OF THE "WESTERN PACIFIC RIM"

JAPAN

Japan and the People's Republic of China have the second and third largest economies of the Pacific Rim. (The U.S. is first.) The U.S.  buys much from these two countries. According to the U.S. Department of Commerce, the U.S. buys an annual average of $12 billion in goods from China and $90 billion from Japan. Projections show these figures will increase.

Japan took two decades to rebuild its economy after World War II. From the 1960's, it grew into a global economic superpower. Its electronics, automotive, and computer products are among the largest selling in the world. Japan leads the world in steel production. Its financial investments dominate the Pacific Rim. Its overseas investment is 22 times that of foreign investment inside Japan. In 1992, for example, Japanese firms invested over $1 billion in China alone.

Japan has much of its wealth spread out globally. In 1990 alone, Japanese firms invested

Japanese Storekeeper, Tokyo

over $83 billion in U.S. business and properties. In 1994, Toyota, Nissan, and Honda produced almost as many cars in their Tennessee, Kentucky, and Ohio plants as they did in their Japanese facilities. Still, this massive worldwide investment makes Japan sensitive to global economic shifts. In the recessions that hit industrial nations in the 1990's, world trade declined. Japan's economic growth slowed.

One reason is the imbalance between imports and exports. Japan lacks natural resources. It has always imported large amounts of low-cost materials and food. Exporting expensive manufactured goods (e.g., autos, electronics) allowed the country to offset its need for imports. Problems in recent years changed this. Compared to imports, its exports declined. Manufacturers began selling more goods at home than abroad. To meet domestic demand, the Japanese increased imports from other countries in the Pacific.

Japanese businesses now face stiffer competition from the outside world, especially from the newly industrializing Pacific Rim countries. The economic slowdown also ended the 38-year rule of Japan's Liberal Democratic Party. For the first time in forty years, Japanese corporations began job and pay reductions. To stimulate the economy, politicians want more reductions in Japan's high income taxes and tariffs. These problems are not Japan's alone. Because it has so many investments in the

Pacific Rim, Japan's economic performance is critical to the region.

CHINA

The People's Republic of China is the second major economic power in the region. Its influence is nowhere near that of Japan's, but it is growing rapidly. Since the death of communist revolutionary leader Mao Zedong in 1976, China has been allowing more economic freedom (not political freedom). The relaxing of economic controls in the communist dictatorship and opening to foreign investment accelerated growth. China's current rate of growth is six times that of the United States. Exports to the U.S. and Europe grew nearly 25% in the first half of 1993. Major exports include silk, cotton, tea, and rice. China's clothing and raw materials exports are increasing.

The **IMF** (International Monetary Fund) recently estimated that a 5% to 6% annual GDP

PhotoDisc Inc. 1994
Silk Weaving Factory, China

ECONOMIC GROWTH & DEVELOPMENT

expansion will allow China to overtake Japan as the second largest economic power by the end of the 1990's. Adding China's output to that of the Four Dragons produces a figure equal to 40% of U.S. output. It is clear why *Business Week* said the Pacific Rim is the "engine that can drive the world out of its slump."(25 Oct. 1993, p.5) Foreign investment, once forbidden in China, is growing rapidly. Available coal, iron, and some petroleum plus a work force of one-half billion people makes it an attractive location. As the most populous nation, a rising standard of living would make China the world's largest market for everything from soap to telephones.

Another bright spot on the Chinese economic horizon is Hong Kong. By treaty with the British, the island city reverts to Chinese possession in 1997. Adding Hong Kong's economic momentum will be a major factor in China's progress (see GDP Chart on previous page).

HUMAN RIGHTS

Yet, experts see China's reactionary political policies as a problem. Democracy fuels most markets. Freedom of choice is critical to a growing economy. Both the United States and the United Nations severely criticize constant human rights violations. The government suppresses dissent harshly. It has executed or kept the 1989 T'iananmen Square protestors imprisoned. Still, the vast market China represents is alluring for the U.S. Despite threats to the contrary, the U.S. renewed China's "Most Favored Nation" trade status, reducing tariffs and other restrictions. Communist China's military power is also a source of concern on the Pacific Rim. Japan and the U.S. devote only 1%-4% of their spending on military goods. China spends nearly 9%.

Despite major political differences, American corporations continue to invest heavily in communist China. Increasing numbers of corporate leaders travel to China and other Pacific Rim countries, seizing the opportunities in the fastest growing global region.

QUESTIONS

1 Which headline would anger nations in Oceania?
1 *"World Bank Cancelling Debts Owed by Developing Pacific Rim Nations"*
2 *"Pacific Rim Nations Hold Summit in U.S. to Discuss World Trade"*
3 *"European Community to Raise Tariffs on Pacific Rim Imports"*
4 *"Japan to Drop Tariffs on Pacific Rim Imports"*

2 Which statement best describes a developing nation in the Pacific Rim?
1 high standards of living
2 high level of industrial production
3 dependence on export crops or raw materials
4 widespread consumption of luxury goods

3 The Pacific Rim nations have
1 adopted subsistence agriculture
2 become the world leaders in peacekeeping efforts
3 shown little concern for natural environment
4 blended Western economic values with traditional social ones

4 Japan and The People's Republic of China have the
1 second and third largest economies in the world
2 largest colonial empires
3 highest consumption of luxury goods
4 most natural resources

5 Economists refer to Singapore, South Korea, Taiwan, and Hong Kong as the "Four Dragons of the Pacific Rim" because they
1 maintain their traditional culture and resist development
2 are the most aggressive military nations in the region
3 are rapidly developing industrial powers
4 dominate the culture of most of the region

6   Which is true of economic systems in the western Pacific Rim? They have
    1   private ownership and no government interference
    2   strict adherence to communist 5-year plans
    3   little or no exportation of products
    4   various mixtures of private and government ownership of industries

7   In Singapore, a person eats lamb from New Zealand, drinks wine from Australia, and uses gasoline from Indonesia. Which idea does this illustrate?
    1   scarcity
    2   ethnic identity
    3   human rights
    4   interdependence

8   The nations in the western Pacific Rim primarily base their growing prosperity on
    1   large labor forces and modern technology
    2   abundant iron and coal deposits
    3   loans from Asian and African nations
    4   military strength

9   Which statement best describes Australia since the end of World War II?
    1   Its economy declined seriously.
    2   It underwent major industrialization.
    3   Its population centers shifted from the coast to the Outback Region.
    4   It adopted communism.

10 Australia's continued economic success depends mainly on its ability to
    1   increase defense spending
    2   increase its colonial possessions
    3   export raw materials
    4   defend its borders against illegal aliens

11 One problem Australian manufacturing faces when competing against the "Four Dragons" is that
    1   labor is more expensive in Australia
    2   all raw materials must be imported
    3   Australia levies heavy export fines
    4   few sources of fuel are found in Australia

12 As economically developing nations become more industrialized and open to democracy, which situation occurs most frequently?
    1   authority of religious leaders increase
    2   the size of families skyrocket
    3   the cost of medical care decreases
    4   traditional roles of women change

13 During the late 1980's and early 1990's, many Pacific Rim nations experienced major changes in their economies that resulted in
    1   military dictatorships
    2   increasing religious fanaticism
    3   the rise of communism
    4   dramatic increases in Gross Domestic Product

ESSAYS

1   Global cooperation can result in dramatic economic improvement for underdeveloped areas.

    Explain the role of *three* of the following in bringing economic improvement to the Pacific Region:
    •   China
    •   Japan
    •   United Nations
    •   United States.

2   Several Pacific Rim nations are enjoying expanded economic prosperity.

    Choose *three* of the following nations and for *each* one explain what has led to its new prosperity:

    •   Australia
    •   South Korea
    •   Singapore
    •   Hong Kong
    •   Taiwan.

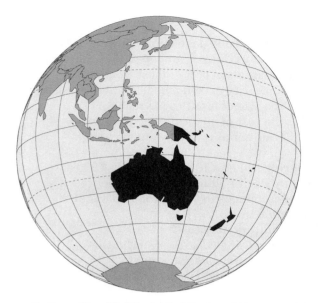

V. OCEANIA IN THE GLOBAL CONTEXT

From the late 15th Century, European nations influenced global life. Today, the sources of power vary. The Pacific Region is evolving. It has potential as a source of power. Current economic and political growth give it a new global importance.

Power and influence in the Pacific Region emerged from many sources. European imperial powers reshaped traditional political and economic life. Later, Japan and the United States added their own influences. After World War II, international organizations altered institutions even more. Commercialism and industrialization brought more change. A review of these complex elements offers perspectives on the region's new global standing.

POLITICAL LINKAGES IN OCEANIA

Affiliations with the United Nations and the United States have shaped the present environment. The influence of the British Commonwealth and the French Community is still present but rapidly fading.

THE UNITED NATIONS

U. N. influence in the region is significant. The devastation left after the brutal fighting in World War II made rebuilding necessary. Trying to rebuild themselves, former imperial powers lacked resources to restore the region. Colonial administration went limp even in areas not touched by battle. In the years after the war, the United Nations launched a global effort to help emerging nations. The U.N. created the Trusteeship Council  to prepare colonies for independence. The Council coordinated U.N. agencies (see table below). Over the next few decades, these organs of the U.N. restored and readied former colonies for independence. In the 1970's Fiji, Papua New

United Nations Agencies Active In Pacific Trust Territories	
Agency	**Activity**
IMF	International Monetary Fund helps new nations coordinate stable money systems and promotes international trade.
World Bank	International Bank for Reconstruction and Development lends money for public works (water and health facilities). Its divisions such as International Finance Corporation, International Development Association, International Fund for Agricultural Development aid private enterprises.
UNESCO	United Nations Educational, Scientific, and Cultural Organization supervises projects to share the developed nations' facilities and talents with developing nations.

Guinea, Western Samoa, and the Solomon Islands became nations. Since then, Vanuatu, the Marshall Islands, and the Federate States of Micronesia gained independence. Of the original trust territories, only Palau remains under U.S. administration.

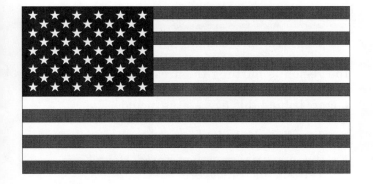

THE UNITED STATES

U.S. trade with China began early (1785). In the first half of the 19th Century, American settlers entered the Hawaiian Islands and Midway. Trade with Japan opened in 1854. The U.S. war with Spain (1898) led to colonies in the Philippines, Guam, and Samoa. In the 20th Century came struggles with Japan and trusteeship administration for the U.N. Later, the collapse of the U.S.S.R. allowed the U.S. to change policies and reduce its military forces. Yet, political and economic interest in the Pacific continues.

- **Hawaii** (Hawai'i) – Admission of the Hawaiian Islands as the 50th state of the Union (1959) gave the U.S. a permanent stake in Polynesia. High living standards and excellent educational and healthcare facilities place it among the most advanced states in the nation. Unemployment is traditionally low. Major industries include agriculture (sugar, coffee, pineapple), food processing, defense, and tourism. Polynesian culture predominates, but recent years have seen an influx of Asian groups. Japan and Korean firms hold large investments in "The Aloha State."

- **Territories** – Guam (133,000) and American Samoa (50,000) are the most populous Pacific territories. Inhabitants are U.S. citizens and have nonvoting delegates in the U.S. Congress. Other small island possessions are either sites of military installations or uninhabited. These include Wake, Midway, Baker, Jarvis, Palmyra, and the Johnston Atolls.

- **Commonwealth Status** – On 3 November 1993, the Northern Marianas Islands became a self-governing commonwealth of the United States. As with the Commonwealth of Puerto Rico in the Caribbean, the inhabitants are U.S. citizens. They have all rights and protections under the United States Constitution. There is a nonvoting delegate in Congress. Still, they cannot vote in national elections and do not pay Federal income tax.

- **U.N. Trust Territory** – Palau is a group of small islands between the Philippines and Indonesia. It is the last of the U.N. World War II Trust Territories. U.S. authorities have nearly completed work in Palau and expect independence soon.

- **Newly Independent Nations** – The Republic of the Marshall Islands and the Federated States of

PhotoDisc Inc. 1994   Waikiki, Hawaii, U.S.A.

Micronesia are both former trust territories. They became independent in 1991. They have special financial aid, defense, and trade arrangements with the United States.

THE BRITISH COMMONWEALTH AND THE FRENCH COMMUNITY

After World War II, both Great Britain and France lacked the resources to rule their overseas empires. Except for the tiny Pitcairn group in the middle of the South Pacific, Britain released its possessions in the region. France retains control of 130 islands with a population of nearly 200,000.

Both set up alliances to maintain close relations with former colonies. Papua New Guinea, Nauru, Tuvalu, Kiribati, and Vanuatu have special economic status with Britain. France's arrangements with its former colonies lean more toward preserving cultural ties through the French Union or Community.

AUSTRALIA AND NEW ZEALAND

While under British influence, Australia and New Zealand had internal self-government early in the 20th Century. They are still ethnically and culturally European. Many people from the British Isles emigrate to Australia and New Zealand each year. As the British Empire disintegrated, both these nations remained  allied with the West. In the Cold War Era, they strengthened ties with the U.S. They became active U.N. members. Both still manage trust territories. Australia joined the U.N. action in the Korean War and supported the United States

in Vietnam. Yet, both moved quickly to grant diplomatic recognition to the People's Republic of China. They supported its entrance into the U.N. They rapidly made major trade agreements with China.

ECONOMIC LINKAGES IN OCEANIA

The great global changes of the last twenty years are clear in Oceania. Economic growth in the region is hurtling the area into an entirely new global status (review section IV). The key factors behind this new status include:

- Japan's industrial power

- the industrial growth of Korea, Hong Kong, Taiwan, and Singapore

- the reopening of China's trade and its accelerated industrialization

- the trade shift of Australia and New Zealand to Pacific neighbors

Two recent events underlined the new economic status of Pacific Rim nations. In 1993, global attention focused on the Asian-Pacific Economic Summit and the conclusion of the GATT's Uruguay Round.

In 1989, several Pacific Rim nations formed **APEC** (**Asian-Pacific Economic Conference**) to promote trade and economic progress in the region. In  November 1993, the U.S. was host to a 15–nation Asian-Pacific Economic Summit in Seattle, WA. For the first time since the rift over the T'iananmen Square Massacre in 1989, leaders of China and the U.S. met to discuss issues. Pacific Rim nations sponsored ideas on trade sanctions against North Korea for continued nuclear build-up. China, Japan, the U.S., Canada, and Australia reduced trade barriers. Yet, not much reciprocation appeared from other new industrial powers. The key result of the summit was recognition of the emerging power of the region.

The U.N. created the **General Agreement on Trade and Tariffs (GATT)** in 1948. It organizes world trade treaties on tariffs and markets. The GATT's Uruguay Round of revisions

Polynesians live on Pacific islands from Hawaii southwest to New Zealand and east to EASTER ISLAND. The mythical homeland of their ancestors was Hawaiki, near Tahiti. Traveling from island to island, they became master shipbuilders. The KON-TIKI expedition (1947, led by Norwegian explorer Thor Heyerdahl) demonstrated that the first Polynesians could have sailed from South America, but not that they actually did. Current views suggest that they came from the direction of Asia.

- Eugene Fairbanks, Artist

began in the 1980's. In December 1993, the negotiations concluded. The latest GATT update cut worldwide tariffs on agricultural products. It also set uniform ideas on patents, copyrights, trademarks, and corporate rights. Additionally, the GATT set some rules to control **product dumping**. This occurs when developed nations intentionally flood a developing country with cheap goods to kill competition.

In relation to the Pacific Rim, the new GATT will allow more open markets and freer trade for the newly industrializing nations. Major food exporters such as Australia and New Zealand will find it easier to export their wares to the smaller nations.

OCEANIA AND TODAY'S WORLD

The industrial emergence of Pacific nations, coupled with the birth of new democratic countries, ushered in a new status for this region. The fading of hostilities between the communist and free nations opens a new stage of global politics. Pacific nations once caught up in European power struggles are now more independent. The new environment is less rigid. Former colonies and satellite countries make decisions on their own. For nearly four decades,

Australia and New Zealand loyally supported Britain and the U.S. in cold war issues in the region. Now in a more secure position, these nations can focus on developing their economic strengths. Like Japan, they are also leaders in the region and can reach out to support LDCs (Less Developed Countries).

In general, developed nations must strengthen economic and political ties among LDCs and NICs (newly industrializing countries). As diverse and  far-flung as Oceania is, there are common concerns. Richer nations must aid poorer ones. Creating regional markets and addressing social needs are important. In a new global situation, they must organize to compete against trade groupings such as those emerging in Europe (**Common Market** or **European Union**) and North America (**NAFTA**).

An area long shaped by other nations, Oceania has begun to act independently. The Pacific Rim has the resources. More than ever before, new technology can provide the infrastructure. If the world can maintain a peaceful political climate, the 21st Century may well become the "Pacific Age."

QUESTIONS

1   Which statement about the population of Australia and New Zealand is most accurate?
    1   The population is most dense in the interior regions.
    2   Most of the people are of European descent.
    3   Wide cultural diversity exists.
    4   Overpopulation threatens prosperity.

2   Since the end of World War II, Oceania has experienced
    1   internal conflicts caused by isolation policies
    2   a rising tide of communist insurrections
    3   steady declines in standards of living
    4   political and economic cooperation among its nations

3   *"Examples of trade in the Pacific Rim today include heavy Japanese investment in Australia, the sale of Australian grain to Russia, and the reliance of many Pacific Rim nations on Indonesian oil."* Which generalization best supports this statement?
    1   Most nations of the Pacific Rim are self-sufficient.
    2   Nations controlling vital resources have lost power.
    3   Subsistence agriculture is growing as an industry.
    4   Interdependence is growing.

4   Which is an accurate statement regarding modern nations of Oceania?
    1   Most nations have rejected membership in the United Nations.
    2   Most nations are military allies of the People's Republic of China.
    3   Most nations are experiencing a decreasing birthrate and falling economic prosperity.
    4   For economic reasons, many nations have maintained ties to their former colonial powers.

5   In relation to the Pacific Rim, the 1993 GATT (General Agreement on Trade and Tariffs)
    1   opens markets for the newly industrializing nations
    2   makes food exportation more difficult for Australia and New Zealand
    3   allows the U.N. to control "The Four Dragons"
    4   destroys the drug cartels of the region

6   Since the end of World War II, Australia has
    1   become a major force in Oceania's regional economy
    2   adopted imperialist policies toward its neighbors
    3   stopped all foreign ownership of business
    4   returned to the pre-WW II isolation

7   Which factor explains why both Japanese and U.S. influence are strong in the Pacific Rim?
    1   They are both members of the British Commonwealth.
    2   Both fear the opening of markets in China will hurt their economic power.
    3   Both nations have large investments in the other nations of the region.
    4   The GATT gives them trusteeships over the smaller nations of the region.

ESSAY

Global organizations and agencies significantly influence the Pacific Rim.

Global Agencies
•   APEC
•   British Commonwealth
•   GATT
•   International Monetary Fund
•   Trusteeship Council
•   UNESCO
•   World Bank

Choose *three* of the agencies. For *each* one chosen, explain the role played by the organization in assisting a particular nation in the Pacific Rim.

UNIT FOUR: OCEANIA ASSESSMENT

ISSUE: ECONOMIC COOPERATION AND GLOBAL INTERDEPENDENCE

This three-part simulation assessment offers individual library research, role playing, cooperative group decision-making, and oral reporting opportunities.

STUDENT TASK

Research and participate in a simulation on interdependence in the Pacific Rim.

DETAILED PROCEDURES

Part One:
Write a briefing for delegates to **APEX–2** (Second Asian Pacific Economic Summit) on an assigned nation.

A   Use library to investigate the nation's economic strengths and weaknesses. List resources, industries, population, import-export data.

B   Add a conclusion on the nation's economic health. Include a judgement about how the nation can help others and what kind of help it needs from others.

Part Two:
Advise and prepare a delegate to speak at **APEX–2.**

A   Teacher assigns students to one of six groups.

B   Each group selects a group chairperson and an **APEX–2** delegate.

C   Each member reads briefing while rest take notes on economic strengths and weaknesses.

D   Chairperson leads a discussion to decide the common needs of the nations in the group.

E   Group writes a speech for its **APEX–2** delegate to deliver at the opening of *Session A*.

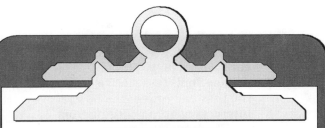

LEARNING STANDARDS

Students should:

• Understand that people's values, practices and traditions are diverse, yet face the same global challenges.

• Understand that different national, ethnic, religious, racial, socioeconomic, and gender groups have varied perspectives on the same events and issues.

• Analyze and evaluate differing views of historic, social, cultural, economic, and political events, eras, ideas, and issues.

• Understand that interdependence requires personal and collective responsibility for the local and global environment.

• Work cooperatively and respect the rights of others to think, act, and speak differently from themselves within the context of democratic principles and social justice.

• Demonstrate civic values and socially responsible behavior as members of school groups, local, state, national, and global communities.

• Monitor, reflect upon, and improve their own and others' work.

Part Three:
Participate in a simulated **APEX–2** meeting.

Session A:
1   Class takes notes as delegates make presentations on the strengths and needs of their countries. Listen for ways to help your group bargain with other groups.

2   Original groups reconvene and share notes. Groups decide offers to make to other groups. Groups write offers and deliver them to other groups.

3   Groups evaluate offers received. Groups can negotiate and bargain with other groups. Each group votes on offers to accept. Groups write a final compromise presentation for group's delegate to deliver at *Session B*.

Session B:
1   Take notes as delegates make presentation. Tally the number of ways each nation helps others.
2   Join in final class discussion analyzing the pros and cons of the new interdependence resulting from **APEX–2**.

EVALUATION

The scoring grid next to the evaluation items (on the following pages) was left blank intentionally. Choice of appropriate category terms is the decision of the instructor. Selection of terms such as "minimal," "satisfactory," and "distinguished" can vary with this assessment. The table on page 10 offers additional suggestions for scoring descriptors that might be inserted in the blank grids.

Part One: Individual Research
Table on page 10 offers suggestions for scoring descriptors.

	Category 1	Category 2	Category 3	Category 4	Category 5
Evaluation Item a Does briefing report contain factual information?					
Evaluation Item b Does briefing report include a judgement about how the nation can help others and what kind of help it needs from others?					
Evaluation Item c Does briefing report cite library sources?					
Evaluation Item d Is plan written clearly and effectively?					

Note: Part Two Evaluation Grid is on the opposite page.

Part Three: Session B – Final Statements
Table on page 10 offers suggestions for scoring descriptors.

	Category 1	Category 2	Category 3	Category 4	Category 5
Evaluation Item a Does the group's final statement solve its country's problems?					
Evaluation Item b Does the group's final statement help solve regional problems?					
Evaluation Item c Does the group's final statement show interdependence?					

Part Two: Session A – Delegate Presentations

Table on page 10 offers suggestions for scoring descriptors.

Evaluation Item a Does delegate's speech clarify nations' problems?	Category 1	Category 2	Category 3	Category 4	Category 5
Evaluation Item b Does delegate's speech clarify nations' strengths?	Category 1	Category 2	Category 3	Category 4	Category 5
Evaluation Item c Does delegate's speech offer a variety of proposals?	Category 1	Category 2	Category 3	Category 4	Category 5
Evaluation Item d Are delegation's proposals realistic, given available resources?	Category 1	Category 2	Category 3	Category 4	Category 5

ADMINISTRATIVE GUIDELINES

1   Survey library resources, discuss project, and arrange library time with librarian.

2   Divide countries being researched into industrialized and LDCs. Depending on size of class, create 2 to 3 groups of industrialized nations and 2 to 3 groups of LDCs.

3   Assign students their countries and groups.

4   Discuss library resources available and research goals with class.

5   After rating individual research reports, return individual research reports and form groups.

6   Outline work expectations for groups during Part Two (individual briefing, common needs discussions, speech writing, note taking).

7   Outline work expectations for APEX-2 general sessions during Part Three (offers to other groups, needs assessment, writing final statement).

8 a   *Option*: Instructor may wish to use peer rating or voting for the Part Three presentations.

8 b   *Option*: Instructor may wish to rate individual delegates' speeches for extra portfolio commendation.

9   Conduct a debriefing discussion to evaluate new levels of interdependence and the degree of cooperation resulting from the APEX-2 simulation.

5 *Latin America*

barrios
caudillo
machismo
assimilation
urbanization

mercantilism
fragmentation
pre-Columbian
Pan–American
encomienda system

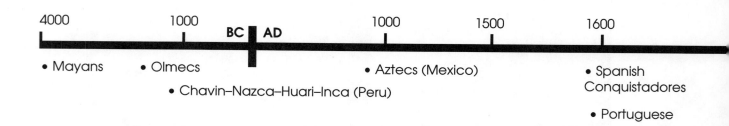

4000		1000		BC ▮ AD			1000		1500		1600

• Mayans   • Olmecs   • Aztecs (Mexico)   • Spanish Conquistadores

          • Chavin–Nazca–Huari–Inca (Peru)

                                                                                    • Portuguese

Time-line is not drawn to scale.

1800   1900   1950   2000

- Independence Movements   • Spanish–American War   • OAS   • Contra Affair
- Gran Colombia   • Panama Canal   • Castro
- Monroe Doctrine   • Mexican Civil War   • Alliance for Progress
- Juarez & Diaz   • Good Neighbor Policy

Time-line is not drawn to scale.

UNIT FIVE:

LATIN AMERICA

I. PHYSICAL AND HISTORICAL SETTING

Latin America influences many other regions of the globe. The physical, historical, political, and social influences that make up the variety of cultures in this vast region are the focus of this unit. Colonization by the nations of Europe's Iberian Peninsula (Spain and Portugal) in the 15th and 16th Centuries A.D. created a cultural shadow that sometimes over-simplifies views of the region.

SIZE AND DIVERSITY

Latin America is located south and southeast of the United States. It is a large region, encompassing almost 8 million square miles (1/6th of the Earth's land surface). It runs nearly 6,000 miles (9,656 km) north to south and is over 3,000 miles (4,828 km) at its widest point.

Latin America consists of 33 independent nations and 3 **dependent states** (colonies). Geographers usually subdivide the region into Mexico, Caribbean America, Central America, and South America.

These subregions are diverse. Each developed cultural and traditional variations. The dominance of the **Latin-based (*Romance*) languages** (Spanish throughout most of the region, Portuguese in Brazil) led to the general description of the region as "Latin America." However, there are areas where English, Dutch, and French are also official languages. The Iberian (Spanish / Portuguese) dominance in the colonial period also accounts for the dominance of the **Roman Catholic** religion.

PHYSICAL FEATURES

Much of the region lies in the tropics. Winters are generally moderate. However, the variety of elevations in its rugged topography reveal nearly every major climate except the polar types. The amount of rainfall varies greatly. These variations in climate and topography have significant influence on the lives of the people.

Distance Scale Latin America

250 Km
250 Mi.

Latin America:
PHYSICAL FEATURES

Tropical & Sub-Tropical Forests	
Savanna	
Desert	
Mediterranean	
Temperate Grasslands	
Temperate Forests	
Mountains	

Distance Scale South America

500 Km
500 Mi.

For centuries, the vast mountain ranges, dense rain forests, and unnavigable rivers separated the people of Latin America. These barriers blocked development of a functional **infrastructure** (transportation and communication system).

The physical features of Latin America include its massive mountain ranges, lengthy river systems, extensive plateaus, and small plains.

The coastal **Sierras** of Central America and **Andes Mountains** of South America form a **cordillera** ("backbone" mountain chain) along the western coast of Latin America. (It extends northward becoming the Rocky Mountains of North America.) The highest peaks in the Andes are over 20,000 feet (6,000 meters) above sea level. Only the Himalayas in Asia are taller. The highest peak is Argentina's **Aconcagua** (22,831 ft; 6,959 m). East-west travel in the Andes is limited to a few narrow passes.

Latin America: CLIMATIC FEATURES

Tropical Rainy: Af Aw Am
Af - highland, wet all-year
Aw - even amount wet & dry
Am - tropical & humid

Dry: Bs Bw
Bs - steppe, low, even rainfall
Bw - hot, low rainfall

Mid-Lat. Rainy: Cs Cw Cf
Cs - even amount wet & dry
Cw - wet & dry, mild winter
Cf - rainy, mild winter

Mid-Lat. Wet/Dry: Dw Df
Dw - wet & dry, cold winter
Df - rainy, cold winter

Polar: ET EF
ET - tundra
EF - ice cap

Most of the population lives on the temperate plateaus that range from 4,000 to 9,000 feet (1,219 m to 2,743 m) above sea level. The latitude, altitude, and prevailing winds have much to do with the patterns of life in the region. The Andes have **vertical environmental zones**. Proceeding up into the mountainous regions, numerous climate and vegetation zones can be found within a few square miles. They are major determinants of human activity.

As in other regions, rivers are a central life support system. The chief river systems of South America are critical to the region's development.

- The **Orinoco River** in the north winds its way from the Guyana Highlands through 1,500 miles (2,414 km) of Venezuela before emptying into the Atlantic.

Aerial view of the rain forest – Guyana, South America

- The **Rio de la Plata** (River of Silver) is actually an **estuary** (broad, shallow bay) in the southern part of the continent. It is formed by two rivers (Parana and the Uruguay) which flow southeasterly draining the Andes. This river system provides a large irrigation basin for one of the most productive agricultural regions in the world.

Two large plateau regions contain rich farmlands and mineral reserves. The **Brazilian Highlands** in the south-central region near the Atlantic coast contain Brazil's major population centers. The **Gran Chaco** is a 200,000 square-mile flatland shared by Argentina, Bolivia, and Paraguay. Cotton and yerba maté (a native tea) are grown extensively on the Gran Chaco.

The region's plains areas are savannas used for raising livestock and grains. They include the **Llanos** of northern Venezuela and Colombia, Brazil's **Mate Grasso**, the huge **Pampas** of Argentina, and the cold, barren **Patagonia** on the southern tip of the continent.

RESOURCES

Latin America is fortunate to have abundant natural resources. Its soils produce 75% of the world's coffee, 60% of its bananas, and 25% of its sugar cane. Other staple crops include cacao, tobacco, cotton, maize, and rice. There is

- The **Amazon River** system drains from the Andes into the vast lowland basin occupying the northern half of Brazil. The Amazon is over 3,000 miles (4,828 km) long and has nearly 200 tributaries. It is second in size only to the Nile River System in Africa. The Amazon River System drains over 2% of the world's fresh water into the Atlantic Ocean. Farming is nearly impossible in Amazonia, but this huge tropical rain forest yields large supplies of natural rubber and carnauba (wax from a Brazilian palm).

David Johnson, 1993

Cattle grazing and birds feeding on the Llanos, Venezuela, South America

PhotoDisc Inc. 1994

Traditional Amerindian Marketplace – Ecuador, South America

the earliest inhabitants, migrating down the American continent from the Asian interior in prehistoric times. Today, they make up the bulk of the population of Mexico, Guatemala, Ecuador, Peru, and Bolivia. Most of the descendents of African slaves brought by Europeans live in Brazil, Colombia, Venezuela, Haiti, Cuba, and the other Caribbean islands.

The original European colonizers intermarried with Amerindians forming a mixed group, commonly called **mestizos**. Mestizos make up about one third of the Latin American population. The major portion of the fifteen million **Caucasians** are found in the southern areas (Argentina, Chile, Uruguay). In recent years, there has also been significant immigration from Asia.

Seventy percent of all Latin Americans live in urban areas. Twenty cities exceed one million in population. The contrast between rich and poor is most dramatic in urban areas where modern high-rise apartments share neighborhoods with squatter slums, called **barrios**.

extensive herding of beef cattle, sheep, llamas, alpacas, and goats for food, hides, and fur. Mexico, Venezuela, and Ecuador are major producers of petroleum and natural gas. From South American mines come great quantities of iron ore, manganese, tin, bauxite, copper, silver, and gold. The region suffers from lack of adequate technology, and many farmers exist at a subsistence level, forcing some Latin American nations to import food supplies.

PEOPLE

CULTURE

Latin America has a variety of racial and ethnic mixtures. Over the centuries, there has been much blending of racial groups. Three main groups dominate the region: Amerindians (Native American Indians), Europeans, and Africans. The Indians were

Children of the Andes – Ecuador, South America

PhotoDisc Inc. 1994

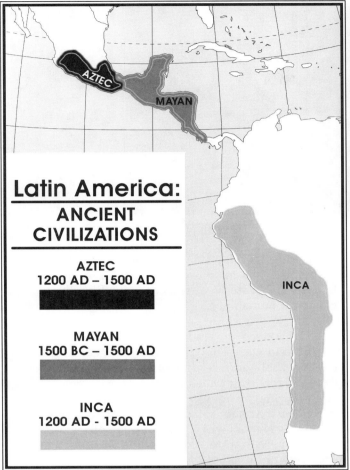

Latin America:
ANCIENT CIVILIZATIONS

AZTEC
1200 AD – 1500 AD

MAYAN
1500 BC – 1500 AD

INCA
1200 AD - 1500 AD

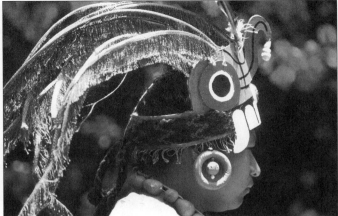

PhotoDisc Inc. 1994
Ceremonial Mayan Headdress – Mexico

Compared to other global regions, race prejudice is less intense in Latin America. Yet, economic discrimination is more evident than in other regions.

EARLY CIVILIZATIONS

Traditionally, Amerindians have suffered the most from discrimination. This is ironic, for these people had high civilizations of amazing accomplishment in **pre-Columbian** times (prior to the first voyages of Columbus in 1492). Three of the most highly developed were the **Mayan**, **Aztec**, and **Inca** civilizations. They developed **pyramidal social structures** (lower to upper classes) that were the forerunners of modern Latin American structures.

Each culture developed in isolation from the others and from the rest of the world. Not until the European Age of Discovery did they become known to the outside world. The cultures disintegrated rapidly once European colonization began.

MAYAN CIVILIZATION (1500 B.C. - 1548 A.D.)

Mayan civilization began in **Mesoamerica** (a region of Central America). It was an agrarian economy, relying on the production of maize. The Mayans shifted their villages frequently because their "slash and burn" farming quickly wore out infertile rain forest soils. The process of slash and burn clears forests fast without concern for the ecological balance of the region.

The great Mayan ceremonial center was the city of **Tikal**. It had a great palace and pyramid temples arranged in a **forum** (mall-like marketplace). A unifying social institution was their polytheistic religion. Its major deities, the Sun, Moon, soil, and rain, guided daily activities such as planting and harvesting.

PhotoDisc Inc. 1994   Chichen Itza – Mayan Ruins, Mexico

Oaxaco, Pre-Columbian Figure, South Mexico

Teotihuacan Figure – Aztec, Mexico

At its peak in 300-900 A.D., Mayan culture was the most advanced of the pre-Columbian civilizations. The Mayans excelled in mathematics, astronomy, architecture, ceramics, and sculpture. They had a complex writing system that combined phonetic symbols with **ideographs** (picture writing). It is still being translated today. Its complexity continues to astound linguistic experts.

AZTEC CIVILIZATION (1200 - 1535 A.D.)

Aztec civilization emerged from a nomadic warrior group that settled in central Mexico about 1200 A.D.

Tenochtitlan (the present site of Mexico City) was the magnificent center of the Aztec state. It had an estimated population of 100,000 people and was built on a lake with an ingenious series of moveable bridges connecting its islands. It became the capital of an empire that ruled over five million people. It had an elaborate legal system, with liberal use of capital punishment.

The Aztecs worshiped **Huitzilpochtli**, god of Sun and war. They frequently waged war to expand their empire and to capture prisoners from neighboring tribes for human sacrifices at their annual religious rites. Recent evidence indicates that the Aztec government was theocratic. Priests were extremely powerful. Historians estimate Aztecs made 20,000 such sacrifices annually.

The Aztecs engineered elaborate reservoirs and floating gardens for their maize production. They adopted many of the cultural advances of their southern neighbors. Mayan artisans created exquisite gold and silver jewelry as well as carved jade, crystal, and wood sculpture. Their most sacred activity was warfare. It led to their downfall when the European colonizers arrived in the 1500's.

Tenochtitlan – Center of Aztec life, present site of Mexico City

PhotoDisc Inc. 1994

Machu Picchu, the famed Inca fortress city, was almost inapproachable because it sat high in the Peruvian Andes. It was the Incas' crowning achievement.

INCA CIVILIZATION (1200 - 1535 A.D.)

The **Inca Empire** (1200-1535 A.D.) was built in the Andes Mountains of Peru. The name means "children of the Sun." From the capital at Cuzco, an emperor ruled over a totalitarian state. At its peak, the empire ruled about 15 million people. It included much of what is present-day Ecuador, Peru, Chile, and Bolivia.

Inca Civilization was known for its vast supplies of gold and silver used in jewelry of stunning quality. The Incas learned about roads, irrigation systems, and imperial administration from previous tribal empires. Yet, their own original achievements were impressive. They used agricultural terracing in the mountainous terrain. They assigned different crops to different elevations, making each dependent on the other. They domesticated llamas and alpacas to transport goods on a magnificent network of roads. Relay runners constantly travelled these roads carrying messages throughout the empire. They kept official records on bundles of knotted and beaded strings called **quipu**. They had a refined spoken language, **Quechua** (also Kechua).They used anesthetics in medicine and developed brain surgery techniques.

Machu Picchu, their famed fortress city, sits in the Peruvian Andes 8,038 feet (12.936 km) above sea level. The city's stone monuments and buildings were the Incas' crowning achievement. Just prior to the arrival of the European colonizers in the early 1500's, a royal family struggle erupted into a civil war. This made the weakened empire easy prey for outside conquest.

The history of Latin America is rich and diverse. A variety of environmental conditions makes this region a fascinating blend of diverse people and culture.

The Incas domesticated llamas and alpacas to transport goods on a magnificent network of roads that included bridges which were engineering wonders.

QUESTIONS

1 Geography has often caused people in Latin America to experience
   1 environmentalism
   2 agrarianism
   3 urbanization
   4 isolation

2 The llanos is an area of South America known for its
   1 grasslands
   2 mountainous terrain
   3 rain forests
   4 deserts

3 The Aztec civilization was known to neighboring people for
   1 irrigation programs
   2 warlike behavior
   3 ritual animal sacrifices
   4 peace efforts

4 The Inca Empire was centered in the
   1 Amazon Basin
   2 Yucatan Peninsula
   3 Gran Chaco
   4 Andes Mountains

5 During the 20th Century, the flow of population into the cities led to
   1 deeper economic class divisions
   2 decreased pressure on rural regions
   3 greater isolation
   4 more European colonization

6 The landform that has been a barrier to cultural and economic development in Latin America is the
   1 cordillera
   2 llano
   3 estuary
   4 savanna

7 Latin America produces three-fourths of the world's supply of
   1 corn
   2 tea
   3 rice
   4 coffee

8 The presence of high mountains (cordilleras) prevented development of
   1 culture
   2 infrastructure
   3 agriculture
   4 religion

9 The dominant cultural characteristics common in Latin America are
   1 English language and parliamentary government
   2 French language and Protestantism
   3 Spanish language and the Roman Catholic religion
   4 African language and the Islamic religion

10 The main racial and ethnic groups in Latin American history have been
   1 Africans, Europeans, and Amerindians
   2 Asians, Muslims, and Europeans
   3 Amerindians, Arabs, and Africans
   4 Europeans, Amerindians, and Asians

ESSAY

Three great Amerindian civilizations existed during the Pre-Columbian era of Latin American history: Inca, Mayan, and Aztec. Choose *one* of these, and discuss the following aspects of the civilization:

   a the major achievements

   b the economic livelihood

   c the influence of geography

II. THE DYNAMICS OF CHANGE

EUROPEAN COLONIALISM

THE AGE OF DISCOVERY

The European Age of Discovery had a dramatic impact on the development of Latin America. In 1492, Christopher Columbus, searching for a shorter water route to the "East Indies" of Asia, discovered the islands of the Caribbean Sea. Numerous explorers followed.

In the 15th and 16th Centuries, Spain and Portugal became major colonial powers because of the strength of their **armadas** (navies). In this Era of Exploration, they were the two nations that led Europe in efforts to colonize the "New World."

European Exploration Of Latin America

Date	Explorer (Country)	Discovery
1492-1504	Columbus (Spain)	West Indies & Cent. Amer.
1500	Cabral (Portugal)	Brazil
1513	Balboa (Spain)	Panama / Pacific Ocean
1519-21	Magellan (Spain)	circumnavigated the globe
1519	Cortes (Spain)	Mexico
1524-35	Pizarro (Spain)	Peru

drawing an imaginary line through the western Atlantic. He based the treaty on primitive maps of the times. It allowed Spain to make claims to the west of this line and Portugal to its east. This explains why Portugal ended up claiming only the large area of Brazil. The rest of the region (including much of the southern area of North America) fell into Spanish hands. Spain also moved more quickly to explore, colonize, and legitimize its claims.

Two factors promoted rapid colonization by Spain and Portugal in the 15th and 16th Centuries. The first was a strong **mercantilist economy** (establishing

COLONIAL DEVELOPMENT

As more knowledge about the Americas emerged, the monarchs of Europe desired more and more control over the new lands. After Columbus' discovery, intense competition emerged between the Catholic sovereigns of Spain and Portugal.

In the midst of the Protestant Reformation and the Counter Reformation, the Church did not want war between the major Catholic nations. Pope Alexander VI intervened. He negotiated the **Treaty of Tordesillas** (1494),

David Johnson, 1993

Procession of St. Augustine - Dance of Conquest, Lanquin Village, Guatemala

Latin America:
COLONIAL VICEROYALTIES

NEW SPAIN
(Spain) — SPANISH

NEW GRENADA
(Spain) — SPANISH

PERU
(Spain) — SPANISH

LA PLATA
(Spain) — SPANISH

BRAZIL
(Portugal) — PORTUGUESE

colonies as government-sponsored private business enterprises to bring wealth to the mother country). The second was high degree of Catholic **missionary zeal**.

During this time, new economic structures influenced Latin America more than racial differences. Amerindian labor was scarce and proved difficult to manage. The colonizers began importing slaves from Africa to work their **encomiendas** and **fazendas** (vast tracts of land). This led to even more racial variety and mixture.

Portugal centered its attention on eastern trade routes around Africa to India and the rest of Asia. Portugal did not start to develop its Brazilian lands until the mid-Sixteenth Century.

Driven by the desire for wealth, Spain sent out fortune seekers and **conquistadores** (conquerors). The Spanish were consumed by Amerindian myths such as **El Dorado**, the fabulous desert city of gold.

Filled with the spirit of the **Counter-Reformation**, Catholic Church officials felt an obligation to Christianize the local population and save them from the **Protestantism** of northern European nations such as England and the Netherlands. Missionaries were sent to build churches and schools in the settlements. They taught Iberian languages and culture to the local people. Because of this, the Roman Catholic Church became the dominant social institution of Latin America.

Mercantilist ventures in "New Spain" involved plantation agriculture, mining, and cattle ranching. They were rural enterprises. The Spanish built few large settlements. Crown authority flowed from colonial governors called **viceroys**. They were assisted by crown appointed **audiencas** (councils) that watched over the viceroys and advised them.

Between 1505 and 1700, Spain divided its New World holdings into four **viceroyalties** (large territories): **New Spain**, **Peru**, **New Grenada**, and **La Plata** (see map opposite page).

The wealth of Spain's huge empire depended on the forced labor of the Amerindians, and few laws protected them. Although some Africans had been with the earlier explorers and conquistadores, in 1522 Spanish colonists began importing African slaves in large numbers to work the mines and land.

POLITICAL AUTHORITY AND SOCIAL CLASSES

A distinct social class system emerged in the early colonial period. It was based on birth and resembled the Hindu caste system. The Spanish crown granted **encomiendas** (vast tracts of land) to Iberian-born nobles (**peninsulares**) or the American-born sons of such nobles (**criollos**). These colonists were pledged to protect the social welfare of the Amerindians on their assigned holdings. This rarely occurred.

Bitter protests surfaced over the mistreatment of Amerindians and African slaves. A notable example was led by a 16th Century Dominican priest in New Spain, **Bartolomé de Las Casas**. However, the Church was generally neutral in such matters or acted as a tool of colonial administrators. As the titled heads of the Church within their empire, Spanish rulers appointed pastors and other church officials. The crown granted permission to collect special taxes to maintain the Church. The Church also accumulated vast wealth through inheritance of estates and the **tithe** (10% of a person's earnings were to be donated).

Initially, there was less colonial domination in the huge Portuguese colony of Brazil. In 1555, the Portuguese defeated a French attempt to move into the area. Afterwards, the Portuguese began to strengthen their rule. They divided the colony into **captaincies** (districts or provinces). Towns, **fazendas** (ranches and plantations), and other business operations emerged along the Atlantic Coast. The Portuguese crown appointed a **Captain-General**, an equivalent to Spain's viceroys.

Sugar cane, grown on the fazendas, was Brazil's first profitable crop. Amerindians did not adjust to plantation life. West African slaves were imported. Intermarriage between Caucasians and Africans became common and led to a high percentage of **mulattoes** in the Brazilian population.

This blurring of racial groups led to class lines of wealth and occupation rather than race. There was slightly more religious toleration in Brazil than in Spain's empire.

Peninsulares
Iberian Aristocrats

Criollos
Descendents of Peninsulares

Mestizos
Caucasian & Amerindian

Mulattos
Caucasian & African

African Slaves

Amerindians

Latin American Colonial Class Structure

Yet, the Roman Catholic Church was still the major unifying force there, as it was in the Spanish territories.

In addition to Spain and Portugal, there were Latin American colonies of other European nations. **England**, the **Netherlands**, and **France** established small, profitable colonies on the northern coast of South America and in the Caribbean. Their economies depended largely on sugar plantations.

INDEPENDENCE MOVEMENTS

The first outbursts against colonial rule came in the late 18th Century. Ironically, rebellions did not occur in the strictly ruled Spanish or Portuguese regions. They began against the French on the island of Hispaniola. **Toussaint L'Ouverture**, a self-educated black slave, led a popular rebellion in 1791 in **Saint Dominique**. The French suppressed it. Yet, it inspired a series of revolts that ended in independence for **Haiti** in 1804.

Spain and Portugal ruled their Latin American empires for 300 years. In the late 1700's, festering resentment of the criollos and wealthy mestizos against the ruling peninsu-

lares boiled over. Also, the ideas of the American and French Revolutions began to penetrate the region. The majority of free people no longer viewed themselves as European. They felt little allegiance to the Iberian crowns.

The Napoleonic Wars of the early 1800's distracted authorities in Europe. In America, criollos "liberators" organized opposition. The first outbreak against Spain came in Mexico on 16 September 1810. A Catholic priest, **Miguel Hidalgo**, signalled the start of the revolution by the famous **Grito de Dolores** (ringing of the bells). Today, Mexico celebrates its independence on this date.

Throughout Latin America, there were many heroes of the independence movements. Perhaps the most famous was **Simón Bolívar**, "The Liberator." He began the quest for freedom in **Gran Colombia** (a short-lived union of Venezuela, Colombia, Peru, Ecuador, and Bolivia).

Jose de San Martín formed an "Army of the Andes." He liberated the area controlled by the Viceroy de la Plata. **Bernardo O'Higgins** led Chile toward independence. The fights for freedom were not easy. It took fifteen years before most of Latin America was free of Spanish control.

Brazil proclaimed itself an independent empire in 1822. Brazil set up a government under **Pedro I** without bloodshed.

Spain was weak and exhausted by 1821. Most Central American countries joined a short-lived federation and achieved independence without a struggle.

The European colonial powers were more resistant to independence when it came to the Caribbean islands. It took several generations more for them to win their freedom.

In a span of 300 years, Latin America experienced dynamic changes. The region endured the Age of Discovery, harsh colonial rule, exploitation, and finally, independence. For all the negative elements of the colonial experience, the Iberian nations left a legacy of cultural unity through their social structure, traditions, language, religion, and the arts.

QUESTIONS

1   Mercantilism was an economic philosophy in which colonies existed for the economic good of the
    1   colony's population
    2   mother country
    3   middle class merchant
    4   Christian churches

2   The king's representative in the Spanish colonies of Latin America was called a
    1   Captain
    2   Viceroy
    3   Mulatto
    4   Criollo

3   The first independence movement in Latin America occurred in
    1   Brazil
    2   Hispaniola
    3   Bolivia
    4   Argentina

4   Mixed marriages of European settlers and Amerindian natives produced
    1   criollos
    2   slaves
    3   mulattos
    4   mestizos

5   The largest racial group of people in Latin America were
    1   African slaves
    2   mercantilists
    3   Mestizos
    4   peninsulares

6   As applied to Spanish colonization in the New World, the term *conquistador* meant
    1   large land grant
    2   plantation owner
    3   expert navigator
    4   military explorer

7   "Grito de Dolores" signifies
    1   a colonial treaty between Spain and Portugal
    2   the beginning of Mexico's revolution
    3   Bolivar's war cry
    4   the conquest of the Aztecs by Cortes

8   Portuguese sugar cane plantations in Brazil were called
    1   fazendas
    2   viceroys
    3   peninsulares
    4   audiencas

9   How long did the Iberian colonial empires in Latin America last?
    1   400 years
    2   300 years
    3   200 years

4   100 years

10   *Encomiendas* were
1   taxes paid to the Roman Catholic
     Church
2   Aztec gold designs
3   land grants to peninsulares
4   early slave revolts

11   Which is one way that Latin American
     traditional colonial society was similar to
     society in Asia?
1   placed great value on public education
2   experienced a surplus of skilled labor
3   was organized according to a class
     system
4   de-emphasized religion

12   In the 16th and 17th Centuries, which
     countries were most involved in colonizing
     Latin America?
1   Spain and Portugal
2   Germany and Spain
3   Russia, Spain, and France
4   France and the Italian States

13   In Latin America, a major reason for the
     importation of slaves from Africa was the
1   scarcity of Amerindian labor
2   development of subsistence farming
3   need for skilled industrial workers
4   desire to promote Christianity

14   Which was a result of the European Age of
     Discovery?
1   Islam spread to the New World.
2   Military dictatorships arose in Europe.
3   War-crimes trials were held in Spain.
4   European culture spread to Latin
     America.

15   Which term best describes the position of
     the Native American Indians in Colonial
     Latin America?
1   landed gentry
2   military dictators
3   exploited laborers
4   political elite

16   Throughout the colonial period, power in
     Latin America was traditionally held by
1   landless mulattoes
2   mestizos
3   poor city workers
4   peninsulares

17   Which man would merit the 20th Century
     term freedom fighter?
1   Toussaint L'Ouverture
2   Hernan Cortes
3   Pope Alexander VI
4   Pedro Cabral

ESSAY

During the colonial period in Latin
American history, a distinct socioeconomic
structure emerged that limited
advancement for a majority of the people.
Certain groups became dominant, while
others suffered.

Groups

- Peninsulares
- Mestizos
- Criollos
- Mulattoes
- Amerindians

a   Use *all* of the groups above to explain
     the social structure that emerged in the
     colonial era.

b   Select *two* of the groups and for *each*,
     discuss their living standards within the
     social structure.

DETERMINATION OF POLITICAL & ECONOMIC SYSTEMS

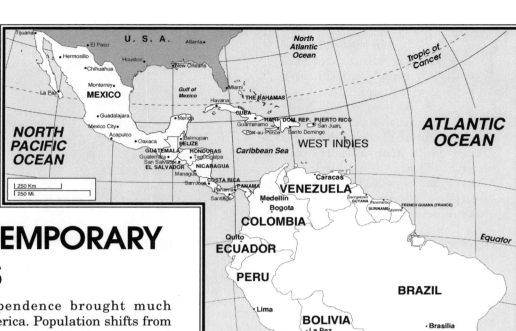

III. CONTEMPORARY NATIONS

Political independence brought much change to Latin America. Population shifts from rural areas to cities, high birth rates, and nationalist movements can both help and hinder progress. Also, regional cultural and geographic barriers can block progress.

Individuals often resist change, but long-standing social institutions are very hard to change. In Latin America, change is blocked noticeably by what critics call an "iron triangle." It is a combination of aristocratic landowners, the military, and the Church. To achieve progress, reform leaders must try to bridge the gap between this entrenched power triangle and the new urban-industrial pattern of life.

INITIAL ATTEMPTS AT UNIFICATION

In the early 1800's, strong nationalism in the new countries prevented leaders from uniting into larger confederations. Simón Bolívar's **Gran Colombia** and the **Central American Federation** crumbled. Poor financing, intense regional jealousy, and internal power struggles among leaders kept Latin America fragmented.

Bolívar himself is symbolic of the contradictory nature of political life in Latin America. He rallied followers against the Spanish with the noble ideals expressed in the *United States Constitution*. Yet, when he assumed the presidency of Gran Colombia, Bolívar had himself declared president-for-life and arranged for power to be concentrated in his own hands. His abandoning of democratic principles led to Gran Colombia's disintegration in civil war.

OBSTACLES TO CHANGE

In addition, the rugged mountainous terrain and great travel distances made unity difficult. The lack of the preparation of people for self-rule also frustrated attempts toward democracy. Power remained in the hands of those who owned the fazendas and encomiendas. They made up a **landed aristocracy** (nobility rich in land holdings) that became the core of the iron triangle **oligarchy** (government controlled by a small, elite group). It had no interest in creating democratic reforms that might undermine its wealth and position. The military and the Church supported this landed elite. This "iron triangle" maintained the **status quo** (the current power structure).

In this triangular alliance of economic, social, and political interests, the military kept law and order so that the other two groups could keep property and wealth. The landowners and Church leaders supported the **caudillos** (strong military leaders) financially and morally. The caudillos managed the few elections to preserve their power. Democratic revolutionary leaders often led opposition to this structure. In recent times, democracy has made gains, but the iron triangle remains effective in many Latin American nations.

Church **hierarchy** (leaders) accumulated land and wealth in return for services to the colonial rulers. The hierarchy lost some of its power after the overthrow of the colonial powers. It did not adjust to meeting the needs of the new societies. Church leaders often allied themselves with the wealthy land owners to support dictatorial caudillos and their **juntas** (military councils). The political systems were built on the personality of the individual caudillos. They were fragile, and **coups d'état** (internal power struggles) became frequent in Latin America.

POLITICAL EVOLUTION SINCE INDEPENDENCE

This is a somewhat generalized view of political structures. Systems varied. A look at situations in Mexico, Argentina, Cuba, Panama, and Nicaragua provides better understanding.

Central Plaza Cathedral – Antigua, Guatemala. Surviving for hundreds of years, this 16th Century church symbolizes the power of the Church in Latin America.

David Johnson, 1993

MEXICO

Some nations have struggled mightily to establish democratic systems. Mexico is a case in point. It became a dictatorship after independence in 1821. From the 1830's to the 1860's, **Antonio Lopez de Santa Anna** ruled the country, losing Texas and most of the northern half of the original nation to the United States.

Benito (Pablo) **Juárez**, a liberal reformer, emerged in the 1860's. Mexicans regard him as their greatest President. He struggled against conservative landholders and the Church hierarchy to gain reforms for the lower classes, especially Amerindians. He gained a new constitution. Yet, foreign intrigue delayed his reform program. In 1863, with the help of local conservatives, the French invaded Mexico. They set up Austrian Archduke **Maximilian** as emperor. He was overthrown shortly afterward with the help of the United States.

Juarez died just after reestablishing independence. After his death, a "law and order" caudillo, **Porfirio Diaz**, became dictator from 1876 until he was forced to resign in 1911. During his rule, there was superficial peace and prosperity, but peasants and factory workers did not share in the prosperity. Living conditions deteriorated for the lower classes.

In a six-year civil war, landholders' private forces fought the national army. By the 1920's, President **Venustiano Carranza's** new consti-

Central America & Caribbean

250 Km
250 Mi.

tution guaranteed all Mexicans the right to vote. In the new government, mestizos began to dominate the country's political life.

ARGENTINA

Political evolution in Argentina occurred differently. Following the dictatorship of **Juan Manuel de Rosas** (1829-1852), a new constitution modeled after that of the U.S. was approved. A period of stability and prosperity followed, attracting a large number of European immigrants.

By 1900, Argentina became the wealthiest nation in Latin America. As happened in Germany, Italy, Spain, and many countries during the worldwide depression in the 1930's, the economic collapse set the scene for political upheaval. A military coup d'état overthrew the civilian government and began a half century of decline.

During World War II, a local caudillo, **Colonel Juan Domingo Perón**, emerged as a favorite of the middle classes and the militant labor unions. He promoted higher wages and fringe benefits for the working classes. At the same time, he blocked opposition by cutting back freedom of speech and the press. His popular wife Eva Duarte de Perón (known to the people as "**Evita**") was his dynamic Minister of Health and Labor. She succeeded in getting women the right to vote. When Evita Peron died at age 33 in 1952, Juan Peron's regime was shaken. Living in fear, he lost considerable support by weakening the power of the Church and then alienating the military. Peron was deposed and exiled to Spain in 1955.

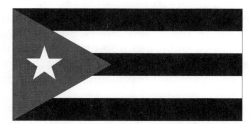

CUBA

The island nation of Cuba also experienced a stormy political evolution. It was liberated as a result of U.S. intervention in the Spanish-American War of 1898. The U.S. granted Cuba independence in 1902, with the reservation that the U.S. would intervene if it felt it was necessary. A series of "do-nothing" dictators ruled until 1933, when **Fulgencio Batista** seized control. Batista catered to American business interests, allowing them to take huge profits in sugar and tobacco, but little of the money earned ever got to the laboring classes.

In 1956, **Fidel Castro** began a revolt against Batista. Castro succeeded in 1959. He then set up the first communist state in the Western Hemisphere. The United States cut off relations. During the Cold War, Cuba used aid from the Soviet Union to build its military. Castro also helped communist rebels elsewhere in Latin America and Africa.

In the 1980's, communism declined in the U.S.S.R. and Eastern Europe. Soviet leader Mikhail Sergeyevich Gorbachev cut foreign aid. Castro's regime ran into trouble. He cut aid to Ortega in Nicaragua, and the communists there lost power (see below). In recent years, Cuba has appeared less hostile to its neighbors. Castro has been trying to improve relations and trade with neighboring countries.

NICARAGUA

The most successful of Castro's foreign revolutionary ventures occurred in Nicaragua. In the late 1970's, a communist guerrilla movement called the **Sandinistas** (after a 1920's socialist rebel, Augusto Cesar Sandino) arose.

The Sandinista National Liberation Front (FSLN) used Cuban-Soviet aid to overthrow the dictatorial Somoza regime. Sandinista leader **Daniel Ortega** (Saavedra) became President. He created a military state with increased aid from Cuba and the Soviets.

In 1981, relations with the U.S. came to a crisis as President **Ronald Reagan** approved a plan to have the U.S. Central Intelligence Agency (CIA) give aid to the **contra** opposition force. The 1990's began with Nicaraguans going to the polls and unseating the Sandinista Party in favor of a moderate coalition party. **Violeta Barrios de Chamorro**, wife of a slain opposition leader, was elected President. The Chamorro government ended the contra rebellion. Still, reviving the war-ravaged economy proved difficult. The Chamorro regime resorted to making alliances with caudillos to retain power.

PANAMA

Panama's history shows the dominance of the United States in Central America. Colombia frustrated attempts by the U.S. to negotiate a treaty to build an interocean canal through its territory of Panama. On 3 November 1903, Panamanian rebels declared independence from Colombia. U.S. President Theodore Roosevelt immediately recognized the new nation. He sent American gunboats to the region in support of the rebels. Panama became an independent nation. Simultaneously, it granted the U.S. the right to create a canal zone through its center.

Japanese freighter in the Panama Canal – Panama, Latin America

Noriega was under indictment for smuggling narcotics into the United States. The U.S. invasion resulted in Noriega's capture and restored civilian control of the government.

These examples show that patterns of national change vary. The experiences of these nations reflect the variety of roles played by the iron triangles and outside forces. Even today, military, church, landowners, labor organizations, and foreign powers engage in struggles over land, wages, working conditions, education, and social, economic, and political equality.

By 1978, the Panama Canal had become less useful to the U.S. A treaty signed by President Carter arranged for a gradual transfer of the Canal Zone back to the Panamanian government by the year 2000.

Over the years, a series of anticommunist military governments in Panama received U.S. support. However, in late 1989, President Bush authorized an invasion of U.S. troops to protect American lives and property in the Canal Zone from the threats of sabotage by forces under a hostile dictator, General **Manuel Noriega**.

DEMOGRAPHIC CHANGE

Over the past two centuries, Latin America experienced rapid population growth caused by high birth rates and improved medical technology. In certain regions, such as the southern countries, European immigration added to this rapid population growth. In Central America and the northern area of South America, Asians have been entering in large numbers. Many of the immigrants have settled in urban areas.

Since World War II, Latin American cities have grown nearly twice as fast as the rest of the other cities of the world. Most of this growth has been caused by internal migration from rural areas. The poor and illiterate, 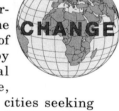 lacking job skills, move to the cities seeking work. Most migrants live in the **barrios** (poor squatter settlements), often in cardboard or tin shacks with no water or electricity.

Recent projections show that, by the year 2000, Sao Paulo, Brazil and Mexico City, Mexico will be the two largest cities in the world with over twenty million people each. (cf. New York City has 7.2 million people.)

Nearly one-third of Latin America's urban population live in the barrios. The consequences

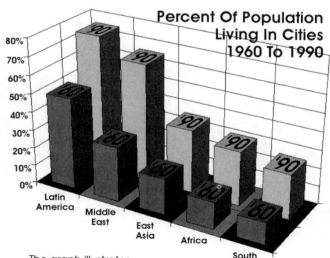

Percent Of Population Living In Cities 1960 To 1990

80%
70%
60%
50%
40%
30%
20%
10%
0%

Latin America — Middle East — East Asia — Africa — South Asia

The graph illustrates the increasing migration of population to cities between the 1960's and 1990's. For comparison, the average of people living in cities worldwide is 43%. In the U.S., it is 75%.

Source: World Bank, 1993

David Johnson, 1988

In stark contrast in the quality of life, the barrio falls in the shadow of the modern middle-class apartments – Caracas, Venezuela.

OTHER SOCIAL FACTORS

Within this growing political and economic gap, the family remains the cornerstone of stability and security. Personal ties are often more important than political affiliations. The extended family is still found throughout the region at all levels of society. Clannish family pride is very strong. The families are **patrilineal** (male-dominated) and a **machismo** attitude (exaggerated sense of masculine dominance) pervades most of the social life.

In the past, marriages were arranged for women. The role of the female was always as support to the male. Some of this male dominance has begun to break down. Economic prosperity among the urban middle and upper classes has opened employment and educational opportunities for females. By 1961, women in all nations of Latin America achieved the right to vote. Conditions vary, but Latin American women generally are behind the progress women achieved in North America and Europe.

Migrations of people always cause upheaval. Industrialization and **mobility** (moving physically and socially to gain better economic and political positions) have enormous impacts on Latin American societies. In the more industrialized nations of Argentina, Uruguay, Brazil, and Mexico, migratory effects on the social structure are evident.

of this urban population explosion are clear. Shortages of food and other goods, congestion, disease, and pollution are ever present in the run-down, overcrowded barrios. Many governments try to relieve the enormous problems by building public housing.

Movement from the farms to cities causes problems. Channeling scarce resources to relieve the cities' pressing problems, governments neglect the farmers. Funds for education and technology to help agricultural production are cut. This policy causes divisions in the society between urban and rural groups competing for the government resources.

David Johnson, 1993

Mezquital District Slum – Guatemala City, Guatemala, July 1993

The middle classes are making their presence known in politics. They challenge the small, elite, landowning families. The urban middle class identifies more closely with the needs of the poorer levels of laboring classes. Expenditures for education are increasing. While few people go beyond elementary levels, literacy is still approaching 75%. This can provide a vital link between the middle and poorer groups seeking justice.

QUESTIONS

1   Elitist groups which exercised great power in the newly independent Latin American republics were the
1   artisans
2   landed aristocracy
3   subsistence farmers
4   intellectuals

2   An oligarchy refers to rule by
1   the majority
2   a small group
3   a single person
4   the military

3   A group of military commanders that reinforces a dictator is called a
1   monarchy
2   commonwealth
3   parliament
4   junta

4   After Fidel Castro came to power, the U.S.
1   supported Cuba against communist aggression
2   broke off relations with Cuba
3   supported Castro's forces in Nicaragua
4   gave aid for a new Caribbean Canal

5   The squatter settlements in large urban centers of Latin America are often called
1   juntas
2   coups d'état
3   barrios
4   contras

6   In Nicaragua,
1   communists overthrew the Somoza regime
2   women cannot run for office
3   the U.S. created a Canal Zone
4   Church hierarchy rules the country

7   Why was Argentine dictator Juan Peron overthrown?
1   He could not defeat the communist guerrillas.
2   He insulted the United States.
3   He alienated the church and the military.
4   He would not allow women voting rights.

8   A major change after Mexico's 1914 - 1917 civil war was that power passed to
1   male-dominated families
2   a committee of military commanders
3   liberals and communists
4   those with Amerindian blood

9   Which happened in most new Latin American nations following the independence movements of the 19th Century?
1   Monarchies were reestablished by European powers.
2   Liberal reform movements began.
3   Communist guerrillas launched counter-revolutions.
4   Dictators called caudillos emerged.

ESSAYS

While the revolutions against European colonialism were successful, most new Latin American countries experienced great difficulties.

a   Explain why the countries were so poorly equipped to govern themselves.

b   Discuss *two* specific instances of Latin American nations struggling to establish democratic government after independence.

IV. ECONOMIC DEVELOPMENT

Latin America's economic development has both great potential and severe limitations.

Uneven distribution of most resources in the area results in uneven patterns of development. There is growth, but there is also a significant gap between economic development and the quality of life for the majority of people. Recent waves of international immigration have had positive and negative effects on these patterns.

Argentina, Brazil, and Mexico account for 70% of the region's industrial output. Added to these are the five nations of Venezuela, Chile, Uruguay, Colombia, and Peru which account for about 22% of total output. All of the other nations combined account for only 8% of the region's output. Thus, eight out of thirty-three nations account for 92% of the production in Latin America.

Stock Exchange – Mexico City, Mexico

PhotoDisc Inc. 1994

FOREIGN INVESTMENT

Economic dependence has haunted Latin America since its colonial period. In the mercantile system, the colonies exported raw materials and cash crops while importing the mother country's finished goods. As Spanish and Portuguese control eroded, trade relationships emerged with the U.S. and Europe (England, France, the Netherlands). It is two centuries since independence, and still most Latin American nations chiefly depend on trade with the United States.

Under the 19th Century trade situation, young Latin American nations remained largely undeveloped and highly dependent on imports, while their trading partners prospered. Only minor industrial development occurred in the areas of tanning, pottery, and weaving.

In the 20th Century, foreign capital brought some industrialization. Investors enjoyed substantial profits in Argentina, Brazil, Chile, and Mexico. However, industrial development actually occurred in very limited areas, and the profits went to foreign owners. In the 1930's, worldwide depression caused foreigners to slow down or halt their enterprises in Latin America.

During and after World War II, European investment declined rapidly. U.S. investors became the dominant source of capital. To continue industrial growth, Latin American nations adopted policies that favored outside investors with tax incentives. They also developed restrictive tariff policies to protect emerging industries. **Tariffs** are import taxes on foreign goods being shipped into a country. **Subsidies** (financial grants) encouraged local manufacturers to produce consumer goods which could be made efficiently in Latin America.

FOREIGN-SPONSORED INDUSTRY

Latin America attracts foreign businesses primarily because of low labor costs. In addition, many companies have moved portions of their manufacturing to take advantage of fewer restrictions on safety, environmental pollution, and working conditions.

In this large furniture factory in San Salvador, El Salvador, local craftsmen are paid low wages compared to their counterparts in the U.S. and Canada. To take advantage of the low wages, fewer restrictions on safety and environmental pollution standards, and poorer working conditions, many companies are moving manufacturing operations to Latin America.

In 1991, Latin America received 69% of U.S. direct investment in developing regions and 17.2% of total overseas investment. The 1993 North American Free Trade Agreement (NAFTA) also increased U.S. and Canadian investment in Mexican industries.

In the 1980's, the **Caribbean Basin Initiative (CBI)** brought together U.S. government aid and private investment. CBI was designed to spur social and economic development in the Caribbean and Central America. The program included tax incentives for U.S. manufacturers that located new plants in the region. It gave duty-free status to many Caribbean exports and millions of U.S. dollars to stabilize their foreign debt and balance of payments.

In Latin America today, foreign capital promotes industries that are primarily labor intensive, requiring many work-hours to complete the manufacturing. This includes factories producing woodworking (such as furniture and sculptured decorative items), shoes, clothing, and custom boat building.

AGRICULTURE

Today, 50% of Latin America's labor force remains engaged in the agricultural sector while agricultural production makes up less and less of each nation's **Gross Domestic Product**

(GDP: sum of all goods and services produced within a nation's boundaries in a year).

Modern technological advancements in agricultural productivity have occurred in connection with export crops. Such advances lag in producing food staples for the local populations. The region supplies 75% of the world's coffee, 60% of its bananas, and 25% of its sugar cane. Yet, like many underdeveloped regions, it is unable to feed its own growing population.

The reason for this can be traced to the peninsulares' **encomienda system** of landholding in the colonial era. Criollos eventually ran the encomiendas for absentee peninsulare landlords in Spain or Portugal. The wealthy landlords across the ocean knew little of conditions on the encomiendas and failed to provide proper support.

Campesinos (paid laborers, peasants) were tenants who lived on the land but did not own it. Poorly treated and without the motivation that  comes from owning their land, campesinos had little desire to produce more than just a bare subsistence.

In no other area of the world has so much land been owned by so few people. The problem continues today. Caudillos grasp at land for themselves and their families as did the Somozas in Nicaragua. There have been only a few successful land-reform programs in the 20th Century. Even in these, results have been mixed. Governments have been quick to break up encomiendas but have not had the resources to educate and equip campesinos to achieve economic and social development.

The climate and topographical variations limit the supply of arable land. Despite the diversity of conditions, most countries lean toward **single cash crop economies** (coffee, bananas, or

sugar). This can be dangerous. An entire economy linked to the fluctuating world market for one commodity is too vulnerable. Also, natural disasters often destroy the entire crop and plunge the nation into long-term debt.

MINERALS AND ENERGY

Mineral and energy resources are another important source of economic development in the area. Vital ores are concentrated in only a few remote areas. Often, they are impossible to develop. Infrastructures are inadequate to move these minerals to industrial processing centers. There is also a lack of high-grade fossil fuels (coal and oil) necessary for industrial development. Most countries import them.

Mexico, Ecuador, and Venezuela have considerable oil reserves. These petroleum resources have been a mixed blessing. In the 1970's when oil prices soared, oil producers borrowed huge sums to develop Latin American sources. When global prices declined in the 1980's, a crisis developed over this foreign debt to international banks. Inflation in other sectors

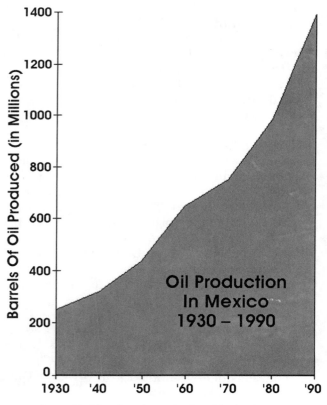

Oil Production
In Mexico
1930 – 1990

As worldwide oil reserves decline, Mexico increases production, tapping into vast crude oil reserves.

of the countries' economies and higher import costs worsened the situation.

Brazil has the world's largest manganese deposits. Chile is the second largest copper producing nation. Raw minerals are **primary resources**. Economists point out that selling them in their raw state generates minimal income. Capital income is greater if they are processed, refined, used in manufacturing, or incorporated in an end product. Thus, even a supply of primary resources does not guarantee wealth.

PATHS TO DEVELOPMENT

Latin American leaders continue to search for a solid path to development. Industrialization is critical to providing the increased employment the rising populations need. Industrialization will fill domestic demands and diversify national exports. Still, finding foreign investment capital for development other than primary resource exports is difficult. Some blame rests with the long reputation for unstable governments. Additional 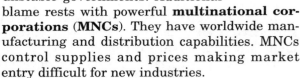 blame rests with powerful **multinational corporations (MNCs)**. They have worldwide manufacturing and distribution capabilities. MNCs control supplies and prices making market entry difficult for new industries.

Since 1950, attempts to achieve regional economic cooperation have been limited. The **Latin American Trade Association**, the **Central American Common Market**, and the **Caribbean Free Trade Association** have not lived up to their founders' expectations. **NAFTA**, the new North American Free Trade Association (Canada + U.S. + Mexico), should be of great benefit to Mexico. But, other Latin American nations are already complaining of economic isolation.

TOURISM

Many areas of Latin America that lack mineral resources or sufficient tracts of arable land have turned to tourism. Sunny climates, beautiful beaches, historic ruins, and cultural festivals such as Brazil's "Carnival" continue to attract foreign tourists. As an economic mainstay, how-

Cruise ships visiting Charlotte Amalie, St. Thomas, U.S. Virgin Islands. Tourism is of great economic importance to Latin American and Caribbean countries.

ever, tourism has its problems. The high costs of advertising, building modern facilities, and the large numbers of people employed in tourism cut profits. Mexico earns the most of any nation from tourism.

MIGRATION

Migration to the cities as well as immigration from other nations is usually motivated by desire for better jobs. Certain patterns have emerged:

Migration Patterns	
From:	**To:**
Mexico & Central America	United States
Central America	Mexico
Colombia	Venezuela
Paraguay	Bolivia, Brazil, Argentina
Caribbean	U.S. and Great Britain

In seeking greater economic opportunity in new lands, immigrants face resentment from groups competing for jobs and discrimination from employers and governments. Those opposing immigrants claim their willingness to work for lower pay keeps wages down and depresses living standards for local lower classes.

New immigrants sometimes resist **assimilation** (blending into a new culture). When they meet with hostility and resistance as they settle in large urban areas, they cope by isolating themselves. They band together in ethnic enclaves (barrios).

An estimated one million people from Mexico, Central America, and the Caribbean attempt to enter the United States illegally each year. Many are caught by the **INS** (U.S. Immigration and Naturalization Service) officials and deported, but many more avoid border patrols and find work as migrant farm workers or in unskilled jobs in cities. U.S. immigration laws, recently revised to deal with this problem, have been ineffective. This wave of immigrant labor is similar to that in other countries of the Western Hemisphere as people seek to break out of the poverty cycle.

Serious economic problems persist in many areas of the region. One problem is **economic nationalism** (the effort to stimulate internal development by using government policies to eliminate outside competition). Nations such as Cuba have learned that **nationalizing** foreign-owned industries (confiscating them) drives out the foreign capital needed to maintain them.

Nations that borrow heavily from foreign bankers at high interest rates often **default** (cannot make debt payments). This earns them ratings as bad credit risks. Even the more prosperous nations like Argentina, Mexico, and

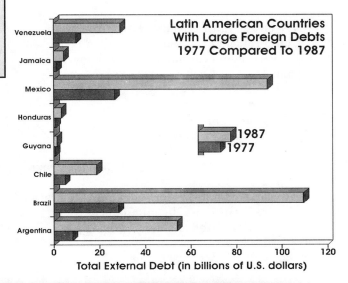

Latin American Countries With Large Foreign Debts 1977 Compared To 1987

1987
1977

Total External Debt (in billions of U.S. dollars)

Brazil have huge debt burdens, widening the gap between themselves and economic progress. Their debt-ridden connection to the wealthier countries makes this problem global in nature.

QUESTIONS

1 The major source of wealth for most Caribbean island nations is in
1 heavy industry
2 tourism
3 mining
4 food processing

2 Unlike the United States, the internal migration pattern in most Latin American nations is from
1 rural to urban areas
2 cities to suburbs
3 urban to rural regions
4 suburbs to rural regions

3 The largest segment of the labor force in most Latin American nations is engaged in
1 governmental work
2 industrial production
3 agriculture
4 mining

4 Even the most effective Latin American land reform programs have failed because governments cannot adequately meet the need for
1 fossil fuels
2 industrial support
3 education
4 military protection

5 Collectively, Mexico, Argentina, and Brazil have
1 formed a union for economic cooperation
2 sent the most illegal aliens to the U.S.
3 nationalized the most industries in Latin America
4 debt-ridden economies

6 Venezuela, Mexico, and Ecuador are major world suppliers of
1 copper
2 magnesium
3 coffee
4 crude oil

7 Which essential industrial resource is generally lacking in Latin America?
1 fossil fuels for export
2 unskilled labor
3 local capital for investment
4 tariffs on imports

8 Capital needed for industrial development has usually come from
1 juntas
2 campesinos
3 encomiendas
4 foreign investment

9 Which is an example of attempted economic cooperation in Latin America?
1 Multinational Corporation
2 Gross Domestic Product
3 Central American Common Market
4 Gran Colombia

10 Latin American campesinos' problems stem from
1 lack of land ownership
2 mechanization of agriculture
3 union strikes
4 refusal to accept church authority

ESSAYS

One-crop economies have often meant disaster for Latin American countries.

a Choose *two* export crops (e.g., coffee, bananas) and explain the problems of single cash crop economies dependent on them.

b Discuss what can be done to broaden the economic base of the nations discussed in part *a*.

V. LATIN AMERICA: GLOBAL CONTEXT

REGIONALISM GROWS TO GLOBALISM

Viewing Latin America in a global context can be difficult. There is considerable geographic, political, and cultural diversity. In addition, long before the industrial era, most Latin American countries adopted policies that involved only their neighbors in the Western Hemisphere, virtually isolating themselves from other global regions. There was outside contact, but it was usually limited to the former colonial powers.

Still, the region has begun to take on an important role in the global economy. Increased interdependence of the entire world has linked the region to more developed nations.

During the Cold War Era, strong anti-imperialist feelings emerged in the region. The global struggle of the two superpowers caused political realignments. Civil wars and border disputes were frequent. For example, Cuba's aid to communist groups led to its exclusion from the OAS and from contact with other nations in the hemisphere. In other cases, there has long been a brittle relationship with the U.S. Its power to intervene has led to fragile relations in Latin America.

INTER-AMERICAN RELATIONS

One positive arrangement that offers a legal channel for resolving international disputes is the **Organization of American States** founded in 1948. It is a mutual defense and peace-keeping union of thirty-two North and South American nations (Cuba was excluded in 1962).

EUROPEAN RELATIONS

Since the beginnings of European settlement in Latin America, interdependence has grown between the two regions. Economic integration emerged through trade relations that centered on exchange of cash crops and primary resources for finished products. As foreign investment grew, returns were substantial. Multinational corporations have a considerable presence in Latin America. Giant MNCs include Unilever, Mitsubishi, ITT, General Motors, Exxon, Philips Electronics, Nestlé, and Royal Dutch Shell. In the past twenty years, Japan increased its investments in Latin America not only for natural resources but for a potentially large market for Japanese industrial products.

U.S. RELATIONS

Although politically independent, most Latin American nations continue to be heavily influenced by the **"Colossus of the North"** – the United States. They share geographic similarities and European heritages, but historically, their relations have not been smooth. There have been a number of U.S. policies toward Latin America over the years.

- **The Monroe Doctrine** – Originally, the U.S. encouraged the early 19th Century independence movements. A policy was formulated in President Monroe's term (1823) that became known as the Monroe Doctrine and warned European nations against trying to reestablish colonies in the area.

- **The Roosevelt Corollary** – The Monroe Doctrine has often been misused as an excuse for intervention in Latin American affairs by the U.S. At the end of the 19th Century, it was used by the U.S. to go to war against Spain over its treatment of Cuba and Puerto Rico. In 1903, President Theodore Roosevelt used it to intervene on behalf of American business interests in Cuba and the Dominican

Republic. He also secretly aided a 1903 revolt in Panama against Columbia so that an inter-ocean canal could be built.

- **Dollar Diplomacy** – Armed intervention on behalf of U.S. businesses became frequent under Presidents Taft, Wilson, Harding, Coolidge, and Hoover. This pattern of "Dollar Diplomacy" convinced many Latin American leaders that the U.S. was practicing a new form of colonialism.

- **Good Neighbor Policy** – In an effort to improve relations, President Franklin D. Roosevelt developed the "Good Neighbor Policy" in 1933. He attempted to create a feeling of "**Pan-Americanism**" by granting favorable trade policies with Latin American countries and halting armed intervention.

COLD WAR POLITICS

After World War II, most Latin American nations joined the U.N. They have since become enthusiastic supporters of the world organization, often voting with LDCs.

During the Cold War era, Latin American nations were caught up in the global struggles between the superpowers. Their long-running dependency and favorable relations with the U.S. moved them into the democratic camp.

Still, the iron triangles and dictatorships attracted certain groups to communism. Fidel Castro's Cuban Revolution in 1959 established the first communist state in the Western Hemisphere.

In the early 1960's, a new policy emerged under President Kennedy's **Alliance for Progress.** It promoted large-scale foreign aid grants in Latin America in hopes of making communism less attractive. Unfortunately, the land-holding aristocracies which dominated politics resisted land reform. Much of the U.S. aid money found its way into the hands of military juntas. They used it to strengthen their power and brutally suppress reform movements. Frustration and suppression drove more people toward revolutionary movements. Some

of these were financed by the Soviets through Cuba. For example, the communist **Sandinista** movement in Nicaragua converted the country into a Marxist state in the 1980's.

POST-COLD WAR EVENTS

Even as tensions of the Cold War faded in the late 1980's, differences among the nations of Latin America led to conflicts. OAS humanitarian efforts have been more successful than its record of resolving disputes. Other regional organizations, such as the **Organization of Central American States** (1951), the **Central American Common Market** (1980), the **Latin American Integration Association** (1980) and the **Contadora Group** (1983), have not stopped the frequent outbreaks of violence in Latin America.

The collapse of the U.S.S.R. cut off aid once funneled to communist insurgents through Cuba. Short on funds, Castro trimmed covert operations in Latin America and tried to open trade with neighbors. At the same time, he increased Cuban government restrictions and rationing. The economic decline led Cubans to flee the country. An estimated 125,000 left in the 1980 "Mariel Boatlift," most fleeing to Florida. Castro again allowed a mass exodus of **balseros** (rafters) in 1994. The U.S. and other area nations rescued them and set up detention camps for over 30,000 Cuban refugees.

A repressive government in Haiti led to another large exodus of refugees. The country's first freely elected president, **Jean-Bertrand Aristide**, was overthrown by a military coup in 1991. The OAS tried to have the exiled Aristide reinstated. The OAS tightened sanctions into a virtual economic blockade, the military junta launched repressive attacks on civilians. To get relief, the junta agreed to restore Aristide in 1993, but abandoned its promise once sanctions eased. Because of intensified repression and atrocities, thousands fled the island. With the apparent failure of strong economic pressures on rich Haitians and military leaders, the U.S. organized an invasion coalition force in the fall of 1994. Facing certain overthrow by the invasion force, the military leaders accepted a last minute deal arranged through a U.S. negotiating team led by former President Carter, to give up power and allow the coalition force to manage a transfer of government to Aristide.

LATIN AMERICAN CULTURAL CONTRIBUTIONS

Beyond its global economic and political connections, Latin America has contributed much to world culture. It blends Native American, African, and European cultures. From the days of colonization to the modern era, Latin American influence has been felt in the world's art, music, and literature. Its contributions are many:

- **Weaving** – Native American patterns are prominent in plain, patterned, loop pile, and tapestry masterpieces.

- **Metalwork** – The silver jewelry of Mexico and the Peruvian Incas are considered by many the best in the world.

- **Music and Dance** – Rhythmic folk compositions on string and percussion instruments are now performed by symphony orchestras and opera companies. Ballroom dances such as the Tango, Samba, Rhumba, Bossa Nova, and Merengue are performed throughout the world.

- **Murals** – Artist Diego Rivera's huge and powerful scenes of Mexican battles, legends, and traditions are admired and imitated worldwide.

- **Architecture** – Unique Hispanic cathedrals blend Native American styles with Iberian, Moorish, and Romanesque traditions of the European past. The ultra-modern forms of the government buildings in Brasilia by Oscar Niemeyer feature magnificent use of concrete, glass, and bronze.

- **Literature** – Oral literature and folk tales of the Incas, Mayans, and Aztecs blend with modern themes in celebrated poetry of Nicaragua's Ruben Dario. Jose Enrique Rodo of Uruguay questions the values of modern life in his essays. The poems of Chile's Nobel Prize winner, Pablo Neruda, express the feelings of common country folk of Chile. Jorge Luis Borges portrays the rugged lives of Argentine gauchos. Another Nobel Prize winner Guatemalan Miguel Angel Asturias writes vividly of the Central American Indians' culture.

In the latter half of the 20th Century, Latin America has been drawn into the global context. There is poverty and underdevelopment, but it is not quite a Third World region. It stands politically and culturally as a bridge between the developed and the underdeveloped regions of the global community.

(left) Petroglyph located on St. Kitts, Lesser Antilles, Caribbean

(below) Mexican Folk Art for sale in the market in Isla Mujeres, Mexico

PhotoDisc Inc. 1994

(left) Procession of St. Augustine – Dance of the Conquest – showing traditional masks and costumes, Lanquin Village, Guatemala.

photo by David Johnson August 1993

QUESTIONS

1 A feeling of "Pan-Americanism" refers to Latin American nations which have
  1   a unified military force
  2   economic tariff agreements
  3   a Good Neighbor Policy
  4   U.S. aid grants

2 The Contadora group refers to a group seeking
  1   a common market for Latin American countries
  2   to coordinate communist revolutionary activities
  3   a mutual defense treaty
  4   to end violence in Central America

3 The United States gained a site for the Panama Canal by helping
  1   victims of famine
  2   in agricultural development
  3   European powers to conquer it
  4   a rebel group to launch a revolution

4 A major cause of quarrels among Latin American nations in the past two centuries has been
  1   language differences
  2   cultural differences
  3   boundary disputes
  4   unfair trade practices

5 Which country became an ally of the Soviet Union during the Cold War?
  1   Brazil
  2   Mexico
  3   Puerto Rico
  4   Cuba

6 The Good Neighbor Policy of Franklin D. Roosevelt was a departure from the policy of
  1   intervention
  2   Dollar Diplomacy
  3   mercantilism
  4   Alliance for Progress

7 Cuba and Puerto Rico came under U.S. control as a result of the
  1   Alliance for Progress
  2   Spanish-American War
  3   Organization of American States
  4   Pan-Americanism

8 The Latin American nations' borrowing from foreign banks has resulted in
  1   an increase in the standard of living
  2   cultural diffusion
  3   a build-up of nuclear weapons
  4   enormous debt problems

9 The Alliance for Progress was President Kennedy's attempt to abolish
  1   the Monroe Doctrine
  2   anti-American feelings in Latin America
  3   Fidel Castro's communist government
  4   the Organization of American States

10 The "Colossus of the North" is a term used to portray
  1   the threat of American interventionism
  2   traditional Latin American isolationism
  3   the power of multinational corporations
  4   the revolution in Latin American architecture

ESSAYS

Despite the great mineral wealth and agricultural production of the region, for the majority of Latin Americans, being able to obtain enough food to avoid hunger is a daily task.

a Use any *two* of the following countries to discuss the validity of the above statement: Brazil, Chile, Cuba, Mexico.

b Choose *two* of the following and explain how they have either helped or hurt the development of Latin American nations.

- United States foreign policy
- United Nations programs
- Regional organizations
- Communism

UNIT FIVE: LATIN AMERICA ASSESSMENT

ISSUE: AWARENESS OF CULTURAL CONTRIBUTIONS

This evaluation offers an individual research report writing opportunity.

STUDENT TASK

Write a detailed 3-5 page report on a person's or period's contribution to Latin American culture.

DETAILED PROCEDURES

Part One:
Research a globally recognized contribution of Latin America in music, painting, literature, dance, or architecture.

Part Two:
Submit a detailed 3-5 page report on a person's or period's contribution to Latin American culture and its effect on world culture. Where possible, the report should contain some annotated graphic illustrations of the contribution. At least 4 resources must be cited in the bibliography.

Extra Credit Option:
Teacher may offer extra credit for an oral presentation on selected reports.

EVALUATION

The scoring grid next to the evaluation items (on the following pages) was left blank intentionally. Choice of appropriate category terms is the decision of the instructor. Selection of terms such as "minimal," "satisfactory," and "distinguished" can vary with this assessment. The table on page 10 offers additional suggestions for scoring descriptors that might be inserted in the blank grids.

LEARNING STANDARDS

Students should:

• Present ideas both in writing and orally in clear, concise, and properly accepted fashion.

• Employ a variety of information from written, graphic, and multimedia sources.

• Analyze and evaluate differing views of historic, social, cultural, economic, and political events, eras, ideas, and issues.

• Understand that different national, ethnic, religious, racial, socioeconomic, and gender groups have varied perspectives on the same events and issues.

• Understand that peoples' values, practices and traditions are diverse, yet they face the same global challenges.

• Analyze the effects of human, technological, and natural activities on societies.

• Monitor, reflect upon, and improve their work.

Research Process and Final Report

Table on page 10 offers suggestions for scoring descriptors.

Evaluation Item a Have a variety of sources been checked and evaluated?	Category 1	Category 2	Category 3	Category 4	Category 5
Evaluation Item b Is list of source citations included?	Category 1	Category 2	Category 3	Category 4	Category 5
Evaluation Item c Are report and bibliography written clearly and effectively?	Category 1	Category 2	Category 3	Category 4	Category 5
Evaluation Item d Are graphic examples included and appropriately annotated?	Category 1	Category 2	Category 3	Category 4	Category 5
Evaluation Item e Is the impact on Latin American culture analyzed?	Category 1	Category 2	Category 3	Category 4	Category 5
Evaluation Item f Is the impact on world culture analyzed?	Category 1	Category 2	Category 3	Category 4	Category 5

ADMINISTRATIVE GUIDELINES

1 Survey library resources and discuss project with librarian. A variety of sources are suggested in the text. (e.g., Diego Rivera, Pablo Neruda, Ruben Dario, Miguel Asturias, Carlos Chavez).

2 Arrange library time for both preliminary student research to decide topics, and depth research on selected topics.

3 Discuss and duplicate examples of desired writing format and style (source citation techniques, etc.).

4 Establish schedule of intermediate checkpoints and final due date.

5 Explain extra credit oral report requirements and selection process.

6

North America

Aztec
Mayan
GATT

Amerindian
49th Parallel
Megalopolis
Coureur de Bois

Viceroy
NAFTA
Quebecois

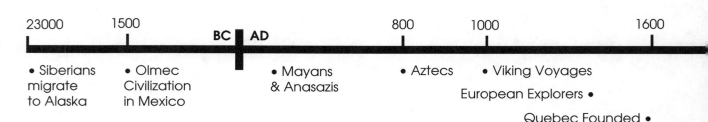

| 23000 | 1500 | BC ┃ AD | | 800 | 1000 | 1600 |

- Siberians migrate to Alaska
- Olmec Civilization in Mexico
- Mayans & Anasazis
- Aztecs
- Viking Voyages
- European Explorers •
- Quebec Founded •

Time-line is not drawn to scale.

1760   1820   1900   1950   1990   2000

- French & Indian War   • Dominion of Canada   • Statute of Westminster   • NAFTA
  - American Revolution   • NATO, OAS
        • Mexican Republic   • Rio Grande Treaty

Time-line is not drawn to scale.

UNIT SIX:

NORTH AMERICA

During the past 400 years, the North American region has had significant influence on the other regions of the globe. That influence flows from the cultures of the variety of people that live in this vast region.

I. PHYSICAL AND HISTORICAL SETTING

The North American Continent lies in the northern half of the Western Hemisphere. The region's territory covers 8.2 million square miles – over 14 % of the Earth's land surface. It is dominated by three large nations: Canada, Mexico, and the United States. Their combined population is nearly 380 million. Many island nations of the Caribbean Sea and seven Central American countries are also geographically part of this continent. However, this unit focuses on the physical, historic, economic, political, and social links of the three largest nations. (See Latin America, Unit Five, for Central America and the Caribbean.)

"BIG THREE" OF NORTH AMERICA

Canada and the United States rank as the 2nd and 4th largest nations in the world.

Canada is a parliamentary democracy that includes ten provinces and two territories. English is the common language except in the French-speaking Quebec Province. The seat of government is Ottawa in the province of Ontario.

The **United States** is a democratic republic with fifty states. It also has the overseas dependencies of Puerto Rico and the Virgin Islands in the Caribbean and Guam and numerous island territories in the Pacific. The seat of government is Washington, DC, on the Atlantic Coast. English is the dominant language. Still, more than 17 million speak Spanish, primarily in Florida, Texas, California, the southwestern states, and many larger metropolitan centers.

Mexico (official name: Estados Unidos Mexicanos – United Mexican States) is a republic with thirty-one states and the Federal District of Mexico City. Spanish is the dominant language, but 25 percent of Mexico's people speak localized Amerindian dialects. Mexico is treated in Units Five and Six because it is culturally linked to Latin America. Yet, it is geographically and economically part of North America.

Under **NAFTA** (North American Free Trade Agreement, 1993), Canada, Mexico, and the United States created a regional trade zone. NAFTA cut **tariffs** (taxes on imports) and created the largest free market area in the world. This

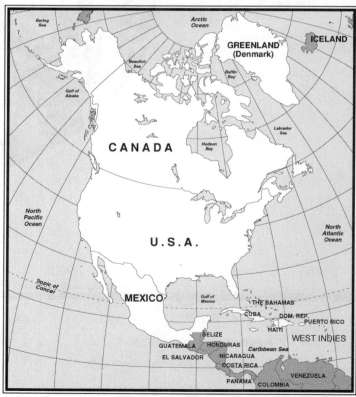

gave the three nations a chance to broaden political and economic cooperation. Vigorous debate over this treaty occurred in each of the national legislatures. Yet, the political and economic realignments of the late 20th Century made it necessary. (Part IV of this unit provides more detail on NAFTA.)

PHYSICAL FEATURES

From north to south, North America extends about 4,300 miles (6,900 km). At its widest point (excluding the state of Hawaii in the Pacific Ocean), the region measures over 5,400 miles (8,700 km). It is a large geographic area with diverse terrain.

Much of Canada's land is uninhabited taiga and tundra. This **Canadian Shield** area extends from Labrador to the Arctic Circle. Most of Canada's population lives in the eastern provinces of Ontario and Quebec near the Great Lakes and St. Lawrence River Valley or in British Columbia on the Pacific Ocean.

The U.S. shares its northern border with Canada, extending over 3,000 miles (4,800 km) from east to west. To the south, the U. S. shares a 2,000 mile (3,200 km) southern border with Mexico. Extending from the Atlantic to the Pacific Oceans, the land area encompasses woodlands, prairies, deserts, and mountains. It also includes the sub-Arctic state of Alaska and the tropical state of Hawaii.

Snapshots of North America. (clockwise from top left) Shrimp boats in Key West, Florida; Rain forest in Southeast Yucatan Peninsula, Mexico; Niagara River between U.S. and Canada linking the Great Lakes, St. Lawrence River, and Atlantic Ocean; Great Plains farmland of Manitoba, Canada; Grand Canyon National Park, Arizona; Mt. Rainier in the State of Washington; and Grizzly Bear and cub on the Alaskan Range, Alaska. Photos by PhotoDisc and Garnsey.

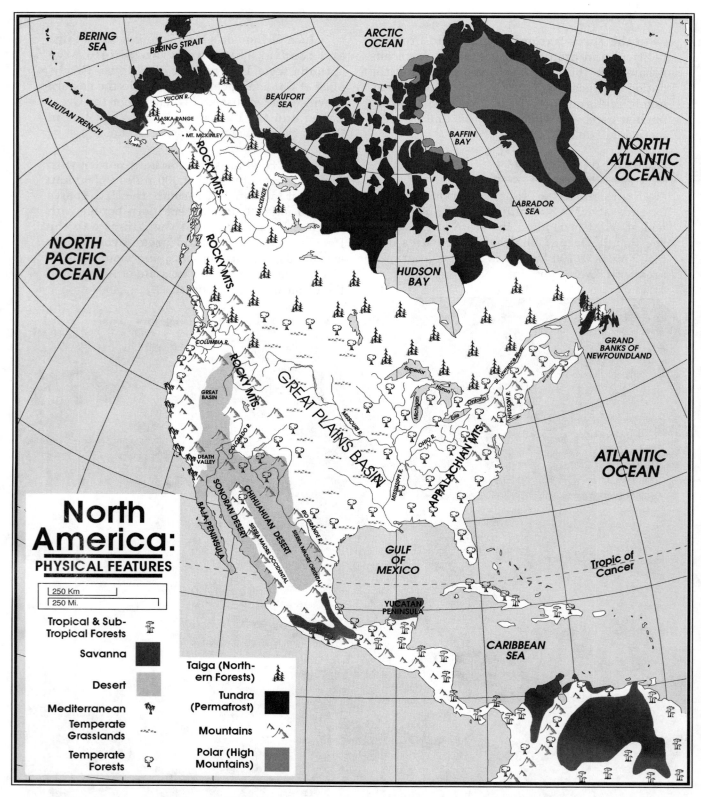

North America: PHYSICAL FEATURES

250 Km
250 Mi.

Tropical & Sub-Tropical Forests

Savanna

Desert

Mediterranean

Temperate Grasslands

Temperate Forests

Taiga (Northern Forests)

Tundra (Permafrost)

Mountains

Polar (High Mountains)

Map labels: BERING SEA, BERING STRAIT, ARCTIC OCEAN, ALEUTIAN TRENCH, YUKON R., ALASKA RANGE, MT. MCKINLEY, BEAUFORT SEA, BAFFIN BAY, NORTH ATLANTIC OCEAN, NORTH PACIFIC OCEAN, ROCKY MTS., MACKENZIE R., LABRADOR SEA, HUDSON BAY, COLUMBIA R., GRAND BANKS OF NEWFOUNDLAND, GREAT BASIN, Superior, Huron, Michigan, Ontario, Erie, St. Lawrence River, GREAT PLAINS BASIN, MISSOURI R., COLORADO R., DEATH VALLEY, MISSISSIPPI R., OHIO R., HUDSON R., APPALACHIAN MTS., ATLANTIC OCEAN, BAJA PENINSULA, SONORAN DESERT, CHIHUAHUAN DESERT, SIERRA MADRE OCCIDENTAL, SIERRA MADRE ORIENTAL, RIO GRANDE R., GULF OF MEXICO, YUCATAN PENINSULA, Tropic of Cancer, CARIBBEAN SEA

Mexico has tropical rain forests along its southern coasts, a temperate central plateau between the **Sierra Madre** mountain ranges, and the Sonoran Desert to the north. The desert extends into Arizona in the U.S.

Every major climate zone (see map) exists in North America, and rainfall varies. Regional population centers are on the coasts and inland waterways. The highest and lowest points of North America are both in the United States:

Mt. McKinley (AK) is 20,230 ft. (32,556 km), and **Death Valley** (CA) is 282 ft. (454 km) below sea level.

Until recently, North America was sparsely settled. In the last 150 years, a modern transportation and communication infrastructure tamed the vast distances between population centers.

River systems have been crucial in North America's development. The major river system draining the interior is the combined **Missouri-Mississippi** that extends over 3,800 miles (6,080 km) to the Gulf of Mexico. It lies within the boundaries of the United States. It serves as a major inland waterway and irrigation basin for one of the most productive agricultural areas of the world.

The St. Lawrence River connects the Great Lakes with the Atlantic Ocean. It serves as a 1,900 mile (3,040 km) border between Canada and the United States. In the 1950's, the two nations developed the **St. Lawrence Seaway**. It connects the Great Lakes with the Atlantic Ocean. Its system of locks permits ocean-going freighters to carry large amounts of mineral ores, oil, grain, and manufactured goods.

The **Rio Grande River** serves as an irrigation source for the southwestern portion of the United States. It extends from Colorado's San Juan Mountain Range over 1,800 miles 2,880 km) to the Gulf of Mexico. For over 1,000 miles (1,600 km), it serves as a boundary between the United States and Mexico.

Other major rivers of North America are the Ohio, Columbia, and Colorado in the U.S., and the Mackenzie and Yukon Rivers in Canada. Canada and the United States also contain many of the world's largest lakes. In the center of the continent, glacial depressions formed the **Great Lakes** (Superior, Michigan, Huron, Erie, and Ontario). They serve as natural boundaries between the two nations and as part of an extensive shipping infrastructure.

North America's key mountains are the **Rocky / Sierra Madre Cordillera** (spine-like mountain range) in the west. Running north to south, they cross the borders of the three countries. The Appalachian Mountains along the Atlantic coast extend from Canada into the southern U.S.

Mexico has two massive mountain ranges: the western **Sierra Madre Occidental** and the eastern **Sierra Madre Oriental**. These ranges extend along the coasts in a north-south direction. A high, fertile valley called the Central Plateau divides them. Most of Mexico's people live on this plateau. It includes the capital, Mexico City – the world's second most populous city with 21 million. (Tokyo is the first with 27 million.) Mexico also has two large peninsulas, the Baja on the Pacific Ocean and the Yucatán on the Gulf of Mexico.

Canada and the U.S. have large coastal plains on the Atlantic and Pacific Oceans. In the central region of these two nations is the **Great Plains Basin**. It produces a large portion of the world's grain and livestock.

The continent plays host to many climates. From the polar region Ice Cap (EF) southward, Canada's Tundra (ET) changes to Mid-Latitude Wet and Dry (Dw/DF). Moving southward, the U.S. ranges among Mid-Latitude Rainy climates (C types). Mexico ranges from warmer Mid-Latitude C climates to Tropical Rainy (A Types) in the Yucatan Peninsula (see Climate Map on the next page).

RESOURCES

Canada, Mexico, and the United States have an abundance of natural resources. Their soils produce significant amounts of the world's grain supply: wheat, corn, barley, and rye. Many fruits and vegetables are grown in the more temperate and sub-tropical climates of the United States and Mexico.

In Mexico, corn is the most widely grown crop and is a dietary staple. Mexico is a leading supplier of coffee and cotton. It also produces 50% of the world's **sisal** (a fiber used to make heavy twine or rope). Mexico markets its cattle, sheep, chickens, and hogs globally. North America's extensive saltwater coastlines and large fresh water lakes support a profitable but shrinking fishing industry.

Mining is significant to all three nations. They have vast natural gas and petroleum reserves. Coal is a major mineral product for

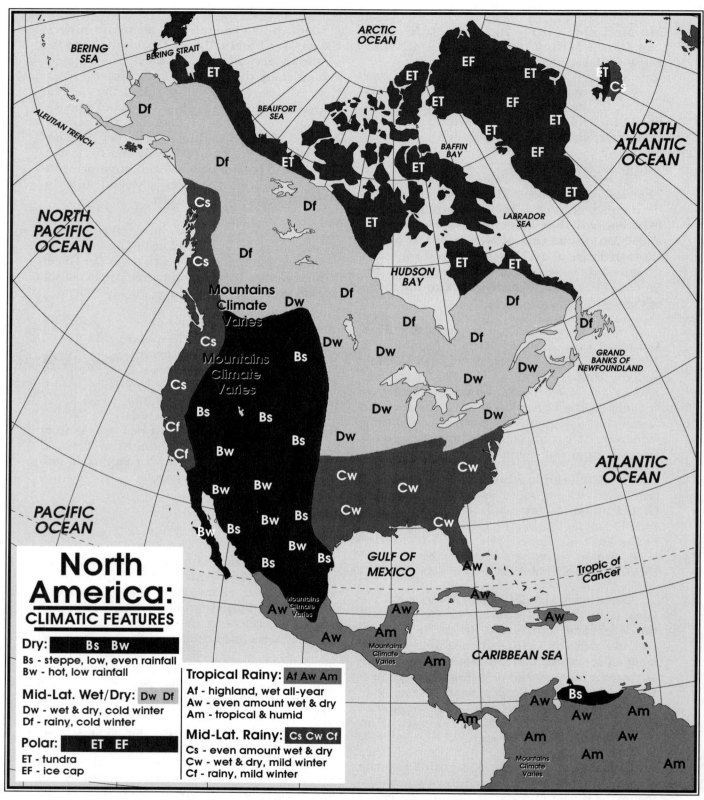

North America: CLIMATIC FEATURES

Dry: Bs Bw
Bs - steppe, low, even rainfall
Bw - hot, low rainfall

Mid-Lat. Wet/Dry: Dw Df
Dw - wet & dry, cold winter
Df - rainy, cold winter

Polar: ET EF
ET - tundra
EF - ice cap

Tropical Rainy: Af Aw Am
Af - highland, wet all-year
Aw - even amount wet & dry
Am - tropical & humid

Mid-Lat. Rainy: Cs Cw Cf
Cs - even amount wet & dry
Cw - wet & dry, mild winter
Cf - rainy, mild winter

the United States as well as gold, copper, and lead. Mexico produces gold, lead, zinc, and copper. It is also the world's fifth leading producer of silver. Mexico mines iron ore and coal basically for its own steel industry. Canada supplies one third of the world's nickel. It also produces copper, lead, zinc, silver, coal, gold, iron, and uranium.

The large taiga region of northern Canada has some of the most extensive timber reserves in the world. It is a global supplier of lumber products and the wood pulp used for paper. Surprisingly, one third of the United States is also forestland. It also has a considerable timber industry.

Advanced technology in Canada and the United States makes both nations leading industrial powers. In recent years, Mexico has shown rapid industrial growth in steel, textile, chemicals and petroleum. All three nations benefit from well-developed infrastructures that aid in efficient production and marketing of their products.

PEOPLE

Nowhere else in the world is there such an intermixing of racial and ethnic groups as in North America. Four major groups of people have formed the historic background of the area: Amerindians, Europeans, Africans, and Asians.

Amerindians were the first to migrate to the region. According to archeological finds, the first Americans came from the Siberian steppe in Asia. About 25,000 years ago, they crossed a narrow land bridge in what is now the Bering Strait. The cold northern climate caused southward migrations. Amerindians are descendents of these earliest settlers. Nations and groups evolved different cultures as they spread out in North America, reflecting the differences in environments. Europeans migrated to the region after 1500 A.D.

Canada and the United States have pluralistic populations. **Immigrants** from all over the world have set-

tled these nations. Canada's dominant ethnic distribution is British (40%) and French (27%). Other early settlers came from the northern European nations of the Netherlands, Germany, and Scandinavia in the 17th and 18th Centuries. These people came seeking better economic conditions and freedom from religious persecution.

In the 19th and 20th Centuries, Canada saw a greater shift to eastern and southern European immigration and from the Pacific Rim nations of China, Japan, and Korea. These new immigrants represent over 25% of the population. Immigrants have made Toronto the major cosmopolitan center in Canada.

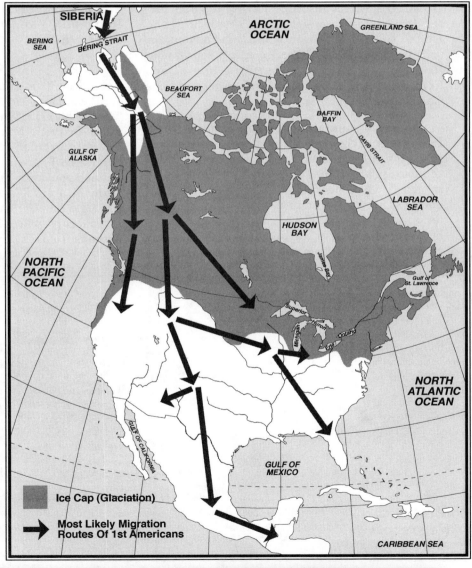

Ice Cap (Glaciation)

Most Likely Migration Routes Of 1st Americans

North American Population Distribution

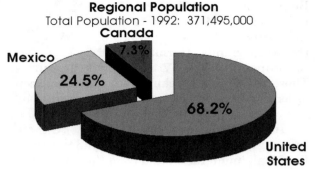

Regional Population
Total Population - 1992: 371,495,000

Canada 7.3%
Mexico 24.5%
United States 68.2%

Source: U.S. Dept. of Commerce, Economics, and Statistics Bureau

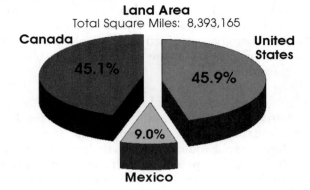

Land Area
Total Square Miles: 8,393,165

Canada 45.1%
United States 45.9%
Mexico 9.0%

The United States is also a **cultural melting pot**. Added to the migrations mentioned is a large African-American population segment (16%). As a direct result of slavery in early history and later immigration, Canada and the United States have been traditional havens for refugees from economic and political repression. Recent examples include refugee migrations from Southeast Asia, the Middle East, and the Caribbean.

Mexico's population is more homogeneous. Its large **mestizo** (mixed European and Indian racial group) population represents over 80% of the total population. This goes back to the early intermixing of people after the Spanish conquests. The widely scattered Amerindian population is a minority (10%). The remaining 10% is largely European, although it also includes recent migrations from the Pacific Rim.

Most of the people of North America live in large metropolitan areas. Seventy-six percent of Canada's 27.4 million people live in urban areas. Toronto (4.0 million), Montreal (3.1 million), and Vancouver (1.6 million) are the largest cities.

In the United States, several **megalopolis corridors** (continuous strips of dense population) contain 75% of its 260 million people. "BosWash" stretches down the Atlantic coast from Boston, MA to Washington, DC. The Pacific Corridor on the California coast runs from San Francisco to San Diego, CA. A less defined southern Sun Belt Corridor is emerging from Miami, FL to Atlanta, GA. The Texas Triangle has San Antonio, Houston, and Dallas at its corners. The Great Lakes Corridor extends from Chicago, IL to Pittsburgh, PA.

In Mexico, 70% of the nation's 92 million people live in cities. In the Central Plateau, Mexico City and Guadalajara contain more than one third of the country's population. Social problems are prevalent in these large urban centers. Dramatic contrasts exist between the rich and poor. Modern, high-rise apartment buildings tower over **los barrios** (poverty-stricken slums).

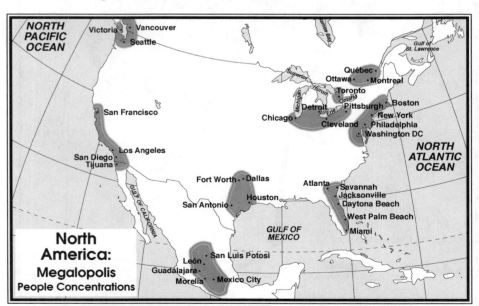

North America: Megalopolis
People Concentrations

OVERPOPULATION

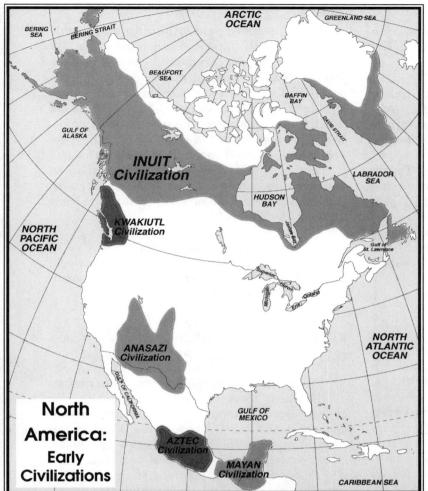

North America: Early Civilizations

THE INUIT (23,000 B.C. - PRESENT)

The group closest to the Siberian settlers who first crossed the Bering Strait is the **Inuit** of Canada and Alaska. While often called Eskimo, an Algonquin name for "eater of raw meat," they prefer the name Inuit. They live in one of the harshest climates in the world. In the polar tundra environment, the Inuit developed a survival culture. Unlike most Amerindian groups, they have no tribal chiefs or organized system of government. Instead, they developed simple rules of moral conduct requiring everyone to help each other and participate in a peaceful method of survival.

Inuit food, clothing, shelter, and ritual evolved from the limitations of the Arctic. Seal, whale, and fish from the sea, plus caribou from the land serve as staples. The early Inuit often ate food raw because of the lack of fuel for fire. Skins and fur were used for clothing and mild weather tent material. During the six-month long sub-zero winters, they built snow houses and traveled by sled. Inuit developed skill carving soapstone into lamps,

EARLY CIVILIZATIONS

Recent history shows how the governments and societies of Canada, Mexico, and the United States repressed the Amerindian. These people developed high civilizations in Pre-Columbian times (before 1492). Yet, they suffered hostile discrimination. Official discrimination is banned, but racial and ethnic inequalities remain in all nations.

Their were hundreds of Amerindian civilizations. Most developed in isolation from the rest of the world. Not until the European Age of Discovery did some of them become known globally. After European colonization began, many Amerindian civilizations disintegrated rapidly. Still, Mexico has labored to preserve the Mayan and Aztec heritage.

Symbols of the Inuit life and culture

cooking pots, and utensils. They carved wooden plates and used whalebone for cups and eating utensils.

When the European whalers and fur traders came into the Arctic region in the 1800's, traditional Inuit culture declined. The Inuit contracted fatal diseases brought by Europeans. In addition, the rifles of European hunters wiped out game in trapping and hunting areas. Today, about 25,000 Inuit live in the northern territories of Canada. Forty thousand live in Alaska. The traditional way of life has ended for most Inuit. They now live in small, government subsidized villages. The Canadian government has encouraged Inuit fishing and handicraft cooperatives.

MAYAN CIVILIZATION (1500 B.C. - 1548 A.D.)

Mayan Civilization developed in the rain forests of Mexico's southern neighbors, Guatemala, Honduras, and Belize. It then gradually moved northward to the Yucatan Peninsula. Mayan agricultural settlements focused on the **míles** (cornfields) from which they grew their staple food, maize. Mayans used "slash and burn" agriculture. This exhausted the soil and forced frequent migration. As a result, cities did not exist in the early stages of Mayan civilization.

PhotoDisc Inc. 1994   Chac Mool – Mayan Sculpture, Mexico

Mayan society paid tribute to many gods associated with planting and harvesting. By 300 B.C., religious ceremonial centers became popular. **Tikal** became a major ceremonial center. It had several large temple pyramids and an impressive palace complex. Historians claim the Mayans constructed more than forty cities, each with populations of more than 20,000 people. Some historians call the Mayans the "Greeks of the New World." They excelled in mathematics, astronomy, architecture, ceramics, and sculpture. Linguists still translate their complex ideographs.

Today, many Mayan descendants live in Mexico. Tourists travel from around the world to marvel at the ruins of Uxmal and Chichen Itza on the Yucatan Peninsula.

KWAKIUTL CIVILIZATION (BEFORE 1492 A.D. - PRESENT)

The **Kwakiutl** people were an Amerindian civilization that emerged in the Pacific Northwest. Their homeland overlaps British Columbia and the United States. Food in the form of marine life from the ocean and many rivers was plentiful. The land provided plant life and game to supplement their diet. The Kwakiutl conducted religious ceremonies honoring the spirits of fish, animals, and plants. Large, upright wooden carvings called "totem poles" symbolized these spirits. Some considered the totem spirit to be an ancestor of the tribe. Totem poles included family and tribal emblems.

People considered wealth more important than valor in battle. Chiefs held tribal feasts called "potlatches." They distributed valuable property, food, and beautiful wooden and shell earrings to guests. Custom bound the recipients to return the property with interest in the future. This practice created a network of loyalty and support within

PhotoDisc Inc. 1994

Kwakiutl Totem – Victoria, British Columbia, Canada

tribal groups. When European settlers abolished this ceremony, the Kwakiutl lost this bond of industry and thrift.

As skilled crafts workers, the Kwakiutl used the plentiful timber of their region to make canoes, boxes, dishes, and masks. Noted anthropologist **Ruth Benedict** studied and wrote extensively about the Kwakiutl in *Patterns of Culture* (1934). Yet, little of their culture remains. Their descendants work in fish canneries or farms on Vancouver Island. Others serve the tourist industry as guides or as wood carvers, trying to preserve their ancient crafts.

ANASAZI CIVILIZATION

(300 A.D. - 1200 A.D.)

A remarkable American culture existed in an area of the southwestern United States commonly called "The Four Corners" (Utah, Colorado, Arizona, New Mexico). The **Anasazi**, commonly called "cliff dwellers," were known for their architectural achievements. The Anasazi built two- to three-story houses in the steep, flat top outcroppings called mesas. They used wooden poles, sandstone blocks, and mud mortar. The dwellings had many rooms for living and food storage. For protection, they often lacked doors at ground level, and the inhabitants had

David Johnson, 1971

Mesa Verde – Cliff Dwellings of the Anasazi, The Four Corners, United States to use ladders to enter through the roof. By building deep inside canyons, the Anasazi allowed for air currents to cool their dwellings during the summer and provide warmth in the winter. These locations also served as protection from enemy attacks. One cliff palace had more than 200 rooms and housed over 400 people.

The dryness of the region preserved many Anasazi artifacts and some mummies. They tell much about the culture of these cliff dwellers. For example, they used an underground chamber called a **kiva** for religious rituals. The Anasazi had clever farming methods, intricately designed black and white pottery, and beautifully constructed baskets for carrying water and crops.

Historians believe a long-term drought forced the Anasazi from the region. Present-day Pueblo tribes are their descendants. The most famous Anasazi settlements are in **Mesa Verde** in Colorado and **Canyon de Chelly National Monument** in Arizona. These are the oldest standing buildings in North America.

AZTEC CIVILIZATION

(1200 A.D. - 1535 A.D.)

The **Aztec** people were a nomadic warrior society that emerged in the central plateau of Mexico around 1200 A.D. Their most sacred activity was warfare. They worshiped Huitzilopochtli, god of Sun and war. Historians estimate the Aztecs made 20,000 human sacrifices annually. They adopted many cultural advances of their southern neighbors, the Mayans. Their artisans crafted beautiful gold and silver jewelry and carved jade and crystal. Aztec clothing often featured bright cotton colors adorned with feathers.

Tenochtitlan (present day Mexico City) became the center of the Aztec Empire. At its peak, Tenochtitlan had more than 100,000 inhabitants. The Aztec rigidly organized their society. They had an elaborate legal system with liberal use of capital punishment.

Historians attribute the fall of the Aztecs to their belief in warfare and human sacrifice. The legend of the coming of the god **Quetzalcoatal** to Earth may have eased the Spanish conquest in 1521. Historians hypothesize that the Emperor Montezuma and Aztec leaders believed Cortes to be Quetzalcoatal. They allowed him access to Tenochtitlan. From there, the conquistadores' European modern weaponry overpowered them.

The early historical development of North America shows its rich cultural heritage. The variety of natural and social environmental forces created an area of diverse peoples and cultures.

Tenochtitlan – Center of Aztec life, present site of Mexico City

QUESTIONS

1   Historians believe that the first North American inhabitants migrated from Asia by way of the
    1   Gulf of Mexico
    2   Baja Peninsula
    3   Bering Strait
    4   St. Lawrence River

2   The only tropical rain forests found in North America are located in
    1   Mexico's southern coasts
    2   Ontario, Canada
    3   the Great Plains
    4   Southeastern United States

3   Which describes the economic status of the Canadian tundra?
    1   a largely unexplored frozen land in the Arctic
    2   the grain growing regions of its prairie provinces
    3   the fishing maritime provinces
    4   the vast lumber region in Ontario

4   Where do the majority of the people of Mexico, Canada, and the U.S. live?
    1   river valleys
    2   urban centers
    3   coastal plains
    4   rural regions

5   Historians call the Mayans the "Greeks of the New World" because of their
    1   ritualistic war ceremonies
    2   subsistence agriculture
    3   development of math, sciences, and architecture
    4   worship of one god

6   Physical barriers often serve as geographic boundaries between nations. Which is an example of this?
    1   Sierra Madre Mountain range
    2   Rocky Mountains
    3   Mississippi River
    4   Rio Grande River

7   Mexico's population is over 80% mestizo, a racial mixture of which two groups?
    1   European and African
    2   European and Amerindian
    3   African and Amerindian
    4   Oriental and European

8   Which item shows that Canada, Mexico, and the United States are pluralistic societies?
    1   Spain conquered the ancient Amerindian societies.
    2   Populations today represent mixtures of African, European, and Amerindian groups.
    3   Population is concentrated in megalopolis strip settlements.
    4   English is the predominant language in all three nations.

9   The Amerindian group that most resembles early Siberian settlers of North America is
    1   Mayan
    2   Aztec
    3   Anasazi
    4   Inuit

10 The Anasazi settlements in Colorado and Arizona are famous for
    1   resemblance to ancient Asian dwellings
    2   the oldest standing buildings in North America
    3   potlatches
    4   gold ornaments

ESSAYS

1   Describe *three* geographic regions that exist in Canada, the United States, and Mexico. For each region selected, describe the following:

    a   the type of climate and vegetation
    b   the economy of the region

2   Discuss the major achievements of *two* different early Amerindian civilizations that developed in North America and explain what may have caused the decline of these societies.

II. DYNAMICS OF CHANGE

Who came to North America after the Amerindians? Archaeologists discovered artifacts and old stone buildings in Labrador and Newfoundland that show the **Vikings** from Scandinavia created settlements as early as 1000 A.D. This verifies the tales of the great Viking explorer, **Leif Eriksson**. Vikings brought nothing of great value back to Europe, and these early settlements did not last. In Pre-Columbian North America, many Amerindian local cultures existed. There were more languages than in Europe. Until the Spaniards arrived, the people of North America lacked horses, domesticated cattle, and wheel and iron implements. Vast oceans isolated them. All this

changed in the Age of Discovery. Christopher Columbus' first voyage to America began a European quest for "gold, glory, and gospel."

THE AGE OF DISCOVERY

In the 15th and 16th Centuries, Spain and Portugal were the major colonial powers because of the strength of their navies. In the Age of Exploration and Discovery, they colonized and dramatically affected the development of the "New World." The two were rivals for control of the Western Hemisphere. War was avoided when Pope Alexander VI negotiated the **Treaty of Tordesillas** (1494). Faulty maps resulted in an unbalanced agreement. Spain was granted a vast empire reaching from the southern United States to the tip of South America. Portugal received only the territory of Brazil.

European Explorations Of North America		
DATE	**EXPLORER/COUNTRY**	**DISCOVERY**
1000 AD	Erikson/Scandinavia	Canada: Labrador/Newfoundland
1492-1504	Columbus/Spain	West Indies and Central America
1497	Cabot/England	Canada: Newfoundland
1519	Cortes/Spain	Mexico
1524	Verrazano/France	East coast US and Canada's Maritime Provinces
1534-1535	Cartier/France	Canada-St. Lawrence River

Spain sent Cortes and other **conquistadores** to crush the Amerindian empires in Mexico and other areas of its new empire. The Spanish gained wealth through a mercantilist economy. The government sponsored private business enterprises that brought wealth from the colonies to the mother country. These economic ventures in **New Spain** involved plantation agriculture, mining, and cattle ranching. **Viceroys** (crown governors) and their **audiencas** (appointed councils) ruled New Spain. Mexico City was the administrative center.

British colonial settlements along the Mid-Atlantic Coast began in 1607 in Jamestown, Virginia. English Protestant separatists such as the **Pilgrims** settled Massachusetts (1620). Great waves of **Puritans** (Anglican Calvinist reformers) entered New England in the 1630's. During the 17th and 18th Centuries, Britain pursued a **mercantilist policy** (managed trade regulations with colonies).

European colonial settlement in Canada began when French fur companies sent **coureurs de bois** (trapper-traders) into the St. Lawrence River Valley and Great Lakes Region. In trading with the Indians, the French did not attempt to conquer them as did the Spanish in Mexico. French missionaries followed the coureurs. Some such as **Father Jacques Marquette** became explorers who sent written accounts to Europe. Marquette's missionary work carried him into the Mississippi Valley.

With poor soil and a short growing season, settlements in eastern **New France** (Canada) grew slowly. Yet, colonial governor **Samuel de Champlain** built a series of forts along the major rivers to protect the fur trade. In 1608, Champlain set up a lasting settlement at Quebec on the St. Lawrence River. New France remained a colony of France until 1760.

Early colonists also came to Canada from the British Isles. They settled in the eastern maritime region of Newfoundland, Nova Scotia (New Scotland), New Brunswick, and Prince Edward Island. The **Hudson Bay Company** controlled the wealthy fur trading region in northern Canada. It forced the French to give up many claims by 1670. By 1713, the British forced the French out of the entire maritime region. British settlers from the thirteen Mid-Atlantic colonies expanded westward into the Ohio River Valley. War between the British and French became inevitable.

Worldwide struggles for trade and larger empires continued for most of the 18th Century. In North America, the **French and Indian War** (1754-1763) was the decisive clash. At Quebec (1759), British General **James Wolfe**'s victory over General **Louis Montcalm** destroyed French control in Canada. *The Treaty of Paris* (1763) gave British control of New France. Yet, this victory cost Britain dearly. Parliament raised taxes on the American colonists to pay war debts. The colonists resisted. The seeds of discontent ripened into the American Revolution.

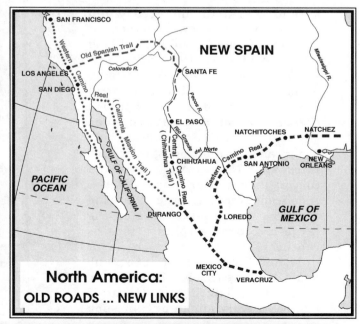

North America:
OLD ROADS ... NEW LINKS

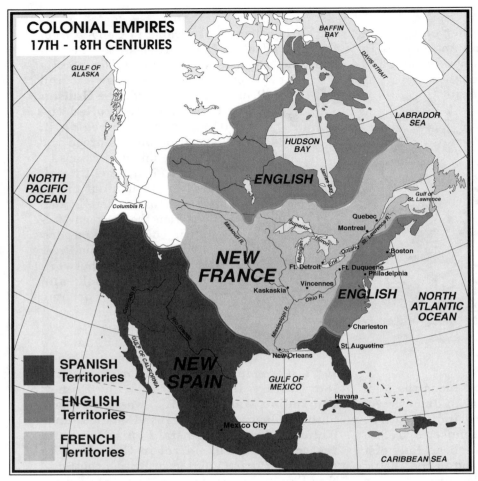

COLONIAL EMPIRES
17TH - 18TH CENTURIES

GULF OF ALASKA

NORTH PACIFIC OCEAN

BAFFIN BAY

DAVIS STRAIT

LABRADOR SEA

HUDSON BAY

ENGLISH

James Bay

Gulf of St. Lawrence

Columbia R.

Missouri R.

Superior

Huron

Quebec

Montreal

St. Lawrence R.

NEW FRANCE

Ft. Detroit

Michigan

Ontario

Erie

Ft. Duquesne

Boston

Vincennes

Philadelphia

Kaskaskia

Ohio R.

ENGLISH

NORTH ATLANTIC OCEAN

Mississippi R.

Charleston

Colorado R.

Rio Grande

GULF OF CALIFORNIA

NEW SPAIN

New Orleans

St. Augustine

GULF OF MEXICO

Havana

Mexico City

CARIBBEAN SEA

■ **SPANISH** Territories

■ **ENGLISH** Territories

■ **FRENCH** Territories

POLITICAL AUTHORITY & SOCIAL CLASSES

The colonial empires of North America evolved distinct social class systems. In Mexico, a feudal system emerged when Spanish monarchs rewarded conquistadors with **encomiendas** (vast land tracts). A **viceroy** (the king's representative in the New World) governed New Spain (Mexico, Central America, Caribbean). The Spanish Crown expected **peninsulares** (Iberian - born nobles) and their American - born offspring (**criollos**) to care for Native Americans and convert them to Christianity. Native Americans were supposed to be paid for work in the mines and on the large **haciendas** (plantations or ranches). This rarely occurred. Nor did the Church often intervene against mistreatment of the Native Americans. The Roman Catholic Church rarely spoke out on such

political issues. Instead, it became a tool of the colonial administrators. The Church did create some cultural unity in New Spain. Still, by catering to the aristocracy, it sustained class lines.

Native Americans far outnumbered the Spanish who settled in Mexico. Many Spanish settlers married Indian women. Their children were called **mestizos**. Today, they are Mexico's dominant population group. Few African slaves were ever brought to Mexico. To the North, many colonists migrated to Britain's Mid-Atlantic Coast colonies because of poor economic conditions. This region offered many economic opportunities. Farming, fishing, lumbering, and commerce provided a livelihood for skilled and nonskilled workers. Other colonists came for greater political freedom from the British government. In England, there were many religious **dissenters** (people whose religion conflicted with the established Anglican Church of England). Over

Spanish influence and the power of the Roman Catholic Church is apparent throughout Southwest U.S. and Mexico. 17th C. San Xavier Mission, Tucson, AZ

Wayne Garnsey, 1974

Spreading French culture and converting Amerindians to Christianity, coureurs de bois – French Canadian trappers, traders – and missionaries explored and established outposts in the Great Lakes region and the Missouri-Mississippi river valleys.

POLITICAL & ECONOMIC REFUGEES

30,000 fled to the colonies for freedom. Still, not everyone who came to British North America was from England. By 1750, one-third of all immigrants had migrated from Ireland, France, Germany, and the Netherlands. They sought the same freedoms as the English immigrants. The remaining population consisted of either Amerindians or Africans originally brought to America as slaves.

Most colonists lived simple farming lives. Only a small elite represented the governments and southern plantation aristocracy. Perhaps 10% of the population were merchants, professionals, or skilled crafts people. Indentured servants and African slaves made up the bottom of the social hierarchy. The British Crown and Parliament loosely controlled the colonies until

1763. Under a policy of **salutary neglect** (limited attention by Parliament), mercantilist regulations were ignored. This laissez-faire approach led the colonies to develop rapidly. Varieties of self-government evolved, based upon rights enjoyed in England. Virginia created its **House of Burgesses** (legislature) in Jamestown in 1619. It was the first example of representative government for Europeans in the New World. New England created its own form of self-government in regularly held town meetings.

By 1680, only 10,000 colonists lived in scattered farm communities along the St. Lawrence River, New France. **Habitant** was the name given the French colonial farmers. **Voyageurs** were the more prosperous colonial merchants. Many of earlier coureurs de bois intermarried with the local Amerindian women and adopted local languages and customs. Montreal became the fur trade center. To keep the French culture alive, the French Crown sent Roman Catholic missionaries to build churches, hospitals, and schools. They converted Amerindians to Christianity as they pushed into the Great Lakes and the Missouri-Mississippi Rivers.

INDEPENDENCE MOVEMENTS

Enlightenment ideas of the 18th Century fertilized the seeds of revolution in North America. Europeans such as Locke, Montesquieu, Voltaire, and Rousseau questioned the idea of the divine right of monarchy. They supported people participating in government. Their words strongly influenced Thomas Jefferson's writing of the *Declaration of Independence* (1776) in America.

For a decade after the French and Indian War, settlers in Britain's 13 Mid-Atlantic Coast colonies rebelled against "taxation without representation." The **American Revolution** (1776-83) resulted in their independence from Great Britain. The new United States of America developed its *Constitution* (1787) with a *Bill of Rights* (1790). The documents guaranteed a separation of power in government and basic civil liberties. Today, the *Declaration of Independence*, the *U.S. Constitution*, and the *Bill of Rights* still inspire freedom-seeking peoples of the world.

The **French Revolution** (1789) soon followed the American Revolution. It incorporated many Enlightenment ideas and rights embraced by Americans. The new French Republic abolished the privileges of the nobility and the Catholic Church. It ended the old feudal order. This frightened the monarchs of Europe. They tried to overthrow the French Republic.

In the late 18th and early 19th Centuries, the French Revolution evolved into the **Napoleonic Wars**. European rulers began neglecting some of their colonies. In Mexico, resistance to Spain began even earlier. Criollos and wealthy mestizos felt little allegiance to the Spanish Crown. Resentment against the ruling peninsulares reached organized levels. In ridding themselves of the crown's officials, Mexicans felt they could gain new economic freedom and social mobility.

In 1810, Father **Miguel Hidalgo** ignited Mexico's lengthy struggle for independence. On 16 September 1810, he urged his peasant parishioners in Dolores to take back their land from their Spanish colonial rulers. His words spread throughout Mexico. "El Grito de Dolores" became a rallying cry. Mexicans still commemorate the date as their Independence Day.

At first, the criollos, mestizos, and Indian peasants supported Hidalgo. When he promised land reform, the criollos broke from his ranks and joined the wealthy Spanish loyalists. Hidalgo's rebellion faltered after he and a fellow priest, **Jose Morelos**, were captured and executed by a loyalist firing squad. A change in Spain's government in 1820 gave the criollos more rights. By then, the wealthy criollos wanted independence. Under military leader **Agustin de Iturbide**, they declared Mexican independence in 1821. Spain was too weak to conquer the colony again, and independence came to the Republic of Mexico in 1823.

In Canada, the route to self-government took longer evolutionary paths. After the signing of the Treaty of Paris in 1763, New France became part of the British Empire. The *Quebec Act* (1774) divided the region into Lower Canada (now Quebec Province) and Upper Canada (Ontario). The act allowed the French colonists to keep their language, culture, and Catholic religion in Lower Canada. It perpetuated the cultural and political differences that continue to exist today.

In the early 19th Century, there were rebellions for self-rule in both the French sector (Lower Canada) and the British-dominated Upper Canada. Parliament unified Upper and Lower Canada in 1840. By 1849, Parliament approved limited self-government in internal affairs. Yet, Britain continued to manage the external trade. In 1867, Britain passed the *British North America Act* granting Canada dominion status (self-governing territory). A confederation of the provinces followed, choosing Sir **John A. MacDonald** Canada's first Prime Minister.

In a period of just over 300 years, the North American region went from colonial empires under Spanish, British, and French rulers to the new nations of Canada, Mexico, and the United States. The empires left each new nation a cultural unity. For Mexico, Spain's social structure, religious traditions, and language continued. For Canada and the United States, multicultural tolerance encouraged diversity.

QUESTIONS

1 Which European group first created settlements in North America that survived and prospered into the present?
1 Spanish
2 French
3 Vikings
4 British

2 The earliest French colonial settlements in Canada began with economic ventures that evolved from
1 fur trapping
2 fishing trade
3 gold mines
4 slave plantations

3 Which document first influenced the overthrow of colonial rule in North America?
1 *U.S. Constitution*
2 *Grito de Dolores*
3 *British North America Act*
4 *Declaration of Independence*

4 Encomiendas were large land tracts given by the Spanish Crown to the conquistadors as
1 fur trading enterprises
2 religious shrines
3 bribes to refrain from exposing corrupt colonial leaders
4 rewards for their loyalty to the Crown

5 Early colonists came to the thirteen British Atlantic Coast Colonies to escape
1 religious persecution
2 conversion to Christianity
3 viceroys
4 the European Enlightenment

6 Which is a reason the protests concerning the inhumane treatment of Indians in New Spain accomplished little?
1 The Church served as a cultural unifying element.
2 Religion was used as a repressive tool of the colonial viceroys.
3 Native American laborers were paid well.
4 Religious leaders required peninsulares and criollos to convert Native Americans to Christianity.

7 Which two groups initially led the fight for Mexico's independence in the early 1800's?
1 peninsulares and criollos
2 criollos and mestizos
3 peninsulares and mestizos
4 Native Americans and peninsulares

ESSAYS

1 In the colonial period in North America, a number of socioeconomic groups helped shape the future of new nations. Some groups dominated and others suffered.

Groups
- Voyageurs (Canada)
- Habitants (Canada)
- Peninsulares (Mexico)
- Mestizos (Mexico)
- Slaves (U.S.)
- New England merchants (U.S.)

a Select *three* of the groups listed above (one from each nation) and explain their role in the colonial social structure.

b Choose *two* of the remaining groups. Explain the economic conditions which would lead them to seek independence from their colonial rulers.

2 In an essay, discuss the social, political, and economic differences in the colonial rule of

a the British in the 13 Atlantic Coast Colonies (U.S.),
b the French in New France (Canada), and
c the Spanish in New Spain (Mexico).

system. The *United States Constitution* took effect in 1789. The new plan gave the United States government critical national powers but allowed individual states control of most local decisions. In 1803, the United States began an expansion policy (later called "Manifest Destiny"). In that year, Congress approved President Jefferson's purchase of the vast Louisiana Territory from France.

By 1900, the United States had expanded from coast to coast and included the territories of Alaska and Hawaii. A strong spirit of nationalism prevailed, and the U.S. government encouraged rugged individualism and free enterprise. Millions of European immigrants came to the United States, and the multicultural, "melting pot" society assimilated them.

For Mexico, political independence brought much change and many power struggles. In

III. CONTEMPORARY NATIONS

Political independence brought distinct changes to each of the three nations. Just as each evolved from different cultural roots, each evolved different political institutions.

INITIAL ATTEMPTS AT UNIFICATION

Unlike Mexico and the United States, Canada did not fight a revolution for its independence. Throughout the 19th Century, Great Britain slowly gave Canada more decision-making power. Yet, it was not until 1931, under *The Statute of Westminster*, that Canada became a truly independent nation. It did not sever its last governmental ties with Great Britain until 1982.

The Middle Atlantic colonies declared independence from Britain in 1776. After fighting the Revolutionary War, they set up *The Articles of Confederation* (1781-1787). This document created a unicameral legislature as its ruling body. It was a weak government and the country changed to a federal

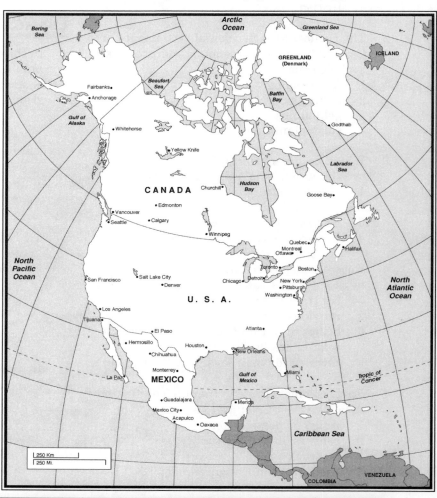

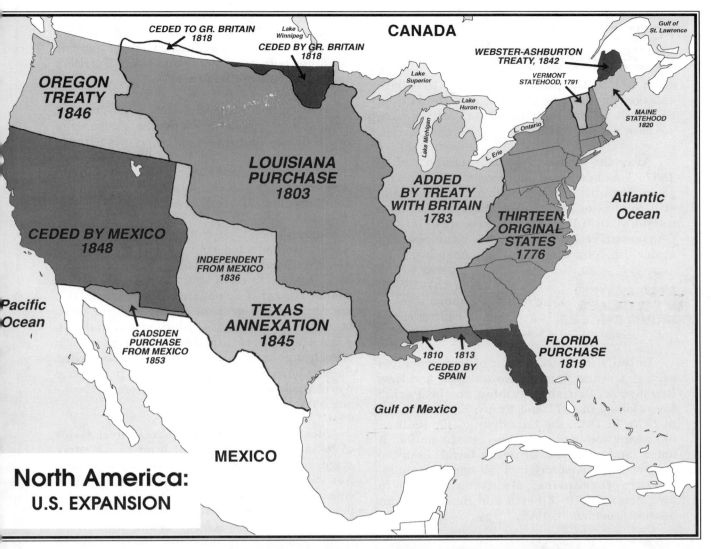

North America:
U.S. EXPANSION

Map labels:
CEDED TO GR. BRITAIN 1818
Lake Winnipeg
CEDED BY GR. BRITAIN 1818
CANADA
Gulf of St. Lawrence
WEBSTER-ASHBURTON TREATY, 1842
VERMONT STATEHOOD, 1791
MAINE STATEHOOD 1820
OREGON TREATY 1846
Lake Superior
Lake Huron
Lake Michigan
L. Ontario
L. Erie
LOUISIANA PURCHASE 1803
ADDED BY TREATY WITH BRITAIN 1783
THIRTEEN ORIGINAL STATES 1776
Atlantic Ocean
CEDED BY MEXICO 1848
INDEPENDENT FROM MEXICO 1836
Pacific Ocean
GADSDEN PURCHASE FROM MEXICO 1853
TEXAS ANNEXATION 1845
1810 1813 CEDED BY SPAIN
FLORIDA PURCHASE 1819
Gulf of Mexico
MEXICO

1821, Mexican dictator **Agustin de Iturbide** declared an empire. In 1824, a new government declared Mexico an independent republic. Between 1821 and 1887, Mexico had two emperors, several dictators, presidents, and provisional executives.

One colorful leader, General **Antonio Lopez de Santa Anna**, was elected president four times between 1833 and 1855. He was noted for his corrupt policies and neglect of the poor people. In his off-and-on thirty years in office, Santa Anna lost the territory now called Texas and most of the northern half of the nation's land to the United States. Democratic reform was difficult for Mexico. A strong combination of traditional institutions such as the close-knit family structure, the landed aristocracy, the military, and the Church slowed the process of democratic reform.

OBSTACLES TO CHANGE

Each North American nation's early history and cultural roots influenced political evolution. Having the British parliamentary political system as a model prepared Canada and the United States for democratic self-rule. In Mexico, power remained with wealthy owners of the encomiendas. This landed aristocracy was left over from Spanish colonial days. Aristocrats felt democratic reforms might  alter their wealth and position. The military and the Roman Catholic hierarchy depended on this landed elite. This "iron triangle" alliance kept the status quo. **Caudillos** (military strongmen or warlords) and their supporters dominated the national life, allowing few democratic elections.

POLITICAL EVOLUTION SINCE INDEPENDENCE

A look at the political structures that have emerged in Canada, Mexico, and the United States shows diversity. Some similarities exist, yet each nation is unique.

After the ***British North America Act of 1867***, Canada enjoyed dominion status as a self-governing unit of the British Empire. Canada still celebrates **Dominion Day** (July 1) as a national holiday. In the late 1800's, the Conservative Party controlled the country under Sir John MacDonald's leadership. The one exception was a six-year span in the 1870's when the Liberals managed to gain control of the Canadian Parliament.

Initially, a confederation of four provinces existed: Ontario, Quebec, Nova Scotia, and New Brunswick. British Columbia on the Pacific Coast joined in 1871 and Prince Edward Island in 1873. In 1885, the Canadian Pacific Railway linked the east and west coasts of the nation. A major land purchase (**Rupert's Land**) from the Hudson Bay Company in 1869 added the midwestern territories. Manitoba became a province in 1870. Alberta and Saskatchewan became provinces in 1905.

Newfoundland became Canada's 10th province in 1949. In addition, Canada has two large northern territories, the Yukon Territory and the Northwest Territory.

Canada has a federal system of government with a prime minister as leader. As a member of the British Commonwealth, it also has a Governor-General appointed by the British crown. A lawmaking Parliament, consisting of the Senate and the House of Commons, meets in Ottawa, Ontario, the nation's capital.

Like its neighbor to the north, the United States also has a federal system of government. After the *Treaty of Paris* (1783) recognized independence, the thirteen states grew to fifty states and the District of Columbia. In Washington, D.C., the national government operates under three branches: Executive, Legislative, and Judicial. A constitutional separation of powers gives each branch unique responsibilities. Yet, the *United States Constitution* also allows each branch the power to check the other two (system of checks and balances).

Mexico's present borders are a direct result of losing large amounts of land in its early stages of development. In the northeast, settlers from the United States rebelled in 1836, won a war against Santa Anna, and set up an independent nation – the **Republic of Texas**. In 1845, Texas agreed to annexation as part of the United States. Mexico lost nearly half its territory in a war with the U.S. (1846-48). In the **Gadsden Purchase** (1853), Mexico sold the United States another 30,000 square miles along the southern borders of Arizona and New Mexico for railroad construction.

In the 1850's, Zapotec Indian reformer **Benito Juarez** launched a campaign to aid Mexico's lower classes. His target was land reform and redistribution of the land holdings of the wealthy

Canadian Parliament, Ottawa

PhotoDisc Inc. 1994

and the conservative Catholic Church. His tenure as President saw a new constitution that favored the lower classes. Power struggles delayed the reform program. Conservatives conspired for intervention from European governments. A civil war broke out. From 1864 to 1867, Austrian Archduke **Maximilian** ruled Mexico with French military backing. U.S. protests forced the French to drop the scheme, and Juarez's forces managed to reinstate him.

Juarez died in 1877, and dictatorial rule returned under the caudillo **Porfirio Diaz**. For the next thirty years, Mexico appeared to have peace and prosperity. In reality, living conditions grew worse for most of the workers and peasants. Relations with the United States deteriorated. Border violence erupted in 1916. President Wilson sent U.S. military expedition in pursuit of **Pancho Villa**, a revolutionary leader. Stability and equality eluded Mexico in its first century of independence.

URBAN VERSUS RURAL CHANGE

Transportation improvements in the latter half of the 19th and 20th Centuries led to continual population shifts in Canada, Mexico, and the United States. Modern machinery and advanced farming methods cut farm jobs. People flowed toward large urban centers. Today, all three nations have many large industrialized metropolitan areas. They contain more

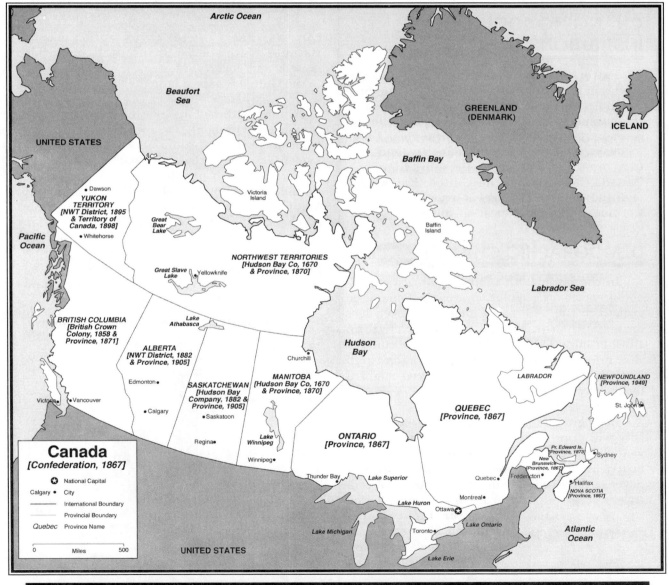

Canada
[Confederation, 1867]

⊗ National Capital
Calgary • City
— International Boundary
— Provincial Boundary
Quebec Province Name

0 — Miles — 500

than 70 percent of each nation's population.

Farmers from poor rural areas migrate to the cities in Mexico by the thousands. There are few jobs available for them. Most migrants live in **los barrios** (slums). They survive on limited government assistance. Wide divisions between the wealthy and the poor are more noticeable in the urban centers. Unrest, disease, crime, congestion, and pollution grow rapidly.

David Johnson, 1993

Poor living conditions are the standard in a barrio in Cuernabaca, Mexico.

CHANGING SOCIAL INSTITUTIONS

Patterns of national change and political evolution have been vastly different in the three North American nations. Social institutions and the pursuit of civil rights have taken different courses. They reflect the powerful roles taken by business, labor, religious, minority, and military organizations. In their short histories, Canada, Mexico, and the United States have endured constant struggles over land, wages, working conditions, education, and equality.

DEMOGRAPHIC CHANGE

In the latter 20th Century, Mexico experienced enormous population growth. Population growth in the U.S. and Canada has been less dramatic than in Mexico, yet each has grown substantially. Demographers attribute much of this growth to immigration in Canada, high birth rates in Mexico, and improved medical technology in both countries.

Demographic projections show that Mexico City will grow to over 23 million people by the year 2000. Mexico's population growth rate of nearly 3% a year is one of the world's highest. Severe overcrowding will continue to be of concern. Guadalajara, a rich agricultural and mining area, and Monterrey, an industrial steel center, are two large Mexican urban

OVERPOPULATION

centers. Each exceeds three million people. Because of its enormous internal population growth and poverty, Mexico's immigration rate to the United States is large.

Canada's three large metropolitan areas are Montreal (Quebec), Toronto (Ontario), and Vancouver (British Columbia). They are cosmopolitan centers that have populations of two to three million people. Seventy percent of Canadians are of British or French ancestry. Yet, Canada has become a nation of immigrants in the 20th Century. Its multiculturalism resembles that of the U.S., including a wide diversity of ethnic and cultural groups. Montreal is the second largest French-speaking city in the world. Vancouver has the second largest Chinese community in North America.

North American Population Growth

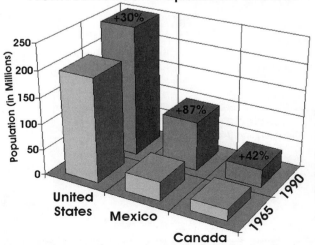

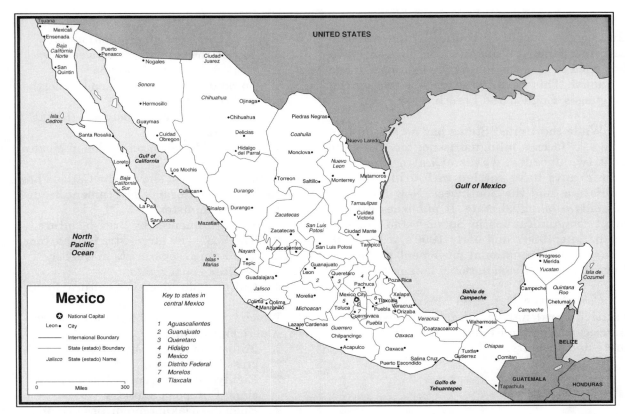

With a population of less than a 1% Amerindians, the United States has become a nation of immigrants. As President John F. Kennedy stated, *"The fact is, the truth is, we all got off the boat."* Of the 60 million people that immigrated to the U.S. between 1820 and 1992, 37.3 million came from Europe, 10.5 million from Latin America, 6.8 million from Asia, 4.2 million from Canada, and 500 thousand from Africa.

The late 20th Century saw an increased rate of immigration from Latin America and the Pacific Rim. In the last thirty years, the number of Mexicans illegally crossing the border reached into the millions. Congress tried to solve the problem in 1986 by toughening penalties for hiring illegal aliens. Yet, failure to fund enforcement actually increased the flow of illegal aliens. **NAFTA** (North American Free Trade Agreement) supporters claim this problem will decline as more factory jobs emerge in Mexico.

OTHER SOCIAL FACTORS

In recent years, the family structure changed more dramatically in Canada and the United States than in Mexico. Canadians and U.S. citizens frequently move from place to place for better jobs, housing, and education. Widespread use of the automobile and an extensive highway system supports this mobility. As a result, families become divided and extended family units are rare. The social function of the family in communicating values diminishes.

In Mexico, life for most of the population still centers on the home and family unit. Extended families influence the social structure. Family pride is very strong. Patrilineal family lines and **machismo** (male dominance) are very strong social forces in Mexico. Mexican women have the right to vote, but their counterparts in Canada and the United States have a greater degree of equality in society and the workplace. Mexico's middle class is gaining strength in the urban industrial areas. It places emphasis on higher education and social justice. As Mexico approaches the 21st Century, the days of the triangular aristocrat-military-Church alliance appear to be declining.

A major challenge to Canadian unity centers on the French-speaking province of Quebec. It is Canada's second largest province with over 7 million people. The **Quebecois** (French-speaking separatists) have used the language issue to preserve their culture. They believe that Quebec should be politically and economically independent. Canada's federal government has tried to ease the tension by making Canada bilingual. This means Canada has two official languages, English and French.

While the United States has no official language, it faces a bilingual issue, too. Over the past two decades, waves of Latin American immigrants have settled in Florida, Texas, California, and the Southwest. New Mexico is officially a bilingual state. It publishes government communications in Spanish and English. In the late 1980's and early 1990's, a backlash occurred with a national movement promoting English as the official national language.

Canada, the U.S., and Mexico are young, multicultural nations. Each of these North American neighbors must address the issue of unity and diversity.

QUESTIONS

1 Canada became an independent nation under the
   1 *Declaration of Independence* (1776)
   2 *Webster-Ashburton Treaty* (1842)
   3 *Treaty of Versailles* (1919)
   4 *Statute of Westminster* (1931)

2 Mexican leader Santa Anna lost much of the country's land in the 19th Century because of
   1 border wars with the United States
   2 poorly negotiated land deals with his Central American neighbors
   3 extensive borrowing from the former colonial ruler, Spain
   4 catering to the peasants with land reform

3 Mexico's caudillos were
   1 democratic reformers
   2 wasteful and corrupt in operating government
   3 powerful champions of Indian and peasant rights
   4 in the forefront of economic advancement

4 Rupert's Land was an acquisition that
   1 settled the boundaries between the United States and Canada
   2 encompassed most of Canada's northern and central regions
   3 resulted from a war between the U.S. and Mexico
   4 provided large encomiendas in Mexico

5 Which reason best shows why Canada has a parliamentary form of government headed by a prime minister?
   1 It was influenced by British culture.
   2 The U.S. is its largest trading partner.
   3 The French separatists in Quebec demand equal rights.
   4 Cultural pluralism is a cultural force.

6 Which is a current problem in the North American Region?
   1 Millions of illegal aliens from the U.S. cross into Canada.
   2 Eighty-three percent of U.S. citizens claim European ancestry.
   3 English-speaking minorities demand representation in Canada's Parliament.
   4 Mexico's annual population growth rate approaches four percent.

7 For a short period in the mid-1800's, Mexico was ruled by a European emperor, Maximilian, in an effort
   1 to reassert Catholic Church control
   2 to strengthen the Juarez regime
   3 by the U.S. to influence Mexican government
   4 by European powers to reinstate a colonial empire

ESSAY

The political structures that emerged in Canada, Mexico, and the U.S. after their independence showed both stability and instability.

a Explain *each* nation's initial framework of government.

b Discuss *two* specific instances of major land acquisition or loss that affected each nation's growth.

PhotoDisc Inc. 1994

and import the mother country's finished products. This control caused a pattern of economic dependence strongly resented by the colonists. Mercantilist policy led to revolutions and independence. Yet, strong European trade continued after each nation attained autonomy.

Industrial development occurred rapidly in the United States in the first half of the 19th Century. Many inventions and power-driven machines led to a factory system of mass manufacturing of goods. Increased production and an improved transportation network made the U.S. the heart of the North American Industrial Revolution. In the last two centuries, Canada and Mexico relied chiefly on the United States as a major trade partner.

Capital from U.S. corporations and private investors stimulated Canadian and Mexican industrial growth in the 20th Century. This created an economic interdependence in the region.

Before 1900, Canada's economic growth stemmed from farming, fishing, lumbering, and mining. The two world wars spurred development of vast natural resources into an industrial-based economy. Today, more than 75% of Canadian exports go to the United States.

Mexico experienced more limited industrial development. Under colonial rule, Spain pre-

IV: ECONOMIC DEVELOPMENT

The North American nations of Canada, Mexico, and the United States comprise one of the world's leading economic regions. Current indicators point to continued economic growth. This is because of its vast natural resources and its regional literacy rate of over 90%. Ever increasing technological development will enable its citizens to maintain above average living standards. Despite recent industrial growth, Mexico is still behind its two northern neighbors. The Mexican economy still relies heavily on its agricultural base.

POWER OF U.S. CAPITAL

Under similar **mercantilist systems**, England, Spain, and France forced their colonies to export raw materials and cash crops

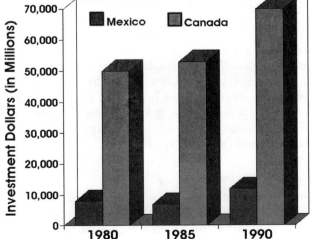

U.S. Investments

Investment Dollars (in Millions)

■ Mexico ■ Canada

70,000 — 60,000 — 50,000 — 40,000 — 30,000 — 20,000 — 10,000 — 0

1980   1985   1990

Source: U.S. Dept. of Commerce, Economics, and Statistics Bureau

Harvesting wheat along the border of North Dakota and Manitoba.

PhotoDisc Inc. 1994

labor force in agricultural production, whereas the United States and Canada have less than 5%. Modern equipment increased agricultural productivity and created large corporate agribusinesses. Mexico is less advanced in this technology. Climate, topographical variations, and availability of irrigation also play a significant role in each nation's agricultural development.

Like their U.S. counterparts, farmers in Canada grow enough food to supply their domestic needs. Both nations export large quantities of food. Canada's harsh climates limit the nation's growing season. Yet, it has rich agricultural resources. The vast prairie provinces of the Canadian Great Plains produce more than half the nation's net farm income from grain (wheat) and livestock production. The fertile southern

vented industry. Spain's mercantilists wanted colonies to buy its manufactured goods. In the late 1800's, U.S. citizens invested in Mexico's infrastructure in an attempt to develop its mining. The investments enabled exportation of minerals but did little to develop Mexican industry. Instead, foreign investment created a form of imperialism. It benefited foreign firms and a few wealthy Mexican families, but most Mexicans remained poor farm peasants.

In 1910, angry Mexicans revolted against long-time leader Porfirio Diaz and his wealthy supporters. After an eleven-year civil war, the new Mexican government developed a **mixed economy**. It helped private firms develop industry in limited areas of the nation. It forbade more than fifty percent foreign ownership in any Mexican company.

In 1938, the government paid off U.S. investors for their wells and refineries and nationalized the oil industry. After World War II, Mexico practiced a policy of **economic nationalism**. It developed its industrial base by offering tax incentives to many foreign investors. Simultaneously, it imposed high tariffs on imports to protect local industries.

AGRICULTURE

Although the North American region produces much of the world's supply of food, there are wide differences in each nation's agricultural labor force. Mexico has almost 30% of its

Typically arid, non-farmland outside of Chihuahua, Mexico

David Johnson, 1993

regions of Ontario and Quebec produce fruits and vegetables. These products support a domestic and an export market. In the eastern and western maritime provinces, potatoes generate significant farm revenue.

Only 10% of Mexico's land is used for agriculture. Much of the soil is too poor and rainfall is minimal. The better farmland is on the southern plateau in the central region. About half the farmers work on **ejidos**. These agricultural collectives were set up by the government under a land reform program in the 1940's. Still, most ejidos barely produce at subsistence level. The government currently encourages commercial farming on large **haciendas**. These plantations and ranches belong to wealthy corporations which produce for export. Modern equipment, irrigation, and a tropical location permit year-round commercial farming on haciendas. The leading export products are coffee, fruits and vegetables, cotton, rice, sugar cane, corn, and sisal (a fiber crop used to make cord and rope). Mexico produces 5% of the world's supply of coffee and 50% of the world's sisal.

Impressive as it is, this exportation of commercial agricultural products creates a problem. Mexico is unable to feed its own population. It must import many basic food products. Corn and beans have always been the staple diet for the poor. To feed the growing population, Mexico imports both food products. There is extensive cattle ranching in the drier northern regions, but it contributes mainly to the upper and middle class diets.

MINERALS AND ENERGY RESOURCES

Mineral and energy resources are other important factors of the economy in the region. A well-developed infrastructure and a worldwide demand for these prod-

Moreau, 1992
Strip mining operation for copper ore – Yukon Territory, Canada.

ucts contribute to the growth of each nation's economy.

Canada has a large supply of mineral and energy resources. It exports many of these because it has much more than its own industries can use. In the 19th Century, mining firms uncovered copper and silver in western and northern Canada. Today, Canada is a world leader in the export of nickel, cobalt, tungsten, potash, zinc, copper, and uranium. Deposits of iron ore and coal in eastern Canada contribute to a growing steel industry in Ontario and Quebec.

PhotoDisc Inc. 1994
Logging operations in Oregon, Northwest United States.

Canada has significant energy reserves. Besides coal, the petrochemical industry shows dramatic growth. Alberta has an abundant supply of crude oil and natural gas. The largest energy resource in Canada is water. Hydroelectric power, a renewable energy resource, is Canada's main source of electrical energy. Canada has over one-third of the world's supply of fresh water. It exports hydroelectric energy to the U.S. Canadian water also irrigates many dry regions in the U.S.

Canada's forests account for over 10% of the world's forest area. They are the nation's most valuable resource. Canada is the world's largest exporter of forest products such as pulp, paper, plywood, and lumber. It is also the world's largest producer of newsprint. The lumber industry contributes more to Canada's positive trade balance than any other industry.

Mexico has diverse mining operations throughout the nation. Mineral exports include gold, lead, zinc, copper, and silver. Mexico is the fifth largest producer of silver in the world. The Monterrey Region supplies much iron and coal used in Mexico's steel industry.

The discovery of large oil deposits in the southern Mexican states of Chiapas and Tabasco in 1974 made Mexico a leading world producer of oil. Mexico enjoyed great prosperity during the world's energy crisis in the mid-1970's. Oil soon accounted for 70% of Mexico's export income. The Mexican government borrowed heavily from foreign nations to strengthen its oil industry. Mexico's economic growth became dependent on the price of oil in the world market. By the early 1980's, the world's supply of oil was greater than the demand. As global oil prices fell, interest rates on Mexico's loans rose. The country went into a debt crisis that plagued it for over a decade.

TOURISM

Tourism is another major revenue source in North America. But, the tourist industry can be very uncertain. A downturn in the global economy, poor weather, natural disasters, and local political unrest can lead to economic problems.

In Canada, tourism accounts for almost 5 % of the Gross Domestic Product. It has an enviable location next to the United States, the world's most affluent travel market. It has scenic, cultural, and ethnic diversity. The developing attractions in its major cities and its historical preservations add to its travel appeal. Canada has an abundance of open space. Its northern territories represent one of the few remaining tourist frontiers for fishing and hunting. Long winters with high snow falls and mountains make Canada a skier's paradise.

PhotoDisc Inc. 1994

Wayne Garnsey, 1993

Tourism is big business in Canada, from the Parliament building in Victoria, British Columbia on the west coast to a quaint fishing village on the rugged eastern coastline of Nova Scotia.

Major resorts in Mexico, such as Cancun, have been built specifically to take advantage of the beautiful weather and waters of the Gulf of Mexico and the Pacific Ocean. The resorts lure hundreds of thousands of American tourists and help Mexico's economy with millions of dollars.

Tourism is also an important part of Mexico's economy. A six billion dollar tourist income ranks eighth in the world. It has a tropical climate and beautiful beaches on the warm waters of the Gulf of Mexico, Caribbean Sea, and Pacific Ocean. Resort hotels dominate the landscape in such locations as Acapulco, Cancun, Cozumel, and Puerta Vallarta. Ancient Mayan and Aztec ruins, plus quaint villages and towns, provide a rich study of Mexico's heritage. High advertising costs and the large number of employees needed in the tourist industry limit profits.

MANUFACTURING AND INDUSTRIAL GROWTH

The North American region is a global leader in manufacturing. Increased industrialization in Canada and Mexico provides critical employment opportunities for each nation's growing population. The United States and Canada have highly developed economies. Both nations rank in the world's top ten nations in terms of GDP (Gross Domestic Product). Much of this can be attributed to vast natural resources and the use of modern technology. Both nations meet their domestic demand and have surpluses for extensive foreign trade.

Strengthened by a large, low-wage labor force, industrial manufacturing in Mexico grew dramatically in the last two decades. High tech, multinational corporations continue to develop Mexico's industries. In the past, state-owned factories were highly inefficient and unprofitable. Private foreign investors bought many of these factories in the 1980's. Declining oil prices, and Mexico's inability to pay large foreign debts to international banks led to this downward trend.

In 1986, the Mexican government dramatically broke from its protectionist policy on manufactured goods. It joined other world nations in **GATT** (General Agreement on Tariffs and Trade). The goal of this U.N.-sponsored treaty group is global free trade. The latest GATT agreement in 1993 enhanced Mexico's global trade.

REGIONAL COOPERATION

The late 1980's witnessed a growth in regional trade agreements. Mexico, Canada, and the United States have been trading partners for years. (See North American Trade 1990 map on page 254).

In 1989, Canada and the United States signed a free trade agreement. When this occurred, Mexico pushed for inclusion in **NAFTA** (North American Free Trade Agreement). This 1993 agreement is being phased in over a 15-year period. It creates the world's largest free trade zone. Extending from the Yukon to the Yucatan, NAFTA links a network of 360 million consumers of the three nations.

NAFTA Partners				
		(figures in U.S. dollars)		**Hourly Wage (Manufacturing)**
Nation	**Population**	**Gross Domestic Product**	**Per Capita GDP**	
Canada	27 million	$521 billion	$21,900	$16.00
Mexico	83 million	$289 billion	$3,400	$1.80
United States	253 million	$5,950 billion	$22,400	$14.75

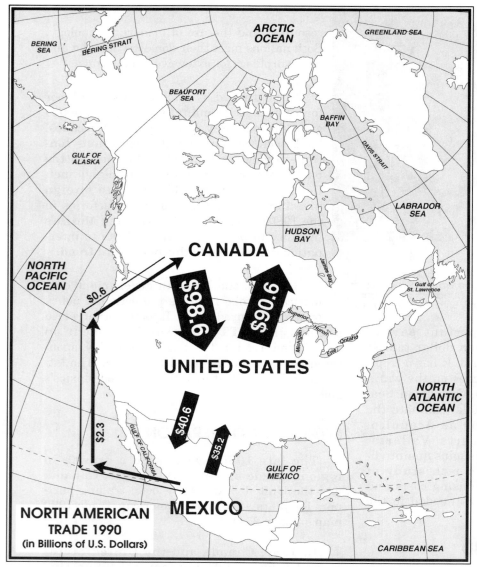

NORTH AMERICAN TRADE 1990
(in Billions of U.S. Dollars)

Critics of NAFTA said passage would:

- lose U.S. manufacturing jobs to low-wage Mexican workers in Maquiladoras (foreign-owned factories on the border)

- increase environmental degradation along the U.S.-Mexico border

- produce unfair competition with fruit and vegetable growers in Mexico, where the growing season is the same, but wages are much lower

In a close vote, NAFTA passed the U.S. Congress in November 1993 and went into effect in 1994. By dismantling regional trade barriers, the nations pursued the liberalized trade agreements within GATT. At the time, Mexican President Carlos Salinas de Gorteri stated, "It is the kind of opportunity that only presents itself once in a generation."

Extensive debate over this free trade plan occurred in the Canadian Parliament, the U.S. Congress, and Mexico's legislature. Fear of losing jobs if manufacturers moved south for cheaper Mexican labor fueled heated debates. Supporters of NAFTA said passage would:

- make North American companies more competitive with Asian rivals by taking advantage of lower wages in Mexico

- open previously closed Mexican markets to automobiles, computers, telecommunications, financial services, etc.

- strengthen Mexico economically by giving Mexicans more money to buy U.S. products and therefore creating more U.S. jobs

MIGRATION

Historically, immigration has been a key factor in the growth of Canadian and U.S. populations. Recently, Mexico witnessed a similar trend with political and economic refugees from its Central American neighbors.

Immigrants often face discrimination and resentment from nativist groups who fear job competition and depressed wages. Debate persists on whether immigrants should adopt the customs and language of their new nation or preserve and honor the culture of their birth.

The United States and Canada are called "nations of immigrants."

PhotoDisc Inc. 1994

The Statue Of Liberty – NYC Harbor – Symbol of Immigration

Traditionally, Americans have debated three views on the immigrant issue:

- **Cultural Pluralism** — to respect and value all cultures, while adjusting to their new nations and allow foreigners to practice bilingualism

- **Melting Pot Theory** — to combine the best elements of all cultures into a gradual blending process

- **Total Assimilation** — to adapt as quickly as possible by learning to speak English and accepting the new culture

The United States has long experienced migration problems along its southern borders. An estimated million people a year illegally cross its borders from Mexico, Central America, and the Caribbean. The U.S. Border Patrol apprehends and deports many illegal aliens. Yet, others find work as migrant farm workers or unskilled laborers in U.S. cities.

In Canada, immigration has been cyclical and directly related to economic conditions. Canada has shown a commitment and compassion for refugees through the acceptance and reunification of their families. Traditionally, Canada's largest immigrant population has come from Great Britain. However, in the past two decades there has been a sharp increase in immigrant diversity. New immigrants now come from Asia, Africa, the Caribbean, Latin America, and the Middle East. Most of these new immigrants settle in three urban centers: Montreal, Toronto, and Vancouver. Canada has an interesting cultural mosaic. Still, the latest census shows more than two-thirds of the population as either British or French in ethnic origin.

Mexico's culture developed from a rich mixture of Spanish and Indian influences. Eighty percent of its people are mestizos, a mix of Spanish and Indian. By U.S. and Canadian standards of living, most rural Mexicans are poor. There is an uneven distribution of wealth in Mexico. Yet, in the last decade, demographers point to a rising middle class in the cities. This trend is a mixed blessing. It attracts migrant labor from Mexico's poorer Central American neighbors. The Mexican government has not encouraged this immigration. The poor compete for the few low wage jobs available. This drives thousands of Mexicans to enter the U.S. illegally in search of employment.

CULTURE

1990's Canadian Immigration

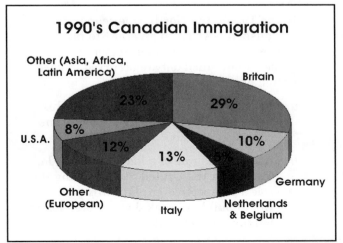

Other (Asia, Africa, Latin America) 23%
Britain 29%
Germany 10%
Netherlands & Belgium 5%
Italy 13%
Other (European) 12%
U.S.A. 8%

QUESTIONS

1 The economic system used by England, France, and Spain in their North American colonies was
   1 laissez-faire
   2 capitalism
   3 mercantilism
   4 socialism

2 Which concept best describes Canadian, Mexican, and U.S. trade relations today?
   1 independence
   2 interdependence
   3 caveat emptor
   4 protectionism

3 In the 20th Century, Canadian and Mexican industrial growth relied heavily on
   1 U.S. corporations and investors
   2 investments from China
   3 their former colonial masters for the technology and funds
   4 their local stock markets for investment

4 Grain is a dominant agricultural product in the Canadian and U.S. economies. In which area is it primarily grown?
   1 the eastern maritime provinces or states
   2 the Great Lakes region
   3 the Great Plains
   4 the Rocky Mountain region

5 Ejidos, large agricultural collectives set up in Mexico, were an effort at land reform but resulted in
   1 great wealth to the middle class
   2 a subsistence level for the farmers
   3 a surplus of food supply for Mexico
   4 a series of small farms for the peasants

6 Each North American nation has major energy resources. Canada's largest renewable energy resource is
   1 oil
   2 coal
   3 hydroelectric power
   4 timber

7 A major revenue source for Canada, Mexico, and the United States is tourism. Yet, it is often undependable because of
   1 unplanned downturns in the economy
   2 poor transportation in the region
   3 lack of information on each nation's key attractions
   4 labor unrest

8 Which is a major reason Mexico is unable to feed its growing population?
   1 overemphasis on mining
   2 too much fertile land to few farmers
   3 commercial farming devoted to export crops
   4 a mass exodus of the rural farm labor force to the cities

9 NAFTA changed Canada, Mexico, and the United States by creating a(an)
   1 union negotiations in each nation
   2 new regional sports competition
   3 new organization to promote the performing arts
   4 large free trade zone

10 While Canada has a diverse culture, more than two-thirds of the population traces its ethnic origins to
   1 United States and Mexico
   2 Great Britain and France
   3 Japan and France
   4 Germany and Great Britain

ESSAY

In the 1990's, the North American nations established NAFTA in an effort to provide economic strength through regional cooperation. Much debate occurred in each nation about its merits.

a Provide *two* reasons in defense of this trade agreement and give two reasons critics opposed it.

b Assume the role of a leader of Canada, Mexico, or the United States. Using the role's perspective, explain why you would build or break down protectionist barriers to free trade.

V. GLOBAL CONTEXT
REGIONALISM GROWS TO GLOBALISM

It is sometimes difficult to see the three major nations of North America comprising a unified region in a global context. North America has such a wide range of political and cultural diversity that policies of each nation have varied. In the nations' early stages, there were isolation and limitations inherited from colonial masters. Later came brief wars and interventions. With the 20th Century came greater cooperation.

The United States is a global superpower both militarily and economically. Despite its comparatively small population, Canada ranks in the world's top ten economic and military powers. Both nations exert powerful forces in the world marketplace.

In the past two decades, Mexico's economy has grown much more rapidly than its Latin American neighbors. Its government policies promoted large-scale industrial development. Previously, Mexico feared the economic power of its northern neighbors. More recently, Mexico intensified its efforts to open its markets to Canadian and American businesses.

INTERNATIONAL AFFILIATIONS

Mexico and the United States are founding members of the **OAS** (Organization of American States). The OAS attempts to settle disputes among the nations of the Western Hemisphere. Although not a permanent member, Canada sends a diplomatic mission to the Washington, D.C.-based organization. The 32 member nations pledge to support peace and justice in North and South America. The OAS provides defense for member nations against outside attack. It also supports economic development in the LDCs of the region.

Canada and the United States were founding members of **NATO** (North Atlantic Treaty Organization) in 1949. Its members agree to collectively support each other in case of outside attack.  Canada is also a member of the **Commonwealth of Nations** based in London. All three of these North American nations were founding members of the United Nations in 1945.

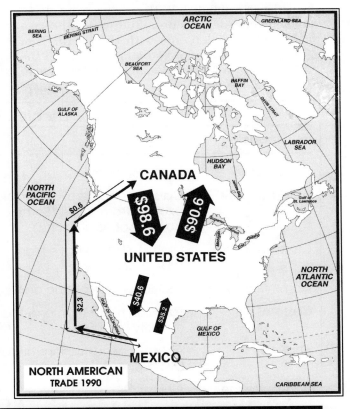

NORTH AMERICAN TRADE 1990

North American Nations

NAFTA

𝔈𝔘

European Union Nations

Pacific Rim Nations

APEC

The Economic Tug-of-war

With the signing of economic treaties, the developed nations of the world have created massive trade alliances. Japan, Australia, Taiwan, and other nations of the Pacific Rim have economically joined into the Asian Pacific Economic Conference (APEC). The former Common Market countries of Western Europe evolved through the European Community (EC) to the newly enlarged European Union. Feeling the international pressure, the United States, Canada, and Mexico formed the North American Free Trade Association (NAFTA).

ECONOMIC INTEGRATION

After World War II, regional economic interdependence expanded. With ever growing global economic interdependence, multinational corporations abounded. Trade with the Pacific Rim nations (notably Japan and other nations of the APEC – Asian Pacific Economic Conference) and the **European Union** (former Common Market or European Community countries) is important to each nation. Under **NAFTA**, Canada, Mexico, and the United States now form the largest free trade alliance in the world. NAFTA integrates the 360 million people of the three nations into a six trillion dollar economic network.

Effects Of NAFTA	
Industry	**Effect**
Agriculture	Duties on farm products phased out over 15-year period.
Automotive	Cars have to be 62% from North American materials and labor to be exempt from tariffs. (Some cars, assembled in North America, have high content of Asian parts.)
Clothing	Clothing has to have high North American textile content. (Some precut fabrics are now only assembled in North American plants.)
Communications	Restrictions on phone and cable companies abolished by 1996.
Customs	Tariffs on more than one-fourth of export products eliminated in 1994, majority by 2000.
Finance	All Mexican restrictions on foreign banks and investment firms eliminated by 2000.
Transportation	All restricted border crossings phased out.

Canadian – U.S. Settlements	
Agreement	**Provisions**
1817 Rush-Bagot Agreement	Each side removed land fortifications and reduced armed ships on Great Lakes. (Full disarmament came in 1871.)
1818 Convention of 1818	Britain and United States agreed to fix boundary from Oregon to Minnesota at the 49° N parallel.
1842 Webster-Ashburton Treaty	Settled Maine, Vermont, New Hampshire, and New York boundaries with New Brunswick, Quebec, and Ontario.
1846 Division of Oregon Territory	Britain and United States agreed to divide the Oregon territory at the 49° parallel.

CANADIAN AND MEXICAN RELATIONS WITH THE U.S.

While Canada is the second largest country (3.8 million square miles) in the world, it has only one-tenth the population of the United States. Two out of three of the 27 million Canadians live within 100 miles (160 km) of the U.S. border.

Similarities abound between the United States and Canada. Most notable are a common English language (with the exception of French-speaking Quebec) and the abundant multicultural heritage. Peaceful relations have existed since the War of 1812. Canada and the United States have the longest unfortified border in the world (much of it along 49° N Latitude). Yet, they came after military struggles of the American Revolution, and the War of 1812.

Since the above agreements, the United States and Canada have cooperated on many programs. Notable was the **St. Lawrence Seaway** that promoted interdependent shipping trade on a channel connecting the Great Lakes with the Atlantic Ocean. Major trade agreements in the 1980's and the recent NAFTA link Canada's future with those of the United States and Mexico.

Canada and the U.S. shared a similar cultural heritage, but Mexico and the U.S. had many different political, linguistic, and theological colonial backgrounds. In the early 1800's, Mexico greatly admired the democratic government of the United States. Independence leaders enjoyed the encouragement from their northern neighbors. In 1823, U.S. President James Monroe delivered a policy address to Congress (later called the Monroe Doctrine). It boldly warned European powers not to reestablish their former colonies. Monroe cautioned them not to seek any further involvement in the Western Hemisphere. The policy was welcomed by Mexicans trying to maintain their independence from Spain.

In the 19th Century, the United States pushed its boundaries westward under an expansionist policy (Manifest Destiny). This policy strained U.S.–Mexican relations. The U.S.–Mexican War of 1846-48 left Mexicans with bad feelings and distrust toward the United States. By the end of the 19th Century, Mexicans lost more than half their land to United States expansion.

The United States continued interventionist policies at the beginning of the 20th Century. In 1916, President Wilson sent a U.S. military force to stop border raids by revolutionary leader Pancho Villa. The unsuccessful expedition clashed with Mexican government troops. Mexico and its neighbors regarded Wilson's policies as "moral imperialism." Wilson even forced an arms embargo, and the American navy captured the Mexican port of Vera Cruz during the Mexican Civil War.

Relations between Mexico and the United States were strained again in 1938. The Mexican government seized and nationalized all foreign-owned oil facilities. American oil companies received compensation in 1941.

Mexican – U.S. Settlements	
Agreement	**Provisions**
1835-1836 Texas War of Independence	Lone Star Republic formed under Governor Sam Houston. Texas annexed to the U.S. in 1845.
1846-48 Mexican – American War	Treaty of Guadalupe Hidalgo (1848). U.S. gained more than a half million square miles from Texas to California. Mexico given $ 15 million.
1853 Gadsden Purchase	U.S. purchased a strip of desert land in southern Arizona from Mexico for $10 million.
1967 Rio Grande Treaty	U.S. ceded El Chamizal Territory to Mexico. (437 acres of land was caused by the Rio Grande River changing its course.)

Under the spirit of NAFTA, a chance looms for the two countries to resolve old problems. These include energy prices, smuggling, and the influx of illegal aliens into the United States. Mexico's economy is only 5% that of the U.S., but NAFTA can accelerate major changes in Mexican business practices.

Mexicans came to resent the Monroe Doctrine. The expansion of U.S. business led to problems. Under an extension of doctrine, the U.S. often sent its forces to protect businesses. This intervention irritated Mexicans. They felt that the U.S. was attempting to become the new imperial master of the Western Hemisphere. To them, the United States was seen as the "Colossus of the North." Mexican poet Octavio Paz said, "Their shadow covers the whole hemisphere. It is the shadow of a giant."

Wal-Mart, Blockbuster Video, and many other U.S. franchises have outlets in every major Mexican city. As Mexican economist Carlos Poza recently stated, "Stores are coming that draw attention by giving special offers. That hasn't been done here, where the problem has been keeping the shelves stocked." Traditionally, Mexican businesses have operated on low volume / high profit sales. U.S. franchises work the opposite way. The Mexican consumer should benefit from lower prices.

CANADIAN AND MEXICAN CULTURAL CONTRIBUTIONS

Beyond their global and hemispheric economic and political connections, Canada and Mexico have contributed much to world culture.

Both have blended Amerindian and European cultural heritages from the days of colonization to the modern era. Their contributions are many.

CANADA'S CULTURAL CONTRIBUTIONS

- **Music, Theater, Dance** – The Canadian Council, an independent agency created and funded by the Canadian Parliament since 1957, actively supports theater, ballet troupes, opera, and symphonies. Toronto and Montreal have world-renowned centers for the performing arts. Two recording artists of world fame are Anne Murray and Gordon Lightfoot. The Canadian National Film Board produces and distributes world-class award-winning films.

- **Literature** – A unique Canadian literary heritage has been promoted by such authors as Lucy Maud Montgomery (*Anne of Green Gables*), Marshall McLuhan (*The Medium is the Message and Global Village Surveys*), and Margaret Atwood (*The Handmaiden's Tale*). The multicultural anthology, *Tales Told in Canada* (Edith Fowke, Ed.), reflects Canada's cultural pluralism and the experiences in both urban and frontier environments.

- **Art** – Wood, stone, and ivory carvings of the Inuit are prized by art collectors from around the world. The Group of Seven, a famous school of Canadian painters in the 1920's, captured the uniqueness of the Canadian wilderness with their paintings.

- **Sports**. A vast national parks system promotes hiking, skiing, fishing, and hunting, but Canada's national sport is ice hockey. (In Canada, it is often said that children can skate before they can walk.) Professional ice hockey teams, such as the Montreal *Canadiens*, have dominated the professional National Hockey League for years. Recently, professional baseball in domed stadiums has captured the hearts of Canadians in summer. The Toronto *Blue Jays* have succeeded in bringing the World Series championships to Canada.

MEXICO'S CULTURAL CONTRIBUTIONS

- **Art** – The best known works of Mexican artists are huge and powerful murals with bright dazzling colors. Artists Diego Rivera, José Clemente Orozco, and David Alfaro Siqueiros, are known as the "Big Three." Each artist's murals adorn the walls of many public buildings in the U.S. and Mexico. Their paintings tell the story of Mexican history from the enslavement of the Indians by the Spanish to the struggles of the modern working class. Frida Kahlo (wife of Diego Rivera) was a leading female artist. Her many paintings depict Mexican culture and the hardships of human survival. Juan O'Gorman created numerous architectural settings and designed Mexico City's impressive central library. Illustrator Jose Guadalupe Posada achieved wide popularity with his cartoon caricatures of Mexico's contemporary leaders and his satiric views of the trials of everyday life.

- **Literature** – Mexicans appreciate writers who address political and social issues. Rosario Castellanos' writings tell of the clash of cultures between the Europeans and the Indians. In the classic novel, *Pedro Parano*, Juan Rulfo described the wide gulf between the rich and poor. Octavio Paz and Carlos Fuentes wrote social commentaries that pertain to the despair and complexities of urban life.

- **Metalwork**, **Pottery**, **and Weaving** – Mexico's skilled crafts workers produce exquisite silver and jade jewelry and colorful pottery with elaborate designs. Native American woven patterns are prominent in plain, patterned, and looped pile tapestries.

- **Music and Dance** – The music of Mexico blends brass, string, and percussion instruments with a rhythmic folk composition of European and Indian culture. Concerts, operas, and symphony orchestras are common in Mexico's large cities. Composers Carlos Chavez and Silvestre Revueltas have international reputations. The Mexican Hat Dance is famous throughout the world.

- **Sports** – The dominant athletic activities in Mexico are *futbol* (soccer), *beisbol* (baseball), bullfighting, and track and field. Mexico City was host to the Summer Olympic Games in 1968.

Cultural activities in Canada and Mexico serve to blend the diversity of social traditions. These traditions have served to bind together the populace of each nation.

QUESTIONS

1   In the last half of the 20th Century, Canada, the United States, and Mexico attribute their economic growth rate to
1   dependency on cash crop farming
2   colonizing areas in Africa and Asia
3   large-scale industrial development
4   deforestation of their vast forests

2   The OAS (Organization of American States) tries to
1   determine the price of oil on the world market
2   mediate disputes amongst member nations in the Western Hemisphere
3   set the rules of international athletic competition
4   establish a quota system on immigration into the region

3   Economic integration throughout the region is evident from the influx of multinational corporations from
1   the Pacific Rim and European communities
2   Middle Eastern and African corporations
3   Russia and China
4   South Africa and Eastern Europe

4   "El Norte" and "Colossus of the North" are terms used by Mexicans who
1   adopt a new musical appreciation of their Canadian and U.S. neighbors
2   suspect new U.S. intervention and neocolonialism in their nation
3   despise the economic power of multi-national corporations
4   support the athletic excellence of their neighbors

5   The St. Lawrence Seaway is symbolic of
1   a U.N. sponsored peace agreement
2   North American interdependence
3   the history of stormy U.S. – Canadian relations
4   American ethnocentrism

6   Which shows why the 49th parallel is significant in both Canadian and U.S. historical development?
1   It eventually served as the land boundary between the two nations.
2   The area had many battles between the two nations.
3   Huge deposits of oil were found there.
4   The main metropolitan centers of each nation developed there.

7   Which U.S. policy strained relations with both Canada and Mexico during the 19th Century?
1   Laissez-faire
2   Isolationism
3   Moral Imperialism
4   Manifest Destiny

8   Which created major friction between Mexico and the United States in the last half of the 20th Century?
1   the influx of illegal Mexican aliens into the United States
2   the heavy shipping of goods on the Rio Grande River
3   the sales of U.S. automobiles in Mexico
4   the U.S. refusal to promote the Mexican tourist industry

9   Canadian and Mexican Native American tribal groups share a similar cultural contribution of
1   religious philosophy
2   craft work of skilled artisans depicting their past heritage
3   opera
4   the sport of ice hockey

10 Which is a powerful media for Mexican history?
1   rhythmic folk music
2   huge, colorful wall murals
3   competitiveness of various athletic events
4   metalwork, pottery, and weaving

ESSAYS

1   Compare and contrast two of the following cultural contributions from Canada and Mexico. Where appropriate, cite specific artists and/or performers.

- Artwork
- Literature
- Music
- Sports

2   Canada and Mexico have had differing foreign relations with their neighbor, the United States. At times, the relations have been cooperative and at other times, strained.

Describe how *three* of the following events affected the course of modern history.

- Rush-Bagot Agreement (1817)
- Texas War of Independence (1836)
- Division of Oregon Territory (1846)
- Mexican-American War (1846-1848)
- Gadsden Purchase (1853)
- NAFTA (1993)

UNIT SIX: NORTH AMERICA ASSESSMENT

ISSUE: THE IMPACT OF WORLD ISSUES ON A REGION

This assessment offers individual research writing opportunity.

STUDENT TASK

Write a summary-analysis of an article from a current periodical that reflects on a contemporary issue and its impact on the lives of people in North America.

DETAILED PROCEDURES

Part One:
Explore current periodicals (*Time*, *U.S. News*, *Washington Post Weekly*, *Scholastic Update*, *MacLeans*, etc.) for articles on a major world issue and how it affects this region. (Emphasis will be on articles about Canada and Mexico. Where relevant, it should include the relationship with the United States.)

Part Two:
Select one article. Have it photocopied to make your personal research easier and more accurate. Read, highlight, and outline it. (Include article, outline, summary, and bibliography with final assessment.)

Part Three:
Write a brief summary and critical analysis. (Length determined by instructor.)

Part Four (optional):
Summaries may be presented orally for extra credit.

EVALUATION

The scoring grid next to the evaluation items (on the following pages) was left blank intentionally. Choice of appropriate category terms is the decision of the instructor. Selection of terms such as "minimal," "satisfactory," and "distinguished" can vary with this assessment. The table on page 10 offers additional suggestions for scoring descriptors that might be inserted in the blank grids.

LEARNING STANDARDS

Students should:

- Present ideas both in writing and orally in clear, concise, and properly accepted fashion.

- Understand that different national, ethnic, religious, racial, socioeconomic, and gender groups have varied perspectives on the same events and issues.

- Analyze and evaluate differing views of historic, social, cultural, economic, and political events, eras, ideas, and issues.

- Understand that interdependence requires personal and collective responsibility for the local and global environment.

- Monitor, reflect upon, and improve their work.

Parts Two & Three: Periodical Article Summary

Table on page 10 offers suggestions for scoring descriptors.

Evaluation Item a Does student's outline reflect article's ideas?	Category 1	Category 2	Category 3	Category 4	Category 5
Evaluation Item b Does student communicate information clearly?	Category 1	Category 2	Category 3	Category 4	Category 5
Evaluation Item c Does student clearly identify and analyze the author's purpose, degree to which purpose is accomplished?	Category 1	Category 2	Category 3	Category 4	Category 5
Evaluation Item d Does student identify global concepts and world issues involved?	Category 1	Category 2	Category 3	Category 4	Category 5
Evaluation Item e Does student display an understanding of the impact on global culture?	Category 1	Category 2	Category 3	Category 4	Category 5
Evaluation Item f Does student summary list sources in the proper form?	Category 1	Category 2	Category 3	Category 4	Category 5

ADMINISTRATIVE GUIDELINES

1 Start with list of key global concepts and world issues in front of this book.

2 Survey library resources. Discuss project with librarian and reserve library time for student research.

3 Give guidance on handling photocopies (highlighting, outlining, note taking) and organizing and formatting summaries, and bibliographies.

4 *Option for extra credit*: Select four of the most enlightening summaries to be presented by the students to the class as part of a review prior to the unit examination.

7

Middle East

4000   **BC** | **AD**   600   1400

- Sumerians   • Hebrews   • Byzantine Empire   • Islamic Empire
     • Egyptian Civilization   • Christianity Begins   • Ottoman Empire

Time-line is not drawn to scale.

Jihad
OPEC
Zionism
terrorism
Monotheism

Islamic fundamentalism
cradles of civilization
Arab socialism

1900   1950   2000

• European Mandates   • Suez Crisis • OPEC   • Iran Revolution

• World War II   • Six–day War   Persian Gulf War •

• Israel   • Camp David Accords

Time-line is not drawn to scale.

UNIT SEVEN:
MIDDLE
EAST

Global civilization owes much to Middle East culture. The region's strategic location in the world makes it a crossroads for the three continents of the Eastern Hemisphere. Like Europe, the region has always been a center of struggles among competing power groups. Many physical, historic, social, and economic forces intermix in the diversity of cultures, and it is important to understand these complex relationships.

I. PHYSICAL AND HISTORICAL SETTING

GEOGRAPHY AND RESOURCES

PHYSICAL FEATURES

Many Westerners view the Middle East as one big desert, but the region has great geographic diversity. It encompasses approximately six million square miles and is twice the size of the United States. It extends from Morocco on the Atlantic Coast of Africa to Afghanistan in Asia. Its unique physical diversity includes:

- **The Sahara Desert** – This region has the world's largest desert which covers an area of 3.5 million square miles in Northern Africa. **Sahara** comes from the Arabic word meaning "emptiness." Yet, only a third of the Sahara is shifting sand dunes. Much of the desert is rocky plateaus and barren plains strewn with pebbles and boulders. The common feature throughout this region is a lack of water. Only a few fertile **oases** (regions where underground water is close to the surface) exist.

- **The Nile River Basin** – Egypt has often been called the "Gift of the Nile." The Nile annually provides Egypt with rich **alluvial soil** and irrigates the four percent of Egypt not claimed by the desert. Along its banks is one of the world's oldest and most fertile agricultural regions. Egyptian civilization could not have existed without the Nile's rich deposits of silt and irrigation.

- **The Arabian Peninsula** – This area has mountain ranges in the west along the Red Sea and a huge desert called the **Rub al Khali** ("empty quarter") in its large interior plateau. Only in the extreme south where monsoons water the region and in the Oasis of the north is the land suitable for cultivation.

- **The Northern Tier** – The **Anatolia Plateau** of Turkey and high plateaus and mountain regions of Iran and Afghanistan are found in this region. Turkey is in a strategic location. It controls the important waterways linking the Black Sea and the Mediterranean Sea. This area has long been

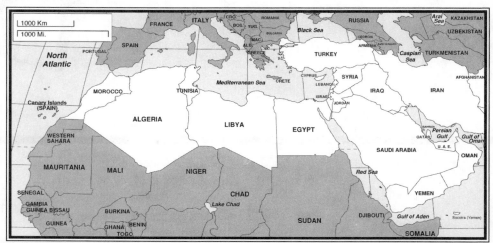

coveted by the Russians who have wanted and needed warm water ports.

- **The Levant** – This rich plateau bordering the Mediterranean Sea is the major agricultural region of Syria, Lebanon, and Israel.

- **The Fertile Crescent** – Some of the best-growing soil of the region is found here, and much of it is irrigated by the Tigris, Euphrates, and Jordan Rivers. This is a region of valleys and plateaus with rich alluvial soil. The Fertile Crescent was home to numerous civilizations such as the Sumerians and Babylonians (see map on page 273).

CLIMATE AND NATURAL RESOURCES

Koppen's **"B" Type** climates (dry hot summers and warm winters) characterize the region. Some areas such as Turkey and Iran have extremes in temperatures, cold winters, and snow in the mountain regions. In the Levant on the Mediterranean Coast, there is abundant rainfall (as high as 40 inches (102 cm) annually) with cool, pleasant spring weather (Cf).

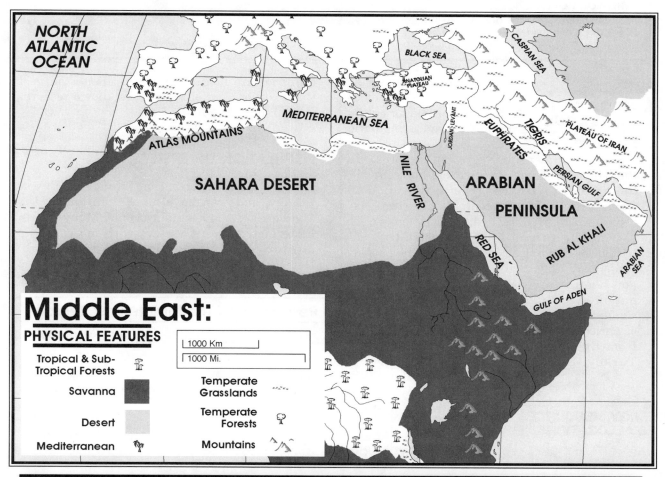

Middle East:
PHYSICAL FEATURES

Tropical & Sub-Tropical Forests	Temperate Grasslands
Savanna	Temperate Forests
Desert	Mountains
Mediterranean	

1000 Km
1000 Mi.

NORTH ATLANTIC OCEAN

BLACK SEA

CASPIAN SEA

ANATOLIAN PLATEAU

MEDITERRANEAN SEA

ATLAS MOUNTAINS

JORDAN-LEVANT

EUPHRATES

TIGRIS

PLATEAU OF IRAN

PERSIAN GULF

SAHARA DESERT

NILE RIVER

ARABIAN PENINSULA

RED SEA

RUB AL KHALI

ARABIAN SEA

GULF OF ADEN

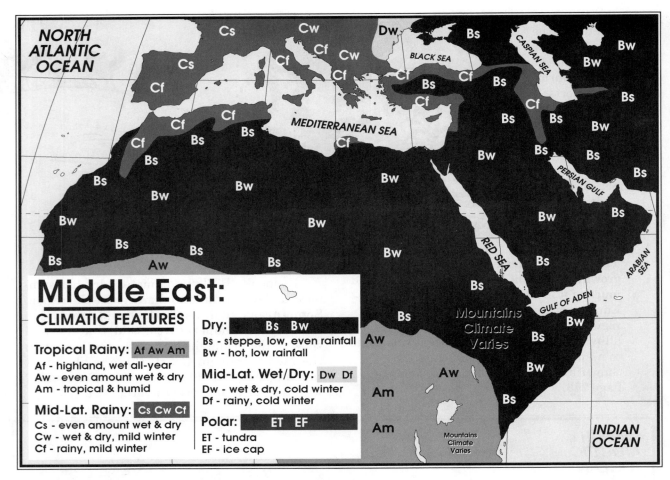

Middle East:
CLIMATIC FEATURES

Tropical Rainy: Af Aw Am
Af - highland, wet all-year
Aw - even amount wet & dry
Am - tropical & humid

Mid-Lat. Rainy: Cs Cw Cf
Cs - even amount wet & dry
Cw - wet & dry, mild winter
Cf - rainy, mild winter

Dry: Bs Bw
Bs - steppe, low, even rainfall
Bw - hot, low rainfall

Mid-Lat. Wet/Dry: Dw Df
Dw - wet & dry, cold winter
Df - rainy, cold winter

Polar: ET EF
ET - tundra
EF - ice cap

ENVIRONMENTAL CONCERNS

Water resources are limited. Only 15% of the land is suitable for cultivation. The main population dwells along the three major river systems in Egypt and Iraq: the **Nile**, the **Tigris**, and the **Euphrates**. For centuries, these waterways have provided irrigation and transportation. More recently, these rivers have been used to produce hydroelectric power. The **Aswan High Dam** in Egypt created both electric power and irrigation control for the people of the Nile Valley. Still, subsistence agriculture and herding are common, and every nation except Turkey has to import significant amounts of food. A variety of agricultural exports include cotton from Egypt and Iraq; tobacco from Turkey, Lebanon, and Syria; and dates (75% of the world's supply) from Iraq.

ENERGY: RESOURCES & ALLOCATIONS

While lacking water, some countries are floating on oil. Estimates suggest that sixty percent of the world's known reserves are found in the Middle East.

POPULATION DIVERSITY

Population distribution is uneven. Egypt, Turkey, and Iran have more than half of the Middle East's 240 million people. Many live in large metropolitan centers with more than a million people such as Baghdad, Cairo, Damascus, Teheran, and Tel Aviv. Rural inhabitants constitute less than 2% of the population.

Mineral Resources Of The Middle East Region	
Nation	**Mineral Resources**
Turkey	Coal, Iron Ore, Chrome, & Copper
Israel	Phosphates
Iran	Iron Ore, Coal
Saudi Arabia	Gold
Egypt	Coal
Morocco	Phosphates
Algeria	Natural Gas

Today, only a few follow nomadic lives. These are the people of the dry plateau regions who follow seasonal migration for water and pastures.

The population has a wide mixture of races, nationalities, religions, and language groups. **Semites** are the largest language group, primarily made up of Arab, Assyrian, and Hebrew peoples. Two other large groups are **Iranians** and **Turks**.

Trade has always been an important vehicle for cultural diffusion. Its effects are most visible in the population centers in the Nile, Tigris, and Euphrates River Valleys. Since the dawn of civilization, these areas have been centers of great cultural achievement. Today, two of the largest metropolitan areas of the Middle East are found at Cairo, Egypt and Baghdad, Iraq.

EARLY CIVILIZATIONS

CITIES AND TRADE

Beginning in 6000 B.C., the culture of the **Neolithic Age** was centered on agricultural pursuits. Technological developments, from stone hunting weapons to farming implements, led to small communities cultivating crops and domesticating animals. The two earliest centers of civilization were the Egyptian and the Sumerian. Both began approximately 4000 B.C.

Trade and commerce developed early in the region because of the scarcity of resources. Commercial enterprise also led to the emergence of a third settlement area along the eastern Mediterranean Coast extending from Turkey south to Palestine. The Phoenicians dominated the area headquartered in what is modern-day Lebanon.

Artifacts Showing The Magnificence Of Egyptian Civilization

Upper Left: Abu Simbel, Ramses Temple.
Upper Right: Sphinx
Lower Right: Great Pyramid of Cheops, Egypt

EMERGENCE OF WRITING SYSTEMS

Knowledge of these three areas of civilization is extensive. This is because each society developed a different system of writing.

- **Sumerians** developed **cuneiform**. It used a wedge-shaped implement to carve designs in clay tablets. More than 350 designs represented syllables, sounds, persons, places, and things.

- **Egyptians** developed **hieroglyphics**. It entailed an elaborate system of picture writing to suggest ideas, objects, syllables, or words.

- **Phoenicians** developed **phonetics**. This was an alphabet code in which each letter stood for only one distinct sound.

Recording information on trade, government, and religion allowed ideas to be transmitted to other regions. More importantly, their languages provided a historical legacy. Furthermore, the invention of writing made more complex civilizations and technology possible. Many of the ancient languages have been difficult to translate. One of the greatest breakthroughs occurred in the early 1800's. **Jean Francois Champollion**, a French scholar traveling with Napoleon's army, deciphered Egyptian hieroglyphics on the **Rosetta Stone**.

CONTRIBUTIONS OF THE EARLY EMPIRES

The chart of Early Middle East Empires shows that numerous peoples shaped the early history and unique identity of the region. The groups in the region of the Tigris-Euphrates River Valley were often overcome by the advanced technology of a neighboring civilization. Conquered people were placed into slavery to build new empires. As civilizations spread, diversity increased. Political codes of law reflected successively more complex societies.

HEBREWS OF ANCIENT ISRAEL

A close examination of the region's first major religion, **Judaism**, demonstrates that

Early Middle Eastern Empires And Their Contributions

People	Area	Contributions
Sumerians	Southern Iraq	Political City-State; Formalized religion with a 7 story temple called a Ziggurat; Cultural Center at Ur; Writing - Cuneiform; Developed the wheel, a numbers system based on 60, and geometrics
Egyptians	Nile R., Egypt	Political kingdoms dominated by the Pharaohs (kings); Religion based on many gods, immortality, and mummification to protect the soul; Huge tombs called pyramids built to preserve honored Pharaohs; Cultural centers – Memphis and Thebes; Writing - hieroglyphics; Skilled engineers demonstrated knowledge of algebra and geometry in architectural art forms
Babylonians	Tigris/Euphrates R., Mesopotamia	King Hammurabi's Code of Laws (an "eye for an eye"); Central City - Babylon: famous Hanging Gardens at Babylon - one of the 7 wonders of the ancient world
Hebrews	Palestine	Monotheism - The belief in one God; The Old Testament - written book of scriptural teachings
Lydians	Western Turkey	Coined money used in place of bartering
Phoenicians	Lebanon	A maritime empire; Commercial center was Tyre; Extensive use of purple dye - indigo; Phonetic alphabet
Persians	Iran	Conquered and united Fertile Crescent

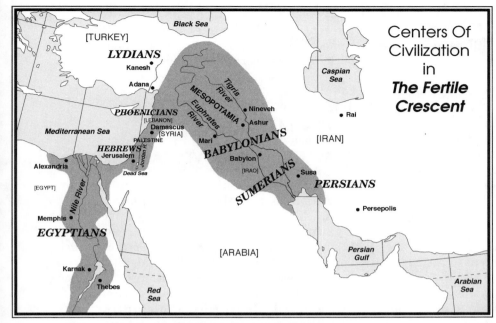

Centers Of Civilization in *The Fertile Crescent*

later years, these teachings greatly influenced both Christianity and Islam.

Judaic ideas included belief in the compassion of God, the *Torah* (first five books of the Old Testament), the *Ten Commandments*, and the dignity of the individual.

However, the Hebrew kingdom was destroyed by the Roman Empire in 70 A.D. This date signaled the beginning of the **Diaspora**, or great dispersion of the Jews from Palestine to all areas of the world.

values play a major role in shaping the character and identity of a culture.

Palestine, on the Eastern Mediterranean coast, became the site of the Hebrew kingdom of Israel about 1400 B.C. It was both a culture and a nation. In its rejection of polytheism, Judaism insisted upon the belief in one God, social justice, and moral law. This distinguished it from the religions of the other ancient Middle Eastern cultures.

The Hebrews called their God *Yahweh*, and believed that this supreme being created the human race and the entire universe. Their religious literature, especially the *Old Testament* of *The Bible*, contained the teachings and laws required for the moral behavior of the Jews. In

To keep their traditions alive in new surroundings, the Jews relied on **rabbis** (religious teachers) to interpret Judaic law and make decisions for the new situations. Rabbinical decisions were written in a multivolume text  called the *Talmud*. It became a repository of Judaic knowledge and ethics. This law established an identity for Jews of the world. Though scattered throughout the world, the Talmud maintained their culture for almost 2,000 years. Although the Jews were without a nation of their own, many remained in the Middle East and eventually established the independent nation of Israel (1948).

THE GROWTH OF CHRISTIANITY

During Roman rule in Palestine, a new religion emerged based on the teachings of a Jew named **Jesus Christ**. Nearly 2,000 years ago, Jesus preached about the way God wanted people to act toward each other. He was crucified by the Romans for his teachings. Much of what is known of his life and teachings can be found in the first four books of the *New Testament* of *The Bible* (the Gospels of Matthew, Mark, Luke, and John). Christianity's basic principles include the beliefs that there is only one God and Jesus Christ is the Son of God and a person of the Holy Trinity. Christians followed Jesus' teachings to love God, promote brotherhood,

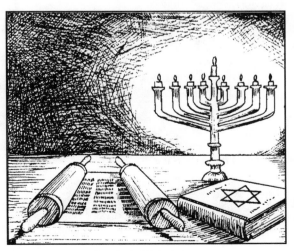

Symbols Of Judaism

acknowledge divine judgment of one's actions on Earth, and accept Christ's death as atonement for sins.

Christianity spread rapidly along the trade routes of the Roman Empire. Many followers were attracted to its teachings by special messengers called apostles and disciples. The universal appeal of the Christian ethic and the promise of salvation was partially a blend of Judaic and Greek philosophy. By the 3rd Century, Christian communities spread from Palestine to Syria, Turkey, Egypt, Greece, and even Rome itself. Initially, Roman authorities persecuted and killed Christians because they worried about the religion's threat to their rule.

In the 4th Century, Christianity's popularity grew even greater among the educated and upper classes. When the Roman Emperor Constantine the Great issued the *Edict of Milan* in 313 A.D., he granted freedom of worship to all Christians. By the end of the century, Christianity became the established religion of the Roman Empire, and worship of all other deities was declared illegal. Over the centuries, the **Judeo-Christian Ethic** continued to shape the values, ideals, and culture of the western world.

THE BYZANTINE EMPIRE (395 - 1453 A.D.)

ROMAN EMPIRE MOVES EASTWARD

Prior to Constantine's rule, his predecessor, Diocletian, divided the Roman Empire into two parts. The Eastern part was centered at **Byzantium** and consisted of Greece, Asia Minor, and the Middle Eastern territory which bordered the eastern end of the Mediterranean Sea. The western part of the Empire remained centered at Rome but declined during the 4th and 5th Centuries. Constantine gave Byzantium the new name of **Constantinople**. As the Byzantine Emperors pushed the Eastern Roman Empire eastward, it became vastly different in culture and language.

In the Byzantine Empire, the emperor presided over church and state and was regarded as God's agent on Earth. Byzantine culture combined **Hellenistic** (Greek/Balkan) and

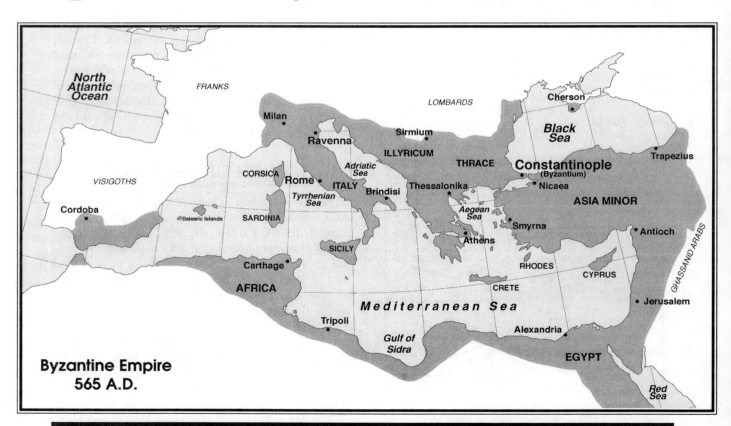

Byzantine Empire
565 A.D.

Hagia Sophia, Constantinople

other Eastern Mediterranean cultures. Christians adopted differing practices in their **Eastern Orthodox Church** from the Roman Church. A formal split between the two churches finally occurred 500 years later. Yet, Christianity continued to experience growth in both regions. While Western Europe fragmented into small feudal units, the political system of Byzantium and the church-state relationships created a model for future power relationships in Russia and the Middle East. Constantinople became the crossroads of global trade and culture.

RULE OF JUSTINIAN I AND THEODORA

The Byzantine Empire reached its peak during the late 5th and early 6th Centuries. Under the rule of **Justinian I** and his wife **Theodora**, great attention centered on Byzantine law, religion, and art. Justinian constructed **Hagia Sophia** ("Holy Wisdom"), the largest and most beautiful church in the Byzantine Empire. It is considered one of the world's architectural wonders. The *Justinian Code* became a written collection of civil law preserving the Roman legal heritage. It was Justinian's great accomplishment. It became a legacy to the judicial systems of Western Europe and Latin America and had great influence on the concept of human rights.

After Justinian's death in 565 A.D., the Byzantine Empire suffered invasions from Eastern Europe, Persia, and the Arab World. These invasions changed the political and cultural institutions of both the conquered and the invader. They left the Byzantine Empire with territories that were primarily Greek and with a diminished international influence.

Although the economy of the Byzantine Empire never recovered, the Eastern Orthodox Church had missionary successes. Most notable was the dispersing of Orthodox Christianity and Byzantine culture into the **Slavic** core-land of Russia, Ukraine, and Eastern Europe. This was accomplished by the use of the Cyrillic alphabet, a modified form of the Greek alphabet. Legend credits two Byzantine missionaries, **Cyril** and **Methodius**, with introducing it to the Slavs. Many Slavs were then converted to the Eastern Orthodox Church.

THE OTTOMAN CONQUEST

By 1453, the Byzantine Empire declined to a point that the Ottoman Turkish Sultan laid siege to **Constantinople**. Shortly after, the Sultan victoriously entered the city. The Byzantine Empire had lasted over 1,000 years. The **Ottoman Turks** followed Islam. When they made Constantinople their new capital, they converted the famous Hagia Sophia into a **mosque** (an Islamic house of worship). The new leaders permitted religious freedom for the Orthodox Christians in Greece and in Eastern Europe but installed a new Patriarch to supervise their religious and political life.

In reviewing the physical and early historical setting of the Middle East, it is evident that the region has a geographic diversity. Its vast heritage is traced through the rise and fall of numerous empires. Beliefs and value systems evolved through the cultural diffusion of many philosophies and cultures. Many of these are incorporated into the cultural patterns of the Western world.

QUESTIONS

1 The land area of the Middle East is
  1 twice the size of the United States
  2 four times the size of the United States
  3 about the same size Russia
  4 twice the size of Africa

2 The Nile River Basin has been a home to civilization since early times because of its
  1 wealth of minerals
  2 rich alluvial soil
  3 temperate climate
  4 access to Africa's interior

3 Because of the Rub al Khali in the Saudi Arabian Peninsula,
  1 settlement has remained along the coast
  2 the country is the major agricultural producer in the region
  3 the people are the most isolated in the world
  4 constant flooding makes permanent settlement difficult

4 Which of the following indicates the importance of cultural diffusion in the Middle East?
  1 the Judaic-Christian tradition
  2 the dominance of polytheism
  3 a single common language for all the diverse people
  4 peace and harmony with little warfare

5 An oasis is a
  1 large oil well
  2 fertile region within a desert
  3 the mouth of a large river
  4 religious shrine

6 Judaism was significantly different from that of civilizations that preceded it because
  1 the religion's prophets became their ruling council
  2 it required worship of a sacred stone called the Rosetta
  3 it rejected polytheism
  4 the central belief was in a three-person divinity

7 The largest ethnic group in the Middle East is called
  1 Bedouin
  2 Arab
  3 Semite
  4 Byzantine

8 The Sumerians' cuneiform was
  1 one of the earliest forms of writing known on Earth
  2 a seven-story temple
  3 a form of government
  4 an ingenious irrigation system

9 Talmudic law held significance for the Hebrew people because it created
  1 an identity and cultural basis despite a 2,000-year dispersal
  2 a major reason for persecution of their culture
  3 a rigid social class structure
  4 the first written code of law in history

10 The *Justinian Code* is significant because it was
  1 an effort to make Roman architecture uniform in design
  2 the first attempt of a civilization to keep laws secret
  3 an attempt to preserve the Roman legal heritage
  4 a collection of the military strategies that built the Roman Empire

ESSAYS

Geographic factors often determine the founding and development of civilizations.

Civilizations

- Egyptians
- Sumerians
- Hebrews
- Phoenicians
- Babylonians

Choose *three* of the civilizations above and for *each* explain why geography played an important role in its development.

II. DYNAMICS OF CHANGE

THE RISE OF ISLAM

Almost 600 years after Christianity, another of the world's great religions began in Arabia. The teachings of **Muhammad** (the Messenger of God) inspired **Islam**. It is an Arabic word meaning "submission to the will of God." Islam has played a major role in shaping the culture and value system of the Middle East. It became one of the fastest growing religions in the world, and by the 1990's, its numbers approached one billion.

Within a few centuries, Muslims (Muhammad's followers) spread the religion throughout the world. Islam played an important role in preserving Greek and Roman cultures and advancing the arts and sciences while Europe was in its feudal age.

Islam promotes cultural identity through a common language and common religious beliefs, values, and ethics. Over the past 1,400 years, Islam shaped Middle Eastern society. In modern history, the unity of Islamic culture allowed the Ottoman Empire to survive into the 20th Century, long after its political structure had declined. To understand the region, it is important to observe the strong grasp that Islam has on its followers.

Islam's prophet, Muhammad, was born in the city of **Mecca**, Saudi Arabia, in 570 A.D. Islamic scripture indicates God selected Muhammad to continue the beliefs of Abraham. He taught that all believers in **Allah (God)** were equal, and that the rich should share their wealth with the poor. His early converts were poor townspeople who focused on his teachings of the one Allah, Creator of all. Wealthy merchants and town leaders opposed Muhammad. They had grown prosperous from the pilgrims who came to Mecca to worship the many gods (in particular, the famous black meteor at the Kaaba Shrine). They feared Muhammad's teachings would take away their power.

Muhammad and his followers were persecuted and forced to flee to a neighboring city, Medina. This **Hegira** (flight) in 622 A.D. signaled the beginning of the Islamic Era. Muhammad's following grew among **Arab** tribes as he established a reputation as both a religious leader and a warrior.

ISLAMIC BELIEFS AND PRACTICES

To his followers, Muhammad was the last in the succession of the great prophets such as Abraham, Moses, and Jesus. Muhammad's revelations are recorded in the *Qur'an* (*Koran*), the sacred book of Islam. Muslims believe the *Qur'an* is the word of Allah spoken to Muhammad by the Angel Gabriel. A key doctrine is *Five Pillars of Wisdom*. These practices govern the conduct of all Muslims:

---

1 **Faith** - reciting of the creed, "There is no God but Allah; and Muhammad is his prophet."

2 **Prayer** - praying five times a day (dawn, noon, mid-afternoon, sunset, and nightfall). Services are held in mosques (houses of worship) at noon on Friday.

3 **Alms-giving (charity)** - sharing to help the poor.

4 **Fasting** - renouncing food, drink, and other pleasures from sunrise to sunset during the ninth month of the year (Ramadan).

5 **Pilgrimage (hadj)** - visiting the sacred Kaaba Shrine at the Great Mosque in Mecca once in one's lifetime.

Muhammad established basic religious obligations for his followers which have remained remarkably intact throughout Islamic history. The *Qur'an* (*Koran*) is a guide to Islamic religious and civil behavior. Islamic moral rules are part of a code of law called the *Shari'a*. It provides guidance for all aspects of private and public life. In Islamic culture, there is no separation of religious and political activities.

By the time Muhammad died in 632 A.D., most of the Arabian Peninsula was under Islamic religious, social, political, and economic control or influence. The question surfaced as to who would succeed him. A group of Islamic leaders met and chose a new type of leader called a **Caliph** ("the successor").

The first Caliph was **Abu Bakr**, the father-in-law of Muhammad, who was elected for life. The Caliphs strengthened the Muslim community by developing strong civil and military governments. The followers of Islam united to spread the religion beyond Arabia in a series of holy crusades called **jihads**. The jihads sought converts as they swept throughout the Middle East and across Northern Africa (see map of Islamic Empire below).

As expansion continued, the Islamic Empire became a rich mixture of cultures. By the end of the 8th Century, the **Umayyad Dynasty** consolidated power over a huge territory covering modern-day Pakistan, across Northern Africa, and into Spain. When this occurred, a religious split developed within Islam.

EXPANSION AND CONSOLIDATION OF POWER

In 661 A.D., disagreements concerning the succession of the Caliph caused a **schism** (split) in Islam. The **Sunnis** believed in orthodox Islamic doctrine. An opposition group believed that Muhammad's son-in-law, Ali, and his descendents should be Caliphs. In this power struggle, Ali was assassinated. His followers founded the minority **Shi'ite** group which was primarily located in Mesopotamia and Persia.

Under **Caliph Muawiyah**, the Sunnis established the Umayyad Dynasty and moved the Muslim capital from Medina to Damascus (Syria). It was a more centralized location for the empire. In their search for additional converts, the  Umayyad Caliphs extended the boundaries of Islam westward to Egypt, across North Africa to Spain, and eastward to the Indus River Valley. This empire was organized into provinces led by governors who reported to the Caliph in Damascus.

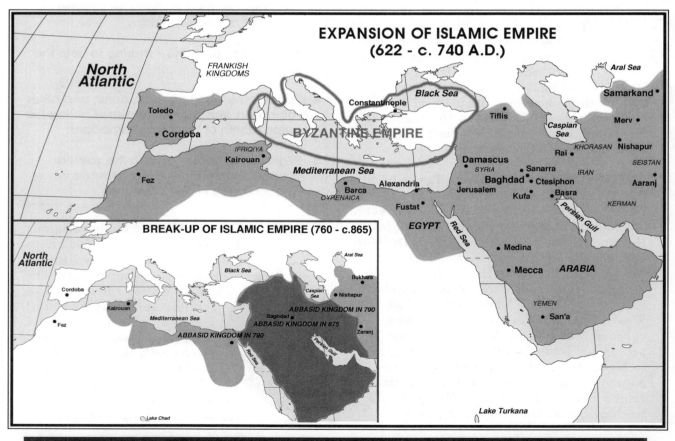

The Umayyad Dynasty employed numerous artists and architects to build beautiful mosques, palaces, and fortresses, and much of their work featured classical Greek and Byzantine architecture.

Jerusalem's famous **Dome of the Rock Mosque** was built during this time. Still, many groups were dissatisfied with the highly centralized rule of the Umayyad Dynasty. In 747 A.D., Shi'ites in Persia and Mesopotamia revolted and brought a new dynasty, called **Abbasid**, to power.

Dome Of The Rock Mosque, Jerusalem

PhotoDisc Inc. 1994

THE GOLDEN AGE OF ISLAMIC CULTURE

The "Golden Age" of Islamic culture occurred during this time (750 - 1258 A.D.). Its second Caliph, **Abu Jafar al-Mansur**, established a new capital at Baghdad (modern-day Iraq). The founding of Baghdad shifted the Muslim Empire's center of power to the eastern part of the Middle East and marked a turning point in Arab control.

Although the religion of Islam and the use of Arabic as the common language brought unity to the empire, other cultures exercised considerable influence. The **Persians** became the most powerful force in the government, the **Turks** dominated the military organizations,

and the **Arabs** continued to control religious institutions and the administration of law.

The 8th through 13th Centuries were an age of toleration. Muslims and non-Muslims alike were given equality. Increased shipping and camel caravan trade brought wealth and luxuries from all over the world. Baghdad hosted a brilliant **cosmopolitan** (diverse) civilization. Tales of this wealth were documented in the famous literary work, ***Arabian Nights*** (a collection of stories told at the Caliph's Court in the 8th and 9th Centuries).

Scholars devoted energy to preserving the earlier cultures of Greece and Rome. This intellectual effort also saw scholars diffusing Persian history and literature and Indian science and

Contributions Of Islamic Civilization	
Discipline	**Achievement**
Medicine	Surgery with anesthetics; Understanding of the functions of internal organs; Science of optics - study of sight; Written medical encyclopedias; Advanced use of drugs and therapy.
Mathematics	The concept of zero, and Arabic numerals (0-9); Algebra and trigonometry.
Chemistry	Laboratory equipment (beakers, vials, etc.); Alchemy - turned base metals to compounds; Distinguished between acids and alkalis.
Astronomy	Mathematical models of the universe with charts giving distances to stars and planets; Described solar eclipses and the moon's effects on ocean tides.

philosophy to the Arab world. With this type of interest and support, scholars and scientists innovated and laid the foundations for today's modern science and mathematics.

In the 8th to the 10th Centuries, Western Europe was in its "Dark Ages." The Islamic world became unique in its religious tolerance and a new-found acceptance of cultural diversity. Muslim cultural advances during this "golden age" eventually reached Europe through increased trade with Spain and Sicily.

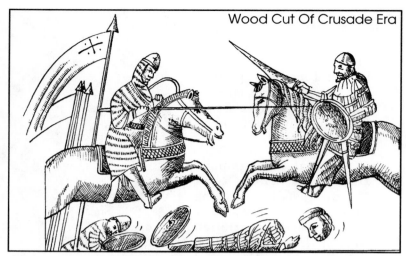
Wood Cut Of Crusade Era

ISLAMIC RULE WEAKENED

SELJUK TURKS

Eventually, the wealth and luxury that accumulated in Baghdad led to corrupt rule by the Caliph and his associates. The Islamic Empire became too large to be governed effectively. Slowly, regional ruling families began to set up their own independent states in Persia, Morocco, Tunisia, Spain, and Egypt.

The Persian **Buyid Dynasty** even went so far as to seize Baghdad and force the Caliph to accept its rule. During the disunity, a nomadic people from Central Asia, called the **Seljuk Turks**, began a conquest of the region. They took control of Baghdad in 1055. They allowed the **Abbasid Caliph** to keep his religious authority but established their own political control through their leader, called the **Sultan** ("he who has authority").

The Seljuk Turks converted to Islam and continued their territorial expansion southwestward to Jerusalem and into Egypt. Their armies crushed the Christian Byzantine forces of the region. Alarmed that the Seljuk Turks controlled the Christian shrines in Palestine and threatened the rest of the Byzantine Empire, the Emperor appealed to the Roman Catholic Pope for assistance.

CRUSADES

In 1095 A.D., a call went out from Pope Urban II for a crusade to drive the Turks out of the **Holy Land**. Religious-military expeditions were organized by European nobles and common people who hoped to conquer Jerusalem and the surrounding area.

Over the next 200 years, Europeans launched eight major crusades to the Middle East. These became holy wars for Christian and Muslim alike. Each side's religious leaders promised supporters that if they were to die in battle, they would go directly to heaven. The Crusades left a  legacy of mistrust between Muslims and the Western Europeans. Many Middle Eastern cities were pillaged and innocent people killed by Crusaders who were more interested in wealth than religion.

Perhaps the most significant impact was the cultural diffusion brought to Western Europe by the returning Crusaders. European trade with the Middle East became important. A demand was created for the luxuries that had been seen such as spices, sugar, exotic foods, and fine fabrics. Also, the Europeans borrowed extensively from the knowledge that the Islamic world had developed in the arts, literature, and sciences.

MONGOLS

Early in the 13th Century, the Seljuk Turks lost control of the Middle East. The **Mongols**, a Central Asian nomadic group, began their conquest of the region. In 1258, the Mongols destroyed Baghdad and ended the Abbasid dynasty. For the next hundred and fifty years, the Mongols' Muslim empire included Iran,

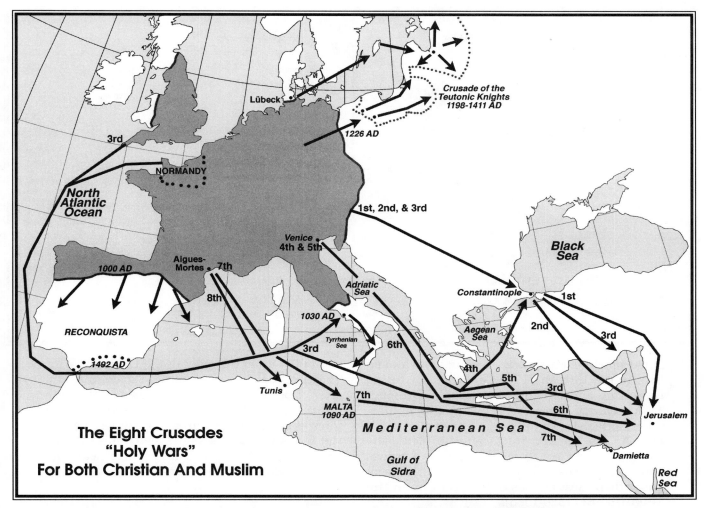

The Eight Crusades
"Holy Wars"
For Both Christian And Muslim

Iraq, Turkey, Syria, Afghanistan, and the Indus River Valley.

OTTOMAN TURKS

In the late 14th Century, the Mongol influence declined. The **Ottomans**, another group of nomadic Turks from the Anatolia Plateau region, began a rise to power. Their rule influenced the Middle East until the 20th Century. The Ottomans established a small, powerful state in Turkey.

Their power increased as the Abbasid Dynasty and the Byzantine Empire declined. They took Constantinople in 1453. This began a land empire which extended far beyond the territories controlled by either of these earlier empires (see Ottoman Empire map on the next page). The Ottoman Turks adopted Sunni Islam as their religion and often assumed the role of defenders of the faith.

THE OTTOMAN EMPIRE (1282 - 1918 A.D.)

Seeking an empire that would connect Europe and Asia, the Ottoman Sultans domi-

16th Century Mosque

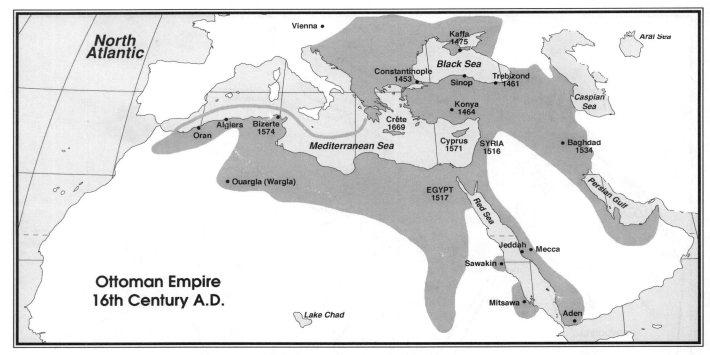

**Ottoman Empire
16th Century A.D.**

nated much of Eastern Europe and the Middle East in the 16th and 17th Centuries. By fusing Byzantine and Muslim cultures, the Ottoman Turks realized important achievements in literature, especially in the field of poetry and civil law. As master architects and builders, the Ottoman Turks constructed beautiful mosques and palaces. The Ottomans reached their peak under their most famous Sultan, **Suleiman the Magnificent** (1520-1566).

Known as "The Codifier," Suleiman organized Ottoman laws and presided over a vast bureaucracy of officials that were promoted by a merit system. This bureaucracy contained a variety of nationalities that represented the other ethnic groups in the Ottoman Empire.

The defeat of the Ottomans in the famous **Battle of Vienna** in 1683 signaled the beginning of their decline. Only intense rivalry among the European nations saved the Ottoman Empire from total collapse. In the 1800's, the Ottoman Empire was forced to withdraw from many territories that it had ruled for centuries. It became nicknamed "the Sick Man of Europe," and other European nations eagerly awaited the opportunity to assert power in their spheres of influence in the Middle East.

At one point in the mid-1800's, Austria and Russia made an agreement to divide the Ottoman Empire, but France, Britain, and the others thwarted this plan in the **Crimean War**. They felt that this would upset the delicate balance of power in Europe. Throughout the 19th Century, Russia fought several wars against Turkey hoping to obtain a warm water port in the Black Sea to its south. Only through the support of England and France was the Ottoman Empire able to survive.

EUROPEAN IMPERIALISM

RUSSIAN - BRITISH RIVALRY

In the 19th Century, European imperialism moved into the Middle East. The Europeans held the upper hand with their modern military technology and administrative organization. However, they did little to change the Islamic culture.

The British wanted to rule over and invest in the less developed regions to obtain raw materials for their factories and markets for their goods. The Russian tsars saw the British ambitions as a threat to their own goal of expanding toward the Mediterranean.

An intense rivalry developed in the region. Britain successfully denied Russian expansion. In 1907, the two powers reached an agreement regarding spheres of influence in Persia (mod-

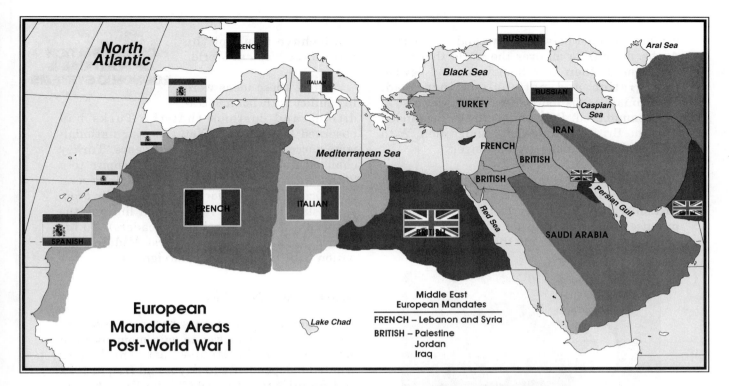

European Mandate Areas Post-World War I

Labels on map: North Atlantic, FRENCH, ITALIAN, SPANISH, RUSSIAN, Black Sea, Aral Sea, TURKEY, RUSSIAN, Caspian Sea, IRAN, FRENCH, BRITISH, Mediterranean Sea, BRITISH, FRENCH, ITALIAN, Red Sea, Persian Gulf, BRITISH, SAUDI ARABIA, SPANISH, Lake Chad

Middle East
European Mandates

FRENCH – Lebanon and Syria
BRITISH – Palestine
         Jordan
         Iraq

ern Iraq). The Russians gained the northern section, and the British operated the southern tier, while the middle of the country remained neutral.

At the close of the 18th Century, local rulers remained in their respective offices in the Middle Eastern States. They were often puppets of Western European nations that exercised true political and economic control.

OTTOMANS: PAWNS IN THE BALANCE OF POWER

The Ottoman Empire collapsed at the end of World War I with the defeat of the Central Powers by the Allies. The British openly encouraged the Arabs to fight against the Ottoman Empire with vague promises of independent nationhood for the Arabian Peninsula. This did not occur. Instead, the League of Nations established **mandates** (territories ruled by the French and British until they were considered ready for independence).

Feeling betrayed, the Arabs reacted bitterly against what they considered imperialism by the Western nations of France and Great Britain. This became a unifying factor among the Arabs, giving rise to nationalist movements in the Islamic world.

RISE OF NATIONALISM

Nationalism has been used as an agent of change in the Middle East. It rallies not only those who favor tradition, but also those that favor modernization and Westernization.

ZIONISM AND THE BALFOUR DECLARATION

Two examples of the rise of Middle East nationalism in the late 19th and early 20th Centuries are Zionism in Palestine and Turkish secularism under Ataturk.

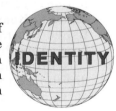

Zionism became an organized movement in 1897 by **Theodor Herzl**, an Austrian who sought a Jewish homeland. Zionism gained momentum in 1917 when the British issued the ***Balfour Declaration***. It was an attempt to gain Jewish support for their war effort. It called for..."*the establishment in Palestine of a national home for the Jewish people...*" The declaration also proclaimed the right of non-Jews to establish a homeland in Palestine.

Ninety percent of Palestinian inhabitants were Arab. When the British set up their mandate government after World War I, a growing conflict emerged between Jews and Palestinian Arabs. Jews from all over the world thought of Palestine as their true homeland, and Jewish immigration and nationalism increased. Palestinian Arabs feared that they would soon be outnumbered. Palestinian Arabs demanded that the British end Jewish immigration. With this, Arab nationalism grew stronger.

World War II interrupted the drive for an independent Arab state in Palestine. The British realized that they had made conflicting promises but could provide no solution acceptable to both the Arabs and the Jews.

ATATURK AND TURKISH NATIONALISM

Ironically, Turkey, the home of the crushed Ottoman Empire, became the first Middle Eastern nation to modernize and create a international identity. **Kemal Ataturk** (formerly Mustafa Kemal), a Turkish war hero, established the Republic of Turkey in 1923. He became its President from 1923-1938, and his "Six Principles" gave his people purpose and direction. Ataturk claimed that for Turkey to survive as an independent nation, the people

would have to adopt the ways of the Western World.

Often, these ideas were in conflict with Islamic traditions and customs that the Turks had observed for centuries Yet, "secular nationalism" succeeded. Within twenty years, Turkey changed from a defeated medieval empire to a 20th Century nation. Ataturk was often severely criticized for his reforms (especially for dropping Islam as a state religion and limiting the authority of Muslim religious leaders). To his credit, Turkey became the first Middle East nation to be independent of foreign control.

ARAB NATIONALISM

Nationalist movements began in the 19th Century but were slower to gain momentum in other areas of the Middle East. The British granted independence to Egypt and Iraq in 1922 and Saudi Arabia in 1927. The French held absolute power in Syria and Lebanon until the end of World War II, and it was only after that war that the region as a whole achieved real independence.

Ataturk's Six Principles

1 **Nationalism** – unification of the Turkish people with common land, culture, and language

2 **Secularism** – separation of religion and government

3 **Populism** – election of officials by the people

4 **Republicanism** – formation of representative government

5 **Statism** – nationalization of industries

6 **Revolutionism** – acceptance of reform in all phases of social, political, and economic life

---

QUESTIONS

1 Muhammad was persecuted because his new religion taught
   1 all believers in Allah were equal
   2 polytheism was better than monotheism
   3 the rich must give up their wealth to the poor
   4 European imperialism must be overthrown

2 Which occurred during the Islamic "golden age" under al-Mansur?
   1 huge sculptures were dedicated to the many gods
   2 Islam's center of culture shifted to Baghdad
   3 Mongols used slave labor to build temples to their gods
   4 Arabs conquered most of Western Europe

3   The *Qur'an (Koran)* contains
    1   over 500 chapters called psalms.
    2   the laws that govern a Muslim's daily life
    3   the legendary stories of the *Arabian Nights*
    4   the history of the Muslim conquest of North Africa and Spain

4   The religion of Islam began in this Middle Eastern country.
    1   Egypt
    2   Iran
    3   Saudi Arabia
    4   Kuwait

5   Which indicates why the Islamic Empire grew rapidly under the highly centralized rule of the Umayyad Dynasty?
    1   An organized political system was established with provincial governors reporting to the Caliph.
    2   A caste system forbade social advancement.
    3   Intense religious persecution began against non-Islamic groups.
    4   Nationalism became a major stabilizing force.

6   Which is the main reason why the Popes organized the Crusades?
    1   They wanted to promote missionary work.
    2   They wanted to drive the Turks out of the Holy Land.
    3   They wanted to expand commercial activities.
    4   They wanted to conquer more land for themselves.

7   "Caliph" was the title given to the chief Muslim
    1   priest
    2   religious leader
    3   tax collector
    4   chanter of prayers

8   The term "Sick Man of Europe" was associated with
    1   the Ottoman Empire
    2   the Holy Roman Empire
    3   the Mongol Empire
    4   the Byzantine Empire

9   In 1917, the British gave support to the creation of a homeland for
    1   Ottoman Turks
    2   Jews in Palestine
    3   a central Islamic mosque
    4   the Byzantine Empire

10 A major change that Ataturk brought to Turkey in the 1920's was
    1   the separation of religion and the government
    2   forced collectivization of farms
    3   the national income tax
    4   adoption of the Cyrillic alphabet

ESSAYS

1   The "golden age" of Islamic culture (7th to 10th Centuries A.D.) demonstrated that the Muslims could contribute many ideas to the rest of the world in science, mathematics, philosophy, literature, architecture, and government.

    a   Explain in detail how contributions in *three* of these fields influenced civilization.

    b   This golden age also saw a serious split in the Islamic religion. Discuss this schism's impact on the Arab world.

2   At the beginning of the 20th Century, European nations were eager to establish spheres of influence in the Middle East.

    a   Identify the leading nations involved in this policy and the territories they controlled.

    b   Discuss what these nations gained from controlling these territories.

III. CONTEMPORARY NATIONS

Prior to World War II, the European powers exerted their influence and control over the Middle East. In the two decades following 1945, most of the countries became independent. In studying the contemporary nations and cultures of the Middle East, it is important to analyze conflicts. In most contemporary societies, groups struggle to maintain their traditional cultures and values while experiencing rapid change. In the Middle East, this process is intense. Ethnic diversity and traditional values have a widespread impact on the region. Shifting power structures have affected nationalism and the struggle for human rights. The rebirth of Israel as a nation-state had an especially significant effect on regional affairs.

POST-WW II INDEPENDENCE

CLASH OVER PALESTINE

Many conflicts in the Middle East since World War II centered on the possession of Palestine. Jewish Zionists and Arab Nationalists saw no improvement when the British withdrew from the area of Palestine and turned the problem over to the newly-formed United Nations.

Worldwide support for the Zionist movement grew as a result of the Nazi persecution of Jews during the Holocaust of World War II. In 1947, the U.N. General Assembly voted for separate Jewish and Arab states in Palestine. A United Nations' supervised international zone was created in the city of Jerusalem. The plan was immediately accepted by the Zionists but rejected by the Arabs.

In May of 1948, Jewish leaders proclaimed Israel a nation. Jews throughout the world began returning to their ancient homeland, yet Arab neighbors refused to recognize the new nation. Neighboring nations immediately provided military aid to Palestinian Arabs to block Israel's independence.

The **Israeli War of Independence** (1948) became the first of a series of Arab-Israeli wars. Outnumbered 50 to 1, the Israelis fought for their survival with vastly inferior military equipment. Surprisingly, the Israelis proved to be more than a match for the Arabs. They held out until the U.N. negotiated

Middle East:
CONTEMPORARY NATIONS

a series of armistices in 1949. Israel gained an additional third of the land in Arab Palestine and control of half of Jerusalem. The conflict resulted in a great loss of prestige for the Arab nations.

POLITICAL & ECONOMIC REFUGEES

Nearly one million Arabs left Palestine and settled in refugee camps in the neighboring Arab nations. Keeping the refugees in the camps intensified Middle East tension. Radical Palestinians used these camps for terrorist training centers. The U.N. could not convince the Arab world to recognize Israel. Arab nations also **boycotted** (refused to buy) commercial products of nations which traded with Israel, but the effort was unsuccessful.

THE SIX-DAY WAR (1967)

In June 1967, war erupted again. Israel retaliated against its neighbors for the continu-

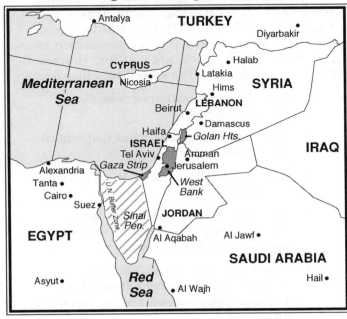

1967 Arab – Israeli War

ous attacks on its borders. Egypt ordered the removal of the United Nations peacekeeping force in the Sinai Peninsula and closed Israel's vital oil supply depots on the Gulf of Aqaba.

With lightning speed, Israel conducted an all-out attack on Egyptian and Syrian targets, capturing vast quantities of the Soviet-supplied equipment from its enemies.

By the time a truce was made in what became known as the **Six-Day War**, Israel occupied a land area four times its original size, including the Gaza Strip, Sinai Peninsula, Golan Heights, the West Bank, and all of Jerusalem.

THE 1973 WAR

Despite diplomatic efforts by the U.N. and major world powers, the Arab nations mounted another military effort to reclaim their lost territories. In October 1973, Egypt attacked Israel's occupation troops in the Sinai Peninsula. Syria attacked Israel's occupation troops in the Golan Heights (see map below left). Israel was caught off guard. Global alarm spread as the U.S. began sending massive aid to Israel, and the U.S.S.R. did the same for Egypt and Syria. Tank warfare continued for three weeks with intense fighting between the Egyptians and the Israelis. Finally, after pressure was exerted by the Soviet Union and the United States, another uneasy cease-fire was arranged through the U.N.

THE CAMP DAVID ACCORDS

In March 1979, the historic Camp David Accords were signed by Israeli Prime Minister **Begin**, Egyptian President **Sadat**, and U.S. President **Carter**. For the first time, an Arab nation had recognized Israel as a nation. The Camp David Accords provided for:

• withdrawal of Israel from the Sinai and a return of the U.N. peacekeeping forces

• normalization of diplomatic and economic relations

• negotiations on Palestinian self-rule

The 1979 agreement was welcomed by most as a positive step. Yet, groups in the Arab and

March 1979 Camp David Accords
signed by (left to right) Egypt's Anwar Sadat,
U.S.'s Jimmy Carter, and Israel's Menachem Begin.

Islamic world looked upon Sadat's actions with disdain since Palestinians had not been involved in the negotiations. For their peace efforts, Sadat and Begin won the 1978 Nobel Peace Prize. Sadat was assassinated in 1981 during a military parade by several gunmen associated with a militant Muslim fundamentalist group. Negotiations on a Palestinian homeland broke down numerous times and kept peace an elusive goal.

For many years, the United Nations issued resolutions that interrupted the Arab-Israeli Wars by cease-fires and truces. The most famous document was **U.N. Resolution #242**, passed by the Security Council in 1967. It called for acknowledgment of the sovereignty, territorial integrity, and political independence of every state in the region.

The U.N. also requested that Israel withdraw from the territory that it attained in 1967's Six-Day War. Israel refused to comply until the Arab nations recognized its existence as a nation in permanent peace settlements.

By the 1990's, there were over three million displaced Palestinian Arabs. In 1964, several groups of Palestinian refugees formed the **Palestinian Liberation Organization** as the political and military arm of Palestinian Arabs. For three decades, the PLO struggled to liberate their homeland from what they viewed as an illegitimate Israeli state. To emphasize their cause, some Palestinian groups launched terrorist attacks against Israel from their refugee camps in Jordan and Lebanon. Miserable living conditions in the Palestinian refugee camps

motivated revolutionary guerrilla fighting and terrorist activities.

Israeli military retaliation was swift and violent. The Israelis wanted security and recognition as a nation from the Arabs. The Arab Palestinians wanted East Jerusalem returned and an independent nation established on the West Bank and the Gaza Strip - regions which Israel claimed as vital to its defense.

PALESTINIAN SELF-RULE

A major development occurred in September 1993 when Israel and the PLO signed a *Declaration of Principles for Palestinian Self-rule*. Various problems and violent incidents erupted as both Israeli and Palestinian opponents to peace tried to stop the implementation of the agreement.

In May 1994, Egypt and the U.S. helped to broker another step toward Palestinian self-rule in the Gaza Strip and town of Jericho, on Jordan's West Bank. PLO Chairman **Yasir Arafat** and Israeli Prime Minister **Yitzhak Rabin** signed the agreement, starting the implementation of the September 1993 accord for limited Palestinian autonomy. The agreement called for:

- Israeli Army to withdraw from Gaza Strip and Jericho

- Palestinians to elect a municipal council to supervise self-rule

- Palestinian police officers to keep order in autonomous territories

- Palestinians to be responsible for taxation, education, health, tourism, and social welfare in the territories

- Israelis and Palestinians to begin negotiating a permanent accord, leading to Palestinian autonomy before summer 1997

POST-WW II ARAB LEADERSHIP

After World War II, the spirit of nationalism grew in Arab countries. It brought new political leadership which has often looked to Western technology to cure social, political, and economic problems. At the same time, the leaders recognized the necessity of maintaining their national culture and values. In trying to hold this delicate balance, revolutions and political instability plagued many of the leaders.

Egyptian President Gamal Abdel Nasser Promoted Arab Unity After WW II

Following World War II, Egypt assumed the early leadership role on the promotion of **Pan-Arabism** (Arab unity) under the guidance of a charismatic military leader, **Gamal Abdel Nasser**. Egypt became independent in 1922. It was ruled by King Farouk and a class of wealthy landowners that were heavily influenced by the British.

In 1952, Nasser led a coup d'état of army officers in ousting the Egyptian monarch and proclaimed a republic. He helped create a modern, mixed economy. One of his first achievements was land reform accompanied by extensive irrigation projects. This significantly increased agricultural production. The Cold War occupied the great powers, and Nasser accepted aid from both democratic and communist nations.

Nasser's social, political, and economic reforms strengthened Egypt's nationalism. Perhaps his greatest project was the construction of **Aswan High Dam**. It was built with Soviet financial aid and technical supervision. The project provided energy for the growth of Egyptian industry. His social reforms promoted education, health care services, and more equality for women. Nasser excited the Arab world when he spoke of **Arab Socialism** (improvement of the social and economic conditions for all Arabs).

In 1956, Egypt established national ownership of the **Suez Canal** and prohibited Israel from using it. Israeli forces then invaded Egyptian territory in the Sinai Peninsula. Within five days, the Israeli military smashed through the Sinai to the Canal. Great Britain and France also invaded claiming that they wanted equal access to the canal. The U.N. stepped in, arranged a truce, and sent in a peacekeeping force to prevent further clashes.

Despite losing two costly wars to the Israelis, Nasser remained a hero to the Arabs. Over two million people joined his funeral procession in Cairo in 1970.

Nasser's successor, **Muhammad Anwar al-Sadat**, broke relations with the Soviets and established closer ties with the United States. In a bold move, Sadat journeyed to Jerusalem in 1977 to negotiate with Israel to resolve the Egyptian-Israeli disputes In 1979, he signed the *Camp David Accords*. He angered the Arab World by making a separate peace and destroying Arab unity. A year later, Sadat was assassinated by gunmen from a militant Muslim fundamentalist group.

In recent years, Islamic fundamentalists in Egypt have exerted pressure on the government to refrain from **secularization** (accepting Western lifestyle). They urged Egyptian political leaders to return to the more traditional Islamic teachings and culture. Into the 1990's, conflicts continue over the roles of men and women in the Muslim society and over guarantees of individual rights.

Iraq's Dictator, Saddam Hussein

In other nations of the Middle East, similar military coups ousted traditional monarchs who favored former European colonial regimes. In Libya, military leader **Muammar al-Qaddafi** successfully overthrew King Muhammad Idris I in 1969. Through the 1970's and 1980's, he used profits from Libya's vast petroleum reserves to promote global terrorism in support of radical Middle East politics.

Military revolutions were also frequent in Syria, Lebanon, and Iraq. In recent times, Iraq's dictator, **Saddam Hussein**, attempted to become the new leader of Arab Nationalism by building his country into the most powerful military force in the Middle East.

THE ISLAMIC REVOLUTION

IRAN'S MODERNIZATION AND FUNDAMENTALISM

In Iran, **Shah Muhammad Reza Pahlavi** ruled as a figurehead until 1953. With the help of his military and the support of Western gov-

ernments, he overthrew the nationalist regime of Prime Minister **Muhammad Mosaddeq** (or Mossadegh).

The Shah repealed many of Mosaddeq's anti-Western measures. He announced plans to modernize his country. His reforms included land reform for the peasants, changing the legal status of women, and improving educational and health standards. Some of these goals were achieved. Yet, he spent much of the money from sale of Iran's oil and natural gas on grand building projects in the cities, lavish government ceremonial events, and armaments.

Poverty continued to plague the nation. Rural villages lacked running water and other basic facilities. The Shah's efforts at Westernization alienated the people. He ignored Iran's Islamic leaders. His government was corrupt. To preserve his hold over the people, his **Savak** (secret police) used terror and torture.

MODERNIZATION V. FUNDAMENTALISM

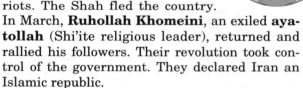
CULTURE

Opposition to the Shah became overwhelming. In 1979, strikes in Teheran became bloody riots. The Shah fled the country. In March, **Ruhollah Khomeini**, an exiled **ayatollah** (Shi'ite religious leader), returned and rallied his followers. Their revolution took control of the government. They declared Iran an Islamic republic.

Iranian Ayatollah, Ruhollah Khomeini

Khomeini's group began reforms that reflected strict Shi'ite teachings and political structures. The new government pursued an anti-Western and anti-modernization policy. The economy weakened in the aftermath of this revolution. Khomeini's Islamic fundamentalist regime abolished Western dress and the sense of freedom Iranian women enjoyed under the Shah's modernization.

PERSIAN GULF CONFLICTS

THE IRAN-IRAQ WAR

For many years, Iran and its neighbor, Iraq, disputed border land on the **Persian Gulf** and its many islands. In 1975, they signed an agreement that seemed to settle these differences. After the Khomeini regime took over in Iran, tension mounted again. Khomeini's agents tried to rally Iraqi Shi'ites in a revolution. In September 1980, Iraq's military leader **Saddam Hussein** launched a full-scale war against Iran.

The war raged throughout the 1980's, straining each nation's economy and claiming more than a half million lives. The U.N. eventually worked out a truce in the summer of 1988.

IRAQ'S INVASION OF KUWAIT

In August 1990, Iraq began a new crisis in the Persian Gulf. Needing to pay debts from the long Iran-Iraq War and rebuild the military,

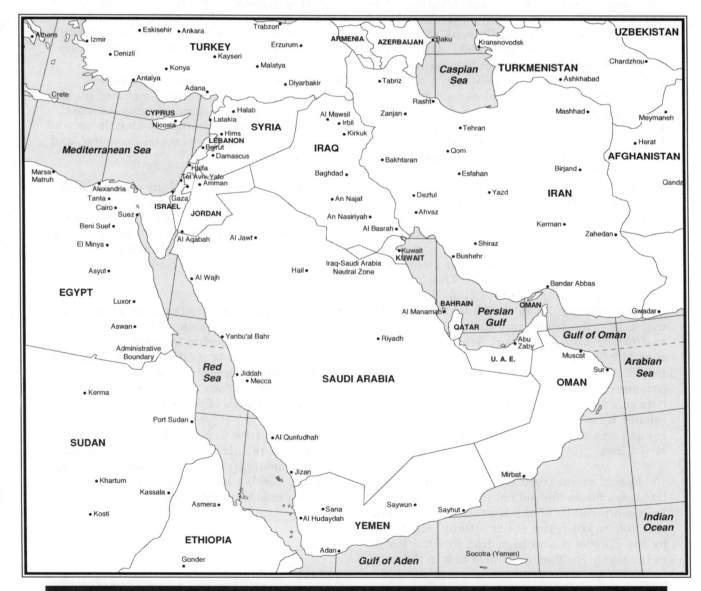

Saddam Hussein wanted OPEC to raise prices by cutting oil production. However, competing OPEC neighbors voted to maintain high production and low oil prices. In retaliation on 2 August 1990, Saddam Hussein used his military power to invade, overrun, and annex Kuwait.

Within a few days, the Arab League, the Gulf Cooperation Council, the U.N., and the U.S. condemned Iraq's invasion. Through international cooperative action, Iraq's export oil piplines were blocked and economic and trade sanctions were imposed. Authorized by the U.N., President Bush organized a coalition of 28 Middle East and other nations. These countries provided financial aid and military support to defend Saudi Arabia from continued Iraqi threats. By late August, **Operation Desert Shield** began. In January 1991, **Operation Desert Storm** began a relentless attack from U.S., British, Saudi, and Kuwaiti aircraft. Saddam answered with Scud missile attacks on Israel and Saudi Arabia. On 24 February, led by U.S. Gen. H. Norman Schwarzkopf, coalition forces attacked along the Saudi-Kuwaiti border launching a 100-hour ground invasion. Iraqi troops, including Hussein's Republican Guard, fled Kuwait being driven out by U.S. army and Marine units, British, French, and Saudi forces, and Pan-Arab troops. The U.N. imposed stiff conditions for a formal end to the hostilities.

The cost of the Kuwait War was great. Total coalition losses were 224 dead. Iraq reported that 1,591 civilians were killed. The Saudi Arabian ambassador to the United States estimated that the Iraqi army had suffered 85,000 to 100,000 killed. General Schwarzkopf said that 300,000 Iraqi troops had been :"endered ineffective for combat." An estimated 50,000 prisoners of war were taken. The war cost between $40 and $50 billion. The price tag to rebuild Kuwait was over $40 billion. Estimates ranged upwards of $100,000 billion to reconstruct Iraq.

Desert Storm freed Kuwait and devastated Saddam's forces but did not unseat the dictator. In the aftermath of the Kuwait War, Saddam was able to crush two major internal rebellions, by the Shi'ites in southern Iraq and the Kurds in the north. Saddam continued to be a threat to peace, steadily rebuilding Iraq's conventional and nuclear military capability.

SOCIAL CHANGE

Today, much of the Middle East is experiencing social changes through industrialization and rapid urbanization. Examples of the impact of these changes include:

- **Role of Women** – Despite the opposition of Islamic fundamentalist, large numbers of women are receiving more education and have become members of the work force. In many nations, they have earned the right to vote and hold political office. In Israel, equality is guaranteed by law, and women serve side by side with men in the military.

- **Democratic Reforms** – Centralized schools provide education. Improved literacy rates create more social equality. In most nations, voting is granted to all citizens, and women have improved social, economic, and legal equality.

- **Religious Conflict** – Many religious leaders of the region (Islamic, Jewish, and Christian) attempt to block modernization and to keep their conservative fundamental value systems. An example is the ongoing legacy of the Ayatollah Khomeini's movement in Iran.

- **Terrorism** – Terrorists represent many different ethnic, religious, and nationalist causes. They resort to frequent surprise attacks to achieve their ends. In coping with these threats, many nations have met violence with violence. Others support terrorist factions as tools of revolution.

Conflicts arise as people try to balance these changes in religious tradition with secular forces of modernization. Revolutionary groups seize any conflict as an opportunity to support terrorism to achieve their goals.

QUESTIONS

1 The nation of Israel was created in 1948 as a homeland for the Jews in Palestine because
   1 this was the only territory the British would give up
   2 Arab Palestinians wanted to help Jewish refugees from Nazi camps
   3 the U.N. recognized a separate Jewish state
   4 the U.S.S.R. needed a place to send Jewish dissenters

2 Egyptian leader Gamal Abdel Nasser nationalized the Suez Canal to
   1 provide the U.S. with a strategic base
   2 reserve it for Caribbean countries
   3 abolish Arab dominance in the region
   4 control Middle East shipping

3 The U.S.S.R. helped Egypt construct Aswan High Dam because it
   1 needed the electric power
   2 wanted a stronger alliance with Nasser
   3 wanted to conquer Central Africa
   4 wished to repay its WW II debts to Egypt

4 In the 1967 War, the Israelis captured the Golan Heights from Syria. This was a valuable area because it had
   1 the richest oil field in the Middle East
   2 uranium for nuclear development
   3 the holy shrines of three major world religions
   4 a strategic observation point to view Syria

5 The 1979 *Camp David Accords* called for
   1 the sovereignty, territorial integrity, and political independence of every state in the region
   2 a joint development project on the Jordan River
   3 withdrawal of Israeli troops from the Golan Heights
   4 negotiations for a new Arab-Palestinian state

6 Yasir Arafat seeks
   1 fundamental Islamic reform
   2 an independent Palestinian-Arab state
   3 Arab socialism
   4 a share of Persian Gulf oil reserves

7 Which is crucial to Libyan leader Muammar al-Qaddafi's success?
   1 a strong nationalist movement
   2 aid from Western leaders
   3 peace with Israel
   4 freedom for women

8 Many Arab nations felt that as a result of the *Camp David Accords,*
   1 President Sadat betrayed them
   2 the United States abandoned support for Israel
   3 Western imperialism would return
   4 Israel endorsed Arab nationalism

9 The Islamic Revolution occurred in Iran as a result of the Shah's
   1 insensitivity to traditional customs
   2 invasion of Iraq
   3 friendship with Khomeini
   4 support for the PLO

ESSAY

Contemporary problems in the Middle East revolve around Israel and Islam.

a Explain why there has been a resurgence of Islamic fundamentalism in the Middle East in recent years. Include an example of a country where this has occurred.

b The key to peace in the Middle East rests in the resolution of the Arab-Palestinian homeland problem. Discuss the reasons why the solution to this problem is so difficult.

c Discuss one other problem that has been caused by modernization of life in the Middle East in the past generation.

IV. ECONOMIC DEVELOPMENT

For centuries, the major economic activity in the Middle East has been agriculture. Today, the region's vast oil reserves generate extensive capital. This money helps to modernize and broaden the industrial base in the region. Major transformations occur with improved educational systems and modern technology. Industrialization increases employment, but problems accompany such radical economic development.

BARRIERS TO DEVELOPMENT

Throughout its long history, arable land deteriorated through overpopulation, overgrazing, and an overall lack of conservation. Turkey is the only nation in the region that is self-sufficient in agriculture. All other nations of the Middle East must import much of their food supplies.

The scarcity of water resources is also a major concern. In certain areas such as the Jordan River Basin water is a more vital issue than oil. In the next century, the need for irrigation and hydroelectric power in Jordan, Israel, and Syria will cause more conflict. This is an area already in constant crisis over the Palestinian homeland question. Population pressures on water supplies call for new technology. Israel, Saudi Arabia, and Kuwait have expensive irrigation and desalinization projects to transform arid desert lands.

Wealth from oil revenue is in the hands of only a few Middle East nations. Power and control of the distribution of this money is critical. It has often been used for political ends. **OPEC** (Organization of Petroleum Exporting Countries) is an example.

OPEC is a **cartel** (an international business group that controls prices and production) created in the 1960's. Its members control 75% of world's estimated oil reserves. Currently, OPEC includes member nations from South America, Africa, and Asia. However, the Middle Eastern nations control 85% of all OPEC's production and have the most influence on its policies.

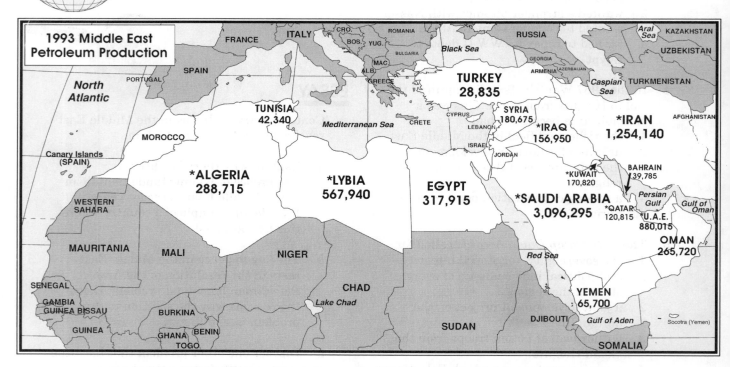

1993 Middle East Petroleum Production

Country	Production
TURKEY	28,835
TUNISIA	42,340
SYRIA	180,675
*IRAQ	156,950
*IRAN	1,254,140
*ALGERIA	288,715
*LYBIA	567,940
EGYPT	317,915
*KUWAIT	170,820
BAHRAIN	39,785
*SAUDI ARABIA	3,096,295
*QATAR	120,815
U.A.E.	880,015
OMAN	265,720
YEMEN	65,700

*Production numbers on the map are in thousands of 42 gallon barrels. A * denotes OPEC member.*
In 1993, total worldwide petroleum production was 22,054,030,000 barrels (42 gallon units). The Middle East totaled 7,479,660,000 barrels (33.9% of world production). United States production was 2,689,320,000 barrels (12.2%).

OPEC's financial reserves grew in the 1970's. Cartel members increased their power in world politics and economics. Global conservation measures, political infighting, and market economic shifts caused OPEC's power to decline in recent years. In addition, many Middle East countries lack the oil resources of their OPEC neighbors. This division deepens regional discord and political instability.

The new and the old of Tel Aviv, Israel   PhotoDisc Inc. 1994

ARAB SOCIALISM

Some countries of the Middle East tried to further their economic development by nationalizing industries, businesses, and resources. An example of this policy occurred in Egypt in the early 1950's under Colonel Nasser. Combining a mixture of ideologies under the title of Arab Socialism, Nasser created a mixed economy. He broke up the large estates the rich accumulated under Egypt's monarchy. He set up public ownership of industry, but encouraged private ownership of farms.

Still, Nasser's new Egyptian economy failed to meet his lofty goals. In 1957, Nasser nationalized many banks and insurance companies. By 1961, the Egyptian government controlled all of the nation's light industry. Nasser provided more and more public services and education for Egyptians. These political moves made Nasser a hero but did not provide for a sound, long-range economic structure.

A MIXED ECONOMY IN ISRAEL

Israel achieved success with limited raw materials and energy sources. Assisted by Western aid, Israel mixed private enterprise and public planning and developed a relatively strong, balanced industrial and agricultural structure.

Israel's economic base rests on an educated work force. It has the highest literacy rate in the region (90% for Jews, 70% for Arabs). Israeli industries include food processing, fertilizer, textile, diamond cutting, and chemical production. It absorbs many skilled immigrants in its labor force and solicits large amounts of foreign investment, loans, and donations.

Israel created gains in agriculture through strict government control of limited water resources. It is nearly self-sufficient in food production. It reclaims desert land through successful irrigation and modern soil management. Cotton and citrus fruits are produced for export.

Israel's agricultural sector involves only ten percent of its population. Government subsidized **moshavs** (cooperative farms) increased Israeli agricultural output. These are settlements where land is rented by the state to individuals. Farmers purchase or rent their supplies through a regional cooperative agency.

Another lesser-used Israeli agricultural system is the **kibbutz**. The government provided early Zionist settlers with collective farmland and equipment. It encouraged shared work and communal living. In return for their labors, members are provided with food, clothing, social services, and education for their children. Unlike arrangements in communist countries, the kibbutz is strictly a voluntary system. Members are free to join or leave. Recently, the government expanded the system to include light manufacturing industries.

Israel has the highest GDP in the region(1992 = $55 billion). Still, its large defense budget causes inflation problems. There are also unemployment problems. A constant flow of immigrants adds to instability in the labor force. To broaden its economic base, Israel promotes tourism, but tension and insecurity in the region make it unpredictable.

DIVERSE ECONOMIC FORCES

Many other influences shape economies in the Middle East. Economists list several causes for the diversity of living standards:

- **Population Growth** – Urbanization takes place very quickly as population shifts from rural areas to the region's cities. As people seek educational and job opportunities, new nations are unable to keep up. They fall behind the demand for housing, education, and health and sanitary conditions. Overcrowding causes food shortages and miserable slum conditions. Exceptions occur in a few newly created cities of the wealthy oil nations.

- **Rise of the Middle Class** – In the large, cosmopolitan urban centers, a new class of highly educated professionals and bureaucrats has emerged. Some have distanced themselves from traditional religious customs and family traditions. Their new-found independence results in marriage by choice and smaller nuclear families. This new secular class demands more progressive political leadership and reform.

- **Impact of Islamic Fundamentalism** – Traditional conservative Islamic leaders voice concern over secular laws and reforms. They urge supporters to return to strict adherence to Islamic law and traditions. Iran's Shi'ite-led revolution (1979) is an example.

- **Impact of Western Values** – Since World War II, Middle Eastern women have achieved greater equality in the large urban centers influenced by the Western world. Women achieved the right to vote. And, in some nations they have become politically active. Through education, many nations moved toward creating a professional work force. Israel guarantees equality by law. While some newly organized political systems of the Middle East borrowed ideas from western nations, Israel remains one of the few successful democracies in the region.

- **Global interdependence** – The world is heavily dependent on Middle East oil, and the Middle East needs the technology and foodstuffs of the industrialized nations. This global interdependence creates a critical linkage that continues to shape affairs in the region.

QUESTIONS

1 A rising middle class has emerged in the Middle East among the
   1   religious leaders
   2   urban professionals
   3   military forces
   4   independent farmers

2 The most rapid change from traditional to modern societies in the Middle East is occurring in Israel because it has
   1   large oil deposits
   2   high mineral wealth
   3   a balanced, planned economy
   4   the most advanced military

3 OPEC is a cartel, a group of nations seeking to control
  1 the Olympic games
  2 the price and production of oil
  3 traditional Islam
  4 nuclear weapons

4 There is intense interest in the Middle East in desalinization, an expensive process used in converting
  1 petroleum to unleaded gas
  2 seawater to freshwater
  3 salt to gold
  4 coal to gasoline

5 Nationalization of an industry means that
  1 the government takes control
  2 it is sold at an auction
  3 a government loan is being guaranteed
  4 the industry has gone bankrupt

6 A moshav is an Israeli economic institution primarily used to organize
  1 agricultural production
  2 military training skills
  3 oil marketing with Arab nations
  4 trade with Western nations

7 One economic consequence of Israel's high-cost defense budget is
  1 loss of traditional values
  2 high inflation rates
  3 decrease in leisure time
  4 decrease in domestic oil production

8 The goal of Islamic fundamentalists in the Middle East is to
  1 revert to traditional Muslim laws
  2 encourage the secular middle class
  3 support Israel
  4 encourage women to be active in politics

9 With the exception of Israel, most of the labor force in the Middle East is involved in
  1 the tourist industry
  2 the oil industry
  3 agriculture
  4 commerce or business

ESSAY

In the last 30 years, oil has been used as a political and economic weapon in various conflicts involving Arab nations and groups

Conflicts

- OPEC v. Western Nations (1970's)
- Iran-Iraq War 1980-1989
- Arab-Israeli War of 1973
- Libya v. the U. S. (1980's)

Choose *three* of the conflicts above and discuss how oil was used as a weapon and how effective its use was in *each* conflict.

V. GLOBAL CONTEXT

COLD WAR POWER STRUGGLES

The Middle East plays a central role in world affairs in modern times. In the decades after World War II, many Cold War issues centered on the region. The U.S. and Soviet Union aligned themselves with various groups. Each  sent foreign, technological, and military aid into the region. The U.S. became the major ally of Israel and the Shah of Iran. By the late 1980's, U.S. aid to Israel was between three and six billion dollars annually. The Soviets aided Egypt, Afghanistan, Yemen, and Syria. During the 1980's and 1990's, the U.S. became involved in the Persian Gulf to protect the industrial world's petroleum supplies.

STRATEGIC LOCATION

The Middle East's strategic location makes it the hub of three continents. Its waterways continue to serve major east-west trade routes. After World War II, Middle Eastern wars, oil, and politics greatly influenced the foreign policies of the world's superpowers.

ARAB-ISRAELI CONFLICTS

Arab-Israeli confrontations constantly endanger the region. In the Cold War, the U.S. and Western democracies tried to balance supporting Israel and maintaining relations with Arab oil producing nations. The Soviets worked to undermine these Western activities. These superpower influences sometimes prevented hostilities, yet they also disturbed the region.

The presence of the nation of Israel remains a problem in the Arab world. As an American diplomat once stated, *"Israel is a blessing and a curse for the Arabs - a bless-*  *ing because it brings the Arabs together, but a curse because its existence demonstrates how ineffective the Arabs usually have been."* After all the Arab-Israeli conflicts, Israel appears to have proven it cannot be driven from the region.

AFGHANISTAN

In 1979, the Brezhnev regime of the Soviet Union invaded Afghanistan. Brezhnev claimed a weak communist government needed reinforcement against Mujahadin rebels seeking an Islamic republic. The Soviets feared such rebellions spreading into their own Central Asian region with large Islamic populations. They also thought the invasion could extend Soviet influence into the Persian Gulf area. In a classic Cold War response, the U.S. sent aid to the rebel groups. Islamic nations also sent aid to the rebels.

As with the U.S. in Vietnam, the Red Army became mired in the **Afghanistan War**. The rebels' guerrilla tactics hit the Soviets with

fury. Then they retreated into the mountainous terrain. Conventional Soviet military forces with high tech weaponry could not make any progress. The Soviets lost thousands of troops and poured millions into the effort to no avail.

The war became more unpopular in the U.S.S.R. When Mikhail Gorbachev came to power in 1985, he struggled with military leaders to pull the Soviet forces out. In 1988, Gorbachev signed a truce agreement. The Red Army withdrew in 1989, but general civil unrest continued to wrack Afghanistan in the 1990's.

CIVIL WAR IN LEBANON

Another source of trouble in the 1980's was a series of bloody civil wars in Lebanon. Many different religious and ethnic groups reside in this Mediterranean area. Lebanon became a republic in 1942. Initially, it had lofty goals such as democracy, a strong economy, and harmony among its diverse groups.

For a short time, these goals seemed to be within reach. The government was balanced by a unique leadership of a Maronite (Eastern Roman Catholic) President, and Sunni (mainstream Islamic) Premier and Legislative President. Initially, the Christian population was the majority and retained the most seats in the legislature. This gradually changed. During the 1940's and 1950's, the nation prospered.

Beirut became the commercial and financial center of the Middle East, even being called the "Paris of the Middle East." A brief civil war occurred in 1958. President Eisenhower sent U.S. troops to aid in a peacekeeping effort.

Serious problems erupted in the 1970's. The the population balance shifted. The Christians declined to 45% of the population, and the Muslims demanded a greater role in governing the nation. The situation grew worse with the additional presence of almost 400,000 Palestinian refugees from Israel who settled in refugee camps in southern Lebanon. The PLO used the camps as  bases for staging terrorist attacks on Israel. The Israelis retaliated by bombing and invading the PLO camps. This caused political strife in Lebanon. Most of the Muslim population supported the PLO, and the Christian (Phalangist) groups supported Israel.

In 1975, a full-scale civil war erupted. The Muslims vowed to fight on until they had the dominant position in the Lebanese government. The nation saw its businesses collapse and its cities ravaged by numerous bombings. In 1976, the Arab nations and the Lebanese government asked neighboring Syria to intervene to restore order. A cease-fire was arranged. The following year, Syria sided with the PLO, and the war resumed.

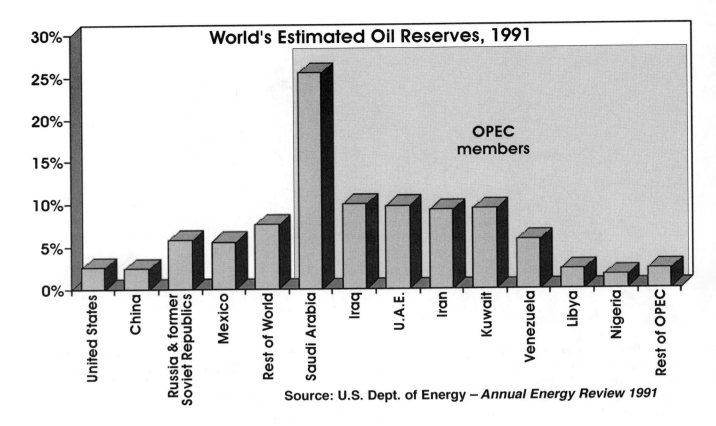

World's Estimated Oil Reserves, 1991

OPEC members

United States | China | Russia & former Soviet Republics | Mexico | Rest of World | Saudi Arabia | Iraq | U.A.E. | Iran | Kuwait | Venezuela | Libya | Nigeria | Rest of OPEC

Source: U.S. Dept. of Energy – *Annual Energy Review 1991*

In 1978, Israel retaliated against terrorist attacks from the PLO camps near its borders. In 1982, Israel launched an all-out invasion against the PLO which drew it into the war. Eventually, the PLO agreed to withdraw from Lebanon. A multinational peacekeeping force of American, French, British, and Italian troops  was sent to Lebanon in an effort to supervise the PLO withdrawal. In 1983, over 250 U.S. Marines died in a suicide bombing of their headquarters in Beirut. Terrorists assassinated the Lebanese President. In 1984, the peacekeepers withdrew and the civil war resumed. Israel withdrew in 1985. Syrian troops remain, and sporadic outbursts continue from PLO guerrillas in the south.

PETRO POLITICS

In the modern world, having oil is synonymous with power. In recent decades, the concerted actions of petroleum producing nations focused attention on the political and economic power of the Middle East. Even though

OPEC includes nations from South America, Africa, and Asia, the Middle Eastern members control 85% of OPEC's production. This gives them the most influence on OPEC's policies. In the mid-1970's, some OPEC member **embargoes** (cutting off supply) sent oil prices skyrocketing. This caused global inflation and recessions. Industrialized countries feared being shut-off because OPEC controls 75% of world's estimated reserves (note the graph on World Oil Reserves, above).

During the 1973 Arab-Israeli War, some Arab members of OPEC forced an embargo on shipments of oil to nations that aided Israel. Global supplies dwindled, and shortages forced prices to rise. By 1979, prices quadrupled. Fabulous wealth came to the OPEC nations, but severe inflation throughout the rest of the world triggered recessions. Conservation became a priority for world consumers. Industrial nations developed energy efficient automobiles, homes, and appliances.

Conservation and high prices lowered demand for oil. OPEC nations wound up with an oversupply. This forced severe budgetary

Dangerous conditions in the Persian Gulf during the Iran Revolution and the Iran – Iraq War led President Reagan to re-flag (reregister the ships as U.S. property) oil tankers of Kuwait in 1987. These ships were given U.S. naval protection.

WORLD TRADE & FINANCE

cuts among the OPEC nations. Even the non-oil producing nations of the Middle East suffered. Some had grown extremely dependent on their oil rich neighbors for financial aid and employment for their people. Arab oil money, previously invested in foreign countries and loaned to foreign governments and corporations, dried up. Oil prices began a long decline and did not stabilize until the late 1980's.

Frequent fighting among Middle East oil producing nations also threatens world supplies. Threats to oil tankers in the Persian Gulf during the Iran-Iraq War prompted unusual U.S. action. In 1987, President Reagan ordered the oil tankers of Kuwait reregistered and reflagged as U.S. property to afford them U.S. naval protection. Saddam Hussein's 1990 invasion of Kuwait and the international war it caused involved nearly every nation in the Middle East and most of the major industrial nations of the world.

The Middle East remains an important crossroads in today's political and economic world. Numerous crises disrupt chances for the region's stability. The Palestinian question, superpower intervention, and religious upheaval are continuing problems.

The leaders in this region face many challenges: poverty, overpopulated urban centers, contrasting values, educational needs, modern technology, and social inequality. The directions chosen will be closely watched by other nations as these actions will shape the future of the world.

QUESTIONS

1 The U.S.S.R. sent its military forces into Afghanistan in 1979 to support
1 the Mujahidin rebellion
2 the power of a rising capitalist class
3 its pro-Soviet Marxist leader
4 the cause of human rights under Camp David Accords

2   OPEC is a cartel, this means that it seeks to dominate
    1   capitalists
    2   communists
    3   production and prices
    4   the import-export business

3   The Phalangists are important religious political figures in Lebanon because they are
    1   a fanatical terrorist group
    2   dominant in the bureaucracy of the Middle East
    3   a nonviolent-pacifist group
    4   representative of the large Christian population there

4   Beirut was given the name "the Paris of the Middle East" because
    1   of its financial and commercial successes following World War II
    2   it has many evidences of Gothic architecture
    3   French is the national language
    4   it is the largest wine producing country in the region

5   Why did the Arab nations ask Syria to intervene in Lebanon's civil war?
    1   It was feared Israel would continue to intervene in the nation.
    2   The major Arab military base is in the country.
    3   Syria wanted to control the mineral wealth of Lebanon.
    4   There was fear of a Shi'ite fundamentalist revolution there.

6   Israel invaded Southern Lebanon in 1982 to stop
    1   the Lebanese from attacking its oil refineries
    2   Jordan from taking its land
    3   attacks by the U.S. and U.S.S.R.
    4   PLO terrorist attacks threatening its security

7   In the 1980's, a multinational peace-keeping force was sent to Lebanon because
    1   multinational corporations wanted oil
    2   the withdrawal of the PLO needed close supervision
    3   it was the center of Arab aggression
    4   it was about to become the site of a nuclear confrontation

8   A 1970's political goal of OPEC was to punish
    1   Islamic fundamentalism
    2   those who supported Israel
    3   the Russians in Afghanistan
    4   Arabs under Libya's Qaddafi

9   Why did the U.S. assumed a major role in keeping oil from the Persian Gulf flowing to the rest of the world?
    1   U.S. oil companies' boycott the area.
    2   The Persian Gulf is the world's only source of crude oil.
    3   Western nations and Japan are highly dependent on Middle East petroleum.
    4   Other Western nations have large forces in the region.

ESSAY

During the Cold War the United States and the Soviet Union became involved in many Middle East conflicts.

a   Explain the importance of this region to each superpower.

b   Select *three* of the following events and discuss a reason why one of the superpowers was concerned:

•   Nationalization of the Suez Canal (1956)
•   Yom Kippur War (1973)
•   Invasion of Afghanistan (1979)
•   Lebanese Civil War (1982)

UNIT SEVEN: MIDDLE EAST ASSESSMENT

ISSUE: GEOGRAPHIC INFLUENCES ON REGIONAL DEVELOPMENT

This two-part assessment offers individual research and cooperative reporting opportunities.

STUDENT TASK

Write a research report on geographic influences in the Middle East and use it for reference in a panel discussion.

DETAILED PROCEDURES

Part One:
Write a detailed, 3-4 page report on an assigned geographic factor's influence on the Middle East. Where possible, the report should contain some annotated graphic illustrations. Cite at least 4 resources.

Part Two:
Work cooperatively with other students who have done the same geographic factor to set up a panel presentation for the class. Each member must present a different idea about the influence of this geographic factor on the people of the Middle East. Each member should prepare to answer questions from the class after the presentation.

EVALUATION

The scoring grid next to the evaluation items (on the following pages) was left blank intentionally. Choice of appropriate category terms is the decision of the instructor. Selection of terms such as "minimal," "satisfactory," and "distinguished" can vary with this assessment. The table on page 10 offers additional suggestions for scoring descriptors that might be inserted in the blank grids.

LEARNING STANDARDS

Students Should:

• Present ideas both in writing and orally in clear, concise, and properly accepted fashion.

• Understand that peoples' values, practices and traditions are diverse, yet all face the same global challenges.

• Analyze and evaluate the effects of human, technological, and natural activities on societies.

• Demonstrate civic values and socially responsible behavior as members of school groups, local, state, national, and global communities.

• Employ a variety of information from written, graphic, and multimedia sources.

• Monitor, reflect upon, and improve their own and other's work.

• Work cooperatively and respect the rights of others to think, act, and speak differently within the context of democratic principles and social justice.

Part One: Individual Research Process and Report

Table on page 10 offers suggestions for scoring descriptors.

	Category 1	Category 2	Category 3	Category 4	Category 5
Evaluation Item a Have a variety of sources been checked and evaluated?					
Evaluation Item b Are report and bibliography written clearly, accurately, and effectively?					
Evaluation Item c Is the effect of geographic factor fully explored?					

Part Two: Group Planning and Panel Report

Table on page 10 offers suggestions for scoring descriptors.

	Category 1	Category 2	Category 3	Category 4	Category 5
Evaluation Item a Group Planning: Does student work effectively within group? Does student appreciate and respect views of others?					
Evaluation Item b Panel: Are effective graphic examples used?					
Evaluation Item c Panel: Is the impact on Middle East culture clearly presented?					
Evaluation Item d Panel: Are audience questions answered effectively?					

ADMINISTRATIVE GUIDELINES

1. Survey library resources and discuss project, especially graphic needs with librarian.

2. Arrange library time for research.

3. Hold class discussion to identify geographic influences on development in the Middle East.

4. Evaluate individual reports and give advice for panel presentations.

5. Allow adequate class time for groups to work cooperatively on panel presentation.

6. Establish schedule for panel presentations. (Suggest one per day.)

7. Combine teacher and peer ratings for panel evaluation.

8 *Western Europe*

Parliamentary system   feudalism
European Union   absolutism
mixed economy   totalitarianism
codified law   market system
Cold War   Industrial Revolution
socialism   consent of the governed

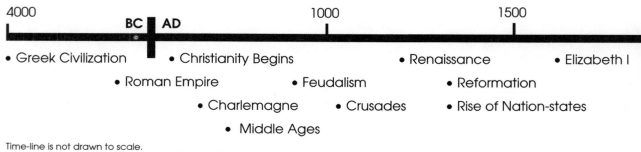

4000		1000	1500
BC **AD**			

• Greek Civilization   • Christianity Begins   • Renaissance   • Elizabeth I

          • Roman Empire   • Feudalism   • Reformation

                    • Charlemagne   • Crusades   • Rise of Nation-states

                              • Middle Ages

Time-line is not drawn to scale.

1800   1900   1950   2000

- Enlightenment   • Industrial Revolution   • WW I   • WW II   • Cold War   E. European •
- French Revolution   • Imperialism   • Hitler   • NATO   Pro-democracy Movements
- Napoleonic Wars   • Bismarck   • Holocaust   • Common Market

German Reunification •

Time-line is not drawn to scale.

UNIT EIGHT:

WESTERN EUROPE

I. PHYSICAL AND HISTORICAL SETTING

Western Europe is a densely populated global region containing two dozen nations and dependencies. It is bordered by the Arctic Ocean on the north, the Atlantic Ocean on the west, the Mediterranean Sea on the south, and the region of Eastern Europe. It is subdivided by mountain ranges into northern, western, central, and southern sections.

THE WESTERN SECTION

The nations of the United Kingdom, Ireland, France, Belgium, the Netherlands, and Luxembourg are included in the western section. While they are above 40° North latitude, the section has milder **Type C climates** (mid-latitude rainy) because of the influence of the **North Atlantic Drift** (warm Gulf Stream currents). The **English Channel**, a narrow strait, separates the British Isles from the European mainland. Historically, it offered England, Scotland, and Ireland unique natural protection from invasion.

- The **United Kingdom's** (England, Wales, Scotland, and N. Ireland) isolation from the mainland of Europe nurtured the U.K.'s development as a seafaring nation that ruled a huge overseas empire. Rich iron and coal deposits helped Great Britain emerge as the

world's major industrial nation in the early 19th Century. In the 20th Century, rapid depletion of these resources spurred development of North Sea petroleum drilling. An infrastructure developed around a series of canals linked to the **Thames River**.

- **Ireland's** rolling terrain, rainfall, and numerous rivers make it a natural agricultural country. Britain's long domination of Ireland and a lack of mineral resources slowed its industrial development until well into the 20th Century.

- **France's** seacoast, rivers, fertile soils, and mineral deposits permitted a balanced economic development. Mountain boundaries inland (**Pyrenees** and **Alps**) have given the French some protection, but a relatively open plain in the northeastern section of the country has been a frequent invasion route.

- **Belgium's**, the **Netherlands'**, and **Luxembourg's** locations on the Northeastern European plain make them lowland countries that have been frequent battlegrounds in Europe's many wars. These countries have excellent harbors and rivers that helped their communication, trade, and cultural development. The Netherlands' low elevations forced the people to build and use dikes, canals, and windmills in constant battles to reclaim and preserve the land from the encroaching seas.

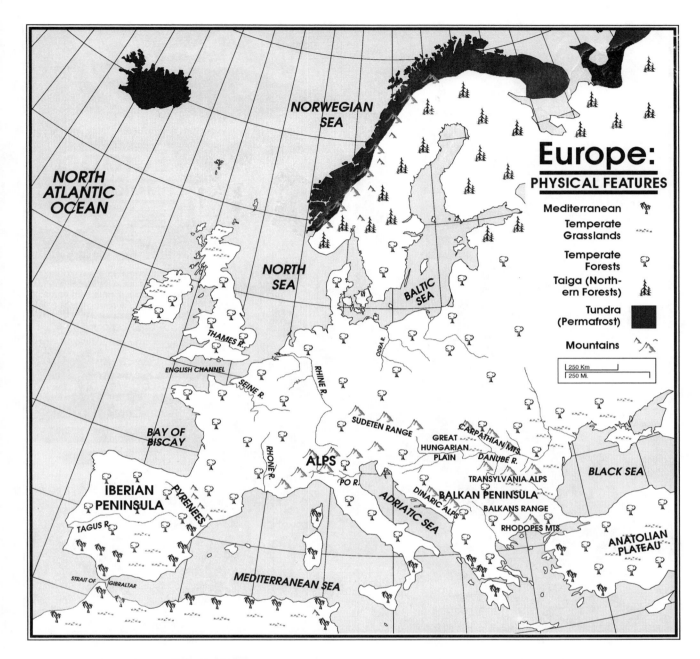

Europe: PHYSICAL FEATURES

Mediterranean

Temperate Grasslands

Temperate Forests

Taiga (Northern Forests)

Tundra (Permafrost)

Mountains

250 Km
250 Mi.

THE CENTRAL SECTION

Central Western Europe includes Germany, Switzerland, Austria, and the tiny country of Liechtenstein. This inland area basically has a **Type D climate** (mid-latitude, wet-and-dry) with cold winters. Yet, the topography modifies the wind currents from place to place within the section.

• **Germany's** Ruhr and Saar areas provide rich coal and iron ore deposits that aided industrialization. The **Rhine River** and its canal system have been a vital communica-

tion and transportation route for centuries. The river also provided some natural protection against invasion from the west.

• **Austria's** mountainous terrain, cut by the lengthy **Danube River**, acts as a major trade route. Because of the river, Austria has a flourishing agricultural economy.

• **Switzerland's** formidable **Alps** have not provided complete protection because of the many passes through them. Today, their rivers are a source of hydroelectric power for the small nation. Despite poor soils, the Swiss

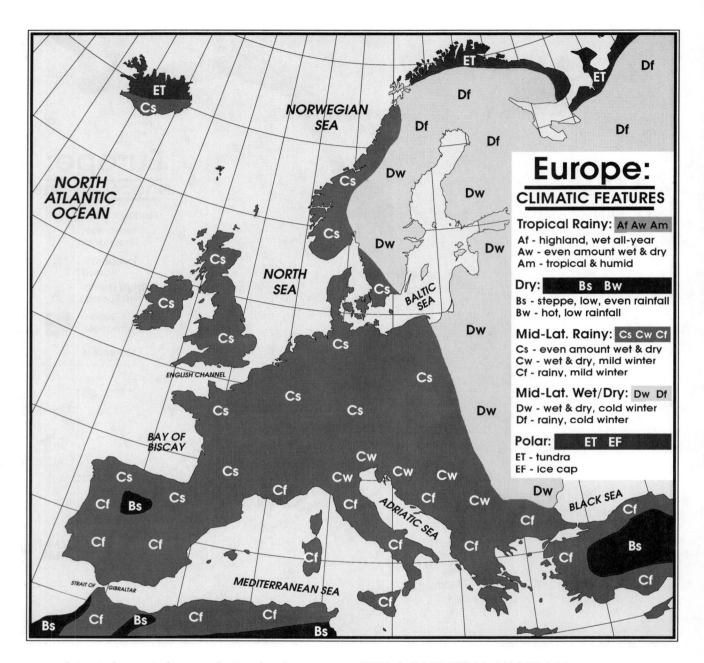

Europe: CLIMATIC FEATURES

Tropical Rainy: Af Aw Am
Af - highland, wet all-year
Aw - even amount wet & dry
Am - tropical & humid

Dry: Bs Bw
Bs - steppe, low, even rainfall
Bw - hot, low rainfall

Mid-Lat. Rainy: Cs Cw Cf
Cs - even amount wet & dry
Cw - wet & dry, mild winter
Cf - rainy, mild winter

Mid-Lat. Wet/Dry: Dw Df
Dw - wet & dry, cold winter
Df - rainy, cold winter

Polar: ET EF
ET - tundra
EF - ice cap

dairy industry is famous. Switzerland's major source of wealth is found in its industrial, financial, and commercial enterprises.

THE NORTHERN SECTION

The **Scandinavian Countries** (Norway, Sweden, Finland, Denmark, and Iceland) have **Type C** and **D climates** except in the extreme northern polar regions (**Type E**). Short, cool growing seasons cause the population to rely more on fishing and shipping for their livelihood. Mining and lumber industries are also sources of income.

THE SOUTHERN SECTION

Spain, Portugal, Italy, and Greece are the major nations in the Southern section. They have hot, dry summers and mild, sunny winters of the **Type C climates** (Mediterranean – Cf predominates).

• **Spain's** and **Portugal's** locations on the **Iberian Peninsula** separate them from the rest of Western Europe by the Pyrenees Mountains. As a consequence, its development has been influenced by Islamic cultures of North Africa. The economy is largely agricultural, although Portugal has large fishing fleets. Spain has considerable mining operations. The strategic **Strait of Gibraltar**, on the southern tip of Spain, controls the entrance to the Mediterranean. It currently lies in British hands.

- **Italy's** mountainous, boot-like peninsula juts out into the central Mediterranean below the Alps. The **Po River Valley** is its most productive farming region. The Northern section has fertile soils and is also industrialized. Southern Italy has poorer soils and is less developed.

- **Greece's** mountainous terrain has limited its agricultural development, but numerous fine harbors and a commanding location in the Eastern Mediterranean have made its people turn to seafaring for their livelihood.

ANCIENT CIVILIZATIONS

GREECE

Between 1500 and 1000 B.C., invading Hellenes married with the people at the tip of the Balkan Peninsula and began the Greek civilization. Unity was difficult because of the mountainous terrain. Therefore, a series of small, autonomous **city-states** emerged. Two of these merit special attention: Sparta and Athens.

Sparta placed its emphasis on military prowess and aristocratic control of the government. Young boys were taken from their families and educated in military schools. Sparta led a coalition of Greek city-states (Peloponnesian League) to victory in the Persian Wars (480-479 B.C.). Later it conquered Athens in the Peloponnesian Wars (431-404 B.C.). Slave revolts and civil wars weakened Sparta, and it declined. In the 4th Century B.C., it fell to Philip II of Macedonia. In the 2nd Century B.C., Rome conquered it. It devoted its energies to military power and made few cultural contributions to Western civilization.

Athens made significant contributions to government and

Western culture. From the 7th to the 5th Centuries B.C., Athens took numerous steps toward a more democratic government. It **codified** (organized and recorded) laws to insure equal treatment. It created jury duty for citizens and allowed commoners to vote in the Assembly. This created a form of **direct democracy**. Citizens had a direct say in making laws rather than being represented by officials. Still, citizenship was very limited. Athens denied citizenship to women, aliens, and slaves. Punishments for crimes were severe.

ATHENIAN CONTRIBUTIONS

Under **Pericles** (461-429 B.C.), all restrictions on office-holding were removed, so that the poor could participate. The responsibility of service in office was taken seriously, and many served to protect their rights as citizens. The democratic environment in the **Age of Pericles** led to a spirit of questioning, individual expression, and creativity.

Of the many philosophers, the three who laid the foundation for modern thought were Socrates, Plato, and Aristotle. They were concerned with questions of justice, morality, government's purpose, and the interrelationship of human beings.

Parthenon, Acropolis – Athens, Greece. The Parthenon, a temple dedicated to Athena Parthenos (Athena, the Warrior Maiden), is the largest building atop the Athenian Acropolis. During the Crusades, portions of the temple and its sculptures were destroyed or moved to Constantinople. In later times, the Parthenon served in succession as a Byzantine church, a Roman Catholic church, a Turkish harem, and a Turkish powder magazine. Photo by PhotoDisc Inc. 1994

- **Socrates** held that individuals should know themselves and gave Plato, his student, a method of seeking truth through constant questioning of life.

- **Plato** wrote his *Dialogues*, including *The Republic*, which described ideal social institutions.

- **Aristotle** preached moderation in life as well as the use of logic and reason in his *Politics* and *Ethics*.

The ideas of these philosophers continue to be studied to this day. Socrates was sentenced to death for encouraging his students to question authority. He accepted his sentence, for he believed that civilization rested on the principle of law and that people should not put themselves above the law.

Modern mathematics and science also developed in the intellectual atmosphere of Athens. Examples include the work of **Pythagoras of Samos** (principles of geometry), **Hippocrates** (medicine - natural causes of disease; the oath physicians take to serve the best interests of their patients), and **Democritus** (elementary ideas about the basic composition of matter).

Greek ideals of simplicity, perfection, realism, balance, and symmetry can be readily seen in the architecture of this age. The Greeks built the **Parthenon** on the Acropolis, the city's highest hill, to honor Athena, the patron goddess of the city. Its ruins still stand, and it is considered one of the most beautiful structures in the world. Its **Doric columns** and decorative friezes (wall sculptures) are still copied in modern structures.

The Greeks of this age also laid the groundwork for modern theater. Plays were performed in outdoor amphitheaters (arenas). It was viewed as a civic responsibility to attend performances. The tragedies of **Aeschylus**, **Sophocles**, and **Euripides** and the comedies of **Aristophanes** are still performed to this day.

The **Olympics**, the international games of today, date to the Greeks. The ancient games were dedicated to the gods, especially **Zeus**. All fighting was stopped for their duration. Athletes who won in foot races, discus throwing, wrestling, and other sports were rewarded with crowns of laurel or olive leaves and received the admiration of the crowds.

Greece's location, with its good harbors, promoted much trade and travel. As a result of the contacts made throughout the Mediterranean, Greek culture was diffused and preserved by others.

THE HELLENISTIC WORLD

The disunity of the Greek city-states led to their eventual conquest by **Philip II of Macedonia** (359-336 B.C.). After Philip's assassination, he was succeeded by his son, **Alexander the Great** (336-323 B.C.).

Alexander conquered a vast region stretching from the Balkan Peninsula, across Egypt and the Middle East, to Persia and the Indus

Hellenistic Contributions		
Field	**Contributor**	**Contribution**
Philosophy	Diogenes	**cynic** – humans should seek truth and not be driven to seek wealth, power, and pleasure
Natural Science	Archimedes	circumference of a circle; use of pulley and lever; principle of buoyancy (flotation)
Philosophy	Epicurus	**epicurean** – the proper end of life is to seek knowledge; seek happiness in moderation
Mathematics	Euclid	Euclidean geometry
Philosophy	Zeno	**stoicism** – humans must rise above misfortunes; seek harmony and equality

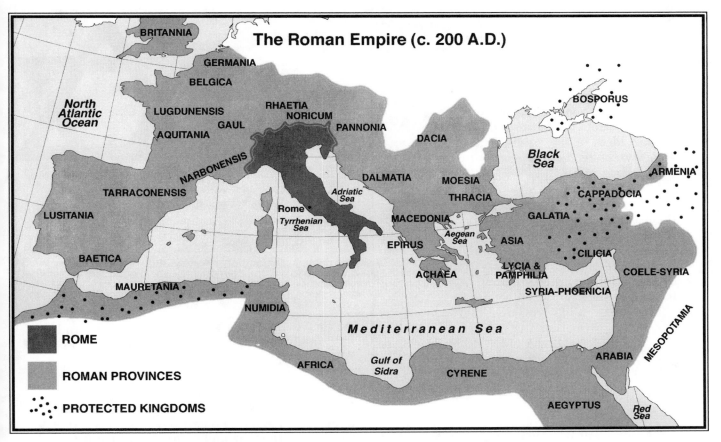

The Roman Empire (c. 200 A.D.)

BRITANNIA
GERMANIA
BELGICA
North Atlantic Ocean
LUGDUNENSIS
RHAETIA
NORICUM
GAUL
AQUITANIA
PANNONIA
NARBONENSIS
DACIA
BOSPORUS
TARRACONENSIS
DALMATIA
MOESIA
Black Sea
ARMENIA
LUSITANIA
Adriatic Sea
THRACIA
CAPPADOCIA
Rome
Tyrrhenian Sea
MACEDONIA
GALATIA
BAETICA
EPIRUS
Aegean Sea
ASIA
CILICIA
MAURETANIA
ACHAEA
LYCIA & PAMPHILIA
COELE-SYRIA
NUMIDIA
SYRIA-PHOENICIA
Mediterranean Sea
MESOPOTAMIA
ROME
AFRICA
Gulf of Sidra
CYRENE
ARABIA
ROMAN PROVINCES
AEGYPTUS
Red Sea
PROTECTED KINGDOMS

River in India. His conquests led to **cultural fusion** between the Greeks and the people of the Middle East. It resulted in a culture that became known as **Hellenistic** and made lasting contributions to civilization in many fields.

Disunity among Alexander's followers made it easy for the ambitious Romans to seize control of the Hellenistic conquests.

ANCIENT ROME

Rome was founded by the **Latins** on the hills above the Tiber River in Italy c. 1500 B.C. Initially, the government was an **aristocracy**. Power rested with the landed **patricians** (nobles). The **plebeians** (common people) had few rights, and they demanded reforms. This resulted in admission of their representatives into the lawmaking assembly. Plebeians gained the right to hold government office and a veto power over the patrician consuls and patrician-dominated Senate. As a result, Rome's aristocracy became a **republic** (representative democracy).

One of the most important achievements of the plebeians was to secure codification of the

The Colosseum is one of Rome's most famous landmarks. Begun in 69 A.D. by the Roman Emperor Vespasian, this massive amphitheater has survived although greatly damaged in many wars. Today, the Colosseum faces its greatest challenge from corrosive air pollution.   Photo by PhotoDisc Inc. 1994

law into *Twelve Tables*. This ensured that arbitrary (unwritten) acts would not be used against them. The modern word justice comes from the Latin *Ius*. The Roman ideal of the "individual's equality before the law" comes to us from this source.

The *Twelve Tables* concerned themselves with civil law, primarily the rights of the individual. For example, a murdered person's family had the responsibility of demanding satisfaction for its loss. Both sides appeared before a judge who decided

whether the murder was deliberate. If the judge decided in favor of the accusers, the accused lost the protection of the gods, and the murdered person's family could legally take revenge.

Around 340 B.C., Rome began to expand. It seized control of all of Italy, then the entire Mediterranean basin, Western Europe, and even England. As a consequence, Greek civilization was absorbed and diffused.

On the negative side, great differences began to separate the rich from the poor and the composition of the Roman army changed from one of citizens to professionals. The common people demanded more reforms, and civil wars broke out in which military men sought control of the empire. As a result of one of these struggles in the 1st Century B.C., **Julius Caesar** emerged as dictator, and the ideas of a republic faded.

Caesar was assassinated in 44 B.C., and after another power struggle, Rome crowned its first Emperor, **Caesar Augustus**. The **Roman Empire** came into existence. The Senate became an advisory group and the government, a military dictatorship. The Roman Empire lasted from 27 B.C. to 476 A.D.

The Romans enforced a **Pax Romana** (Peace of Rome) for over 200 years by using

Hadrian's Wall crosses northern England at its narrowest point, between the River Tyne and the Solway Firth, and was the permanent northern boundary for Roman-held territory. Construction of the ancient fortress was begun about 121 A.D. by order of the Roman emperor Hadrian and reflects his conservative policy of consolidating Rome's imperial acquisitions. Photo by PhotoDisc Inc. 1994

their armies, road systems, language, and broadened citizenship to unify the Mediterranean World.

Progress was made in many fields. Individual rights were protected by organizing imperial laws. The Roman codes specified the freedom of thought and expression, placed the burden of proof on the accusers, and considered age in sentencing punishments.

During the early years of the Empire, Christianity spread rapidly despite government persecutions. Its emphasis on the Judeo-Christian belief in one God, human brotherhood, and the immortality of the soul won converts among the common people. It became the official religion of the Empire in 392 A.D.

The achievements of the Romans in the practical art of engineering are noteworthy. Even today, their roads, aqueducts, and buildings (employing the round arch, dome, and Greek columns) stand as reminders of their skill. However, in terms of sculpture, painting, drama, and literature, Romans tended to imitate Greek patterns.

THE DECLINE OF THE ROMAN EMPIRE

The Roman Empire in Western Europe declined due to a combination of internal weakness and attacks by outside peoples. Politically,

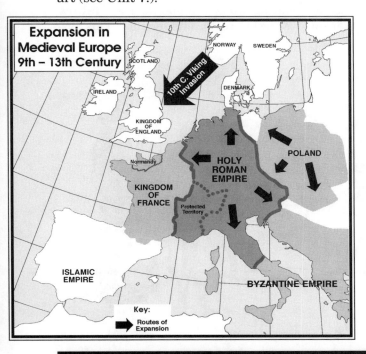

the military dictatorship left little room for citizen participation and slowly failed to provide effective protection.

Economically, expensive imports undermined the value of currency and led to a barter system. Large estates in the outer parts of the Empire became more self-sufficient and began to break away from the Empire. Socially, a rigid class structure developed, crime increased, and the population declined. Under these circumstances, Rome became easy prey for raiding **Germanic tribes**. The last emperor was overthrown in 476 A.D., and the Roman Empire disintegrated.

In the 4th Century A.D., the problems stated above caused the Eastern area of the Roman Empire to break away from Rome's control and set up its capital in **Byzantium** (in modern Turkey). The Eastern Emperor dominated both the government and the **Eastern Orthodox Church**. The Byzantine Empire's active commerce with India and the Orient led to substantial riches. Its craftsmen made luxury items that were exported to the West and into the interior of Eastern Europe. It continued the Greek classical heritage. Many manuscripts were preserved for later generations. The Byzantine Roman Empire also made many of its own cultural contributions, especially in mosaic art (see Unit 7.).

Expansion in Medieval Europe 9th – 13th Century

NORWAY SWEDEN

SCOTLAND

10th C. Viking Invasion

IRELAND

DENMARK

KINGDOM OF ENGLAND

Normandy

POLAND

HOLY ROMAN EMPIRE

KINGDOM OF FRANCE

Protected Territory

ISLAMIC EMPIRE

BYZANTINE EMPIRE

Key:

Routes of Expansion

MEDIEVAL TIMES

After the collapse of the Roman Empire, Western Europe fell into a period of disorder and chaos marked by the lack of a strong central government and a decline in trade with little cultural progress. Central Asian (Huns), Nordic (Vikings), and Germanic tribes (Saxons) constantly invaded Western Europe during this period. They founded many small kingdoms and trading centers, and they assimilated and diffused Western culture. The period became known as the **Dark Ages**, or the **Early Medieval** period. It lasted from 500 to 1000 A.D.

CHARLEMAGNE

There were some notable exceptions to this general period of decline in Western Europe. In the 8th Century A.D., the Franks' chieftain, **Charles Martel**, turned back a Muslim invasion at the **Battle of Tours**. A strong Frankish kingdom emerged in the central and western sections of Europe. It reached its zenith under **Charlemagne**. His empire extended from the Pyrenees and northern Italy, north to the English Channel, and eastward to the modern Czech Republic.

Charlemagne divided his large empire into provinces governed by loyal nobles. His power rested on traveling investigators, or **missi dominici**. These agents kept the emperor informed of the actions of the provincial nobles. Conquered people were forced to convert to Christianity under the penalty of death. His conquest of the Lombards of Northern Italy provided lands for the Pope who crowned Charlemagne the first **Holy Roman Emperor** in 800 A.D. Charlemagne established a palace school for the children of his loyal nobles. He was only partially successful in getting monasteries and churches to start schools for the young. His empire disintegrated amid struggles by his heirs.

FEUDALISM

A series of violent invasions by raiders from the northern regions of Europe (**Norsemen** or **Vikings**) in the 9th and 10th Centuries destroyed the larger kingdoms and principalities of Western Europe. Local lords who

DETERMINATION OF POLITICAL & ECONOMIC SYSTEMS

could defend their small holdings drew loyalty from local people. Frequently, landholders signed over their lands to these local lords in exchange for protection. These interrelated local loyalties evolved into a political, economic, and social structure called **feudalism**. It provided strong local government, a connected system of self-sufficient manors with a rigid class structure. Feudalism provided military protection in a perilous time of disorder, but it came at the expense of freedom.

Sue Ann Kime, 1974

Warwick Castle, England, built by Richard Neville, Earl of Warwick, b. Nov. 22, 1428, d. 1471. He became known as the Kingmaker because of his great wealth and power.

Land-holding nobles became **knights** (fighting men). They provided defense for those who worked their lands. They usually allied themselves with some powerful **overlord**. They served in his army in exchange for the lord's protection of their manors. Thus, the knights became **vassals** of the overlords and swore oaths of **fealty** (loyalty) to them.

On the individual manor (fief), people were bound to the land as **serfs** giving their labor in exchange for land to work and protection. As the feudal system evolved, it considered a serf property to be passed on as part of a noble's inheritance. Serfs could not leave the estate, marry, or change their trade without the noble's permission. In this rigid class structure, the only way serfs could possibly change status was to enter the service of the Church.

The feudal **manor** was self-sufficient. Trade was minimal since travel was dangerous. In agriculture, a rotating **three-field system** evolved. Each season, two fields were planted with alternating crops and one field left **fallow** (vacant, resting) to restore its fertility. This sys-

tem reduced the wear on the limited land. Tools were crudely fashioned of wood because metals were scarce and needed for battle weapons. The substance level farms offered low yields. The serf maintained some personal livestock on the lord's pastures, gathered firewood, and fished. However, hunting game was restricted for the lord. The **manor house** was usually a walled castle for protection. These fortresses were sometimes surrounded by a moat or built on high ground. Under siege, the people of the manor would gather behind the castle walls.

On his lands, the knight was absolute. For the serf, justice often took the form of a trial by some brutal **ordeal**. Survival indicated God's blessing of the innocent, but often badly injured the serf. The social needs of the manor were often met by the Church's ceremonies, services, and festivals. Manor lords were sometimes entertained by traveling bands of troubadours, jesters, jugglers, and wandering theater groups.

THE CHURCH

In many respects, the Church was the main social institution of the Middle Ages. Its governmental structure survived the fall of Rome, and its teachings provided some sense of universal law and order. Church courts and canon law provided a background for the inevitable clashes between the Church's spiritual power and the secular power of local overlords.

The Church controlled literature. Monks decorated Latin manuscripts with artistic flare and beautiful illumination.

The Cathedral of Our Lady of Chartres looms high above the small town of Chartres, southwest of Paris, France. Constructed between 1194 and 1220 A.D., no other Gothic church of comparable size has the harmonious nature and quality of architecture, sculpture, and stained glass. Photo by Sue Ann Kime, 1974

The Church also had economic power. The **tithe** (10% of one's wealth was donated to the Church) and **Peter's Pence** (obligatory donations to the Pope) yielded vast amounts. Much of this wealth was used to benefit others, particularly monks in monasteries. In turn, they provided care for the sick and lodging for travelers, copied ancient manuscripts, chronicled events, and introduced new farming techniques.

Wealth was rather static because the Church forbade **usury** (lending money at interest). Since Christians could not engage in such financial dealings, many of the Jews of Europe became moneylenders and later established banking houses. This often led to prejudice and jealousy against Jews since they were able to accumulate wealth. They were often expelled from regions where nobles who had borrowed did not wish to repay them.

To Christian Europe, the Church provided the services necessary for the faithful to achieve eternal life. The Mass and the sacraments were important rituals in these times. **Excommunication** was greatly feared because it denied the Church's services to a person. The cultural role of the Church is evident when one views the enormous Romanesque and Gothic cathedrals built in Medieval times. The donations of wealth, artisanship, and creativity in these structures, which sometimes took centuries to build, indicate the powerful position of the Church as a social institution. The painting, sculpture, and writing of the age had God or Church teachings as major themes.

The Abbey of Saint Peter and the Convent of Nonnberg, founded about 700 A.D. and remodeled in the 15th Century. They present architectural splendor that shows such an Italianate influence that Salzburg, Austria has been called the "German Rome." Photo by PhotoDisc Inc. 1994

QUESTIONS

1 Which of the following contributed most to the industrial development of Great Britain?
1 iron and coal deposits
2 Rhine River
3 lumber industry
4 mild, sunny winters

2 The Great Northern Plain played a significant role in European history because it
1 provided France with access to Spain
2 blocked German expansion to the east
3 allowed the spread of industrial development
4 was a major invasion route into France

3 The Ruhr and Saar areas of Germany are
1 Western Europe's major agricultural region
2 areas of mineral wealth
3 on the border with Russia
4 along the Danube River

4 Which of the following rivers is correctly associated with a country through which it flows?
1 Po River – Great Britain
2 Danube River – France
3 Rhine River – Germany
4 Thames River – Austria

5 Southern Europe is an area which
1 depends on large-scale industry as its major source of wealth
2 has fallen behind other areas of Europe in industrial growth
3 derives little of its income from agricultural production
4 has a moist, cool climate during the summer months

6 Which is true of a direct democracy?
1 The people elect representatives who make decisions.
2 Government officials are appointed by a groups of elders.
3 Citizens vote on laws themselves.
4 Juries are selected by the defendants.

7 The diffusion of Greek culture was aided by
1 a series of rivers linked by canals
2 location and good harbors
3 a lack of mountain barriers
4 widespread acceptance of the Greek religion

8   In *The Republic*, Plato wrote about
1   a system for international peace
2   monotheism
3   new methods of scientific farming
4   ideal governmental forms

9   The Parthenon is noted as
1   the site of a major European battle
2   a Roman government building
3   a Spartan monument to dead warrior heroes
4   a symbol of the ancient Greek ideals

10   Preservation of the classical heritage, the use of mosaic decorations, and the spread of the Eastern Orthodox religion can be attributed to
1   the Byzantine Empire
2   the Roman Empire
3   Alexander the Great
4   Charlemagne

11   Which was true of early Christians in the Roman Empire?
1   They were exempt from taxes in the Roman Empire.
2   They first attracted followers among the common people.
3   They were basically polytheistic.
4   They denied the existence of life after death.

12   A fighting man, head of the local government, and major landowner are all terms that could be used to describe a medieval
1   noble
2   merchant
3   serf
4   troubadour

13   Feudalism might best be described as a system designed to
1   oppose the spread of Christianity
2   increase the power of absolute monarchs
3   provide protection through interdependence of classes
4   protect the trade of merchants

14   Alexander the Great's conquests led to
1   development of the Hellenistic culture
2   the spread of Christianity
3   the establishment of feudalism
4   a cultural decline called the "Dark Ages"

15   The *Twelve Tables* were
1   a statement of religious doctrine
2   an important Greek archeological find
3   written by the Greek philosopher Plato
4   a written statement of Roman law

16   Tithes, usury, and canon law are terms connected with
1   Charlemagne
2   feudalism
3   the medieval Church
4   architecture

ESSAYS

1   Select *three* major geographic features of Western Europe from the list below. For *each* one selected, explain how it affected the development of the area in which it is located.

•   The Great Northern European Plain
•   The English Channel
•   The Alps
•   The North Atlantic Drift

2   Select *three* of the fields listed below. For each one selected, discuss two contributions that the ancient Greeks and/or Romans made in that field to modern civilization.

•   Philosophy
•   Science and Mathematics
•   Government
•   Architecture
•   Sculpture
•   Literature

3   Feudalism and the Roman Catholic Church were the dominant institutions in Western Europe in the Middle Ages.

a   Explain how *each* affected the economic, political, and social structures of the era.

b   Explain why the Church also dominated the cultural achievements of the age.

II. DYNAMICS OF CHANGE

CROSS CULTURAL CHANGE

THE CRUSADES

In 1095, Pope Urban II called for a crusade to take control of the Holy Land from the Muslim Turks. But, the Crusade had other purposes:

- to increase the Church's power

- to reunite the Roman and Eastern Orthodox Churches

- to unify the warlike nobility of Western Europe in a Church cause

Impression of a woodcut from Crusade Era

Over the next 200 years, there were eight Crusades by Europeans to the Eastern Mediterranean. They obtained the right for Christian pilgrims to visit the area. There were also minor crusades to drive the Turks out of Central Europe and the Muslims out of Spain ("Reconquista"). The Crusades brought about far-reaching social, political, and economic results that moved Europe from the Middle Ages into modern times.

Byzantine and Muslim artisans and scholars preserved much ancient Greek and Hellenistic culture. They used it as a starting point for their own contributions, including advances in mathematics, medicine, and science. The Crusades also brought the Europeans into contact with the spices, silks, and porcelains of the Far East as well as block printing, gunpowder, and the compass. The increased knowledge, desire for the new products, and wealth gained from the resulting trade did much to bring about the Renaissance in Western Europe.

CULTURAL CHANGE: THE RENAISSANCE

The Renaissance (14th – 17th Centuries, A.D.) first appeared in the Italian city-states which had extensive contacts with the Middle East. Genoa, Venice, Florence, and other cities acted as intermediaries for the rest of Western Europe. Popes and powerful families such as the **Medici** of Florence used the wealth to sponsor artisans.

St. Mark's Church, Venice, Italy houses one of Europe's richest collections of treasures, including the Pala d'Oro (a huge Byzantine altarpiece of gold; 976) as well as magnificent reliquaries, book covers, and statues, which were among the rich booty taken from Constantinople in 1204 by the Venetian-inspired Fourth Crusade.   PhotoDisc Inc. 1994

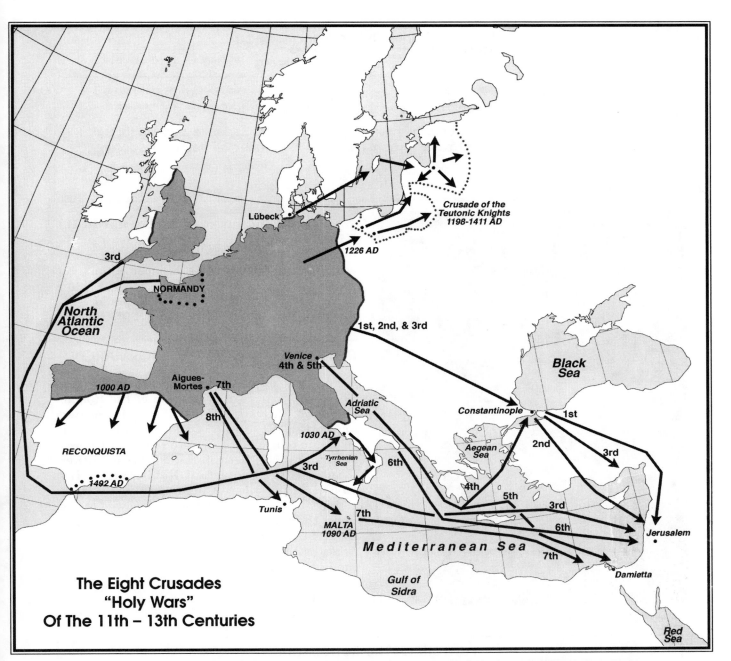

**The Eight Crusades
"Holy Wars"
Of The 11th – 13th Centuries**

Map labels: Lübeck; Crusade of the Teutonic Knights 1198-1411 AD; 1226 AD; 3rd; NORMANDY; North Atlantic Ocean; 1st, 2nd, & 3rd; 1000 AD; Aigues-Mortes; 7th; Venice 4th & 5th; Adriatic Sea; Black Sea; Constantinople; 1st; 2nd; 3rd; RECONQUISTA; 8th; 1030 AD; Tyrrhenian Sea; 6th; Aegean Sea; 4th; 5th; 3rd; Jerusalem; 1492 AD; 3rd; Tunis; 7th; MALTA 1090 AD; 6th; 7th; Mediterranean Sea; Damietta; Gulf of Sidra; Red Sea

Renaissance means "rebirth." This time period was one in which people once again became interested in education and learning. Classical Greek and Roman civilizations inspired artists to follow interests in humankind, nature, and individualism.

The Renaissance was also a period of transition. Characteristics of ancient times, medieval, and modern times mixed. The interest in humankind was particularly evident in the movement called **humanism**. It placed an increased emphasis upon individuality and personal worth. Both characteristics were reflected in the literature and art of the period.

Magnificent pieces of sculpture such as **Moses**, the **Pieta**, and **David** by **Michelangelo** were known for their accurate rendition of human anatomy and their expressive portrayal of people. In addition to this work, Michelangelo was responsible for much of the planning of **St. Peter's Basilica** in Rome. It was closely modeled on Greek and Roman buildings, but with the addition of a Renaissance touch, the **cupola** (domed roof, ceiling, or surmounting structure).

Literary Works Of The Renaissance

Writer	Work	Ideas
Danté	*Divine Comedy*	Described imaginary trip through Hell, Purgatory, and Paradise using people such as the Roman poet Virgil as guides.
Erasmus	*In Praise of Folly*	Satirized the professions, but reserved special criticism for the clergymen whom he found to be uneducated and worldly.
More	*Utopia*	Proposed an ideal society in which there was no unemployment and everyone had equal possessions.

Michelangelo's statue of *David* – Florence, Italy

PhotoDisc Inc. 1994

Many historians consider **Leonardo Da Vinci** the epitome of the Renaissance. He excelled as an artist, writer, scientist, inventor, sculptor, and engineer. He designed a tank, an airplane, a parachute, and the bicycle chain drive, but no technology existed to produce his inventions.

RELIGIOUS CHANGE: THE REFORMATION

As change spread, Europeans began to question the practices and doctrine of the Roman Catholic Church. People placed increased emphasis on the role of the individual with regard to religion. Voices were raised for Church reform. In 1517, German cleric **Martin Luther** formalized the **Protestant Reformation**. His **95 Theses** questioned Church practices such as selling indulgences, the role and power of the Pope, the way to attain salvation, the value of some of the sacraments, the interpretation of the *Bible*, and the role of clergy. His protests led to the **Lutheran** Christian sects.

John Calvin, a Swiss religious reformer, went further than Luther in proposing changes.

Artwork Of The Renaissance

Artist	Work	Characteristics
Da Vinci	*Mona Lisa*	Used triangular composition and landscape background, famous smile and expressive eyes.
	Last Supper	Depicted Last Supper at moment when Christ announced betrayal by Judas. Famous for portrayal of apostles' characters, triangular composition, and perspective.
Michelangelo	*Sistine Chapel*	Combined the Bible story from the creation to the flood with figures from ancient Greece.
Raphael	*Disputa*	Showed Greek philosophers holding a discussion. Used overlapping figures and extended limbs to hold multifigured picture together.

Cathedral of Notre Dame de Paris on the Seine River at night. Typical of the Early Gothic style, Notre Dame was begun in 1163 and completed in 1200. The formidable structure symbolized the power of the Roman Church in Medieval Europe.

increase his power, he gave some to important nobles to win their support.

The Roman Catholic Church responded to these threats to its power with the **Catholic Counter Reformation** in the 16th Century. The Church convened the **Council of Trent**. It reaffirmed basic doctrine and took steps to eliminate abuses within the Church.

The Reformation had far-reaching results that affect Europe even today. Protestant reformers emphasized self-interpretation of the *Bible* and a return to the simple beliefs and ideas of early Christians. The invention of the movable-type printing press by

His followers later founded the Presbyterian, Congregational, Puritan, and Dutch Reformed churches.

CHOICE Protestant reformers contested the power of the Pope and Church hierarchy. Most believed that faith alone was sufficient to achieve salvation and accepted only the sacraments of Baptism and the Lord's Supper. They encouraged self-interpretation of the *Bible* and believed in the priesthood of all believers.

Along with the religious debates, many rulers began to question the political power of the Church. They saw it as competing with their attempts to centralize their governments.

For example, in order to obtain a male heir for the throne of England, **Henry VIII** wished to annul his marriage to Catherine of Aragon in order to marry **Anne Boleyn**. The Pope refused. Thomas Cranmer, Archbishop of Canterbury, helped King Henry secure a divorce independently of the Pope. Cranmer helped Henry persuade Parliament to pass the *Act of Supremacy* (1534). It established the **Anglican Church** (Church of England). After the American Revolution, the Church of England became known as the Episcopalian Church in America. The act made Henry head of the Church in England. The king was able to seize the Church property. Keeping some to

Martin Luther protested the authority and practices of the Roman Church by posting a series of grievances on the door of the Roman Catholic Church in Wittenberg, Germany.

Johann Gutenburg (1447) helped them greatly. Availability of inexpensive printed books increased the literacy rate. Publishing the *Bible* in **vernacular form** (everyday languages) instead of scholarly Latin allowed more individuals to read the scriptures. This broadened self-interpretation and intensified the Reformation.

The strong religious unity of Western Europe disappeared. For two hundred years, devastating religious wars wracked every section. Uneasy toleration settled in after the last of these wars ended (1648). Still, in parts of Europe, the animosity among religions continues today.

POLITICAL CHANGE: NATION-STATES AND ABSOLUTE MONARCHS

The rise of nation-states and the development of **absolutism** (all power in hands of a single party) evolved during the Renaissance and accelerated during the Protestant Reformation.

Bases for these political philosophies can be found in the writings of Nicolo Machiavelli of Florence, Bishop Jacques Benigne Bossuet of France, and other writers. **Machiavelli (1469-1527)** wrote ***The Prince*** to give advice on how to increase and hold power. Later rulers frequently followed his advice. He stated that "the end justifies the means" (anything that a ruler does to keep or increase power is justified). He suggested that a ruler use citizen armies as opposed to less reliable mercenaries. Machiavelli believed that rulers should be seen as cruel and tight-fisted (as opposed to kindly and generous). Numerous rulers used these ideas as justification for increasing their power.

The **Tudor** rulers of England never claimed to rule by **divine right** (ruling power bestowed on a person or family by God) as did the French monarchs. Yet, they did come very close to absolute power. Henry VIII's younger daughter, **Elizabeth I** (1558-1603) was very powerful and popular. However, she had difficulty living within the income Parliament granted her. Because she feared a loss of power, she seldom called Parliament to meet or to give her more money.

The popular Elizabeth I, Queen of England

Religion continued as a controversial issue during her reign. Elizabeth provided secret aid to Protestant groups fighting the Catholics. Still, she wisely followed a policy of limited toleration for the private practice of religion as long as no threats were made to her power. Her encouragement of trade won her support from the vital middle class. She masterfully negotiated with foreign monarchs, even arranging marriages for her nobles to cement temporary alliances.

By 1588, **Philip II** of Spain tired of Elizabeth's plots and intrigues. In his eyes, Elizabeth's cousin, **Mary, Queen of Scots**, was the legitimate Catholic ruler of England. After Elizabeth had Mary executed, Philip sent his Armada against the English. Their navies engaged off the English Channel. A combination of storms, English seamanship, and the use of fire-ships resulted in the defeat of Spain. Elizabeth began mercantile policies encouraging overseas adventures. This was the groundwork for the British Empire. During her reign, English nationalism developed. Its beginnings were reflected in the literary works of **William Shakespeare**, **Edmund Spenser**, and **Christopher Marlowe**.

Louis XIV of France (1643-1715) is considered to be the best example of a Machiavellian, absolute, divine right ruler. He never called the

Beefeaters, the Warders of the Tower of London (established in 1669), and Yeomen of the Guard (established in 1485) wear picturesque Tudor costumes of red and gold. Now ceremonial, they originally had a distinct function as bodyguards of the British monarch.

Louis also gained control over the economy by the use of mercantilist policies. His able minister, **Jean Baptiste Colbert**, increased the revenues of the government to pay for the king's frequent wars. Louis fought several wars to eliminate the Netherlands as a commercial rival. He also tried to gain the Rhine River as a boundary for France. Colbert could not stimulate enough revenue to cover the heavy costs of these wars. Louis' expulsion of the economically important **Huguenots** (middle class Calvinists) made the financial situation worse.

France gained little from Louis' wars. He obtained a few small territories near the Rhine. A French prince was allowed to rule Spain on the condition that the two countries would never unite. France emerged from Louis XIV's wars heavily in debt. It also lost valuable colonies on the North American Continent to England. French nationalism developed during Louis' reign, and many European rulers imitated his life style. French cultural influence spread. The French language, fashion, and cooking became popular throughout the Continent.

POLITICAL CHANGE: LIMITS ON ABSOLUTISM

England became dissatisfied with the nearly absolute power of monarchs after Elizabeth I. Parliament began to assert itself. There had been earlier attempts to limit the power of English monarchs.

Estates General (the French Parliament) to meet. He appointed middle class officials to replace nobles who could challenge his power.

Louis built the magnificent **Palace of Versailles** to serve as a "gilded cage" for an elaborate court life to control his nobles. He drew the nobles to the Palace by the lifestyle that involved banquets, dances, gambling, fireworks, and theatrical performances. They relished the prestige of being in the presence of the **Sun King** (the absolute center of French life). In the meantime, the nobles' estates were often mismanaged. The nobles decreased income limited their ability to challenge the power of the king.

Sue Ann Kime, 1974   The Palace of Versailles, France

DETERMINATION OF POLITICAL & ECONOMIC SYSTEMS

For example, in 1215, rebellious nobles, who thought King John infringed on their rights, forced him to sign the *Magna Carta*.

The **Model Parliament** (1295) under Edward I established the concept of the **power of the purse**. Later Parliaments used this weapon to decrease the power of kings who were ever in need of additional revenues. In the 17th Century, Parliament used it against the **Stuart Dynasty**.

Scotland's Stuart family succeeded the Tudors after Elizabeth I died. They did not fully understand the English system of government. **James I** and his son, **Charles I**, tried to rule without consulting Parliament. They claimed divine right authority. They also had Puritans persecuted. **Puritans** were Anglicans who sought to reform the Church of England along Calvinist lines. They had power in the House of Commons, yet various groups persecuted them as too radical.

The Stuart kings also became involved in expensive political struggles on the European Continent. They were unable to live within their income. They frequently clashed with Parliament over these issues. Charles I had to call Parliament to meet in 1628 because of his need for funds. Parliament forced him to sign the *Petition of Right* in exchange for new revenues. This act strengthened some of the principles of the *Magna Carta*. Charles continued to rule without Parliament until a revolt in Scotland forced him to do so. He arrested some opponents among House of Commons' Puritan leaders. His actions triggered a revolution.

The **Puritan Revolution** (1642-1653) ended in the defeat of **Cavaliers** (the king's supporters) at the hands of the **Roundheads** (Puritan supporters). The Roundheads executed Charles, abolished the monarchy, and established a new commonwealth form of government. Puritan leader **Oliver Cromwell** became **Lord Protector**. An interesting result of this government was the first modern written constitution, the *Instrument of Government*. It later became a model for the framers of the *Constitution of the United States*.

Cromwell's Puritan Commonwealth was not popular with the English people. It imposed a severe form of Puritanism on the Anglican population. Richard Cromwell became Lord Protector after his father's death in 1658. The younger Cromwell could not hold the commonwealth together. In 1660, Parliament voted to restore the Stuart heir, **Charles II** (son of the executed king), to England's throne.

Charles II wished to avoid the fate of his father. In the **Restoration Period**, he did little to interfere with Parliament. Parliament passed the *Habeas Corpus Act*, further expanding individual rights. It guaranteed arrested persons a statement of charges, bail, and a fair and speedy trial.

Charles' brother James succeeded him in 1685. **James II** claimed divine right rule, flaunted his Catholicism, and disobeyed English law by appointing Catholics to high positions. His harsh suppression of minor uprisings also brought Parliamentary protests. In 1688, the birth of a son displaced his daughters as Protestant heirs to the throne. James defied Parliament and had his son baptized a Catholic. Parliament deposed James in the **Glorious Revolution** of 1688.

Parliament asked James' older daughter and her husband, **William and Mary of Orange**, to rule England.  This unmaking of one ruler and making of a new one marked the supremacy of Parliament. To further ensure its power, Parliament required the new rulers to sign the *Bill of Rights* in 1689. This document combined with the earlier *Magna Carta* and *Petition of Right* became cornerstones in limiting the power of the monarchy in England.

Cornerstones of Political Reform and Democracy

Document	Justice Provisions	Financial Provisions
Magna Carta 1215	Guaranteed judgment by peers for all freemen. Justice may not be denied, delayed, or sold.	Taxes levied only with the advice of the Great Council (Parliament).
Petition of Right 1628	Cannot be imprisoned without a charge and provision for trial by jury.	No taxes levied without the consent of Parliament.
Bill of Rights 1689	Guaranteed a speedy trial. Protected against excessive fines, and bail, as well as protected from cruel or unusual punishment.	No taxes levied without the consent of Parliament.

Progress toward democracy in England was evolutionary. It involved minimal violence compared to revolutions seen in France and other countries. Still, the evolution provided a philosophical basis for later revolutions in the American colonies, France, and elsewhere. In fact, some provisions of the English *Bill of Rights* were duplicated in the U.S. *Bill of Rights*. American revolutionaries claimed they were simply seeking their rights as Englishmen when they took up arms against George III (1776).

ECONOMIC CHANGE: THE AGE OF EXPLORATION AND DISCOVERY

The Age of Exploration and Discovery was an extension of the Renaissance and the Crusades. It reflected the improvement of life and the Renaissance spirit of questioning authority and institutions. The Crusades introducted Europeans to the goods of Asia. A demand emerged for the new products. Muslim rulers dominated overland routes through Asia. They demanded tribute from the caravans. In addition, Italian city-states controlled the sea routes of the Mediterranean. All this complicated trade and made goods expensive. The fall of Constantinople to the Ottoman Turks in 1453 made the situation worse. Consequently, European rulers desired finding an all water route to Asia.

The Portuguese intensified the search for such a route to Asia in the 15th Century under **Prince Henry**. Improved navigational devices such as the astrolabe and compass as well as better ways of rigging ships encouraged Europeans to support exploration ventures. Gradually, the Portuguese inched their way down the African coast and around the Cape of Good Hope to the Indian Ocean. They claimed good harbors as supply stations as they went. Finally, **Vasco da Gama** reached India in

Age of Discovery

Explorer	Country	Area Claimed Or Discovered
Diaz	Portugal	Cape of Good Hope – 1488
da Gama	Portugal	India– 1498
Columbus	Spain	Caribbean islands, parts of northern South America and Central America – 1492 - 1498
Cortes	Spain	Mexico – 1519 - 1521
Pizarro	Spain	Peru – 1531 - 1534
Magellan	Spain	Philippines – 1519 - 1522
Cartier	France	St. Lawrence River (Canada) – 1534 - 1536
Champlain	France	Eastern Canada and northern U.S. – 1608
Cabot	England	Northern U.S. and Labrador – 1496 - 1497
Hudson	Netherlands	Hudson River – 1609

1498. The goods that he brought back paid for the voyage several times over.

The Spanish began looking westward across the Atlantic for a route to Asia. In 1492, Isabella of Spain agreed to finance the first voyage of an Italian mariner, **Christopher Columbus**. England, France, and the Netherlands also joined in the search for sea routes for trading. Explorers sought passages through North America and Russia. As they went, these adventurers claimed territories for their respective countries.

Dreams of "Gold, God, and Glory" motivated European explorers. Conflicts arose. They frequently seized each others' colonies. The greatest conflict involved England and France (1667 - 1763). This series of global wars ended with the **Seven Years' War** (1756-1763). In North American history, it was known as the "French and Indian War." France lost Canada and all claims east of the Mississippi (now the U.S.) and was all but pushed out of India. Britain emerged as the world's dominant colonial power.

ECONOMIC CHANGE: COMMERCIAL REVOLUTION

A far-reaching **Commercial Revolution** resulted from the global exploration. To finance exploration and colonization, a new form of business organization emerged, the **joint stock company**.

Selling stock (ownership shares) made it possible to raise small amounts of money from many backers. The combined capital financed exploration and colonial ventures. To meet the needs of the emerging **capitalist system** (private enterprise), modern banking and insurance companies also began in this era.

As demand for European products increased, some areas abandoned the medieval **guild system**. Guilds were small associations of highly trained craftsmen. Highly independent, the guilds could not coordinate large-scale production. The **domestic system** (also called the "putting out system") emerged. Private capitalist financiers coordinated simple piecework production done in employees' homes.

In England, much of the domestic system revolved around the production of textiles. Investors, trying to organize the production of wool, pressed Parliament to pass the ***Enclosure Acts***, allowing fenced pastures. Enclosure led to unemployment among agricultural laborers, since fewer were needed to manage livestock. Some went into the new domestic system, but economic hardships were frequent.

Monarchs who had been centralizing national power now tried to do the same with the economy. Many nations adopted **mercantilism** as their economic policy. This policy aimed at increasing the gold and silver that a country possessed. Nations limited imports and encouraged exports with subsidies (support grants) for trading companies. Mercantilism led to national conflicts such as the Seven Years' War (1756 - 1763).

As in France under Louis XIV and Colbert, governments sometimes helped commerce by improving infrastructures (harbors, roads, bridges, canals). Some governments regulated standards of quality. They sought colonies as sources of raw materials and controllable markets for finished products. Mercantile regulations made colonies serve the economic interests of the mother country. Some of these mercantile restrictions led to the revolutions in the Americas.

POLITICAL REVOLUTIONS
THE ENLIGHTENMENT

The spirit of the Renaissance and Reformation slowly evolved into the intellectual revolution in the 17th and 18th Centuries. It was called the **Enlightenment**. European scholars began a search for natural laws that governed human existence.

In his ***Universal Law of Gravitation***, England's **Sir Isaac Newton** presented a blending of science and reason accumulated over centuries of Western civilization. Enlightenment scholars came refer to it as **natural law**.

Some Enlightenment thinkers, called **Deists**, embraced the idea that God created the first life, established the laws governing the

Enlightenment Philosophies

Philosopher	Work	Ideas
Locke 1690	*Two Treatises of Civil Government*	People establish government to protect their **natural rights** of life, liberty, and property. If the government fails to do this, the people have the right to revolt.
Voltaire 1753	*Letters on the English*	Rulers should govern through **enlightened despotism**: use of power for the benefit of people. Admired the relative freedom of speech, press, and religion in England.
Montesquieu 1753	*The Spirit of the Laws*	Power should be separated among the branches of government and preserved through a checks - and - balance system.
Smith 1776	*The Wealth of Nations*	Government should keep its hands off business (**laissez-faire**). The natural laws of supply and demand would do the best job of meeting the needs of the people and properly allocating economic resources.
Paine 1776	*Common Sense*	Hereditary monarchy created the problems of the American colonists. Urged independence from England. Promoted natural human rights of humankind .

universe, and then left it to run according to established rules. They believed that if humans were allowed to use reason, they would uncover the natural laws that governed existence, and progress would result.

Most Enlightenment **philosophers** (scholars seeking truth through logical reason) believed that humans were rational, thinking beings. They felt that governments and the Church often interfered with people's ability to use their power of reasoning. They questioned the idea of divine right rule. Some felt that people should participate in their government. Many questioned the authority and rules of the Church but continued to believe in God.

THE AMERICAN REVOLUTION

The political impact of these new ideas was enormous. People began to seek freedom from old lines of authority. The Enlightenment influenced not only the American and French Revolutions but also many later ones. In the U.S. *Declaration of Independence* (1776), Thomas Jefferson reflected the ideas of English Enlightenment thinker John Locke. Locke claimed denial of natural rights justified revolution. The framers of the *Constitution of the United States* used French Enlightenment

philosophe Baron de la Brede et de Montesquieu's ideas of separation of powers and a checks–and–balance system.

THE FRENCH REVOLUTION

The ideas of Enlightenment philosophers inspired the downtrodden French people to seek reform. The **French Revolution** (1789) had many causes. Among them were the ideals of England's Glorious Revolution (1688) and the American Revolution (1776). They inspired members of the rising **bourgeoisie** (urban middle class) to challenge the Old Regime (absolute monarchy and the privileged nobles and clergy).

Resentment within the lower and middle classes grew despite the fact that the economy of France was on the upswing and many bourgeois were wealthy. Still, they resented the fact that their lack of a noble birth denied them status. In  1789, the monarchy under **Louis XVI** and Marie Antoinette found itself unable to meet its financial obligations. King Louis called the **Estates General** (the parliament) to meet for the first time in 175 years. This gave the bourgeois a chance to air their dissatisfaction.

In *The Anatomy of Revolution*, historian Crane Brinton examined the patterns of modern national revolutions. He noted that the early leadership of the French Revolution (1789 - 1793) was in the hands of the moderate bourgeoisie. It successfully demanded that the three-chamber Estates General (nobles, clergy, and bourgeoisie) be replaced by a more democratic **National Assembly**, with one vote per representative. Shortly, this body was replaced by the **Legislative Assembly**, still under the control of the moderate middle class. The Legislative Assembly created a limited, or constitutional, monarchy. Yet, domestic economic problems and hostile reactions by monarchs in Prussia and Austria resulted in the rise of radical leaders.

Violence-prone *sans-culottes* (urban workers) with radical bourgeoisie such as Maximilien Marie Isidore Robespierre, Georges Jacques Danton, and Jean Paul Marat took control. They created the **National Convention** government. During this period, the **Committee of Public Safety** conducted the **Reign of Terror**. It resulted in the execution of fifteen to forty-five thousand supposed opponents of the revolution. Included among the victims of the guillotine were Louis XVI and his queen.

The French people grew tired of the violence and bloodshed and themselves executed the leaders of the Committee. Control returned to a group of moderates called **The Directory**. The most violent period of the Revolution subsided.

For a decade, France experienced revolutionary turmoil. It had five governments, the Reign of Terror, and foreign invasion. Yet, both the National Assembly and the National Convention passed numerous reforms (see chart below).

Napoleon Bonaparte

Despite these important reforms, the French people reeled from violence and upheaval of these ten years. They wanted stability. Brinton indicates that when revolutions come to this point control shifts to a central figure. In 1799, military hero **Napoleon Bonaparte** seized power in a **coup d'état** from the Directory. To the weary French, he seemed

French Revolution Reforms		
Government	**Control Group**	**Reforms**
National Assembly 1791 - 1792	Moderate bourgeoisie	• *Declaration of the Rights of Man* • *Civil Constitution of the Clergy* • Reforms of Night Session of August 4th • Le Chapelier Law
National Convention 1792 - 1794	Radical workers and bourgeoisie	• Abolished imprisonment for debt • Established a citizen army leadership • Established the First French Republic • Planned a system of public education • Granted women the same property rights as men.

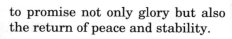

to promise not only glory but also the return of peace and stability.

Within France, Napoleon created a government with a facade of democracy. In reality, he held most of the power. Where he made changes such as the establishment of the **First French Empire**, Napoleon allowed the people to have a voice in voting on issues.

In Napoleon's early reforms, he appeared to be a true son of the French Revolution. He created a merit system for government advancement and the **Legion of Honor** for those who performed important services for France. The **Bank of France** stabilized the currency, and the **University of France** provided for a government controlled public education system. His *Concordat of 1801* established amicable relations with the Catholic Church.

Perhaps the most significant reform was the ***Napoleonic Code***, or *Code Civil* (1804). This legal system has been widely copied since that time. It reflected the ideas of the Enlightenment, proclaiming such things as equality before the law, religious toleration, and equality of inheritance.

Napoleon was very successful in dealing with other nations. Despite the strong efforts of the British, European monarchs were unable to unite against him. In 1806, Napoleon created the **Continental System**. It was a series of trade regulations that established French economic supremacy on the Continent. It was also designed to hurt British trade. The British retaliated with their **Orders in Council**. These measures organized embargoes and boycotts against Napoleon and his allies. The British eventually won this economic war because their powerful navy effectively enforced its sanctions.

In 1812, Russia's **Tsar Alexander I** also challenged Napoleon. He refused to abide by the terms of the Continental System. This disagreement led to Napoleon's ill-fated invasion of Russia. Alexander's forces were no match for the French Emperor's army. Yet, the brutal Russian winter, guerrillas behind French lines, and the Russians' **scorched-earth policy** (destroy and retreat) led to a disastrous defeat for the French. Close to 500,000 men lost their lives in this campaign.

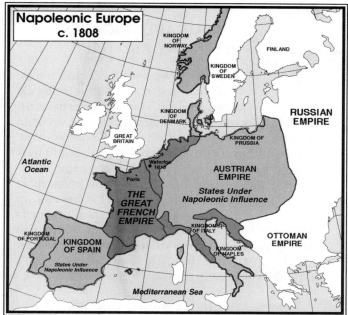

French Sphere Of Influence During The Napoleonic Era

This defeat on the Russian steppes encouraged Napoleon's enemies to join forces. They defeated Napoleon's army at the **Battle of Nations**. They exiled him to the Mediterranean island of Elba. Later, Napoleon escaped and returned to  power for the "Hundred Days." He assembled an army but was defeated by the **Duke of Wellington** at the **Battle of Waterloo** (1815). This time, he was exiled to the island of St. Helena in the South Atlantic, where he died in 1821.

The French Revolution's ideals of nationalism and democracy spread through Europe as Napoleon's armies crisscrossed the continent. Areas which came under French control enacted reforms similar to France's. They adapted the *Napoleonic Code* to their legal systems, abolished feudalism, and instituted education systems.

The monarchies of Europe moved to stem this tide of democracy. They met just before Napoleon's final defeat at Waterloo. At the **Congress of Vienna** (1815), they returned many of the pre-1789 rulers or their heirs to power. With them came the return of Old Regime conditions. Yet, the people did not forget the French ideals, and a number of revolutions broke out in the 19th Century.

NATIONAL UNIFICATION: GERMANY AND ITALY

The Napoleonic Period began reforms and a desire for self-rule that had universal repercussions. It also affected overseas areas under European influence. It unleashed an Era of Nationalism. **Nationalism** is an emotional force which binds people with the same or similar language, history, religion, institutions, beliefs, and geographic area. It unifies people, but it also breaks up empires. Nationalism's most extreme form is **chauvinism**, a powerful obsession which can sweep people into abnormal acts of aggression. In the 20th Century, for example, Hitler's Germany was consumed with chauvinism.

During the 19th Century, this new force of nationalism led to the formation of two new nation-states, Germany and Italy. In both cases, the French Revolution and Napoleonic reforms accelerated the process. Just the presence of the French occupying countries aroused patriotic sentiment that helped unify people. Patriotic literature aroused nationalism. Writers such as **Johann Gottlieb Fichte** in Germany and **Guissepe Mazzini** in Italy spurred nationalists toward unification. (The chart below reveals other parallels between the countries.)

In both Germany and Italy, wars were important means of achieving unification and creating a sense of national pride among previously divided people. Still, **plebiscites** (national votes) added a democratic element in Italy that was not present in Germany.

Prussia's "Iron Chancellor," **Otto von Bismarck**, used the **autocratic tradition** (power concentrated in a single person) to forge the German nation. To unify the nation, Bismarck needed additional tax revenue to increase and update the army. Without authorization from Prussian Parliament, he simply collected the monies. Bismark claimed he forged the German nation "by blood and iron." The phrase revealed his autocratic philosophy of making decisions on his own, ignoring parliamentary majorities.

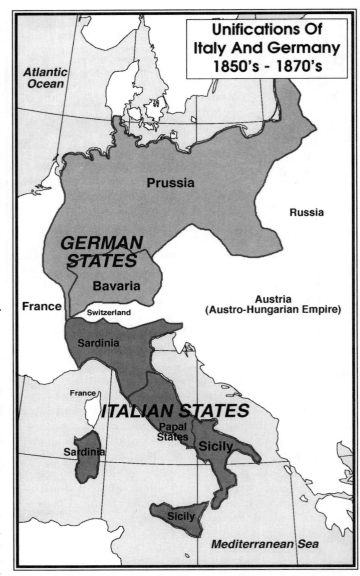

Unifications Of Italy And Germany 1850's - 1870's

The emergence of the unified German states upset the balance of power in Europe. The new German Empire was considerably stronger than France in terms of manpower and resources. Still, Bismarck feared France's desire to avenge

National Unification Of Italy And Germany 1850's - 1870's		
Parallel Factors	**Germany**	**Italy**
Nucleus State	Prussia	Sardinia-Piedmont
Leader	Bismarck	Cavour
Means of Unification	Wars: Danish War Austro-Prussian War Franco-Prussian War	Wars: Austro-Sardinian War Austro-Prussian War Franco-Prussian War Plebiscites

Bismarck's German Empire

| Zollverein Trade and Tariff Unions | Danish War 1864 | Austro-Prussian War 1866 | North German Confederation 1867 | Franco-Prussian War 1871 |

Common Language, Customs, Race, and Historic Traditions

its humiliation in the Franco-Prussian War (1871). At the end of the 19th Century, the Iron Chancellor set up the system of protective alliances that later caused World War I.

THE INDUSTRIAL REVOLUTION

The rise of new nations paralleled the **Industrial Revolution**. Industrial development began much earlier in England (about 1750). England had a unique combination of conditions that made economic transformation possible:

- **An agricultural revolution** led to better methods of planting, crop rotation, and scientific breeding of cattle. It resulted in an increased production per person. Fewer people were needed to supply food for the nation. Unemployed agricultural workers provided a labor force for newly developed industries

- **Coal and iron resources** needed for industrialization were available

- **Capital** gained from colonial ventures was available for investment

- **A positive government attitude** led to subsidies and protections for new factory investments

- **Good harbors, traditional sea power,** and **overseas colonies** opened global markets

- **Technological innovation** provided production alternatives that the domestic system could not provide. Creative people began looking for new ways to produce goods, particularly in textiles, the first area to be affected by the new methods of production and transportation

Technological Innovation Brought About By The Industrial Revolution		
Inventor	**Invention**	**Effect**
Kay	flying shuttle	doubled the speed of weavers – 1733
Hargreaves	spinning jenny	could spin 8 to 20 threads at once – 1764
Arkwright	water frame	used water power; required development of factories; could spin 48 to 300 threads at once – 1769
Crompton	spinning mule	combined jenny and water frame; could spin fine thread – 1779
Cartwright	power loom	first application of power to weaving – 1785
Watt	steam engine	new source of power to run factory machines and to power land and marine vehicles – 1760's
Stephenson	steam locomotive	Faster land transportation – 1829
Telford and McAdam	hard surfaced roads	Faster land transportation in all kinds of weather – 1780

In 1750, the Industrial Revolution began in England. Along with a gradual improvement in the standard of living and the technological advances that it brought, the Industrial Revolution rapidly increased air, water, and land pollution which, in turn, caused health hazards such as lung cancer, infant death, children with malformations, and many assorted diseases.

England's Industrial Revolution also had negative effects. It was not unusual to have young children 5 to 6 years old working 14 to 16 hours in factories where the machines had no safety devices. There was poor ventilation, brutal heat, and physical punishment for minor errors. Subsistence wages completed the picture. The *Sadler Report* on factories and *Ashley Report* on mines brought these conditions to the attention of the public.

In the mines, conditions were no better, and there were frequent explosions. Workers suffered from lung diseases, back deformities, and miscarriages from pulling coal carriages through the mine tunnels. Eventually, some political leaders empathized with the workers. This led to investigations and laws such as the *Factory Act of 1833*, the *Mines Act of 1842*, and the *Ten Hours Act of 1847*.

Suffrage Reform In Britain	
Reform Bill of	**Group Gaining Right To Vote**
1867	City workers
1884	Farm workers
1918	Universal male suffrage and all women over 30
1928	Universal suffrage
1969	Lowered voting age to 18

Economic changes fostered broader political reforms. In 1832, Parliament passed the *Great Reform Bill*. It lowered property requirements for suffrage and gave members of the middle class the right to vote. It abolished most **rotten boroughs** (areas with little or no population and with representation in Parliament). The Act also gave seats in Parliament to newly developed industrial areas with enlarged populations.

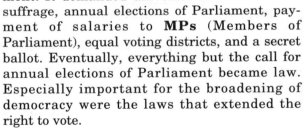

Still, the working class was left out of this reform. Workers started the **Chartist Movement** to demand suffrage and other rights for themselves. A giant charter (petition) was drawn up and presented to Parliament. It demanded universal male suffrage, annual elections of Parliament, payment of salaries to **MPs** (Members of Parliament), equal voting districts, and a secret ballot. Eventually, everything but the call for annual elections of Parliament became law. Especially important for the broadening of democracy were the laws that extended the right to vote.

SOCIALISM

Improvements in the standard of living did not affect the working class until after the mid-19th Century. In part, it was the great sacrifices by workers that brought about the industrialization of England. It took a long time for reform to come because the government was dominated by the upper classes. It followed

Marxist Theories		
Theory	**Explanation**	**Criticism**
Economic interpretation of history	Economic factors determine the course of history and those who control the means of production will control the government and the society.	Cannot explain such things as the Crusades, religious wars, and the unifications of Germany and Italy.
Class struggle	Throughout history, there have been the "haves" and the "have nots." In a modern industrial society, the struggle is between proletariat and capitalists.	Does not consider the cooperation between the proletariat and capitalists to increase production or profit.
Surplus Value Theory	Price of product minus the cost of labor equals surplus value. Here, Marx says the value goes to the capitalist, but should go to the workers that produce the value.	Does not provide a return for capitalists who risk financial capital and provide management services.
Inevitability of Socialism	Over a long period of time, overproduction will result in bankruptcies and depressions. Conditions will get so bad that the proletariat will revolt and establish a dictatorship of the proletariat.	This has not come true. Communism has not gained control in highly industrialized nations.

Adam Smith's **laissez-faire economic policy**. Business interests made sure the government kept regulations to a minimum. Businesses tried to avoid the costs of providing for the safety and well being of the workers.

People such as Robert Owen, Karl Marx, and Frederick Engels condemned the capitalist system for maintaining such industrial class evils. They argued for alternative economic systems.

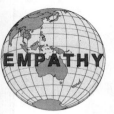

Robert Owen was a **utopian socialist** (idealistic social reformer) who tried to set an example for capitalists. He believed working conditions could be improved and businesses could still make profits. He purchased the industrial town of **New Lanark**, Scotland. In his factory, he decreased hours, increased wages, and forbade the employment of young children. Instead, Owen set up rudimentary schools for children. He built decent housing for his workers and even provided small garden areas.

Owen proved he was able to make a profit, but few of his fellow factory owners followed his example. Later, he invested in a new enterprise in **New Harmony** (Indiana, USA) that operated according to the principle, *"from each according to his ability, to each according to his need."* Unfortunately, New Harmony was a dismal failure. Owen's last project was an attempt to organize English workers into one gigantic union.

Other voices for the workers promoted a more radical brand of **"scientific socialism"** (a workers' government controls and manages all productive resources and means of production). **Karl Marx** and **Frederick Engels** proposed a revolutionary approach in their 1848 pamphlet, ***The Communist Manifesto***. Marx later expanded his ideas in the multivolume work, ***Das Kapital***. He merged past history and current conditions in industrializing countries to predict what might happen in the future.

Marx scorned idealistic utopian socialists such as Owen. While he claimed his ideas were **scientific socialism**, he left no clear description of what his communist society would be. He said that initially the government would commandeer the means of production. Then, a **dictatorship of the proletariat** (working class) would gradually abolish classes. Eventually, government would "wither away." However, he gave no indication of how long this process might take.

Ironically, Marx's predictions of violence during change may have been responsible for the failure of his ideas to come true in industrialized countries. Governments slowly began to alleviate poor working conditions, limit the role of big business, make provision for labor organizations to exist, and decrease "boom to bust" business cycles.

All of these actions helped to keep conditions from reaching the stage that would cause Marx's proletarian revolution.

IMPERIALISM

In the 1870's, around the time the Industrial Revolution was making itself felt in Britain, France, and Germany, a new wave of imperialism arose. Japan and the United States, both beginning to industrialize, joined the movement to acquire new territory. Many factors contributed to the movement to acquire colonial empires:

- the demand for raw materials and new markets

- the unifications of Italy and Germany

- France's desire to restore prestige after the Franco-Prussian War

- the emergence of Japan as a power in international affairs

- the desire of humanitarian groups to help others

In 1859, Charles Darwin put forth the biological theory of natural selection in his book, ***The Origin of Species***. Nationalists and imperialists adapted natural selection into **Social Darwinism**. They claimed certain groups among the human race were naturally

superior to others. This belief developed into an elaborate ethnocentric excuse used by Europeans to control the resources of the less developed regions. The combination of the technological supremacy of the Europeans and the weak, disunited governments they encountered made it easy for them to gain control.

Conflicts rapidly developed among the imperialist countries over control of key areas. Britain's ambition to control East Africa from "Cape to Cairo" (north - south corridor) brought it into conflict with both the Germans and French. France's desire for North African colonies also led to clashes with both Italy and Germany. Imperialistic disputes among European countries were among the many causes of World War I.

In the 1890's, the United States abandoned its traditional isolationism to become a player in

Europe:
IN WORLD WAR I

ALLIED POWERS
CENTRAL POWERS

the world of international politics. American nationalism led to armed conflict with Spain over Cuba.

WORLD WAR I (1914 - 1918)

A variety of forces caused World War I. Key among them were:

- competition for raw materials and markets

- acquisition of colonies for national prestige

- struggles for national independence in Eastern Europe

- competition among powers to build military power (militarism)

Mounting tensions made countries feel increasingly insecure and mistrustful. A shaky **balance of power** rested on two opposing alliance systems:

- **Triple Alliance –** Fear of French retaliation for its loss of the Franco-Prussian War led Germany to create the **Triple Alliance** in 1882 with Austria-Hungary and Italy.

WAR & PEACE

Later, a secret agreement with Russia to eliminate the possibility of a two-front war strengthened this pact.

- **Triple Entente –** When Bismarck was forced out of office by **Kaiser Wilhelm II**, the German agreement with Russia lapsed. The French took advantage of the break, establishing the **Triple Entente** in 1907. Later, France and Russia persuaded the British to side with them. (The Entente was not a firm commitment for action. Some uncertainty remained about the British position right up until the outbreak of World War I.)

A series of crises preceded the outbreak of World War I. Relations worsened between the two alliances. Two crises involving Morocco pit-

Europe: AFTER WORLD WAR I

New States (Results of WWI Peace Treaties)

Russia (U.S.S.R. after 1922)

ted France against Germany. Two wars in Eastern Europe's Balkan Peninsula earned the area the nickname of the "tinder box" or the "powder keg" of Europe.

Austria–Hungary wanted power over the Balkans in order to insure its existence. The Russians wanted to help Slavic people establish independent states under their influence. They backed Serbia, the leader of the Slavic movement. The Russians encouraged the small countries to revolt against the Ottoman Empire in two Balkan wars. This further increased tension with Austria-Hungary.

In 1914, a Slav who belonged to a Serbian nationalist organization assassinated **Archduke Franz Ferdinand** (heir to the throne of Austria–Hungary). The act was the spark that set off the European powder keg.

Austria asked for German support, and the Germans pledged that support. The German leaders encouraged Austria to attack Serbia. They were willing to aid Austria against Russia and France if the war broadened. However, Britain's position concerned them. The British did not make their stand clear until the War began. Mobilization began in Russia. Austria declared war, setting up a chain reaction that activated the network of alliances. A regional crisis grew into a worldwide war.

Italy claimed its allies were the aggressors. It refused to honor its alliance with Germany and Austria–Hungary. In 1915, Italy accepted promises of land and entered the war on the side of the Triple Entente (Britain, France, and Russia).

On the Eastern Front, the Russians fought valiantly. Yet, their failure to modernize and their lack of equipment resulted in heavy losses. The outbreak of revolution, the abdication of the Tsar, and the rapid switches in governments led to Russian withdrawal in 1917.

However, most of the action occurred on the Western Front. A defensive war quickly bogged down the fighting. The front lines, stabilized in 1914, hardly changed for the next three years. Thousands of men died for less than a mile or two of land. New technologies emerged. Yet, their strategic use did not develop at the same speed. The full impact of new weapons such as tanks, mobile artillery, airplanes, and submarines was not realized until 1939. They made possible the high mobility of World War II.

Despite early attempts to remain neutral, the United States was drawn into World War I in 1917. Unrestricted submarine warfare by the Germans, loans made to the Allies, and the idea of the democracies (Allies) fighting the autocratic powers (Central Powers) drew America into the conflict.

During the course of World War I, U.S. President **Woodrow Wilson** drew up his *Fourteen Points*. They were designed to settle the issues that had caused the war and to pre-

vent wars in the future. He stressed the self-determination of nations, freedom of the seas, equal access to trade, and the return of Alsace-Lorraine to France. The Allies accepted most of Wilson's ideas as the basis for a peace settlement. Still, they demanded **reparations** (money payments) for the war costs from Germany.

By the fall of 1918, the German military knew it could not win the war. The Kaiser abdicated, and the government signed an **armistice** (truce) based on Wilson's Fourteen Points. The Germans were not allowed to be present at the Paris Peace Conference. The basic decisions were made by Lloyd George of Britain, Clemenceau of France, Orlando of Italy, and Wilson. The resulting *Treaty of Versailles* required the Germans to:

• accept responsibility for the war (war guilt clause)

• pay reparations

• reduce its military

• surrender all of its colonies

• return Alsace-Lorraine to France

• accept the loss of various territories in Europe

Under protest, but with the Allies threatening to resume fighting, the Germans signed the treaty. German resentment of the Treaty's harsh terms was a major cause for World War II. The loss of lives resulting from World War I upset the demographic patterns in Europe. It left a large surplus of females over males. It also brought younger people to national leadership earlier than in the past.

Outside of Europe, the war resulted in an increase in a nationalist spirit in colonies. It aroused the expectation of independence or self-government.  European global domination weakened after World War I, but it was World War II that dealt the fatal blow to colonial empires.

QUESTIONS

1 In Europe, the Crusades helped begin the Renaissance because they
1 opened trade with the Western Hemisphere
2 brought contact with the ideas and products of other people
3 increased the power of the Roman Catholic Church
4 freed the Byzantine Empire from Muslim control

2 The Renaissance occurred first in Italy because
1 wealth from trade made sponsorship of art possible
2 the feudal system clearly dominated Italian life
3 censorship of new ideas was strong
4 there were many different religions

3 Political developments in 17th Century England are important because they
1 established a direct democracy
2 made England a republic
3 influenced the American and French revolutions
4 resulted in an absolute monarchy

4 Which resulted from Henry VIII's actions regarding the Roman Catholic Church?
1 establishment of the Anglican Church in England
2 flight of most Protestants from England
3 a series of major religious wars
4 a loss of power for the English monarchy

5 Rulers following Machiavelli's advice would most likely
1 listen to legislative bodies carefully
2 be merciful when handing down punishments
3 hire mercenaries to do the fighting
4 do anything necessary to keep or increase power

6 Which of the following correctly associates a writer with his work?
1 Dante – *Divine Comedy*
2 More – *In Praise of Folly*
3 Erasmus – *The Courtier*
4 Marx – *Utopia*

7 Leonardo Da Vinci represented well the ideals of the Renaissance because he was
1 extremely wealthy
2 an excellent athlete
3 multitalented
4 very religious

8 The Roman Catholic and Protestant religions differed in regard to
1 monotheism
2 the role of Jesus
3 life after death
4 the value of some of the sacraments

9 Which enabled Elizabeth I to establish England as an international power?
1 defeat of Philip II and the Spanish Armada
2 passage of the *Act of Supremacy*
3 defeat of the French in America
4 implementation of religious toleration

10 To increase power, a Machiavellian ruler would most likely try to
1 call the legislature to meet frequently
2 decrease the power of the nobles
3 support the power of the Roman Catholic Church
4 encourage free trade

11 The English *Magna Carta*, *Petition of Right*, and *Bill of Right*s all
1 limit the taxing power of the king
2 provide for universal male suffrage
3 prohibit excessive fines and bail
4 guarantee complete freedom of religion

12 Which of the following characteristics of the Renaissance do the Protestant Reformation and the Age of Exploration and Discovery best illustrate?
1 interest in Greece and Rome
2 progress in math and science
3 questioning of formerly accepted authority
4 attention to realism and detail

13 The Scientific Revolution helped start the Enlightenment because
 1 people began to search for universal laws in many fields
 2 the Roman Catholic Church supported the findings of Luther and Calvin
 3 men were willing to accept the teachings of the Church
 4 scientists accepted the findings of the early Greeks

14 The need for markets, raw materials, and nationalism led to
 1 the Napoleonic Wars
 2 imperialism
 3 the unification of Germany
 4 the Industrial Revolution

15 An absolute monarch, privileged nobles and clergy, and an unfair tax structure for the Third Estate best describe
 1 pre-1789 France
 2 post-1688 England
 3 pre-1776 America
 4 post-1789 France

16 In *The Anatomy of Revolution*, Crane Brinton states that
 1 conservatives control the early phases of revolutions
 2 peasants provide revolutionary leadership
 3 revolutions often result in a return to one-person rule
 4 a revolution's initial result is a democratic government

17 Two European nation-states emerging in the 19th Century were
 1 England and France
 2 Russia and Austria
 3 Spain and Portugal
 4 Germany and Italy

18 Napoleon might be called a "son of the revolution" because he
 1 established an absolute monarchy
 2 supported equality of law and religious toleration
 3 used birth as the criteria for advancement
 4 gave the Roman Catholic Church control of religion

19 Which is a result of the French Revolutionary and Napoleonic Eras?
 1 a spread of ideas of nationalism and democracy
 2 a strengthening of religious forces
 3 the expansion of communism
 4 a new race for colonies

20 An agricultural revolution, world-wide markets, and good supplies of iron and coal made it possible for England to
 1 begin the Commercial Revolution
 2 establish the guild system
 3 start the Industrial Revolution
 4 begin mercantilism

21 Which did the British *Great Reform Bill of 1832* achieve?
 1 It abolished rotten boroughs.
 2 It established universal male suffrage.
 3 It set up annual elections of Parliament.
 4 It gave women the right to vote.

22 Karl Marx believed that
 1 capitalists would improve working conditions voluntarily
 2 bad conditions would cause the proletariat to revolt
 3 governments would act to improve working conditions
 4 large labor unions would protect worker interests

23 Locke believed that
 1 there should be a separation of powers in government
 2 rulers should have absolute powers
 3 the people have the right of revolution
 4 government power comes from God

24 Bismarck established the Triple Alliance of 1882 because he
 1 feared the power of the British navy
 2 wished to avoid war in the Pacific
 3 was afraid of an attack by France
 4 needed help against Austrian aggression

25 The Commercial Revolution established
 1 the factory system
 2 modern trade unions
 3 a capitalist economic system
 4 a self-sufficient economy

26 The immediate cause of World War I was the
1 Moroccan Crisis
2 British-French naval cooperation
3 Balkan Wars
4 assassination of Archduke Franz Ferdinand

27 Which statement is true about the Treaty of Versailles?
1 It placed no blame for starting the War.
2 It forced Germany to pay reparations.
3 It failed to return Alsace-Lorraine to France.
4 It allowed Germany to keep all its colonies.

28 Which statement is true of World War I?
1 It was a highly mobile, offensive war.
2 It produced new weapons technology used during World War II.
3 It resulted in few casualties.
4 It was fought mainly on the Eastern Front.

29 Which of the following pairs is correctly matched?
1 Watt – steam engine
2 Crompton – spinning jenny
3 Kay – cotton gin
4 Arkwright – sewing machine

30 The bourgeoisie supported the French Revolution because they
1 believed in divine right
2 could not own property under Old Regime
3 resented their lack of political power
4 wanted socialism

31 Emphasis on individual uniqueness and worth during the Renaissance is known as
1 isolationism
2 nationalism
3 manorialism
4 humanism

32 In the 1800's, a major cause of European imperialism was the
1 desire to spread democracy
2 emergence of Marxism as an economic system
3 desire for raw materials and markets
4 religious wars between nations

ESSAYS

1 The Renaissance is characterized as the Age of Transition, or the Age of Change. Major changes took place in many fields.

- Religion
- Art
- Science
- The Economy
- Government or Politics

Choose *three* of the fields listed. For *each*, discuss *two* changes that occurred during the Renaissance. Be sure to use specific examples for each change.

2 European political philosophers have profoundly influenced the governments and social patterns of the Western World. Below are some major ideas of these philosophers:

- *Governments must protect the natural rights of the people or the people have the right to revolt.*

- *Governments should not interfere with the economic affairs of the country.*

- *Governments should be separated into three branches with a check and balance system.*

a Name the philosopher most closely associated with *each* of the ideas expressed.

b Explain the meaning of *each* idea.

c Discuss how *each* idea, properly implemented, could contribute to the development of democracy.

III. CONTEMPORARY NATIONS

Exhausted from World War I, Europe fell into a period of disorientation. Governments rose and fell. Totalitarian regimes replaced fragile democracies. Military aggression fomented a second world war. The era of European dominance ended, and a Cold War began. As the century closed, the danger of communist aggression subsided, and new patterns of national power emerged.

THE TOTALITARIAN STATE

POSTWAR GERMANY

In the period after World War I, Germans resented their punishment under the Treaty of Versailles. Oddly, they did not blame their dire state on the autocratic German Empire but on the new **Weimar Republic**. Economic problems occur at the end of any war; yet, the reparation payments required by the Treaty heavily burdened the Germans. The final sum had been set at $33 billion.

ANTI-SEMITISM

Migration of large numbers of war-displaced Jews from Eastern Europe further inflamed the situation. **Anti-Semitism** (anti-Jewish feeling)

was not new in European history. The Middle Ages evidence frequent episodes of it. Jews were expelled from a number of countries at various times.

Russia, in particular, had a long history of anti-Semitism. Russian Jews were often required to live in **ghettos** (segregated areas). When they needed scapegoats to deflect attention from other problems, the Tsars subjected Jews to **pogroms** (violent purges). Jews were often forced to wear the Star of David as a means of identification.

Anti-Semitism also had a long history in Germany. Some 19th Century writers such as **Friedrich Wilhelm Nietzsche** extolled the nationalistic virtues of the German people. Such writing rein-

forced the idea of racial superiority that led to anti-Semitic campaigns. They precipitated the Nazis' fanatical drive to keep the Germanic race "pure" by attempting to annihilate the Jews.

PROBLEMS OF THE WEIMAR REPUBLIC

The unhappy political situation in Germany made it easy for a movement such as Nazism to develop. The democratic Weimar Republic won little respect from the Germans. They were used to an autocratic (domineering) government. The Weimar leaders were very tolerant, even when opposition bordered on treason. Movements from both the right and the left shook the Republic in its early years. **Adolf Hitler's** attempt to seize control of the state of Bavaria with his 1923 **Beer Hall Putsch** (uprising) is an example. His prison sentence for the attempted overthrow was five years, but he served only about eighteen months.

The 1923 **Ruhr Crisis** highlighted the Weimar Republic's difficulties in handling economic problems. France and Belgium claimed that Germany had fallen behind in reparation payments. French troops occupied the industrial Ruhr region. The Weimar government weakly suggested Germans in the Ruhr refuse to work for France. It issued large amounts of printing press currency. The action backfired when massive inflation wiped out savings and seriously affected people on fixed incomes. The action devastated the middle class in particular. New currency was issued and some relief from the reparation payments schedule was obtained. Still, the vital middle class support of the government eroded.

From 1924 to 1929, German politics and finance stabilized. The economic problems eased and international respect for Germany rose with the signing of the **Locarno Pacts** (border settlements), admission to the League of Nations, and the signing of the **Kellogg-Briand Pact** (renouncing war). However, the Great Depression changed the growing positive outlook completely.

NAZI RISE TO POWER

When the Great Depression hit Germany in 1929, people looked to radical groups of the far

Europe: Contemporary Nations

left (communists) or the far right (the Nazis) for answers to their problems. Extremist parties' seats in the **Reichstag** (lower house of the German parliament) increased. The multiparty system kept any majority from instituting a strong government. President von Hindenburg had to govern by decree.

In early 1933, the right wing **National Party** leaders persuaded Hindenburg to appoint a new chancellor. Hindenburg chose the leader of the **National Socialist German Workers' Party** (**Nazi Party**), Adolf Hitler.

THE NAZI STATE

Chancellor Hitler's first move was to call for new elections. He hoped the Nazis could win an outright majority in the Reichstag. During the campaign, Hitler's staff showed a mastery of political techniques. Great outdoor rallies were carefully arranged by Nazi leaders. Hitler's aides used mass psychology skillfully. They whipped crowds into emotional frenzies with cheers and songs. When Hitler entered the stadium to speak, the crowd fell silent. His speeches were simple with only a few themes: abolish the Treaty of Versailles, restore German prestige, establish the supremacy of the Aryan Race.

During the election, fire destroyed the Reichstag building. The Nazis claimed the event was a Russian sponsored communist conspiracy. They tried to use paranoia to rally voters to their side. The election disappointed the Nazis. Their coalition with the Nationalist Party represented a narrow 52% of the vote. They never won the support of a majority of the people in a free election.

Still, Hitler gained dictatorial powers by using Nazi Storm Troopers to deny communist opponents access to the rebuilt Reichstag. He used these powers to centralize the government and wipe out any effective opposition. Next, he set up a **totalitarian government** (total control over all aspects of the lives of the people) with himself as **Der Führer** (leader).

To deal with the problems of the Depression, Hitler announced plans to rebuild the German Army. He enlarged the armaments industries with government subsidies. He removed most women and Jews from the work force. He began public works projects such as the autobahns. He set up compulsory work service for all young people. Largely because of massive defense spending, the number of unemployed workers declined from six million to one million by 1936.

To control the people psychologically, Hitler gave extensive power to **Joseph Goebbels** and his Ministry of Propaganda and Enlightenment. Goebbels launched a censorship and book-burning campaign. Later, Goebbels set up **Reich Culture Chambers** to control the work of artists, sculptors, and others in the fine arts. Schools placed emphasis on physical education and obedience to the state. They discouraged young people from thinking for themselves. More than anything else, the presence of Storm Troopers and the hated *SS* (secret police) put fear in the hearts of the people. Their terror tactics violated human rights and discouraged the opposition.

Der Führer – Adolf Hitler

The Nazis persecuted many groups such as the Jehovah's Witnesses, gypsies, the handicapped, and Eastern European Slavs. The group that suffered most was the Jews. Hitler believed that the German people were a part of the Aryan Race, a superior group that must be kept pure to rule the world.

The Nazis regarded Jews as subhuman and not fit to survive. They drove Jews out of the main stream of German life.

Nazi death trains took Jews by the thousands to the concentration camps.

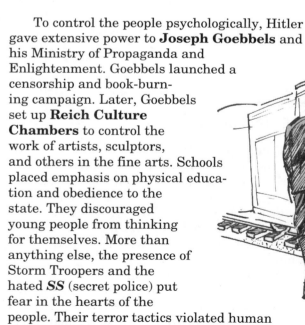

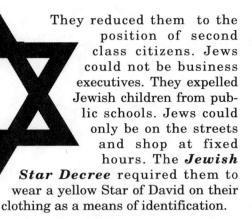

They reduced them to the position of second class citizens. Jews could not be business executives. They expelled Jewish children from public schools. Jews could only be on the streets and shop at fixed hours. The *Jewish Star Decree* required them to wear a yellow Star of David on their clothing as a means of identification.

After World War II started, the Nazis developed the **"Final Solution."** It called for all Jews and dissidents to be rounded up and forced to work in war related industries as long as they were capable. Later, Jews were sent to concentration camps such as **Treblinka** and **Auschwitz**. Some received a short reprieve when they arrived at the camps. They were assigned to work crews or became the subjects of medical experimentation. Still, the Nazis executed millions in the death camps. This treatment was applied not only to German Jews but also to the Jews of all nations under Nazi control.

By the end of World War II, the Nazis had killed six million Jews and three million others in what is now known as **The Holocaust**. After the war, the **Nüremberg Trials** pronounced Nazi leaders responsible for crimes against humanity. Their acts were not considered normal under the accepted rules of warfare. The judges at the international trials said wholesale violations of human rights were really Nazi state-sponsored crimes. Since that time, **genocide** (extermination of an entire people) has been condemned and declared illegal by the **U.N. Commission on Human Rights**.

WORLD WAR II

CAUSES

Some of the same factors that caused World War I helped to bring about World War II. Militarism arose with dictators such as Hitler and Mussolini, and economic problems arose with the depression. Nationalism and imperialism were especially evident in the Axis nations' goals:

- **Lebensraum** – ("living space") the German desire to push into Eastern Europe

- **Mare Nostrum** – ("our sea") the Italian desire to expand their influence in the Mediterranean

- **Asia for the Asiatics** - Japanese goal to rid Asia of European and American influence

Recall that the French concern about the loss of the Franco-Prussian War was a cause of World War I. Similarly, the dissatisfaction of Italy, Germany, and Japan with the treatment they received at the Paris Peace Conference of 1919 was a cause of World War II. Between the two wars, the League of Nations proved incapable of dealing with the aggression of major powers or keeping a balance in world affairs. As in the pre-World War I period, there were a series of crises that contributed to the outbreak of war (see chart below).

However, there were some differences in what caused the two wars. There was no real arms race until war was about to break out in 1938-1939. This was largely because the democracies were not willing to acknowledge that another world war was possible. They were also busy fighting the effects of the Great Depression and lacked the economic resources for an arms build-up. Also, there was only one formal alliance

Pre–World War II Crisis		
Crisis	**Aggressor**	**Results**
Manchurian 1930	Japan	League of Nations sent Lytton Commission to investigate. It condemned Japan for aggression but no further action was taken by the League. Japan established puppet state of Manchukuo.
Ethiopian 1935	Italy	Italian aggression condemned by League. Ineffective economic sanctions imposed and later lifted.
Austrian 1938	Germany	German invasion and takeover condemned by League. No further action was taken.

system, that of the **Axis** powers. Germany, Italy, and Japan formed the **Rome-Berlin-Tokyo Axis** (1939) presumably to fight the spread of communism.

The episode that most revealed the weakness of the Western democracies was a crisis over Czechoslovakia in 1938. Hitler demanded self-government for the Sudetenland, an area of Czechoslovakia inhabited by a large German population. Benito Mussolini of Italy persuaded him to hold the **Munich Conference** to discuss the problem. Present were Mussolini, Hitler, Neville Chamberlain of Great Britain, and Edouard Daladier of France. No representatives of Czechoslovakia were present nor of the Soviet Union which had an alliance with the Czechs. Essentially, the decision was made by those present to give in to Hitler's demands.

Historians consider the Munich Conference to be the most notorious modern example of **appeasement** (the policy of giving in to aggressors to avoid war). Shortly after the Munich Conference, Britain and France gave assurances of their support to Poland in case it became the next target of Hitler's aggression.

Hitler stunned the Western democracies by forging an agreement with Soviet Premier **Josef Stalin** of the Soviet Union. A Nazi-Soviet non-aggression pact was signed in August 1939 to avoid the possibility of a two-front war. Hitler and Stalin then began the invasion of Poland on 1 September 1939. France and Britain declared war, and World War II began.

THE WORLD AT WAR

World War II was fought in Europe, Asia, Africa, and Oceania. It resulted in the loss of approximately 40 million people and cost more than one trillion, one hundred billion dollars (not including the cost of destroyed civilian

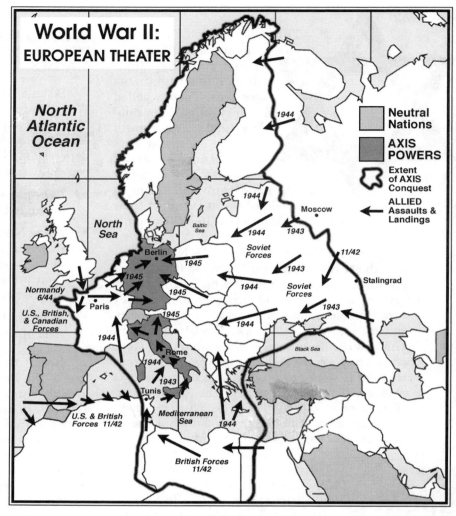

properties). It was very different from World War I because it was largely an offensive war.

The Nazi **blitzkrieg** (lightning war) offensive led to the defeat of Poland in approximately one month. Motorized vehicles, tanks, and airplanes made it possible. Their military value was just beginning to be apparent during World War I. Technological and scientific warfare advanced enormously during World War II. The warring sides turned jungles into airports. They constructed roads across impossible terrain. Pontoon (floating) bridges were built across rivers overnight. Harbors were made where there had been none.

The British developed **radar** to locate approaching objects. It was a vital factor in helping the British Royal Air Force to win the **Battle of Britain**. **Sonar** helped the Allies control the Atlantic against German U-boats. The Nazis developed **V-1** and **V-2** jet-propelled bombs to terrify the British. They were forerunners of today's guided missiles.

Other developments included **magnetic sea mines** and the **Schnorchel device** allowing submarines to remain submerged for longer periods. The **atomic bomb** was developed by the U.S. and dropped on the Japanese cities of Hiroshima and Nagasaki. It was the beginning of a new technological age in warfare.

GLOBAL IMPACT OF THE WAR

By the end of World War II, a very different picture of international power became apparent. Europe was devastated by its war effort. The old global powers declined, and the world polarized between two **superpowers**: the United States and the Soviet Union.

Nationalist rebel movements took advantage of the European powers' inability to devote the necessary resources to hold their colonies. During the post-war period, many of the colonies gained independence. In some cases, the European countries struggled to hold their colonies. They became involved in long wars which further drained their resources. Eventually, the colonies gained independence.

BRITISH GOVERNMENT

By the end of World War II, Britain completed a long evolution toward parliamentary democracy. The modern British government is the product of countless changes that occurred without major bloodshed. Therefore, the change is considered to be evolutionary, as opposed to the revolutionary process.

Great Britain is a democracy. The laws guarantee human rights and limit the power of the government. Historic acts and **precedents** (past actions and decisions that act as models) compose the **unwritten constitution** (see chart below). In technical form, Britain is a **constitutional** or **limited monarchy**. For example, the British ruler has the power to appoint the Prime Minister. Yet, by precedent, the ruler must appoint the leader of the majority party in the House of Commons. No bill can become law without the signature of the ruler, but no ruler has refused to sign a Parliamentary bill since the early 18th Century.

The British Parliament has a **bicameral** legislature (two houses): the **House of Commons** (elective) and the **House of Lords** (hereditary or appointive). Since the passage of

EVOLUTION OF PARLIAMENTARY DEMOCRACY

Event	Change
Establishment of royal court system (11th Century)	Provided an alternative to feudal justice and Church courts. Began development of grand juries, trial juries, and common law.
Signing of Magna Carta (1215)	King could not tax without advice of Great Council. Freemen guaranteed trial by jury for the first time. Provided for power of purse.
Model Parliament (1295)	Led to the establishment of the Houses of Lords and Commons.
Glorious Revolution (1688)	Established supremacy of Parliament over king.
Cabinet system (17th-19th Centuries)	Provided for cabinet ministers to be selected from Parliament and to be responsible to it.
Reform Bills: 1832, 1867, 1884, 1918, 1928, and 1969	Extended the suffrage.
Parliament Acts: 1911 and 1949	Limited the power of the House of Lords to veto legislation.

The Houses of Parliament (Westminster Palace on the Thames) are topped by the famous clock tower, Big Ben. Westminster Abby stands beside them. PhotoDisc Inc. 1994

East of the heart of London and its financial district, Tower Bridge, a distinctive Victorian structure, crosses the Thames beside the Tower of London. PhotoDisc Inc. 1994

the *Parliament Acts*, power clearly rests with the House of Commons. The **Prime Minister** is the majority leader of the House of Commons. Other administrators, or members of the **Cabinet**, are selected from the House of Commons. Occasionally, a cabinet member may be chosen from the House of Lords. There is a **unitary** (single) power structure. (Executive and legislative branches are not separated as they are in the United States Federal government.) Parliament also has certain judicial functions.

The cabinet government is directly responsible to the House of Commons and indirectly responsible to the people. Each cabinet member heads a department, draws up legislation to be presented, and defends it before Parliament. If a major piece of cabinet sponsored legislation is defeated in Commons, or if Commons votes "no

confidence" in government policy, the cabinet must either:

• **resign** – in which case the opposition party forms a cabinet; or

• **go to the country** – an election is held within weeks to determine the reaction of the country to the issue involved.

If the people support the cabinet, it continues in office. If they do not, the cabinet resigns and the opposition takes over.

The parliamentary system of government has worked well in Britain. This is because there are only a few parties with any political strength, and there is almost always a party with a majority. This avoids the chaos of government by constantly changing coalitions (such as in postwar Italy). Currently, there are three major parties in Great Britain:

- The **Conservative Party** is closely allied with the U.S. and generally follows a capitalist economic policy with some government ownership and regulation

- The **Labor Party** favors socialist programs in Britain and opposes the American nuclear presence in the British Isles

- The new **Social Democratic Party** includes many former Liberals and Labor Party members

PROBLEM OF NORTHERN IRELAND

The issue of Northern Ireland continues to plague Great Britain. The problem goes back 800 years to the first British attempts at conquest. In order to control the rebellious Irish, a number of English rulers (including Mary Tudor and Oliver Cromwell) set up large plantations with English and Scots as landowners. Many of these new landowners were Protestant who dispossessed the Irish Catholics. The Catholics became landless tenant farmers or laborers. This has been the basis of the religious and socioeconomic problems in Northern Ireland. During the 19th Century, Prime Minister **William Gladstone** partially rectified some of these problems.

After the bloody **Easter Rebellion** of 1916, Catholics in the south proclaimed the **Irish Free State** (Eire). In 1948, it became the Republic of Ireland. The north was given a separate government under Protestant control. Civil disorder resumed in the 1960's with the outlawed **Provisional Wing of the IRA** (Irish Republican Army) and various Protestant groups responsible. The British government sent in troops and assumed emergency powers to deal with the situation in 1976, but the violence continued.

In 1985, Britain signed an agreement giving the Republic of Ireland a voice on violations of the human rights of the Catholic minority in the North. Northern Ireland's Protestants balked. Their leader, **Reverend Ian Paisley**, resigned from the British Parliament. Another attempt to solve the deeply divided country's problems took place under Prime Minister John Major in the early 1990's. In 1994, the Irish Republican Army declared a unilateral end to the fighting between the IRA and the British and Protestants opening the door to negotiations again.

CONTEMPORARY LIFE

ETHNIC AND RELIGIOUS MINORITIES

Western Europe is an area with many different ethnic and religious groups. While this diversity adds to the rich cultural identity of the continent, it also leads to many problems.

The **United Kingdom** of Great Britain (England, Wales, Scotland) and Northern Ireland, remains 90% native. In recent times, immigration increased from former colonies, especially the Caribbean, India, and Pakistan. The immigrant competition for jobs prompted periodic riots in major cities. In 1962, Parliament passed the *Commonwealth Immigrants Act* that restricted immigration for those without means of support or likely employment. Further legislation established three categories of British citizenship (two of which may not live in Britain) and applied quotas for immigrants of different areas. Although most of the population of Britain is Protestant, there are large Catholic and Jewish minorities. A new controversy for Britain concerns admission of immigrants from the crown colony of Hong Kong slated to return to Chinese control in 1997.

France has the fourth largest Jewish population in Western Europe. During the last two decades, France experienced new waves of anti-Semitism. In the 1980's, international terrorist groups attacked synagogues. The French have not been totally sympathetic to the plight of the Jews. Like Britain, France also has a sizable number of immigrants from former colonies. There are large numbers of Vietnamese, Algerians, and Moroccans. In addition, Portuguese, Italians, and Spanish come as temporary immigrants because of seasonal employment.

Germany's work force has large numbers of "guest workers" from Turkey, the Balkans, Italy, and Greece. It has moved to integrate these large numbers of foreigners. Yet, there is ethnic strife. Pressure mounted as the country reunified after the East German communist regime collapsed. The dislocations also led to anti-Semitic outbursts and agitation to deport Kurdish guest workers in the 1990's.

Spain is ethnically homogeneous in three-fourths of the country, but there are considerable differences between the north and the south. The government gives ethnic groups such as the Basques, Galatians, and Catalans considerable self-rule. The Basques remain dissatisfied and sometimes resort to terrorism. Population movements to urban areas, the coasts, and island possessions helped decrease problems.

Italy also has a high degree of ethnic homogeneity. There are Germans in the northern Tyrol area and Slavs in the area of Trieste. However, there are major socioeconomic differences between the industrial north and the poor farm area of the south. These differences are decreasing with movement to the north and with the rural–to–urban migration.

RELIGION

There is a basic sense of shared values in Western Europe. Most people share the Judeo-Christian tradition even though they belong to different religious groups.

The Roman Catholic Church has a strong influence on the region. Beginning with Pope John XXIII in 1959, the Church actively pursued **ecumenism** (seeking harmony among various religions). Recent Popes have met with representatives of the Orthodox Church and Anglican Churches. The Church has taken steps to improve relations with Jews. Pope John Paul II continued these dialogues both in the Vatican and on frequent visits to global regions.

Critics see an inconsistency in Vatican policies. While encouraging Roman Catholic clergy's involvement in prodemocracy movements in Poland, the Vatican warned priests in Latin America against using "liberation theology" and becoming involved with violent political movements.

URBANIZATION

European countries saw a considerable rural-to-urban movement in the period after World War II. It brought about a number of concerns about pollution of the environment, causing governments to react.

The Ruhr River Valley, center of the coal and steel industry of Germany, was an area of lung and bone diseases. The Ruhr was so polluted that few fish could live there. With help from the government, the **Ruhr Association** began an anti-pollution program. Dues in the Association are paid by businesses in proportion to the amount of pollution they create. The cost of

St. Peter's Basilica, the principal church of Roman Catholicism, is located in the Vatican, an independent state within the borders of Italy. The Pope resides in the Vatican Palace, that includes Michelangelo's frescoes on the ceilings of the Sistine Chapel. PhotoDisc Inc. 1994

keeping the river clean is in excess of $14 million per year. Today, it is one of the cleanest rivers in Europe.

In Great Britain, the **Control of Pollution Act of 1974** and other laws decreased environmental pollution substantially. Since the 1950's, pollution of the Thames River has fallen by approximately 25%. Well over 75% of the population have sewage treatment facilities available. A developing problem for the British, however, is control of oil spills in the North Sea fields.

THE FINE ARTS

The arts reflect Europe's changing political, social, and economic values. During the 19th Century, works of art and music reflected romanticism and nationalism. **Romanticism** idealized the beauties of nature and looked back on the Middle Ages with fondness. Strong feelings of nationalism were particularly evident in the music of the time.

Late in the 19th Century, the **impressionist** school of art survived considerable criticism. Impressionist artists tried to capture a moment in time and painted scenes of everyday life. They painted pictures full of light and color, but the subjects appeared somewhat blurred. In the 20th Century, artists moved even further from reality. After World War I, this tendency increased, and art seemed to reflect the turbulence and uncertainty of the

The Eiffel Tower, named after its French structural engineer, Alexandre Gustave Eiffel, was erected for the Paris Exposition of 1889 to celebrate the science and engineering achievements of its age. PhotoDisc Inc. 1994

times. **Surrealism** emphasized the unconscious and was a totally subjective approach to art.

Modern architecture began to move away from traditional styles in the 1920's under the leadership of people such as the American **Frank Lloyd Wright**, the Swiss **Le Corbusier**, and the German **Walter Gropius**. These architects have done much to establish

an **international style** of architecture in the 20th Century. Much effort has gone into the design of skyscrapers which emphasize design with the efficient use of expensive urban land. Extensive use of glass, steel, and reinforced concrete is evident in the simple and strikingly designed structures which carefully consider function and the modern life style.

European Art Movements			
Artist	**Country**	**Movement**	**Work**
Delacroix	France	Romanticism	Abduction of Rebecca – 1858
Constable	England	Romanticism	Salisbury Cathedral – 1817
Monet	France	Impressionism	St. Lazare RR Station – 1891
Renoir	France	Impressionism	The Rower's Lunch – 1886
Braque	France	Cubism	The Table – 1930
Picasso	Spain	Expressionism	Guernica – 1937
Dali	Spain	Surrealism	Persistence of Memory – 1939

City planning has also played a major role in architectural design as architects work with governments to redesign cities to fit modern needs.

TOWARD POLITICAL UNIFICATION

As a consequence of post-World War II problems, European nations began to realize that cooperation was necessary. Moves to establish a uniform European driver's license and increased educational exchanges were designed to increase the feeling of unity among the people.

The **Council of Europe** sets policy for the European Union (see section IV). The **European Court of Justice** handles controversies among the various branches of the European Community and interprets its agreements and treaties.

QUESTIONS

1 Factors which contributed to the rise of Nazism include
1 unequal treatment of women
2 the autocratic Weimar Republic
3 economic problems of the Depression
4 religious differences

2 The Holocaust in Europe and the actions of the Khmer Rouge in Cambodia (Unit 2) both illustrate
1 interdependence
2 cultural diffusion
3 empathy
4 genocide

3 The unification of Germany in 1990 *best* illustrates the strength of
1 religious fundamentalism
2 nationalism
3 collapse of collective security
4 isolationism

4 The Reich Culture Chambers, the Storm Troopers, and persecution of the opposition were all used by Hitler to
1 control the population
2 win support of the German Army
3 obtain foreign acceptance
4 show his support of religion

5 The Nazi "Final Solution" involved a plan to
1 deport all European Jews
2 eliminate the Jewish population of Europe
3 invade the Soviet Union
4 achieve economic self-sufficiency

6 World War II was caused by
1 many circumstances similar to those prior to World War I
2 religious differences among the European countries
3 the Soviet desire to spread communism
4 the expansionist goals of France

7 To avoid war during the 1930's, the democracies gave in to Hitler's demands. Which of the following is associated with this policy?
1 balance of power
2 détente
3 imperialism
4 appeasement

8 A result of World War II was that
1 Britain and France emerged as the major world powers
2 power shifted to the Southern Hemisphere
3 power was spread evenly among a number of countries
4 the U.S. and U.S.S.R. emerged as the major world powers

9 The British government has
1 always been a republic
2 no written constitution
3 a one-house legislature
4 a monarch with absolute power

10 In terms of population composition, Britain and France have
1 almost no Jews
2 substantial colonial minorities
3 a rapidly increasing birth rate
4 a declining number of senior citizens

11 After World War II, the rise of independent nations in Asia shows the
1 decline of European power
2 failure of nationalism
3 success of capitalism
4 importance of urbanization

Base your answers to questions 12 and 13 on the reading below.

"Young people in Germany often receive contradictory information about the true conditions of life in the Third Reich. History books, documents, films, and magazines describe it as ugly and horrible... Their elders, on the other hand, often tell them that most people lived well in the Third Reich."
— Hannah Vogt, *The Burden of Guilt: A Short History of Germany, 1914 - 1945*

12 The "ugly and horrible" aspect of the Third Reich might *best* be supported by the
1 mass rallies and speeches
2 Nazi control of culture
3 the Holocaust
4 Beer Hall Putsch

13 The idea of the elders "that most people lived well in the Third Reich" might *best* be supported by the
1 *Jewish Star Decree*
2 establishment of Reich Culture Chambers
3 decline in unemployment
4 rebuilding of the Reichstag building

ESSAYS

1 Modern British government has had a long period of evolution.

- *Magna Carta*
- Glorious Revolution
- Model Parliament
- Use of precedents
- Government or Cabinet responsibility to Commons

Select *three* of the factors listed above which contributed to the development of British democracy. For *each*, briefly identify it, explain why it occurred, and state why it helped to make Britain more democratic.

2 The rise of Hitler to power in Germany and his establishment of a totalitarian government had a profound effect on the history of the 20th Century.

a Discuss the problems of the Weimar Republic which allowed the Nazi movement to take control of Germany.

b Explain how the methods employed by Hitler to control the German people fit the definition of totalitarian government.

c Describe the role played by Germany in causing World War II.

3 Contemporary Europe has faced many changes and problems brought about by modern technology and a changing global world.

- Problems in Northern Ireland
- Urbanization
- Diverse populations
- Political unification
- Environmental pollution
- Decline in power

Select *three* of the above areas. For *each*, explain the nature of the change or problem, and how contemporary Europe has dealt with it.

The interdependent economic and trade relations between the United States and Western Europe was shaped following World War II. Named for U.S. Secretary of State George C. Marshall, the Marshall Plan, formally known as the European Recovery Program, provided U.S. economic and technical assistance to 16 European countries. In early 1947, the Cold War between the United States and the Union of Soviet Socialist Republics began to heat up. Washington, DC policymakers became concerned that Western Europe would need major economic aid in order that those nations attain political stability. The Plan was designed to stimulate economic growth and trade among the major non-Communist countries and to restore the war-ravaged West European economy.

IV. ECONOMIC DEVELOPMENT

WORLD WAR II RECOVERY

World War II devastated Western Europe's economy. Much of the physical damage was repaired within a short time, but rebuilding the industrial base and infrastructure took much

longer. The war also shattered Eastern Europe, a major market for the West before the war. The U.S.S.R. converted Eastern European nations into isolated communist dependencies and closed them to Western business. During the war, Western Euro-

peans lost their overseas investments and could not afford to pay for vital imports. Many overseas territories were damaged by the war or developed their own industries during the war. Also, because the U.S. economy gained strength during the war, it had picked up some of the markets Western Europe lost.

The question for the United States was how to best help Europe recover. U.S. Secretary of State **George C. Marshall** proposed an answer. Under the *European Recovery Act* of

1947, the U.S. Congress made available approximately 12.5 billion dollars in aid and technical assistance to the war-torn nations of Europe. The ERA became known as the **Marshall Plan**. It required European nations to develop their own plans for economic recovery. The Cold War was beginning, and while the United States Congress offered the aid to all nations, the Soviet Union put pressure on its Eastern European satellites to turn down the offer. The U.S.S.R. launched a scaled down aid package of its own under **COMECON** (Council of Mutual Economic Assistance).

The Marshall Plan also aided American industry, because much of the money for supplies and equipment was spent in the United States. The ERA program was successful. Western Europe recovered economically. U.S. – Western European trade increased. With restored economic strength, the communist threat in Western Europe diminished. As the Marshall Plan drew Western nations together, many began to think in terms of economic cooperation.

EUROPEAN SOCIALISM

European economies became more **mixed** (capitalist and command) after World War I. By the Great Depression years, a third form of

socialism emerged in addition to the utopian and scientific (Marxist) types discussed earlier in section II. Sometimes called **democratic socialism**, it began to appear in a variety of forms. Governments subsidized capitalist ventures and assumed greater roles in economic development and planning.

Most West European countries have extensive social welfare programs, and many have substantial economies. Some nationalized major industries and resources. In Britain and France, the governments nationalized some major industries and resources while leaving the smaller concerns in private hands.

Great Britain is an example of democratic socialism. Its social welfare program dates from the early 20th Century. After World War II, the Labor Party won election and Parliament expanded the system. As a result of the *Beveridge Report*, Parliament developed the **National Insurance Service and National Health Service**. The program provides benefits for sickness, accident, old age, maternity, and disability. It is financed by contributions of employers, employees, and the self-employed. The National Health Service provides medical and dental care.

Britain's mixed system combines private, government, and cooperative industrial ownership. The national government supervises the transportation, communication, fuel, power, coal, and steel industries. Most other manufacturing industries remain in private hands. Both the Conservative and Labor parties support the social welfare program.

Britain's democratic socialism is fluid in nature. The amount of government-owned industry varies depending on the party in power in Britain. When in power, the Conservative Party frequently acts to undo nationalization or slow the process. The reverse has been true of the Labor Party. During the 1980's

and early 1990's, the Conservative government diminished its strong role in the economy and allowed more private enterprise to operate.

France's economic system also moved toward more socialism after World War II. Communists became a strong force in the nation's politics. Moderate socialists attempted a series of economic plans to decrease reliance on imported oil, increase the use of advanced technology, and decrease unemployment and inflation. When these plans falter, the government implements austerity measures. It cuts wages in nationalized industries and often levies new taxes. The country sees frequent demonstrations and national strikes over these policies.

ECONOMIC GROWTH & DEVELOPMENT

REDEVELOPED ECONOMIES

As Europe rebuilt, government involvement and world events changed economic structures. Britain, for example, now lives largely from manufacturing and trade. Before World War II, Britain produced coal and low-grade iron ore. Other mineral resources vital to its industry were imported. Since the end of the War, traditional British mineral industries have decreased in importance. North Sea oil deposits

Representing the free market side of Britain's mixed economic system (socialism and capitalism), the London Stock Exchange is one of the world's largest trading centers.   PhotoDisc Inc. 1994

The economy of Western Europe is diverse. (clockwise from top left)
Offshore oil workers in the North Sea; Olive groves in Andalusia, Spain;
Clockmaker in Schaffhausen, Switzerland; Shipyards of Bremen, Germany;
TGV Rail Transit in Paris, France; and vineyards at Tuscany Castle, Italy.
PhotoDisc Inc. 1994

WORLD STUDIES – *Global Issues & Assessments* **N&N©**

have been intensely developed, but other industries replaced mining. Electronics, chemicals, and commercial services such as banking and insurance lead the list. Britain is far less self-sufficient today. In terms of agriculture, Britain currently produces only about two-thirds of its needs. The remainder must be imported.

France has a better balance between industry and agriculture. It is among the leading producers of coal and iron in Europe. It leads the world in the production of bauxite (aluminum ore). Its industry increased considerably since the end of the World War II. Electronics, transportation, and construction are the leading industries. French industries tend to be smaller in scale and less inclined to use mass production techniques. Fashions, wine, cosmetics, and perfume are important. Agriculture employs only 9% of the population. Yet, France is the only country in Europe self-sufficient in food production. The quality of the agricultural products is undoubtedly a factor in the famous French cuisine. France also exports products such as wine, sugar, wheat, and beef.

Germany has the most significant coal deposits in Western Europe, but its iron ore is low in quality. Industry is well developed and diversified. Chemicals, iron and steel production, and engineering play important roles. Because agricultural production does not come close to meeting consumer demand, Germany is a major importer of food products. In 1990, reunification of the weak former communist nation of East Germany strained West Germany's strong industrial economy. Converting former East German state industries presented more difficulties than leaders expected. Unemployment rose, and a serious recession plagued the nation in the early 1990's. Experts feel Germany is one of the world's strongest economies but will struggle for most of the 1990's with the problems of reunification.

Southern Europe provides a contrast with the north. Farming is a larger component of the economy, and industry is less well developed. After World War II, governments took strong measures to improve both industry and agriculture. In Italy, the resource base is poor, but industry continues to grow, especially in the northern part of the country. Automobiles, precision machinery, chemicals, and rubber prod-

ucts are important. Still, much of the industry remains small and involves artisan-type production. Attempts to attract industry to the poorer areas of the south are showing some results.

Italian agriculture declined in recent years. It is the world's largest producer of wine and olive oil and has good climatic conditions for two annual crops. While it is a major cereal producing nation, wheat yields dropped in the last decade. Competition from abroad forced many farmers out of business and production fell.

Spain has a considerable mineral base, but mining is declining because of competition from LDCs (developing nations). Industrially, textiles and chemicals are significant. In agriculture, the use of fertilizers and mechanization has increased. Spain's economy is mixed. A government agency regulates about 25 million acres of land and encourages the use of irrigation and new cultivation methods to increase productivity. This has caused the number of farm workers to decline, but agriculture's importance in the economy has also declined.

ECONOMIC COOPERATION

After World War II, Western European leaders began to see economic cooperation as critical. Loss of colonial resources, the diversity of the industry, and the uneven distribution of resources made cooperation imperative. They knew West European countries have economies that compliment each other. The **Marshall Plan** made this evident. European statesmen launched the European communities movement.

In 1951, the **European Coal and Steel Community** was established by Belgium, Netherlands, Luxembourg, France, and West Germany based on a plan proposed by Robert Schuman of France. The **Schuman Plan** removed barriers to the movement of iron and steel and the relocation of industry workers among member countries. In 1957, the same six nations established **EURATOM** (European Atomic Energy Community) to coordinate nuclear research and aid in the development of nuclear power.

In the 1950's, the original six members of the European Coal and Steel Community formed the **European Economic Community**, also called The Common Market, and later known as the European Community (EC). Beginning in the 1970's, the Common Market expanded to include Ireland, Denmark, Greece, Portugal, Spain and Great Britain, and in 1993, it became known as the **European Union**.

Economic growth and political stability are intertwined. For example, the European Community played a major role in seeking solutions on the Balkan civil wars.

CONTEMPORARY ISSUES

Despite the international cooperation, the increased government economic role, and the establishment of the "safety nets" of social welfare programs, Western European nations face a variety of contemporary economic problems.

Serious inflation (rapidly increasing prices) plagued Europe in recent decades. In the 1970's, much of the inflation was a result of the increase in oil prices. Governments sponsored programs to increase fuel conservation. In the 1980's, the British inflation rate reached 21.9 percent. By 1991, several recessions and government efforts lowered it to 4.5 percent.

International trade balances aided Europe. In the 1980's, a rise in U.S. interest rates led to increased value for the U.S. dollar. This made European exports more attractive and helped to reduce inflation. In the early 1990's, a still lower U.S. dollar value kept European inflation at about twice the U.S. rate.

Unemployment continues to be a serious problem. In the early 1990's, British, French, and German unemployment remained high

EUROPEAN UNION 1994

(around 9%). Most countries felt the burden of increased unemployment compensation costs.

Recent developments present the region with many challenges. Economic conditions change often. Situations influencing economics include:

• **Dependence on oil from the troubled Middle East** – With the exception of Britain, Middle East oil price increases during the 1970's adversely affected West European countries. Recessions or depressions occurred. The decline in oil prices between 1981 and 1985 improved economic conditions, but Europe is heavily dependent on that volatile region. The recent opening of Russian and Eastern European oil reserves to the West may reduce the dependency on Middle East oil.

European Union (Common Market) – Economic Goals	
Goals	**Actions**
• Raise member nations' standards of living. • Equalize competition in world markets. • Strengthen competitive position with Japan and U. S.	• Abolish trade barriers (tariffs, quotas) among its members. • Create standard trade rules for entire membership region. • Set up single money and credit system. • Allow free movement of workers into countries where needed. • Create standard worker benefits and protections.

ECONOMIC GROWTH & DEVELOPMENT

- **The Soviet collapse and transforming Eastern Europe from communism** – Trade with former communist bloc countries is increasing. Yet, there is an imbalance. The West's desire for most Eastern European manufactured products is limited. Polish hams, Russian vodka, and Czech glass are popular, but the quality of Eastern manufactures is lacking. Trade should increase with a new Russian natural gas pipeline to Europe. Yet, economic problems hampered progress. Internal problems in the old communist bloc hinder free enterprise and cut the size of its market.

- **Behavior of MNCs** (multinational corporations) – Massive global corporations such as European-based Phillips and Nestlé are large enough to move operations easily to advance their profits. They can alter economic life, and governments and regional trade alliances have little control over them.

- **Unification of Germany** – When unity came in October 1990, German leaders underestimated the cost of integrating the feeble East German economy with West Germany's strong industrial economy. East German state enterprises collapsed, and a recession hit the reunified nation. Most economists feel it may take until the year 2000 to restore the German economy. In addition, Germany's strength is at the heart of the European Union. Competing with other global powers was also a setback.

- **Global trade alliances** – West European countries must strain to remain competitive in the changed world market. The European Union is only minimally united. The upsurge of the Pacific Rim and NAFTA plus the equalizing force of GATT present challenges to Europe. Costly government programs subsidize certain industries (autos in Britain and agricultural products in France). Those costs must rise to keep Europe competitive. In the 1993 GATT negotiations, France desperately held out for trade protection for its farmers and its film industry.

GLOBAL TRADE

West European countries that belong to the European Union do most of their trading with fellow members. Britain, for example, carries on close to half its foreign trade with the European Union members. Less than 15% of its foreign trade is now with the Commonwealth of Nations. Spain trades extensively with European Union nations and with the United States and Latin America.

The 12-member European Union produces one fourth of the world's output. On their own, Switzerland, Norway, Germany, and Sweden are among the world's highest per capita GDP nations.

The European Union must deal with other economic powers. In critical industries such as electronics and automobiles Japanese products offer strong competition. Japanese and U.S. firms have factories in Europe which allow them to trade within the European Union and not worry  about tariffs and other trade barriers. Powerful Japanese and North American MNCs have enough strength to quickly expand into new Eastern European markets and absorb losses longer than some Western European firms.

Today, the European Union is one of the three great centers of economic power with Japan and North America. Yet, in *Preparing for the Twenty-First Century*, historian Paul Kennedy notes that Europe's internal problems endanger its global capabilities. Within the European Union, cooperation is not easy. The British government recently vetoed the plan of a British corporation to purchase Norwegian gas. The 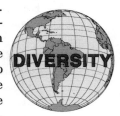 Norwegians had to investigate other European sources of investment. Such difficulties are rooted in Europe's long history of divisiveness. Kennedy says if national leaders can overcome ancient rivalries, Europe's future can be very bright.

QUESTIONS

1 At the end of World War II, Europe's economy was
   1 extremely prosperous
   2 able to live off colonial investments
   3 in a state of chaos
   4 denied aid by the United States

2 Since 1945, North European countries' economies have
   1 increasingly relied on agriculture as a source of income
   2 experienced few unemployment problems
   3 increased their "high tech" industries
   4 discovered large new sources of coal and iron

3 Which best describes the current economic system of most Western European countries?
   1 laissez-faire capitalist
   2 communist
   3 mercantilist
   4 mixed

4 The European Union, EURATOM, and the European Coal and Steel Community are all examples of
   1 European economic cooperation
   2 plans to limit weapons production
   3 European foreign aid programs
   4 postwar American aid plans

5 Democratic socialist countries usually have
   1 complete government ownership of industry
   2 extensive social welfare programs
   3 very low tax rates
   4 little overseas trade

6 A major economic problem for most European countries in the 1970's was
   1 the spread of communism
   2 the failure to subsidize industry
   3 an increase in oil prices
   4 an insufficient supply of labor

7 During the early 1990's, which of these was the strongest trading partner for most of Western Europe?
   1 the Pacific Rim
   2 the U.S.
   3 Saudi Arabia
   4 Eastern Europe

8 Why do MNCs (multinational corporations) present a challenge to national economies?
   1 They dictate Middle Eastern oil prices.
   2 Governments have little control over them.
   3 They cannot operate in mixed economies.
   4 They will not pay taxes.

9 Which is affected most by global trade alliances such as the European Union and NAFTA?
   1 economic competition
   2 communist power
   3 government subsidies
   4 democratic socialism

10 The Marshall Plan aided Western Europe's post-World War II recovery with
   1 social welfare "safety nets"
   2 financial and technical assistance
   3 national health insurance
   4 forming multinational corporations

ESSAY

Economic cooperation is essential to the future development of Western Europe.

a Discuss the success of the Marshall Plan and the role it played in promoting European economic cooperation.

b Using specific examples, explain why economic cooperation is essential in contemporary Europe.

c Explain the role of the European Union (former EC or Common Market) and evaluate its success.

V. GLOBAL CONTEXT

After the Axis Powers surrendered in 1945, the period of European global dominance ended. The U.S., by virtue of its atomic monopoly and powerful economy, was the world's major power. The Soviet Union's military power and dominance of Eastern Europe placed it in opposition. In 1949, the U.S.S.R. exploded its first atomic bomb. The period of the Cold War began. A tense era ensued with the world frequently in danger of nuclear holocaust. Wedged between the superpowers, Europeans always saw themselves as the great battlefield of the Cold War.

In the final decades of the 20th Century, forty years of Cold War ended. The Soviet Union collapsed, and communism declined as a major ideology in Europe. Like other regions, Western Europe had to make adjustments to a new global landscape. A look at the events of the late 20th Century lends some perspective on that new landscape.

NUCLEAR POLITICS

Western Europe became the center of the Cold War struggles between the superpowers. At mid-century, both atomic powers continued nuclear testing and developed hydrogen bombs with many times the explosive power of those used against Japan. Atomic weapons were also miniaturized for use by troops under battlefield conditions. By the 1950's, people all over the world were concerned about the military threat posed not just by the use of such weapons but also the environmental threats resulting from nuclear tests.

Tensions sometimes brought the world to the brink of nuclear war, but diplomacy avoided direct confrontation. In 1963, the *Limited Nuclear Test Ban Treaty* outlawed tests in the atmosphere. In 1967, the *Outer Space Treaty* prohibited the spread of nuclear weapons to outer space.

In 1970, the *Nuclear Nonproliferation Treaty* attempted to end the spread of nuclear weapons to countries not already possessing them. The treaty was not successful in disarming a number of nations (India and China) which tested nuclear weapons. Also, it has not dissuaded a number of other nations driven to acquire nuclear capability (Iraq, Pakistan, Israel, and North Korea).

The *SALT Treaty* (Strategic Arms Limitation Treaty) of 1979 began a decade of serious reduction in nuclear capability by the superpowers. In 1992, the *START Treaty* (Strategic Arms Reduction Treaty) continued the reduction momentum begun by the U.S. and the republics of the former Soviet Union. Yet, the danger of multiple nuclear powers is still a matter of concern to people of all nations.

COLD WAR POLITICS IN EUROPE

"BIG THREE" AGREEMENTS

During World War II, a number of conferences were held by "The Big Three." Joseph Stalin represented the Soviet Union, Franklin Roosevelt (and later, Harry S Truman) represented the United States, and Winston Churchill spoke for Great Britain. The decisions made at these wartime conferences shaped the postwar world.

Wartime "Big Three" Conferences	
Conference	**Significant Decisions**
Teheran – 1943	Agreed to open a second front against Germany on the continent of Europe and attack from all directions.
Yalta – 1945	Divided Germany into four occupation zones and pushed democratization and due punishment for war criminals. Guaranteed the Poles a broader based democratic government and free and fair elections. Russia promised to enter war against Japan in exchange for territory in the Far East.
Potsdam – 1945	Confirmed Yalta agreements and virtually gave the Soviet Union control of Eastern Europe.

THE IRON CURTAIN

During World War II, the Allied decision to open a second front on the Italian Peninsula rather than the Balkan Peninsula left the way open for the Soviet Red Army to liberate most areas in Eastern Europe from Nazi occupation.

The Red Army also established "puppet governments" in the nations they occupied. In fact, if one were to draw a line around the advances of the Red Army, it would coincide almost exactly with the areas later controlled by communists. In describing the situation, Churchill later coined the phrase, **"Iron Curtain."** It came to symbolize the prevention of the free flow of ideas between the West and the communist-dominated East.

THE BERLIN CRISIS

There was no peace treaty at the end World War II. Immediately after the War, the Big Three divided Germany into four occupation zones. The U.S., France, Britain, and U.S.S.R. each controlled one zone. The capital, Berlin, was completely inside the Soviet Zone. The allies also divided the city into four occupation zones. **West Berlin** (the U.S.–French–British half), prospered and enjoyed a better standard of living as did West Germany. It became a constant source of irritation for the communists.

In 1948, the Russians closed off all surface routes to Berlin in an attempt to force the Western powers out of the city. The Allies responded with the **Berlin Airlift**. They supplied the needs of the city by cargo flights for approximately a year. The embarrassed Soviets finally reopened access, but there were periodic closings until the reunification of the two Germanies in 1990.

In 1949, the Soviet Union established the **German Democratic Republic** (East Germany) as a communist satellite country. In 1955, the Western Allies combined their occupation zones to form the **Federal Republic of Germany** (West Germany) which they recognized as an independent republic. They also recognized West Berlin as a part of the West German nation. In 1961, Soviet leader

Following the defeat of Hitler in World War II, the Allies divided both the capital city of Berlin and the country of Germany into four occupation zones.

Nikita Sergeyevich Khrushchev became so angered by the continued migration of educated people to West Germany that he ordered the East German government to erect the **Berlin Wall**, cutting the city in half. It became a symbol of the division of the world during the Cold War.

Communist activities and Soviet power moves in Berlin rekindled fears of totalitarianism. War-weakened Western European nations turned to the United States for help.

SUPERPOWER BEHAVIOR

The United States responded with a policy of **containment**. It promised to block communist expansion. The Marshall Plan (see section IV) and the Truman Doctrine were part of this policy. **The Truman Doctrine** (1947) gave financial aid and weapons to Greece and Turkey to resist communist insurgency. Containment eventually became a global policy. Americans gave aid and fought the spread of communism in every global region.

After World War II, Soviet occupation established communist governments in other countries of Eastern Europe. The continued

presence of Russian troops, economic dependence, and various treaties and alliances combined to give the Soviet Union control in these **satellite countries** (subservient near-colonies).

In some satellite countries, groups revolted against Soviet control. Reaction was swift and often involved invasion. An uprising in 1968 in Czechoslovakia is an example. **Alexander Dubcek** emerged as leader of the Communist Party. He promised a reform program of improved ties with the West and greater freedom for the people. The Soviets mobilized its **Warsaw Pact** allies, invaded Czechoslovakia, and forced Dubcek from power. Not only the West but also several communist-dominated countries denounced the Soviet action. After the Czech uprising, the Soviets announced the

Brezhnev Doctrine. It said the U.S.S.R. would intervene if rebellions threatened communist regimes.

Due to superpower diplomacy, the 1960's and 1970's were periods of relative peace in Europe. Khrushchev and his successor, Brezhnev, were less aggressive after the Cuban Missile Crisis (see Unit 9). They sought "peaceful coexistence." In the 1970's, a more cordial relationship emerged under "détente."

By 1989, economic problems weakened the power of the Communist Party in many Eastern European nations. In addition, Soviet leader **Mikhail Gorbachev** diminished Soviet influence over the satellite countries. Gorbachev's *glasnost* and *perestroika* reforms inside the U.S.S.R. encouraged reformers in the satellite nations. Mass demonstrations for reform began throughout Eastern Europe. In Poland, Lech Walesa led the **Solidarity** labor movement that challenged communist authority.

By November of 1989, weeks of demonstrations weakened the hard-line communist regimes. In East Germany, demonstrators with hammers and chisels broke openings in the infamous Berlin Wall. The East German communist leaders allowed free movement through the wall for the first time in twenty-eight years. Afterwards, the governments cleared political and economic barriers rapidly. The two Germanies reunited into one nation in 1990.

COLLAPSE OF COLONIALISM

World War II delivered a death blow to European imperialism. It led to freedom for almost all of the prewar colonies.

Some colonies fought for their independence. In 1954, the communist Vietminh won the critical **Battle of Dien Bien Phu** against the French in Indochina. Later that year, France, Britain, the Soviet Union, Red China, and the Indochinese states signed the *Geneva Agreements*. They provided for an independent and neutral Cambodia and Laos. Vietnam was divided at the 17th Parallel. The North was under communist control, and the South had an anti-communist government. Plans were made to reunify the two Vietnams with elections in 1956 under U.S. supervision. The elections were not held. In the 1960's, American involvement escalated into the Vietnam War. Following the end of the U.S. involvement in the war in 1973, the communist regime united the country.

The situation in the **Suez Canal Crisis** (1956) was somewhat different. Britain and France, former colonial powers in the Middle East, were angered by Egyptian leader Gamel Abdel Nasser's nationalization of the Canal. They feared that the Egyptians would not be able to run the vital waterway properly. The Israelis wanted to stop guerrilla raids into their country and open the Gulf of Aqaba to shipping. The three invaded the Egyptian canal region. The U.N. (with the affirmative votes of both the Soviet Union and the United States) condemned the attack and demanded the withdrawal of the invading forces. The countries complied, and a U.N. Emergency Force was sent in to keep the peace.

Despite early hostility between newly independent countries and their former colonial masters, many established cordial relationships. In fact, many former colonies looked to the colonial power for economic and military aid. Recent French aid to the government of Chad, fighting Libyan incursions, is one such example.

Before World War II, Britain established the **Commonwealth of Nations** for former colonies. It is still a viable organization. Members voluntarily choose to join the organization. Certain economic and trade benefits are extended to the members, and regular conferences are held to discuss joint problems. The French established a similar French Union (later called the **French Community**) to retain ties with former colonies. However, many members later chose to withdraw, and the French Community no longer functions.

PEACE ORGANIZATIONS

THE UNITED NATIONS

At the end of World War II, the **San Francisco Conference** (1945) made the provisions for the charter (constitution) of the **United Nations**. The purpose of the organization was to promote:

- international peace and security
- settlement of disputes between nations by peaceful means
- development of friendly relations
- international cooperation to solve world social, economic, and cultural problems

The United Nations charter gave the **Security Council** the power to deal with threats to international peace and security.

There are five permanent members of the U.N. Security Council. They are China, France, Great Britain, Russia, and the United States. Each permanent member has a veto power over the Council's actions. There are also ten non-permanent members elected by the General Assembly for two-year terms. Strong efforts are made to insure that various groups and areas are represented on the Council on a rotating basis.

The **U.N. General Assembly** includes all member nations each having one vote. It holds discussions and makes recommendations on world problems. The **Secretariat** handles the day-to-day operations of the organization, calls conferences and meetings, and distributes information.

The **U.N. Secretary General** has the responsibility of calling Security Council attention to threats to world peace. The Secretary also undertakes special missions and heads U.N. emergency forces.

The **U.N. Economic and Social Council** coordinates the activities of specialized agencies and tries to improve global economic and social conditions. The **U.N. Trusteeship Council** prepares areas for self-government under the supervision of major powers. This council has done its job so well that few areas remain under its supervision today. Finally, the **U.N. Court of Justice** decides disputes that member nations voluntarily submit to its jurisdiction. It also gives other U.N. agencies advisory opinions on international law.

The U.N.'s greatest successes have been in the social and economic fields. It has dealt with health problems, famine relief, crop production, labor conditions, and women's rights.

Politically, it has had difficulty with nations and their claims of sovereignty (independent self-rule). Numerous times, nations have refused to obey United Nations' resolutions. Examples include the Soviet invasion of Hungary (1956), India's seizure of Portuguese Goa (1961), or South Africa's apartheid struggles. However, in the case of the Korean War (1950-53), it did raise a U.N. force to protect the independence of South Korea. It also used emergency forces numerous times to keep warring nations or factions apart. Its activities during the early 1990's in Somalia, Rwanda, and Bosnia are examples.

Financially, the U.S. has accepted the largest burden for supporting the United Nations. Some countries (including the U.S.) have refused to contribute for U.N. actions of which they disapprove. Sometimes, major powers have used forums other than the U.N. to settle their differences. These actions have weakened the U.N.'s ability to deal with international problems.

THE LEAGUE OF NATIONS

There were earlier formal attempts at world peace. The most famous was the **League of Nations**. The Treaty of Versailles established the League at the end of World War I. It was one of U.S. President Wilson's Fourteen Points. Its structure was very similar to that of the U.N.; however, its Council required a unanimous vote of the members in order to act. Isolationists in the United States Senate prevented its joining. Countries such as the Soviet Union, Germany, and Japan joined late, left early, or were expelled for aggression as World War II approached. As a consequence, it never gained adequate global support.

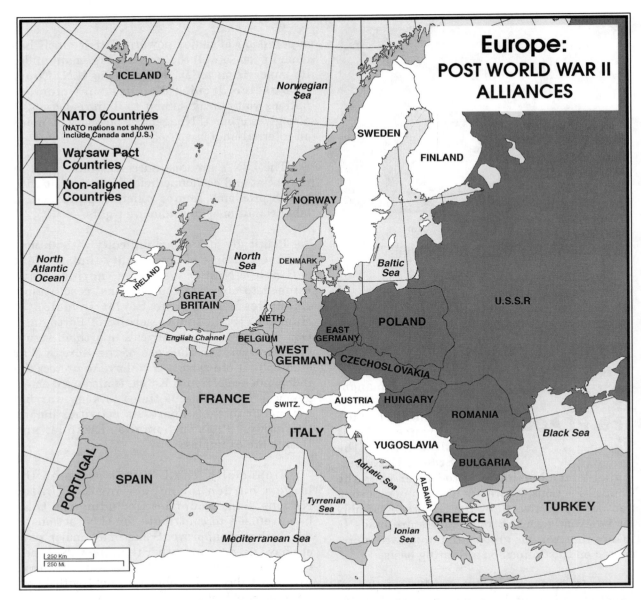

Europe: POST WORLD WAR II ALLIANCES

NATO Countries
(NATO nations not shown include Canada and U.S.)

Warsaw Pact Countries

Non-aligned Countries

The League had the power to use diplomatic, economic, and military sanctions to punish those who disobeyed its resolutions. It never attempted to use military power. As is true for the U.N., its most effective work was in the economic, social, and cultural fields. The League dissolved in 1945 when the U.N. came into existence.

THE HAGUE

Prior to World War I, the **Hague Conferences** tried to limit the arms race without success. They did, however, establish "humane rules of warfare" that outlawed things such as bombing civilian populations. They also established the **Hague Tribunal** to settle international disputes. It worked under both the League and the U.N. and still exists today.

THE CONCERT OF EUROPE

Going back to the 19th Century, after the Congress of Vienna in 1815, the major powers set up the **Concert of Europe**. It was a periodic conference of monarchs' delegates. It attempted to preserve the peace in the face of potential revolutions by people seeking democracy and self-determination. For a brief period, the countries involved did cooperate to achieve these objectives, but the more liberal British, and at times the French, refused cooperation. By the time of the revolutions of 1848, the Concert of Europe no longer functioned.

The history of international organizations and their success in preventing wars or major incidents is not outstanding, but they have provided the opportunity for nations to discuss differences.

EUROPEAN DEFENSE

In addition, alliance systems were used to preserve peace. They sometimes balanced power and deterred aggression.

Two major alliances balanced power in the post-World War II period. In 1949, twelve nations formed a **collective security agreement** (mutual defense). Britain, France, Belgium, the Netherlands, Luxembourg, Italy, Portugal, Norway, Denmark, Iceland, Canada and U.S. formed the **North Atlantic Treaty Organization**. They pledged to come to the aid of any member attacked, if required. In the years that followed, Greece, Turkey, Spain, and Germany joined **NATO**.

To balance power, the Soviets answered by forming the **Warsaw Pact** alliance in 1955. It joined the U.S.S.R. in a mutual assistance defense agreement with most of the Eastern European nations (see map on opposite page).

NATO has a unified command and a military force that integrates units from the armies of member nations. The Supreme Allied Commander has traditionally been an American. However, disagreements have damaged the unity of NATO at different times. Examples include the Greek-Turkish dispute over Cyprus, and President Charles de Gaulle's withdrawal of French forces from the unified NATO command in the 1960's.

The question of U.S. strategic weapons in Germany became a problem for NATO. Nations such as Switzerland maintained security by a position of neutrality. However, as Belgium unfortunately learned in both World Wars, neutrality is not a protection if you stand between hostile powers.

The alliances changed in the mid-1980's when Cold War tensions eased. Gorbachev and Reagan (and later Presidents Yeltsin, Bush, and Clinton) agreed to missile and troop cuts. In the 1990's, the rise of democratic governments and economic problems led the Soviet Union to dissolve the Warsaw Pact (February 1991).

In response, Western nations reorganized and streamlined NATO. The **Council of Europe**, organized under the European Community organization, appeared ready to take on some of its regional security duties. Critics wondered if NATO was needed due to the collapse of communism and the dissolution of the Soviet Union. Yet, NATO's supporters argued that instability in Russia and the Balkans required a united military presence in Europe.

Poland, the Czech Republic, and Hungary petitioned NATO for membership. NATO responded with a **Partnership for Peace**, offering East European nations associate status in NATO. Russia, wary of a NATO presence in Eastern Europe, has also explored ways to co-operate with NATO and the West.

SUMMARY

Throughout history, different regions of the world seemed to dominant world events. For 2,000 years, the dynasties of China perceived themselves as being the center of civilization and power, the "Middle Kingdom." For 700 years, Rome considered itself the center of the Mediterranean world. Following them, the spread of Islam influenced four world regions.

However, from the Age of Discovery to World War II, European civilization held center stage in world affairs. In the early 20th Century, Europe ignored the rise of newly industrialized powers such as Japan and the United States, because they existed outside the European center of global affairs. Historians refer to this as a "Eurocentric World."

That came to an end with the Cold War. Weakened European powers lost their empires and their ability to influence world affairs. Power gravitated to the two superpowers. With the disintegration of the Soviet Union, the global power structure changed again. Decisions made by Western European nations, acting as a community, are key to the new shape of global affairs.

QUESTIONS

1 Decisions made at the Teheran, Yalta, and Potsdam Conference initially led to
   1 the spread of communism
   2 a democratic government for Poland
   3 a united Germany
   4 a Soviet withdrawal from the war against Japan

2 Which was true of the Soviet suppression of the 1968 Czech revolt?
   1 It was supported by the entire communist world.
   2 It established limits beyond which liberalization could not go.
   3 It led to revolt against the communist leadership in the U.S.S.R.
   4 It led to serious disruption of the Czech economy.

3 In the immediate post-World War II period, the U.S. policy toward communism was called
   1 détente
   2 containment
   3 collective security
   4 peaceful coexistence

4 The Suez Canal Crisis was unusual in post-World War II history because
   1 a U.N. force was sent in to protect Egypt
   2 the Canal was peacefully internationalized
   3 the U.S.S.R. and the U.S. voted together to condemn the attack
   4 Britain and France refused to obey the U.N. resolution

5 Which was a major reason for the success of Soviet domination in Eastern Europe after World War II?
   1 Eastern Europeans accepted the Brezhnev Doctrine.
   2 The democracies of Western Europe needed greater security.
   3 The Soviet Union had military forces in Eastern Europe as a result of WW II.
   4 Western Europeans feared Nazism would be rekindled in Eastern Europe.

6 Benefits of membership in the Commonwealth of Nations include
   1 access to British atomic weapons
   2 governmental control from London
   3 economic and trade benefits
   4 representation in the British Parliament

7 The agency of the U.N. charged with keeping world peace is the
   1 Security Council
   2 General Assembly
   3 Economic and Social Council
   4 Trusteeship Council

8 The U.N., the League of Nations, and the Concert of Europe all sought to
   1 return prewar governments to power
   2 preserve international peace
   3 use military force to defeat aggression
   4 establish an international military force

ESSAYS

1 The results of World War II have had a lasting impact upon European history and the global power structure. Discuss *three* of the following:

   • European attempts to coordinate defense
   • impact of WW II on colonial empires
   • the impact of the atomic age on the postwar world
   • changes in the international power structure

2 The Cold War dominated European affairs for a generation after World War II.

   a Explain how decisions made at the wartime conferences reshaped Europe.

   b How did the behavior of the superpowers govern affairs in Europe?

   c What role should Europe play in world affairs now that the Cold War is over?

UNIT EIGHT: WESTERN EUROPE ASSESSMENT

ISSUE: EVALUATING PRIMARY SOURCES

This two-part evaluation offers individual research and cooperative reporting opportunities.

STUDENT TASK

Organize a set of notes on a primary source and its time period and use it to produce a group report.

DETAILED PROCEDURES

Part One:
Examine a primary source provided by teacher. Prepare a set of notes.

A Cite the source in proper form.

B Identify the period associated with the source.

C Tie the source to key events and characteristics of its time period.

Part Two:
Produce a combined report with other students who read the same source.

A Select a spokesperson who will orally present the group's report.

B An open question period will follow the report. Other members of the group should be prepared to help the spokesperson answer questions from the class after the presentation.

EVALUATION

The scoring grid next to the evaluation items (on the following pages) was left blank intentionally. Choice of appropriate category terms is the decision of the instructor. Selection of terms such as "minimal," "satisfactory," and "distinguished" can vary with this assessment. The table on page 10 offers additional suggestions for scoring descriptors that might be inserted in the blank grids.

LEARNING STANDARDS

Students should:

• Analyze and evaluate differing views of historic, social, cultural, economic, and political events, eras, ideas, and issues.

• Analyze and evaluate the effects of human, technological, and natural activities on societies.

• Present ideas both in writing and orally in clear, concise fashion.

• Work cooperatively and respect the rights of others to think, act, and speak differently from themselves within the context of democratic principles and social justice.

• Demonstrate civic values and socially responsible behavior as members of school groups, local, state, national, and global communities.

• Employ a variety of information from written, graphic, and multimedia sources.

• Monitor, reflect upon, and improve their own and others' work.

Part One: Individual Reading and Notes

Table on page 10 offers suggestions for scoring descriptors.

	Category 1	Category 2	Category 3	Category 4	Category 5
Evaluation Item a Are notes and bibliography written clearly and organized effectively?	Category 1	Category 2	Category 3	Category 4	Category 5
Evaluation Item b Are text and library sources used to prepare notes shown?	Category 1	Category 2	Category 3	Category 4	Category 5
Evaluation Item c Is the period accurately noted?	Category 1	Category 2	Category 3	Category 4	Category 5
Evaluation Item d Are key events and characteristics of the era connected to the source noted?	Category 1	Category 2	Category 3	Category 4	Category 5
Evaluation Item e Are notes and bibliography written clearly and organized effectively?	Category 1	Category 2	Category 3	Category 4	Category 5

Part Two: Group Planning and Report

Table on page 10 offers suggestions for scoring descriptors.

	Category 1	Category 2	Category 3	Category 4	Category 5
Evaluation Item a Group Planning: Does student work effectively within group? Does student appreciate and respect views of others?	Category 1	Category 2	Category 3	Category 4	Category 5
Evaluation Item b Report: Are the period, the key events, and characteristics of the era clearly associated with the source?	Category 1	Category 2	Category 3	Category 4	Category 5
Evaluation Item c Report: Is the significance of the source clearly presented?	Category 1	Category 2	Category 3	Category 4	Category 5
Evaluation Item d Report: Are audience questions answered effectively?	Category 1	Category 2	Category 3	Category 4	Category 5

ADMINISTRATIVE GUIDELINES

1 Obtain pictures and excerpts from primary sources from different eras in European history. (Suggestions: pictures of Notre Dame, Michelangelo's *David*, Versailles, Sadler Report excerpt, Kipling's *White Man's Burden* excerpt, Treaty of Versailles excerpt, Picasso's *Guernica*, preamble to the U.N. Charter).

2 Survey library resources and discuss project with librarian.

3 Arrange library time for research.

4 Allow adequate class time for groups to work cooperatively on report.

5 Establish schedule for presentations. (Suggest one per day.)

9

Eastern Europe Russia & Central Asia

500		BC	AD		1000		1500	1700

- Slavic migrations
  - Romans in E. Europe
- Varangian Bulgar & Magyar Invasions
  - Kiev City-state
    - Mongols
  - Eastern Orthodox Church
- Ivan the Terrible
  - Peter the Great

Time-line is not drawn to scale.

revolution
Soviet Bloc
communism
Westernization
ethnic populations

Glasnost
proletariat
Perestroika
dictatorship
command economy

| 1800 | 1900 | 1950 | 1990 | 2000 |

- Duchy of Warsaw
  - Napoleonic Invasion
- Austro-Hungarian Empire
- WW I
  - U.S.S.R. Formed
  - Bolshevik Revolution
- WW II
  - Hitler Invades U.S.S.R.
- Stalin
- Cold War
  - Hungarian Revolt
- *Glasnost*
- U.S.S.R. Collapses •
- E. European • Pro-democracy Movements

Time-line is not drawn to scale.

UNIT NINE:

EASTERN EUROPE, RUSSIA, & CENTRAL ASIA

I. PHYSICAL AND HISTORICAL SETTING

Geography plays an important role in the life and development of every region. Mountains, deserts, and climate can protect or expose people to aggressors. However, the steppes of Central Asia and the plains around the Danube have been natural invasion routes. Constant invasions led to an enormous ethnic diversity in the Eastern Europe, Russia, and Central Asia region. There is a long history of struggles among various groups.

CHARACTERISTICS OF THE REGION

CLIMATE AND TERRAIN

This region is more than 12 million square miles and is more than 2.5 times the size of the United States. It contains over two dozen nations, large and small. Among them is the Russian Federation, physically the largest nation in the world. The region occupies nearly all of the northern Eurasian land mass. Most of it has **Dw** or **Df** (mid-latitude wet and dry cold winter) climates.

The northernmost regions have **ET** (Tundra) or **EF** (Ice Cap) climates with long winters and short summers. The severity of the climate has rendered some protection against invaders.

Milder climates also exist in the region. Beginning with the Caspian Sea and moving east, there is a cool desert area (**Bw** and **Bs** climates). The area along the north coast of the **Black Sea** is closer to a temperate (**D** or **C**) climate. It is able to produce crops such as citrus fruits and grapes.

The **tundra** region (see map opposite page) is a land of long, harsh winters. It has short, cool summers. Much of the land is permafrost and not arable. Herding reindeer is the chief occupation. South of the tundra is the **taiga**, a large evergreen forest area encompassing nearly 50% of the region. The people earn their living from timber and furs.

The **steppe**, or plains area, is south of the forested region. It stretches 3,000 miles (4,828 km). It is a vital area for the economy of the region because it is where much of the farming occurs, especially wheat. It is also a major industrial area. Unfortunately, the flat grasslands have proven to be a popular invasion route.

The most southerly area in Central Asia is the desert. It is very dry and inhabited by nomads. However, modern irrigation techniques are helping yield crops such as cotton. At the same time, the projects are severely damaging the region's ecology.

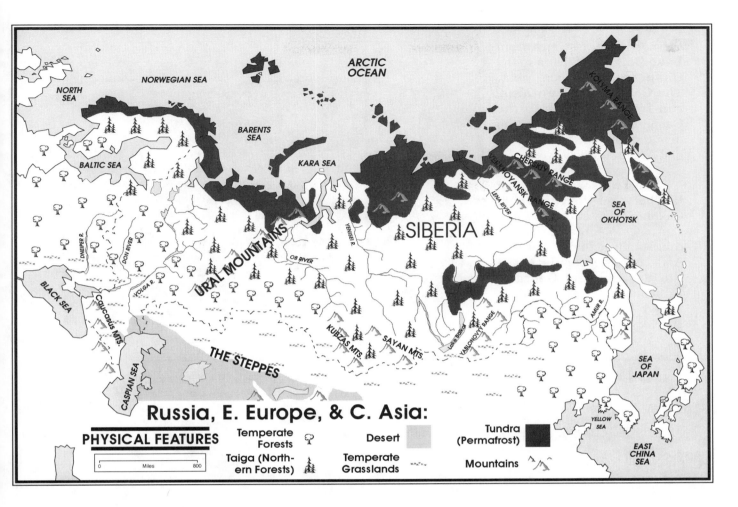

Russia, E. Europe, & C. Asia:

PHYSICAL FEATURES

Temperate Forests

Taiga (Northern Forests)

Desert

Temperate Grasslands

Tundra (Permafrost)

Mountains

The rivers of Russia and Central Asia are a vital source of inland transportation and communication. Their importance is accentuated by the fact that the region is largely landlocked. The North Pacific and Arctic coasts are frozen almost year round. The Caspian, Black, and Baltic Seas are almost totally landlocked, and other nations can control their exits. In Central Asia, the **Ob**, **Yenisei**, and **Lena** rivers flow northward in Siberia toward the Arctic Ocean. In the east, the **Amur** forms part of the border with China and empties into the Pacific in the Sea of Okhotsk. In the west, the **Dnieper**, **Don**, and **Volga** are vital arteries of trade and commerce. The Volga, with its interlocking system of canals to other rivers, is the most important of Russia's rivers.

SUBREGIONS: RUSSIA & CENTRAL ASIA

European Russia extends from its western border with Eastern Europe to the **Ural Mountains**. Geographers consider the Urals

the dividing line between Europe and Asia. However, the mountains are low. They are not much of an impediment to travel, and the people on both sides are very similar.

Siberia occupies the Northern part of the Asian region and is an area of extremes. The far north is tundra. Moving southward there is forest area, the grasslands of the steppe, and finally, an area of fertile farmland. Development of Siberia has been slow. From the tsars to the communists, it has been a place of exile for political opponents. It was not until the completion of the **Trans-Siberian Railroad** in the 20th Century that real development began. The former Soviet communist government took strong steps to promote the development of the area because of its natural resources, industrial potential, and location that make it less vulnerable to attack.

To the south of Siberia lies **Central Asia**. It is a rugged area with fertile steppes and some deserts. It is surrounded by mountains except on the north. They stretch from **Lake Baikal** in Siberia to the **Caspian Sea** on the west. The **Caucasus Mountains**, run from the Black to the Caspian Sea. They form the dividing line between Europe and Asia in the southwest.

The **Transcaucasus** area lies between the Black and Caspian Seas and below the Caucasus Mountains. Transcaucasus is actually a part of Asia, but the population of the Republics of Georgia, Armenia, and Azerbaijan are mixed Asian and European people.

Sue Ann Kime, 1993
Children playing in the Siberian village of Listvyanka near Lake Baikal, Russia

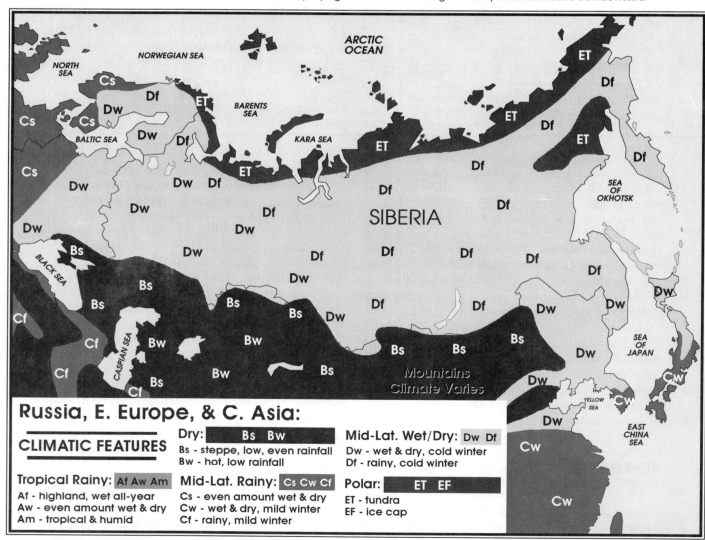

Russia, E. Europe, & C. Asia:

CLIMATIC FEATURES

Dry: Bs Bw
Bs - steppe, low, even rainfall
Bw - hot, low rainfall

Mid-Lat. Wet/Dry: Dw Df
Dw - wet & dry, cold winter
Df - rainy, cold winter

Tropical Rainy: Af Aw Am
Af - highland, wet all-year
Aw - even amount wet & dry
Am - tropical & humid

Mid-Lat. Rainy: Cs Cw Cf
Cs - even amount wet & dry
Cw - wet & dry, mild winter
Cf - rainy, mild winter

Polar: ET EF
ET - tundra
EF - ice cap

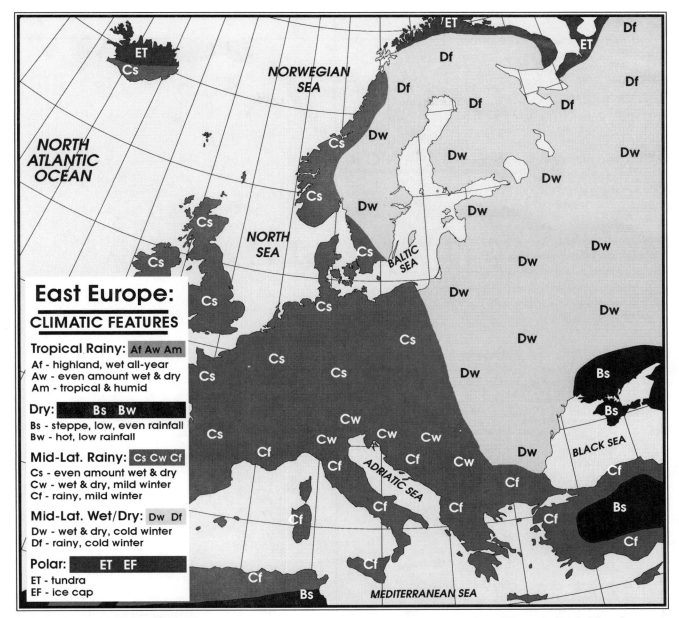

East Europe:
CLIMATIC FEATURES

Tropical Rainy: Af Aw Am
Af - highland, wet all-year
Aw - even amount wet & dry
Am - tropical & humid

Dry: Bs Bw
Bs - steppe, low, even rainfall
Bw - hot, low rainfall

Mid-Lat. Rainy: Cs Cw Cf
Cs - even amount wet & dry
Cw - wet & dry, mild winter
Cf - rainy, mild winter

Mid-Lat. Wet/Dry: Dw Df
Dw - wet & dry, cold winter
Df - rainy, cold winter

Polar: ET EF
ET - tundra
EF - ice cap

NATURAL RESOURCES :

RUSSIA AND CENTRAL ASIA

The area has one of the best natural resource bases in the world and is self-sufficient in many important raw materials. It is the world's leading producer of platinum, nickel, and iron. Somewhat surprisingly, the Soviet Union was the leading producer of oil, much of which was sold to Eastern Europe. It has enormous coal reserves and 40% of the world's known natural gas reserves. Russia's Siberian gas pipeline supplies Eastern and Western Europe.

Nuclear power generators supply a considerable amount of the region's electricity. However, after the **Chernobyl Nuclear Power Plant Accident** in Ukraine (1986), questions arose about safety. Hydroelectric power is still the most significant source of electricity.

SUBREGIONS: EASTERN EUROPE

Eastern Europe makes up nearly 1.3 million square miles of the region. It is located between Western Europe and the interior of Eurasia. It has been a convenient route for invaders.

In Eastern Europe, mountains play an important role. They serve as barriers to invaders. The **Carpathians** are the longest

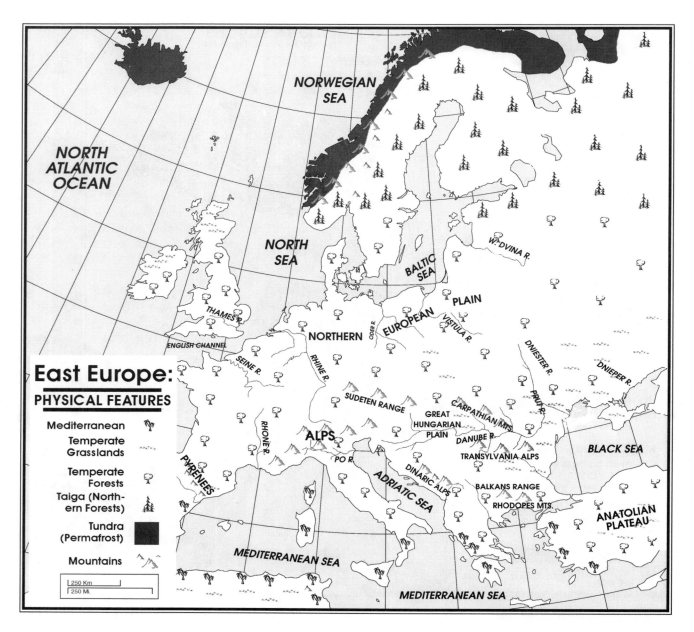

East Europe:
PHYSICAL FEATURES

Mediterranean

Temperate
Grasslands

Temperate
Forests

Taiga (North-
ern Forests)

Tundra
(Permafrost)

Mountains

250 Km
250 Mi.

mountain range. They cross Romania, Hungary, Slovakia, and Poland. Other ranges include:

- **Balkans** in Bulgaria and Serbia

- **Sudetens** in the Czech Republic and Austria

- **Dinaric Alps** stretch along the Adriatic Coast from Slovenia through Croatia and Bosnia into Albania

- **Rhodopes** in southern Bulgaria

- **Transylvania Alps** in Romania

Eastern Europe is also an area of vast plains, some of which have been historic invasion routes. This is particularly true of the **Northern European Plain** which crosses Poland into Belarus, Lithuania, Latvia, Estonia, and Russia. The **Great Hungarian Plain** is in the middle of Eastern Europe and is an agricultural and horse-raising region. It stretches from Hungary into Romania, Moldova, and Ukraine. Other, smaller plains are located among the various mountain ranges. There are also a number of scenic lakes located in the mountain areas such as Lake Balaton in Hungary.

WORLD STUDIES – *Global Issues & Assessments*   N&N©

Rivers are important in the life of the area. By far, the **Danube** is the most vital waterway. It winds its way eastward from Germany past major cities in Austria, Hungary, Serbia, Bulgaria, and Romania on its way to the **Black Sea**. It is used not only for trade and commerce- but also as a source of irrigation water, fish, and hydroelectric power. Other important rivers are Poland's **Vistula** and **Oder**.

NATURAL RESOURCES: EASTERN EUROPE

Eastern Europe does not have the abundance of natural resources that the republics of the former Soviet Union have. Poland's **Silesia** has significant coal and iron ore. They are vital to the country's industrial development. The **Czech Republic** also has important coal and iron deposits which make it an important industrial country. (Czechoslovakia split into the Slovak Republic and the Czech Rep. in 1992.)

Balkan Peninsula nations have rich mineral resources such as iron ore, lead, copper, and zinc. The Yugoslav Federation formed after World War I disintegrated in the early 1990's. **Slovenia**, **Croatia**, **Bosnia**, and **Macedonia** declared independence. Serbia, Kosovo, Montenegro and Vojvodina remained together under the name of the **Federal Republic of Yugoslavia**. However, the Balkan countries' disintegration and constant civil wars weakened the industrial and economic development.

Romania is the only country of Eastern Europe with significant deposits of oil, a resource which made it a target during World War II. However, the country remains industrially. underdeveloped **Bulgaria**, **Hungary**, and **Albania** lack strong mineral resource bases and are largely agricultural producers. All three are attempting to develop more industry.

EARLY PEOPLES

THE SLAVS

Of the many tribal groups that migrated into what is now Russia, the dominant group was the eastern **Slavs**. They originated in what is now eastern Poland, Belarus, and Ukraine. One Slavic group migrated to the forest areas of Russia, settled along the rivers and became traders developing routes from the Baltic to the Black Sea. The **Poles**, **Czechs**, and **Slovaks** are descendants of another group. The **Croats**, **Serbs**, and **Slovenes** of the Balkans claim a third group as their ancestors.

Kiev and **Novgorod** became important trading centers for Slavs who settled along the rivers in Russia and Ukraine. These Slavic centers were constantly threatened by invaders

Eastern Europe:
POLITICAL CHANGES

from Central Asia. Among them were the **Khazars** who demanded tribute from the Slavic traders. The Slavs were not prepared to fight and turned for protection to a Viking warrior-merchant group, the **Varangians**. They came from what is now Sweden and established firm control over many of the Slavic routes to Byzantium. **Oleg**, one of their chiefs, took Kiev around 862 A.D. The Slavic and Varangian cultures fused, providing the basis for the modern Russian culture.

NON-SLAVIC PEOPLE

Although most areas of Eastern Europe were also under Slavic control, Hungary, Bulgaria, Albania, and Romania had additional influences. The **Magyars**, a nomadic tribe, established itself in Hungary about 900 A.D. The **Bulgars**, an invading group from Central Asia, combined with the Slavs to form Bulgarian civilization. Albanians and Romanians are descendants of people who settled the area long before the Slav, Magyar, and Bulgar people arrived. As a consequence of this variety, significant cultural differences are still apparent in the entire region today.

A MIX OF CULTURES

By about 900 A.D., the city-states from Novgorod to Kiev established a loose confederation with the **Grand Prince of Kiev** at its head. Local princes were expected to protect  their city-states and administer justice. In return, they received part of the town's profit from trade. **Veches** (assemblies) of all adult male citizens dealt with local affairs. The society was divided into several classes including the Grand Prince and nobles, **boyars** (merchants and landowners), and peasants (the largest group).

A prosperous trade developed between the Kievan Rus cities and the Byzantine Empire. After the Muslims gained control of the Mediterranean Sea in the 8th Century, the only safe route between the Byzantine Empire and Western Europe was through Russia. As a consequence, the Russians came into contact with the cultures of both areas. But, the Byzantine culture appealed to them most.

Eastern Orthodox Catholic Churches are easily identified by their "onion" shaped domes.

One of the most significant effects of the exposure to the Byzantine culture was the conversion of **Vladimir**, the Grand Prince of Kiev, to the **Eastern Orthodox Catholic** faith. Tremendous cultural diffusion resulted. In 988 A.D., the Orthodox religion became the official religion of Russia. It provided the basis for beginning the establishment of a Russian identity. Church architecture, onion-shaped domes, the painting of icons, and the Cyrillic alphabet resulted from this diffusion. This strengthened Russian ties with the Byzantine Empire and led to greater differences with Western Europe.

Even when the Russian government failed to function, the Orthodox Church continued to act in much the same fashion as the Roman Catholic Church acted during and after the decline of the Roman Empire. Some westerly areas of Eastern Europe were Christianized from Rome, and their culture reflected that of

Western Europe. They developed substantial cultural differences from the Russians.

THE MONGOL LEGACY

Kiev reached its height under **Yaroslav I** in the 11th Century and had a "golden age." Yaroslav's successors were not able to preserve the peace. Civil wars divided the people. When the **Mongols** entered Russia in the 13th Century, there was no one strong enough to oppose them. Unfortunately, Mongol conquest denied Russians access to the advances of Western Europe's Renaissance. The fall of Constantinople to the Ottoman Turks in 1453 A.D. completed the isolation. As a consequence, Russia was slow to enter modern times.

Initially, the Mongols devastated Russia and burned cities such as Kiev. The peasant population became their serfs. Later in the 200th-year of Mongol rule, Russians were allowed to practice the Orthodox religion and control local affairs. Still, they had to pay tribute to the **Khan** (Mongol leader). The Mongols allowed Russian princes to keep their positions if they collected taxes and kept law and order. Thus, systems resembling the **feudalism** and **absolutism** of the West developed in Russia.

Later, Russians did join together against the Mongols. This gave them a sense of unity, but their long isolation caused development of a unique culture which would make interaction with others difficult.

QUESTIONS

1   Real development of Siberia began with the
   1   Russian Revolution of 1917
   2   exile of tsarist opponents
   3   completion of the Trans-Siberian Railroad
   4   Russo-Japanese War

2   Russia has
   1   few strategic natural boundaries that provide protection
   2   long, hot summers and cool, moist winters
   3   its chief vacation area along the Pacific Ocean coast
   4   small rivers of little economic significance

3   Which of the following climate and vegetation zones is accurately paired with its description?
   1   *tundra* – long, harsh winters with permafrost
   2   *forest* – major industrial and farming area
   3   *steppe* – produces fur and lumber products
   4   *desert* – arid rain forest

4   Rivers are vital in Russia because they
   1   all flow south
   2   are avenues of transportation and communication
   3   connect Siberia with the west
   4   form the major route from Moscow to Leningrad

5   During the 1980's, the Soviet Union was the world's leading producer of
   1   gas
   2   gold
   3   oil
   4   diamonds

6   The most important river in Eastern Europe is the
   1   Amur
   2   Ob
   3   Danube
   4   Rhine

7   Most Eastern European countries have
   1   excellent mineral resources
   2   largely farming economies
   3   major oil reserves
   4   no industrial development plans

8   Which is an example of cultural diffusion from the Byzantine Empire to Russia?
   1   modern technology
   2   the Latin alphabet
   3   feudalism
   4   the Eastern Orthodox Church

9   The Slavs were
    1   the dominant rulers of Russia in
        medieval times
    2   members of the Islamic faith
    3   the major cultural group of Eastern
        Europe
    4   chiefly of the boyar class

10 Which was a result of the 13th Century
    Mongol invasion of Russia?
    1   Russia was brought into contact with
        Western Europeans.
    2   Russia was unable to take part in the
        Renaissance.
    3   Russia was formed into a modern
        industrial society.
    4   Russia began to establish a democratic
        government.

11 Which happened under the Mongols' rule of
    Russia?
    1   No Russians were allowed in the
        government.
    2   The practice of the Eastern Orthodox
        religion was denied.
    3   Tribute was paid in exchange for control
        of local affairs.
    4   The peasant population became free.

12 Early Russian culture reflected the
    contributions of the
    1   Byzantine Empire, Orthodox Church,
        and Mongols
    2   Orthodox Church, Mongols, and Persians
    3   Germans, Mongols, and Magyars
    4   Western Roman Empire, Byzantine
        Empire, and Mongols

13 Early Russia resembled Western Europe in
    its
    1   use of Renaissance ideas
    2   use of classical architecture
    3   adoption of a feudal system
    4   acceptance of Protestantism

14 The geography of the Balkans has generally
    led to
    1   social cohesion
    2   cultural diversity or different ethnic
        groups
    3   political unity
    4   widespread democracy

15 Areas of Africa and parts of Siberia are said
    to be "gems-in-the-rough," because they
    have
    1   extensive tracts of permafrost
    2   well-developed coastal ports
    3   many undeveloped natural resources
    4   decreasing populations

16 Parts of Eastern Europe and Russia
    developed differently because
    1   rivers were more important in Russia's
        development
    2   the Eastern Orthodox branch of
        Christianity took hold in Russia, while
        much of Eastern Europe adopted Roman
        Catholicism
    3   the Russians were not subject to
        invasions, while Eastern Europe was
        conquered many times
    4   Eastern Europe was more influenced by
        the Asian civilization and Russia was
        more influenced by Western Europe

ESSAY

Geography has had a significant impact on
the development of Russia and Eastern
Europe.

a   Explain how Russian historical
      development was influenced by
      geography.

b   Discuss the economic role of rivers in
      Russia and Eastern Europe.

c   Discuss the extent to which a resource
      base helps to make the economies of
      Russia and Eastern Europe
      interdependent.

II. DYNAMICS OF CHANGE

RISE OF TSARIST POWER

EARLY TSARS

While the Mongols ruled Russia, the princes of Moscow began to increase their power. One of these princes, Ivan I, persuaded the Orthodox Church to move its headquarters to Moscow. Ivan also convinced the Mongols to name him "Grand Prince of All Rus." Subsequent Moscow princes further increased the territory under their control. **Ivan III** (1462-1505) eventually "threw off the Tartar yoke" in 1480 by refusing to pay tribute to the Mongols.

Ivan IV, called Ivan The Terrible, oppressed opposition.

Ivan III, later known as Ivan The Great

Ivan III strengthened ties between the church and the state. He married Zoe, the niece of the last emperor of Byzantium. By virtue of this marriage, Ivan claimed his power to rule directly from God (divine right). He assumed the title of "**tsar**" (emperor). The Turks cut off Russian contact with Byzantium (Constantinople). Eastern Orthodox Church leaders in Russia could no longer get direction from Constantinople. They found a ready ally in the tsar. For his considerable achievements in consolidating power and strengthening Russia, Ivan III was later known as **Ivan the Great**.

His grandson, Ivan IV (1533-1584), was known as **Ivan the Terrible**. He suppressed noble opposition to his power, encouraged the development of a new class of nobles (who were given land in return for military service), and began a policy of tying the peasants to the soil, thus establishing systems similar to feudalism and serfdom in 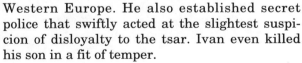 Western Europe. He also established secret police that swiftly acted at the slightest suspicion of disloyalty to the tsar. Ivan even killed his son in a fit of temper.

Ivan IV continued the expansion of Russian territory. He failed to gain territory on the Baltic Sea. Still, he gained the middle Volga area, the Caspian Sea, and the steppe area of Siberia. As the borders of Russia expanded, the tsars began a **Russification** policy. To unify the country, the government forced conquered people to adopt the Russian language, culture, and religion. In addition, Ivan increased communications with the West.

Weak tsars ruled the country after Ivan. Russia suffered foreign invasions, natural disasters, peasant revolts, and civil wars. In 1613, an assembly of nobles selected **Michael Romanov** as ruler. He began the **Romanov Dynasty** that reigned until 1917. During the 17th Century, the Romanov tsars became more interested in Western Europe. The tsars welcomed European merchants, engineers, and doctors. Still, most Russians were suspicious of them, and they were forced to live in segregated areas.

Peter the Great, student of Western European civilization

PETER THE GREAT

Western European civilization fascinated **Peter the Great** (1682-1725). He learned about fighting wars and ship and artillery building from foreigners. He was determined to use European technology to strengthen Russia. Peter undertook a tour of Western Europe as a private citizen to learn what he could of Western ways. He worked in a shipyard in the Netherlands and visited England. A revolt of nobles forced him to return to Russia. On his return, he quickly suppressed the uprising and executed those involved.

Peter then began a program of **Westernization**. He was determined to modify Russian life. Tsar Peter ordered men to shave off their beards and wear short coats. He ordered nobles to wear Western dress at court. Peter expected women to socialize with men. He sent Russians to study Western technology and offered high salaries to European experts to come to Russia. The government started schools, constructed canals, established a navy, and reformed the army. Military roads were built between major cities. These changes irritated conservative Russians.

In his government, Peter used people of different backgrounds. He developed a civil service system to allow advancement into the ranks of the nobility. To control the Church, he established a **Holy Synod** and replaced the **Patriarch** (church leader) with his own appointee. Peter designed these reforms to increase Russian prestige. They reflected the actions of Western European rulers.

Tsar Peter continued the search for access to the sea. It later grew into a desire for warm water ports. He fought the **Great Northern War** (1708-21) against Sweden to get a "window on the west" – an outlet on the Baltic Sea. Sweden controlled the Baltic. A major victory at Poltava gave Russia land along the southern shores of the Gulf of

Sue Ann Kime, 1989

Large cannon built during Peter the Great's reorganization of the Russian military resulting from his study of Western technology.

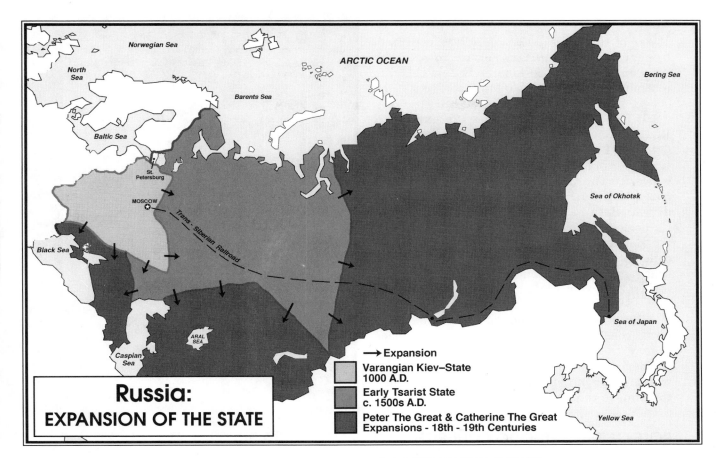

Russia:

EXPANSION OF THE STATE

→ Expansion

Varangian Kiev–State
1000 A.D.

Early Tsarist State
c. 1500s A.D.

Peter The Great & Catherine The Great
Expansions - 18th - 19th Centuries

Finland. Peter failed to duplicate his Baltic success against the Persians in the Caspian Sea area.

Peter turned his attention to the construction of a new capital on the Baltic coast, the city of **St. Petersburg**. This large marsh was not the best place to build the great capital city Peter envisioned. It proved costly in terms of money and lives. Like France's Louis XIV, the Tsar expected nobles to construct homes in the new city and spend at least part of the year there.

Tsar Peter's policies changed and strengthened Russia. He set precedents that later rulers followed. Still, there were real questions concerning his westernization reforms. There was industrial progress, but the government remained in the hands of the aristocracy, subject to the tsar's control. The Patriarch was changed, but the Church functioned much as it had before. Peter's moves also created a deep division between the **Westernizers** (those who favored the adoption of western ways) and the **Slavophiles** (those who favored the traditional Russian values).

CATHERINE THE GREAT

The Romanovs that followed Peter were insipid and had short-lived reigns. Not until **Catherine the Great** (1762-1796) assumed the throne were conditions right for further progress. Catherine came to the throne under unusual conditions. Her weak husband was assassinated. There is some evidence that she had prior knowledge of the murder. Catherine was a former German princess well known for her intellectual interests. She corresponded with Voltaire, Diderot, and other leaders of the Enlightenment.

Initially, she introduced some reforms earning her the reputation of an **enlightened despot** (one who uses absolute power to improve life). She changed the government structure, codified the laws, limited the use of torture, and allowed some religious toleration.

Deteriorating conditions for serfs led to a peasant insurrection in 1773. Afterwards, Catherine became repressive. She increased the power of the noble landlords. She freed them from compulsory military service to keep the serfs under control. Serfdom in Russia began to resemble slavery in the United States.

In foreign affairs, Catherine expanded Russia at the expense of Poland and the Ottoman Empire. Both were very weak at this time. During the 1770's, while Russia was at war with the Ottoman Empire, Austria proposed that Russia join Prussia and Austria to divide Poland. Austria hoped to distract Catherine from campaigns against the Turks in the Balkan Peninsula, an area that it hoped to control. This was the first of three partitions that removed Poland but not its people from the map of Europe in 1795.

Ultimately, Catherine gained control of the north coast of the Black Sea through a peace treaty with the Ottoman Sultan. Thus, Catherine continued the Russian search for warm water outlets to the sea and expansion, this time in the direction of the west.

ROLE OF THE ORTHODOX CHURCH

The Russian Orthodox Church played a major role in the history of Russia and in the daily lives of the people. Peter placed it under Tsarist control. The close government ties increased the influence of the clergy. Monasteries received gifts of land which sometimes led to special favors and corruption.

Still, parish priests remained very close to the people and lived in very similar circumstances. Frequently, they were not well educated, and their practices included superstitions. At times, priests led revolts against the government. However, the hierarchy of the Church  usually supported the tsars. Much of Russia's cultural development centered on the Church. Magnificent Russian Orthodox churches with onion-shaped domes dot the landscape. They are reminders of the pervasive influence of religion.

After the communists assumed control in 1917, there was a period of violent religious persecution. In 1927, the leader of the Church pledged absolute loyalty to the government and established a quiet church-state relationship.

Uspenskii (Assumption) Cathedral, where Tsars were crowned, located within the walls of the Kremlin, Moscow.

Sue Ann Kime, 1989

The support given by the Church during World War II led to an easing of restrictions and improved relations with the communists.

DEVELOPMENT OF EASTERN EUROPE

The West had greater influence on Eastern Europe than it did on Russia. Poles, Czechs, Slovaks, and Hungarians followed the Roman Catholic Church or, in some later cases, one of the Protestant sects.

POLAND

Roman Catholicism probably played the greatest role in Poland. The Church developed the close ties with Polish nationalism that it retains to the present. During the 17th Century, the leadership of **King John Sobieski** made Poland a strong nation. Still, its system of nobles that elected the king left the country vulnerable to foreign interference.

Interference in the late 18th Century led to three partitions (land divisions) by Austria,

Prussia, and Russia. These annexations split up the country. Emperor Napoleon briefly reconstructed a small Polish state, the **Grand Duchy of Warsaw**.

However, the 1815 Congress of Vienna placed Poland under the indirect control of the Russian tsar. After revolts by the Poles, the Tsar Alexander I abolished their constitution and took direct control. An intense Russification campaign followed, but it only increased the Polish sense of nationalism. Polish leaders wanted an independent nation-state. This goal was finally realized at the end of World War I.

HUNGARY

The **Magyars** invaded the Carpathian Basin from south and west of the Ural Mountains. They became Christians under **King Stephen I** (1001-1038). They gradually developed a constitution requiring every Hungarian ruler to swear loyalty to the **Golden Bull** (1222). This charter provided basic liberties. During the Middle Ages, both the Mongols and the Turks threatened Hungary. The **Hapsburg** kings of Austria defeated the Turks in 1683 and finally gained control of the area.

In the aftermath of the French Revolution and Napoleonic Era, Hungarian nationalism increased. The Austrians needed Russian help to put down a strong revolt in 1848. After its defeat in the **Austro-Prussian War** (1866), Austria gave more recognition to the Hungarians. The *Compromise of 1867* created the dual monarchy of Austria-Hungary and gave Hungary a large degree of self-government and more prosperity.

OTTOMAN EMPIRE

By the time the **Ottoman Turks** conquered Constantinople in 1453, they had already

gained control of Bulgaria, parts of the Balkan Peninsula, and Hungary. Later, they conquered all of the Balkan Peninsula. The Ottoman Empire reached its height under **Suleiman** (1520-1566), who conquered much of Hungary and panicked Christian Europe. However, Suleiman failed to conquer Vienna. After Spain defeated the Turkish fleet (1571), Ottoman power declined. In the Balkans, the Ottomans allowed religious toleration and self-rule over local affairs. The Ottomans taxed the people heavily but exempted those who converted to Islam.

BULGARIA

Internal problems and European wars weakened the Ottoman Empire in the 19th Century. Its hold on the Balkans declined, and gradually, countries gained independence. The *Treaty of San Stefano* (1877) and the **Congress of Berlin** (1878) gave Bulgaria some self-rule, but full independence did not come until 1908.

ROMANIA, ALBANIA, AND THE BALKANS

The Turks gave up parts of Romania in the 17th Century, but not until the Congress of Berlin did it receive total independence. Sections of the Balkan Peninsula received and lost independence at various times. The central area of Serbia received technical independence after the **Russo-Turkish War** (1877-1878). Yet, Austria-Hungary exercised enough control to arouse Serbian nationalism to the point of being a major cause of World War I.

Following World War I, Serbia became a part of Yugoslavia. The last state, **Albania**, was created after the **Balkan Wars** of 1912-1913 at the insistence of Austria to deny Serbia access to the sea.

Eastern Europe: c. 1920

19TH CENTURY REFORMS

France's **Napoleon Bonaparte** is an important figure in Russian history. In helping the Grand Alliance defeat him, Russia emerged as a major power in international affairs. It played a significant role at the **Congress of Vienna** (1815). In the Napoleonic era, many Russian soldiers learned of nationalism, democracy, and the ideals of the French Revolution as they marched through Europe. These factors had a substantial impact on 19th Century Russia.

ALEXANDER I

Alexander I (1801-1825) was the grandson of Catherine the Great. He was tsar at the time of the defeat of Napoleon and the Congress of Vienna. Raised by his grandmother, Catherine II, and taught by the French Enlightenment thinkers, he absorbed some liberal ideas, but at the same time, Alexander believed in the autocratic power of the tsars.

Prior to the Napoleonic invasion, Alexander instituted a program of reforms but were abandoned because of the invasion. After the wars, advisors urged him to return to his reform pro-gram. It would have established a constitution, freed the serfs, and placed limits on the tsarist power, but he refused. Turning in a conservative direction, Alexander limited freedom of speech and press. Secret societies developed to press for reforms.

NICHOLAS I

On assuming power, Alexander's successor, **Nicholas I** (1825-1855), faced the **Decembrist Revolt**, a palace coup d'état. Nicholas suppressed the revolt and followed a policy that involved censorship and repressive use of the secret police (cheka). He insisted on the principle, *"one church, one government, one language."* Also, it has been said that he refused to allow the importation of sheet music, because he feared that the musical symbols were a special code for communication among secret revolutionary societies. In foreign policy, Tsar Nicholas warred against the Ottoman Empire to expand Russian territory in the Balkans. Britain, France, and Austria opposed further Russian expansion. This clash of interests brought about the **Crimean War** (1854-56).

ALEXANDER II

Nicholas' son, **Alexander II** (1855-1881), assumed the throne during the Crimean War. The fighting went against the Russians. In defeat, Russia lost much of its earlier gains in the Balkans. The loss of prestige made the new Russian tsar unpopular.

Alexander realized that changes were needed to keep Russia a great power. In 1861, the tsar signed an **Emancipation Act**, which freed the serfs. The government also pursued land reform. It purchased some land from noble landowners to provide former serfs with a living. The land was turned over to the **mir** (village community council). The mir collected payments from the peasants. Peasants could not leave the community without the mir's permission. Peasants were disgruntled because of the lack of sufficient private land and personal freedom. Gradually, some of the peasants became landless farm laborers and others moved to towns to obtain work. A small number purchased land and expanded their holdings, increasing class differences.

Alexander II allowed elective assemblies to govern local affairs. He reformed the courts to include more Western principles of justice. He provided public primary schools and established a banking system. Because the reforms were long overdue, they opened the door to agitation. Many critics felt they had not gone far enough. They demanded a **Duma** (national legislative body). A terrorist killed Alexander II in 1881.

The new tsar, Alexander III (1881-1894), became a reactionary. He blamed his father's liberalism for the assassination. While Alexander III did not abolish his father's reforms, his own reign was repressive in terms of human rights.

ECONOMIC CHANGE

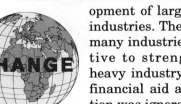

The economy of Russia changed significantly in the 19th Century. The expansion of Russian railroads in the 1870's led to the development of large-scale iron and steel industries. The government financed many industries. With is chief objective to strengthen the military, heavy industry received most of the financial aid and consumer production was ignored.

The most spectacular industrial feat was the construction of the **Trans-Siberian Railroad**. Foreign loans, especially from France, made the railroad possible.

Switching yard along the Trans Siberian Railroad near Irtusk, Russia   Sue Ann Kime, 1993

In fact, by 1914, one-third of the national debt was for railroad construction. The railroad opened Siberia to settlers. Approximately five million people moved into the area within ten years, beginning the development of what became one of the most important industrial areas of Russia.

RUSSIAN CONTRIBUTIONS TO THE ARTS

During the 19th and 20th Centuries, Russian musicians and writers made major contributions to European culture. In doing so, they reflected European cultural trends such as nationalism and romanticism. In many instances, they were critical of the government. Composers produced many ballets, symphonies, and operas in which their love of the motherland and its people was apparent. Novelists tried to capture the essence of life in Russia in their works.

An overview of Russian contributions to the arts would not be complete without an acknowledgment of their contributions to ballet, a field in which they have excelled. The **St. Petersburg Ballet Company (Kirov Ballet)** produced some of the greatest dancers of all time including **Anna Pavlova** and **Vaslav Nijinsky**. The dances were choreographed to display the tremendous technical skill of the dancers. Later,

Russian Music	
Musician	**Works**
Tchaikovsky	*1812 Overture, Nutcracker Suite, Swan Lake*
Rimsky-Korsakov	*Scheherazade, Flight of the Bumblebee*
Mussorgsky	*Boris Godunov*

Russian Writings	
Writer	**Works**
Pushkin	*Eugene Onegin, Boris Godunov*
Tolstoy	*War and Peace, Anna Karenina*
Dostoyevsky	*Crime and Punishment, The Brothers Karamazov*

the dances, dramatic scenes, and stories were blended together in works such as *The Firebird* and *Prince Igor*. In recent years, the **Bolshoi Ballet** has become the best known of the Russian companies, largely because of its foreign tours.

THE REVOLUTION OF 1905

Pressures mounted in Russia in the early years of the 20th Century. Slow industrialization, peasant land hunger, and rising political opposition plagued Tsar Nicholas II. He undertook a war against Japan to distract the attention of the people from their grievances. Nicholas' advisors favored the war to gain much desired warm water ports in Manchuria and Korea. To achieve this, Russia had to confront Japan, which also desired these areas.

Nicholas' scheme backfired. Japan soundly defeated Russia in the **Russo-Japanese War** of 1904-05. Russia's prestige suffered at home and abroad, since Japan was supposedly a third rate military power. Opposition to the Tsar intensified just as it had after Alexander II's defeat in the Crimean War. Yet, Nicholas did not move toward reform as his grandfather had. In this instance, the opposition culminated in the **Revolution of 1905**. There were three main groups seeking reform at this time.

- **Kadets** (Constitutional Democrats) were members of the middle class who favored a constitutional monarch in Russia with a role in the government for the educated.

- **Social Revolutionaries** were the strongest party. They drew most of their support from the peasantry. Their program called for "land socialism" with the land controlled by the mir (community council) and distributed to the peasants based on their ability to cultivate the land.

- **Social Democrats** followed the ideas of Karl Marx. In 1903, this group broke into two parties. The **Mensheviks** believed that Russia would have to develop an industrial society and have a prolonged period of bourgeois democratic government before the revolution of the proletariat could occur. The more radical **Bolsheviks** were under the leadership of **N. (Nikolai) Lenin** (pseudo name for Vladimir Ilyich Ulyanov) and later, **Leon Trotsky**. The Bolsheviks believed that the period of bourgeois democracy could be brief and be followed quickly by the proletarian revolution.

The best known episode of violence during the Revolution of 1905 was **Bloody Sunday**. A group of workers led by an Orthodox priest, **Father Gapon**, staged a peaceful march to the Winter Palace in St. Petersburg. They were to present a petition to Tsar Nicholas. Someone ordered the soldiers protecting the Palace to fire on the workers, killing and wounding hundreds. This sparked strikes and mutinies throughout the country. Finally, a general strike forced the tsar to act.

Nicholas II issued the *October Manifesto*. It promised a national Duma and granted basic civil liberties. This satisfied the Kadets. They supported the government and helped suppress the Revolution. Later, the Tsar limited the power of the new Duma. He also deflected some of the remaining hostility in a pogrom against the Jews. However, life did become somewhat freer in Russia, and a land reform program decreased some peasant dissatisfaction.

WORLD WAR I AND THE RUSSIAN REVOLUTIONS

A wide variety of factors was responsible for the outbreak of World War I (see Unit 8, p. 337). One of the key causes was the nationalistic feel-

ings of the East European nations. Russian policy supported nationalism in the Balkans to decrease the power of Austria-Hungary and the Ottoman Empire and possibly to win access to warm water ports. Russia actively encouraged **Pan-Slavism**, a kind of ethnic super nationalism. Russia sponsored the **Balkan League** which attacked the Ottomans in the Balkan War (1912).

In 1914, a Slavic nationalist from Serbia assassinated **Archduke Franz Ferdinand** of Austria-Hungary. Russia shielded Serbia in the face of the Austrian threats, encouraging Serbia to stand firm. Finally, Austria declared war, beginning the chain reaction leading to World War I.

RUSSIAN ARMY MOBILIZATION

Surprising everyone, the Russian Army mobilized speedily. It entered the field against Austria-Hungary and Germany before the Germans could conquer France. The Germans withdrew part of their army from the Western Front to face Russia in the East. This led to the stalemate in the West that continued for most of the War.

However, neither the Russian government nor its economy were strong enough to sustain the war effort. Russia sent troops to the front lines without weapons or supplies. Casualties mounted. In the **Battle of Tannenberg** (1914), the Russians suffered so many casualties that the Russian commander committed suicide.

On the Russian home front, increased mechanization could not make up the serious shortages of consumer goods and food. Old problems of the 19th Century such as the autocratic government, limitations on civil liberties, and land hunger continued to create dissatisfaction. Finally, in March 1917, demonstrations broke out in St. Petersburg. Russian soldiers refused to fire on the people, so the tsar acceded to the demands of the Duma. On 15 March 1917, Nicholas II abdicated the Russian throne, bringing the 300-year rule of the Romanovs to an end. In July 1918, Nicholas and his family were assassinated by the Bolsheviks.

PROVISIONAL GOVERNMENT

The Kadet leaders of the Duma formed the **Provisional Government**. It was recognized by Russia's wartime allies as the official government. During the same time, the Social Revolutionary and Social Democratic Parties founded the St. Petersburg Soviet (a workers' and soldiers' government council). It refused to cooperate with the Provisional Government. And yet, the Soviet had the support of many of the people because its program appeared to meet their demands.

Clash Of The Parties		
Demands	**Provisional Gov't.**	**Bolshevik Program**
Peace	Continue the war	Immediate peace
Land	Eventual land reform	Immediate land reform
Bread	No real plan	Proposed rationing

Between January and September 1917, the leftists (socialists) of the St. Petersburg Soviet gained strength. Bolshevik leader N. Lenin returned from exile and rallied his party. Major war defeats during the summer further disillusioned the Russian people with the Kadet war effort.

The people placed the blame on the Provisional Government. The Bolsheviks helped the Provisional Government defeat an attempt to gain control by conservative military leaders. By November 1917, Lenin thought that the right time had come for a **revolution of the proletariat**.

NOVEMBER REVOLUTION

In St. Petersburg, Lenin, Trotsky, and the Bolsheviks swiftly and effectively carried out their **November Revolution** with only a minimum loss of life. Prince Lvov and Aleksandr Kerensky, leaders of the Kadet Provisional Government, fled into exile, and other government members were arrested. In a week, the Bolsheviks gained a secure hold on Moscow. Opposition was stronger in the countryside, including former tsarist army officers, landowning nobles, and members of the middle class. From 1917 to 1921, a civil war raged in the south and central regions of the country.

During this period of upheaval, many of the ethnic groups tried to establish their independence. The Bolsheviks signed the *Treaty of Brest-Litovsk* with the Germans in March 1918. Russia withdrew from World War I and agreed to honor the independence of Finland, Estonia, Latvia, Lithuania, and Poland. In Ukraine, the Transcaucus, and Central Asian regions, Leon Trotsky and the Bolsheviks' **Red Army** defeated revolts for independence.

LENIN AND MARXISM

By 1922, the Bolsheviks shifted the capital to Moscow and renamed the country the **Union of Soviet Socialist Republics** (U.S.S.R., or the "Soviet Union"). Bolshevik leader N. Lenin tried to adapt the ideas of Karl Marx to a soci-

ety that did not fit Marx's idea of proletarian revolution. Lenin believed that a small, revolutionary elite must lead the masses. Russia was far from an industrial society ready for a proletarian revolt against capitalists, so Lenin became creative. He claimed the peasantry, as well as the proletariat could be a revolutionary class. Lenin preached that Russia could move to proletarian revolution without a long period of industrialization. He claimed the Bolsheviks had already overthrown a corrupt, bourgeois regime when the Bolsheviks defeated the Provisional Government.

To avoid being labeled a utopian socialist, Marx never wrote much about what the society and government would be like after the proletarian revolution. Lenin was a **pragmatist** (a practical theorist); he freely interpreted the few general statements made by Marx. Lenin modified Marx's ideas to fit the situation that existed in the new Soviet Union. In classic autocratic fashion, Lenin claimed anyone who disputed his approach was a "**revisionist**" (one who changed the purity of Marxist dogma). Lenin's policies led to many power struggles among the Bolsheviks during the formation stages of the Union of Soviet Socialist Republics and in years after his death in 1924.

QUESTIONS

1 Ivan the Great unified and strengthened Russia through his refusal to pay tribute to the Mongols, his marriage to the niece of the last Byzantine emperor, and
1 his adoption of the divine right theory
2 adoption of Western European culture
3 the abolition of feudalism
4 defeat of German invaders

2 Peter the Great is known for his policy of
1 Westernization
2 religious freedom
3 peace
4 traditionalism

3 The policy of Russification forced the people to
1 emigrate from Russia if they were Jewish
2 adopt the Russian language, culture, and religion
3 accept the government's policy of economic control
4 allow foreign ownership of industries

4 Catherine the Great's attempts at reform were ended when
1 Poland invaded Russia
2 she was overthrown
3 a peasant insurrection occurred
4 the power of the nobles decreased

5 Which did Catherine the Great achieve?
1 She conquered France and ended the French Revolution.
2 She conquered Austria and Prussia.
3 She helped to divide up Poland.
4 She took over a large area of territory from China.

6 Poland has
1 a long history of independence
2 accepted the Russian Orthodox religion
3 never been ruled by foreigners
4 struggled to establish itself as a nation

7 When did Hungary have a large degree of self-government?
1 immediately after the Turks were defeated
2 during the French Revolution
3 after the Austro-Prussian War
4 during the time of the Mongol conquest

8 Under Ottoman control, the people of the Balkan Peninsula were
1 forcefully converted to Christianity
2 allowed religious toleration
3 freed of tax obligation
4 denied control of local affairs

9 Which was the achievement of Ivan the Terrible?
1 He expanded Russian borders to the Volga and Caspian Sea areas.
2 He made the Orthodox Church move to Moscow.
3 He freed the serfs from control by noble landlords.
4 He began the industrialization of Russia.

10 Alexander I of Russia refused to
1 follow a reactionary policy
2 enforce Russification
3 increase Russian territory
4 allow complete freedom of speech and press

11 Alexander II's *Emancipation Act* in 1861 established
1 freedom of speech
2 freedom of the press
3 freedom for the serfs
4 a national Duma

12 In which artistic field are Russian contributions most widely acknowledged?
1 painting
2 sculpture
3 ballet
4 opera

13 During the late 19th Century, which was true of the Russian economy?
1 It began to industrialize.
2 There was no railroad construction.
3 Agriculture declined as a peasant way of life.
4 Communists took over the government.

14 The Bolshevik reform group believed Russia
   1 would have proletarian revolution after a brief bourgeois period
   2 did not need peasant support for revolution
   3 could eliminate all government control immediately
   4 was not ready for revolution in 1917

15 The *October Manifesto* provided for
   1 pogroms against the Jews
   2 a Duma and civil liberties
   3 an absolute monarchy
   4 the start of the 1905 Revolution

16 During the pre-World War I period, Russia opposed
   1 Pan-Slavic movements
   2 the Balkan League
   3 Austria's influence in the Balkans
   4 East European nationalism

17 The Bolsheviks established their control of Russia
   1 without any bloodshed
   2 with allied help
   3 only after a civil war
   4 despite German opposition

18 World War I helped to cause the 1917 Russian Revolutions because
   1 the government was incompetent and casualties were high
   2 Russia was abandoned by its allies
   3 unemployment among farm laborers was high
   4 the Russian Army was unable to mobilize

19 A policy of the Provisional Government was
   1 a rationing plan for bread
   2 an immediate land reform
   3 continued participation in World War I
   4 support of the Bolsheviks

20 Which was Lenin's belief?
   1 Marx's ideas could be adapted to apply to Russia.
   2 Only the proletariat could be revolutionary.
   3 Communists should have a large, democratically organized party.
   4 A long period of bourgeois, democratic government was needed.

ESSAYS

1 Change in Russian history has been caused by many different factors.

Select *three* of the following pairs. For *each*, explain how the factor cited first contributed to reform during the reign of the ruler with whom it is paired.

- *Drive for Westernization* – Peter the Great
- *The Enlightenment* – Catherine the Great
- *Loss of the Crimean War* – Alexander II
- *Loss of the Russo-Japanese War* – Nicholas II

2 Several factors have significantly affected the development of Russia.

- Russification
- Autocracy
- Pan-Slavism
- Search for warm water ports
- Drive for Westernization

Select *three* of the factors listed above and for *each* one selected, discuss one significant impact that it had on Russian history.

3 The Russian Revolutions of 1917 are among the most significant events that have occurred in modern history. Discuss *all* of the following:

a 19th and 20th Century causes of the 1917 revolutions

b Reasons for the increase in support for the Soviet between March and November 1917

c Lenin's modifications of Marx's ideas to fit the situation in Russia

III. CONTEMPORARY NATIONS

The Twentieth Century witnessed great changes which reshaped Eastern Europe, Russia, and Central Asia. The 1917 Russian civil war gave the communist totalitarian regimes much control over the region. But, seventy years later, pro-democracy movements again changed the region as radically as the Bolsheviks had during the World War I Era.

COMMUNISTS CREATE A TOTALITARIAN STATE

CIVIL WAR

The 1917-1921 Russian civil war pitted the **Reds** (Bolsheviks) against the **Whites**. The Whites included former tsarist army officers, landowning nobles, members of the middle class, Russia's former World War I allies, and some of kulaks (wealthier peasants). However, the White effort was not coordinated. It frequently consisted of isolated resistance on the fringes of the country.

DETERMINATION OF POLITICAL & ECONOMIC SYSTEMS

Bolshevik leader **Leon Trotsky** built a well-trained **Red Army** that controlled the interior of the country. Fighting for independence was fierce in Ukraine. Among the victims of the civil war were Tsar Nicholas and his family. The Bolsheviks executed all of them to keep them from becoming symbols to rally the White cause.

During the civil war, Lenin and the Bolsheviks followed a policy called **War Communism**. It turned control of industries over to the workers, called for peasant ownership of the land, and seized farm surpluses for distribution to the cities. By 1921, Russia's production fell to less than 50% of its pre-World War I level. To silence opposition just like the tsars, the Reds used a ruthless secret police, the **Cheka** (later called OGPU-1922, NKVD-1934, MGB-1946, and KGB-1954).

E. Europe, Russia, & C. Asia CONTEMPORARY NATIONS

Lenin promotes his New Economic Policy before a gathering of the proletariat, 5 May 1920. Soviet Government Photo

LENIN'S NEW ECONOMIC POLICY

At the end of the civil war, Lenin decided to "take one step backward" to revive the ailing economy. He proclaimed the *New Economic Policy* (**NEP**). It allowed some capitalism in the economy. The government kept ownership of the "commanding heights of the economy" (major natural resources and industries). Other businesses were turned over to private ownership. Farmers were allowed to sell their surpluses in a free market and to keep the profits. By 1928, production returned to pre-World War I levels.

STALIN AND TROTSKY STRUGGLE FOR POWER

Lenin died in 1924 before he had the opportunity to see the full effects of the NEP. His death led to a struggle for power between Josef Stalin and Leon Trotsky.

Stalin had been in charge of ethnic minorities under Lenin. Later, he became **First Secretary** of the Communist Party. This gave him access to all Party records, intimate knowledge of the background of Party members, and the ability to appoint followers to high positions. A ruthless Machiavellian, Stalin believed it was possible to have a proletarian revolution, rebuild the country and eventually export communist revolution to other areas.

Trotsky had his base of power in the Red Army that he created. He was a brilliant orator and known for his command of Marxist ideology. He believed in immediate global revolution.

Stalin emerged as the victor. He had control of the main policy-making groups and the Cheka. Trotsky was exiled in 1929. He was murdered in Mexico in 1940 (perhaps by the NKVD on the orders of Stalin). The position of General Secretary of the Communist Party became an extremely important position in the Soviet hierarchy. Subsequent Soviet rulers all held this position.

STALIN'S TOTALITARIAN STATE

PURGING THE LEADERSHIP

Trotsky was not the only one to suffer at Stalin's hands. During the 1930's, Stalin carried out a massive **purge** (cleansing) of Communist Party officials. He drove to eliminate any opposition or suspected opposition. Leftists with leanings toward Trotsky's teachings were executed. He eliminated others who favored less severe policies in dealing with kulak resistance. Recent research estimates as many as twenty million died in Stalin's purges of the 1930's.

Josef Stalin

Also significant was Stalin's elimination of Red Army leaders in the period right before World War II. This purge is one of the reasons for his agreeing to a nonaggression pact with Hitler in 1939. Stalin needed time to train new military leaders.

A COMMAND ECONOMY

Stalin decided to abandon the NEP for a totalitarian command economy. In 1928, he began the first of the **Five-Year Plans**. He ordered government ownership of all the means of production. **Gosplan** became the powerful central planning agency for economic decision-making.

Even under the early 5-year plans, Gosplan continued some capitalistic practices. There were personal incentives. Factory workers were paid on a piecework basis. Meeting government-specified production quotas led to rewards for factory managers.

Stalin's plans focused on the development of heavy industry and neglected consumer or light industry. One aim was to build up exports to earn foreign currencies and buy industrial technology that the Soviets could not produce themselves.

In order to achieve Stalin's industrial objectives, radical changes were made in the agricultural sector. He needed high agricultural productivity to feed the bulk of the population working the factories and mines. To achieve these objectives, he ordered that small peasant farms be merged into large **collective farms**. They would be government directed and cooperatively farmed by the peasants. He hoped that this would free even more peasants for factory work and permit increased mechanization and production.

Collectivization gave the government more control over farm production. Also, there were capitalist incentives, and peasants were to share in the profits. Also, they were allowed private plots of about one acre in size that they could farm on their own time for their own profit.

Tremendous opposition to collectivization arose among the peasants, especially kulaks in Ukraine. Most peasants supported the communists based on the pledge to give them land. Stalin ruthlessly crushed the opposing peasants. Kulaks killed cattle and burned crops. For that, Stalin killed thousands of kulaks and exiled thousands to Siberian. It took nearly 20 years to bring the herds back to the levels of the 1930's.

Over time, Stalin's industrial conversion succeeded. No Western country had ever shown as much growth in a period comparable to the first two 5-year plans. Between 1928 and 1938, "The Russian Miracle" quadrupled iron and steel production, and more than tripled coal output.

By 1939, only Germany and the United States exceeded the Soviet Union in gross industrial output. Much of this development was east of the Ural Mountains in new industrial centers. This proved to be a wise move when Hitler later invaded the older industrial areas of the western U.S.S.R.

A TOTALITARIAN GOVERNMENT

In 1922, Russia became the **Union of Soviet Socialist Republics** (U.S.S.R.). There were four republics at first – the Russian Federation, Ukraine, Byelorussia, and Transcaucasia. By World War II, there were fifteen. The 1922 Constitution gave ethnic groups in the republics some self-rule. As time went on, Stalin centralized power in Moscow. He created a new authoritarian constitution in 1936, in which the republics lost their powers. In 1977, Brezhnev changed the constitution slightly to give different groups more rights on paper, but not in practice.

Spasskaya (Savior) Tower, main public gate from Red Square, near St. Basil's Cathedral, into the Kremlin. Sue Ann Kime, 1989

Lenin's 1922 Constitution created a bicameral national legislature – the **Supreme Soviet**. Representatives of the people served in the Soviet of the Union, and representatives of the republics and territories served in the Soviet of Nationalities. These houses became "rubber stamp" bodies that merely endorsed decisions of Communist Party leaders.

The Supreme Soviet appointed a **Council of Ministers**. It ran the country's daily operations. The leader of the Council was the **Premier**, the real head of the government.

The U.S.S.R. became a one-party totalitarian state. From Lenin through Gorbachev, party leaders and government leaders were the same people. Real power rested in the party's leadership committee, the **Politburo**, that conducted business in Moscow's Kremlin fortress built by the tsars. The leader of the Politburo, the **First Secretary**, usually became the Premier of the government. Periodically, the government held elections. However, there was usually only one candidate, the Communist Party candidate. As a result, the U.S.S.R. became a totalitarian state ruled by the elite oligarchy of the Communist Party.

TOTALITARIANISM AFTER STALIN

KHRUSHCHEV

Stalin died in 1953. A struggle for power took place in the Politburo. **Nikita S. Khrushchev** won the struggle. He was a strong, clever man but not as ruthless as Stalin. In fact, Khrushchev shocked the nation by denouncing Stalin. He reviled the late dictator for a variety of crimes: personal cowardice, foreign policy mistakes, and terrorizing citizens. The attacks on Stalin's reputation boosted Khrushchev's popularity with younger party leaders. Stalin's old-line supporters were angered. They avoided open criticism of Khrushchev but quietly sabotaged his policies.

Khrushchev wanted to improve the people's standard of living. He said government spent too much on heavy industry and military production. He tried to increase agricultural production and consumer goods and tried to reduce the power of central economic planners.

In 1958, Soviet Premier Nikita Khrushchev proudly boasted to the world of Soviet economic superiority by "demonstrating the success" of the collective farms. Soviet Government Photo

Khrushchev also tried to open new lands in Central Asia to settlers. This *"Virgin Lands Program"* failed, because the climate was poor for the crops the government ordered the settlers to grow. This failed policy eventually helped to topple his regime.

Khrushchev's worst blunders came in foreign policy. At heart, he wanted to prove that communist societies gave people a better life. To do this, he wanted to diminish the costly arms race with the U.S. and its allies. It drained resources from producing consumer products. Khrushchev spoke of **"peaceful coexistence"** with the Western democracies. However, his construction of the Berlin Wall, placement of nuclear missiles in Cuba, and disputes with Red China's Mao Zedong hurt the chances for his policies. Khrushchev's old enemies in the Politburo forced his retirement in 1964.

BREZHNEV

In the mid 1960's, **Leonid Brezhnev** emerged from another Politburo struggle in the Kremlin. By the 1970's, Brezhnev was First Secretary and Premier. Like Khrushchev, he first tried to cut down central planning to produce more consumer goods. The quality of goods improved, but quantities fell short of needs. By the early 1980's, military and heavy equipment production once again received economic priority.

Brezhnev's foreign policy was uneven. Friction with China continued. He ordered an invasion of Czechoslovakia (1968) to stop democratic reformers from taking power. World leaders denounced his 1979 Afghanistan invasion.

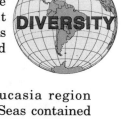

Yet, relations with the United States and Western democratic nations generally improved. Brezhnev signed several treaties on arms and human rights (see SALT and Helsinki Accords). There was more cooperation on Middle East problems. **Détente** (a warmer, more cordial atmosphere) resulted. The Cold War thawed in the 1970's. However, in 1979, it froze again. Angered by the Afghanistan invasion, the U.S. and other Western nations embargoed grain sales to the Soviets and boycotted the 1980 Summer Olympic Games in Moscow.

On May Day 1980, Soviet Premier Leonid Brezhnev waves a salute to troops from the Kremlin balcony overlooking Red Square.   Soviet Government Photo

Brezhnev died in 1982. His two successors continued his policies. Both Konstantin Chernenko and Yuri Andropov died soon after taking control. Neither had much of an impact on domestic or foreign affairs.

LIFE AND CULTURE IN THE TOTALITARIAN STATE

THE DIVERSITY OF THE SOVIET PEOPLE

Lenin's U.S.S.R. drew together the many diverse people of the Tsars' Russian Empire. The country had over 90 ethnic groups speaking 80 different languages. The Slavs were the largest single group. Within it were many subgroups such as Russians, Ukrainians, and Byelorussians.

The mountainous Transcaucasia region between the Black and Caspian Seas contained more than forty ethnic groups, mostly of Turkic or Persian origin. East of the Caspian Sea, Central Asians formed several ethnic republics of their own with the Islamic religion remaining a strong cultural force in these regions.

In the early days of the U.S.S.R., some of the major ethnic groups controlled their own

republics. They designed their own constitutions that guaranteed the preservation of their languages, cultures, and local governments. Moscow gave smaller ethnic minorities similar guarantees.

As time went on, the central government in Moscow took more control in the republics. The original ideals of individual rights and local rule faded as the country became more totalitarian. As with the old Tsarist "Russification Policy," Moscow ordered the Russian language taught in all the republics. Communist leaders moved Russians into the different republics to "homogenize the nation" (blend the culture).

DIVERSITY OF RELIGION

The communists proclaimed the Soviet Union officially **atheist** (denied the existence of God). However, the national constitution guaranteed freedom of religion, and the **Russian Orthodox Church** remained the largest organized religion. However, communist leaders were suspicious of any organizations that would undermine their control. The government watched and regulated all religions.

In Transcaucasia and Central Asia, millions of people followed Islam. Again, communist leaders feared the power of any cultural force such as Islam. They knew it could unify people and spur independence movements along the southern borders.

There were also about three million Jews throughout the U.S.S.R. Anti-Semitism was common in Russian history. Under tsarist rule, Jews were often victims of **pogroms** (violent raids and brutal resettlements). Tsarist troops overran and destroyed Jewish **pales** (isolated settlements, ghettos). Under the totalitarian rule of the communists, Jews had few rights. The communists sentenced those who protested to forced labor in **gulags** (remote prison camps). Jews found it nearly impossible to **emigrate** (leave the country).

URBANIZATION

At the time of the Bolshevik takeover, Russia was largely rural. The bulk of the people were peasants, living in small rural villages. Lenin and the communists knew they had to build an industrial society to succeed. Extensive urban development resulted from Stalin's forced industrialization. The government offered housing and paid incentives to spur urban growth in Siberia and Central Asia. In general, urbanization and resettlement were poorly planned and occurred too rapidly. The government built factories but neglected housing for workers. Even in the 1970's and 1980's, insufficient and substandard housing remained problems in major cities.

ROLE OF WOMEN

Social changes under the communists included new roles for women. Women became equals to men in most respects and composed over 50% of the Soviet work force. Women outnumbered men in the fields of education and medicine and equalled men in technical fields, assembly line work, and manual trades. Women received equal pay for equal work. However, men still outnumbered them in administrative, supervisory, and managerial positions.

Stalin's daughter, Svetlana, once lived in similar "upper middle class" apartments in Moscow.   Sue Ann Kime, 1989

The huge loss of lives in the Soviet Union during World War II (estimates exceed 20 million) left many jobs to fill and widows with families to support. The government actively encouraged women to join the work force. It provided day care centers for their children and guaranteed job security after pregnancy and maternity leaves.

Legally, men and women were equal in Soviet society. Divorce became a simple administrative procedure if there were no children. Streamlined court proceedings decided custody of children and property division. In reality, women were still primarily responsible for child care, cleaning, and household management, but the economy made few modern appliances available. As in the old Russia, the culture did not expect husbands to help around the house.

TOTALITARIAN CENSORSHIP OF THE ARTS AND SCIENCES

Totalitarian governments try to control all social activity. In the Soviet Union, communist leaders blocked free expression in art and insisted art reflect what they called "social realism." They expected artists to paint themes which glorified work and supported patriotic goals. Some artists fled the country. Ironically, the communists preserved much art and treasure of the Russian past in tsarist palaces that they converted to museums.

The totalitarian government also controlled literary expression. Under Stalin, official censors blocked publication of any works critical of communism. Authorities censured, exiled, or imprisoned writers frequently. Even after Stalin's death, strict censorship remained. **Boris Pasternak** received global recognition for his novel **Dr. Zhivago**. Yet, the Soviet censors claimed it contained ideas critical of the Bolshevik Revolution. The government refused to publish the book and forced Pasternak to decline the Nobel Prize for Literature in 1958.

In the 1970's, dissident author **Aleksandr Solzhenitsyn** wrote about the forced labor camps of the Stalin Era. When his friends published **Gulag Archipelago** outside the U.S.S.R., communist censors banned all of his works inside the country. Solzhenitzyn left his homeland in protest. In the West, he became a critic of Soviet human rights policies and the weaknesses of democratic societies. Solzhenitzyn returned to his beloved Russia in 1994.

From tsarist times, Russians were scientific leaders. Many scientists and technicians left the country when the communists seized control. The communist government sponsored research programs. However, they were subject to strict control by the renowned **Soviet Academy of Sciences**. Its bureaucrats directed and monitored all major research programs. Western critics felt that this limited scientific innovation and free exchange of ideas.

The government funded research projects for military and space research. Its medical research opened the field of laser eye surgery. However, the U.S.S.R. fell behind in most other areas: medical technology, microelectronics (computers) and automotive technology.

DECLINE OF TOTALITARIAN RULE
GORBACHEV BRINGS CHANGE

A younger leader emerged from the Politburo in 1985. **Mikhail Gorbachev** began to change the governmental structure. His

Soviet Reformer, Mikhail Gorbachev

Glasnost, "a new openness," was like opening a window, bringing in an era of "freshness."

glasnost policy allowed people more freedom to criticize and try to reform the government. He allowed dissidents to leave the country, permitted more Jews to emigrate, and freed some political prisoners.

Under Gorbachev, constitutional reforms gave more power to a new national legislature (**Congress of the Peoples' Deputies**) and created a stronger Presidency. The control of the Communist Party diminished, and Gorbachev's reforms allowed rival parties.

DETERMINATION OF POLITICAL & ECONOMIC SYSTEMS

Gorbachev was less successful at reforming the command structure of the economy. His ***perestroika*** policy allowed the people to explore market principles such as self-interest, competition, credit, and profit. *Perestroika* promoted privately owned, small business and encouraged local plant managers to decide about the quality and quantity of consumer goods.

In foreign policy, Gorbachev reduced Soviet influence in Eastern Europe. In the 1980's as democratic reforms spread, Poland's outlawed Solidarity movement regained strength. Mass demonstrations and protests toppled communist regimes in Eastern Europe. In 1989, Germans tore down the Berlin Wall and in 1990, reunified their country. The Warsaw Pact dissolved in 1991. Summit meetings with Western leaders reduced missiles and military presence in Europe. With the Cold War over, Gorbachev received the Nobel Peace Prize in 1990.

While Gorbachev became a hero abroad, his cautiousness toward reform created instability at home. Anti-reform Politburo members launched a coup against him in the summer of 1991. However, supporters of democratic reform defied the coup leaders by demonstrating in the streets of Moscow. Russian Federation President **Boris Yeltsin** rallied democratic resistance to the coup. Red Army soldiers refused the coup leaders' orders to fire on civilians demonstrating at the Russian Parliament building (the "White House"). The coup disintegrated and so did the Soviet Union.

The world supported Gorbachev's reforms and gave him the 1990 Nobel Peace Prize. But, was he a hero at home?

At home in Russia, reforms brought frustrations to Gorbachev and social pain to the Russians. His popularity and power diminished and he resigned. Yeltsin took over.

Boris N. Yeltsin, President of Russian Federation

Party ranks with Gorbachev's help. By 1987, he had become convinced Politburo leaders would not permit Gorbachev to reform the U.S.S.R. Yeltsin resigned from the Communist Party. He won the Presidency of the Russian Soviet Federal Socialist Republic (SFSR) Parliament as an independent reform candidate. Soon after, he won the first democratic election for President of the Russian SFSR. In 1991, while the coup leaders held Gorbachev prisoner in the Crimea, Yeltsin led public demonstrations defying the coup.

When the coup fell apart and Gorbachev returned, he had to share power with Yeltsin. They ended armed confrontations in the Baltic Republics and recognized the independence of Estonia, Latvia, and Lithuania. As the Baltic Republics gained independence, Ukraine and other republics prepared to leave the sinking Soviet Union.

Just before the coup, Gorbachev prepared a new *Treaty of Union* to return real power in local and regional matters to the republics. After the coup, republics began to declare independence. Gorbachev could not hold the country together and resigned as President. The totalitarian state created by Lenin in 1917 faded into history.

Yeltsin took actions on his own. With the leaders of Belarus and Ukraine, he negotiated a loose military and economic alliance of former republics, the **Commonwealth of Independent States** (CIS). After this, Gorbachev resigned, but his reforms had ended Lenin's dream of a Marxist paradise.

YELTSIN BEGINS A NEW ERA

After the aborted coup against Gorbachev, Boris Yeltsin emerged as a key personality. Yeltsin originally rose through Communist

NEW POWER STRUCTURE

The CIS was a vague alliance. Each of the new republics wanted its sovereignty above all. Most were powder kegs and civil strife wracked Georgia and others. The CIS had no authority to coordinate affairs. Critics compared it to the weak U.S. government under the *Articles of Confederation* (1781-1789). CIS members minimally agreed on only a few policies.

The Grand Kremlin Palace, as viewed from Moscow River and completed in 1849, housed large reception halls and the imperial family's private chambers.

The U.N. gave Russia the Security Council seat that belonged to the former U.S.S.R. Other republics applied for U.N. membership. Yeltsin continued Gorbachev's pattern of foreign policy. He shared some control of the nuclear arsenal with other CIS members but began negotiations to reduce nuclear power. The republics still oversee the former Soviet bases on their soil. There is little cooperation among the former republics concerning the military, foreign policy, currency, and trade. Each acts independently and negotiates with other nations separately.

As in Russia, new leaders arose in Ukraine, Belarus, and Kazakhstan to control their new governments. Civil struggles plagued the new nations in the Transcaucasian and Central Asian regions. In some areas, the Communist Party retained power.

However, the economic chaos concerns leaders. Most market systems work on trial and error. It takes time before consumers and producers achieve price equilibriums. In Russia, the government ended some price controls, but shortages of most products kept inflation high. Crime and extortion threatened free enterprise. When some Russians became fearful and angry, critics demanded a return to the communist system. Western aid helped stem the threat, but Yeltsin sought more. In 1993, he had to use force to overcome a revolt by Parliamentary leaders. He sent troops against leaders barricaded in the "White House" (Russian Parliamentary building in Moscow). Instability frightened private foreign investors away from long-term investment in the region's development. Later, Yeltsin's supporters failed to gain a majority in Parliamentary elections, but opponents could not form a coalition. Government reform suffered in the stalemate.

FORCE OF NATIONALISM IN THE REGION

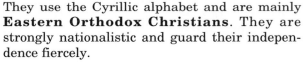

In the western areas of the region, Slavic groups dominate Russia, Belarus, and Ukraine. They use the Cyrillic alphabet and are mainly **Eastern Orthodox Christians**. They are strongly nationalistic and guard their independence fiercely.

In the Baltics, the Latvians, Lithuanians, and Estonians differ linguistically and culturally from the Slavic groups. The Baltics share a long history of struggles for their existence. They use the Latin alphabet and are mainly Roman Catholics and Protestants. The Baltic Republics have strong national identities. As coastal nations, their sea links with Poland and Western Europe are vital to survival.

The Transcaucasian region is in turmoil. There are more than forty ethnic groups with diverse languages, traditions, and religions. **Christian Armenians** and **Muslim Azerbaijanis** have been in an armed struggle over territory for many years.

The forces of tradition and modernization threaten the Central Asian republics. Islam and

Muslim culture predominate. Turkish and Iranian influences are strong. Political possibilities range from a new federation to further fragmentation.

FORCE OF RELIGION IN THE REGION

Gorbachev's *glasnost* policy eased religious restrictions. In addition to the rise of Islam's strength in Central Asia, Orthodox Churches reopened. Training of the clergy increased, and many young people attended services. Baptisms and marriages in the Orthodox Church increased. Some Catholic and Protestant sects also saw increased activities. However, anti-Semitism also returned. Disturbing news reports said that the Pamyat, a local racist group, frequently attacked Jews.

FORCE OF DEMOCRACY IN THE REGION

Glasnost awakened a new generation of people to freedom. It unleashed a pro-democracy movement that astonished the world. Its force surprised the older generation, trained under totalitarian regimentation. Long silent, the people participated passionately in criticizing their government and the poor quality of their lives. They joined campaigns and ran for office. New regional parliaments bristled with political and economic reform proposals.

The success of democracy in the region became entwined with setting up free economies.

Glasnost worked far better than *perestroika*. *Glasnost* opened a repressive government to criticism and let people participate. *Perestroika* promised free economies; yet, the people have little skill or experience making complex economic decisions. Markets are risky and insecure, but without direct government controls, a free economy may make democracy work.

TOTALITARIANISM IN E. EUROPE

PATTERNS AFTER WORLD WAR I

At the end of World War I, both the Ottoman and the Austro-Hungarian Empires disappeared. For leaving the war, Russia lost considerable territory in Eastern Europe. The region's many ethnic groups desired national autonomy. The 1919 Paris Peace Conference tried to satisfy those desires. At the Conference, diplomats signed treaties creating new nations (the three Baltic Republics, Czechoslovakia, Hungary, Poland, and Yugoslavia) from the rubble of the old empires (see map below).

The new national boundaries dissatisfied many of the smaller minorities. Power struggles among opposing groups made the new governments unstable. Most of the new nations began as democracies. The need to solve land reform problems, ethnic clashes, and inexperience with self-government overwhelmed the new nations. In little more than a decade, all except Czechoslovakia fell into some form of totalitarian dictatorship.

SOVIET DOMINANCE AFTER WORLD WAR II

During World War II, either the Nazis or Soviets held the Eastern European nations. As the war ended, the Red Army pushed the Germans westward. The Soviets set up communist puppet governments backed by Red Army occupation forces. After the war, the military remained to make the nations **satellites** (near colonies). The **Warsaw Pact** and **COMECON** bound the nations to the U.S.S.R. militarily and economically (see Sections IV and V).

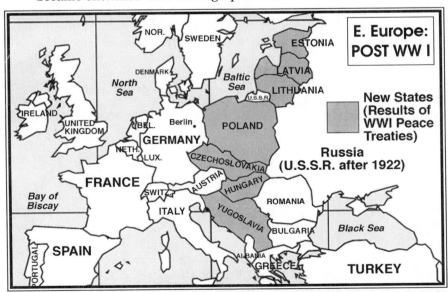

E. Europe: POST WW I

New States (Results of WWI Peace Treaties)

Russia (U.S.S.R. after 1922)

Despite this Soviet control, there was resistance. When Khrushchev denounced Stalin's brutal rule in 1956, he triggered democratic revolutions in Hungary and Poland. Soviet troops crushed those revolts. In 1968, Warsaw Pact nations joined in suppressing a revolt in Czechoslovakia. Afterwards, the *Brezhnev Doctrine* declared the Soviet Union would intervene in any nation where communist rule was threatened.

PRO-DEMOCRACY MOVEMENTS

When Gorbachev unleashed *glasnost* in the U.S.S.R., he allowed it to flow into the Eastern European nations. In some cases, he urged the communist regimes to copy his *glasnost* and *perestroika* reforms. He did not order Soviet troops to help faltering communist regimes. Pro-Democracy movements unseated communists and set up freer governments. Gorbachev played a major role in allowing the two Germanies to reunite.

Poland's Solidarity Leader, Lech Walesa

In the early 1980's, the move toward democracy in Poland caused nationwide strikes by labor unions under the **Solidarity** organization. Led by **Lech Walesa**, Solidarity received backing from Roman Catholic Church leaders. The government outlawed Solidarity and imprisoned some of the strike leaders. But, in the mid 1980's, Gorbachev's policies revived the Solidarity movement. In 1989, Poland held free elections with Solidarity candidates winning 99 of 100

senate seats. In 1991, Walesa won the presidency. The government replaced the command system with a free market structure. The Walesa government began **privatizing** (selling to private businesses) former state factories and production facilities. This has not been a simple task, as Poland has deep economic problems. Difficult negotiations with the West have not stabilized the shaky economy.

The influence of pro-democracy movements in Yugoslavia reopened age old ethnic feuds. Ethnic nationalist movements of Balkan minorities arose as they had before World War I. President Milosevic's communist regime could not stop bloody outbursts. The pro-democracy movement led to Yugoslavia's disintegration.

Intervention by the European Community and the U.N. led to a truce in the ethnic and religious civil war in 1991. Slovenia, Croatia, Bosnia, and Macedonia became independent. Serbia and Montenegro remained united under the name Yugoslavia.

In 1992, strong Serbian nationalist groups began fighting Croats and Muslim groups for power in Bosnia. The insurgents received aid from Yugoslavian Serbs. Deaths, destruction, and dislocation of people mounted. The European  Community (Union), N.A.T.O., and the U.N. diplomats tried to end the fighting. In 1993, U.N. peacekeeping missions could not control Serb guerrilla attacks on Sarajevo in Bosnia. Threats of NATO air strikes kept another Sarajevo truce intact while leaders from the area negotiated a settlement. Yet, the U.N./NATO presence failed to protect Muslim enclaves such as Gorazde from attacks by Bosnian Serbs.

In Czechoslovakia, former political prisoner and playwright **Vaclav Havel** led the nation toward democracy. The country's 1948 constitution recognized two major ethnic regions, the **Czech Republic** in the west and the **Slovak Republic** in the east. By 1992, the pro-democracy movement led to the two regions to quietly separate (the "**Velvet Revolution**"). The Czech

Republic emerged as a strong industrial nation, while the poorer agricultural east became the **Slovak Republic**.

The reunited Germany, Poland, the Czech Republic, Slovak Republic, and Hungary appear to have good chances for democracy. However, elections in countries such as Lithuania, Hungary, and Poland have shown moderate communists regaining status. Dissatisfaction with economic progress and loss of the socialist "safety net" benefits appear to be the source of the voters' turnabout. Global concerns with the breakup of the Soviet Union have deflected attention from the struggling Eastern European nations. Global recessions have diminished foreign political and financial support, and the decline of former Soviet markets presents additional economic problems for the former satellites.

QUESTIONS

1 War Communism called for
   1 a revolution of the peasantry
   2 worker control of industries
   3 free markets for agricultural produce
   4 suppression of Lenin and the Bolsheviks

2 The New Economic Policy (1921-1928) called for
   1 government ownership of all the means of production
   2 some elements of capitalism in the economy
   3 forceful sale of agricultural produce to the government
   4 collectivization of farms

3 To aid the troubled Soviet economy in the 1980's, Gorbachev
   1 increased the role of central planners
   2 created large numbers of collective farms
   3 permitted private ownership of small businesses
   4 decreased production of consumer products

4 During the 1930's, Stalin strengthened his hold on the U.S.S.R. by
   1 purging many of his opponents
   2 increasing the civil rights of the people
   3 encouraging the development of capitalism
   4 signing an alliance with the democracies

5 The major goal of Stalin's first Five-Year Plan was
   1 expansion of consumer industry
   2 establishment of private farms
   3 strengthening of heavy industry
   4 increasing imports

6 The collectivization of farms
   1 failed completely
   2 was opposed by peasants
   3 increased livestock production
   4 increased farm employment

7 Josef Stalin was
   1 the founder of the Red Army
   2 a brilliant orator
   3 General Secretary of the Party
   4 a believer in immediate worldwide revolution

8 During the 1930's, industrial development of the Soviet Union might best be described as
   1 a slow steady increase
   2 a period of tremendous growth
   3 largely centered west of the Ural Mountains
   4 slowed by insufficient coal and iron

9 As General Secretary and Premier of the U.S.S.R., Nikita Khrushchev
   1 expressed strong support of Stalin's regime
   2 did not expand the farm area
   3 faced no major foreign crises
   4 followed a policy he called "peaceful coexistence"

10 During the period between the two world wars, the countries of Eastern Europe
   1 successfully dealt with their minority problems
   2 carried out comprehensive land reform programs
   3 frequently fell victim to dictatorships
   4 remained under the loose control of the Austrian Empire

11 Under General Secretary Leonid Brezhnev, the U.S.S.R.
    1 returned to Stalin's foreign policy
    2 began a policy of détente with the West
    3 decreased attention in war industries
    4 refused to negotiate on arms reductions

12 In the early 1990's, the Orthodox Church in Russia
    1 closed churches
    2 opposed the Yeltsin government
    3 had an increase in baptisms and marriages
    4 attracted only the elderly

13 Gorbachev's policy of *glasnost* involved
    1 increased cultural exchanges
    2 restrictions on Jewish immigration
    3 ending all capitalist activity in the economy
    4 freedom of the press

14 During the period of totalitarian rule in the Soviet Union, which group had the most political power?
    1 the Supreme Soviet
    2 the Russian Orthodox Church
    3 the Communist Party
    4 the Commonwealth of Independent States

15 The general pattern for treatment of dissenting groups in the Soviet Union under communist control was one of
    1 persecution
    2 encouragement of religion
    3 protection of civil rights
    4 toleration

16 Before the U.S.S.R. disintegrated, women were
    1 in the highest positions in the country
    2 receiving equal pay for equal worth
    3 encouraged to remain in the home
    4 not allowed to become doctors or teachers

17 Which of the following happened after World War II?
    1 Soviet leadership of the communist countries was only challenged by Cuba.
    2 There was little evidence of dissent among the communist countries.
    3 There were several attempts at revolution in Eastern Europe.
    4 The Soviet Union never interfered in the affairs of its satellites.

18 Which is an area of weakness in Russian technological development?
    1 space program
    2 development of computers
    3 military hardware
    4 atomic weapons

19 Under the U.S.S.R.'s totalitarian regime, artists were
    1 allowed complete freedom of expression
    2 denied access to the necessary tools of their trade
    3 expected to portray themes of "social realism"
    4 limited by their lack of an artistic heritage

ESSAYS

1 Leaders of the U.S.S.R. (and now Russia) showed an ability to change policies to fit shifting conditions. Choose *three* of the following pairs. For *each*, explain the circumstances surrounding the event and how it affected the policy of the paired leader:

   a Post-civil war economic conditions – Lenin

   b Purge of the Red Army – Stalin

   c World-wide emphasis on human rights – Gorbachev

   d Change to democracy – Yeltsin

2 Economic dissatisfaction has been a source of many problems in Russian History. Discuss any *three* of the following:

   a Economic problems in 19th Century Russian history

   b The economic causes of the Russian Revolutions of 1917

   c The problems caused by the implementation of the Five-Year Plans

   d The economic problems faced by Yeltsin

IV. ECONOMIC DEVELOPMENT

Today, the republics of Eastern Europe, Central Asia, and Russia struggle to change **command economies** (run by central decision-making). A **market system** (individual decision-making) can replace official agencies such as the old Soviet Gosplan. Ideally, personal choice and the profit motive can become the driving forces of the economy as they are in the West.

Classical economists claim free markets work best with **laissez-faire** (minimal government regulation). Yet today, even the strongest market systems mix government roles with private enterprise. At minimum, people need some protections when today's interdependent industrial economies falter. Still, over regulation and control can deaden incentive and innovation. Mixing entrepreneurship and experimentation with too much command drains the life from economic activity.

In recent times, the sickly command systems of Eastern Europe and the Soviet Union malfunctioned. The Cold War pressures of competing with the technologically advanced military production of the West overstrained the central planners. Economic conditions brought down communist regimes. A look at this region's contemporary economic history reveals why its problems are complex and not easily solved.

COMMAND ECONOMY

Lenin's command system, called **War Communism**, was used during the civil war of 1917-1921. Economic scarcities resulted from the chaos of this period. After the war, Lenin converted to his **NEP** (New Economic Policy). It allowed some capitalist incentives to encourage production while the government maintained ownership of the major means of production.

GOSPLAN'S PRIORITIES

The NEP brought the country back to its pre-1914 levels of production. Once Stalin was in control, he accelerated Soviet economic production. He instituted the first **Five-Year Plan** in 1928. It placed primary emphasis on the development of heavy industry. Communist planners recognized that industrial advancement depended on an increase in agricultural production.

Gosplan bureaucrats made the economic decisions based upon national goals established by the Party. The goals rested on estimates of needs sent from local factory managers up Gosplan's bureaucratic mountain. Guesswork and estimates changed as the paperwork moved through the layers of planning offices. Frequent problems occurred with underproduction or overproduction of a particular product. Still, there had never been an industrial plan in the nation, and early organization yielded spectacular growth especially in areas such as coal, iron, and steel production.

Under the communists, G.U.M., the government's department store (the Moscow store shown here), was designed to impress the capitalistic West. Costs for consumer goods were fixed by the State Committee on Prices and kept artificially low. However, due to shortages caused by overemphasis on military production, many shelves were usually empty in the "peoples' showcase department store." Sue Ann Kime, 1989

SCARCITY OF CONSUMER GOODS

There was a price paid for the emphasis on heavy industry. Consumer goods production languished. Sacrifice of consumer goods was the **opportunity cost** (economic "trade-off") of heavy industry. Food, clothes, and personal care items were always scarce. Also, there were frequent complaints of poor quality of goods because quotas were more important than quality. In effect, the communists demanded people make sacrifices for future generations. Planners and Party leaders showed little sympathy for the human costs in the relentless drive for rapid industrialization. It was deemed unpatriotic to criticize the government. Stalin's **NKVD** (secret police, later called the KGB) repressed opponents as "enemies of the state."

Private enterprise, as observed at the Farmers' Market in Khabarousk, gives evidence of the economic reforms of perestroika.   Sue Ann Kime, 1993

In the 1960's, Brezhnev **decentralized** (localized) some planning. There was a brief period when Gosplan put a higher priority on production of consumer goods. By the 1970's, high military production and poor agricultural yields reversed this trend on consumer production.

PROBLEMS IN AGRICULTURE

COLLECTIVIZATION

The most troubled part of the Russian economy has traditionally been agriculture. In the 1930's, Stalin's first Five-Year Plan forced collectivization of small farmers. Kulaks launched vigorous and sometimes violent protests. The peasants met brutal repression. Many, especially in Ukraine, were executed, imprisoned, or exiled to Siberia. About 50% of the country's livestock was slaughtered in protest. Sporadic famines plagued the country.

Soviet planners hoped collectivization would release farm workers for factory jobs, give the government increased control over production, and increase efficiency. Initially, all farm products except those from private plots were sold to the government. It then set prices and established **allocation priorities** (decided who received the goods).

One measure of the failure of Soviet agriculture is astonishing. Private plots on collective farms accounted for only 2-3% of the land. Still, they accounted for nearly one-third of the dairy products, vegetables, and meat in the Soviet Union. Khrushchev set up most of the large state farms under his Central Asian "virgin lands policy," but, the land and climate were unsuitable for this ambitious project. Its failure was a major factor in forcing him from office.

DECENTRALIZATION

In the 1950's and 1960's, Khrushchev made a weak attempt to **decentralize** (localize authority) agricultural planning. Local incentives increased farm production slightly. Later, Brezhnev and Gorbachev put more money into farm machinery and transportation. Production increased. However, the spending programs were inconsistent and so was production.

Russia still imports food, because market reorganization and breakdowns in the transportation system caused production to drop in the 1990's. There were critical food shortages; thus,

humanitarian food supplies flown in from Western nations helped Russians survive.

PERESTROIKA

In the 1980's, Gorbachev's *perestroika* was aimed at serious production of consumer goods. The government abandoned Five-Year Plans in most industries. Ownership, management, and profit sharing arrangements changed drastically in factories and farms. *Perestroika* called for **privatization** (placing government facilities under private ownership) and reducing government regulation of businesses. *Perestroika* programs included:

- **increasing incentives** to state farms and factories

- **internationalizing the ruble** to be traded as a currency outside the U.S.S.R.

- **allowing more foreign investment** and businesses to operate in the U.S.S.R. (a McDonald's Restaurant opened in Moscow in late 1989.)

- **allowing more small private businesses** to be owned and operated by the people

These economic changes encouraged Westerners and invited direct investment by foreign companies and individuals. Still, Gorbachev had opposition. For more than two generations, the communist system educated and conditioned the Soviet population. Many people were suspicious. Many officials did not wish to give up the security of socialist benefits for the risks of competitive capitalism.

Old, entrenched government bureaus dragged out the reform process, because some bureaucrats feared loss of power. Many life-long communists resented market reforms. Many workers and managers simply did not understand or trust the new incentives; so, confusion mounted and distribution systems collapsed. Production dropped. Agricultural production nearly halted. Shortages grew worse. Anger and resentment against Gorbachev mounted as suffering increased. To balance the nation's finances, Gorbachev reduced the military forces overseas and cut foreign aid.

On the other side of *perestroika* were more radical reformers such as Russian Federation President **Boris Yeltsin**. The radicals claimed preserving the communist command system was useless. They called Gorbachev's moves timid, wanting a faster conversion to a free market.

These divisions led to the August 1991 coup by those who wished to restore the communist system. Yeltsin and his followers helped Gorbachev retain power, but afterwards, Gorbachev still remained too cautious for Yeltsin's group. Yeltsin prodded and finally took actions that led to Gorbachev's resignation and the collapse of the U.S.S.R.

QUALITY OF LIFE

For nearly three generations, the Soviet economy produced a vast war machine and miraculous growth in heavy industry. It turned a peasant country into an industrial power. Still, the economy never rewarded the sacrifices made by the people.

Russia's 1992 per capita GDP was less than $4,000 (cf. U.S. = $23,292). Food and adequate housing are in short supply. Basic consumer items (clothes, cosmetics, pharmaceuticals, paper goods) are smuggled into the country by profiteers who gouge the public in "black market operations." Organized crime rings extract protection fees from merchants and control the smuggling of Western goods into the country.

Comparison of Collective and State Farms		
Farm Type	Size	Method Of Paying Workers
Collective	Varied, but smaller than state farms	Shared in the profits of collective and kept after tax profits from private plots.
State	Average size was 75,000 acres	Paid as factory workers with similar benefits.

Government housing complex in Siberia. Approximately two thirds of Russians live in state built and maintained apartments in urban areas.   Sue Ann Kime, 1993

Both actions raise prices for consumers. In general, the quality of life has declined since Gorbachev began reform in the mid 1980's. Unrest became violent in 1993. Parliamentary leaders attempted to overthrow Yeltsin. They were defeated, but reformers supporting Yeltsin lost power in the Parliamentary elections later that year.

HOUSING

A scarcity of decent housing, especially in major cities, is a weakness of the economy. In the aftermath of World War II, the government built housing speedily, without much concern for quality. As a consequence, much of what does exist is in poor condition. For those in lower income brackets, state housing is predominant. The government controls rent. Usually it is fixed at 4 to 5% of income. The average number of rooms is 2.3. Most state housing has indoor plumbing. Statistics in rural regions fall below the numbers for urban dwellings.

EDUCATION

The Soviets placed a high priority on education. This continued after the U.S.S.R. collapsed. State-operated kindergartens and nursery schools also serve as day care centers. Compulsory education begins at age 6 and continues until 17, six days a week. The system is centralized, and the same textbooks are used throughout the country. Major emphasis is placed on mathematics, science, and foreign languages.

At age 15, students take a state examination that determines whether they prepare for a university or go to a trade school. Those who train for a university must take an additional examination at the end of their high school careers to qualify. Only one in five students is accepted by a university. University education is free and students are given a special living allowance.

TECHNOLOGY

The U.S.S.R. was a world leader in technological development. The space program was an outstanding example of its progress. Its "firsts" included the first space satellite in 1957, first manned space orbit in 1961, the first space walk, the first space station, and two Venus probes in 1982. However, outside of these

Teachers and students awaiting classes at High School #659, a math and science school in Severno Chertanovo, a suburb of Moscow.   Sue Ann Kime, 1989

Russian Education in 1990's

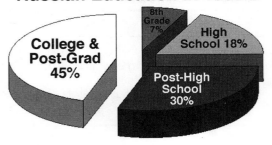

College & Post-Grad 45%

8th Grade 7%

High School 18%

Post-High School 30%

Russian Employment in 1990's

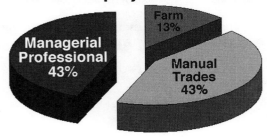

Farm 13%

Managerial Professional 43%

Manual Trades 43%

programs, bureaucrats traditionally discouraged technological innovation. Since Gorbachev, new programs have begun to provide financial incentives for advances in technology.

EASTERN EUROPE AND CENTRAL ASIA

With the pro-democracy movement came the collapse of communist regimes in the former U.S.S.R. Political struggles and inexperience with free enterprise have plagued the new countries. Ties with the West have helped a few attract foreign investment and aid, but many have deteriorated. Most still trade with former COMECON nations (see page 419) most of whom are now part of the CIS (Commonwealth of Independent States).

WORLD TRADE

Until recently, Russia's trading partners were the COMECON members in Eastern Europe. Gorbachev's *glasnost* and *perestroika* policies allowed Eastern European nations to turn toward trade with Western Europe. The policies encouraged Western businesses to broaden trade inside the U.S.S.R.

Multinationals such as Occidental Petroleum, PepsiCo, McDonald's, and others responded. The August 1991 coup slowed the momentum, but economic ministers are working to encourage foreign investment. Instability under Yeltsin in 1993 saw many foreign ventures decline. Western nations sent aid and experts to shore up global confidence in the faltering reform movement.

Russia has tremendous wealth in natural resources and could lead the world in the production of such vital resources as coal, iron ore, and oil. It also has a greater variety of mineral resources than any other country in the world, and there is a global demand for these resources. In the past, the government devoted much effort to developing mineral resources. Recent reports show organized crime has penetrated the export business, and corrupt officials engage in smuggling of raw materials. Controlling the criminal organizations may be the main hope for Russia's survival.

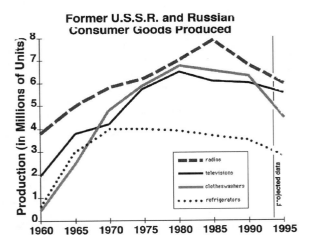

Former U.S.S.R. and Russian Consumer Goods Produced

- — — radios
- ——— televisions
- ▨▨▨ clotheswashers
- • • • refrigerators

SUMMARY

Problems continue with the inadequate quantity and poor quality of life in the region. There is dissatisfaction and frustration with rising prices, shortages of food and everyday items, and street crime. With the economy performing poorly, governments lose tax revenues. Without money, cleaning up corruption and stimulating

Economic Conditions After The Soviet Collapse

Area / Nation	Situation / Products	Trade Partners
Balkan Area		
Albania	One of the poorest nations in Eastern Europe; weak industrial base; trades mainly in raw materials	Germany, Italy, Austria, France, CIS*
Yugoslav Fed. (former)	Mineral rich; plagued by civil wars	CIS, Austria, Italy, Czech Rep.
Central Asia		
Kazakhstan	Strong dependence on mineral exports; little manufacturing; dairy and farm products	Uzbekistan, Ukraine, Kyrgyzstan
Kyrgyzstan	Strong dependence on agriculture; some electronics manufacturing	Kazakhstan, Uzbekistan, Ukraine
Tajikistan	Poorest of all CIS countries; former communist command system still in place; trades agricultural products, cotton; some aluminum exports	Russia, Uzbekistan, Ukraine, Kyrgyzstan
Turkmenistan	Perhaps strongest economy of new Central Asia republics; oil, gas, petrochemical, textiles exports; relies heavily on imported food	Russia, Uzbekistan, Ukraine,
Uzbekistan	Strong dictatorship remains and blocks progress; natural gas, chemical, textile, vegetable oil exports	CIS
Russian Border		
Belarus	Natural resources and food imports; electronics, farm machinery exports	CIS
Estonia	Strong but aging industrial base; highest per capita GNP of all new republics; grain imports; dairy, meat, electricity, forest products exports	CIS, Western Europe
Latvia	Strong industrial base; galloping inflation; exports processed food, clothing, and transportation equipment	Ukraine, Germany, Sweden, Russia, CIS
Lithuania	Strong industrial base, galloping inflation; exports home appliances and meat	CIS
Moldova	Landlocked; exports wine, fruits, grains, some metal products	CIS
Ukraine	One of the strongest of new republics; exports coal, electricity, minerals, and grain	Russia, Belarus, Kazakhstan
Eastern Europe		
Bulgaria	Weak industrial base; some agricultural exports	CIS
Czech Rep.	Fading productivity due to aging industrial base	Germany, Austria, Switzerland,
Hungary	One of the best chances for move to market economy; some mineral resources; strong agricultural exports	CIS, Germany, Austria
Poland	Strong manufacturing of steel and chemical products; taming employment and inflation from 1980's; expanding exports; problem with pollution	Germany, Czech Republic, Slovak Republic
Romania	Former communist command system still in place; oil and natural gas exports	CIS, Germany, Italy, U.S.
Slovak Rep.	Poor, agrarian economy; some iron ore exports	CIS, Austria
Transcaucasus		
Armenia	Strongest economy in this region; border disputes with Azerbaijan drain economy; raw minerals, fruit exports	CIS, Turkey
Azerbaijan	Civil war and border disputes with Armenia drain declining economy; oil, petrochemicals, tobacco, fruit exports	CIS, Turkey
Georgia	Civil war and difficulties with neighbors hurt trade in agricultural products, wine, steel and heavy machinery	Turkey, Bulgaria, Romania

* CIS = Commonwealth of Independent States (trade alliance of former Soviet republics)
Source: U.S. Department of State and Commerce

business is difficult. History shows that economic frustrations lead to political upheaval. Russia and other new republics could turn toward dictatorships. Some Eastern European countries have returned moderate communists to office.

Even with all the internal tensions, the move toward democracy eased stress between East and West. Western governments revamped trade policies. Some changed bans on exporting new technology to the former Soviet republics. The new countries have more access to computers and hi-tech. More than anything else, economic affairs will determine the future of the region.

QUESTIONS

1   Until Gorbachev, Soviet leaders hoped that collectivization of farms would
    1   establish a market economy
    2   increase the number of farm laborers
    3   make the entire economy more productive
    4   eliminate problems of overproduction

2   Which most hurt Gorbachev's attempts at economic reform?
    1   KGB actions
    2   incentives on the collectives
    3   bureaucratic resistance
    4   foreign investors

3   Most of the region's new republics trade within the
    1   the United Nations
    2   LDCs
    3   CIS
    4   NATO

4   In terms of mineral resources, a major problem Russia has is
    1   corruption and smuggling
    2   a lack of most minerals
    3   a lack of technology
    4   inadequate irrigation

5   Which Soviet economic priority eventually hurt the quality of life?
    1   a free trade approach
    2   export of grain
    3   oil pipeline construction
    4   emphasis on military and heavy industries

6   Which is a correct conclusion based on the information on the graph below?

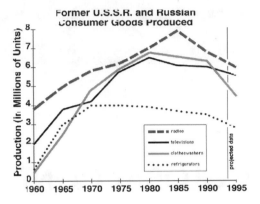

Former U.S.S.R. and Russian Consumer Goods Produced

Production (in Millions of Units)

legend: radios, televisions, clotheswashers, refrigerators — projected data

1   Soviet production of consumer goods peaked between 1970 and 1975.
2   The Soviet government placed more emphasis on production of clothes washers than on radios.
3   Production of consumer goods since the time Yeltsin took power has declined.
4   The Soviet government emphasized production of radios for propaganda reasons.

ESSAY

Discuss *each* statement below, using specific information to prove the validity of each statement.

a   Communist economic goals ignored the needs of individuals.

b   *Perestroika* used capitalist incentives to solve economic problems.

c   Agriculture presents the most critical economic problem for the region.

V. GLOBAL CONTEXT

The two-headed eagle once adorned the imperial insignia of Russia's Romanov Dynasty. It looked both East and West. Throughout history, Eastern and Western civilizations influenced the region. This attests to the difficulty of ruling the region. The Eastern tradition of centralized, autocratic rule clashes with the Western preference for personal freedom. The region stands astride both cultures and remains an enigma (mystery) to the outside world.

A hybrid of two cultures, Russia viewed both East and West with suspicion. From Central Asia came the Mongols, Tartars, and Cossacks to dominate the early history of the region. In modern times came major invasions and threats from the West's Napoleon, Kaiser Wilhelm II, Hitler, and NATO.

In the Cold War, the Soviet Union tried to lead the region toward a new communist order but eventually faltered. The years since the disintegration of the U.S.S.R. have witnessed a new struggle to blend Western and Eastern economic and social systems.

Today, the two-headed eagle is once again the symbol of the Russian Federation. The region has long struggled with the dual vision of its destiny. Global affairs will be reshaped as the eagle changes focus.

SOVIET FOREIGN POLICY: 1917-1945

In the aftermath of World War I, the spread of communism alarmed the Western European countries and the United States. Communists attempted to seize power in Germany. They succeeded in Hungary. Western coalition troops penetrated Russia to aid the Whites in Russia's Civil War. The Red victory made Western nations reluctant to establish normal relations with Lenin's new Soviet Union.

The U.S.S.R. did not join the League of Nations until 1932. Not until 1933 did the United States recognize the existence of the Soviet  Union. However, the increasing power of the Soviets forced the Western nations to acknowledge their presence. During the mid-1930's, Soviet leaders raised warnings as Hitler built his military colossus in Germany. Still, the Western Powers ignored Soviet requests for collective security arrangements.

By the late 1930's, the threat of Nazism was clear. Because Stalin had grown distrustful of the West, he fashioned a temporary arrangement with Nazi Germany. The *Nazi-Soviet Non-Aggression Pact* (1939) was the result. This agreement recognized Soviet interests in Finland, the Baltic states, and parts of Romania. Stalin agreed to divide Poland with Germany. Also, he promised to stay out of any war between Germany and Poland or Germany and the democratic nations of the West. This agreement permitted Germany to attack Poland without fear of a two-front war. It led directly to the outbreak of World War II.

In June 1941, Hitler reneged on the Pact. He turned on the U.S.S.R. and attacked, but it was not totally unexpected. The Nazis needed the agricultural areas as a compliment to their industrial base. Also, they feared Soviet expansion into Eastern Europe. Nazi blitzkriegs allowed the occupation of Romania, Bulgaria, Hungary, and Yugoslavia. Hitler then moved on the grain producing area of Ukraine and the oil wells of the Caucasus.

Late in 1941, the German Army advanced to the outskirts of Moscow and Leningrad. The

Effects Of Wartime Conferences

Conference	Participants	Major Decisions
Teheran 1943	Stalin, Roosevelt, and Churchill	To open a second front on the continent to ease the pressure on the Russian front
Yalta 1945	Stalin, Roosevelt, and Churchill	To hold free elections in Russian occupied Eastern Europe; to divide Germany into four occupation zones; to enter the USSR in the war against Japan in exchange for territories lost in 1905; to give all major countries veto power in U.N. affairs
Potsdam 1945	Stalin, Truman, and Churchill (later - Atlee)	To make agreements on demilitarization and de-Nazification of Germany; to hold war crimes trials for Nazis; to make Germany pay reparations with the Soviets to receive the most

Red Army held its positions. Yet, the "scorched earth" policy of the Soviets deprived the Germans of any ability to live off the land. The Germans began an all-out assault on Stalingrad (Volgograd). The Kremlin ordered the city held at all costs. With the aid of the Russian winter, General Georgy Zhukov began a counteroffensive that did not end until the war was over.

The arrival of aid from the United States contributed to the Soviets' stand at Stalingrad and their counteroffensive. American war materials and supplies reached the Soviet Union along routes through the Persian Gulf and the Arctic Ocean. The Allied help was indispensable to the Soviet war effort, and yet, the Soviet Union lost more military troops in the Battle of Stalingrad than the United States lost in the entire war.

During the war, the leaders of the United States, Great Britain, and the Soviet Union met at a series of wartime conferences to discuss strategy and postwar plans.

SCORCHED EARTH: In 1812, the Russians retreated beyond Moscow and burned their land to defeat Napoleon who lost nearly 80% of his forces. In 1942, the Russians repeated the same tactic, forcing Hitler to retreat with over 280,000 casualties.

Unfortunately for the Western nations, these wartime agreements laid the basis for much of the Soviet power in the postwar world. By the end of the war, the Western European nations lost much of their power. They could no longer counterbalance the Soviet Union's power. The United States and the U.S.S.R. had become the two world **superpowers**.

COMMUNISM IN EASTERN EUROPE

The postwar exhaustion and economic desolation of Western Europe made Eastern Europe vulnerable to the Soviet military. As the Soviet Red Army pushed the Germans back across Eastern Europe, it installed communist governments dependent on the U.S.S.R.

The Soviet leaders were determined to create a **buffer zone** between themselves and Western Europe. A series of military and economic treaties made the economies of the countries dependent satellites of the Soviet Union. Eastern Europe's "puppet regimes" and their people disappeared behind what Churchill called the "**Iron Curtain.**"

Some of the satellites attempted to regain full national independence (Hungary in 1956,

Czechoslovakia in 1968, and Poland on several occasions). In these cases, the Soviets used force and the denial of human rights to suppress these movements.

CHURCH INFLUENCE

The Roman Catholic Church led protests against Soviet-directed rule. In 1949, the Hungarian government seized Church lands, nationalized Church schools, and dissolved Church organizations. Cardinal Jozsef Mindszenty encouraged demonstrations, so the communists sentenced him to life imprisonment. The 1956 Revolution freed him, and the U.S. Embassy gave him asylum. Later, the Vatican removed Mindszenty from his position of leadership in Hungary. This paved the way for a 1964 accord that led to an improvement in Church-state relations.

In Poland, the Church led the dissidence against the communist regime, continuing the centuries-old link between religion and nationalism. In 1978, the election of the first Polish Pope, **John Paul II**, enhanced this relationship. It called international attention to the position of the Church in Poland.

At times, the Church tried to be an intermediary between the people and the state. Some local parish priests defied their Church hierarchy. In the 1970's and 1980's, many declared

their support for the outlawed Solidarity union. As the government yielded to popular calls for reform, Church leaders joined with Solidarity. They rallied people to push for the downfall of the communist totalitarian government.

COMMUNISTS LOSE POWER

As the decade of the 1980's closed, every Eastern European state was the scene of some open opposition to communist authority. In Poland, East Germany, and Czechoslovakia, pro-democracy movements forced resignations of communist leaders. Constitutional changes allowed coalition governments. Romanians violently overthrew the harsh dictatorship of **Nicolae Ceausescu** and executed him. However, in both Romania and Bulgaria, communists remained entrenched as the main political group.

The U.S.S.R. tightly controlled the nations of Eastern Europe economically, militarily, and diplomatically. **COMECON** (Council of Mutual Economic Assistance) served as the Soviet answer to the Marshall Plan of the United States. COMECON developed an interdependence between the economies of the Soviet satellites and the Soviet Union. Eastern European dependence on Russian oil and markets is still strong. Still, the economic pattern is changing as the Eastern European nations move toward modifying their economic structures (see chart sec. IV on page 414).

In 1955, the Soviets created the **Warsaw Pact Alliance** to balance the NATO alliance. It combined the military forces of the satellite nations under Soviet command. It gave the Soviets control of the armed forces of the Eastern European nations.

COLD WAR CONFRONTATIONS

During the Post-World War II Era, the U.S. and the Soviet Union were adversaries in many fields. There were constant military competition, a space race, a struggle for the loyalty of the Third World LDCs, and an economic competition designed to prove the worthiness of their respective economic systems. As a consequence, the Cold War developed. The two superpowers conflicted in every way short of direct military engagement. The competition included:

- **Arms Race** – Military strategies and technology changed often. It was difficult to tell which nation had more power. In the 1980's, tensions relaxed. **SALT** (**Strategic Arms Limitation Treaty**) and **START** (**Strategic Arms Reduction Treaty**) limited nuclear arms, troops, and conventional weapons. After the collapse of communism and the disintegration of the U.S.S.R. in the 1990's, the situation changed, but Russia and the republics continued to work for reductions. Ukraine is the world's third largest nuclear power and is using its status to reach new security and aid agreements with the U.S. and Russia.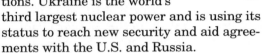

- **Space Race** – Initially, the Soviet Union had the lead in the space race with the first cosmonaut to orbit the Earth. The U.S. was able to accomplish the spectacular feat of landing men on the moon in 1969. Both nations still deploy military spy satellites as well as communications satellites.

- **Third World** – Both sides in the Cold War used economic and military aid to gain support in the Third World. LDCs quickly learned the art of playing one superpower against the other to get more aid.

- **Economy** – The U.S.S.R. made tremendous economic progress after World War II. It led the world in the production of many vital resources. However, the Soviets lagged in industrial output and standard of living. The failure to advance in productivity and the computer lag led to the nation's collapse.

- **Cultural Programs** – Despite intense Cold War competition, the superpowers set up valuable cultural exchanges. Students, farmers, and cultural groups exchanged visits. The **Bolshoi Ballet** drew large American audiences. American musicians and stage performers often toured the Soviet Union. Technological exchanges included joint space ventures.

- **Foreign Policy Differences** – Cold War tensions eased considerably in the 1980's. Diplomatic summit meetings often decreased the tensions between the super-powers. However, the Soviets still had problems with China. Each considered itself the leader of world communism. Both sought to influence less developed nations. Border disputes continued along the Amur River and in Central Asia.

- **Problems in Central Asia** – In the late 1970's and throughout the 1980's, Soviet

leaders became concerned with the growth of Islamic fundamentalism in the southern border regions of Central Asia. The religious movement opposed the atheism of communism and revitalized Muslim traditionalism. The Soviets invaded Afghanistan in 1979 to support the communist regime. They also aimed at checking the spread of Islamic fundamentalism in the southern border republics.

SUMMARY

Gorbachev's *glasnost* policies led to changes in the diplomacy of the Soviet Union. He

reduced the Soviet presence in Eastern Europe, allowed the reunification of Germany, withdrew from Afghanistan, and released dissidents such as Nobel Prize winner Andrei Sakharov. These moves opened doors to negotiations with the U.S. and the Western Allies. Economic changes under his *perestroika* opened the U.S.S.R. for foreign investment and trade.

In 1991, Gorbachev was nearly overthrown by reactionaries. Yeltsin's assumption of power and the people's loss of faith in the government led to the dissolution of the Union of Soviet Socialist Republics and President Gorbachev's resignation. The new confederation called the Commonwealth of Independent States did not function well. President Yeltsin reassured the world that the new arrangement is stable; yet, discontent runs deep throughout Russia.

Pessimists in the Western World now fear nuclear control is in doubt. Western governments fear that nations such as Libya, Iran, and Iraq may try to purchase technology with military applications or recruit trained personnel involved in these programs. All the newly independent republics have leaders with different ambitions. Optimists say the Cold War Era is over. A whole new era of foreign policy is at hand.

QUESTIONS

1. In 1989 and 1990, Lithuania's declaration of independence, the overthrow of Romania's Ceausescu, and the election of Walesa in Poland reflect
   1. strengthening of the Warsaw Pact
   2. increasing self-determination in Eastern Europe
   3. increasing militarism of Russia
   4. the failing of Eastern European nationalism

2. What was the importance of the Nazi-Soviet Non-Aggression Pact?
   1. It freed Hitler to attack Poland.
   2. It made the Germans supreme in the Baltic Sea area.
   3. Stalin promised to help Germany in its war against the democracies.
   4. The Soviet Union remained neutral throughout World War II.

3. Which was true of the economic status of the Soviet satellite nations of Eastern Europe during the Cold War?
   1. They were self-sufficient in agriculture.
   2. They were very dependent on Soviets for vital resources.
   3. They were interdependent with Western European economies.
   4. They were free market systems.

4   Hitler attacked the Soviet Union because
    1   it threatened his ally, Italy
    2   he needed Soviet grain and oil
    3   he feared Stalin's foreign policy in Asia
    4   it expanded into Greece

5   The turning point of Hitler's Russian campaign was
    1   Moscow
    2   Leningrad
    3   Stalingrad
    4   Kiev

6   Under Gorbachev, the Soviet Union pursued the foreign policy of
    1   refusing to allow dissidents to emigrate
    2   ignoring Western proposals on arms limitations
    3   increased cooperation and communication
    4   isolation from the West

7   After World War I, the Western powers feared the Soviet Union would
    1   build a Third World empire
    2   spread communism
    3   be allied to the U.S.
    4   never join the League of Nations

8   The return of communists to office in some Eastern European countries in the early 1990's may have been the result of
    1   pressure from Boris Yeltsin
    2   increasing economic problems
    3   dislike of human rights protection
    4   anger at the U.S. and Western nations

9   In the communist satellite countries of Eastern Europe, the Roman Catholic Church was
    1   destroyed by the government
    2   treated with complete toleration
    3   often in opposition to the government
    4   free from control by the Pope

10 Which was true of the superpowers' attempts to limit the arms race during the Cold War?
    1   They failed.
    2   They succeeded from time to time.
    3   They destroyed all nuclear weapons.
    4   They only agreed to limit conventional arms.

11 Which area of Cold War competition most strained the Soviet Union?
    1   the increase in cultural exchanges
    2   technological cooperation in space
    3   the military arms race
    4   aid to LDCs

12 The Islamic fundamentalist movement concerned the U.S.S.R. because
    1   it depleted oil reserves
    2   broke up the Warsaw Pact
    3   traditionalist ways conflicted with communist authority
    4   it outlawed freedom of religion

13 The Warsaw Pact was the communist equivalent of
    1   NATO
    2   United Nations
    3   League of Nations
    4   COMECON

14 After World War II, Soviet domination of Eastern Europe resulted from
    1   Germany's victory
    2   the growth of democratic movements
    3   peace agreements supported by the United Nations
    4   Soviet occupation of the region

15 The unification of Germany in 1990 can be interpreted as the
    1   rise of religious fundamentalism
    2   collapse of NATO
    3   failure of a communist system
    4   rejection of democratic ideas

16 A problem of Mikhail Gorbachev's was
    1   ethnic minorities demanded self-determination
    2   agricultural production created huge surpluses
    3   Eastern Europe demanded more Soviet military forces
    4   West Europe refused to trade with the Soviet bloc

ESSAYS

1 Major trends in Russian (and Soviet) foreign policy for centuries have included expansionism and the search for warm water ports.

   a Briefly develop the pre-20th Century historical roots for this statement.

   b Discuss Stalin's foreign policy in light of the above statement.

   c Describe the policies of Soviet (and Russian) leaders after Stalin in relation to this statement.

2 A major result of World War II was the emergence of the U.S. and the Soviet Union as the two superpowers. The rivalry between them extended far beyond their opposing ideologies.

Fields

- Economics
- Technology and space
- Military
- Third World nations

Choose *three* of the above fields. For *each* one, explain their rivalry and the impact of the rivalry in the fields selected in the global context.

Use the political cartoon below for the following essay.

3 This political cartoon illustrates the relationship between the Soviet Union and the Eastern European bloc nations during the Cold War.

   a Briefly describe what led to the domination of the Soviet Union over the Eastern European bloc nations following World War II.

   b Discuss *two* specific ways the U.S.S.R. exerted power in Eastern Europe during this time period.

   c In words or by drawing a cartoon, describe how the relationship between the former Soviet Union and Eastern European nations has changed in the 1990's.

UNIT NINE: E. EUROPE, RUSSIA, & CENTRAL ASIA

ISSUE: UNDERSTANDING DIFFERENT PERCEPTIONS OF ECONOMIC POLICY

This three-part assessment offers individual research, analytical role playing, and cooperative learning opportunities.

STUDENT TASK

Take notes that can be used to present a view of government economic policy through the eyes of a fictitious person in Russia. Include a bibliography of sources used.

DETAILED PROCEDURES

Part One:
Take notes to explain a fictitious person's position and views and write a bibliography of sources used.

A   Use a variety of sources: newspapers, magazines, books, computer software, etc.

B   Librarian or teacher must verify the types of sources used.

C   Use the notes and sources to prepare arguments for the position the person might take on the government's economic policy.

Part Two:
Participate with others playing the same role (ex., all entrepreneurs) in a panel discussion before the class. Through the eyes of the person assigned, state the arguments for and/or against the government's policy.

Part Three:
Participate in the class discussion to develop conclusions about the similarities and differences among the various persons.

EVALUATION

The scoring grid next to the evaluation items (on the following pages) was left blank intentionally. Choice of appropriate category terms is the decision of the instructor. Selection of terms such as "minimal," "satisfactory," and "distinguished" can vary with this assessment. The table on page 10 offers additional suggestions for scoring descriptors that might be inserted in the blank grids.

LEARNING STANDARDS

Students should:

• Analyze and evaluate different national, ethnic, religious, racial, socioeconomic, and gender groups that have varied perspectives on the same events and issues.

• Understand that ideals of democratic principles and human rights constantly evolve in the light of global realities.

• Analyze and evaluate the effects of human, technological, and natural activities on societies.

• Present ideas both in writing and orally in clear, concise, and properly accepted fashion.

• Understand that peoples' values, practices, and traditions are diverse, yet they face the same global challenges.

• Work cooperatively and respect the rights of others to think, act, and speak differently from themselves within the context of democratic principles and social justice.

• Demonstrate civic values and socially responsible behavior as members of school groups, local, state, national, and global communities.

• Employ a variety of information from written, graphic, and multimedia sources.

• Monitor, reflect upon, and improve their own and others' work.

Part One: Individual Research and Bibliography

Table on page 10 offers suggestions for scoring descriptors.

Evaluation Item a Is the bibliography in the proper form?	Category 1	Category 2	Category 3	Category 4	Category 5
Evaluation Item b Does the library check sheet show a variety of sources?	Category 1	Category 2	Category 3	Category 4	Category 5
Evaluation Item c Do notes support conclusions?	Category 1	Category 2	Category 3	Category 4	Category 5

Part Two: Round Table Presentation

Table on page 10 offers suggestions for scoring descriptors.

Evaluation Item a Group Planning: Does student work effectively within group?	Category 1	Category 2	Category 3	Category 4	Category 5
Evaluation Item b Group Planning: Does student appreciate and respect views of others?	Category 1	Category 2	Category 3	Category 4	Category 5
Evaluation Item c Presentation: Does student offer appropriate and comprehensive arguments for the role assumed?	Category 1	Category 2	Category 3	Category 4	Category 5
Evaluation Item d Presentation: Does student show an understanding of the government's economic policy?	Category 1	Category 2	Category 3	Category 4	Category 5

Part Three: Class Discussion

Table on page 10 offers suggestions for scoring descriptors.

Evaluation Item a Are student's comments accurate for assigned person?	Category 1	Category 2	Category 3	Category 4	Category 5
Evaluation Item b Does student contribute on long range effects?	Category 1	Category 2	Category 3	Category 4	Category 5
Evaluation Item c Does student adequately back position with reasons?	Category 1	Category 2	Category 3	Category 4	Category 5

ADMINISTRATIVE GUIDELINES

1 Survey library resources. Discuss project with librarian. May want to have librarian initial student notes or develop a resource verification sheet. Reserve library time for student research.

2 Select people for students to research and role-play. (entrepreneurs, factory workers, farm workers, pensioners, university students, etc.). Give students fictitious Russian names along with their occupational identities.

3 Discuss round table presentation format, and rules, and set presentation schedule.

4 To avoid confusion, have no more than one or two groups (ex. factory workers or soldiers) in a class period.

5 Conduct a final class discussion to review role differences and reasons for them. Use class roster with roles noted to tally responses. May wish to enlist one or two students to help with tracking responses.

6 Collect and evaluate bibliography and library verification sheet.

10

The World Today

WORLD STUDIES – *Global Issues & Assessments* N&N©

population pressures
world trade and economic development
changing power structures
environmental issues
human rights
technology
interaction of cultures

UNIT TEN:

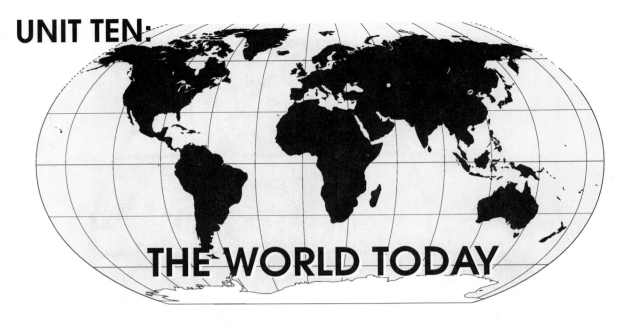

THE WORLD TODAY

This world studies course stresses global interdependence. More than ever, people have the ability to investigate, analyze, and discuss the issues that affect them and the future of the human race. Present behavior influences the future, and people can no longer pretend that their actions have no global consequences. It is not just official international policies that shape life in the 21st Century; it is every person's behavior, every moment of every day. In the mid-1980's, futurologist and author Alvin Toffler wrote in *The Third Wave*:

> *"...asking the very largest of questions about our future is not merely a matter of intellectual curiosity. It is a matter of survival..."*

Survival for the global community means facing rapid changes that underscore its interdependence. Key areas of concern include:

- population pressures
- economic development
- changing political power
- environmental issues
- human rights
- technology

I. POPULATION PRESSURES

POPULATION GROWTH

After World War I, the global population stood at 2 billion. In fifty years, it doubled. In the 1990's, it exceeded 5 billion. Population growth has a dramatic effect on world hunger and on achieving improved standards of living.

In the race between the human population growth rate and the ability of the world to produce sufficient food, food production is falling behind.

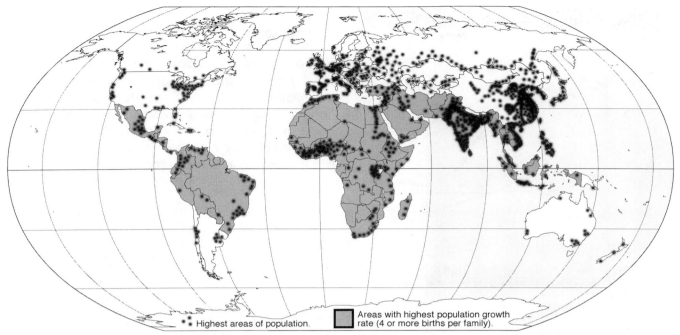

Highest areas of population. | Areas with highest population growth rate (4 or more births per family).

This location map shows that the regions of the world with the fastest population growth rates are also the poorest regions of the world, already having the greatest population. For the most part, these regions consist of the "have not" or Third World nations.

Global issues such as urban crowding, resource depletion, environmental pollution, and political unrest result from overpopulation. In *Preparing for the Twenty-First Century*, Paul Kennedy indicates population pressures in **LDCs** (less developed countries) cause overgrazing in Africa, erosion of Amazonian rain forests, and ruination of Asian croplands just when these resources are most needed.

In 1800, only 3% of the world's people lived in cities. Today, over 40% live in urban centers. LDCs contain more than 80% of the overcrowded cities. Most of the increase in LDC cities is rural villagers seeking better economic opportunities. As this migration continues, life-styles change. Traditional rural, agrarian, extended family units become urban, industrial-based, nuclear family units.

These transitions are difficult and costly. Nothing in traditional life prepares people for the changes they must make. Slums grow rapidly in the LDCs. Availability of housing cannot keep up with the rapid increases and migrations. The United Nations estimates that more than half of the urban population in LDCs live in slums. This creates an ever widening gulf between the "haves" and "have nots."

Solutions are not easy. U.N. and other international efforts try to help the poor. Volunteer efforts such as the U.S. Peace Corps, religious missions, and Live Aid concerts also help. Inspiration also comes from efforts such as those of **Mother Teresa**. This Albanian Catholic nun founded Missionaries of Charity in the 1940's. The Missionaries treat the sick and starving in countries such as India. Mother Teresa received the Nobel Peace Prize (1979) for her lifelong efforts to relieve global suffering.

The rising birth rate in LDCs is partially due to religious objections to birth control. In addition, large families are a traditional  norm in rural communities. Where agriculture is on a subsistence level, children work the fields and care for elders in extended families.

Not all population growth has a negative economic effect. Having a younger population means a larger potential work force. This is good for economic potential if the nation can feed their young as they mature. However, LDCs have high infant mortality. In Somalia, the infant mortality rate is 127 deaths for every 1000 births (U.S. = 10/1000). Many of these children die from malnutrition. Older children, poorly nourished, cannot resist diseases.

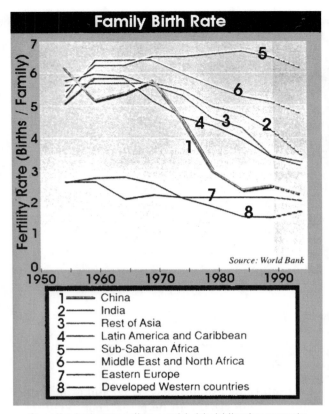

Family Birth Rate

Fertility Rate (Births / Family)

Source: World Bank

1950   1960   1970   1980   1990

1 —— China
2 —— India
3 —— Rest of Asia
4 —— Latin America and Caribbean
5 —— Sub-Saharan Africa
6 —— Middle East and North Africa
7 —— Eastern Europe
8 —— Developed Western countries

Over the last generation, worldwide birthrates seem to be slowing. However, SubSaharan Africa leads the world in highest birthrate. China, with mandatory birth control, has the greatest reduction. Developed nations maintain a lower and more steady birthrate.

The war against hunger is truly mankind's war of liberation...There is no battle on Earth or space more important (for) peace and progress cannot be maintained in a world half-fed and half-hungry... We have the capacity to eliminate hunger from the face of the Earth. Victory will not come in the next year... but it must be in our lifetime.

To fight hunger, the U.N. created **FAO** (the Food and Agricultural Organization). Agronomists (agricultural economists), nutritionists, and even philosophers staff the FAO. They develop strategies to combat world hunger. They say the battle can be won with science, technology, good will, and common sense. Most FAO experts agree the first and most critical step is curbing population growth. Yet, they point out that hunger does not always result from food shortages. In many cases, the causes are unequal distribution of wealth, mass migration to cities, insufficient knowledge, inadequate technology, and natural disasters.

Conversely, too few people can sometimes present problems, as well. The U.S., Germany, and some other Western European nations are moving toward having more older than younger people. In years to come, the fewer young workers will strain to support the elderly. Higher Social Security tax burdens in the U.S. and Western European countries already indicate this kind of human resource problem.

WORLD HUNGER

Hunger exists in every nation. Observers agree that population growth must be slowed to avoid famine and hunger. Many political, environmental, economic, social, and technological factors contribute to worldwide hunger. However, U.S. President John F. Kennedy may have said it best when he addressed the World Food Congress in Washington, D.C. in June, 1963:

HUNGER & POVERTY

This TIME cover illustrates the concern for the problem of world hunger which was heightened through news media attention in the African country of Somalia. Thousands of babies, children, and adults died from starvation. At food stations such as Baidoa, thousands of lives were saved.

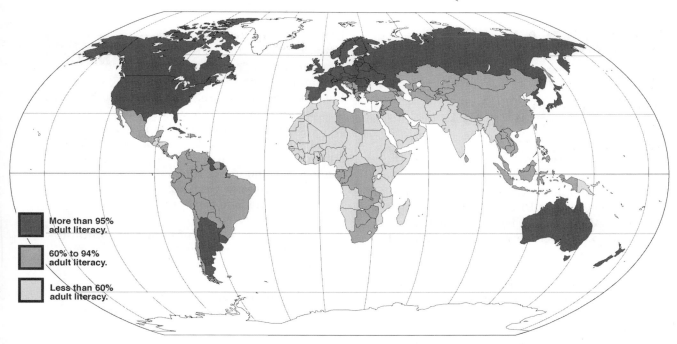

This location map shows literacy in regions of the world. In general, the highest illiteracy is found in the "have not" or Third World nations. These are the poorest nations, often with the highest birthrates and lowest standards of living.

More than 95% adult literacy.

60% to 94% adult literacy.

Less than 60% adult literacy.

EDUCATION GAP

Better education could ease many problems stemming from overpopulation. Global illiteracy declined measurably in the last twenty years. Still, the gap between those who have access to information and those who do not continues to widen. Twentieth Century British historian Arnold Toynbee claimed life on Earth was a struggle between education and catastrophe. For an LDC to survive, it needs an educated citizenry. Yet, literacy rates in LDCs lag while those in industrial nations exceed ninety percent.

NIEs (newly industrialized economies) such as South Korea succeed because of education. In the last generation, the literacy rate tripled (1992 = 96%; U.S. = 98%). South Korea's labor force is prepared to handle the knowledge and to learn the skills needed to grow.

Education levels in LDCs reveal why growth is elusive. Afghanistan's literacy rate is only 29%. Worse, female rates are far lower than males. The female rate in Afghanistan is less than 8%. In Somalia, the male rate is 18%, and the female rate is 6%. Bringing these areas into the technologically advanced age rapidly is impossible. Education is needed to comprehend how the world is changing. Basic skills are needed to convert a nation to meet change. Understanding why increased birth rates are perilous is beyond the majority of people in LDCs. Most LDCs do not have the means to create functional education systems.

Mrs. Regans's 4th Grade class in Southern California poses for a group picture after learning about the food groups, a topic that according to the World Health Organization is not often taught in LDCs.   PhotoDisc Inc. 1994

II. GLOBAL ECONOMIC DEVELOPMENT

INTERDEPENDENCE

Economic interdependence means decisions made in one place have consequences for all regions. When the OPEC (oil) cartel reacted to Western nations' aid to Israel in the 1970's, the cost of oil to the average Western consumer doubled. Petroleum is critical to the manufacture or delivery of nearly every product. The rise in the price of crude oil caused galloping inflation on a global scale.

The needs of people in LDCs are interrelated with those in developed nations. The people of

LDCs struggle in a "Revolution of Rising Expectations." Modern communications tell them

life is better elsewhere. They strain to balance traditional values and modernization while they look to the economically advanced nations for assistance. Balancing the needs of developing and advanced nations is not easy. Cross cultural connections and unequal benefits create frustrations and internal conflict. Today, LDCs ask industrial nations to assist in:

- Equalizing the value of **primary commodities** (raw materials) with that of manufactured goods

- Financing **infrastructure** (transportation and communication networks) and training skilled workers

As LDCs struggle with indebtedness, their financial problems threaten global stability. Attracting private foreign investment capital in such an atmosphere is difficult. Generating domestic capital takes savings and sacrifice. Yet, real economic growth hinges on these two internal factors as much as getting outside aid.

KEYS TO INDUSTRIALIZATION

Some LDCs successfully break out of poverty. NIEs such as the Pacific Rim's "Four Dragons" transformed themselves through key internal actions. They encouraged savings, focused government commitment, and people made significant sacrifices in their lives to encourage a better future.

South Koreans and Taiwanese save over 30% of their national income (U.S. rate = 12%). This provides "home-grown investment capital" for industrial growth. It makes NIEs more stable in the eyes of industrial nations. Investors willing to risk capital to back new enterprises are more important than lenders who expect repayment with interest. A country's high savings rate portrays a clear desire to break away from poverty and subsistence. That strong desire creates an atmosphere that attracts more overseas investment and fosters real growth.

Because of huge debts, the Third World (Less Developed) Countries find themselves on the edge of survival. Being so dependent on foreign money threatens global economic stability.

Most LDCs have subsistence economies, and savings are nearly nonexistent. That condition cannot attract outside investment; so, they rely on grants of aid in "welfare packages" from the U.N. and prosperous nations.

The aid money is siphoned off by dictators and aristocrats. It never trickles down to businesses. Breaking the cycle of poverty is very difficult.

Many LDCs are run by deep-rooted oligarchies and aristocracies bent on self-enrichment. They want only to hold onto their status quo. These regimes frighten overseas investors and stifle development.

The Four Dragons broke the poverty cycle, because their people and governments were committed to economic change. These Pacific Rim NIEs accepted that their lives, traditions, and cultures would have to change.

Lastly, Japan gave the NIEs of the Pacific Rim a regional role model. Like Japan, they focus on export products rather than domestic ones. People sacrifice satisfaction and comfort now to build for the future. Most Asian and African LDCs do not have a model for such direction.

THE RICH / POOR GAP

Most LDCs remain highly dependent on the developed nations for trade, foreign aid, investment, and food. This has often led to frustration, bitterness, and resentment. The comparison chart of the life expectancy and GDP (Gross Domestic Product) statistics (on the next page) illustrates the gap between rich and poor nations.

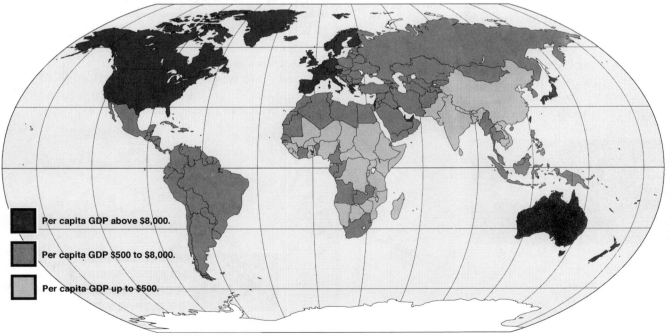

Per capita GDP above $8,000.

Per capita GDP $500 to $8,000.

Per capita GDP up to $500.

This location map shows the per capita Gross Domestic Product in world nations. In general, the lower the per capita GDP, the lower the standard of living and the poorer the country is. In most cases, the low GDP countries are the "have not" or Third World nations.

Socioeconomic Differences			
Nation	1992 GDP (in billions)	Life Expectancy Male	Life Expectancy Female
UNITED STATES	$5,954	72.0	79.0
JAPAN	3,705	76.0	82.0
GERMANY	1,643	73.0	79.0
FRANCE	1,033	74.0	82.0
GREAT BRITAIN	916	73.0	79.0
AUSTRALIA	281	70.0	80.0
PEOPLE'S REP. OF CHINA	415	65.5	69.4
BRAZIL	358	61.6	65.7
INDIA	328	57.0	59.0
EGYPT	39	60.0	61.0
SOMALIA	1.7	56.0	56.0
IRAN	90	64.0	65.0

Source: U.S. Dept. of State, 1993

TRADITION V. MODERNIZATION

Resettled rural migrants also create urban congestion. Overwhelmed cities cannot provide vital public services. The "Westernized existence" in cities leads to frustration and turmoil. As much as industrialization is attractive to leaders, not all people desire such upheaval.

Cultural conflict restrains economic development in many LDCs. The clash between tradition and pressure to adopt Western ways leads to social unrest. Economic opportunity lures people from African and Indian villages, and their traditional culture weakens in the urban environment.

Trying to drag a reluctant population toward radical change is next to impossible. This was part of the reason for the Iranian Revolution in the late 1970's. Shi'ites wished to restore Islamic traditionalism to a rapidly modernizing underdeveloped nation. In NIEs such as South Korea, culture is more pragmatic. The people adapt to change. The contrast between South Korea's development and Iran's deterioration underscores this point.

III. CHANGING POLITICAL POWER
POST-COLD WAR ORDER

World War II weakened the 19th Century global powers (Germany, France, and Britain). Their economies and colonial empires virtually collapsed. Two newer nations filled the power vacuum: the Soviet Union and the United States. These two nations became the poles for

a new political competition: capitalism v. communism. Each superpower grouped a bloc of smaller allies around itself (Warsaw Pact, NATO, and SEATO). Many emerging nations in Africa and Asia tried to remain neutral. Sometimes called the "Third World," they often played both sides of the bipolar structure.

The two superpowers engaged in many diplomatic, military, economic, and ideologic confrontations. They occurred in every global region. Many times, the superpowers were behind the scenes while small allies engaged in open warfare. Occasionally, there were direct confrontations (Berlin Airlift, Cuban Missile Crisis) that came close to the brink of nuclear war. This tense era of history seemed to fade with the collapse of the Soviet Union in 1991 and the fall of communist governments worldwide.

POSITION OF LDCs

The changing global order places LDCs in a fluid position. During the Cold War, most LDCs gained maturity on the world stage. They now become important in keeping the balance of peace. Their majority role in the U.N. General Assembly is evidence of this.

Still, most LDCs are poor and weak. They have so many internal problems that they cannot offset major powers. The passing of Cold War confrontations does not mean the globe is free of threats. Russia and other members of the CIS (Commonwealth of Independent States) have authority over the military and nuclear arsenal of the former U.S.S.R. Other nations have nuclear weapons. Among them are Britain, France, China, India, Israel, and Pakistan. U.N. inspection teams say Iraq and North Korea have deadly nuclear capabilities, too.

Many other countries have impressive conventional military forces. They often commit acts of aggression. Libya's campaigns in Chad and Sudan and Iraq's attack on Kuwait are examples. In 1993, the U.N. had 80,000 peacekeeping troops deployed in 19 global trouble spots. Economic and political competition among LDCs is sometimes fierce. Many have military forces far beyond their needs. Some LDCs specialize in selling arms, although the

U.S. is the number one weapons merchant. According to *U.S. News and World Report*, its $13.6 billion in sales accounted for 57% of all arms sold in 1993. France was second with $3.8 billion. Some nations encourage terrorists. Some wish to overthrow their neighbors by supplying arms to rebel forces. Keeping the peace in the new world arrangement is not easy.

LDCs do not often share the same sense of responsibility for keeping the balance of peace. Many critics feel they present great potential for upsetting the balance in their drive to gain national interests. For example, Iraq invaded Kuwait in 1990. Ethiopia's 1980's war with Somalia brought on the 1990's civil wars and famine in Somalia. The wars drew the U.N., U.S., and other nations into the conflict.

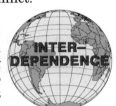

LDCs and developed nations must forge a cooperative approach to peacekeeping. As the remaining superpower, the U.S. struggles to define its role in the new order. It reduced its draining military spending and shrank its overseas military operations. It hoped to redirect the military savings toward renewing its aging industrial base and infrastructure. Still, its desire to keep peace is costly. The United States supports the U.N., NATO, the European Union, and others dealing with regional crises. Engagements in the Persian Gulf, Bosnia, and Somalia have shown how difficult it is to forge a new world order.

ARMS CONTROL

For most of human history, empires and nations postured about condemning war as a means of settling conflict. Yet, nations' fears and suspicions have made forging meaningful arms control agreements difficult. The *Limited Nuclear Test Ban Treaty* (1963) and its counterparts for space and underwater have been relatively successful. Still, nations such as France and China ignore them.

A number of nations refused to sign the *Nuclear Non-Proliferation Treaty* (1968). Some have gone on to develop nuclear capability. The U.S. and other nuclear countries aided nations such as India, Pakistan, Israel, and Libya with peaceful uses of nuclear energy. Tragically, those countries then developed

Détente – a precarious perch

nuclear weapons. As these nations became involved in disputes, the potential of nuclear war increased.

As the Cold War wore on, détente allowed the superpowers to make several attempts at arms limitation. The series of treaties in the 1970's known as the **SALT** agreement, (*Strategic Arms Limitation Treaty*) cut certain types of missiles and numbers of warheads. Problems arose over inspection procedures. The security of new weapons and technology always concerned them.

In the 1980's, **START** (*Strategic Arms Reduction Talks*) continued limiting nuclear arms. Summit meetings between the superpowers reduced troop levels in Europe. Diplomats hinted at an end to the Cold War by the time Mikhail Gorbachev resigned and the Soviet Union ceased to be (1991). Leaders of the new republics in Eastern Europe and Central Asia declared that the former Soviet arsenal was under control. Later, Russia's President Boris Yeltsin traveled to Western capitals with assurances that arms reduction would continue. Yet, Ukraine, with the third largest number of nuclear weapons, resisted giving up its nuclear arsenal.

TERRORISM

Groups struggling to achieve their political and economic goals have turned to terrorism. These groups include the **PLO** (Palestine Liberation Organization), the **IRA** (Irish Republican Army), the **Red Brigades** in Italy, and assorted other small groups. They have used terrorist attacks to bring attention to their demands. For example, the 1994 attack by a Jewish radical Kach leader on worshippers in a Hebron (Israel) mosque sent peace negotiations into a tailspin. Global outrage led to more bloodshed and riots. The Israeli government outlawed the group, driving it underground. Yet, it has strong support even in the United States.

To compound the problem, terrorist groups sometimes work together. Japanese terrorists, working with the PLO, attacked Israel's Tel Aviv airport in 1973. Investigations into the attempted assassination of Pope John Paul II (1981) revealed that terrorist networks operate with great freedom through countries of Eastern Europe.

Global attempts to stop terrorism have not met with great success. The 1993 bombing of New York's World Trade Center showed how vulnerable society is to unexpected violence. The U.N. has been relatively ineffective. Still, some measures taken by individual countries have some deterrent effect (protecting likely targets, increasing travel security, and training antiterrorist units). Terrorism, coupled with the array of conflicting global frustrations, will make forging any new world order difficult in the Post Cold War Era.

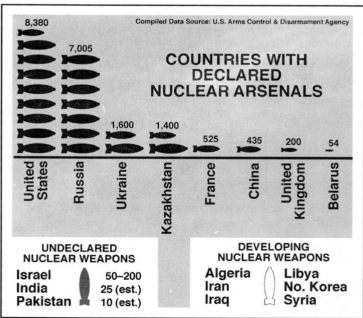

Compiled Data Source: U.S. Arms Control & Disarmament Agency

COUNTRIES WITH DECLARED NUCLEAR ARSENALS

United States	Russia	Ukraine	Kazakhstan	France	China	United Kingdom	Belarus
8,380	7,005	1,600	1,400	525	435	200	54

UNDECLARED NUCLEAR WEAPONS

Israel	50–200
India	25 (est.)
Pakistan	10 (est.)

DEVELOPING NUCLEAR WEAPONS

Algeria	Libya
Iran	No. Korea
Iraq	Syria

IV. ENVIRONMENTAL ISSUES

According to American biologist René Dubos, the Earth's people behave as if there are infinite amounts of air, soil, water, and other natural resources. The results are shocking. Gradually, the environment has deteriorated into filthy water, foul air, and eroded land. Life depends on the protective tissue called the **biosphere** (the thin, integrated layer of air, water, and soil surrounding the Earth). Establishing a compromise between the strain of growth and environmental deterioration is critical.

POLLUTION: WATER, LAND, AND AIR

Throughout history, human activity did little to damage the environment. As the Earth's population increased and technology improved in the 20th Century, the situation changed. As more people use more of the Earth's resources, pollution of the air, water, and soil increase. Consider some of the consequences:

- **Sewage and dangerous toxic wastes** have been dumped into rivers, lakes, and oceans. The water cycle has suffered. Many contaminants find their way into drinking water supplies.

- **Chemical pesticides and fertilizers** increase agricultural production. Yet, groups such as

Copyright 1989, 1991, 1992, U.S. News. reprinted by permission

the Rachel Carson Council consider them "environmental time bombs." Their contaminants build in the soil year after year. In addition, there is the difficulty of disposing of chemical **toxic waste**. Industrial nations now seek disposal sites in LDCs. There is concern that this will make entire subregions uninhabitable.

- **Acid rain** (air pollutants that travel in precipitation) is severe. Industries spew millions of tons of waste into the atmosphere each day. Smoke, smog, soot, and ash from factory smokestacks emit carbon monoxide, hydrocarbons, and other toxic wastes. Distant lakes, forests, and plant and animal life suffer from rain carrying these substances. Great landmarks of the past (sculptures and historical buildings) suffer from the corrosion caused by this contamination. Acid rain scars marble and corrodes bronze, destroying art as well as life. Cultural as well as environmental groups now join forces to promote legislation to prevent the burning of sulfuric coal. It is estimated to cause over 80% of the acid rain.

Remedies falter in the political arena. Lobbies and other special interest groups use bribes or election funds to convince politicians that environmental protection assaults industrial growth and causes job losses. Politicians shy away from actively

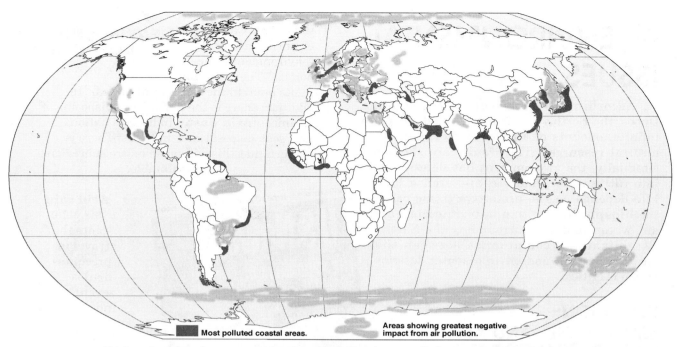

This location map shows areas of major pollution and areas with the greatest negative impact from air pollution. Note that it is not just the areas near the industrial nations that have major pollution problems but also around some of the less developed areas of the world.

Most polluted coastal areas.

Areas showing greatest negative impact from air pollution.

promoting protective legislation. Failure to act causes unnecessary human suffering (lung disease) and billions of dollars in often irreparable damages to natural as well as physical resources.

DESERTIFICATION AND DEFORESTATION

Maintaining an ecological balance is necessary to prevent disasters like the widespread famine that has recently occurred in the African Sahel. Desertification (loss of arable land to the spreading desert) is not entirely a natural phenomena. Too many people, too many herds, and overcultivation of the dry areas of our world cause soil erosion. The World Watch Institute (Washington, DC) claims 283 million Africans relied on 272 million livestock in 1950. Today, there are 604 million Africans and almost equal animal herds. Since growing feed crops is difficult on the desert fringes, these livestock graze on natural growth. With that many animals eating away at the scrub, the desert grows and poverty and hunger worsen.

Another devastating act that contributes significantly to soil erosion is **deforestation** (overcutting of timber resources). This is occurring in Brazil's Amazon rain forests and in India, and Southeast Asia. Destruction estimates run between 1 and 2 billion acres per

David Johnson, 1993

With little or no green vegetation and water, the devastating effects of desertification are evident in the appearance of the emaciated cattle around Keur Mibarick, Senegal.

year. The ecological strain makes the land unsuitable for human or animal habitation. It also increases carbon dioxide and affects global warming and weather patterns. More careful environmental planning by national and international leaders in areas of rural development is essential to prevent unnecessary disasters (see Earth Summit information on page 441).

GLOBAL WARMING

Another controversial issue arising from poor environmental management is the "Greenhouse Effect" (see illustration below). Some scientists feel it is already changing air quality, rainfall, and climatic patterns worldwide.

In *Preparing for the Twenty-First Century*, Paul Kennedy says scientists differ on the effects of global warming, but they agree average global temperatures have risen 0.4° Celsius in the last 100 years. Kennedy cites estimates that show rising carbon dioxide levels may cause a 1 to 4 degree rise in temperatures in the next 100 years.

News magazines such as the well respected *U.S. News & World Report* brought the debate over the reality of global warming to the forefront of public discussion and opinion.

Kennedy's sources say warming from rising carbon emissions and ozone layer loss could cause the oceans to rise and threaten coastal lands. They indicate flooding of low lying LDCs such as Bangladesh could send environmental refugees into India and Myanmar. Experts predict hurricanes, typhoons, and other storms may threaten previously safe, but low, islands in Oceania and fresh water supplies elsewhere. They forecast increased dangers from skin cancer and city smog.

Technological and engineering solutions may save some developed areas, but LDCs would not be able to afford such solutions. Experts feel the solution is not in such costly engineering projects. They say the best hope is reducing destruction of the rain forests and reducing waste gasses. Strong international efforts to carry out agreements such as those of the 1992 Earth Summit are needed (see Earth Summit on page 441).

URBAN ENVIRONMENT

Massive traffic jams, polluting factories, garbage and sewage problems, and a lack of **green space** (parks and gardens) characterize many of the world's urban centers. In many LDCs, poorly managed

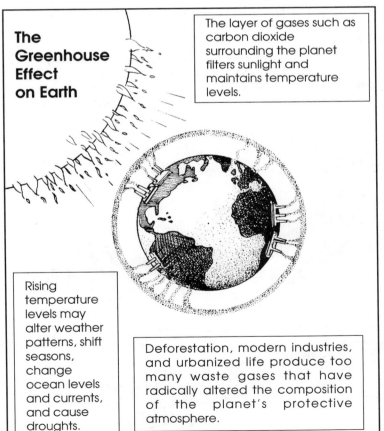

The Greenhouse Effect on Earth

The layer of gases such as carbon dioxide surrounding the planet filters sunlight and maintains temperature levels.

Rising temperature levels may alter weather patterns, shift seasons, change ocean levels and currents, and cause droughts.

Deforestation, modern industries, and urbanized life produce too many waste gases that have radically altered the composition of the planet's protective atmosphere.

The poor of Caracas, Venezuela live in the barrios. These overcrowded houses (several families per one to three room units) are built of cheap materials, often having poor or no sanitation, running water, or electricity.   David Johnson, 1993

provide for the millions that seek a better life.

How can cities cope and be revitalized? Mayur advises urban planners to use available resources judiciously and distribute them equitably. He says efforts must be made to develop alternative resources. Role model cities such as Zurich and Edinburgh demonstrate positive alternatives for desirable urban living.

THE SEA ENVIRONMENT

urban growth causes severe ecological damage. Air and water quality and traffic pollution (noise and air) menace the quality of life.

In *Supercities – The Growing Crisis,* Bombay (India) urban planner Rashmi Mayur wrote that some cities are becoming so large that life has become a nightmare. Cities are

exploding in the developing world as poor people migrate from villages and towns to search for opportunity in the cities. Often, they trade one wretched condition for another. Shanty towns, barrios, and slums continue to grow in alarming numbers. The cities do not have enough resources to

Oceans are another environmental concern. Garbage and sewage disposed in our oceans, seas, and bays endangers marine life.

The world's major fishing grounds have been overexploited. Treaties designed to conserve them have been ignored, especially by Russia and Japan.

A new danger, called **anoxia** (oxygen depletion), has wiped out shellfish in many areas. Environmental groups are closely monitoring the effects on aquatic life exposed to anoxic water. Fish are a significant source of protein in people's diets. It is important to preserve these fishing areas from pollution and overexploitation.

THE EARTH SUMMIT

International efforts to deal with ecological issues grind to a halt when nations cannot balance economic and environmental interests. In June 1992, 172 nations met at the **U.N. Conference on Environment and Development** in Rio de Janeiro, Brazil. It was called the "**Earth Summit**." Its goal was to promote environmentally safe alternative paths to development for newly developing nations. Maurice Strong, Secretary General for the conference, said newer nations must see "the path taken by the older industrial nations is no longer viable." The Earth Summit promoted the concept of **sustainable development**. It means careful use of the natural resources now must include the realization these same finite resources must provide for 10 billion people in the 21st Century. Sustainable development allows growth to improve the quality of life, but does not abuse resources and ecosystems.

The Earth Summit produced five international agreements to achieve sustainable development:

- ***The Rio Declaration*** – Contains 27 principles on the rights and obligations of countries concerning the environment. *The Rio Declaration* promotes international responsibility for the **Global Commons** (biospheric elements such as the oceans and the atmosphere that no one nation owns).

- ***Agenda 21*** – Implements the *Rio Declaration*. This 800-page action plan focuses on social goals such as elimination of poverty and management of human settlements to protect all forms of life.

- ***The Climate Convention*** – Seeks to have nations reduce or hold greenhouse gas emissions to 1990 levels.

- ***The Biodiversity Convention*** – Protects plants, animals, and marine microörganisms. Proposes sharing of environmentally safe biotechnology between the "haves" and "have nots." Calls for each industrialized nation to contribute a small percentage of its GDP to a fund the U.N. will distribute to LDCs for environmentally safe development assistance.

- ***Statement of Agreement on Forest Principles*** – Protects forests in a broad statement. It was not signed by many of the LDCs, including Malaysia and India that feel their forests are keys to their development and not Global Commons.

© U.N. Photo, 1992. Used By Permission

United Nations Conference on Environment and Development (UNCED), Earth Summit, Rio de Janeiro, Brazil, 3rd - 14th June 1992. A small portion of the delegates from 172 nations at a discussion of Agenda 21. In the foreground are Norway's Prime Minister Brundtland and Sweden's King Karl XVI Gustaf.

Not every nation signed every agreement. For example, U.S. representatives declined to sign the *Biodiversity Convention*. President Bush and Environmental Protection Agency Administrator Reilly felt it placed too much financial burden on developed nations. They claimed it also reduced incentives for research in biotechnical companies. A year later under President Clinton, the U.S. signed the convention. German Chancellor Helmut Kohl later said Germany's recession would prohibit it from contributing its share to the U.N. fund on LDCs' sustainable development. Coordinating a global environmental effort is not easy.

René Dubos cautions it will be expensive to protect and restore the rapidly deteriorating environment. If humans are to survive, he says they must accept a *"Stewardship of the Earth,"* protecting it while using it. This will be difficult. For industrial nations, it means accepting reduced living standards, sharing technology, and reimbursing others for precious resources. For LDCs, it may mean never achieving the living standards of developed nations.

V. HUMAN RIGHTS

Attitudes about human rights differ greatly among nations. Achieving universal justice, even after the tragic experiences of totalitarian rule in the World War II Era, still escapes humankind.

UNIVERSAL DECLARATION
OF HUMAN RIGHTS

The foundation of modern thinking on human rights is found in the U.N.'s *Universal Declaration*. It was pioneered by the efforts of Eleanor Roosevelt in the opening years of the United Nations. It contains the fundamental statement that all human beings are entitled to dignity and possess natural political, social, and economic rights such as freedom of speech, assembly, and a decent standard of living.

The *Declaration* is an ideal, a goal toward which humankind aspires. Still, Amnesty International's annual index of freedom shows that a majority of people live under regimes that deny basic rights.

HELSINKI
ACCORDS, 1975

In 1975, the United States and the Soviet Union joined 33 other nations to sign a treaty in Helsinki, Finland. It pledged security and cooperation in Europe and formalized post-World War II territorial arrangements. It also stated mutual respect for basic human rights and encouraged travel among the citizens of the signing nations. On the basis of violations of this agreement, the U.S. later refused to sign several treaties with the Soviets. The United

---

Human Rights Misery

During the last half of this century there have been waves of mass killings and mass refugee exodus, few as great as the 1994 ethnic cleansing in Rwanda, Africa. The following list represents best research estimates of some of the most horrendous violations of human rights.

Mass Killings

China – Mao's Cultural Revolution, 1966-1976 .... 20 million
U.S.S.R. – Stalin's reign of terror, 1936-1953 .... 20 million
Europe – The Holocaust, 1933-1945 .... 11 million
Pakistan – Reprisals against Bengalis, 9 months in 1971 .... 3 million
Cambodia – The Khmer Rouge killing fields, 1975-1979 .... 1.6 million
Rwanda – Ethnic cleansing, Tutsis, 3 months in 1994 .... 1 million
Indonesia – Killing of communists and Chinese, 1965-1966 500,000
Bosnia – Ethnic cleansing, 1992-1994 200,000

Refugees

Afghanistan – After Soviet invasion, 1979-1994 .... 6 million
Rwanda – Ethnic cleansing, 3 months in 1994 .... 2.4 million
Mozambique – Civil war and famine, 1975-1992 .... 1.5 million
Iraq – Kurds flee after Gulf War, 6 weeks, 1991 .... 1.4 million
Somalia – Civil war, 1988-1994 .... 1 million

Source: U.N. data and *Newsweek*, 1 August 1994

States continues to use it as a basis for trade negotiations with Communist China.

RECENT VIOLATIONS OF HUMAN RIGHTS

Slavery, a denial of basic human rights, still exists in forced labor camps in totalitarian states and in some underdeveloped areas of the world. Heinous acts of autocratic governments and oppression of critics still cause anguish in many countries. Recent and historic examples include:

At United Nations Site 2 Rithysen Refugee Camp, Thailand, a young boy holds papers showing a photograph of his missing father, Phan. Thousands of such political refugee children have been left to survive on their own. David Johnson, 1991

- **Apartheid in South Africa** – Until the agreements between the ANC and the de Klerk government, constant protest and defiance of apartheid laws, international trade sanctions, divestiture, and world public opinion created pressure on South Africa. In 1994, free elections and a new constitution promised an end to the long denial of the black majority's basic rights. Still, there is deep dissension. Observers point out that the open elections were only a first step. They will not make racism and violence subside. South Africa has long been a troubled country. The real revolution has only begun.

- **Dissidents And Forced Labor Camps in the U.S.S.R.** – During the 20th Century, the Soviet Union often denied Jews permission to emigrate. The government condemned **dissidents** (outspoken critics) as disloyal. It denied them work and decent housing. It exiled some dissidents to gulags (Siberian work camps) or to mental institutions. This happened to the late Nobel Prize winning physicist **Andrei Sakharov** in the 1970's.

- **Political and Ethnic Massacres in Cambodia, Uganda, and Rwanda** – Mass political executions were carried out under the communist government in Cambodia. From 1977 to 1985, Premier Pol Pot conducted bloody purges resulting in nearly 4 million deaths. Between 1971 and 1979, Colonel Idi Amin Dada executed an estimated 300,000 of his political opponents in Uganda. In 1994, ethnic warfare in Rwanda between Hutu and Tutsi people led to hundreds of thousands of killings and more than 2.4 million refugees.

OPPRESSION IN THE CONTEMPORARY WORLD

Human rights are denied across the globe. Student protestors who sought free speech in

T'iananmen Square in China in 1989 still languish in jails. In Sri Lanka, the Tamil minority fights the Sinhalese majority for political rights. Yet, both sides ignore basic rights, killing innocent people, wiping out families and villages. In Northern Ireland, Protestant majority groups deny representation to Catholics who have often fought back through the radical terrorist attacks of the Provisional Wing of the Irish Republican Army.

POLITICAL & ECONOMIC REFUGEES

Human rights issues are universal. In varying degrees, they exist in every country, developed or not. Yet, agreement on proper, ethical treatment of people varies. Even the *U.N. Declaration* is not accepted as a base. Islamic fundamentalists claim it conflicts with the *Qur'an* on the status of women, corporal punishment, and the death penalty. In 1992, video news of treatment of Bosnian Muslim captives in Serbian POW camps horrified the world.

In early 1994, ethnic slaughter continued in the Balkans. Bosnian Serb guerrilla forces ravaged the Muslim population of Gorazde in contempt of the U.N. and its peacekeeping forces. The tragedy demonstrated the weakness of international resolve in the face of genocide. Equality, freedom to speak, to worship, to move about, and simply to live are not things to be taken for granted. Ignoring human rights violations strengthens those who commit them.

VI. TECHNOLOGY

Technological changes dramatically alter human existence. In modern times, the commercial age and the scientific and industrial revolutions changed daily life in the industrialized world. Recent advances in computers, agriculture, medicine, transportation, and space change life from moment to moment.

TECHNOLOGY

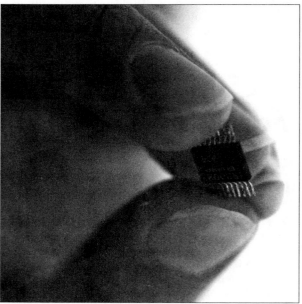

The silicon chip, "brain" of the technological revolution, gets smaller and smaller, year after year.   PhotoDisc Inc. 1994

COMPUTERS

Silicon chips demonstrate how modern technology can be packaged into low cost, mass-produced intelligence data gatherers. These single tiny chips are made of material that can be easily mass-produced for a low cost. Computers continue to change every aspect of our global society. They have made it possible to open a world market of low cost computers for home, schools, industry, medicine, and government activities.

Government leaders speak of getting their countries on "the information highway." Computer expert Jon Roland of Texas foresees such technological breakthroughs and economic consequences as:

Computers, the key factor in the communications highway, have changed the nature of business, government, and life in general.   PhotoDisc Inc. 1994

- **Instant Information** — pocket sized units accessing universal communications data bank networks

- **Home Banking** — financial business conducted by tamper proof personal computers

- **Self-Guided Planes and Cars** — computers piloting vehicles safely to their destinations

- **Classroom Computers** — computer-assisted instruction is impartial and adapts to the individual's needs

AGRICULTURE

There is an old Mexican saying, *"A full belly, a happy heart. An empty stomach, be careful."* World population will exceed six billion by the year 2000. At that rate, agricultural production must increase two-fold. Yet, today, there is a great debate over how to produce food. Technology provides many answers, but it also damages the environment. Opponents of chemical fertilizers and pesticides advocate **sustainable organic agriculture** as the alternative.

In the late 1960's, the **Green Revolution** developed wheat and rice seeds with extremely high yields. To obtain the best results, it required high cost petrochemical fertilizers and pesticides. In LDCs, neither farmers nor governments have the funds for this fertilizer. Very often, the Green Revolution has only benefited large plantation farmers who can afford both the irrigation and fertilizers.

In 1965, Norman Borlaug, Nobel laureate and founder of the Green Revolution, stated, *"We have the possibility of keeping up with the world food situation. But it's going to mean a reallocation of resources – use of fuel for agriculture instead of the family car."* The years since Borlaug made this observation have not fulfilled his wish. The reallocation did not occur. The "Have Nations" continue to waste fuel and resources. Americans consume more fuel than they did before the energy crises in the 1970's. The U.S. has 4% of the world's population. It consumes 25% of the world's fuel.

There is another side to using technological advances in agriculture. Every economic decision involves **real costs** (costs other than money). In this case, there are ecological costs. Opponents of chemically intense, synthetic farming claim it results in environmental damage. They campaign for

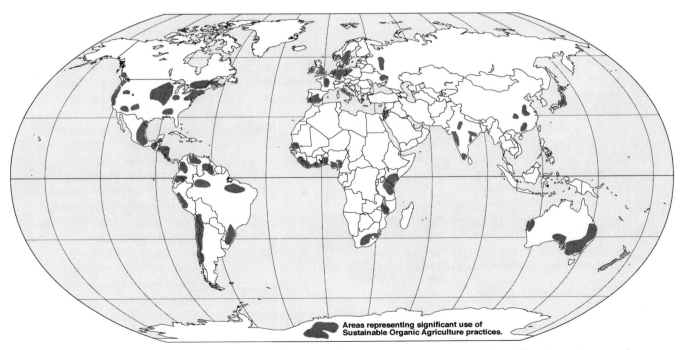

This location map shows areas of the world where sustainable organic agriculture is being practiced on a large-scale. Many "green" scientists and environmentalists are encouraged by widespread cooperation among many nations.

Areas representing significant use of Sustainable Organic Agriculture practices.

safer organic techniques. They press national and international authorities to ban toxic pesticides such as Mirex, Chlordane, and DDT.

Prohibiting such chemicals is not a simple matter of safeguarding human life. Economic needs often displace human needs. Global companies based in the developed nations make huge profits selling chemicals in LDCs. Agronomist Thomas B. Harding says ten multinational corporations dominate the global agribusiness (*Earth Journal 1993*, page 118). They use large scale techniques to produce chemically-saturated foods that ruin the soil and the atmosphere. Harding claims taxes, subsidies, and laws in many nations grant special privileges to these giant firms.

As with most problems facing humankind, technology alone cannot solve the global food crisis. It must be a rational approach to economic and social equity.

MEDICINE

Advanced medical knowledge and technology are changing the quality and length of human life in many places. Still, the question arises: can medical technology cure such diseases as cancer, AIDS, and senility?

AIDS

The current AIDS problem, transmitted through sexual contact and blood contamination, is a frightening example of the limits of medical knowledge. World conferences have been called, and concerted international medical efforts have been launched by the U.N. Still, a cure for HIV virus eludes medical science. It continues to infect large numbers of people around the globe. Public education aimed at prevention is still the main defense, but in underdeveloped and illiterate societies, educating the public is so difficult that there is fear their populations may be devastated in far worse proportions than even the recent famine in Africa. In the early 1990's, nearly two million cases had been diagnosed just in the U.S. Recent estimations predict 25% of Thailand's population may be infected by the year 2000.

GENETICS

In the next century, people can expect to live longer, healthier lives as medical scientists discover new genetic treatments for major disorders. Genetic research produced humulin, an artificial insulin for use by diabetics. Humulin is closer to human insulin than that derived from animals. The artificial virus to combat Lyme disease is a product of genetic research.

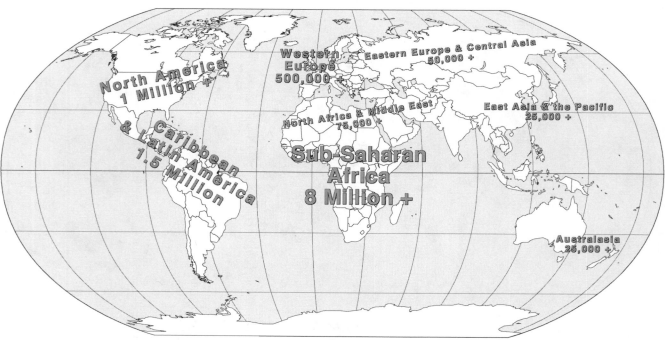

This location map shows the areas of the world where the retrovirus HIV, which causes AIDS, has had the greatest effect. Based on these 1993 statistics, the World Health Organization expresses real concern for the worldwide spread of the disease.

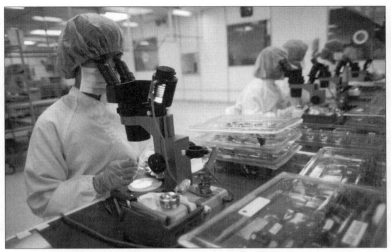
This research lab is working on the development of a vaccine against a potentially deadly strain of Hepatitis. *PhotoDisc Inc. 1994*

Still, the genetic frontier is a controversial area of medical research. It presents the power to manipulate genes and tamper with nature. Any power can be intentionally abused and unwittingly misused. For example, bovine growth hormones increase cows' milk production but make the animals more susceptible to disease. Dairy farmers protect their cows by increasing the use of antibiotics. The presence of these antibiotics in the milk and their being passed on to consumers is controversial. Technological progress is never purely positive.

PROHIBITIVE COSTS

Organ transplants have created a major breakthrough in surgery and the use of artificial parts in the human body is common today. Drug treatments will continue to unlock cures for terminal diseases. Problems not easily solved are astronomical health costs and ethical decisions concerning who will receive expensive medical treatment. High costs widen the gulf between the economic "haves" and "have nots" in the world.

TRANSPORTATION AND COMMUNICATION

Economic advancement requires sophisticated infrastructures. Faster, easier, more comfortable travel and vast communications networks controlled by powerful computers and laser beams are needed. The automobile remains a primary means of travel in the developed world. Today's advanced cars have more on-board electronics and pollution controls. Still, high speed rail, air, and water transportation is needed to move people and products and to reduce urban **gridlock** (enormous time-consuming traffic congestion).

In addition, in many corporate communication laboratories throughout the developed world, modern technology has created computers that talk, televisions that (with satellites) provide hundreds of channels, and telephones that are carried in pockets.

PhotoDisc Inc. 1994

PhotoDisc Inc. 1994

United States astronauts work from the cargo bay of the space shuttle during the repair of a satellite.   PhotoDisc Inc. 1994

As physicist Thomas Emerson stated, *"The limits won't be on technology but on peoples' imagination."* The challenge for the world's leaders will be finding a positive use for all of this creative knowledge.

SPACE EXPLORATION

Technology accelerated the Age of Exploration in the 17th Century. Twentieth Century technologies have developed a new frontier: space. Many scientists and historians predict that space exploration will carry Earth from its infancy to adulthood. It fosters new knowledge, products, and international cooperation. It has already unlocked secrets to help a resource depleted and strife-ridden world.

Through international cooperation, the resources of space can be used to create new-found wealth for all the Earth's people.

Although skeptics disagree, some claim advancements in space will avoid imposing negative effects on the environment in our world.

The people of our globe have a love-hate affair with technological advancement. They are both fascinated and horrified by the world that modern technology has shaped.

In *Megatrends*, John Naisbitt offers the optimistic view that a technological renaissance could free humankind from much of life's drudgery. The resulting economic boom could promote the highest standards of living in world history.

In *Preparing for the Twenty-First Century*, Paul Kennedy presents a more sobering view. He acknowledges that the rapid technological development is transforming economically advanced nations at a bewildering pace. Yet, he says the wealth and technology is of little help to LDCs. The great struggle with population pressures and environmental catastrophes is in the LDCs. Yet, their depleted resources discourage multinational corporations and other investors. Kennedy is pessimistic about the developed world's desire to sacrifice to help the LDCs. In the long run, technology may fall victim to human frailty. Political and economic apathy, ignorance, and insensitivity may ruin the promise of global technological progress.

VII. INTERACTION OF CULTURES
LANGUAGES

As the world becomes increasingly global in outlook, various cultures have significant impacts on others. Nowhere is this more obvious than in language. During the Age of Imperialism, the languages of Europe were taught in colonial possessions. Knowledge of them was a necessity for colonial inhabitants wishing economic, political, or social advancement. As a consequence, English is spoken by more Indians than any other language in that diverse country. Many people educated in former French and Portuguese possessions speak those languages.

After World War II, global communications in the form of radio, movies, and television accelerated the development of an almost international language. Words or terms such as "Levis" and "rock" are commonly used throughout the world. Technical language involving computers and electronic equipment of various types has entered many languages in the mother tongue of the country responsible for its development.

Increased communication in earlier eras led to the establishment of national languages. Today, it appears that an international language is developing in some fields.

INSTITUTIONS

Governments are often seen by people as vehicles for achieving progress. Colonies imitated Western styles of government after their independence. They hoped it could accelerate economic and social development. Many former colonial areas developed parliamentary systems modeled on those of Britain and France. Later, some found that their circumstances did not fit the system adopted.

Most young countries lacked skilled labor and capital to develop rapidly. Still, some groups in them felt democracy was too unstable. They sought firmer government control. Many younger nations' parliaments fell under military-backed dictatorial rule.

Other young countries drifted into socialist structures as government commandeered enterprises to manage resources. Kenya, for example, allows a broad degree of individual capitalist activity and investment. Yet, its neighbors, with greater government control of their economies, have not done as well. Since the collapse of the U.S.S.R., foreign investment in socialist economies increased. Hotels, offices, factories, and even fast-food franchises appear more frequently now in socialist countries.

TRADITION

Many countries want to increase the level of their technology. Yet, they face a dilemma of trying to maintain their traditional culture in the face of rapid change. This was a problem experienced by tsarist Russia under Peter the Great. It also triggered the Islamic Revolution in Iran in 1979.

Today, multinational corporations often nudge tradition aside for modernization. International trade is often a brutal contest with few rules. Time-honored local or regional traditions and regulations are ignored in the name of competition. Methods used by a global corporation to win customers in one place are repeated everywhere the corporation competes. For example, patents issued by national governments are copied and used elsewhere by competing multinationals. Countries sometimes try to protect investments by blocking export of technology others can use. This can lead to boycotts and sanctions by other nations, trade alliances, and multinationals. Preserving tradition and sovereignty is very difficult under wide-open, free-for-all conditions.

Commerce and communications foster **assimilation** (blending) of many customs and beliefs among regions and cultures. Some actions by the European Union (Common Market) illustrate this. The EU encourages a European cultural market. Clothing style is becoming globalized. High fashion designers select their inspiration from all historic periods and cultures. For example, the traditional British Victorian style of women's blouses and dresses is popular as are the fabric designs from African civilizations.

As more people come into contact with other cultures, increasing numbers in urban areas blend Western fashions with their own native styles. Purity of native fashions is usually retained for cultural ceremonies, but otherwise, assimilation is evident. Sports are especially internationalized. Baseball is enormously popular in Japan, tennis in the Czech Rep., gymnastics in Eastern Europe, and soccer in the U.S.A.

Religious beliefs are also spread easily in the modern world. Islamic fundamentalism is a force well beyond revolutionary Iran. It is evident in Saudi Arabia, Egypt, Afghanistan, and parts of Central Asia. Western churches seek to spread their doc-

trines as they send young missionaries to do humanitarian work in developing nations.

SUMMARY

All this cultural and technological change is truly astonishing. Still, it is not universal. Human rights are not enjoyed globally. For all the rhetoric about globalism, regions and nations vary. People in LDCs do not enjoy the quality of political or economic life of those in the developed nations. For many people, prospects for advancement in living standards are dim. Population growth and environmental problems could cause a decline in lifestyle in advanced nations in the future. The world is at a crucial point in its history. Decisions made locally and internationally in the next generation cannot assure human advancement. There are no guarantees. What is certain is that no one can isolate themselves from global events. Destiny is in the hands of those who learn and confront problems with courage, empathy, and common sense.

QUESTIONS

1 From 1945 into the 1990's, which was primarily responsible for keeping world peace?
  1 the Security Council of the United Nations
  2 many nations
  3 the United States and the Soviet Union
  4 Western Europe

2 Which is true of LDCs?
  1 They always follow the policies of the superpowers.
  2 They always vote as a unified bloc in the United Nations.
  3 Self-interest guides their loyalties.
  4 They take no responsibility for keeping world peace.

3 During the Cold War Era, the superpowers were unable to agree on
  1 questions involving nuclear tests
  2 limits on long range nuclear missiles
  3 Strategic Defense systems for outer space
  4 the permissible number of warheads

4 Since the end of World War II, means of communication have
  1 increased the possibility of global war
  2 increased similarities among people
  3 decreased internationalism
  4 decreased the spread of technology

5 Which is a major reason for higher birthrates in the LDCs?
  1 promotion of birth control devices
  2 religious objections to practicing birth control
  3 a highly educated population
  4 political leaders need large populations for military power

6   A major factor contributing to the rapid growth of urban centers in the 20th Century is
    1   the search for better economic opportunities
    2   the influence of village elders
    3   peoples' love of crowded conditions
    4   the development of the automobile

7   Many global issues such as pollution of the environment are a direct result of
    1   high unemployment
    2   a farm-based economy
    3   overpopulation
    4   a balance of world trade

8   Which of the following is a negative side of using pesticides and chemical fertilizers?
    1   They increase crop yields.
    2   They reduce the size of most vegetables.
    3   They may contaminate the soil.
    4   They encourage urban dwellers to move into farm country.

9   A major contributor to the creation of acid rain has been the
    1   underground nuclear testing
    2   burning of sulfuric coal
    3   emissions control testing of nations
    4   wood-burning stoves

10 In which world region has desertification caused widespread famine and death?
    1   Asia's Gobi Desert
    2   Africa's Sahel
    3   India's Punjab
    4   Australia's Outback

11 Which area of modern medical technology raises heated philosophical debates?
    1   artificial human organs
    2   genetic experimentation
    3   wonder drugs as cures for terminal diseases
    4   increasing life expectancy

12 Aside from overfishing many of our oceans, seas, and bays, humans also kill many shellfish through a process called
    1   anoxia
    2   pneumonia
    3   erosion
    4   deforestation

13 A major reason for the success of the Silicon Chip in today's computer revolution is
    1   its low cost
    2   its impressive large size
    3   its limited ability to store information
    4   the limited changes it can bring to human life

14 A negative aspect of the Green Revolution has been the
    1   production of too much food
    2   high cost of petrochemical fertilizers
    3   socialism in LDCs
    4   advancements in communications

15 The great struggle with population pressures and environmental catastrophes is in the LDCs. Why are some experts pessimistic about their chances of winning the struggle?
    1   Their depleted resources discourage multinational corporations and other investors.
    2   They overproduce food.
    3   They burn too much sulfuric coal.
    4   They vote as a bloc in the United Nations.

ESSAYS

1   Discuss the effect *three* of the following 20th Century events have had on the Earth's environment.

    •   The nuclear accident (1986) at the Chernobyl plant in Ukraine (former U.S.S.R.)
    •   Desertification in the Sahel
    •   British industrial air pollutants causing acid rain
    •   Deforestation of the Amazon rain forest of Brazil

2   Discrimination has been a problem faced by many groups of people throughout the world.

   a   Identify *two* groups that have experienced discrimination, and show how they *each* experienced discrimination. (Include the location, time period, and historical events.)

   b   Describe a specific action taken by *one* group to overcome the discrimination.

   c   Discuss how successful the group was in overcoming discrimination.

3   A definite economic gap exists between the developed nations and LDCs. Describe *three* major factors which have contributed to this problem, and give *one* suggestion that might help narrow the imbalance.

4   In 1948, the United Nations General Assembly unanimously approved the *Universal Declaration of Human Rights*. The Declaration included the following rights:

   •   Every person has the right to leave any country, including his/her own, and to return to that country.
   •   No one shall be subjected to torture or to cruel, inhuman, or degrading treatment.
   •   Everyone has the right to work and protection against unemployment.
   •   No one's basic rights shall be violated on account of sex, race, or religion.
   •   No one shall be subjected to arbitrary arrest, detention, or exile.

   a   Select *three* of the above human rights. For *each*, discuss a specific example of a nation's violation of that right since 1948. Use a different nation for each right violated.

   b   Discuss *one* reason why the United Nations has been unable to protect the rights listed in the Universal Declaration.

5   Many problems can be considered global because they affect people and nations beyond any one nation's borders.

   •   Scarcity of energy sources
   •   Lack of investment capital
   •   Spread of nuclear arms
   •   Terrorism
   •   Poverty

   a   Choose *three* of the problems listed above. For *each*, show how the problem is global in nature.

   b   Discuss an attempt to deal with *each* of the problems analyzed in *a*.

6   Technology has opened up new frontiers for humankind in the 20th Century. Select *three* areas listed below. For *each*, describe a significant benefit that technology can give to the world's peoples.

   •   Computer Revolution
   •   Green Revolution
   •   Medical Breakthrough
   •   Infrastructure
   •   Space Exploration

7   The development of a global perspective has been increasingly apparent in many fields since the end of World War II.

                    Fields
   •   Arms Control
   •   Technology
   •   Customs and beliefs

   a   Identify one way in which *each* of the above fields has been affected by the global outlook.

   b   Explain how the "globalizing" of these fields will affect the future.

UNIT TEN: THE WORLD TODAY ASSESSMENT

ISSUE: PERSPECTIVES ON GLOBAL PROBLEMS

This two-part assessment offers individual research and oral reporting opportunities.

STUDENT TASK

In consultation with teacher, choose a global problem, research it, and present an oral report to the class.

DETAILED PROCEDURES

Part One:
Select a problem from the list compiled by the teacher. Use recent magazine articles to develop a set of notes for an oral report. Notes will be reviewed by the teacher. (Include list of articles in proper bibliographic form.)

Part Two:
Present an organized oral report on the problem in class. The report should:

- explain why a problem exists

- discuss the global effects

- assess possible solutions. (Instructor may wish to employ peer rating for this part of the evaluation.)

EVALUATION

The scoring grid next to the evaluation items (on the following page) was left blank intentionally. Choice of appropriate category terms is the decision of the instructor. Selection of terms such as "minimal," "satisfactory," and "distinguished" can vary with this assessment. The table on page 10 offers additional suggestions for scoring descriptors that might be inserted in the blank grids.

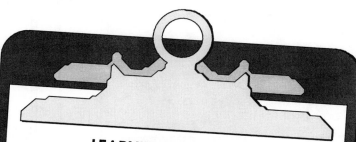

LEARNING STANDARDS

Students should:

- Understand that peoples' values, practices, and traditions are diverse, yet they face the same global challenges.

- Understand that different national, ethnic, religious, racial, socioeconomic, and gender groups have varied perspectives on the same events and issues.

- Analyze and evaluate differing views of historic, social, cultural, economic, and political events, eras, ideas, and issues.

- Analyze and evaluate the effects of human, technological, and natural activities on societies.

- Understand that interdependence requires personal and collective responsibility for the local and global environment.

- Present ideas both in writing and orally in clear, concise, and proper fashion.

- Monitor, reflect upon, and improve their work.

Part One: Research and Articles' List

Table on page 10 offers suggestions for scoring descriptors.

Evaluation Item a Do research notes define the problem?	Category 1	Category 2	Category 3	Category 4	Category 5
Evaluation Item b Do research notes discuss global effects?	Category 1	Category 2	Category 3	Category 4	Category 5
Evaluation Item c Do research notes evaluate solutions?	Category 1	Category 2	Category 3	Category 4	Category 5
Evaluation Item d Do research notes include an article list in the proper bibliographic form?	Category 1	Category 2	Category 3	Category 4	Category 5

Part Two: Oral Presentation

Note: Part Two evaluation is based on combined peer and teacher ratings.

Evaluation Item a Content: Does student express ideas clearly for audience?	Category 1	Category 2	Category 3	Category 4	Category 5
Evaluation Item b Content: Does student explain the global meaning of the problem?	Category 1	Category 2	Category 3	Category 4	Category 5
Evaluation Item c Content: Does student offer and explain the possible solutions for the problem?	Category 1	Category 2	Category 3	Category 4	Category 5
Evaluation Item d Delivery: Is student enthusiastic?	Category 1	Category 2	Category 3	Category 4	Category 5
Evaluation Item e Delivery: Is student aware of audience (eye contact, responsive)?	Category 1	Category 2	Category 3	Category 4	Category 5

ADMINISTRATIVE GUIDELINES

1. Survey library resources. Discuss project with librarian and reserve library time for student research.

2. Provide a list of global problems according to this chapter. A brief list of major library periodicals might be added.

3. Set aside brief time slots each day to check students' note taking progress.

4. Review elements of effective oral reporting with class and explain peer rating system. Decide weighting of student ratings for total evaluation.

5. Set up a time schedule for oral presentations (limit number per day).

6. Collect student rating sheets.

The Appendices

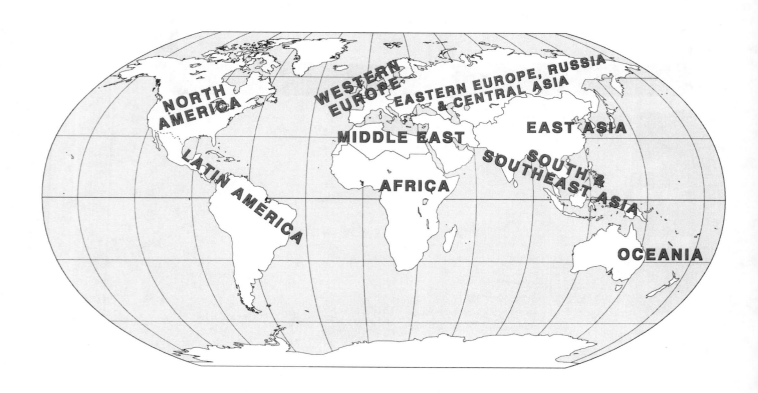

NORTH AMERICA

LATIN AMERICA

WESTERN EUROPE

EASTERN EUROPE, RUSSIA & CENTRAL ASIA

MIDDLE EAST

AFRICA

EAST ASIA

SOUTH & SOUTHEAST ASIA

OCEANIA

CONTENTS

GLOBAL CONCEPTS
Definitions and Examples

Variation or alteration of an existing situation...

- Independence for India [70-73]
- Effects of the Crusades [320]
- French Revolution [329-331]
- Mao's Revolutionary China [108-110]

Determination of a preference for a particular idea or system, usually applies to economic decisions...

- Perestroika in U.S.S.R. & Russia [411]
- Israel's mixed system [295]
- Deng Xiaoping's Four Modernizations [114-115]

Recognition of the duties, rights, and privileges of a member of a state or nation...

- Direct democracy under Pericles in Athens [311]
- Forces that have kept political participation from developing in Latin America [203-204]

Combination of the common concepts, habits, art, and institutions of a group of people...

- Influence of Confucian philosophy on Chinese civilization [97]
- Russian contributions to the arts [389-390]
- Golden Age of Muslim Culture [279]

Characterization of differences between many groups or situations...

- Variation of South American landforms leads to a variety of life styles, crops, and separate cultures [188-192]
- Geographic factors have promoted diversity in Western Europe [308-311]

Identification with other people's problems and points of view...

- Spanish missionary priests sought to understand and act to alleviate mistreatment of African slaves and Amerindians [199]
- Industrial Era reforms for workers [334-335]

GLOBAL CONCEPTS
Definitions and Examples

Integration and sharing of the ideas and experiences of others...
- Force of Nationalism in Russia, Central Asia [404]
- Myths and legends in African history [23-24]

Position of being mutually influenced or controlled by similar forces...
- Australia and New Zealand needed political and economic support from U.S. & Europe in Cold War Era [180]
- Marshall Plan aided post-World War II recovery in Europe [354]
- NAFTA correlating Canadian/Mexican/U.S. trade [253-254, 258]

Administration of laws in a fair and reasonable manner; equitable behavior...
- Romans' Laws of the Twelve Tables [314]
- Napoleonic Code (Code Civil) [331]

Execution of a willingness and ability to act decisively in situations...
- Japan's pre-World War II expansion [131]
- Rise of the Nazi State [342-344]

Limitation of resources necessitating allocation and choices...
- Japan's dependence on other nations because of lack of critical petroleum and other natural resources [141-142]
- Middle East's economic development [294]

Application of scientific principles for productive uses...
- India's future tied to technological development [81]
- Europe's industrialization and major inventions [333-334]

WORLD ISSUES
Definitions and Examples

Economic and political conflicts and accommodations often have far-reaching consequences because of the intricate network of global relationships.
- Europe and the prelude to World War I [337]
- Oceania and the post-World War II changes [164-167]
- Arab – Israeli Conflicts [286-288]
- Cold War politics in Europe [361-364]
- Discussion of changing political power structures in today's world [434-36]

Overpopulation not only has serious implications for the nation or region in which it occurs, but also strains resources of others. Conflicts arise as crowded nations seek more territory, or as people migrate to more sparsely populated areas.
- African problems [44]
- India's population problems [73]
- Discussion of world population pressures [428-431]

Forces of industrialization, urbanization, and environmental depletion reveal inadequate food and resource distribution.
- Hunger in Africa [45]
- Poverty in Latin American cities [207-208]
- Discussion of world hunger [430]

Resettlement of groups uprooted by wars, natural disasters, and industrialization causes stress and conflict throughout the globe.
- Transition and urbanization [439-440]
- European refugees help establish Israeli state after WW II [283-84, 286-87]
- Palestinians [284, 288]
- Kulaks under Stalin [397

Technological progress brings increased contact among people. It forces re-evaluation of traditional lifestyles. A mixture of systems for making economic decisions has resulted from international contacts.
- India's economic development [80-82]
- Latin American development [210-214]
- A mixed economy in Israel [295-296]
- The economic conversion from communism in Russia [411-415]
- Discussion of economic development in today's world [432-434]

Devastation of the land and sea by natural and human forces has repercussions beyond a particular region because the scarcity of critical resources intensifies competition for those resources elsewhere.

- Desertification of Sahel in Africa [43, 45-46]
- European efforts and the Ruhr Association [350-351]
- Discussion of 1992 Earth Summit [441]

Just and fair claims to natural, traditional, or legal powers, freedoms, and privileges are not shared by all. As international contact broadens, common expectations for human decency and justice rise.

- Apartheid in South Africa [37]
- Jews in Nazi Germany [342, 344]
- Pro-democracy Movements in Eastern Europe [406-407]
- Stalin forced collectivization in Ukraine [397]
- Discussion of human rights in today's World [442-444]

Interaction of economic needs and desires demonstrates the interdependence among nations.

- OPEC influences [300-301]
- Economic development of the Four Dragons of the Pacific Rim and Japan's trade [172-174]
- Discussion of economic development and world trade [432-434]

Transfer of decision-making power among groups alters internal and external structure.

- U.S. & Post-World War II Japan [136-137]
- Mao's Great Leap Forward [108-110]
- Evolution of British Parliamentary system [347-349]
- Power of the Communist Party in totalitarian U.S.S.R. [396-401]

Competition of industrially developed and LDCs for limited supplies of fossil fuels creates global political and economic strains. The danger and limitations of artificially produced fuels create worldwide stresses.

- OPEC and Petro Politics [300-301]

As the use of violence as a political weapon to intimidate others becomes commonplace, governments and individuals are drawn into issues that were once only national or regional in scope.

- PLO [287-288]
- Anti-Semitism [342]
- Discussion of human rights in today's world [436]

GLOSSARY OF TERMS
With Page References

Abbasid (8th C. Shi'ite revolt set up separate Muslim region in Persia), 279-280

Abolitionist movement (19th C. anti-slavery movement in Western Europe & U.S.), 31

Aborigine (first prehistoric inhabitants of Australia), 155, 159

Abraham (ancient Hebrew prophet), 277

Absolutism (concentration and exercise of ruling power usually by a monarch), 324-327, 381

Abu Bakr (7th C.; father-in-law of Muhammad; first Caliph, religious leader of Muslims), 278

Abu Jafar al-Mansur (second Caliph, established Islamic capital at Baghdad, 8th C. A.D.), 279

Acid rain pollutants that travel in precipitation), 437

Aconcagua (highest peak in Andes), 189

Act of Supremacy (Anglicanism official religion of England, 1534), 323

Afghanistan, 87, 118, 268, 298-299, 420, 431

Africa: 18-55; agriculture, 24, 43, 45-46; colonial exploitation, 31-33; culture, 23-27; economics, 43-47 [economic case study examples, Zaire-38, Nigeria-39, Kenya-40, life in transition, 41; nationalism, 35-36; population, 44; physical features, 20-23; slave trade, 30-31; role in world affairs, 49-51; unifying influences, 24-27, 33; urban growth, 46

African National Congress (ANC; South African civil rights party), 37

African Kingdoms (Ghana, Mali, Songhai, ancient states had high cultural and economic development), 24-25 [chart], 29 [map]

Afrikaaners (Boers, original Dutch colonists in South Africa), 36-37

Age of Discovery (period of global exploration and colonization by Europeans in 15th and 16th C.), 158, 197, 327-328

Age of Enlightenment (18th C. European age of scientific and philosophical development), 31, 159, 328-329, 385

Age of Imperialism (19th C. African and Asian colonization by European industrial nations for raw materials), 31-33, 158-162, 336-337, 448

Agenda 21 (1992 U.N. Earth Summit document; implements *Rio Declaration*'s global environmental principles), 441

Agrarian (farm-based economy and lifestyle), 82, 429

Agronomists, (agricultural economists), 430

AIDS (epidemic of Acquired Immunodeficiency Syndrome from retro virus HIV), 446 [+map]

Akbar (Mughal ruler of India [1555-1605] began golden age), 61, 63

Albania, 378, 379, 388

Alexander I (Tsar, Napoleonic Era; d. 1825), 331, 387, 388

Alexander II (Tsar; emancipated serfs, established Duma; d. 1881), 388-389

Alexander the Great (Hellenistic conqueror & unifier of ancient Middle East, d. 323 B.C.), 61, 312

All-India Muslim League (Bengali independence movement; 1906), 66-67

Allah (Islamic name for God), 277

Alliance for Progress (U.S. assistance policy for Latin America in 1960's), 216

Alluvial soil (rich in minerals from mountains' drainage), 58, 268, 269

Alps (mt. range in Central Europe), 309 [+map]; (also New Zealand's South Island mt range), 155

Amazon River (massive basin in the center of South America), 191

American Revolution (as extension of European Enlightenment thinking), 200, 237, 240, 242; 329

Amerindian (also Native American or American Indian; descendants of original North Asian groups migrating to North America), 192, 193-195, 229, 231-234, 236

Amin Dada, Idi (Ugandan dictator; massacred thousands bet. 1966 to 1985), 443

Amritsar (Sikh holy city in Punjab Province of NE India), 73

Amulets and charms (ornaments used in African religions to spiritually protect individuals), 25

Amur River (river in East Asia, forms disputed part of Russian - Chinese border), 375

Analects (Confucius' sayings - guide to correct behavior), 97

Anatolia (central plateau of Turkey), 268

Anasazi (Amerindian civilization of southwestern U.S.; cliff dwellers; ancestors of Pueblo People), 233-234

Anatomy of Revolution (Crane Brinton: examines patterns of modern national revolutions), 330

Ancestor worship (in African religions, forbearers are considered a living part of the tribal community), 24-25

Andes Mountains (major north-south cordillera of South America), 189, 195

Andropov, Yuri (succeeded Brezhnev as U.S.S.R. leader, 1983-84), 399

Anglican Church (Church of England), 238, 323, 326

Animism (belief that objects contain a spirit), 50, 126

Anoxia (oxygen depletion), 440

Anthropology (study of origins and development of human culture), 23

Anti-imperialism (strong desire for freedom from foreign control), 31, 35

Anti-Semitism (anti-Jewish feeling), 342, 350

Apartheid (South African policy of total racial separation), 37, 365, 443

APEC (Asian-Pacific Economic Conference; promotes trade cooperation for greater Pacific Rim), 145, 180, 258 [illust.]

Appeasement (policy of giving in to aggressors to avoid war), 346

Aquino, Benigno, (Philippine leader, assassinated 1983), 77

Aquino, Corazon (deposed Marcos regime; President of Philippine Republic, 1986-1992), 77

Arab-Israeli Conflicts, 286-288, 289, 298

Arabian Nights (collection of stories told at the Caliph's Court in the 8th and 9th C.), 279

Arab Nationalism (movement to unify Arab nations), 284

Arab Socialism (improvement of the social and economic conditions for all Arabs), 289, 295

Arable (land useful for agriculture), 110, 294

Arafat, Yasir (Chief spokesman & negotiator of Palestine Liberation Organization), 288

Architecture: African, 27; Lat. Amer., 194, 217; Greek, 311; Roman, 313 [photo], 314 [photo]; 314; Modern, 351

Archeology (study of human existence by means of its physical remains), 23

Archipelago (island chain: peaks of undersea mt. ranges), 60, 76, 123

Argentina, 188 [map], 189, 191, 205

Ariel (Jose Rodo, modern Latin American literature), 217

Aristide, Jean–Bertrand (President of Haiti, overthrown 1991 by military junta, restored to power by U.S. military forces in 1994), 216

Aristocracy (government by a small, privileged class), 203, 313

Aristotle (Greek philosopher, d. 322 B.C.), 311-12

Aristophanes (ancient Greek dramatist, d. 380), 312

Armada (Spanish naval fleet), 197, 324

Arts: African 26-27; European, 321-322, 351; Latin Am., 217; North Am., 260-261; Oceanian, 155-156; Russian, 389-390, 401

Articles of Confederation (first organized government for U.S. 1778-1789 replaced by *U.S. Constitution*), 240, 404

Aryans (early conquerors of India, c. 1500-500 B.C.), 61

Ashanti (ancient African kingdom), 29

Ashikaga Shogunate (feudal Japanese rulers, 1338-1567), 127

Ashley Report (mine safety in British Industrial Revolution), 334

"Asia for the Asiatics" (desire to rid Asia of European & Amer. influences), 345

Asoka (3rd C.B.C. Mauryan ruler of India), 61, 63

Assimilation (being absorbed into a new culture), 213, 255, 449

Association of Southeast Asia (Economic council formed in 1961 to make regional economic plans), 169

Asturias, Miguel (Guatemalan writer–Cent. Amer. Indian culture), 217

Aswan High Dam (Egypt controversial project on the Nile River under Nasser), 270, 289

Ataturk ("Father of Turks," honorary name given Mustafa Kemal, WW I hero who established the Republic of Turkey in 1923), 284

Atheism (belief that there is no God), 400, 420

Atlantic Age (world trade and commerce dominated by Atlantic nations 15th-20th C.), 152

Atlantic Charter (Allies World War I aims became basis for United Nations Charter in 1945), 35

Atlas Mountains (North Africa), 20, 21 [map]; 269 [map]

Atomic Bomb (dropping by U.S. on Japan), 134

Atwood, Margaret (20th C. Canadian author, *Handmaiden's Tale*), 260

Audiencas (crown-appointed advisory to viceroys in colonial Lat. Am.), 199, 237

Cairo, Egypt, 270
Caliph (title for successor to Muhammad as leader of Islam), 278-280
Calvin, John (Swiss theologian, Eur. Protestant Reformation, c. 1560's), 322-323
Cambodia (S.E. Asia mainland nation), 59, 74, 75, 86, 87, 443
Camp David Accords (1979 Middle East peace agreements), 287-288
Campesinos (paid laborers, tenant farmers, or peasants of Lat. America), 211
Canada, (North American democratic nation; 2nd largest country in landmass), 222-265
Canadian Council, The (Canada's national endowment for the performing arts), 260
Canadian Shield (largely uninhabited tundra / taiga regions of Arctic Canada; mineral wealth), 225
Cape Colony (Dutch colony of South Africa, 1652-1806), 36
Cape-to-Cairo Railroad (Cecil Rhodes project for linking British territories in E. Africa), 37
Capetown (capital of South Africa), 37
Capitalism (economic structure based on free [private] enterprise; also free market system), 81, 328, 396, 410
Captain-General (colonial governors of Portuguese Brazil), 199
Caribbean, 188, 192, 224
Caribbean Basin Initiative (CBI; 1980's U.S. agreement to aid Caribbean nations' economic development), 211
Carnuaba (Brazilian rainforest palm by-product used in wax), 191
Carpathians (mountain range crosses Eastern Europe), 377-378 [+map]
Carranza, Venustiano (early 20th C. Mexican statesman), 204-205
Cartel (combination of economic units to limit competition), 50, 294
Carter, Jimmy (U.S. Pres.; 1970's: Panama Canal and Mid-East Camp David peace agreements, Haiti crisis negotiator), 207, 257, 287-288,
Cartier, Jaques (16th C. explorer, made France's claims to St. Lawrence in Canada), 236 [chart]
Castellanos, Rosario (Mexican author, themes of Euro-Indian cultural clashes), 261
Castes (rigid Hindu system of hereditary social groupings dictating one's rank and occupation), 62, 72
Castro, Fidel (Cuban communist leader), 206, 216, +WT

Catherine the Great (Catherine II, absolutist Russian Tsarina, 1762-1796; destroyed nation of Poland), 385-386
Catholic Counter Reformation (Church movement in the 16th C. offset the Protestant Reformation), 199, 323
Caspian Sea (large environmentally impacted, lake in central Asia;), 375-376
Caucasians (members of the white race), 192
Caudillo (Latin America; local ruler with dictatorial power), 204, 205, 211, 245
Cavaliers (king's supporters, English Puritan Revolution, c. 1650), 326
Ceausescu, Nicolae (ruthless communist dictator of Romania, 1970's to execution in 1990), 419
Central America, 188, 205 [map], 224
Central American Federation (post-independence attempt at unification, c. 1820), 203
Central Intelligence Agency (CIA–U.S. espionage network), 206
Central Treaty Organization (CENTO: multi-lateral defense agreement with Middle East and British, c. 1950's), 86
Chad (north central Africa, Saharan nation) 435; Chad Basin, 20
Chamorro, Violeta Barrios de (Nicaraguan president, 1990, unseated Sandinistas), 206
Champlain, Samule de (17th C. explorer, founded Quebec, Governor of New France, 1608), 237
Champollian, Jean Francois (18th C.Fr. archaeologist found Rosetta Stone), 272
Chao Phraya (river basin in Thailand), 60
Charlemagne (8th C. A.D, leader of the Franks; Holy Roman Empire), 315
Charles I (British king, dethroned & beheaded in Puritan Revolution, mid-1600's), 326
Charles II (British king, restored to monarchy after Cromwell's death in 1658), 326
Charter companies (private trading enterprises licensed by government; outposts became bases for colonies), 31
Chartist movement (19th C. movement by British workers to demand the suffrage for themselves), 334
Chauvinism (nationalist extremism in 19th and 20th C. Germany), 332
Chavez, Carlos (Mexican composer), 261
Cheka (tsarist secret police, then the 1st Soviet secret police; later called OGPU in the 1920's, NKVD in the 1930's, MGB in the 1940's, then KGB), 388, 395

Culture (a people's whole way of living: language, traditions, customs, institutions, religions, and folkways), 12-13

Cultural diffusion (cultural patterns spreading from one people to other), 12, 271

Cultural diversity (existence of many cultural groups in a region), 188, 192, 229-230, 260-261, 270-271, 399-400

Cultural pluralism (also cultural diversity), 255

Cultural Revolution (internal power struggle in Maoist China in the mid-1960's), 109-110

Cuneiform (ancient Sumerian system of writing), 272

Cyrillic alphabet (modified form of the Greek alphabet basis for Russian and some Slavic languages), 275, 380

Czar (see "tsar")

Czechoslovakia, 346, 363, 379, 405 [+map], 406, 418, 419

Czech Republic (western half of former Czechoslovakia, independent 1992), 378, 379 [+map], 406-407, 414 [chart], 449

Daladier, Edouard (French premier represented France at the 1938 Munich Conference appeasing Hitler), 346

da Gama, Vasco (15th C. Portuguese explorer; reached India via Cape Horn in Africa in 1498), 327

Daimyo ("Great Lords" of Japan's feudal era, 1300-1600), 128

Dante (Italian Renaissance writer: *Divine Comedy*), 322 [chart]

Danton, Georges Jacques (leader of the radical Committee of Public Safety during the French Revolution's Reign of Terror), 330

Danube River (major European trade route), 309, 379

Dario, Ruben (Nicaraguan poet), 217

Dark Ages (Early European Medieval period; 500 to 1000 A.D.), 315

"Dark Continent" (name popular in 19th C. Europe for Africa because its vast interior sections were unknown to European colonial powers), 20

Darwin, Charles (19th C. British naturalist, artist, and biological theorist on evolution; *Origin of Species*, 1859), 336

Das Kapital (Marx's 1867 elaboration of communist philosophy), 335-336 [+chart]

da Vinci, Leonardo (central figure of Italian Renaissance), 322 [+chart]

"Day of Infamy" (President Franklin Roosevelt's reference to the Japanese attack on U.S. naval forces at Pearl Harbor in 1941), 133

Death Valley (lowest point No. Amer.), 227

Deccan Plateau (occupies most of the peninsula area of India and holds much mineral wealth), 58-59

Decembrist Revolt (a palace coup d'état against the Tsar in 1825), 388

Declaration of Independence (U.S. revolutionary document by Thomas Jefferson reflected the ideas of John Locke), 240, 329

Declaration of Rights of Man (Thomas Paine's French Revolution document justified overthrow of monarchy with Enlightenment ideas), 330 [chart]

Default (cannot make debt payments), 213

Deforestation (over-cutting of timber resources), 438

Deists (Eur. Enlightenment philosophy: God established the laws governing the universe, and then left it to run according to established natural laws), 328-329

de Gaulle, Gen. Charles (French WW II leader; president in the 1950's and early 1960's), 367

de Klerk, F.W. (Prime Minister of Republic of South Africa, 1989-1994), 37

Democratic socialism (mixed economic systems in European nations with extensive welfare systems), 355

Democritus (Greek thinker who expounded elementary ideas about the basic composition of matter), 312

Demographic maps, 11

Deng Xiaoping, (reformist Chinese leader after Mao), 111, 114-115

de Niero, Alváro de Mendàna (16th C. Port. explorer, discovered Solomon Is. in Pacific), 158

Denmark, 310

de Quiriós, Pedro Fernandez (16th C. Port. explorer, discovered New Hebrides Is. and New Guinea in Pacific), 158

De Rosas, Juan Manuel (Argentine dictator, 1829-1852), 205

Desertification (loss of available land to the desert), 45-46, 438

Desert Shield / Desert Storm, Operation (see Persian Gulf conflict), 292

Deserts (climatic classification having little or no rainfall), 21-23, 268-270

Dependent states (colonies), 188

Détente (lessened diplomatic tension), 399, 436

Dharma (sacred duty one owes to family and caste), 62, 65

Diaspora (dispersion of the Jews from Palestine into world, c.70 A.D.), 273

Diaz, Porfirio (Mexico dictator, 1876-1911), 204, 245

Dictatorship of the Proletariat (Marxist dogma that indicates working classes will eventually rule society for the benefit of all), 336, 392

Dien Bien Phu (final defeat of French colonialism in Vietnam, 1954), 74, 364

Diet (two-house legislature of Japan), 136

Dinaric Alps (mountain chain in Yugoslavia and Albania), 378

Diocletian (Emperor who divided Roman Empire into 2 parts, 3rd C. A.D.), 274

Direct democracy (citizens having direct say in the making of decisions), 311

Dissenters (views conflict with established institutions; see dissidents), 238

Dissidents (those who disagree with institutional authority), 401, 402, 420, 443

Divesting (termination of investments in South Africa enterprises as an economic protest against apartheid policy), 37, 44, 51

Divine right (absolute power coming from God), 240, 324

Divine Rulers (African chieftans considered lesser gods or priests), 25

Division of Oregon Territory (1846 British-U.S. treaty, border at 49º N lat.), 259 [chart]

Dneiper River (river system in western Russia and Ukraine), 375

"Dollar Diplomacy" (interventionist U.S.- Latin American Policy of early 20th C. based on protection of commercial investment), 216

Dome of the Rock Mosque (Islamic shrine in Jerusalem), 279 [photo]

Domestic system (commercial production done in homes and coordinated by an entrepreneur), 328

Dominican Republic, 216

"Domino Theory" (communist victory in one small, weak state would lead to other nations falling), 86 [illust.]

Don River (river system in western Russia, Transcaucasia), 375

Doric columns (Ancient Greece), 312

Drakensberg Mountains (Southern Africa), 20, 21 [map]

Dubcek, Alexander (leader of the Communist Party of Czechoslovakia, c.1968), 363

Dubos, Rene (American biologist), 437, 442

Duma (national legislative body under tsars in 19th and 20th C.), 389

Dumping (international trade war tactic; increasing supply to drive price down and undermine competition), 80, 181

Earth Summit (1992 U.N. sponsored global meeting on environmental issues), 439, 441-442

Eastern Europe: physical features, 377-379; natural resources, 379; people, 380; history 386-388, 405-407; religion 418-419; economic conditions, 414, communism, 418-420

Easter Island (E. Pacific), 152, 155, 167, 181

Easter Rebellion (1916 uprising against British, leading to independence for Ireland), 349

Eastern and Russian Orthodox (Catholic) Church, 275, 315, 320, 380 [+photo], 383, 384, 386, 400, 405

ECAFE (Post-World War II U.N. comission for Asia and Far East) 169

Ecology (preserving the natural environment), 142

Economic nationalism (stimulation of internal development using government policies to eliminate outside competition), 213, 250

Ecuador, 192 [+photos]

Ecumenism (movement to seek unity among different religions), 350

Edict of Milan (granted freedom of worship to all Christians in Roman Empire, 313 A.D.), 274

Edo (center of Japan's Tokugawa government, later called Tokyo), 128

Ejidos (Mexican government collective farms in 1940's), 251

Egypt (called "Gift of the Nile"), 268, 270-272, 287-288, 289, 294 [map], 295

Eightfold Path (Buddhism's basic concepts), 62

El Dorado (Spain's conquistadores explored the New World seeking this mythical city of gold), 198

El Salvador, 211 [photo]

Elizabeth I (absolute monarch of England in 16th C., established the nation as a power in Europe), 324, 325

Emancipation Act (1861, Tsar Alexander II abolished Russian serfdom), 389

Embargo (refusal to sell or trade), 133, 300

Emerson, Thomas (American physicist), 448

Empress Dowager (ruler of China in late 19th and early 20th C. under Western imperialists influence), 103

Enclosure Acts (British farm lands fenced for pasture purposes), 328

Encomiendas (vast Latin American plantations), 198, 199, 211, 238, 243

England (see Great Britain, or United Kingdom)

Engels, Frederick (collaborator with Karl Marx on *Communist Manifesto*, 1848), 335

English Channel (narrow strait separates the British Isles from the European mainland), 308 [+map]

Enlightened despot (tyrant who uses autocratic power for the benefit of the people), 385

Enlightenment (intellectual movement in 17th and 18th C. Europe), 159, 240, 328-329 [+chart]; 385, 388

Environment (the habitat or setting in which people live), 11

Environmental concerns (problems over deterioration of the natural ecology), 45-46, 350-351, 437-442

Erasmus (Renaissance writer, *In Praise of Folly*), 322

Erikson, Leif (early Scandinavian explorer, expeditions to North America, c. 1000 A.D.), 236

Estates General (French Parliament under Bourbon monarchs), 329-330

Ethiopia, 31, 51

Ethnocentrism (viewing all cultures as inferior to one's own) 40, 96

Euphrates River, 269, 270, 269, 271, 272, 273 [map]

EURATOM (European Atomic Energy Community; post-WW II consortium of Western European nations to deal with nuclear power management), 357

European Coal and Steel Community (1951 co-op plan [R. Schuman, Fr.] by 5 W. European nations; forerunner of "Common Market"/European Union), 169, 357

European Community (EC; see renamed European Union [1994]; originally "Common Market")

European Russia (extends from the western border to the Ural Mountains - dividing line between Europe and Asia), 375

European Union (originally the "Common Market," then the European Community; ongoing attempt to unify European nations' trade and commerce), 43, 49, 169, 181, 258 [+ illust.], 357, 359 [+chart], 361, 435

Excommunication (depriving a person of church membership), 318

Explorers (Age of Discovery 15th and 16th C.), 158, 197 [+chart], 236 [+chart], 327

Extended Families (three or more generations under one roof), 40

Extraterritoriality (foreigners not subject to a host country's laws), 102

*F*actory Act (1833, protection for British workers), 334

Family: group associations, 24; clans, 25; nuclear, extended, 40

Family Planning Program (India), 72

Family Responsibility System (China; began in 1981, allows the peasants some produce to be sold for profit), 114

FAO (Food and Agricultural Organization, U.N. agency fighting hunger), 430

Faza (8th C. A.D. Kenyan city-state), 39

Fazendas (Brazilian ranches), 199

Federal Republic of Germany (official name for West Germany before reunification in 1989; official name of unified Germany, 1990), 362

Federation of Malaya, 76

Fertile Crescent (Middle East region between the Tigris and Euphrates Rivers considered to be the Cradle of Civilization), 269, 273 [map]

Feudalism (landholding-based lord / vassal economic-political-social system), in medieval Europe, 315-317; in Russia, 381, 383; in Japan (1185-1600), 126-128

Fichte, Johann Gottlieb (1762-1814, early theorist on German nationalism), 332

Fief (self-sufficient feudal manor granted by a lord to a vassal), 316

Finland, 310

First French Empire (Napoleonic Empire, c.1800-1815), 331

Five Human Relationships (basic Confucian structure), 97 [chart]

Five Pillars (basic beliefs and duties of Muslim faith), 62, 277

Five Year Plans (government command in socialist economies [as opposed to free market], India, 81; China, 109, 113-114; U.S.S.R., 397, 409. 410

Food shortage (economic problems of India), 81-82 [chart]

"Four Dragons of the Pacific Rim" (nickname for newly developed economies of Singapore, Hong Kong, Taiwan, and South Korea), 172-174, 432, 433

"Four Modernizations" (revision of China's economic priorities under Deng Xiaoping), 111, 114

Four Noble Truths (basic beliefs of Buddhism), 62

Fourteen Points, The (WW I peace plan for Europe drawn up by U.S. President Wilson, 1918), 338

Fowke, Edith (Canadian writer-editor, *Tales Told in Canada*), 260

Fragmentation (societal divisions by regional culture and geographic barriers)

France: 283 [map], 308 [+map], 324-325, 327, 328, 329-331, 336, 337, 338, 346, 349, 355-357, 359, 364, 365, 366, 367, 435, 449; & Africa, 50; & S.E. Asia, 67-68, 73-74, 75, 86; & Latin America, 200, 204; & Oceania, 160 [+chart], 162, 166 [chart], 167, 180; and Russia, 388

Franco-Prussian War (1871; Bismarck used conflict enhance prestige of new German state), 333 [+ chart], 336, 345

Franks (people of the central and western sections of France in the 8th Century A.D.), 315

Franz Ferdinand, Archduke (heir to Austrian throne; 1914 assassination fomented WW I), 337, 391

Free market systems (economy that operates according to the relationship of supply and demand), 81, 409, 411

French Community; (also French Union; retained ties with former colonies; similar to British Commonwealth), 50, 180, 364

French Revolution (rebellion against Bourbon monarchy c. 1789 transformed the country into a republic), 240, 329-330, 331, 332

FSLN (Sandinistas national liberation front - Nicaraguan communists), 206

Fuehrer, der (Fuhrer, German title for leader used by Hitler), 344

Fuentes, Carlos (Mexican writer), 261

Fuji (large Japanese —owned multinational corp.), 141

Fujiwara family (ruled Japan from the 10th-12th C.), 125

Gadsden Purchase (U.S. bought territory in S.W. AZ & NM from Mexico for rail construction, 1853) 243 [map], 260 [chart]

Gandhi, Indira (Indian Prime Minister: 1966-1984), 73

Gandhi, Mohandas (non-violent Indian independence movement leader, assassinated 1948), 31, 66-67, 70, 71

Gandhi, Rajiv (Indian Prime Minister 1984), 73

Gang of Four (power struggle in China after Mao's death), 111

Ganges (major river system in India), 58, 59

Gapon, Father (Russian Orthodox priest staged a peaceful march fomenting Bloody Sunday massacre in 1905), 391

GATT (General Agreement on Trade and Tariffs; ongoing treaties sponsored by the U.N. to ease international trade), 49, 180-181, 253-254, 359

Gautama, Siddhartha (founder of Buddhist faith, 6th C. B.C.), 62

Gaza Strip (Mediterranean coastal territory taken from Egypt by Israel in the 1967 war), 287[+map], 288

GDP (Gross Domestic Product; total value of goods and services produced annually within [even by foreign owned firms] a particular nation; excludes income from foreign business operations by firms owned by that nation), 80-81 [chart], 115, 136, 170, 211, 253 [chart], 296, 411, 433-444 [+map and chart]

Genetics (biological research to improve life), 446-447

Geneva Agreements (after French defeat at Dien Bien Phu in 1954, provided for an independent and neutral Indochinese states), 74, 76, 364

Genocide (deliberate elimination of a racial or cultural group), 345, 444

Geographers, (includes map makers), 12, 22

German Democratic Republic (name of East Germany, 1949-1990), 362

Germanic tribes (overran Europe in the 5th-7th C.), 315

Germany (official name, after Treaty of Final Settlement 12 Sept. 1990: Federal Republic of Germany, also German Empire, and Third Reich), in Africa—32 [map], in Oceania, 152, 160 [+map and chart], 161, 166 [chart]; 332-333, 336, 337-338, 342-347, 357, 359, 362, 364, 365, 391, 416, 417, 418, 419, 420, 430

Ghali, Bhutros (6th U.N. Secretary General, 1992–)

Ghana (West African empire 7th-11th C. A.D.), 24-25, 29 [map]; Ghana, Republic of (1st Sub-Saharan European Colony to achieve independence after WW II), 36

Ghettos (ethnic or cultural area or neighborhood; also see *barrios*), 342, 400

Ghuru Mahavira (founded Jainism in India in the 6th C. A.D.), 63

Ghuru Nanak (founded Sikhism in India in the 15th Century), 64

Gladstone, William (19th C. British Prime Minister), 349

Glasnost ("openness"- Gorbachev's political reform policies), 402, 405, 406, 413, 420

Global Commons (biospheric elements owned by no single nation, preservation urged at 1992 Earth Summit), 441

Glorious Revolution (Catholic James II deposed; placed Protestant William III [of Orange] & Mary II on English throne in 1688), 326

GNP (total value of goods and services produced annually by a nation at home <u>and</u> <u>abroad</u>), 81

Goebbels, Joseph (Hitler's minister of propaganda), 344

Golan Heights (taken from Syria in 1967 Arab-Israeli War), 287 [+map]

Golden Age of Chinese culture (T'ang Dynasty, 618–907 A.D.), 99

Golden Age of Islamic culture (Abbasid Dynasty, 750–1258 A.D.), 279-280 [+chart]

Golden Bull (Hungarian charter 1222; provided basic liberties), 387

Golden era of India's culture (Mughal Empire, 1526–1857 A.D.), 61

Good Neighbor Policy (F. D. Roosevelt's Latin American policy, c.1933), 216

Gorazde (central Bosnian town, site of Serbian massacres of Muslims in 1994 civil war), 444

Gorbachev, Mikhail (reformer became Soviet leader 1985; negotiated end to Soviet dominance of Eastern Europe; resigned Soviet Presidency in 1991), 118, 299, 364, 401-404, 405, 406, 411, 413, 420, 436

Gosplan (Soviet Union's central economic decision-making agency sets production goals), 397, 409-410

Government of India Act (British Parliament began structure for home rule, 1935), 67

Gran Chaco (200,000 square-mile flatland shared by Argentina, Bolivia, and Paraguay), 191

Gran Colombia (short-lived union of Venezuela, Columbia, Peru, Ecuador, and Bolivia, c. 1820), 200, 203

Grand Duchy of Warsaw (a small Polish state briefly constructed by Napoleon, early 1800's), 387

Great Barrier Reef (major coral formation along the east coast of Australian) 153, 155 [photo]

Great Britain (Island off the NW coast of Europe; nation formed by 1707 union of England, Wales, and Scotland; built world empire from 16th to 20th C.; also England and United Kingdom), 308, 314, 316 [photo], 323, 324, 325-327, 328, 329, 331, 333-334, 336, 337-338, 434, 435, 449; & Africa, 32 [map],36, 37, 39, 49; & S/SE Asia, 65-68, 70-71 [chart], 73, 76, 80, 82, 86; & China, 102, 103, 120-121; & Oceania, 152, 159-161, 164, 166 [chart], 167, 170, 171, 178, 180; & Lat. Am., 200, 213 [chart]; & North Am., 229, 237, 238-239, 240, 242, 244, 246, 255; & Middle East, 282-284, 289, 300; & Russia, 417

Great Depression (1930's worldwide economic collapse; cause of social and political upheaval), 167, 345

Great Dividing Range (inland mt. range in Australia), 154

Great Hungarian Plain (an agricultural and horse-raising region in the middle of Eastern Europe), 378 [+map]

Great Lakes (major lakes of North America, form part of U.S. and Canada boundary), 227

Great Leap Forward (Mao's major economic reorganization of the late 1950's in China), 108-109, 114

Great Northern War (Peter the Great v. Sweden, 1708-21), 384

Great Plains Basin (extensive prairie of North America, produces most of the grain and cattle for Canada & U.S.), 227

Great Reform Bill (1832 British reform gave middle classes the right to vote), 334

Great Rift Valley (canyons of Eastern Africa), 21

Great Trek (1836;Boer migration from South African coast to interior after British took Cape Colony), 31, 36

Great Wall of China (built as an invasion defense on northern borders of China in Qin period, c.220 B.C.), 98 [map], 99 [+photo]

Hippocrates (Greek father of medicine; studied natural causes of disease; originated oath physicians take to serve best their patients), 312

Hiroshima (U.S. atom bomb target at end of World War II), 134, 164, 347

Hispaniola (Caribbean island contains Haiti, Dominican Republic), 200

Hitler, Adolf (Nazi leader of Germany 1933-45), 332, 342-346, 397, 416

Hittite Empire (North Africa; skilled crafts were widely diffused in Africa after its fall, c.1200 B.C.), 23

HIV virus (known cause of AIDS disease), 446 [+map]

Hoarding (international trade war tactic; holding back supplies to drive prices up), 80

Ho Chi Minh (1890-1969, communist Viet Minh leader), 74

Hokkaido (Northernmost major Japanese island), 123

Holocaust (Nazi genocide against Jews), 286, 344-345

Holy Land (Israel / Palestine), 280

Holy Roman Emperor (Charlemagne crowned in 800 A.D.), 315

Holy Synod (Russian Orthodox Church placed under direct control of Tsar Peter in early 18th C.), 384

Homogeneous (same or similar in kind), 95

Homo Habilis (able man earliest human remains in Africa), 23

Hong Kong, 102, 120-121, 173-174, 176, 349

Honshu (largest and most developed island of Japanese group), 123

Hottentots, (central African people), 23

Huguenots (French Calvinists), 325

Huks (Post-independence Philippine communist guerrillas), 77

Huitzilpochtli (Aztec god of sun and war), 194

Hungarian Revolution (harshly suppressed by Red Army in 1956), 406, 418

Hungary, 378, 379, 380, 387, 405, 406, 418

Human Rights (World Today): 442-444

Humanism (European Renaissance revival of classical studies and critical spirit), 321

Humanitarianism (promotion of human welfare and social reform), 31

Hussein, Saddam (President of military council of Iraq; launched 1980's wars in Persian Gulf region), 290, 291-292, 301

Iberian Peninsula (Spain and Portugal), 188, 199, 310

Ibo people (Biafra secessionists in 1960's Nigerian civil war), 39

Iceland, 310

Ideographs (pictures used for concepts or ideas), 117, 125, 194

IMF (see International Monetary Fund)

Immigrants (settlers moving from one country to another), 229, 254-255, 349-350

Imperialism (extension of political and economic control of a nation over other groups or territories), 31-33, 65-68, 160-161 [map and chart], 282-283, 336-337, 448

Impressionist (school of art popular in Europe in 19th and 20th C.), 351

Inca (highly developed Amerindian civilization in Peruvian Andes of S. America, c.1200-1600 A.D.), 193 [+map], 195

India, 58-59, 61-64, 65-67, 70-73, 80-82, 86-87, 95, 119 [map], 429, 430 [chart] 435, 436 [chart], 439

Indian Constitution (British Parliamentary base), 70-71 [+chart]

Indian Ocean, 20, 58-60

Indirect rule system (colonial government which allowed some local autonomy in internal affairs), 31, 161

Indochina (peninsula of Southeast Asia; also French colony that later became Vietnam, Laos, Cambodia), 74-76

Indo-Gangetic Plain (north central India, stretches from Pakistan to Bangladesh), 58

Indonesia, Republic of, 77-78, 82, 87 [chart]

Indo-Pakistani wars (border disputes over Punjab, Kashmir since 1948), 73

Indus River (India - site of early civilizations), 58-59, 61 [+chart]

Industrial Revolution (socio-political change occurring when production of basic necessities becomes organized mechanically; began on large scale in England about 1750), 333-334

Inflation (a period of significantly rising prices without a counterbalancing rise in production; demand outweighs supply, causing prices to rise), 358

Infrastructure (a society's total transport [roads, bridges] and communication system), 130, 189, 212, 251, 432

Instrument of Government (England under Cromwell's Puritan rule in the 1650's, first modern written constitution), 326

Insular (separateness in Japanese culture due to island geography), 123

Interdependence (mutual dependence of people on each other), 11, 43, 215, 253, 258, 296, 354, 432

International Monetary Fund (IMF works through the U.N. to coordinate global currencies and exchange rates), 49, 170, 175, 178 [chart]

Inuit (large Amerindian people living in northern reaches of Alaska, Canada, Greenland; a.k.a. Eskimo), 231-232

Iran, 86, 268 [+map], 270 [+chart], 290-292, 294 [map], 300 [graph], 301, 434 [chart]

Iran-Iraq War (1980-1988), 291, 301

Iraq (Persian Gulf nation; site of Persian Empire, Ancient Mesopotamia, and Abbasid Islamic Empire), 270, 290, 291-292, 294 [map], 300 [graph], 301, 435

Ireland, 308, 349

Irish Free State (Eire; independence from British rule achieved in WW I period), 349

Irish Republican Army (IRA; militant group seeking independence for Northern Ireland), 349, 436, 444

Iron Chancellor (see Bismarck), 332

"Iron Curtain" (After WW II, Churchill coined phrase describing the prevention the free flow of ideas between the West and communist E. Europe.), 362, 418

Irrawaddy (major river system in Burma region), 60

Isabella, Queen of Spain (financed voyage of Christopher Columbus, 1492), 328

Islam (major world religion founded in Middle East by prophet Muhammad, 7th C. A.D.), 277-282, (also see Muslim culture in Africa, 25-26; in S/SE Asia, 63, 73, 434

Islamic fundamentalist movement, 73, 290, 292, 296, 344, 444, 449

Isolationism (avoiding relations with other nations) 128, 130

Israel (ancient Mid-East kingdom of Hebrews; independent nation - 1948), 273, 283, 286-288, 295-296, 298, 299-300, 435, 436 [chart]

Italy, 311, 313, 332, 320, 345-346, 357

Iturbe, Augustin de (Mexican dictator c. 1820's), 243

Ivan III (Ivan the Great; 1462-1505; overthrew Tartars in 1480), 383

Ivan IV (Ivan the Terrible; Russian ruler, 1533-1584), 383

Jahangir (4th Indian Mogul ruler, 1605-1627, continued golden age of father Akbar), 61

James II (English king deposed in Glorious Revolution 1688), 326

Jammu (Muslim state claimed by India and Pakistan), 70

Japan: 123-145; Constitution of 1947 outlawed war 144; cultural origins, 124-128; dependence on imported petroleum, 142; economy, 140-143; educational system 137; food supply, 142; imbalance in trade relationships, 142-143; industries & S.E. Asia, 82, 83, 174-175; population characteristics, 136; social conditions, 137; topography, climate and resources, 123-124; in World War II, 74, 75, 76, 105, 132-134; & Oceania, 164-165 [+map/chart], 167, 170, 171, 172, 173, 174-175

Jainism (religious sect founded by Guru Mahavira in 6th C. A.D.), 63

Jehovah's Witnesses (religious group persecuted by Nazis), 344

Jericho (oldest Mid-East settlement to be uncovered by archeologists), PLO enclave, 288

Jerusalem (center of Islamic-Christian conflicts, see Crusades), 287-288

Jesus Christ (founder Christianity; major world religion), 273, 277

Jews (see Hebrews, Judaism), 272-273, 283-284, 286-288, 292, 295, 342, 344-345, Russia, 400, 443

Jewish Star Decree (Nazis required wearing a yellow Star of David on Jews clothing in 1930's), 345

Jiang Qing (China: led group in power struggle after Mao's death in 1976), 111

Jihad (Muslim crusades to spread faith through armed conquest), 26, 63, 278

Jinnah, Muhammad Ali (founder of Pakistani independence movement), 67, 73

Johnson, Lyndon B. (U.S. President, 1963-69; escalated Vietnam War), 51, 74

Joint stock company (private enterprises used by English to finance exploration and colonization projects, 16th-19th C.), 328

Jordan (E. Mediterranean kingdom), 288

Juarez, Benito Pablo (Mexican reformer, 1850s-60s), 204, 244-245

Judeo-Christian ethic (religious synthesis of values, ideals, and standards of the western civilization), 314

Junta (committee of military rulers, oligarchy - usually in Lat. Am.), 204, 216

Justinian Code (6th C. A.D. collection of civil law, preserved the Roman legal heritage), 275

K

Kaaba Shrine (Islamic holy place in Mecca, Saudi Arabia), 277

Kabuki (traditional Japanese dramatic form originated in the 16th century), 127

Kadets (Constitutional Democrats; middle class party favored a constitutional monarch in Russia, c.1917), 390, 391

Kahlo, Frida (Mexican artist), 261

Kaiser Wilhelm II (German monarch, c. WW I), 337, 416

Kalahari (desert basin wasteland in southern Africa), 20, 23

Kami (in Japanese tradition, the gods who created the islands), 125, 127

Kamikaze (WW II Japanese suicide pilots), 127, 133

Kampuchea (Cambodia renamed briefly in 1980's; see Cambodia)

Kanem-Bornu (Islamic state northeast of Lake Chad destroyed by French in 19th C.), 29

Karma (idea that a person's actions carry un-avoidable consequences and determine the nature of subsequent reincarnation), 62, 65

Kasavubu, Joseph (Military commander involved in Zaire's early power struggles and civil war, early 1960's), 38

Kashmir (territory in N.W. India claimed by both India and Pakistan), 70, 86

Keiretsu (large, powerful Japanese corporations; often multinational in scope; called zaibatsu prior to the 1960's), 140, 141

Kellogg-Briand Pact (1928 Pact of Paris proposed a worldwide non-aggression structure), 342

Kennedy, John F. (U.S. President in 1960's: set up Peace Corps, new Latin American policy), 51, 216; quoted on immigration, 247; quoted on world hunger, 430

Kennedy, Paul (Yale historian, *Preparing for the 21st Century, The Rise and Fall of the Great Powers,* 1994), 359, 429, 439, 448

Kenya (Republic of), 39-40, 449

Kenyatta, Jomo (nationalist leader; 1st President of Kenya), 36, 41

Kerensky, Aleksandr (Kadet premier of Russian provisional gov't. after the abdication of the Tsar overthrown by Bolsheviks[Nov.1917]), 392

KGB (post WW II name for espionage group and secret police in U.S.S.R. & Russia; see also Cheka [pre-1924], OGPU [1920's], NKVD [1930's], MGB [1940's]), 395, 410

Khan, Ayub (1950's/'60's Pakistani leader), 73, 86

Khan, Genghis (13th C. Asian conqueror est. Mongol Yuan Dynasty in China), 99-100

Khazars (invaded Russia from Central Asia, demanded tribute from the Slavic traders, c. 700 A.D), 380

Khmer Empire (Southeast Asian civilization c. 800 A.D.), 61

Khmer Rouge (communist insurgent group in Cambodian civil war, 1960-80), 75

Khomeini, Ruhollah (leader of Iranian Shi'ite Muslims who over threw Shah in 1978), 290-291, 292, 296

Khrushchev, Nikita S. (First Secretary and Premier, U.S.S.R. 1956-64), 362, 364, 398-399, 406, 410

Kibbutz (Israeli collective), 296

Kiev ([Kyiv] Ukraine; important trading center for the Slavs; a loose confederation of city-states established under the Grand Prince of Kiev in 900 A.D.), 379, 380, 381

Kikuyu (Kenya's largest tribal group), 39-40

Kinshasa (Zaire's capital), 38

Kirov Ballet (produced some of the greatest dancers of all time including Anna Pavlova and Vaslav Nijinsky), 389-390

Kiva (underground ceremonial chamber of Anasazi), 234

Knights (land-holding nobles became fighting men under Europe's medieval feudal system), 316

Kongo (ancient African kingdom; modern Angola), 24-25 [chart]; 28 [map], 29

Koppen, Wladimir (19th C. Austrian geographer, created a system of classification of climates), 12, 22.

Koran (Qur'an, Islam's sacred text), 63, 277, 444

Korea: 97, 99, 117, 123, 125, 131 [+map], 435, 436 [chart]; Korean War (1950-53), 117-118 [+map], 140, 144, 145, 170, 171, 172, 173 [graph], 174

Kremlin (ancient Moscow fortress of the tsars used as center of government power by communists and later rulers of Russia), 398 [+photo], 399

Kshatriya (Hindu warrior caste), 62

Kublai Khan (Mongol emperor of China, launched armadas against Japan in 1274 and 1281), 99, 127

Kulak (Russia– wealthier peasants and landowners who resisted the Bolsheviks and later Stalin) 395, 397

Kuomintang (Nationalist Party in 20th C. Chinese Civil War), 104-105

Kush (ancient African kingdom), 24-25 [chart], 29 [map]

Kuwait, 218, 291-292, 435

Kwatiutl (Amerindian civilization of Pacific Northwest), 232-233

Kyoto (served as Japan's capital until 1868), 125

Kyushu (one of the four major islands of Japan), 123

Labour Party (favors socialist programs in Britain), 71, 349, 355

Lagos (capital of Nigeria), 39

Landed aristocracy (oligarchy; governing power of elite group in Latin American nations), 203, 433

Laos (Lao People's Democratic Republic), 59, 75-76

Latin America: 186 -221; agricultural production, 191-192, 211-212; architecture, 193-195, 217; communism, 205-206, 216; colonial period, 197-201 cultural contributions, 217; U.S. influence, 210-11, 212-214; 215-216; Encomiendas system, 198; industrialism, 210-211; literature, 217; migration, 212-213; post independence era, 203-204; resources, 191-193; tourism, 212-213

Latin-based languages (dominance colonial Spanish and Portuguese [Brazil] culture led to general title of "Latin America"), 188

Latins (European people who founded Rome, c. 1500 B.C.), 313

LDCs (Less Developed Nations; "Have—Not," "Third World," or poorer nations), 43, 45, 46, 49, 80-81, 87, 118, 181, 216, 357, 429, 431, 432-434, 435, 437, 439, 442, 445-446, 450

Leached soil (minerals and nutrients are washed away by constant rainfall), 23

League of Nations (world peace organization established after WW I), 132, 144, 161-162, 283, 342, 345, 356-357, 416

Leakey, Mary, and Richard (Anthropologists uncovered earliest human remains in Africa, 1972), 23

Lebanon, 269, 299-300

Lebensraum (Hitler's expansionist policy of "living space"), 345

Lee Kwan Yew (Singapore's Prime Minister, led the anti-British movement in the late 1950's), 76

Legalism (3rd C. B.C. Chinese philosophy - punishment should be very severe for even minor offenses), 97

Legion of Honor (award established by Napoleon for those who performed important services for France), 331

Lena River (U.S.S.R.), 375

Lenin, Vladimir Ilyich (a.k.a. Nikoli Lenin; Marxist leader of Bosheviks in 1917 Russian Revolution), 390, 392, 395, 396, 398, 399, 403, 409

Leopold II (King of Belgium; established Belgian Congo colony; began the imperialist "Scramble for Africa," c. 1880's), 31, 38

Levant (a rich agricultural plateau of Syria, Lebanon, and Israel bordering the Mediterranean Sea), 269

Liberal Democrats (Japan, political party), 136-137

Liberia (West Africa), 31

Libya (North Africa), 50, 290, 435

Limited Nuclear Test Ban Treaty (1963; outlawed tests in the atmosphere), 361, 435

Lineage (social bonds created by one's ancestry, relationships based on a common ancestor), 24, 40, 41

Li Peng (Chinese Premier unleashed troops on T'iananmen Square student demonstrators, 1989), 111

Literacy, 431 [+map]

Liu Shao-qi (Chinese President in 1960's; later opponent of Mao), 109

Llanos (Spanish word for plains; region of northern South America), 191 [+photo]

Locarno Pacts (helped establish European boundaries after WW I), 342

Locke, John (English Enlightenment philosopher), 240, 329 [+chart]

Lok Dal (one of two major parties in India), 71 [chart]

Lome Convention (economic trade agreements for African nations, 1975), 49

L'Ouverture, Toussaint (led 1791 insurrection established Dominican Republic), 200

Lon Nol (Cambodian General led coup 1963), 75

Long March (1934 general retreat of Mao's communist forces), 104, 105 [map]

Louis XIV of France (17th C. French devine right ruler), 324-325

Louis XVI of France (18th C. French ruler, executed by the French Revolutionaries), 329, 330

Lumumba, Patrice (Marxist leader in Congo [Zaire] civil war, c. 1960's), 38

Luther, Martin (German cleric began Protestant Reformation c.1517), 322, 323 [illust.]

Luxembourg, 308

Lydians (ancient civilization of Western Turkey), 272 [chart], 273 [map]

M

MacArthur, Douglas (American commander, WW II & Korea; post-war occupation of Japan), 118, 134

MacDonald, Sir John A. (first prime minister of Canada, 1867), 240, 244

Macedonia (3rd Cent. B.C. Balkan kingdom of Philip & Alexander the Great; independent nation broke from Yugoslavia in 1991), 312, 379 [+map], 406

Machismo (exaggerated sense of masculine dominance in Latin American culture), 208, 247

Machiavelli, Nicolo (wrote *The Prince,* c.1530; advice on how to increase and hold power), 324

Machu Picchu (Incas' famed fortress city in the Peruvian Andes), 195 [+photo]

Magna Carta, (guarantee of rights signed in 1215 by English King John), 326, 347 [chart]

Magsaysay, Ramon (Philippine President, 1953-57), 77

Magellan, Ferdinand (16th C. Spanish explorer; expedition circumnavigated globe, claimed many Pacific Islands), 158, 197 [chart], 327 [chart]

Magyars (Eastern European nomadic tribe that established itself in the region c. 900 A.D.), 380

Mansa Musa (most famous of the Muslim rulers of Mali, 14th C. A.D.), 25

Malaysia (former federation of Malaya, Singapore, North Borneo, and Sarawak formed in 1963 [Singapore now independent]), 59, 76, 170

Malayan Peninsula (S.E. Asia), 60

Mali (West African Islamic kingdom, c.1200 A.D.), 24-25 [chart]; 29 [map]

Manchu-Ching (Chinese dynasty, 1644 - 1912 A.D.), 100

Manchuria (territorial conflict: Japan & Russia. c. 1905, and 1930's), 131-132; (pre-WW II Sino-Japanese crisis), 345; (Russo- Japanese War in), 390

Mandate (right or command), 97; League of Nations authorized rule of former territories of Central Powers by Allies, to prep. for independence in Post-WW I Era), 164, 283 [+map]

Mandela, Nelson (So. African anti-apartheid leader; elected President, 1994), 37

Manifest Destiny (nationalist spirit justifying 19th C. U.S. territorial expansion drive), 242, 259

Manor house (European noble's feudal walled compound [castle]; on high ground for protection of estate's people), 316-317

Mansa Musa (legendary 14th C. ruler of Muslim Hausa Empire in central Africa), 25

Maps, 11

Mao Zedong (Chinese leader, established communist regime, 1949, d. 1976), 108-110, 113-114, 117-118, 119, 120

Maori (Polynesian people originally settled New Zealand) 155, 161

Marat, Jean Paul (leader of the radical Committee of Public Safety during the French Revolution's Reign of Terror), 330

Marco Polo (Italian visitor to the court of Kublai Khan, 13th C.), 100

Marcos, Ferdinand (Philippine dictator, 1965-1986), 77

Mare Nostrum (Mussolini's expansionist program to restore Italy as a power in Mediterranean, c. 1930's), 345

Marquette, Fr. Jacques (16th C. French missionary and explorer; expeditions to interior North America, Mississippi Valley), 237

Market System (economic decisions based on free interaction of consumers and producers, minimal government regulation; also capitalism), 81, 409

Marlowe, Christopher (Elizabethan England, poet, dramatist), 324

Marshall, George (U.S. Sec'y. of State, responsible European Recovery Act), 117, 354, 357, 362, 419

Marshall Plan (European Recovery Act gave U.S. assistance in rebuilding Europe after World War II; named for Gen. George C. Marshall, U.S. Sec'y. of State, also aided in containing communist expansion),354, 357, 362

Nairobi (Kenya's capital), 40 [+ photo]

Naisbitt, John (Am. author, futurist, *Megatrends*), 448

Namib (desert in southern Africa), 23

Namibia (former German South-West Africa; U.N. trusteeship of South Africa granted independence, 1990), 38

Napoleon Bonaparte (ruler of France in early 1800's), 330-331, 388

Napoleonic Code of Laws ([Code Civil] legal system for 19th C. French Empire), 331

Napoleonic Wars (periodic warfare in Europe c. 1802-1815 Britain, Austria, Russia v. France), 200, 240, 331, 388

Nara (Japan's earliest capital city), 125

Nasser, Gamal Abdel (nationalist leader of Egypt in 1950's), 289, 295

National Congress Party (ruling party in India), 71 [+chart]

National Convention (legislature in midst of French Revolution), 330

National Front (or National Union, power group struggling in 1980's Angola civil war), 50

National Insurance Service and National Health Service (British welfare system), 355

National Party (German right wing group aided Nazis in early 1930's), 343

National Socialist German Workers Party (Nazi Party), 343

Nationalism (a strong feeling of unity for people who desire to control their own destinies) in Africa, 34-36; in China, 103, in Mid-East, 284, 286, 289; in Europe, 332-333

Nationalization (gov't. takeover of private enterprises), 38, 44, 82, 213, 259, 289, 295

Native Land Act (1913 apartheid rule forbade black South Africans to own land off reservations), 37

NATO (see North Atlantic Treaty Organization)

Natural Law (philosophical theories developed out of Sir Isaac Newton's discovery of the universal law of gravitation), 328

Natural Rights of Man (basic human rights theories growing out of Enlightenment Era), 31, 328-329

Nazi Germany (1920's-1940's), 342-345, (persecution of Jews) 286, 344-345

Nazi-Soviet Non-Aggression Pact (1939), 346, 416

Nehru, Jawaharlal (disciple of Gandhi in the Congress Party, became the first Prime Minister), 71, 76, 80, 86

Niemeyer, Oscar (Latin American architect), 217

Neocolonialism (a new outside control of African economic life), 43

Neolithic Revolution (life began centering on agriculture), 156, 271

Neruda, Pablo (Chilean author), 217

Netherlands (includes references to Dutch colonialism), 30, 36, 65 [map], 68, 77, 200, 308

New Economic Policy (NEP; Lenin's socialist economic structure for the U.S.S.R.), 396, 397, 409

New France (northern sector of France's N. American colonial empire to 1763), 237-240

New Harmony (utopian living experiment by English socialist Robert Owens in Indiana, U.S.A., 19th C.), 335

New Lanark, Scotland (utopian living experiment by English socialist Robert Owens, 19th C.), 335

New Spain (northern sector of Spain's American/ Caribbean empire 15th to 19th C.), 198 [map], 199, 237-238

New Testament (Christian scripture – the Gospels of Matthew, Mark, Luke, and John), 273

New Zealand, 152-155, 158, 159-161, 164, 166 [chart], 167 [+map], 170-172, 180, 181

Newton, Sir Isaac (universal law of gravitation, 18th C.), 328

Ngo Dinh Diem (President of the Rep. of South Vietnam, 1955-62), 74

Nicaragua, 206

Nicholas I (repressive Russian Tsar 1825-1855), 388

Nicholas II (last Romanov Tsar [1894-1917] during Revolutions & WW I, abdicated, killed w/ family by Bolsheviks), 390-391

NIEs (abbr. Newly Industrializing Economy such as So. Korea, Singapore, Taiwan in the Pacific Rim), 172, 431, 432, 433, 434

Nietzsche, Friedrich Wilhelm (19th C. German philosopher), 342

Niger (major West African river basin), 20

Nigeria (Federal Republic of), 39

Nihongi (*Chronicles of Japan,* 8th C. history of the Yamato Clan), 125

Nile River Basin (Egypt), 20, 268, 270, 271

Ninety-Five Theses (Martin Luther and reformation), 322

Nirvana (Hindu cycle of reincarnation broken when one achieves a perfect state of mind), 62

Nixon, Richard (U.S. president 1969-73, involvement in Vietnam, reopen relations with Red China), 74, 118

Persian Gulf (center of oil production in Middle East), 56, 142, 291-292. 298, 301, 435

Persians (center of ancient Mid-East civilization, modern-day Iran), 272 [chart]

Peru, 192, 195, 197 [chart], 200, 210

Peter the Great (Tsar, 1682-1725, Westernized Russian culture and economy), 384-385, 449

Peter's Pence (obligatory donations to Pope: Medieval Europe), 317

Petition of Right (1628 act strengthened British Parliament), 326, 327 [chart]

Philip of Macedonia (ruler of Hellenes; father of Alexander the Great; 359-336 B.C.), 312

Philippines (Republic of the), 76-77, 172

Philip II of Spain (defeated by Elizabeth I of England in famous English Channel battle 1588), 324

Phnom Penh (capital of Cambodia), 75

Phoenicians (Mediterranean traders; developed an alphabet code in which each letter stood for only one distinct sound), 272 [+chart], 273 [map]

Pictographs (pictures used for writing), 117, 125

Pierce, Franklin (U.S. President authorized Perry's mission to open Japan, 1854), 130

Pilgrims (17th C. Protestant separatists driven from Anglican Church to settle Plymouth Plantation, MA, c. 1620), 237

Plato (philosopher of Ancient Greece, d.347 B.C.), 311-312

Plebians (common people of ancient Rome), 313

PLO (see Palestinian Liberation Organization)

Pogroms (violent purges, often against the Jews), 342, 391, 400

Point Four Program (U.S. Pres. Truman's foreign aid program to assist LDCs as part of a global strategy to contain communism, c. 1948-1953), 86

Pol Pot (Cambodian Premier and violent purges of 1970's), 75

Polish Silesia (significant amounts of coal and iron ore vital to the country's continuing industrialization), 379

Political philosophers (17th-18th C. European Enlightenment: Locke, Voltaire, Montesquieu, Smith, Paine), 240, 328-329

Politics and Ethics (Aristotle's work advised moderation in life as well as the use of logic and reason), 312

Polygamy (having more than one wife), 40

Polynesia (eastern sector of Oceania), 152 [+map], 155-156 [+illust.], 166 [independence chart]

Polyrhythmic (African music using two or more rhythms at once), 27

Polytheism (belief in a multiplicity of gods)

Pontoon (floating bridge suspensions), 346

Pope Urban II (called for a crusade to regain control of the Holy Land from the Muslim Turks in 1095), 280, 320

Popular Movement (Soviet-backed Angolan civil war group), 50

Population density (number of people per square mile), 95

Population problems: Africa, 44-45; India, 72, China, 95; Latin America, 207-208; Middle East, 296; World Today, 428-431

Po River Valley (Italy), 311

Portugal, 26, 30, 31, 32 [map], 78, 188, 199, 200, 310

Posada, Jose Guadalupe (Mexican illustrator), 261

Potlatch (Kwatiutl ritual feast), 232

Potsdam Conference (1945, disagreements among WW II Allies), 289 [chart], 361 [chart], 417 [chart]

Power of the purse (financial control British Parliaments used to decrease the power of kings in need of additional revenues), 326

Poza, Carlos (Mexican economist), 260

Pre-Columbian times (before the first voyages of European discovery by Columbus in 1492), 193-195, 231-234, 236

Presbyterian (Calvinist Christian sect), 323

Precedents (past actions and decisions that act as models), 347

Pretoria (administrative capital of South Africa), 37

Primary commodities / resources (raw products usually sold by LDCs for minimal profit as opposed to processed products), 49, 212

Prime Minister a parliamentary nation's chief executive), 71 [chart], 136, 348

Prince Henry (15th C. Portuguese ruler encouraged voyages of exploration), 327

Privatization (market economic reforms turn government-operated facilities into private businesses; opposite of nationalization), 411

Protestant Reformation (16th - 18th C. Europe religious reform), 322-324

Punjab (Indian province troubled by religious strife), 70

Purge (eliminated any opposition; ex. Stalin brutally purged Soviet Communist Party in 1930's - 20 million est. dead), 396, 442 [chart]

Puritan Revolution (1642; overthrow of British monarchy), 326

Puritans (Calvinist Anglican reformers, C. 16th-17th C.), 237, 326

Pygmy (people of African rainforest), 23
Pyramidal social structures (the forerunners of Latin American class systems), 199 [chart]
Pythagoras of Samos (ancient Greek mathematician; principles of geometry, d. 500 B.C.), 312
Pyrenees Mts. (French-Spanish border), 308, 310

Qaddafi, Muammar al- (Libyan leader, overthrew monarchy, 1969; involved in terrorism), 290
Quebec Act (Divided Canada into Upper and Lower areas, 1774; allowed Quebec inhabitants to keep French culture and religion), 240
Quebecois (Canadian French speaking separatist movement), 247-248
Quechua (spoken language of Inca), 195
Quipu (Inca civilization; official records), 195
Quotations of Chairman Mao (Mao's communist philosophy), 110
Qur'an (*Koran* – Islam's sacred text), 63, 277, 444
Qutb-ud-Din Aybak (Mongul/Mughal conqueror of India established the Sultanate of Delhi, c. 1206), 63

Rabbis (Jewish religious teachers), 273
Radio-Carbon Dating (scientific method of determining the age of dead organic matter by measuring its Carbon-14 emissions), 23
Ramos, Fidel (succeeded Corazon Aquino as Pres. of Philippines, 1992), 77
Raphael (Renaissance painter, *Disputa*), 322
Reagan, Ronald (U.S. President 1981-89), 50, 206, 301
Real cost (economic concept of looking at total cost of a decision, beyond money value such as lost alternatives uses of scarce resources; see also "opportunity cost"), 445
Red Army (successful in stabilizing and securing Russia for the Bolsheviks 1917-21, under the leadership of Leon Trotsky), 392, 395, 396
Red Brigades in Italy (leftist terrorist activities), 436

Red Guards (Chinese students mobilized in 1960's Cultural Revolution), 110
Red River (Vietnam), 60
Reef (coral buildup on undersea land forms slightly submerged ridge), 153, 155 [photo]
Re-flagging (registering other nation's ships as U.S. vessels to insure the safe transportation of vital supplies), 301 [+illust.]
Refugee camps, 75 [photo], 287, 288, 443 [photo]
Regions (areas with common physical, political, economic, and / or cultural traits), 11-12
Reign of Terror (French Revolution in 1790's; resulted in the execution of between 15-45,000 presumed opponents of the French Rev.), 330
Reich Culture Chambers (Nazi agencies established to control the work of artists, sculptors and all others in the fine arts), 344
Reichstag (lower house of the German parliament c. 1930's), 342, 343
Reincarnation (Hindu belief in rebirth of the soul in another form of life), 62
Renaissance (13th -17th Centuries European revival of classical culture), 320-322
Republic (form of government, people elect representatives to make decisions), 313
Republic, The (most famous of Plato's *Dialogues*), 312
Republic of Biafra (eastern region of Nigeria which seceded, 1967, reclaimed 1970), 39
Republic of China, 103-104; (Taiwan gov't.: 106, 117, 118)
Republic of Indonesia, 59, 77-78, 82, 87 [chart]
Republic of South Africa, 36-38, 443
Republic of South Vietnam, 74,
Republic of Singapore, 59, 76, 83, 173
Republic of the Philippines, 76-77
Restoration Period (rule of Charles II in 1660's after the English Puritan Revolution), 326
Revisionist (one who attempts to change accepted views of Marx), 392
Revolution of the proletariat (uprising and control of society's productive resources by the working classes), 335 [chart], 336
Revolution of Rising Expectations (LDCs seeking better standards of living), 432
Revueltas, Silvestre (Mexican composer), 261
Rhine River and its canal system (vital Western European communication-transportation route for centuries), 309
Rhodes, Cecil (British imperialist in Africa), 37
Rhodopes Mountains (southern Bulgaria), 378
Rio Declaration, The (1992 U.N. Earth Summit; global environmental principles, 441

Rio de la Plata (River of Silver in South America), 191

Rio Grande (No. American river forms part of border between U.S. and Mexico), 227

Rio Grande Treaty (1967 border agreement between U.S. and Mexico), 260 [chart]

Ritual ceremonies (of African tribal religions), 25

Rivera, Diego (Mexican mural artist), 217, 261

Robespierre, Maxmilien Marie, Isidore (leader of the radical Committee of Public Safety during the French Revolution's Reign of Terror), 330

Rocky/Sierra Madre Cordillera (western No. American mountain chain extends from Canada into Central America), 189, 226, 227

Roggeveen, Jacob (18th C. Dutch explorer of Pacific, discovered Samoan Is.), 158

Roland, Jon (U.S. computer expert–predictions of technological breakthroughs), 444-445

Role model cities (Zurich, Edinburgh, demonstrate positive alternatives for desirable urban living), 440

Roman Catholic Church, 26, 188, 203-204, 238, 240, 317-318, 320, 322-334, 380

Roman Empire, 273-275, 313-315

Romanesque and Gothic cathedrals, 318

Romania, 378, 379 [+map], 388 [+map], 405 [map], 414 [chart], 416, 419

Romanov, Michael (established the dynasty that ruled Russia from 1613-1917), 384

Romanticism (19th C. European literary and artistic movement), 351 [+chart]

Rome-Berlin-Tokyo Axis (1939; pre-WW II alliance of Italy, Germany, and Japan), 132, 346

Roosevelt, Eleanor (U.N. crusade for human rights), 442

Roosevelt, Franklin D. (U.S. President, 1933-45), 35, 133, 216, 361, 417 [chart]

Roosevelt, Theodore (U.S. President, 1901-09), 206, 216

Rosetta Stone (aided in deciphering Egyptian hieroglyphics), 272

Rotten boroughs (Britain - districts with little or no population and representation, 19th C.), 334

Roundheads (see Puritan Revolution in England), 326

Rousseau, Jean-Jacques (18th C. French Enlightenment writer, opposed divine right, promoted government as a social contract), 240

Royal Niger Company (private British charter company set up trading enclaves along sea routes to the Orient), 31

Rub al Khali ("empty quarter" huge Saudi desert region), 268

Ruhr Crisis (1923; highlighted Weimar Republic's economic problems), 342

Rulfo, Juan (Mexican novelist, *Pedro Parano*), 261

Rupert Land Purchase (British gov't. bought No.and Cent. Canada territories from Hudson's Bay Co., 1869), 244

Rush-Bagot Agreement (1817 U.S.-British treaty disarmed Great Lakes fleets), 256 [chart]

Russia (ancient civilization of easternmost Europe; spread into Central Asia under Tsars; overthrown by Bolshevik revolution, 1917; also see U.S.S.R. and Russian Federation), 374-420, 435, 436

Russian/Soviet-American Confrontation (since WW II), 419-410, 435-436

Russian-British Rivalry (in Middle East), 282-283

Russian civil war (1917-1921, Bolshevik Reds v. anti-communist Whites), 395

Russian dancers (Anna Pavlova, Vaslav Nijinsky), 389

Russian Federation (independent nation [1991] in E. Europe and Asia; formerly largest of the 15 republics of the Soviet Union and its center; one of the original members of the Commonwealth of Independent States [CIS]; Moscow [cap.]), 397, 402, 403, 404-406, 409-411, 412, 413, 416

Russian music (Tchaikovsky, Rimsky, Mussorgsky), 389-390

Russian Orthodox Church, 380, 383, 384, 386, 400, 405

Russian Revolution of 1905, 390-391

Russian Revolutions of 1917, 391-392

Russian writers (Pushkin, Tolstoy, Dostoyevsky), 389-390, 401

Russification (conquered people forced to adopt Russian language, culture and religion to increase unity within the country), 383, 400

Russo-Japanese War (1904-1905), 131, 390

Russo-Turkish War (1877-78), 388

Rwanda and Burundi (civil wars, E. Africa), 36, 443

Sadat, Muhammad Anwar al- (Egyptian President, Camp David Accords, assassinated 1981), 287-288

Sadler Report (19th C. British industrialization), 334

Sahara (world's largest desert), 21-22, 268

Sahel (a drought-stricken area of West Central Africa), 43, 45-46, 438

Sakharov, Andrei (Soviet physicist/ dissident, Nobel Prize, critic of gov't., exiled to Siberia), 420, 443

Saigon (Vietnam capital), 74, 75

Saint Lawrence Seaway (Eastern Canada - U.S. border canal system, c. 1958), 227, 259

Saint Peter's Basilica: Rome, (center of Roman Catholic religion), 321

Saint Petersburg (Peter the Great's westernized imperial Russian capital on Baltic; also called Leningrad under communists), 385, 391, 392

SALT agreements (U.S.-U.S.S.R. arms limitation treaties, 1970's), 361, 398

Salt March (Gandhi's non-violent protest of British tax system), 67

Salutary neglect (lax enforcement of British mercantile rules led to laissez-faire in colonial America), 239

Salween (major river basin in Burma), 60

Samurai (warrior class in feudal Japan), 126-127

Sandinistas (Nicaraguan communist guerrilla movement, ruled 1979-1990), 206, 216

San Martín, Jose de (19th C. South American liberator), 201

Sanskrit (ancient language of India), 61

Santa Anna, Antonio Lopez de (four-time Mexican president/dictator; 1821-55), 204, 243

Sao Paulo (Brazilian city projected pop. over 20 million by 2000 A.D.), 207

Satellite (nation dominated by an outside power; Eastern Europe under Soviets 1945-1990), 405, 418

Saudi Arabia, 270 [map], 277, 292

Savak (Iran: Shah's secret police), 290

Savanna climate (Tropical grassland [Bs]), 23

Savimbi, Jonas (Angolan rebel leader), 50

Scandinavia (Norway, Sweden, Finland, Denmark, Iceland, and Greenland), 310

Schism (a serious split – usually applies in religious matters), 278

Schuman Plan (French plan to remove economic barriers in post WW II W. Europe; first moves toward Common Market), 357

Scientific socialism (see Marxism), 334-335

Scorched-earth policy (Russians' destroy and retreat tactics defeated Napoleon, Hitler), 331, 417

Scramble for Africa (European imperialism in 19th C.), 31, 38

S.E.A.T.O. (see Southeast Asia Treaty Organization)

Seko, Mobutu Sese (a.k.a. Joseph Mobutu; leader of Zaire), 38

Seljuk Turks, 280

Semites (ethnic group made up of the Arab, Assyrian, and Hebrew people), 271

Sepoy Mutiny (India, 1858:Hindu and Moslem mercenaries v. British), 65

Serbia (central Balkan nation in 1990's, part of Yugoslavia), 379, 388, 391, 406

Serbs (dominant ethnic group in central Balkans), 388, 406, 444

Serfs (peasants legally bound to the land), 316, 381, 383, 386, 389

Seven Years' War (worldwide Anglo-French colonial struggle; called French and Indian War in America 1757-1763), 158, 237, 328

Shah Jahan (1629-58; Mughal Indian ruler, continued golden age begun by Akbar), 61, 63

Shakespeare, William (Elizabethan England, dramatist), 324

Shanghai (major port of the Yangtze, China), 95

Shari'a (Islamic moral rules are incorporated into a code of law), 277

Sheep stations (large sheep ranches in Australia), 171 [+photo]

Shikoku (major island of Japan group), 123

Shintoism (Japan: trad. religion), 126

Shi'ites (Muslim fundamentalist sect), 278, 290-291, 296, 434

Shiva (Hindu deity), 62

Shogun (Japanese feudal military ruler), 127-28

Shotoku (Japanese regime blended Chinese culture, 592-621 A.D.), 125

Siberia (Northern part of Asiatic region of U.S.S.R.), 229 [+map], 375 [+map]

Sierra Madre (cordillera in Mexico and Central America), 189, 226 [map], 227

Sihanouk, Norodom (Cambodian ruler 1942-63), 75

Sikhs (Hindu sect founded in the 15th Century), 62, 64, 70, 73

Silicon chip (low-cost electronic computer technology), 444

Sinai Peninsula (conquered by Israel in 1967 War; returned to Egypt by Camp David agreement), 287

Tsunami (undersea earthquake), 154

Tutu, Bishop Desmond (S. African anti-apartheid leader; awarded 1984 Nobel Peace Prize), 37

Tuareg (nomadic people of N. African desert), 21

Tudors (English dynasty, 1485-1603), 324

Tundra (type ET climate; sub arctic treeless plain), 298

Turkey, 86, 274 [Asia Minor], 284, 350, 362, 367

Turks (nomadic people of southwest Asia; rose as dominant Mid East group 1450-1915 A.D.; see Ottoman Empire), 271, 280, 281-282-284, 320, 327, 381, 386, 387

Twenty—One Demands (Japanese attempt to subjugate China in the Pre-WW I period), 131

Twelve Tables (codified laws of the ancient Romans), 314

Uhuru (rallying cry for African independence movement), 35

Ukraine (independent nation [1991] in Eastern Europe; a former republic under U.S.S.R.; original member of the Commonwealth of Independent States [CIS]; Kiev [cap.]), 377, 378, 379 [+map], 395 [+map], 397, 399, 403, 404, 410, 414 [chart], 419, 436

Umayyad (also Omayyad; Muslim dynasty, 632 A.D.), 278-279

Union of South Africa (semi-autonomous British dependency unified Cape Colony, Transvaal, and Orange Free State, c.1910; independent Republic of South Africa, 1961), 36-37, 443

Union of Soviet Socialist Republics (1917-1991, U.S.S.R., or Soviet Union; also see Russia), 50-51, 82, 86, 87, 118-119, 131, 206, 216, 287, 289, 298-299, 347, 354, 361-364, 367, 392, 395-406, 409-413, 416-420, 434,-436, 442-443

UNITA (party in Angolan civil war; also the National Union), 50

United Kingdom (union of England, Scotland, Wales, and N. Ireland; see Great Britain)

United Nations 35, 38, 49, 118, 166 [chart], 167, 178-179, 180, 286-288, 289, 292, 364-366; 429, 430, 433, 435, 441-442, 444; Court of Justice, 365; Economic and Social Council, 365; Food and Agricultural Organization, 430; General Assembly, 49, 365; Resolution #242, 288; Resolution #435, 38; Secretariat, 365; Secretary General, 365; Trusteeship Council, 166, 167, 365; Universal. Decl. of Human Rights, 442, 444

United States: & Africa, 50-51; *Constitution*, 201, 240, 242, 244, 326, 329; & Cuba, 205-206; & Europe, 338, 354, 358-359, 361-365, 367; Immigration and Naturalization Service (INS), 213; & India, 86, 87; & Japan, 132-134, 140-143, 144; & Latin America, 206-207, 210-211, 212, 213,215-216; & Middle East; 287-288, 298-301;& North America, 222-265; & Oceania, 160 [map/chart], 164-168, 170, 171 [graphs], 172-176, 178-181; & People's Republic of China, 117-118; & Philippines, 77; & Russia [USSR], 397, 399, 417-418; & S.E. Asia, 86; U.S.-Japanese Mutual Security Pact (1951), 144; & World Today, 429, 430, 432, 434, 435, 436, 442, 449

Ural Mountains (traditional dividing line between Europe and Asia), 375

Usury (lending money at interest), 317

Utopian socialist (Robert Owen, others in 19th C. attempted to set up ideal societies run by workers), 335

V-1 and V-2 (jet-propelled bombs developed by Nazis in WW II), 346-347

Varangian (Slavic warrior group protected Kiev state in Russia), 380

Vassals (knights swearing oaths of loyalty to the more powerful nobles in Medieval European feudal system), 316

Veches (in early Russian society, citizen assemblies dealt with local affairs), 380

Velvet Revolution (quiet, voluntary 1992 separation of Czechoslovakia into the Czech Republic and Slovak Republic), 406

Verrazano, Giovanni de (16th C. explorer, established France's Claims to St. Lawrence Valley in Canada), 236

Versailles (Louis XIV's Palace outside Paris, Fr.), 325, 338, 342, 343

Viceroys (Spanish crown-appointed colonial governors of Spain's New World administrative regions), 198 [map], 199, 237, 238

Vienna, Battle of (Ottoman expansion into Europe checked, 1683), 282

Vietnam, Socialist Republic of, 74-75, 82, 170